NATIONAL
GEOGRAPHIC
TRAVELER

germany

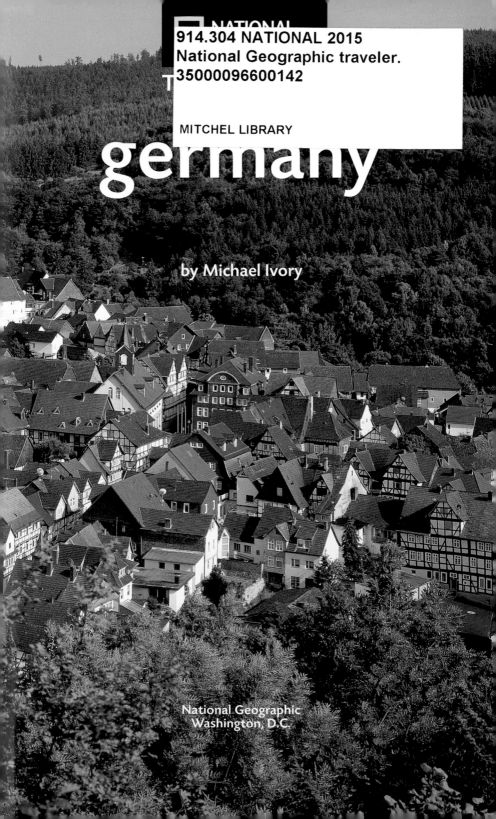

germany

by Michael Ivory

National Geographic
Washington, D.C.

CONTENTS

Pages 2–3: Spangenberg in Hesse
Opposite: Fun at a Munich fair

TRAVELING WITH EYES OPEN

Alert travelers go with a purpose and leave with a benefit. If you travel responsibly, you can help support wildlife conservation, historic preservation, and cultural enrichment in the places you visit. You can enrich your own travel experience as well.

To be a geo-savvy traveler:

- Recognize that your presence has an impact on the places you visit.

- Spend your time and money in ways that sustain local character. (Besides, it's more interesting that way.)

- Value the destination's natural and cultural heritage.

- Respect the local customs and traditions.

- Express appreciation to local people about things you find interesting and unique to the place: its nature and scenery, music and food, historic villages and buildings.

- Vote with your wallet: Support the people who support the place, patron-izing businesses that make an effort to celebrate and protect what's special there. Seek out shops, local restaurants, inns, and tour operators who love their home—who love taking care of it and showing it off. Avoid businesses that detract from the character of the place.

- Enrich yourself, taking home memories and stories to tell, knowing that you have contributed to the preservation and enhancement of the destination.

That is the type of travel now called geotourism, defined as "tourism that sustains or enhances the geographical character of a place—its environment, culture, aesthetics, heritage, and the well-being of its residents." To learn more, visit National Geographic's Center for Sustainable Destinations at *nationalgeographic.com/travel/sustainable.*

germany

ABOUT THE AUTHORS

Before studying modern languages at Oxford University, **Michael Ivory** perfected his German by spending the best part of a year at a Rhineland boarding school. He subsequently taught in Germany and, after qualifying as a landscape architect and urban planner, took student groups there to learn from the country's considerable achievements in these fields. He has traveled extensively in central and eastern Europe, and has watched with particular interest as the peoples and countries of the former Soviet bloc have adapted to the post-communist world. Ivory is also the author of *National Geographic Traveler: Canada.*

Jeremy Gray wrote the updates and sidebars for this edition. Born of English parents in Louisiana, Gray grew up with an equal affinity for crumpets and Southern fried chicken. After a university scholarship took him to Mainz, Germany, he worked as a journalist and author in Amsterdam, Frankfurt, and London, contributing to 20-odd travel guides along the way. He now lives in the heart of Berlin's Mitte district, in a converted butter factory.

Josephine Grever wrote the Travelwise section. Born in Aachen, she now works as the London correspondent for the German magazines *Architektur & Wohnen* and *Feinschmecker.*

Charting Your Trip

This varied and beautiful country of 82 million inhabitants stretches from the Rhine to the Polish border and from the coasts of the North Sea and Baltic to the Alps. Yet even for short-term visitors, Germany can be broken down into enjoyable, bite-size chunks.

You have a huge variety of landscapes from which to choose, and each region offers its own cultural specialties and cuisine. Much depends on your interests and favorite activities, and to a lesser extent the time of year. Want to keep your planning flexible? Your best bet is to rent a car or get around on Germany's excellent and efficient network of national railways (see Travelwise p. 350).

For outdoor enthusiasts, the southern states of Bavaria and Baden-Württemberg draw the most vacationers thanks to scenic highlights like the Bavarian Alps, Lake Constance, and the Black Forest. Apart from the popular Rhine and Moselle Valleys, the northern half of the country is far less frequented but offers a wealth of attractions in the Harz Mountains, Saxon Switzerland, and the Baltic island of Rügen for skiing, cycling, and hiking. Virtually every region has its own areas of natural beauty, and it's easy to get off the beaten track.

If You Have Only A Week

Lovers of history, urban culture, and architecture should begin with a city tour starting in **Berlin.** The German capital mesmerizes visitors with its world-class museums, sizzling nightlife, and eclectic buildings ranging from stately to audacious (two days). Some 120 miles (190 km) to the south, through Saxony's rolling hills, is the next stop, **Dresden,** the baroque arts center on the Elbe (two days). After that you could spend a day in classical **Leipzig,** 70 miles (111 km) to the northwest, where Bach and Mendelssohn conducted. Then, hop on a fast ICE train down to the Oktoberfest city of **Munich,** some 279 miles (423 km) south, for a celebration of beer, bratwurst, and BMWs (two days). The Bavarian capital is an ideal base for excursions to the World War II memorial in nearby **Dachau** and to the **Alps** for skiing. Another recommended

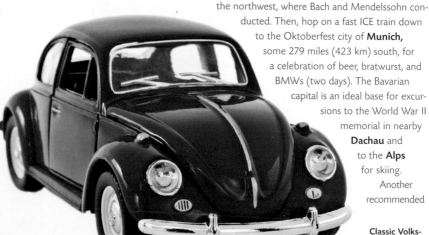

**Classic Volks-
wagen Beetle**

weeklong itinerary takes in northern Germany's unique charms, blending city experiences with Baltic flair. Start in the go-ahead port of **Hamburg** for wonderful museums, shopping, and the lights of the St. Pauli district before hitting the picturesque ancient trading hub of **Lübeck,** just 42 miles (65 km) away on the North Sea coast (two days total). One hundred and thirteen miles (180 km) west toward Holland, the free city of **Bremen** is a gem of the Hanseatic trading era that's stuffed with historic sights (one day).

From there, you're not far from the Rhineland and its fun-loving metropolis of **Cologne,** some 198 miles (314 km) to the south, for outstanding museums, a towering cathedral, and cozy beer pubs (two to three days). For a complete change of scenery, wend your way another 111 miles (177 km) down the lovely **Rhine Gorge,** between Bingen and Koblenz, passing by breathtakingly steep vineyards and the legendary Loreley (sirens!) to reach the Romanesque church town of **Mainz** (one day). Be sure to get on a boat if you have the time.

If You Have More Time

Longer stays allow you to tackle more activities and delve deeper into a province. You might wish to put down stakes in Berlin or Hamburg, and spend your additional time exploring the surrounds in excursions; or you may wish to break off and explore a new region entirely.

If you wish to stay in the vicinity of Berlin, outdoor activities lie within easy reach: the glistening lakes of **Müritz National Park,** 105 miles (166 km) to the north; the **Spreewald's** punt-filled canals starting at Lübben, 53 miles (85 km) in the southeast; and the bird-lover's paradise of **Lower Oder Valley Naturpark,** on the Polish border 60 miles (97 km) to the northeast (one day each). You could

NOT TO BE MISSED:

The museums of cosmopolitan Berlin **62–70**

Frederick the Great's Potsdam palaces **83–85**

Cologne's Gothic cathedral and old town **148–156**

The Rhine Gorge's sensational cliffs and fortresses **180–183**

The embarrassment of riches in Dresden's Green Vaults **233–234**

The sustained heritage of beautiful Bamberg **254–255**

Partying at Munich's famous Oktoberfest **300–301**

Visiting King Ludwig's fairy-tale castles **305–307**

Hiking through the fabled Black Forest **336–339**

The beautiful beaches, orchards, forests, and vineyards around Lake Constance **340–342**

Visitor Information

For pre-departure planning, the German National Tourist Board (germany.travel) is your go-to source for overviews of key travel details, regional destinations, major festivals, and seasonal events. One nice feature is the online travel planner, which enables you to browse places you'd like to visit and organize your personal itinerary. Just about every German town has a Verkehrsamt (tourist office), where you can pick up maps and brochures or book hotel rooms for a small fee—see contacts listed throughout this book. Is your spoken German a little rusty? Most offices have at least one employee who speaks English.

Dos & Don'ts

Germans tend to be formal in everyday situations. Shaking hands is common among both men and women, at least at first meeting. Friends and acquaintances will exchange a hug and peck on both cheeks. Do not use first names or the informal *du* unless invited to do so, although younger people may dispense with the formal *Sie* right away. People who introduce themselves as *Herr* or *Frau* (perhaps even *Frau Doktor*) want to be addressed that way. If invited to someone's home, take along a little something like flowers or a bottle of wine.

also admire the Bauhaus classics of **Dessau,** some 77 miles (123 km) from Berlin, and its whimsical neighbor, the folly-filled **Wörlitz Park** (one day total). Another must-see are Frederick the Great's magnificent Sanssouci palaces, 19 miles (30 km) to the east in **Potsdam** (one day).

You can take the same tack after a stay in Hamburg. It's a pleasure to ramble through the tranquil landscapes, old-fashioned resorts, and harbors of the Baltic coast such as **Wismar,** 79 miles (125 km) to the northeast, or nearby **Bad Doberan** (one day). With water, water everywhere, you might treat yourself to a sailing course in maritime **Rostock,** 36 miles (57 km) farther on (one to three days). The nature reserves along the North Sea are outstanding, a particular highlight being the **Nationalpark Vorpommersche Boddenlandschaft,** 42 miles (66 km) east of Rostock, for trails through woods, dunes, and bogs (one to three days).

Another approach would be to spend a week in Berlin or Hamburg as described above, then shift gears for the second week and explore a different region. The **Black Forest** in southwest Germany, for example, beckons with upscale resorts and spas centered around celebrated natural thermal pools. Base yourself in the exclusive resort town of **Baden-Baden** or the Black Forest capital of **Freiburg,** with its charming old town and towering cathedral. Be sure to hike through gorgeous Hell's Valley or go skiing on the Feldberg, the region's highest point.

Or you might prefer the country towns and scenic landscapes of the **Romantic Road,** which winds between Würzburg and Füssen along northern Bavaria's western edge. You'll need four or five days to explore such charming villages as Rothenburg ob der Tauber and Dinkelsbuhl. Try to avoid peak season.

Another option is to explore some of Germany's wildly romantic castles. Driving southwest of Munich, visit such fairy-tale spectacles as **Schloss Neuschwanstein,**

When to Visit

Germany has its charms any time of year, so choosing when to go depends much on your priorities. Weather-wise, the most reliable months for warm sunshine are May to September, although tourist favorites such as the Rhine Valley are usually overrun in July and August. Spring and fall are therefore often the best times for exploring Germany's historic monuments, medieval walled towns, and fairy-tale castles. A fall visit also rewards you with the chance to experience Oktoberfest, the planet's largest beer festival. In winter, the crowds thin and the Alps, Black Forest, and Harz Mountains are perfect for skiing, while the famous Christmas markets will charm the most determined scrooge with a cozy conviviality that's truly unique.

An East German border guard greets a West Berliner atop the Berlin Wall in 1989.

King Ludwig II's proudest landmark; his royal retreat of **Schloss Linderhof;** and the palatial **Schloss Herrenchiemsee,** his attempted one-up on Versailles (two days for all three castles). You can continue on to the magical Bavarian outpost of **Lindau,** some 92 miles (147 km) west on beautiful Lake Constance (two days).

As you can see, the possibilities are seemingly endless. You can make a complete holiday out of skiing or hiking in the Alps, celebrating Oktoberfest or visiting the magical Christmas markets, or focusing solely on wine-tasting . . . and the list goes on and on. ∎

History & Culture

Black, red, and gold—the German flag
Opposite: A statue of Roland,
Bremen's guardian of civic liberties,
in the city's central square

Germany Today

The prosperity and modernity built up since the end of World War II coexist almost everywhere with historic towns and villages, more castles than can be counted, and a countryside of impeccably managed farmland, deep forests, and a patchwork of nature parks and reserves. The country's cosmopolitan cities are crammed with galleries, museums, and entertainment of all kinds.

People

Few peoples are as fond of their homeland—their *Heimat*—as the Germans, and this exceptional heritage is both appreciated and lovingly maintained. Excellent cultural facilities abound, and it is rare to find an uncared-for building. Visitors flock here from all over the globe, but the country's most enthusiastic visitors are the Germans themselves, with all kinds of agreeable results: e.g., the consistently high standards in hotels, bed-and-breakfast establishments, and restaurants.

Germans love a good time, whether it be in a raucous beer hall, a cozy wine tavern, or an animated street café. To really see them at their most uninhibited, join them at one of the country's countless festivals, the most exuberant of which are Fasching in Munich and Karneval in Cologne (see pp. 158–159). Among the world's great popular folk festivals, these are the equivalent of Mardi Gras in other countries and take place in the run-up to Lent.

> Few peoples are as fond of their homeland . . . as the Germans, and this exceptional heritage is both appreciated and lovingly maintained.

Local identity is expressed in all sorts of ways. Dialects have survived longer in Germany than in many European countries: The everyday language spoken along the lower Rhine has more in common with Dutch than with the German spoken by Bavarians. The media tend to be locally based, with regional newspapers concentrating on the news that affects their particular readership. Some of the country's 1,300 breweries have achieved national prominence, but most people are perfectly happy with the beer brewed locally. With traditional ideas of nationhood debased and disgraced by the Nazis, many Germans have been inhibited about putting too much enthusiasm into anything smacking of nationalism.

Yet increasingly, many yearn to regain a modicum of pride. In 2006, Germany's hosting of the soccer World Cup surprisingly shifted views on patriotism. As the German team advanced, the colors of the national flag popped up on cars, housefronts, and the cheeks of young followers around the country.

Still, such frothy spontaneity is more the exception than the rule. A liking for order and security in personal and working life can perhaps be explained by the traumas of history, when the country's very shape seemed uncertain and there was an unthinkable burden of guilt. Germans study for their careers, often at great length, and plan them down to the final pension contribution. Correct procedures govern many aspects of life; timekeeping is meticulous; jobs are done properly and standards are defined and adhered to.

In the last few decades, there has been a reaction against what were seen as repressive, "traditional" values. Levels of tidiness and cleanliness slipped (but not too much), and people cultivated a deliberately casual manner, with the young defiantly flouting the strict standards of their elders. Germany has in consequence become a country of greater contrasts than before; smaller towns and their inhabitants still have that impeccably groomed look, while parts of the bigger cities and sections of their population almost flaunt their scruffiness.

Berliners meet at the East Side Gallery amid a colorful stretch of the Berlin Wall.

Lifestyle

Traditionally, German women were expected to devote themselves to *Kinder, Küche, Kirche* (kids, kitchen, and church), while men . . . well, many men found great satisfaction in buttoning themselves up in some sort of uniform. To be a *Beamter* (any kind of public official, from diplomat to railway man) guaranteed status and a pension.

Nowadays there is a far greater variety of roles to choose from, and Germans show great determination to make the most of them. Punks seem more outlandish here than elsewhere in Europe, squatters more militant, skinheads more deliberately repulsive. At the other end of the scale, there are probably more would-be English gentlemen in tweeds and Burberry than in England itself, and Germany is easily the biggest market in Europe for the expensive casual look in suede and leather. Those with nothing to hide (and plenty who do) opt for nudity when relaxing in urban parks as well as on the beach.

Nevertheless, German manners still tend to formality. It takes longer to get on first-name terms in Germany than in English-speaking countries, and there is more use of titles like *Herr Doktor* or *Herr Professor.* The distinction between the informal *du* ("thou") and the polite *Sie* ("you") still exists. It's good manners to wish people *"guten Tag"* and *"auf Wiedersehen."* By contrast, public behavior can sometimes seem crude and unfeeling. There is no concept of taking your turn in line, nor mutual apologies when people collide with one another on the sidewalk. At the same time, you now hear phrases like *"Schönen Abend noch*–Have a nice evening"–something that only a few years ago would have earned an uncomprehending stare.

> Concern for the environment is high on the national agenda. . . . German towns and cities have extensive networks of pedestrian-only streets, most of them models of attractive urban design.

Environmental Concerns

Concern for the environment is high on the national agenda. As well as a wonderful system of parks and open spaces (see pp. 204–205), German towns and cities have extensive networks of pedestrian-only streets, most of them models of attractive urban design, beautifully paved with natural materials and embellished with statuary and fountains. The lavish provision of bicycle paths means that cycling is a pleasure, and many town dwellers make their local trips by bike.

People here are as car-crazy as anyone, but they have made sure that virtually every destination is served by superlative public transportation. There are still trams in German towns–in fact the networks have been extended, with trams going underground in congested city centers or gliding gondola-like through the shopping streets. Getting about can be great fun, too–on no account should you miss a relaxing trip aboard a gleaming white riverboat or an exhilarating ride in a chairlift to some giddy viewpoint.

The private car remains a great German icon. On the autobahn, where the recommended speed limit is 75–85 miles an hour (110–130 kph), the car is given its head, but in town it has been tamed by severe parking restrictions.

At a national level, environmental politics are taken seriously. The Green Party entered national government in the 1990s, and although it is no longer part of the

Beer, a brass band, and good company are the essentials of Munich's Oktoberfest.

ruling coalition, it can still influence key issues. A commitment has been made to phase out nuclear power, and Germany has taken a lead in environmentally friendly forms of energy generation, notably in the use of wind and solar power. Wind farms are a prominent feature in the countryside, particularly along the coasts of the North Sea and the Baltic. Remarkably, more than 25 percent of Germany's energy needs are covered by renewables, a figure set to rise to 40 percent by 2025.

Frankfurt's sleek skyline provides a modern backdrop for the classic Old Opera House.

East Is East

Once the euphoria over the opening of the Berlin Wall in 1989 had died down, East and West Germans settled down to digest the implications of reunification. The German Democratic Republic (GDR) had collapsed, as had its former markets in the communist world, so the West German state was in effect taking over a bankrupt economy. Despite Chancellor Kohl's promises that taxes would not be increased, huge amounts of taxpayers' money are still being channeled east more than two decades later, and the eastern industrial landscape blossoms only in places.

In the East, or what are referred to as *Die neuen Länder* (the New States), Germany's unemployment problem is particularly severe, although its true extent is masked by subsidies and job creation schemes. Some Easterners (slightingly referred to by Westerners as *Ossis*, from *Ostdeutsche*, meaning East Germans) feel that their country has become a kind of colony of West Germany. Today the infrastructure almost matches that of the West, and visitors can be sure of finding most of the services and facilities they are used to. But there are still crumbling buildings (sometimes because their ownership is disputed between their Eastern occupants and Western claimants), and whole sections of some towns have been abandoned as the population has moved away westward, in search of jobs.

Some Germans feel that, although the Berlin Wall has physically disappeared, it is more present than ever in people's minds. Certainly the *Wessi* (the Easterners' disparaging term for West Germans, or *Westdeutsche*) and Ossi stereotypes are well established. Easterners think of Wessis as arrogant, spoiled, self-centered, materialistic, and patronizing, while many Westerners feel that Ossis are passive, lack initiative, and grumble instead of being grateful for all the help they have received. After living under a system that, oppressive as it was, provided security and predictability, many Easterners have found it difficult to adapt to Western ways, particularly in an era when social welfare systems are in crisis and individual ambition and willingness to take on responsibility are crucial. It may be that true reunification will only take place once the older generation has passed away.

Government & Politics

Under Allied supervision, the modern German state was given a bulwark of democratic checks and balances that, with the Cold War on the horizon, safely embedded the country into NATO defense structures. Outside the government in Bonn, the capital from 1949 to 1990, key state institutions were dotted around the country to thwart power grabs. The country was run under Basic Law, a quasi-constitution meant to be replaced when Germany was reunited. A slightly modified Basic Law remains in force today, suggesting how robust the original blueprint was.

The Bundestag, the key lower house of the Federal Parliament, is dominated by the CDU/CSU (Conservatives) and the SPD (Socialists). In 2005, they joined forces in a "grand coalition" after Angela Merkel, an Easterner and former physicist, narrowly defeated Gerhard Schröder to become Germany's first female chancellor. Her government has won respect abroad, especially for her deft diplomatic footwork in dealings with Germany's NATO and EU partners. At home, critics have been less generous, citing stagnation in health, labor and tax reforms as well as Germany's hefty bill incurred by the Euro crisis. Many voters have migrated to the Greens and the left-wing Die Linke party. Elections in 2013 returned Merkel to power, although the CDU/CSU again fell short of an absolute majority and renewed their pact with the SPD.

For many years, West Germany was regarded as an economic giant and a political pygmy, inhibited about playing a decisive role in the international arena. It underwent moral agonies about deploying its troops beyond its borders, refusing altogether in the Gulf War of 1991. But in 1999, Bundeswehr tanks were in the vanguard of the NATO formations rolling into Kosovo. Germany did not back the U.S.-led invasion of Iraq but has deployed forces to Afghanistan, the Horn of Africa, and Bosnia-Herzegovina.

The Land

Covering a total area of 137,899 square miles (357,104 sq km), Germany is endowed with the fine natural frontiers of the North and Baltic Seas to the north and the Bavarian

Place-names

These German words often occur in place-names:

Au(e)	meadow or pasture
Bach	creek
Bad	bath
Berg	mountain
Burg	castle or fortress
Dorf	village
Feld	field
Meer	sea or lake
Palast	palace
Rathaus	town hall
Schloss	castle, palace, or manor house
See	lake
Stadt	town
Tor	gate

Alps to the south. To east and west, there are few such barriers. The North European Plain extends into Germany from Holland and continues all the way across the north of the country into Poland. The highlands around the border with the Czech Republic look formidable on the map, but they are easily penetrated and have never inhibited movement and exchange. In the west, upland massifs continue into Belgium and Luxembourg, while the valley of the Upper Rhine is shared with France.

Northern Plain & Coastlands: Like much of eastern Germany, the coastlands facing the Baltic were shaped in the last Ice Age, although the broad and shallow inlets known as *Bodden* were created in the post-glacial period. Long sandy beaches backed by dunes have made it an important vacation area, including the island of Rügen with its pristine chalk cliffs. Inland, Germany's largest lakeland is now Müritz National Park. Upstream from Berlin the Spree River divides into a multitude of tree-shaded streams, and people still get around the Spreewald in flat-bottom boats.

Fjords provide natural harbors for fishing ports and seaside resorts on the east coast of Schleswig-Holstein, while the exposed west coast and the islands of Lower Saxony boast sandy beaches and dunes, a bracing climate, and sunshine. Grand rivers such as

In the cool green jungle of the Bavarian Forest near Waldkirchen

EXPERIENCE: Taking a Chilly Cure

A pioneer in alternative therapy, the Bavarian priest Sebastian Kneipp (1821–1897) forever highlighted the link between ice-cold water and healthy circulation. After contracting tuberculosis in 1849, Kneipp banished the sickness with cold-water baths in the Danube. In the years that followed, and despite attempts by the authorities to ban his methods, he drew a mass audience, especially after successfully healing victims of a cholera outbreak in 1854. His seminars in the Bavarian town of Wörishofen, one of the earliest spa resorts, attracted thousands of eager listeners. By the early 1890s, word of the miraculous Kneipp method had spread throughout Europe, and he was invited to Rome to treat the pope.

Today, with more than 600 Kneipp associations in Germany, his fame appears undiminished. In southern forests you will find the characteristically frigid wading pools where hikers, pants legs rolled up, can splash through an invigorating circuit. **The Kneipp Association** (Adolf-Scholz-Allee 6–8, Bad Wörishofen, tel 08247 30 02 102, kneippworldwide.eu) helps you locate facilities throughout Germany.

the Elbe, Weser, and Ems reach the sea in broad estuaries, and all have given rise to harbor cities, of which Hamburg is the greatest.

Inland from the North Sea, the Münsterland is famous for its array of moated castles and country houses, while the rolling Lüneburger Heide (Lüneburg Heath) is one of Europe's most extensive heathlands. To the west, Germany's greatest water highway, the Rhine, rolls majestically toward Holland, where it reaches the sea in multiple outlets.

Central Uplands & Valleys: A series of massifs divided by river valleys stretches across the middle of Germany. Farming has shaped some of the landscape, but the main crop is trees. This is the heartland of the German forest, an important part of German life and the setting for many tales and legends. As the land rises, oak gives way to beech, then to spruce and fir. Occasionally there are glorious open summits like the Brocken (3,744 feet/1,141 m) in the Harz Mountains, the Feldberg (4,899 feet/1,493 m) in the Black Forest, and the Arber (4,777 feet/1,456 m) in the Bavarian Forest. Pleasure boats are ideal for exploring the river valleys, above all the Rhine Gorge, where the river flows swiftly beneath vineyards and a succession of crag-top castles. Farther upstream, the Rhine flows in a broad rift valley, bounded by the Odenwald and Black Forest to the east and to the west by parallel ranges, the Palatine Forest in Germany and the Vosges Mountains in France.

In the 19th century the presence of coal in the valley of the River Ruhr gave rise to Germany's greatest industrial area, but medieval miners had exploited minerals in the Ore Mountains (Erzgebirge) in Saxony long before. The Erzgebirge continue eastward into Saxon Switzerland (Sächsische Schweiz), a striking landscape of sandstone cliffs and columns cut through by the Elbe upstream of Saxony's capital, Dresden. The Bavarian Forest and the Bohemian Forest between the Danube and the Czech border possess that rarity in Europe, true primeval forest, forming the basis for a national park.

Alpine Lands: Germany possesses only a fraction of the Alps, but they make a formidable, north-facing wall, which reaches its highest point in the summit of the

Zugspitze (9,718 feet/2,962 m), overlooking the town of Garmisch-Partenkirchen, one of many popular mountain resorts. From the Alps, rivers like the Lech and the Isar hurry down toward the Danube. Closer to Salzburg than to Munich, the Berchtesgadener Land runs deep into Austria, and the Königssee area contains some of the most glorious Alpine scenery anywhere, including the country's second highest peak, the Watzmann (8,901 feet/2,713 m). At their western extremity in Bavaria, the Alps descend to Germany's largest lake, Lake Constance (the Bodensee), shared with Switzerland and Austria. Here, a warm climate encourages orchards and vineyards.

Food & Drink

German food is wholesome and satisfying, if a bit on the heavy side. The flair of French or Italian cuisine may be lacking, but food is usually prepared with good ingredients. Great strides are being made with modern twists on traditional favorites such as *sauerbraten* (marinated pot roast).

Hearty breakfasts get the day off to a good start. There's usually a choice of cheeses, cold meats, and hard-boiled eggs, as well as marmalades, jams, and honey, all of which go well with a wonderful selection of breads, ranging from crisp white rolls to tangy rye bread or gloriously rich and heavy pumpernickel. Fruit and cereals are supplemented by yogurt and creamy *Quark* (curd cheese). Lunch is often the principal meal of the day, with soup and a main course, while the evening meal, if eaten at home, may be a modest affair more like breakfast. *Kaffee und Kuchen* (coffee and cakes) is a German institution, offered in smart patisseries cum coffee shops, rather like afternoon tea in the U.K.

Vegetarianism has made some progress in recent years, but this is still a nation of meat-eaters. Beef, game, and poultry all appear on the menu, but the king of the kitchen remains the pig. Pork is served in many forms, of which the most ubiquitous is the *Schnitzel,* a slice of lean meat in bread crumbs or served with a sauce. Pork is the main ingredient in many a *Wurst* (sausage); made from pork, bacon fat, and spices, frankfurters have conquered the world. *Bockwurst* is similar, but more interesting smaller sausages come from Nuremberg (served several at a time on sauerkraut). Thuringian sausages are bloodred, and Munich's are white, made from veal. *Bratwurst* is the generic name for coarse-textured sausages, fried rather than boiled.

Restaurant Lingo

I'd like to reserve a table for ... people.
  Ich möchte einen Tisch für ... Personen reservieren.
A table for ... please.
  Einen Tisch für ... bitte.
I'd like to order. *Ich möchte bestellen.*
We'd like something to drink.
  Wir möchten etwas trinken.
Do you have a menu in English?
  Haben Sie eine Speisekarte auf Englisch?
What do you recommend?
  Was empfehlen Sie?
I'm a vegetarian. *Ich bin Vegetarier.*
I can't eat sugar/wheat/dairy/nuts.
  Ich vertrage keinen Zucker/Weizen/ keine Milchprodukte/Nüsse.
The bill, please. *Die Rechnung, bitte.*
(See also Menu Reader, p. 390.)

As for vegetables, the most common are cabbage (white or red) and potatoes. The latter come in all forms, from purée to pancake, but the best are *Bratkartoffeln,* sautéed with bacon cubes and onion. In southwestern Germany potatoes give way to *Spätzle,*

Salt-studded pretzels, onion bread, and cheese straws are offered for sale at a kiosk.

chewy noodles, or dumplings. The country's favorite vegetable is asparagus, fat and pale; whole regions cultivate it, and the harvest season (in May) is keenly anticipated.

Beer & Wine: Since 1516 the composition of German beer has been governed by the Reinheitsgebot (Purity Law), which forbids the use of ingredients other than hops, malt, yeast, barley, and water. Most of the country's myriad breweries turn out a lager-type product and usually a specialty or two. *Alt*, not unlike British bitter, is drunk in Düsseldorf and *Kölsch* in Cologne. Beers such as the famous Dortmunder from the Ruhr industrial area, originally intended to slake the thirst of hard-working miners, tend to be stronger than their equivalents in Bavaria. Bavarian breweries produce seasonal beers such as *Märzenbier* (see sidebar p. 273), while in Berlin a summer treat is *Berliner Weisse*, a pale brew with a shot of acidic fruit juice.

The reputation of German wine has improved in recent years as a taste for drier, subtler wines has emerged. The principal grape is the versatile Riesling, although varieties such as Müller-Thurgau, Silvaner, Grauburgunder (Pinot Gris), and Weissburgunder (Pinot Blanc) also feature. Many German wines are grown on terraces chiseled out of the steep slopes rising from the Rhine and its tributaries. But the greatest quantities come from the flat, sunny countryside of Rhine-Hessen and the Palatinate. In eastern Germany, the valley of the Elbe around Dresden has a long wine-making tradition. Most German wine is white, but there are good reds too. The highest quality wine is labeled *Qualitätswein*, then comes *Landwein*, and finally *Tafelwein*, which is basic table wine. German sparkling wine, *Sekt*, should not be sniffed at, but quaffed! And there are excellent spirits, ranging from ginlike *Steinhäger* in the north to good grape brandy along the Rhine (Asbach) and fiery fruit brandies *(Kirschwasser, Himbeergeist)* in orchard country. ■

History of Germany

Today's Germany seems a fixed and stable state. Yet historically the country's identity, its governance, and its borders have been subject to constant change. Even today, many German speakers live in Austria, Switzerland, Alsace in France, and Silesia in Poland, echoing the fragmentation that has characterized much of the country's history since the Romans colonized "Germania."

Germans & Romans

The area we now call Germany was settled in prehistoric times. The jawbone of *Homo heidelbergensis*, unearthed near the south German city of Heidelberg, is thought to be nearly 400,000 years old, and Neanderthal Man is named after the Neander Valley near Düsseldorf, where the first remains of this early form of *Homo sapiens* were found in 1856. These discoveries have greatly contributed to our understanding of the early evolution of the human race. In the last millennium B.C., the area was settled by Celtic peoples. They left few traces, although remains of their lakeside stilt dwellings survive on the shores of Lake Constance.

The life of the Celts was increasingly disrupted by the incursions of restless Germanic tribes closing in on them from the east and north. These ancestors of today's Germans eventually came up against the power of a Rome expanding its empire eastward from conquered Celtic Gaul (today's France). In 58 B.C., Julius Caesar checked an attempt by Ariovist, leader of the Swabians, to move into Alsace and flung his forces back across the Rhine. There Caesar halted his legions, believing the land across the river to be nothing more than barren forests. Later expeditions did cross the Rhine, marching as far east as the Elbe. All seemed set for the incorporation of Germania into the Roman Empire, when, in A.D. 9, three of Rome's crack legions were annihilated at the Battle of Teutoburg Forest by warriors led by Arminius ("Hermann" to much later Germans looking for national heroes). The Romans gave up their attempts at subjugating the lands beyond the Rhine and settled for the Romanization of the western and southern parts of the country.

Within the area now protected by the *limes,* a continuous line of defenses roughly following the course of the Rhine and Danube, the Romans made themselves at home. Cities, lesser towns,

> Neanderthal Man is named after the Neander Valley near Düsseldorf, where the first remains of this early form of *Homo sapiens* were found in 1856.

and military bases arose, some of which survive today, including Cologne ("Colonia"), Augsburg, named after Emperor Augustus, and Trier (originally Augusta Treverorum), also honoring the name of Augustus and rich in Roman remains.

In 275, Trier was sacked by Germanic invaders, but it recovered, becoming the capital of the reorganized Western Empire and, under Emperor Constantine, a great center of Christianity. But the end of the empire was approaching; great movements of people in eastern Europe put pressure on the always restless Germans, and during the fifth century various groups moved westward, overwhelming the already weakened Roman defenses.

The Romans departed and their empire collapsed, but they left a heritage that influenced much of the country's subsequent history. Christianity consolidated itself,

The greatest monument of Roman Germania is the Porta Nigra at Trier.

and urban life continued. Even today, the previously occupied lands along the Rhine have a distinct identity, with a joie de vivre not always present elsewhere.

Imperial Revival

Known in German as the *Völkerwanderung* ("migration of the peoples"), the period following the demise of the Roman Empire, from the fourth to the early seventh century A.D., saw a complex redistribution of the populations of Europe. The Franks, who settled in the land around the lower Rhine and Moselle Rivers with Aachen as their base, became increasingly powerful.

Their greatest leader, Charlemagne—Charles the Great— became king of the Franks in 768. On Christmas Day in 800, he was crowned emperor in Rome, in keeping with his view of himself and his realm as successors to the Romans. Both ruthless and enlightened, he subjugated enemies on all sides and promoted literacy, learning, and the arts. His greatest visible monument is his cathedral at Aachen.

After Charlemagne's death, his kingdom was split into three parts, the basis for what were later to become separate French and German states. Central authority continued to diminish, and it was left to local lords to attempt to maintain order and fend off attacks from Vikings and Magyars. From their successes, great dukedoms developed such as Saxony, Franconia, Bavaria, and Swabia. Duke Henry of Saxony, known as Henry the Fowler, succeeded in placating the other dukes and restoring a degree of unity to the realm.

Charlemagne's son Otto, known as "the Great," arranged a glittering ceremony for his coronation as king of Germany in Aachen in 936, consciously presenting himself as heir to Charlemagne. Otto's greatest achievement was finally to eliminate the threat to European stability posed by the marauding Magyars from the east, routing them at the Lechfeld

A reliquary bust from the Treasury in Aachen Cathedral expresses the power and prestige of Emperor Charlemagne.

near Augsburg. In 962, Otto was crowned emperor by the pope in Rome; this union of German and imperial crowns was to persist for hundreds of years, causing endless strife, since German kings constantly had to intervene in the affairs of Italy and contend with the temporal and spiritual power of popes.

Eastward Moves

In the early years of the second millennium, emperors also had to keep an eye on the growing power of the nobility and of bishops who were territorial lords as well as church leaders. In 1077 this balancing act led Emperor Henry IV into a bizarre act of humiliation. With his authority undermined by unrest among the German princes, and fearful that Pope Gregory VII would assert his power in

Germany, he traveled to the castle of Canossa in Italy. Here, dressed in nothing but a hair shirt, he humbly waited until granted an audience with the pope, then prostrated himself, his arms held out in the form of a cross. Satisfied, Gregory granted him absolution and confirmed his authority, although this did little to prevent further conflicts. Imperial power and prestige were constantly challenged by ambitious rulers.

Emperor Frederick I, who ruled from 1152 to 1190, was the outstanding member of an outstanding dynasty, the Hohenstaufens. His glittering court with its poets and troubadours—the eloquent *Minnesänger*—was the high point of medieval chivalry. Despite the continuing political fragmentation of Germany and the lack of a central bureaucracy and armed forces, the empire persisted, becoming known toward the end of the Middle Ages as the Holy Roman Empire of the German Nation.

In principle, the office of German king and emperor was not hereditary. Selection was in the hands of seven Electors, rulers of some of the most important German states, among them the archbishoprics of Trier, Mainz, and Cologne. But eventually the office of emperor became a more or less hereditary possession of the Habsburg dynasty, rulers for considerable periods of time not only of Austria but also of other German provinces, the Netherlands, and Spain. Again, this meant that emperors could often focus only part of their energies on German affairs, a constant temptation for local rulers to assert themselves against imperial authority.

> **Frederick I, who ruled from 1152 to 1190, was the outstanding member of an outstanding dynasty, the Hohenstaufens. His glittering court with its poets and troubadours ... was the high point of medieval chivalry.**

The Reformation

The 95 Theses nailed to the door of Wittenberg church by the young monk Martin Luther in 1517 set in motion a train of events that forever changed the political and spiritual landscape of Europe (see sidebar p. 28). The Church resisted calls for change, preferring to send reformers like Jan Huss to the stake than take heed of his message. Huss was put to death at Konstanz in 1415. Luther was excommunicated, and the Church issued dire threats against anyone coming to his aid. But more was at stake than the freedom of a monk to defy pope and emperor. Many German rulers found his teachings a convenient peg on which to hang their own political ambitions. After his excommunication, Luther was apprehended by followers of the Elector of Saxony and spent a year translating the Bible into vernacular German.

In the years that followed, one peasant uprising after another arose, although all were more or less brutally suppressed. The 1555 Peace of Augsburg was in effect an agreement to disagree, and the principle of *"cuius regio, eius religio"* was adopted, allowing the ruler of a territory to determine its religious confession without outside interference. This still holds today, despite the population upheavals of the 20th century, with central and eastern Germany predominantly Protestant, Bavaria and the Rhineland mostly Catholic.

Luther & the Reformation

It seems unlikely that Martin Luther could have envisioned the religious and European political upheaval that ensued when he nailed the 95 Theses to the door of Wittenberg church in 1517.

Well before Luther, some had condemned the worldliness of popes and prelates and attempted to return the Church to the people, cut through excessive ceremony, and assert the original teachings of the Bible. A particularly flagrant abuse was the sale of indulgences, fundamentally a device for extracting funds from credulous congregations in order to finance the political ambitions of high churchmen.

In 1521, Luther was summoned to the imperial Diet meeting at the city of Worms, where he was condemned and excommunicated. Spirited off to Wartburg Castle, high above the town of Eisenach, Luther spent the best part of a year in disguise, devoting himself to translating the Bible into a form of German that could be understood by everyone, thereby helping lay the foundations of modern German.

In the turbulent years that followed, religious sects rose and subsided. Well before the middle of the 16th century, many princes and free cities had adopted Lutheranism, and attempts by Emperor Charles V to crush the Reformation ended in compromise: the 1555 Peace of Augsburg, which allowed the ruler of any given territory the right of religious self-determination.

Thirty Years of War

Between 1618 and 1648, Central Europe was the theater of a complex sequence of conflicts that came to be called the Thirty Years War, often involving external powers like France and Sweden. It was precipitated by the famous incident called the Defenestration of Prague, when Protestant noblemen, enraged by the emperor's attack on their privileges, threw two of his representatives from the windows of Prague Castle. Imperial revenge followed in 1621, when the forces of the Bohemian nobles were routed by the emperor's army at the Battle of the White Mountain outside Prague. There was fighting from one end of Germany to the other, with armies often composed of rapacious mercenaries whose prime interest was in plunder. Whole cities like Magdeburg were wiped out, peasants fled the land, harvests went uncollected, and epidemics raged. After the Peace of Westphalia in 1648, the German lands slowly recovered, but in economic terms had now fallen way behind countries like France and England. The Peace of Westphalia confirmed the fragmented political map of Germany and allowed territorial rulers much more sovereignty, further limiting the powers of the emperor. Alsace was ceded to France, parts of the Baltic coast to Sweden.

Absolutism & Enlightenment

In the late 17th century and throughout the 18th, the key political actors in Germany were the rulers of the larger states, above all the kings of Prussia. Following the example of France, and impressed by the ruling style of the Sun King Louis XIV, they reorganized their realms on absolutist lines, centralizing power, governing through bureaucracies, and creating standing armies. Rulers often abandoned their cramped medieval castles and built themselves spacious baroque palaces set in formal gardens. Some of the most ambitious and extravagant rulers were powerful churchmen, so-called prince-bishops, such as the Schönborn dynasty, which held sway from its sumptuous Residenz in Würzburg. Many princes strove to enhance their prestige by cultivating whatever intellectual, artistic, and musical talent was available. One of the greatest prizes was the presence of French writer and thinker Voltaire, whose wit and erudition graced several courts, notably the Potsdam of Frederick the Great of Prussia. Use of the French language was de rigueur in all the best circles. Frederick was an exceptionally cultured man, his talent as a flutist celebrated in a famous 19th-century painting by Adolf von Menzel. Johann Sebastian Bach's "Musical Offering" was based on a theme given him by the king, but the great composer (see p. 45) spent most of his creative life as the director of music of one of the free cities, Leipzig, where his employer was no king but a town council.

Frederick the Great was a Hohenzollern, the family that had built up the state of Prussia, centered on Brandenburg and the then small city of Berlin. Relatively liberal at home, Prussia pursued an aggressive foreign policy, regularly expanding its territory, particularly at the expense of its great rival Austria, from whom it took the province of Silesia after the Seven Years War (1756–1763). The other German states watched the rise of Prussia with apprehension, perhaps sensing that in the next century it would be

The destruction of the city of Magdeburg by imperial troops led by Count Tilly in 1632

this militaristic state that would lead the struggle for German unity and impose its style on what was still a highly fragmented country.

Revolutions & Restorations

The outburst of energy released by the French Revolution of 1789 soon led to France's confrontation with Germany, and by 1794 all of the country west of the Rhine was in French hands. Napoleon pushed French conquests farther still, eventually bringing the whole of Germany into a continental system dominated by France and run on French lines. Many much-needed reforms were introduced, including partial emancipation of the Jews. The political map of Germany was tidied up: Church states were abolished, while others such as Baden and Bavaria, which both became kingdoms, were greatly extended. In 1806 that long-lived but now meaningless institution, the Holy Roman Empire, was finally laid to rest.

German unification was eventually achieved, not through rational discussion . . . but through the ruthless diplomacy and the judicious use of force favored by Otto von Bismarck.

Resentment at foreign domination fanned patriotic feelings. In the spring of 1813, anti-French rioting broke out all over Germany; in October, at the so-called Battle of the Nations outside Leipzig, the allied armies of Russia, Austria, and a revived Prussia defeated Napoleon's army. But there was to be no new order in Central Europe. The victorious powers meeting at the Congress of Vienna in 1814–1815 were determined to forestall any further possibilities of revolution. Although much of the Napoleonic reorganization of Germany remained in place, Russia, Prussia, and Austria combined to reinstate authoritarian regimes. Nevertheless, disturbances and protests took place. At a great festival at Wartburg Castle in 1817, students first raised the black, red, and gold banner, later to become the national flag. It was flown again at a rally attended by 30,000 at Hambach Castle in the Palatinate, where passionate speeches were made demanding democracy and national unity. In 1848, a year of revolution throughout Europe, it looked as if the old order might at last crumble. Fearful governments made significant concessions, and a national parliament met in St. Paul's Church in Frankfurt (see sidebar p. 200). The conservative forces finally regrouped, dismissed the parliament, and ruthlessly put down further protests.

Unification Prussian Style

German unification was eventually achieved, not through rational discussion and with the participation of all interested parties, but through the ruthless diplomacy and judicious use of force favored by Otto von Bismarck (see sidebar opposite). The new Kaiser, Wilhelm I, thought it would mean the end of the Prussian monarchy, and many of the other German rulers were fearful for their position; the consent of King Ludwig II of Bavaria had to be bought with a huge bribe. Nevertheless, Germany as a whole was filled with nationalistic euphoria, and the next few years saw an explosion of economic activity; industry flourished, there was a building boom, and Germany soon had Europe's most

Bismarck's Legacy

More than any other single figure, Otto von Bismarck (1815–1898) is credited with the unification of Germany. Appointed chancellor of Prussia in 1862, Bismarck used Austria to help him acquire Schleswig-Holstein, then in 1866 turned on his ally. The victory of the Prussian army over the Austrians at the Battle of Königgrätz (Sadova) in Bohemia finally closed the door on potential Austrian interference in German affairs and meant that Prussia alone would lead Germany to unity. In 1870 the south German states honored the alliances with Prussia into which they had been coerced and joined in the Franco-Prussian War, which ended with a resounding German victory. France was forced to pay a huge indemnity, and the largely German-speaking provinces of Alsace and Lorraine, which had been part of France since the 17th century, were incorporated into what was now known as the Second Reich (the Holy Roman Empire having constituted the First Reich). On January 18, 1871, the king of Prussia was proclaimed German emperor. Bismarck became his "Iron Chancellor," brokering further deals between European powers and overseeing the founding of one of the world's first national health care schemes—ironically, as the elite-minded Prussian was an avowed antisocialist.

extensive rail network. Germany caught up and overtook Britain in coal and steel production and inaugurated a second industrial revolution with its innovative electrical and chemical industries. Social welfare provision included unemployment and sickness benefits and was maintained at a high level, partly to preempt the emerging socialist movement, dominated by the Social Democratic Party, which maintained a constant presence in the Reichstag (parliament). But the Reichstag's powers were few; policy was made first by Bismarck, then after his dramatic dismissal in 1890, by Kaiser Wilhelm II and the small clique around him, which increasingly consisted of military men.

The Great War

Germany came late to the "scramble for Africa," and its colonial aspirations irritated its rivals Britain and France, while its determination to build a naval force could only be interpreted as a deliberate provocation. During the first years of the 20th century, the great European powers became more and more suspicious of each other's intentions and sought security by piling up armaments. When in June 1914 the Austrian heir to the throne, Archduke Franz Ferdinand, was assassinated at Sarajevo by a Serbian student, Germany rashly encouraged Austria to settle scores with her unruly Serbian neighbor. Europe's interlocking alliances were activated, with Germany and Austria facing Russia, France, and Great Britain. When the long-prepared knockout blow against France failed to work, Germany could not, in the long run, hope to survive the attrition of the trench warfare that ensued, least of all once the United States, provoked by reckless submarine attacks on its shipping, had entered the fray with its limitless material resources and reserves of manpower. By late summer 1918, the German military leadership realized the war was lost, but it cleverly managed to evade blame by shifting responsibility onto a civilian government that had requested an armistice.

German troops leave the trenches in the ill-fated final offensive of World War I.

Weimar Interlude

Germany's new republican government—Kaiser Wilhelm II had abdicated and fled to Holland—met initially in Weimar because of revolutionary disturbances in Berlin. Its first task was to accept the harsh terms of the Versailles peace settlement: admission of war guilt, onerous reparations, the occupation of the Rhineland, the return of Alsace and Lorraine to France, and the loss of parts of Prussia in order to give Poland a corridor to the Baltic. Its acceptance was construed by many as treachery. The government also had to contend in 1923 with hyperinflation, which destroyed the savings of millions of middle-class people, and with French occupation of the Ruhr industrial area. But cultural life flourished, freed from the stifling atmosphere of the Second Reich, and Berlin's more than colorful nightlife drew in cosmopolitans from all over Europe. For a few short years in the late 1920s there was a degree of prosperity, while social reforms seemed to be laying the foundation for a more hopeful future. But the Weimar Republic was dealt a fatal blow by the Great Depression starting in 1929. By 1932 there were six million unemployed, and the German National Socialist Workers' Party (the Nazis) was the biggest party in the Reichstag. After a second, inconclusive round of elections in 1932, the aging President Hindenburg was persuaded to make Adolf Hitler chancellor to lead a coalition government. Hitler was sworn in on January 30, 1933.

The Third Reich & World War II

On the night of February 27, 1933, the Reichstag was burned down, supposedly by a Dutch communist, but possibly by Nazi storm troopers. Hitler then had an excuse to imprison his opponents, and he consolidated his power in March elections. He had an uncanny ability to tap into the fears, frustrations, and ambitions of all sorts of Germans and a masterly understanding of how to exploit them. Apart from the excluded Jews and other "undesirables," there was something for everyone in the Nazi grab bag. Industrialists profited from a revived economy and a rearmament that also kept the military on Hitler's side. Provided they abandoned any allegiance to communism, workers no longer feared unemployment. The middle classes had to tighten their belts but no longer feared inflation, while many small businessmen rejoiced at the elimination of Jewish competition. Once Hitler had started on his string of foreign policy successes, beginning with the reoccupation of the Rhineland in 1936, nearly all Germans rejoiced that the shame of defeat and the humiliation of Versailles were being overcome. It seemed to many that the nationalist dreams of the 19th century were coming dramatically true. Opponents were crushed or fled abroad, and the army, the sole center of power that could have stopped Hitler, was reluctant to act.

In 1939, Britain and France declared war on Germany in response to the latter's invasion of Poland. Enthusiasm for war was not unbounded, but as one Blitzkrieg victory succeeded another, many Germans felt that Hitler was invincible. Doubts came with the invasion of the Soviet Union in June 1941 and with the entry of the United States into the war later that year. They were confirmed by the disaster at Stalingrad in January 1943, but by then there seemed no way out, particularly when the Allies declared their policy of unconditional surrender. Nevertheless, resistance elements within the army went ahead with their plans to assassinate Hitler, and in July 1944 nearly succeeded. But Hitler survived, and Germany fought on for nearly another year, during which time more physical destruction took place than during all the previous years of war. Some 15 million Germans either fled or were expelled from lands where many of them had lived for generations—from Poland, Hungary, Yugoslavia, Czechoslovakia—and from those parts of Germany proper which now passed into other hands: East Prussia, Silesia, most of Pomerania.

Recovery & Division

Physically devastated, half-starved, shivering in terrible postwar winters, full of displaced people, utterly demoralized and discredited, and ruled by foreign armies, Germany seemed as if it might never revive.

At the end of the war, the country was formally divided into separate zones of occupation. The British, American, and French zones became the Bundesrepublik Deutschland (Federal Republic of Germany), lifted out of its postwar misery by an ingenious currency reform that destroyed the black market and cleared the way for the *Wirtschaftswunder* ("economic miracle") that made the country one of the wealthiest nations of the Western world. The Soviet zone became the Deutsche Demokratische Republik or DDR (German Democratic Republic or GDR). This was run on Soviet lines by the Socialist Unity Party, a merger forced on the Social Democratic Party by its once bitter rival the Communists.

> [After World War II] the country was formally divided into separate zones of occupation. . . . Germany became the principal theater of the Cold War.

Germany became the principal theater of the Cold War. By 1948, the fragile alliance between the Western powers and the Soviet Union had completely collapsed. In May of that year, the Soviet Union blockaded all routes into Berlin by rail, road, and waterway. The decision was eventually made to defy the one-time ally by flying essential supplies into the western sectors of Berlin. Over the following months British and American

On May 30, 1942, waves of British bombers caused massive damage to Cologne.

aircraft brought in almost 2.5 million tons of supplies, including vast quantities of coal. Nearly a year later the Soviets abandoned the blockade. The Berlin airlift marked a turning point in the Cold War and in a short space of time had transformed Western perceptions of Berlin from Nazi capital to outpost of freedom.

Despite remarkable progress in some areas—low rents, lavish social provision, guaranteed employment—the GDR could only ever command limited allegiance from its population. By 1961, some three million of its citizens had left for the West, passing through what was still a permeable frontier. The construction of the Berlin Wall in that year was a desperate measure, a reaction to the exodus that was crippling the country's economy.

From Division to Reunification

The GDR liked to proclaim that it was on the way to becoming one of the world's leading industrial powers, but its triumphs were based on careful manipulation of statistics, and its industries mainly produced goods that only captive consumers could be persuaded to buy, like the bone-shaking and polluting little Trabant automobile In reality, like its patron the Soviet Union, it was falling further and further behind the West. When Mikhail Gorbachev began to relax the iron certainties of the Soviet system in the late 1980s, General Secretary Erich Honecker thought that the GDR could carry on regardless, but once Soviet support

was removed, the regime started to collapse. In 1989, popular pressure built up, and eventually hundreds of thousands filled the streets demanding change.

Die Wende & Beyond

Meaning "the change" or "the turning point," *die Wende* is the term Germans use to describe the momentous events of 1989–1990 that led to the reunification of their country. A united Germany was not the inevitable outcome of the collapse of the hard-line Communist regime in the GDR; many urged a lengthy transition period while the country digested the implications of its newly found freedom.

The opening of the Berlin Wall on November 9, 1989, was an event of huge symbolic significance, yet it represented only one stage in the slow-motion collapse of East Germany. Many members of the Communist leadership thought the dismissal of figures such as General Secretary Honecker and the implementation of reforms would preserve the shape of the regime. And once the hated barrier of the Wall had been breached, far from fleeing, the majority of East Germans were content to take day trips to the West, do some shopping, and return home. But as details emerged of the extent of *Stasi* (secret police) surveillance and control and of the corruption and privilege of the regime and its servants, more and more Easterners looked to the West for salvation.

Chancellor Helmut Kohl of the Federal Republic quickly understood their mood, and in December declared to a huge crowd in Dresden: "My goal ... is the unity of the nation!" All the government of the GDR could do was to prepare for its first free elections, paving the way for reunification in 1990. Nearly three decades of division ended almost overnight.

Despite the huge financial burdens of unity, today's Germany continues to reap the benefits of sociopolitical stability and its performance as an *Exportmeister*. The country has emerged from the global financial crisis in surprisingly fine fettle, underscoring its de facto economic leadership of the Eurozone. But it still shies away from taking the lead politically on the world stage, a legacy of its Nazi past. Despite a history that is anything but ordinary, recent change has brought Germany a step closer to an elusive goal: social and political normalcy. ∎

> ## Top Five German History Books
>
> **The Roman Empire and Its Germanic Peoples** by Herwig Wolfram and Thomas Dunlap (1997). Spans five centuries of Germanic migrations and the roots of Roman rule.
>
> **The German Empire 1871–1918** by Hans-Ulrich Wehler (1985). A seminal work covering Bismarck to the Weimar Republic.
>
> **A Train of Powder** by Rebecca West (1955). One of the best volumes on the Nuremberg trials.
>
> **Berlin and the Wall** by Ann Tusa (1996). A gripping saga about the Cold War, the Wall, and its effects on the city's people.
>
> **Stasiland** by Anna Funder (2003). Interviews with former Stasi agents with insights into their post-GDR lives.

The Arts

Germany's artistic contributions include sumptuous baroque and rococo palaces and churches of the 17th and 18th centuries, which mark a high point in German architecture, and the music of Bach and Beethoven, while writers like Goethe and Schiller were at the forefront of the Classical and Romantic movements. The early 20th century saw an explosion of artistic talent.

Architecture in Germany

Architectural influences from other countries abound throughout Germany, France's Gothic and Italy's Renaissance revival styles in particular. But Germany has contributed to the world's architectural scene too, most notably with modernism in the early 20th century. Also prevalent in Germany is a rich tradition of vernacular architecture, apparent in the unique local styles of farmsteads and town houses in old German

The late 19th-century Berliner Dom is a salute to the Italian High Renaissance.

villages. Wooden frameworks were common, since timber has historically been more available than good building stone. One recognizable trait you'll see throughout Germany's villages are the carved wooden decorations on houses.

Carolingian to Romanesque: The Romans erected town walls, baths, villas, and places of worship, but the story of German building really begins around A.D. 790 with the construction of the Palatinate chapel, the Münster, at Aachen (see pp. 160–161) by Emperor Charlemagne. This 16-sided, stone-built structure with a central octagon and rounded arches was inspired by the Byzantine church of San Vitale in Ravenna, Italy, but Charlemagne's edifice is bolder and simpler. Part of a great imperial palace (Kaiserpfalz), long since destroyed, it was one of several used by Charlemagne's court. The chapel at Aachen served as a model for other churches in Carolingian style, of which parts have survived in the minster at Essen (see pp. 167–168) and the monastery church of St. Peter in Bad Wimpfen (see p. 327). A characteristic feature of early churches was the westwork,

a fortress-like entrance vestibule with a chapel above; there is a fine example on Reichenau Island in Lake Constance (see pp. 340–342).

Architecture of greater ambition and complexity appeared in the revived empire after the tenth century, of which the outstanding example is St. Michael's Church at Hildesheim (see p. 144), built between 1001 and 1033, a richly satisfying composition of simple geometrical forms: semicircular apses at both ends, two square central towers, and a quarter of cylindrical staircase towers. The later flowering of the German Romanesque style produced magnificent multitowered cathedrals in the Rhineland at Mainz, Trier, Worms, and Speyer (see pp. 178–179, 187–188, 191, & 194), their austere appearance relieved by decorative patterns based on the repeated use of rounded arches, while Cologne (see pp. 148–157) boasts Germany's greatest heritage of Romanesque churches.

Architectural influences from other countries abound throughout Germany, France's Gothic and Italy's Renaissance revival styles in particular.

Gothic: Tentative beginnings of the Gothic style can be seen at Limburg an der Lahn (see p. 207), where the exterior of the cathedral begun in 1211 is exuberantly Romanesque, while the interior incorporates characteristically Gothic rib vaulting. The first fully fledged Gothic structures in Germany are the Liebfrauenkirche at Trier and St. Elisabeth's Church at Marburg (see p. 206), both begun in the 1230s. The latter is a hall church—with a nave and aisles of the same height—a pattern common in Germany. Work started in 1248 on the greatest German Gothic building, Cologne Cathedral (see pp. 150–153), but proceeded slowly. Cologne's cathedral was one of several great churches that had to wait until the 19th century for completion—sometimes because the daring vision of their Gothic designers was beyond the technology of the time.

The 12th and 13th centuries were a great period of monastery building. At Maulbronn in Baden-Württemberg (see p. 345) a near-perfect example has survived of the whole townlike complex.

Most Gothic structures were built in stone, but, along the Baltic coast and elsewhere in northern Germany, a variant developed called *Backsteingotik* (Brick Gothic). You can see this brick-built style in churches and city halls, where they lend great distinction to the centers of Hansa trading cities such as Lübeck and Stralsund.

Renaissance: The architectural forms of the Italian Renaissance, at first often misunderstood in Germany, were used only for decorative effect, or incongruously combined with Gothic features. For instance, the Fugger family chapel of 1512 in St. Anne's Church in Augsburg (see p. 273), Germany's first Renaissance-style structure, was given a Gothic net vault. Munich saw the finest Renaissance construction, especially St. Michael's Church (Michaelskirche; see p. 288), completed by the Jesuits in 1597, and the rulers' palace, the Residenz (see pp. 286–287 & 290). In northern, largely Protestant Germany, Dutch and Flemish influences found their most striking expression in the "Weser Renaissance" style, characterized by extravagant ornamentation with gables, oriels, scrolls, spikes, obelisks, and statuary.

Baroque & Rococo: The baroque style originated in Italy but, in the hands of German architects and craftsmen, took on distinctive characteristics, particularly in the Catholic south. Here Counter-Reformation worship was given a theatrical setting of great sensual appeal. This reached an extreme of opulence and fantasy in the rococo pilgrimage church of Vierzehnheiligen (see pp. 256–257), begun in 1744 to designs by Johann Balthasar Neumann (1687–1753). Neumann also built or contributed to the palaces of the Schönborn dynasty of prince-bishops at Brühl, Bruchsal (see p. 346), and Würzburg (see pp. 261–262), where a grotto-like space on the ground floor leads to a formal garden. The most spectacular baroque garden in Germany was at Wilhelmshöhe outside Kassel (see p. 203), where an immensely long cascade led downhill from a temple topped by a giant statue of Hercules. First laid out at the end of the 18th century, Wilhelmshöhe was later transformed, like most German baroque gardens, into an English-style naturalistic park.

> In the hands of German architects and craftsmen, [the baroque style] took on distinctive characteristics, particularly in the Catholic south. Here Counter-Reformation worship was given a theatrical setting of great sensual appeal.

Baroque opulence and rococo fantasy were not entirely confined to southern Germany, however. The courtyard and pavilions of the Zwinger in Dresden, for example, are among the most ambitious settings for court festivities ever devised, while the gracious rococo interiors of Frederick the Great's lavish Sanssouci Palace at Potsdam contradict all assumptions about Prussian austerity.

The rococo church of Würzburg's Residenz was a sumptuous setting for princely worship.

From Classicism to Confusion: In the 18th century the classical architecture of antiquity was reinterpreted as an appropriate style for state capitals. At Potsdam, Sanssouci was given a classical colonnade by Frederick the Great's court architect Georg Wenzeslaus von Knobelsdorff (1699–1753). In 1791 the approach to Berlin was ennobled by the colossal Brandenburg Gate (see pp. 58–59), directly inspired by the Propylaea on the Acropolis in Athens.

The greatest Prussian architect of this period, and also director of the kingdom's Department of Public Works, was Karl Friedrich Schinkel (1781–1841). He transformed the face of Berlin and its surroundings, with museums, palaces, and country houses in a restrained, but wonderfully inventive, neoclassic style. His counterpart in Bavaria was Franz Karl Leo von Klenze (1784–1864). He gave Munich an appropriately regal air (Bavaria had recently become a kingdom) with buildings like the Glyptothek (see p. 290), the world's first public sculpture museum. He also designed monuments intended to give the rising tide of German nationalism a noble focus—Walhalla (see p. 278) high above the Danube and the Befreiungshalle near Kelheim (see p. 271).

Further national monuments rose in many parts of Germany after unification in 1871. Effort went into looking for an architectural style appropriate for the Second Reich, but much late 19th-century building was little more than a dull rehash of historical styles.

Modernism: At the turn of the 20th century, *Jugendstil*, the German variant of art nouveau, flourished briefly—most notably in the setting of the Mathildenhöhe in Darmstadt (see p. 209). An artists' and architects' colony was established here in 1899. The first decades of the century saw an extraordinary efflorescence of architectural styles and new directions. Strange, organic-looking structures, such as Erich Mendelsohn's Einstein Tower at Potsdam, were grouped under the same heading of expressionism as the shiplike offices of the Chilehaus in Hamburg or the circular Rheinhalle in Düsseldorf. In contrast, the pioneering Fagus Factory at Alfeld by Walter Gropius (1883–1969), with its flat roof, glass curtain-walling, and boxy outline, foreshadowed the things to come. In 1919, Gropius founded the Bauhaus in Weimar (see sidebar p. 43).

The Nazis took up the monumental style of imposing buildings like the superb station at Stuttgart. They also favored a "stripped classical" style exemplified by the Haus der Kunst in Munich. One lasting achievement of the 1930s, a fine synthesis of engineering, architecture, and landscape design, was the autobahn network of strategic highways.

The epic scale of wartime destruction was matched in the 1950s and '60s by a rebuilding program of similar proportions. Much of it was carried out in a rather bland but inoffensive mainstream modernist style. However, there are outstanding individual structures such as the crisply elegant Thyssen tower in Düsseldorf. Germany probably has more modern churches than any other country; the Kaiser Wilhelm Memorial Church in western Berlin is a poignant synthesis of a contemporary setting for worship and wartime ruins. When the Olympic Games returned to Germany in 1972, Günther Behnisch surpassed his predecessors of 1936 by designing a stadium of inspired originality, harmoniously integrated with the surrounding parkland and covered by a joyously swelling tentlike canopy.

> **The world has discovered what Germans have long known—that their country's painting and sculpture embraces some of the finest art ever created.**

Painting & Sculpture

German paintings and sculptures have tended to stay in the country. English aristocrats on the Grand Tour would take home expensive souvenirs from Italy and France rather than Germany, and in the 19th century the development of public collections and museums coincided with the rise of nationalism and a concern for the country's artistic heritage. Then, at the beginning of the 20th century, the prestige of the work of Paris-based artists was so great that it overshadowed the art of other countries. More recently, however, the world has discovered what Germans have long known—that their country's painting and sculpture embraces some of the finest art ever created.

Beginnings: Early examples of German sculpture include the Halle museum's relief panel of an early eighth-century Saxon horseman trotting into battle with shield and lance and, in Cologne Cathedral, the expressive tenth-century Cross of Gero. Painting at this time was largely confined to manuscript illumination, carried out by skilled craftsmen at monastic centers such as Trier and Reichenau Island on Lake Constance. In St. George's Church on Reichenau, wall paintings date from about 1000.

Romanesque sculptors gave Germany symbols that still resonate today: The Brunswick Lion of around 1166 symbolized the power and determination of Duke Henry the Lion, and the sculptures created in the 1230s for Bamberg Cathedral, particularly the equestrian statue known as the "Bamberg Rider," portray the ideals of medieval chivalry.

Fifteenth & Sixteenth Centuries: In the Middle Ages the production of church altarpieces reached a high point of achievement in Cologne, where Stefan Lochner (died 1451) was unsurpassed in depicting spiritual grace and sweetness, as in his "Madonna in the Rose Garden" of 1445. Late medieval piety of this kind combines with the beginnings of Renaissance humanism in the masterly linden-wood carvings of Veit Stoss (ca 1447–1533) and Tilman Riemenschneider (ca 1460–1531), both of whom worked mostly in Franconia (northern Bavaria).

The early 16th century was a golden age in German painting. No one has conveyed human suffering more intensely in the form of Christ crucified than Matthias Grünewald (ca 1470–1528). Albrecht Altdorfer (ca 1480–1538) was a pioneer of landscape painting, subordinating conventional subjects to their setting as in his "St. George and the Dragon," set in the primeval forest of southern Germany. Lucas Cranach the Elder (1472–1553) specialized in female nudes of great sensuality and in portraits, including a famous one of Martin Luther.

The outstanding figure of the era was Albrecht Dürer (1471- 1528), who mastered drawing and engraving as well as oil painting and virtually invented watercolor. Travels in Italy gave him a deep understanding of Renaissance ideals, to which he added a characteristically German expressiveness; his portraits, such as the one of Oswolt Krel in Munich's Alte Pinakothek (see pp. 291–292), seem to reach into the soul of his sitters. The great portraitist Hans Holbein the Younger (1497–1543), on the other hand, concentrated on the detailed physical appearance of his subjects and their typical surroundings, as in his "Portrait of Georg Gisze" in Berlin's Gemäldegalerie (see p. 69)

Must-See German Art Collections

A subjective list of places to start:

Old National Gallery, Berlin. Landscapes by Caspar David Friedrich crown an array of 19th-century greats. (See pp. 64–66.)

Hamburger Kunsthalle, Hamburg. Medieval portraits to modern classics such as Kokoschka and Munch. (See p. 115.)

North-Rhine Westphalia Art Collection, Düsseldorf. Features Klee and masterpieces by Picasso, Matisse, and local enfant terrible Joseph Beuys. (See p. 165.)

Museum Ludwig, Cologne. A postmodern mecca that touches on all genres of the 20th century. (See pp. 156–157.)

Pinakothek art galleries, Munich. Exquisite collections of old European masters, 19th-century art, and Germany's largest trove of modern works. (See pp. 291–294.)

Staatsgalerie Stuttgart, Stuttgart. Choice 14th- to 20th-century works including Cézanne, Monet, Rembrandt, Rubens, and Tiepolo. (See pp. 321–322.)

Seventeenth & Eighteenth Centuries: Artistic production was affected by both the Reformation and the disturbances of the Thirty Years War (1618–1648). A short-lived but influential painter, Adam Elsheimer (1578–1610) produced subtle effects of dark and light in pictures like "The Flight into Egypt." He worked on a small scale, but the proliferation of baroque churches and palaces required artists able to cover vast surfaces with illusionistic paintings and to work in close collaboration with craftsmen like plasterers, gilders, and stucco workers as well as with architects. The Bavarian Cosmas Damian Asam (1686–1739) and his brother Egid Quirin (1692–1750) combined more than one of these roles; their masterpieces are the church named after them in Munich (see p. 286) and Kloster Weltenburg (see pp. 277–278) on the Danube. Another team of brothers, Dominikus (1685–1766) and Johann Baptist (1680–1758) Zimmermann collaborated in similar fashion on the pilgrimage church of the Wieskirche (see p. 316) in the Bavarian Alps foothills.

The sun sets over Albrecht Altdorfer's vision of the "Battle of Alexander" (1529).

Outstanding German baroque sculptors were Andreas Schlüter (ca 1660–1714), whose dynamic equestrian statue of the Great Elector stands in front of Charlottenburg Palace (see pp. 74–75) in Berlin, and Balthasar Permoser (1651–1732), who populated Dresden's Zwinger (see pp. 230–233) with stone cupids, maidens, and other figures.

Nineteenth Century: The major painter of Germany's Romantic movement was Caspar David Friedrich (1774–1840), whose canvases show dreamlike landscapes, often inhabited by a solitary figure apparently contemplating the mystery and melancholy of the universe. It is almost impossible to look at Rügen Island, the Baltic shore, and the Elbe Valley without seeing them through this visionary artist's eyes.

By mid-century, artists were concentrating on the detail of life, exemplified by Carl Spitzweg (1808–1885), who evoked small-town Germany with humor and compassion. Famous for his depictions of high society and idealized history, Adolf von Menzel (1815–1905) also painted scenes of industry. The specialty of Wilhelm Leibl (1844–1900) was country folk painted in the meticulous manner of the old masters. The idea of a "good and simple life" in the countryside led to the establishment of rural artists' colonies. The best known of these, at Worpswede (see p. 139) near Bremen, numbered Paula Modersohn-Becker (1876–1907) among its members; her pictures of village life are still much loved today.

At the end of the century, French Impressionism found an important echo in Germany in the work of Max Liebermann (1847–1935) and Lovis Corinth (1858–1925), but it was with the expressionism of the early 20th century that German art made its own, startlingly original contribution.

Twentieth Century & Beyond: Early in the century, two distinct groups of artists came together to find new ways of expressing a characteristically German preoccupation with feeling. In 1905, *Die Brücke* (The Bridge) was formed in Dresden. Its leading member, Ernst Ludwig Kirchner (1880–1938), used simplified forms and the boldest of colors to convey dynamic meaning in pictures like "Nude With Hat" of 1911. Glorious colors pervade the palettes of both August Macke (1887–1914) and Franz Marc (1880–1916), members of Der Blaue Reiter (The Blue Rider), a group established in Munich in 1911. With something of the quality of medieval stained glass, Marc's sensitive pictures of animals in their habitat have remained extremely popular. The group's most influential member was the Russian-born Wassily Kandinsky (1866–1944), who pioneered abstraction, as did Paul Klee (1879–1940). After World War I, Klee became one of the leading figures in the Bauhaus.

To deal with the horrors of war and the social chaos and misery of the Weimar years, *Neue Sachlichkeit* (New Objectivity) advocated a return to a form of realism. Its foremost exponent, Otto Dix (1891–1969), had served in the trenches in Flanders; his apocalyptic Dresden triptych "War" has an impact equal to that of Grünewald's late medieval Crucifixion. The Dada movement rejoiced in absurdity, with the Hanover artist Kurt Schwitters (1887–1948) making collages from found objects and rubbish. The surrealist Max Ernst (1891–1976) anticipated the coming catastrophe of World War II in some of his unearthly landscapes.

The Bauhaus

Founded by Walter Gropius (1883–1969) in 1919, the Bauhaus school became one of the most influential currents in modernist architecture. Its subtle melding of art, craft, and technology had been partly explored in Germany earlier, but it took the Bauhaus to distill and mass-market the results. Public housing in Berlin and Frankfurt reflects the striking utopian aesthetic that had a similar impact on furniture design. After the Nazis seized power in 1933, most of the school's kindred spirits fled Germany but continued to spread the modernist message. (See also pp. 214–217.)

George Grosz (1893–1959) was perhaps the most bitingly satirical chronicler of the 1920s. Like many artists, he escaped the Nazi clampdown on all but the most slavishly conventional art by emigrating to the United States. Max Beckmann (1884–1950) left Germany after listening to Hitler's speech opening the Nazi exhibition of "Degenerate Art," held in Munich in 1937 with the intention of humiliating their artistic adversaries.

The Nazis' favorite sculptor was Arno Breker (1900–1991), whose muscle-bound supermen adorned public places like the Berlin Olympic Stadium and Reich Chancellery. In contrast, profound feeling is simply expressed in the figures of Ernst Barlach (1870–1938), such as "Hovering Angel" in Güstrow Cathedral.

In the second half of the 20th century, German art seemed to hesitate between re-establishing connections with the vitality of the 1920s and making its own contribution to international trends. The outstanding figure in West Germany was Joseph Beuys (1921–1986), who sculpted in such unorthodox materials as fat, felt, blood, and honey and organized happenings and performances. Germany's most famous contemporary painter is Gerhard Richter (1932–), the Dresden-born photo-realist. In 2013 his 9-by-9-foot (2.7 x 2.7 m) "Domplatz, Mailand" (1968) sold for $37 million, the highest auction price ever paid for the work of a living artist.

Music

Music continues to be important in the German-speaking world, which has produced far more than its share of great composers and performers. Germany has an exceptional number of orchestras, including the world-class Berlin Philharmonic and Leipzig Gewandhaus, and opera houses can be found in the most unlikely of industrial towns. Festivals abound, the most prestigious being Bayreuth's annual celebration of the works of Richard Wagner.

Beginnings to Baroque: The earliest German musicians seem to have performed on long, curved horns of bronze known as *Luren,* which date from the first half of the first millennium B.C. And we know from the Romans that the later Germanic tribesmen went into battle singing. In the early Middle Ages, music was the preserve of the Church, with Gregorian chant sung in Latin. German song really begins in the 12th century, when *Minnesänger,* lyric poets influenced by the troubadours of Provence, celebrated courtly love, sometimes to the accompaniment of fiddle, lute, or harp. The greatest Minnesänger was Walter von der Vogelweide (ca 1170–1230), who is supposed to have participated in the legendary "Contest of the Troubadours" at Wartburg Castle (see p. 223). The Minnesänger also dealt with religious, social, and political themes, as did the wandering songsters known as *Vaganten;* earthier altogether, some of the latter's efforts were collected in the "Carmina Burana" of around 1280, rousingly reworked by Carl Orff in 1937. The successors to the Minnesänger were the *Meistersinger,* singers organized into guilds. The most prominent mastersinger was Hans Sachs (1494–1576), celebrated by Wagner in his opera *The Mastersingers of Nuremberg.*

Martin Luther, who wrote the words of hymns such as *"Eine feste Burg"* ("A Stronghold Sure"), understood the importance of music to true devotion. The chorales of his time developed into the later cantata, one

EXPERIENCE:
Tuning in to Classics

These German stations are renowned among locals for quality classical music:

Bayern 4 Klassik in Munich (103.2 FM)
br.de

hr2 kultur in Frankfurt (87.9 FM)
hr-online.de

Kulturradio rbb in Berlin (92.4 FM)
kulturradio.de

MDR Figaro in Dresden (95.4 FM)
mdr.de

NDR Kultur in Hamburg (99.2 FM)
ndr.de/ndrkultur

SWR2 in Stuttgart (105.7 FM)
swr.de

WDR 3 in Cologne (93.1 FM)
wdr3.de

of the specialties of Johann Sebastian Bach (1685–1750). The outstanding master of all the musical forms of the baroque age, he is perhaps best remembered for developing polyphony. Bach served the courts at Weimar and Köthen before becoming musical director for the city of Leipzig in 1723, where he remained until his death. Bach's reputation has continued to grow, although at the time it was Georg Philipp Telemann (1681–1767) who enjoyed greater acclaim. The other towering figure of baroque music was Georg Friedrich Händel (1685–1759), many of whose greatest works, like his oratorio *The Messiah,* were composed for the Hanoverian court in England. The ducal court at Mannheim was a fruitful environment for musicians from all over the German lands, and it was here that the foundations were laid for the development of the symphony.

Classical to Romantic: The evolution of the symphony and the establishment of the string quartet owed much to the Austrian composers Joseph Haydn (1732–1809) and Wolfgang Amadeus Mozart (1756–1791), but German Ludwig van Beethoven (1770–1827) took these forms to a new level. His nine symphonies gave musical expression to profound human emotions, and his ability to probe the deep recesses of individual experience pointed the way for the next generation of German composers, generally classified as Romantics.

German composer Ludwig van Beethoven

The greatest achievement of Franz Schubert (1797–1828) was his *lieder,* songs in which the lyric, the voice, and the piano fuse in exquisite harmony. A virtuoso pianist, Robert Schumann (1810–1856) also wrote intensely expressive lieder, although he himself considered his C-minor symphony to be his greatest work. Opera in German had reached early glories in Mozart's *Magic Flute* and Beethoven's *Fidelio,* while Carl Maria von Weber's *Freischütz* of 1821 created musical and dramatic harmonies anticipating the work of Richard Wagner (see p. 260). Johannes Brahms (1833–1897) successfully fused Romanticism with the Classical tradition, and he was seen by supporters as counterbalancing the trend to formlessness of Wagner's work. Richard Strauss (1864–1949) drew on all musical traditions with equal virtuosity; he is best known for his symphonic poems, such as *Don Juan,* and operas, including the popular *Der Rosenkavalier.*

The Past Century: Germans and Austrians were responsible for many of the musical innovations of the 20th century, including the use of atonality (Arnold Schönberg, 1874–1951) and electronic techniques (Karlheinz Stockhausen, 1928–2007). The satirical operas of Kurt Weill (1900–1950), such as *The Threepenny Opera* and *The Rise and Fall of the City of Mahagonny,* are among the most popular and accessible music of the century. An emigrant to the United States, Weill was much influenced by jazz.

Literature

Germany has one of the world's great literary traditions, and writing in German spans a vast range, encompassing medieval epic and troubadours' love poetry, Luther's Bible and the heights of Weimar Classicism, right up to the novels of modernism.

The Middle Ages: The spirit of medieval Germany is epitomized by the late 12th-century anonymous epic poem *Das Nibelungenlied (Song of the Nibelungs),* a rich compound of myth, human passions, and historical reality, which furnished Richard Wagner with material for his *Ring* cycle of operas. In an epic poem of the early 13th century, Wolfram von Eschenbach told the tale of the quest for the Holy Grail in *Parzifal.* Like the love songs of the Minnesänger (see p. 44), these epics were written in Middle High German, the predecessor of the modern version of the language, New High German. As the 16th century began, a wave of comic and satirical writing culminated in the figure of the jester and practical joker *Till Eulenspiegel,* whose pranks were recounted by a Brunswick revenue man, Hermann Bote.

Luther & After: Martin Luther's greatest contribution to German culture was his translation of the Bible, completed in 1534. The first translation freed from the bonds of regional dialect, it could be understood by all Germans, while its simplicity and clarity made an immense contribution to the development of German as a literary language. The turbulence of the Reformation and the Thirty Years War inhibited literary production, although out of the war came the picaresque novel *Simplicissimus* of 1669 by Jakob Christoph von Grimmelshausen, whose antihero experiences everything the chaos of the time can offer.

> Writing in German spans a vast range, encompassing medieval epic and troubadours' love poetry ... up to the novels of modernism.

From Enlightenment to "Storm & Stress": Gotthold Ephraim Lessing (1729–1781) put drama on a new footing. He pleaded for religious and social tolerance and, in defiance of theatrical convention, drew his characters from the rising middle classes. As the old European order crumbled, a dynamic literary movement arose that took its name from a German play dealing with the American War of Independence; *Sturm und Drang (Storm and Stress)* preached liberation from tyranny and the supremacy of the emotions. The greatest German literary figure, Johann Wolfgang von Goethe (1749–1832) was an adherent in the early days, but its most representative figure was his friend Friedrich Schiller (1759–1805), some of whose plays, including *Die Räuber (The Robbers),* continued to upset dictatorial regimes well into the 20th century. Goethe used his enormous talent in many fields, but it is for his lyric poetry, his historical dramas, and above all his definitive rendering of the tale of Faust that he is most remembered. Folk and fairy tales provided inspiration for some Romantics, including E. T. A. Hoffmann (1776–1822) and Clemens Brentano (1778–1842), who in 1805 published an anthology entitled *Des Knaben Wunderhorn (The Boy's Magic Horn).* The greatest collectors of such material were the Brothers Grimm (see p. 203), who believed passionately in the accumulated wisdom expressed in folk songs and stories.

Naturalism & Realism: A wonderful writer of lyric poetry in a folk manner *(Die Loreley),* Heinrich Heine (1797–1856) also wrote about the injustices and inequalities of his time. Sensitivity to place and landscape was a prominent theme in later 19th-century literature. No one has evoked the scenery of Brandenburg and the Baltic provinces so tellingly as novelist Theodor Fontane (1819–1898), particularly in his masterpiece *Effi Briest,* the story of an ill-fated marriage. *Der Schimmelreiter (The Rider on the White Horse)* by Theodor Storm (1817–1888) is compulsory reading for visitors to the Schleswig-Holstein coast. A critical social realism pervades plays such as *Die Weber (The Weavers)* by Gerhart Hauptmann (1862–1946).

Twentieth Century & Beyond: In the novels of Thomas Mann (1875–1955), the changing times are reflected in the fate of the individual. *Buddenbrooks* (1901) chronicles decaying upper-middle-class life in Lübeck, while half a century later, *Doktor Faustus* faces the agonies of the Hitler era. Mann's brother Heinrich (1871–1950) is best known for his portrait in *Der Untertan (Man of Straw)* of the spiritual emptiness of a typical citizen of the Second Reich; his *Professor Unrat* formed the basis of the film *Blue Angel.* The Prague German writer Franz Kafka (1883–1924) hit a vein with nightmarish short stories and novels such as *Der Prozess (The Trial),* while Carl Zuckmayr (1896–1977) satirized a German tendency to blindly obey authority in *Der Hauptmann von Köpenick.*

Works dealing with the great issues came from the minds of Günther Grass, famous for his novel *Die Blechtrommel (The Tin Drum)* of 1959 and Rolf Hochhuth, whose 1963 play *Der Stellvertreter (The Representative)* questioned the ambivalent role of the papacy in World War II. Internationally, the most acclaimed dramatist remains Bertolt Brecht (1898–1956), who established the prestigious Berliner Ensemble theater. In West Germany, writers such as Heinrich Böll (1917–1985) strove to keep moral issues alive, as did Christa Wolf (1929–2011) and Stefan Heym (1913–2001) in the East. The latest German-language author to win the Nobel Prize is Herta Müller (1953–), whose 2009 novel *Atemschaukel (The Hunger Angel)* recalls the deportation of Romania's German minority to Soviet Gulags.

EXPERIENCE: Learning German

There are dozens of language schools offering German language courses taught by qualified instructors. The best known is the **Goethe-Institut** *(goethe.de),* a non-profit institution that has promoted the study of German abroad for more than 60 years. The organization is also a key source of information on German culture, society, and politics, with reading rooms and other useful facilities available to walk-in visitors. The institute offers courses at 13 German locations and dozens of branches worldwide.

Cinema

German cinema enjoyed a golden age in the 1920s and early '30s, when Ufa Studios in Babelsberg (part of Potsdam) made films that were not only commercial successes but also high points of cinematic art and technique. As early as 1919, Robert Wiene directed *The Cabinet of Dr. Caligari,* a silent film using expressionist

Apotheosis of the silent movie: Robert Wiene's *The Cabinet of Dr. Caligari* (1919)

devices (unusual camera angles, dramatic contrasts of light and shadow, stylized sets) to tell a tale of madness and murder. Fritz Lang's *Metropolis* of 1926, an evocation of the horrors of the future city, put the science fiction film on a sound footing, just as F. W. Murnau's *Nosferatu* (1921) established the vampire film genre. Erich Pommer's *Blue Angel* (1930) made an instant star of Marlene Dietrich.

The German High Commission had originally established Ufa as a propaganda machine. The cinema again became a propaganda tool after 1933, when Josef Goebbels used it to excite, entertain, and misinform the masses. Leni Riefenstahl's documentaries turned the Nazi Party's Nuremberg Rally of 1934 and the Berlin Olympics of 1936 into enthralling spectacles.

Much of the film industry's talent (Dietrich, Wilder, Zinnemann) fled to Hollywood in the 1930s, and it was many years before German cinema regained a degree of international credibility. Wolfgang Staudte's *The Murderers Are Among Us* (1946) dealt with the aftermath of Nazi rule, but the characteristic genre of West German cinema was *Heimat* ("homeland") movies, romantic comedies in nostalgic rural settings. From the 1960s, inspired by the French *nouvelle vague,* young German directors like Werner Herzog (*Young Törless,* 1966), Volker Schlöndorff (*The Lost Honor of Katharina Blum,* 1975, and *The Tin Drum,* 1979), Rainer Werner Fassbinder (*The Marriage of Maria Braun,* 1978), and Wim Wenders (*Paris, Texas,* 1984) achieved international recognition.

Recent filmmakers include Wolfgang Becker, whose 2003 *Good Bye Lenin!* tapped a vein of *Ostalgie,* or nostalgia for the bygone GDR. Tom Tykwer scored with the kinetic *Lola Rennt (Run Lola Run)* in 1997, followed by the chilling *Perfume* (2006). Florian von Donnersmarck's award-winning *The Lives of Others* (2006) depicts a world saturated by Stasi informants. ■

The vibrant spirit of reunited Germany surrounded by the jewel-like palaces of royal Potsdam

Berlin &
Brandenburg

A helmeted Berlin bandsman

Berlin & Brandenburg

Since 1990, the capital once more of a united country, Berlin has recovered a proper relationship with the towns and countryside of the region now known as the Land of Brandenburg. Nevertheless, fearful of domination by the metropolis, in 1996 the people of Brandenburg forcefully rejected a proposal that would unite Brandenburg with Berlin and elected to stay a separate entity.

A Berlin bear with his organ grinder

From this core grew a principality, then a kingdom, ruled for 500 years by the Hohenzollern dynasty, who built splendid residences at Berlin and Potsdam. As Berlin grew into a great metropolis in the late 19th and early 20th centuries, it drew people from all over Germany and beyond, molding them into characteristic big-city dwellers, with their own acerbic sense of humor. Brandenburgers, by contrast, are held to be loyal and rather slow moving. Their region tends to be ignored in the rush to get to the capital, yet the superlative palaces and parks of Potsdam are only some of the region's many attractions. ∎

Putlitz

Karstädt

NATURPARK
BRANDENBURGISCHE
ELBTALAUE

Elbe

LOWER
SAXONY
p. 125

Perleberg

Wittenberge

Bad
Wilsnack

△
A

The glaciers and meltwater channels of the Ice Age formed the landscape of Berlin and Brandenburg. Water lies everywhere, in the form of lakes, streams, and rivers, as well as the great canals that link Berlin to the rest of Germany. Great forests of pine and oak grow on the sandy, infertile soils that cover much of the area; one of the most extensive woodlands is the Grunewald, western Berlin's green lung. Brandenburg's countryside has its own charm; between Berlin and Potsdam, generations of gardeners and architects transformed the banks of the River Havel into a region of such beauty that it was awarded World Heritage status by UNESCO.

This is indeed the heartland of Prussia. Brandenburg was originally the *Mark*, the border territory seized from the Slavs as the German eastward movement began in the tenth century.

NOT TO BE MISSED:

Area of map detail

Berlin

0   50 kilometers
0   25 miles

◁5

MECKLENBURG-WEST POMERANIA
p. 87

A24
Meyenburg
A21
A19
Pritzwalk
Wittstock
Schönebeck
Rheinsberg
A24
E26
Kyritz
Neuruppin
Bückwitz
Ruppinersee
Herzberg
E55
Rhinkanal
Rhinow
Briesen
Kremmen
Oranienburg
Havel
Plaue
Rathenow
Nauen
Premnitz
Olympiastadion
Sanssouci
Brandenburg
Potsdam
Ziesar
A2
E30
Golzow
A10
Beelitz
Belzig
Görzke
A9
Treuenbrietzen
Wiesenburg
Marzahna
SAXONY-ANHALT
p. 211

Dosse
Gransee
Zehdenick
Löwenberg
Liebenwalde
E251
Oder-Havel Kanal
Hennigsdorf
Falkensee
120m
Teufelsberg ▲
Wannsee
Wannsee
Rangsdorf
Mittenwalde
Trebbin
Zossen
Jüterbog
Golssen
Dahme
Brandis
Schlieben
Herzberg
Falkenberg
Schwarze Elster
Elsterwerda

Ravensbrück
Fürstenberg
Templin
Joachimsthal
Werbellinsee
A11
A28
Birkenwerder
Bernau
BERLIN
Jagdschloss
Grunewald
Eichwalde
Königs
Wusterhausen
A12
Baruth
Märkisch
Buchholz
A13
Lübben
Lübbenau
Luckau
Calau
A13
Finsterwalde
Bad
Liebenwerda
Lauchhammer

Prenzlau
A20
Unterucker-see
Hassleben
Gramzow
Oberückersee
A11
NATIONALPARK
UNTERES
ODERTAL
Schwedt
Angermünde
Kloster
Chorin
Eberswalde
Bad
Freienwalde
Wriezen
Prötzel
Strausberg
Neuenhagen
Rüdersdorf
A10
Fürstenwalde
Storkow
Scharmützelsee
Beeskow
Schwielochsee
Lieberose
BIOSPHÄRENRESERVAT
SPREEWALD
Spreewald Museum
Vetschau
E36
A15
Schloss
Branitz
Drebkau
E55
Talsperre Spremberg
Finsterwalde
Senftenberg
Schwarze
Pumpe
SAXONY
p. 227

Gartz
POLAND
◁4
Alte Oder
Oder
Seelow
Müncheberg
Manschnow
Frankfurt
an der Oder
E30
Oder-Spree Kanal
Müllrose
Eisenhüttenstadt
◁3
Spree
Guben
Peitz
◁2
Cottbus
Forst
Spremberg
◁1

△
B
△
C
△
D
△
E

Berlin

Berlin air—*Berliner Luft*—is supposed to be especially exhilarating, possibly because 30 percent of the city is devoted to green space. These days, the refreshing aura might also come from the sense that the rapidly developing capital, having survived the trauma of Cold War division, is on its way to becoming the focal point of 21st-century Europe.

Berlin is a big city, less in terms of its population—half that of London or Paris—than in its area of nearly 560 square miles (1,450 sq km). A good way to learn its layout, and see how various points of interest are linked, is to use the excellent transportation system.

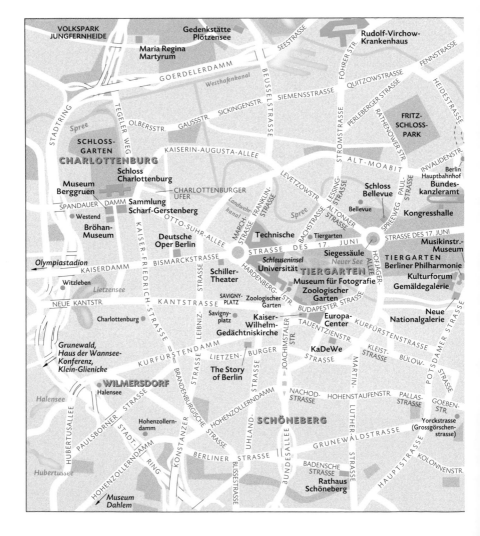

Board the No. 100 double-decker bus (see sidebar p. 66) at Bahnhof Zoo and you start in the center of what was West Berlin, with its fashionable shops and prestigious residential quarters. The bus heads east through the greenery of the Tiergarten, the old royal hunting park, skirting the Reichstag and the burgeoning new government quarter. To the south you get a glimpse of the sparkling modern structures around Potsdamer Platz, reviving an area that was left divided and derelict by the building of the Berlin Wall. The nearby Forum of Culture groups world-class modern museums, galleries, and concert halls.

Beyond the Brandenburg Gate, the bus enters what was East Berlin, the historic core of the city. Although a good deal of its heritage was

Berlin
▲ 51 C3

Visitor Information
✉ Hauptbahnhof (Main railway station, Europaplatz entrance); Pariser Platz (Brandenburg Gate)
☎ 030 25 00 23 23

visitberlin.de/en

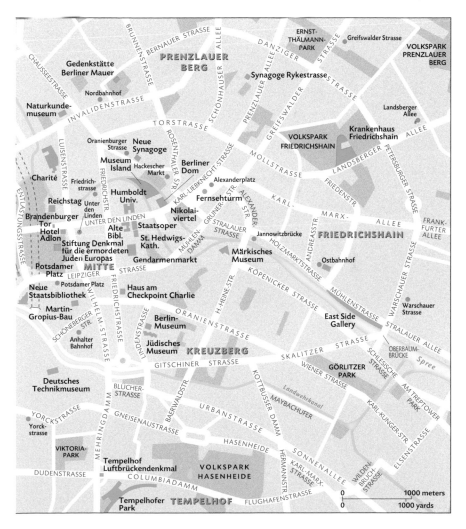

Sir Norman Foster created a people's dome for the Reichstag—home to the national parliament.

Reichstag

 Map p. 53

✉ Platz der
Republik 1

☎ 030 22 70

🚌 Bus: 100

bundestag.de

destroyed by bombing and the advance of the Red Army in 1945, much was preserved and restored, even under communism—which left its mark in the shape of the tall TV tower, the Fernsehturm, the bleak spaces of Alexanderplatz, and the monumental boulevard of Karl-Marx-Allee.

Beyond the city center is a ring of semi-independent boroughs. Kreuzberg has a heady mix of Turkish immigrants and alternative lifestylers, although its role as trendsetter in inner-city living seems to have been taken over by Prenzlauer Berg and to a certain extent, Friedrichshain. Schöneberg and Tempelhof keep memories of the airlift (see pp. 33–34) and Cold War alive, while Charlottenburg has the boulevard

of the Kurfürstendamm and its own restored *Schloss* and museum district. To the west, the prestigious residential areas of Wilmersdorf and Zehlendorf extend into the belt of forests, lakes, and parkland linking Berlin with Potsdam.

The Reichstag

Since it reopened in 1999, the massive Reichstag (Deutscher Bundestag) building has regained its role as the seat of the Bundestag, Germany's parliament, and, crowned by British architect Sir Norman Foster's glittering steel-and-glass cupola, it has become a powerful symbol of the country's unity. Designed to express the openness of the political process and to be welcoming to the public,

INSIDER TIP:

Try using the cylinder mirror in the middle of the Reichstag dome to create some quirky and artistic photographs.

—ELIZABETH BARRETT
National Geographic contributor

it attracted more than three million visitors in the first year of its reopening.

Imperial Germany had been united for more than 20 years before its parliament building was finally completed in 1894, its every detail watched over jealously by Kaiser Wilhelm II, no great friend of parliamentary democracy. Even so, the great neo-Renaissance building failed to gain his approval. He called it "the height of tastelessness" and characterized the activity that went on inside as "the monkey-house." The Reichstag had its revenge; in November 1918 it was from here that the end of the Hohenzollern dynasty was announced and the German Republic proclaimed.

In 1933 the building was set on fire; the ostensible culprit, a feeble-minded Dutchman, was sentenced to death, but Hitler's storm troopers may well have been the real perpetrators. In any event, the Reichstag Fire was used by the Nazi regime as an excuse to terrorize and imprison its opponents, among them many parliamentary deputies.

As the Red Army fought its way into Berlin in April 1945, the Reichstag became a fortress, its formidable walls standing up to all but the heaviest artillery fire. But it was stormed on April 30, and the raising of the hammer and sickle banner over its gaping roof yielded one of the most unforgettable photographic images of World War II.

In the postwar period, the area in front of the ruined Reichstag remained a focus for mass demonstrations of all kinds. In 1948, as the Soviet blockade of Berlin began (see p. 33), it was here that a huge crowd assembled to hear the mayor, Ernst Reuter, hurl an eloquent appeal to the people of the free world to "Look on this city—*Schaut auf diese Stadt*—and know that it and its people must

Look Upon This City: Best Berlin Vistas

Savor the finest views of Berlin at these spots:

- **The Reichstag's sparkling glass cupola (see p. 54)**
- **Atop the television tower at Alexanderplatz (see p. 61)**
- **The Tiergarten from the Siegessäule (Victory Column, see p. 71)**
- **The Kreuzberg district from the Viktoriapark memorial (see p. 77)**
- **On the dome terrace of Berlin Cathedral (see p. 79)**
- **The panorama observation deck at Potsdamer Platz (see p. 80)**

not be abandoned!" Berlin was not abandoned, but the construction of the Wall in 1961 immediately to the east of the Reichstag cut off the great building from the city center. In the 1970s, the interior was made usable again, although Soviet pressure meant that it could not host sessions of the West German parliament. Instead, it housed an exhibition, "Questions on German History," a compulsory stop for school parties from the West.

With reunification accomplished, not everyone wanted the seat of government moved back to Berlin, and not everyone wanted to revive the Reichstag. Its isolated, ponderous mass of darkened stone seemed too heavily symbolic of the

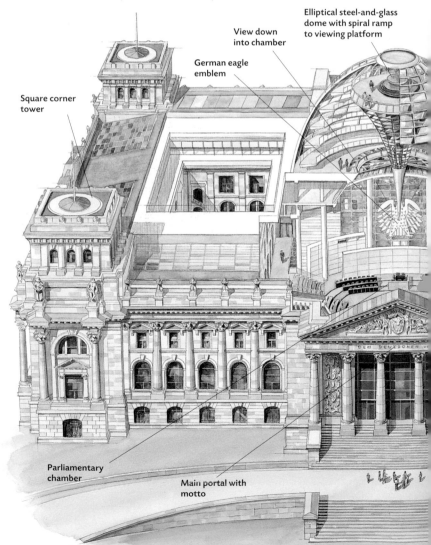

Square corner
tower

German eagle
emblem

View down
into chamber

Elliptical steel-and-glass
dome with spiral ramp
to viewing platform

Parliamentary
chamber

Main portal with
motto

darker aspects of German history. But the Bulgarian environmental sculptor Christo's "Reichstag Wrapping" of 1995 (he encased the building in silver plastic sheeting) transformed people's perceptions of it. Cleaned, reconstructed, thrown open to the people, and with its workings made visible, it now seems the only possible choice.

An elevator whisks you to the visitors dome, where you can peer into the parliamentary chamber and admire Berlin's skyline. To avoid long lines, book online or check for available time slots at the visitors pavilion.

New Government Quarter

Foster may have breathed new life into an old building, but

Internal courtyard

The Reichstag

Rusticated pedestal facade

Brandenburger Tor
Map p. 53

Berlin architects Charlotte Frank and Axel Schultes have remodeled an entire tract of the city around the Reichstag to make a setting for the whole business of modern government. A ribbon of new buildings cuts across the base of a meander in the River Spree, then boldly leaps the river itself into what was East Berlin, providing accommodations for deputies, their staff, and government employees. The most prominent single building is the Bundeskanzleramt, the Federal Chancellor's Office, completed in early 2001 and currently occupied by Angela Merkel.

Farther to the west, the Spree was redirected to create room for a splendid new central railroad

INSIDER TIP:

Make like Marlene Dietrich and take afternoon tea at Berlin's elegant Hotel Adlon (she was discovered here); you'll feel like a movie star relaxing in the beautiful foyer bar.

—JEANNE HORAK-DUFF
National Geographic contributor

station. Unveiled in 2006, this cathedral-like marvel of German engineering was constructed in a gentle bend so that each of its 9,000 glass panels had to be cut individually. Suburban, long-distance, and underground trains cross at three levels, and a north–south tunnel beginning here emerges much farther south, near Potsdamer Platz.

Brandenburger Tor

Right on the fault line between East and West during the decades of the Cold War, the Brandenburger Tor (Brandenburg Gate)—incorporated into the Berlin Wall during the communist reign—was recognized the world over as the most potent symbol of the division of Germany and its capital city. In October 1990, it gained new meaning as a backdrop to scenes of joy as countless thousands celebrated the country's newfound unity.

Inspired by Athens's Propylaea on the Acropolis, the gateway with its sextet of Doric columns on each side—Berlin's only remaining city gate—was completed in 1791.

Tear Down This Wall!

When Ronald Reagan visited Brandenburg Gate in 1987, he addressed the Soviet president: "General Secretary Gorbachev, if you seek peace, if you seek prosperity for the Soviet Union and Eastern Europe, if you seek liberalization: Come here to this gate! Mr. Gorbachev, open this gate! Mr. Gorbachev, tear down this wall!"

Other American presidents who have made memorable speeches here include John F. Kennedy in 1963 (the Soviets hung red banners blocking JFK's view into the East), Bill Clinton in 1994, and Barack Obama in 2013.

Strollers in the dappled sunlight of the Tiergarten

It marks the boundary between the historic core of the city to the east and the royal hunting preserve of the Tiergarten to the west. None but the Kaiser and his family were allowed to pass through the central opening. Crowning the gate is the Quadriga, a chariot drawn by four horses and driven by the goddess Victory. She survived being carried off to Paris by Napoleon, but fell victim to the bombardments of World War II. Luckily a plaster cast had been made, and she was replaced in 1958 in a rare act of East–West cooperation.

South of the Brandenburg Gate stands the sobering **Stiftung Denkmal für die ermordeten Juden Europas** (Memorial to the Murdered Jews of Europe). This field of 2,700 granite slabs, each one unsettlingly askew, is the work of American architect Peter Eisenman, unveiled in 2005 on the former site of Hitler's chancellery. A rear ramp descends to an information center with labels in English and German.

Unter den Linden

The linden trees and carriageways of Unter den Linden, central Berlin's most prestigious thoroughfare, run for more than half a mile from Pariser Platz by the Brandenburg Gate in the west to Museum Island (see pp. 62–67) in the east. Over the centuries, Prussian kings converted what had been a dusty track leading to the countryside into a grand avenue lined with splendid structures. The storied **Hotel Adlon Kempinski** on the south side of Pariser Platz is a remake of one of Berlin's great traditional hotels, long a kind of neutral meeting place for foreign diplomats.

(continued on p. 62)

Stiftung Denkmal für die ermordeten Juden Europas

✉ Cora-Berliner-Strasse 1

☎ 030 200 76 60

🕑 Open daily; information center closed Mon.

holocaust-mahnmal .de

A Walk Through Red Berlin

Taking in some of the key sites of Cold War history, this walk reveals how the old center of Berlin, from the Brandenburg Gate in the west to Alexanderplatz in the east, was marked by more than four decades of communist rule.

Start a few hundred yards west of the Brandenburger Tor (Brandenburg Gate), at the **Sowjetisches Ehrenmal** (Soviet War Memorial) **❶**, built from marble and granite taken from Hitler's Chancellery headquarters. A brace of T34 tanks, supposedly the first to break into the city in April 1945, flanks a colonnade dominated by the figure of a Red Army soldier. More than 20,000 Soviet servicemen perished in the battle for Berlin. Until the fall of the Wall in 1989, the memorial was guarded by Red Army soldiers.

Before passing through the Brandenburg Gate (see pp. 58–59), veer south to see the **Stiftung Denkmal für die ermordeten Juden Europas** (Memorial to the Murdered Jews of Europe) **❷**. The undulating lines of dull granite blocks evoke the pre-communist World War II horror that is both individual and collective. Back on Unter den Linden, pause at the corner of Friedrichstrasse. To the north, the overpass carries the tracks of the S-Bahn, which was one of the few ways in which visitors could pass from East to West. **Friedrichstrasse Bahnhof** (Train Station) **❸** was a dingy place of poignant arrivals and partings, its customs hall known as the Palace of Tears (Tränenpalast).

Turn right and walk south along Friedrichstrasse. The building boom of the 1990s has given back the long straight street something of its prewar bustle after the German Democratic Republic (GDR) rulers' neglect. A cornucopia of consumer goods unimaginable to communist shoppers is available in the fine arcades and in great stores such as the Berlin branch of Paris's Galeries Lafayette. **Checkpoint Charlie,** farther down Friedrichstrasse, is the world-famous crossing point where American and Soviet tank crews eyeballed each other as the Wall went up. The crowded exhibits in the

NOT TO BE MISSED:

Memorial to the Murdered Jews of Europe • Haus am Checkpoint Charlie • Gendarmenmarkt • Fernsehturm • Alexanderplatz

museum of the **Haus am Checkpoint Charlie** **❹** *(Friedrichstrasse 43–45, tel 030 253 72 50)* tell the story of the Wall.

Go back up Friedrichstrasse and turn right along Mohrenstrasse into the

Gendarmenmarkt ❺, perhaps the finest classical square in Berlin. Cross Französische Strasse and Behrenstrasse into **Bebelplatz,** the square flanked by St. Hedwig's Cathedral (St. Hedwigs-Kathedrale), the Old Library (Alte Bibliothek), and the Opera (Deutsche Staatsoper). A memorial recalls that this is the spot where, in 1933, the Nazis organized their bookburning ceremony.

Walk eastward over the bridge into Domplatz, the grassy square bordered by the enormous **Berliner Dom** ❻ (see p. 79). Taller than St. Paul's in London, the cathedral holds the remains of the royal Hohenzollerns. On nearby Schlossplatz stood the Palast der Republik, the GDR's parliament cum social center that has been razed to make way for a copy of a Prussian palace.

Beyond the bridge over the River Spree lies the heart of what was intended to be the showpiece Socialist metropolis of "Berlin, Capital of the GDR." The immense scale of the area is hardly relieved by the presence of one or two surviving old buildings such as the Marienkirche and the **Rotes Rathaus** ❼. The "Red City Hall" got its name from its skin of warm red brick. In the center of this area are surprisingly modest bronze figures of Marx and Engels. The dominant structure is the 1,197-foot-high (365 m) **Fernsehturm** (TV Tower) ❽, completed in 1969 and nicknamed the "Pope's Revenge" because of the crosslike reflection that appears when the sun shines on its top.

Beyond the overhead railway tracks is **Alexanderplatz** ❾, a focal point for eastern Berliners. On the square's eastern side, a mural painted in Social Realist style proclaims the merits of Marxism. Beyond it, miles of Stalinist neoclassic facades stretch along Karl-Marx-Allee, the "First Socialist Boulevard."

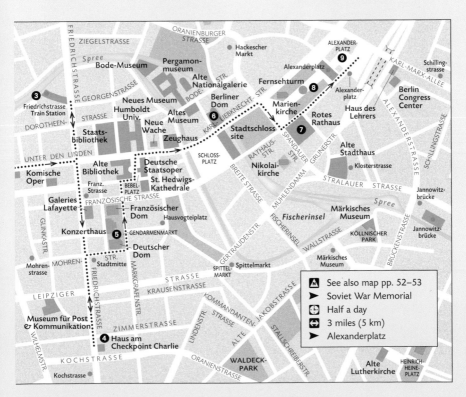

Museumsinsel

Maps pp. 53, 61, & 64–65

smb.museum

The truly monumental part of the Linden begins on the far side of Friedrichstrasse, with great institutions such as **Humboldt University** (to the left) and the magnificent trio of buildings (Old Library/Alte Bibliothek, St. Hedwig's Cathedral, and State Opera) defining the **Forum Fredericianum** or **Bebelplatz** (to the right).

In the middle of the street is a fine equestrian statue of Frederick the Great. Next to the university stands a small but perfect

been restored to house the German Historical Museum.

Museumsinsel

Sometimes called the "Prussian Acropolis" and now a World Heritage site, Berlin's central complex of five museums on Museumsinsel (Museum Island) occupies the northern tip of the island in the River Spree. Nineteenth-century Germans were pioneer archaeologists and antiquarians who unearthed

The Pergamon Museum houses such great ancient monuments as Babylon's Ishtar Gate.

neoclassic temple, the **Neue Wache** (New Guardhouse), an early work by Karl Friedrich Schinkel (1781–1841), venerated as the greatest of all Prussian architects. It is now a memorial to victims of war and tyranny. The imposing building beside it is the baroque **Zeughaus** (Arsenal), which has

the heritage of the ancient world. The incomparable spoils they brought home include the Pergamon Altar and Babylon's Ishtar Gate.

Many of the island's buildings suffered severe damage during World War II, followed by neglect under communism. An ambitious

No visit would be complete without trying Currywurst—grilled, sliced sausage in curry sauce—Berlin's version of German-Indian street food.

—LARRY PORGES
*National Geographic
Travel Books editor*

and extremely expensive master plan is under way, aimed at restoring the building fabric and reassembling in this key location many of the city's treasures. If all goes well, the project, including a fancy new visitor center and an underground passageway connecting all the museums, will be completed in 2017.

Altes Museum: Prussia's royal architect, Karl Friedrich Schinkel (see p. 39), considered the Altes Museum (Old Museum) his finest work. The long colonnaded facade of his neoclassic temple,

which looks south to where the royal Schloss once stood, symbolized the high cultural aspirations of the Prussian state (see p. 30). On completion in 1830, it was one of the world's first public museums. The central feature, inspired by the Pantheon in Rome, is a harmonious rotunda lined with classical statues. Even if time is short, be sure not to miss the lovely figure known as the "Praying Boy" ("Der betende Knabe"), created by an unknown sculptor on the island of Rhodes circa late 300 B.C.

Neues Museum: Erected in the 19th century to keep up with the Prussians' buying sprees of historic artifacts, the Neues Museum (New Museum) was unveiled in 2009 after a painstaking restoration. The building presents two fabulously ornate courtyards in Greek and Egyptian style, as well as treasures going back to the dawn of civilization. Ancient Egypt is the star, most notably for its array of papyrus texts and the celebrated bust of Queen Nefertiti dating

Altes Museum
- Maps pp. 61 & 64–65
- Lustgarten
- 030 20 90 55 77
- Closed Mon.
- $$$ Combination Area Ticket ($$$$) or Museum Pass ($$$$$) also available
- U-Bahn/S-Bahn: Friedrichstrasse or S Hackescher Markt; Bus: 100

Neues Museum
- Maps pp. 61 & 64–65
- Behind Old Museum
- 030 20 90 55 77
- Closed Mon.
- $$$ Combination Area Ticket ($$$$) or Museum Pass ($$$$$) also available
- U-Bahn/S-Bahn: Friedrichstrasse or S Hackescher Markt; Bus: 100

Best Museum Values

Planning on exploring the treasures of Museum Island, you'll pay €10–€12 for individual tickets. But if you want to take in two or more on a given day, the best-value Area Ticket opens doors to all five of the island's museums for €18. Visiting collections across the city? Consider the three-day Museum Pass for €24 (but remember, many museums are closed on Monday).

Some of the more popular exhibitions, such as the Neues Museum (see above) or Pergamon Museum (see p. 66), suggest booking in advance. A welcome bonus: A €1 discount is given on tickets booked on Berlin's state museum website *(smb .museum)*, and visitors under 18 years of age get in free at each museum. Exhibit labels are primarily in German, but you can pick up an excellent audio guide in English.

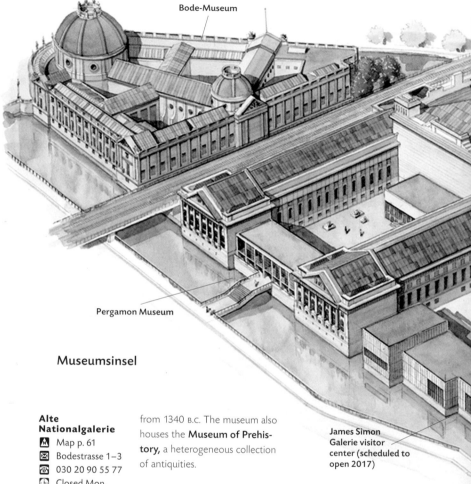

Bode-Museum

Pergamon Museum

Museumsinsel

James Simon Galerie visitor center (scheduled to open 2017)

Alte Nationalgalerie

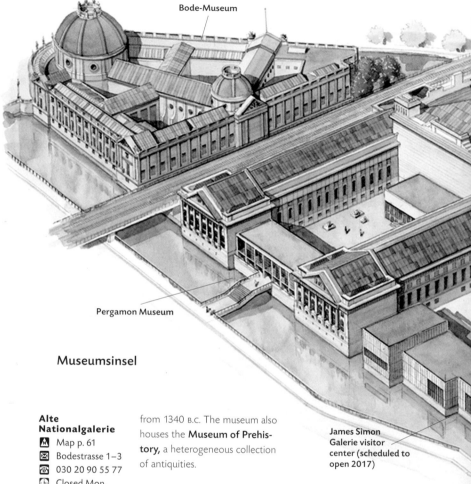 Map p. 61

Bodestrasse 1–3

030 20 90 55 77

Closed Mon.

$$$
Combination Area Ticket ($$$$) or Museum Pass ($$$$$) also available

U-Bahn/S-Bahn: Friedrichstrasse or S Hackescher Markt; Bus: 100

from 1340 B.C. The museum also houses the **Museum of Prehistory,** a heterogeneous collection of antiquities.

Alte Nationalgalerie: The Alte Nationalgalerie (Old National Gallery) vies with the Altes Museum in proclaiming Germany's love of culture and determination to display its devotion in as imposing a setting as possible. Completed in 1876, it, too, is a neoclassic temple, though of a very different kind. It is raised on a substantial podium and approached via a double stairway. After a building and refurbishment program lasting

three years and costing 68 million euros ($97 million), the Alte Nationalgalerie now forms a magnificent home for 19th-century German art.

The gallery is easily the best place to admire the country's particular contribution to Romanticism; there are no fewer than two dozen works by Caspar David Friedrich (1774–1840), including his atmospheric "Monk by the Sea" and "The Lonely Tree." Here, too, are paintings by the versatile

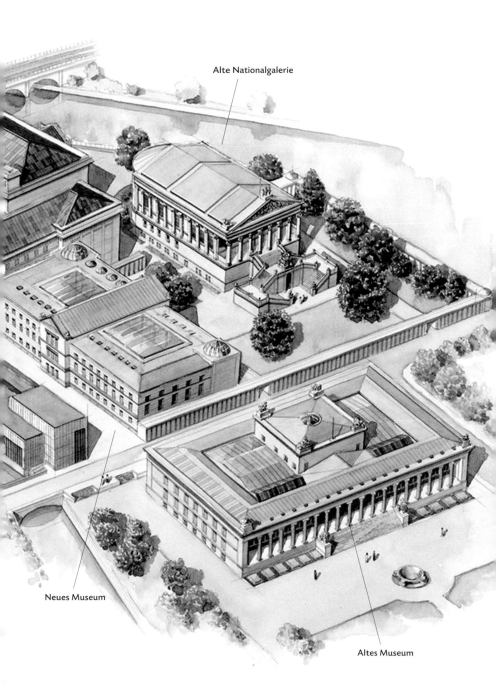

Alte Nationalgalerie

Neues Museum

Altes Museum

Pergamonmuseum

🅰 Map p. 61

✉ Am Kupfergraben 5

☎ 030 20 90 55 77

💲 $$$
Combination Area Ticket ($$$$) or Museum Pass ($$$$$) also available

🚇 U-Bahn/S-Bahn: Friedrichstrasse, S Hackescher Markt; Bus: 100

Karl Friedrich Schinkel, visionary architectural depictions of an idealized classical or Gothic world.

Most of the other great German artists of the century are represented: Philipp Otto Runge's (1777–1810) intensely realized portraits; Carl Spitzweg's (1808–1885) humorous evocations of placid small-town life; and, in contrast, Adolph Menzel's (1815–1905) hymn to the country's burgeoning heavy industry, "The Rolling Mill." Works by late 19th-century painters such as Max Liebermann and Lovis Corinth bear comparison with the paintings of their French Impressionist contemporaries.

EXPERIENCE:
Take a Rolling Tour

An excellent way to see Berlin is on board a public double-decker bus. Lines 100 and 200 of the BVG, the city's transportation authority, cover most major landmarks of the city center for a mere €2.60, the price of a single fare.

Bus 100's half-hour journey from Bahnhof Zoo to Alexanderplatz takes in the **Gedächtniskirche, Tiergarten, Victory Column, Reichstag, Brandenburg Gate,** and **Unter den Linden.** Line 200's route runs south of Tiergarten. There's no audio commentary, so pick up a tour description from **BVG service centers** (Alexanderplatz & Bahnhof Zoo, tel 030-194 49, bvg.de).

Pergamonmuseum: No rival to Schinkel's masterpiece in architectural terms, the Pergamonmuseum (Pergamon Museum) was built between 1912 and 1930 specifically to house the reconstructed

second-century altar from the Greek city of Pergamon in Asia Minor, now Turkey, but its collections of antiquities from the ancient world are almost inexhaustible. The first artifacts were gathered by the Electors of Brandenburg as far back as 1698, although the displays were made accessible to the public only in the 19th century. The scale of the **Pergamon Altar** is overwhelming, as is its frieze depicting the struggle of gods and giants (section closed for a revamp until 2019). Almost equal in impact is the **market gateway,** dating from the second century A.D., from the city of Miletus. Largest of all, the mighty **Ishtar Gate** from Babylon, with its processional way, is adorned with glazed bricks and figures of bulls and dragons. An imposing remnant of an eighth-century desert palace, the **Mshatta Facade** was a gift from the Ottoman Empire to Wilhelm II and today forms the centerpiece of a permanent exhibition of Islamic art.

Bode-Museum: Separated from the Pergamon Museum by the tracks of the elevated S-Bahn, the Bode-Museum is a superb neo-baroque edifice dating from 1904. Its clever design with a dome and rounded elevation enhances the promontory between the two arms of the Spree. Originally called the Kaiser-Friedrich-Museum, its present name honors Wilhelm von Bode, the great director of the Prussian State Museums in the early 20th century. A total refurbishment was completed in late 2006, providing much-needed space for several of the museum's prime collections.

The **Münzkabinett** (Coin Collection) includes coins—several thousand of them—banknotes, seals and medals, minting equipment, and an array of objects used for exchange and barter by people who did not use metal coinage.

The outstanding **Skulpturensammlung** (Sculpture Collection), ranging from the Middle Ages to the 18th century, contains both Italian and German masterpieces. Highlights include works by the talented court sculptor Tilman Riemenschneider, including *Noli me tangere* ("Touch me not"), a meticulously carved relief of Christ appearing before Mary Magdalene.

The **Museum für Byzantinische Kunst** (Byzantine Art Museum) shows sculpture, textiles, ceramics, and paintings from Italy, Greece, the Near East, and the Balkans, plus a collection of religious icons dating from the 14th to the 19th centuries.

Bode-Museum

- Map p. 61
- Monbijoubrücke
- 030 20 90 55 77
- $$$
  Combination Area Ticket ($$$$) or Museum Pass ($$$$$) also available
- U-Bahn/S-Bahn: Friedrichstrasse, S Hackescher Markt; Bus: 100

The Bode-Museum houses an extensive collection of traditional European sculpture, including this bust of St. John the Baptist by 15th-century Italian sculptor Matteo Civitali.

Kulturforum

-  Map pp. 52 & 60
- ✉ Matthäikirchplatz
- ☎ 030 266 42 42 42

smb.museum

Berliner Philharmonie

- Map pp. 52 & 60
- ✉ Herbert-von-Karajan-Str. 1
- ☎ 030 254 88 0
- 💲 Varies based on season & show
- 🚇 U-Bahn: Potsdamer Platz or Mendelssohn-Bartholdy-Park; Bus: S1, S2, S25

berliner-philharmoniker.de

Kulturforum

When, in the 1950s, the city's division looked permanent, the city fathers of West Berlin decided to implement the idea of a major cultural center on wasteland by the southeastern corner of the Tiergarten. It was hoped the Kulturforum could form a link in an eventual East–West cultural axis that would help bring the city together. This ambition has yet to be achieved: The Kulturforum still feels like a collection of individual buildings well off the beaten path. But for visitors with the slightest interest in the arts it has become an essential destination.

Music & Art: The first structure to take shape was a new home for the Berlin Philharmonic Orchestra, directed by Herbert von Karajan from 1954 to 1989. Designed by the city's architect-in-chief, Hans Scharoun, the asymmetrical, tentlike **Berliner Philharmonie** was opened in time for the Berlin Festival of 1963. Book tickets for a concert as far in advance as you can.

Scharoun also drew up the plans for the **Musikinstrumenten-Museum** next door, where the superlative collection of about 3,000 musical instruments dates back to the 16th century.

Opposite the Philharmonie, a

The distinct exterior of Scharoun's Berliner Philharmonie

sloping plaza leads to a complex of bunkerlike buildings with a vast foyer shared by several museums. There's the **Kupferstichkabinett**, with an outstanding collection of prints and drawings, and the **Kunstgewerbemuseum**, covering the decorative arts from the Middle Ages to art nouveau, art deco, and beyond. However, most visitors come here principally for the **Gemäldegalerie**, containing some of the world's great old master paintings. About 1,000 are on display in the main part of the gallery. How to choose between Botticelli, Titian, Raphael, Caravaggio, Claude Lorrain, and Poussin; Rembrandt, Rubens, Brueghel, and Franz Hals; Gainsborough and Reynolds? One way would be to concentrate on the galleries of German greats: Dürer ("Portrait of Hieronymus Holzschuher"), Cranach the Elder ("Fountain of Youth"), Baldung Grien ("Crucifixion"), and Holbein the Younger ("Portrait of the Merchant Georg Gisze") give an idea of the range of German painting in the 13th to 16th centuries.

Leave time to walk the short distance past the delicately detailed 19th-century brick Church of St. Matthew on the way to the **Neue Nationalgalerie** (New National Gallery). Designed by onetime Bauhaus director Ludwig Mies van der Rohe, this steel-and-glass gallery has one of the best collections anywhere of 20th-century German art.

Most of the modern German masters are well represented, including Kirchner and fellow expressionists Klee and Kandinsky,

INSIDER TIP:

After a day at the Kulturforum, catch a movie at nearby Cinestar in the Sony Center on Potsdamer Platz, where films are shown in their original version and beer is available at the snack bar.

—ELIZABETH BARRETT
National Geographic contributor

both teachers of the Bauhaus school. The collection also boasts gems by surrealist Ernst and social commentators Dix and Grosz.

The building is shut for a

Musik-instrumenten-Museum
- Map pp. 52 & 60
- ✉ Tiergartenstrasse 1
- ☎ 030 25 48 11 78
- ⊕ Closed Mon.
- 💲 $
- 🚇 U-Bahn/S-Bahn: Potsdamer Platz; Bus: 200, M48, 347

Gemäldegalerie
- Map pp. 52 & 60
- ✉ Matthäikirchplatz 4/6
- ☎ 030 266 29 51
- ⊕ Closed Mon.
- 💲 $$

EXPERIENCE:
Art Gallery Hopping

In the warmer months, Berlin's art scene hits the streets with a series of open gallery nights. The nexus of the action is the **Mitte district,** peppered with dozens of exhibition spaces ranging from rough, hole-in-the-wall studios to smart designer showrooms. To get a taste, start at the Oranienburger Strasse U-Bahn station in Mitte (map p. 53) and work your way east down Linienstrasse and back on the parallel-running Auguststrasse. These are popular events, and the masses typically spill out onto the sidewalks to chat and sip wine, as it's customary for hosts to offer free drinks. The biggest, best known dates are organized by **Open Gallery Weekend** (gallery-weekend-berlin.de) in early May and **Galerien Berlin Mitte** (galerien-berlin-mitte.de) in late summer. This being a spontaneous, artsy town, many other events materialize at short notice.

Neue Nationalgalerie

- Map pp. 52 & 60
- Am Kulturforum, Potsdamer Strasse 50
- 030 266 29 51
- Closed until 2018

Central-Western Berlin

- Map p. 52

face-lift through 2018, but until then, key works will be displayed elsewhere in town. Some treasures will eventually migrate to a new contemporary art museum, the Museum der Moderne, to be raised on a lot to the rear.

Central-Western Berlin

Running for 2 miles (3.5 km) from the heart of West Berlin toward the countrified suburbs around the Grunewald (Green Wood), the boulevard of the Kurfürstendamm is still the city's liveliest shopping street and the place to see and be seen. In contrast, Berlin's great central park, the Tiergarten, is somewhere to relax. This old royal hunting park is now a much-loved green space where you can find seclusion, or families setting up Sunday barbecue.

Long ago the "Ku'damm" was the route taken by princes and kings to their hunting lodge in the Grunewald, but in its present form it dates from the 1870s, when Bismarck ordered a Parisian-style grand avenue to be laid out. At its eastern end stands the **Kaiser-Wilhelm-Gedächtniskirche** *(Breitscheidplatz, tel 030 218 50 23),* completed in 1895 to honor the first emperor of newly united Germany. In 1943 the church was almost completely destroyed in a bombing raid; a new belfry and church were erected around the shell of the old tower, known to sardonic Berliners as the "hollow tooth."

Breitscheidplatz around the church is one of the busiest spots in Berlin, with constant traffic and a mixed population of punks, skateboarders, and all sorts of idlers. Inside the new octagonal church, however, all is tranquil; calming light filters through the honeycomb of double-glazed stained glass, its deep blue shot with intense flashes of other colors, and a golden figure of Christ hangs serenely over the scene. The square's eastern side is dominated by the 22-story tower of the **Europa-Center,** built in

Battered by war, Berlin's great landmark, the Kaiser-Wilhelm-Gedächtniskirche, still stands.

the early 1960s as Berlin's first American-style shopping complex.

Farther east from the square along Tauentzienstrasse is a very different kind of retail experience. The **Kaufhaus des Westens** *(Wittenbergplatz),* known simply as KaDeWe, is one of the world's great department stores, opened in 1906. More shops extend westward along the Ku'damm, where the street's trademark showcases stand in the middle of the broad sidewalks, although more exclusive outlets line the side streets.

West of Breitscheidplatz, there are galleries and luxury shops on Fasanenstrasse, a street running south off the Kurfürstendamm, while, just to the north, the area around **Savignyplatz** is particularly atmospheric, with restaurants, antique shops, and book dealers. On Ku'damm-Karree, trace Berlin's convoluted history by immersing yourself in **The Story of Berlin.** Don a headset (English version available) and listen to the events of each period of the city's history as you walk through a series of historically themed rooms.

Zoo Station & Around:

Just northwest of Breitscheidplatz, **Bahnhof Zoo** (Zoo railroad station) was the main point of arrival until 2006, when the new Hauptbahnhof opened in Mitte. In the 1970s it became synonymous with dinginess, drug dealing, and street crime, but subsequent facelifts have made it more salubrious. The nearby **Zoologischer Garten** is one of the world's finest zoos, home to 19,000 animals. Highlights include a walk-through aviary and a

The West Rises Again

After the Wall fell, parts of West Berlin began to fade as the Mitte district—the 19th-century city center, in the former East—regained its luster. Now, the Breitscheidplatz area has staged a comeback. Two 1950s showpieces, the Zoo-Palast cinema *(Hardenbergstrasse 28a)* and the curvy Bikini-Haus shopping mall *(Hardenbergplatz 2),* have been restored, while a new Waldorf Astoria hotel tower *(Hardenbergstrasse 28)* graces a once-grungy street by Zoo station.

giant tank filled with tiger sharks.

The zoo merges into the **Tiergarten,** which is bisected by Strasse des 17 Juni, the triumphal avenue widened in the 1930s to link the city center with the Olympic Stadium in the west. Other avenues join it at the roundabout dominated by the **Siegessäule,** the victory column originally erected in front of the Reichstag to commemorate victorious 19th-century Prussian campaigns, and moved here in 1939. One avenue leads northeast toward **Schloss Bellevue,** a modest neoclassic palace built in 1785 as a princely residence and now the official home of the German president.

Farther to the east, on the banks of the Spree, the **Kongresshalle** looms over the trees. It was built in 1955–1957 by the United States, not just as a congress hall but as a symbol of progressive

(continued on p. 74)

The Story of Berlin
▲ Map p. 52
✉ Ku'damm-Karree, Kurfürstendamm 207–208
☎ 030 88 72 01 00
$ $$$
🚇 U-Bahn: Uhlandstrasse; Bus: 109, M29, X10

story-of-berlin.de

Zoologischer Garten
▲ Map p. 52
✉ Hardenbergplatz 8
☎ 030 25 40 10
$ $$$$$ (zoo & aquarium), $$$ (zoo only)
🚇 U-Bahn/S-Bahn: Zoologischer Garten

zoo-berlin.de

The Wall

For 28 years, this most baleful symbol of the Cold War separated West Berlin from the eastern part of the city and from the GDR proper. By the time it crumbled in 1989, the 96-mile-long (155 km) Berlin Wall—called by its creators the "Anti-Fascist Protection Rampart"—had claimed the lives of at least a hundred would-be escapers. The first instinct of Berliners was to destroy the hated barrier. Few traces of it remain today.

Jubilant Berliners sit astride the hated symbol of Germany's division in November 1989.

Before 1961, nothing hindered movement between the eastern and western parts of the city. West Berliners and tourists freely moved around East Berlin, where prices were low and an evening at the opera with Russian champagne could be enjoyed for the price of a movie ticket in the West. Every day, more than 50,000 East Berliners commuted to well-paid jobs in the West. Far more serious, the economy of the GDR was slowly grinding to a halt as the country's labor force—particularly its more skilled members—moved to the West.

By the summer of 1961, more than 3.4 million GDR citizens had decamped, and the regime had become desperate. On the night of August 13, all movement between East and West was halted, and, in an operation of military thoroughness, a temporary wall was thrown up, consisting in some sections of barbed wire, in others of crudely laid building blocks. Official reaction from the West was mostly verbal, although there was a standoff between American and Soviet tanks at Checkpoint Charlie when GDR guards attempted to block Allied access to the East.

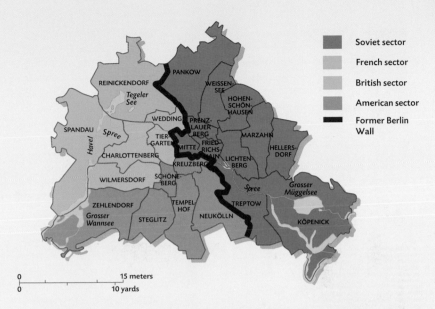

■	Soviet sector
■	French sector
■	British sector
■	American sector
▬	Former Berlin Wall

```
0 ———————————— 15 meters
0 ———————————— 10 yards
```

The hastily laid initial barrier was succeeded by more sophisticated defenses. Eventually there was the Wall itself, a pale concrete structure 13 feet (4 m) high, with a curved top offering no purchase for hands or grappling irons. Behind it came the "death strip" that not even the border guards were allowed to enter, an anti-vehicle ditch, a patrol track, trip wires, a guard-dog run, tank traps, and then a further high fence. A total of 300 watchtowers with machine-gun openings and an array of bunkers provided cover for the border guards.

The Wall became a grisly attraction for Westerners. Platforms were erected so that visitors could peer over the top and catch a glimpse of East Berlin. Western graffiti artists found the smooth concrete irresistible. In 1989, when the Wall was demolished, the most prized souvenirs were those with the best graffiti. The longest intact section of the Wall, running over half a mile (0.8 km) along the Spree in eastern Berlin, is the graffiti-covered so-called East Side Gallery, though this was decorated post-1989 by artists from around the world. Another section remains on Bernauer Strasse. The scene of last-minute escape attempts in 1961, it now hosts the Berlin Wall Memorial (berliner-mauer -gedenkstaette.de) with a documentation center.

EXPERIENCE: Ride Around the Wall

Berlin on Bike! (*Knaackstrasse 97, tel 030 43 73 9999, berlinonbike.de*) takes you on a 9-mile (15 km), 4-hour bicycle tour of the Berlin Wall and other Cold War–era sites. Pedal through the old East German neighborhood of Mitte and its boarded-up subway stations, shop for souvenirs at Checkpoint Charlie, and visit the few remaining sections of the Berlin Wall and its notorious death strips. Marvel at the Chausseestrasse plaque commemorating the rabbit that died unknowingly crossing hostile human borders, a reminder of the innocence of nature. It is best to reserve space in advance. Tours leave from Prenzlauer Berg (*English offered Tues., Thurs., & Sat. at 11 a.m., $$$ including bike rental*).

Schloss Charlottenburg

- 🗺 Map p. 52
- ✉ Spandauer-damm 10–22
- ☎ 030 32 09 11
- 🕐 Closed Mon.
- 💲 $$$ incl. guided/audio tour
- 🚇 U-Bahn: Sophie-Charlotte-Platz, Richard-Wagner-Platz; S-Bahn: Westend; Bus: 109, 309, M45

spsg.de

Museum Berggruen

- 🗺 Map p. 52
- ✉ Schlossstrasse 1
- ☎ 030 266 42 42 42
- 🕐 Closed Mon.
- 💲 $$
- 🚇 U-Bahn: Sophie-Charlotte-Platz, Richard-Wagner-Platz; S-Bahn: Westend; Bus: 109, 309, M45

smb.museum

Sammlung Scharf-Gerstenberg

- 🗺 Map p. 52
- ✉ Schlossstrasse 70
- ☎ 030 266 42 42 42
- 🕐 Closed Mon.
- 💲 $$
- 🚇 U-Bahn: Sophie-Charlotte-Platz, Richard-Wagner-Platz; S-Bahn: Westend; Bus: 109, 309, M45

smb.museum

architecture and of the West's attachment to Berlin. In 1980 it suddenly collapsed, but reconstruction was successful. The building now serves as a multicultural meeting place, the **Haus der Kulturen der Welt** (*John-Foster-Dulles Allee 10, tel 030 39 78 71 75, hkw.de*), with changing exhibitions on globally cultural themes.

Charlottenburg

The graceful tower of **Schloss Charlottenburg** is one of Berlin's landmarks, rising proudly over the western borough of Charlottenburg

INSIDER TIP:

In winter, the pond behind Schloss Charlottenburg turns into an ice-skating rink. Even if you don't have skates, the backdrop of the Schloss makes for a scenic glide.

—LARRY PORGES
National Geographic Travel Books editor

and acting as a beacon for a group of first-rate museums. The palace was severely damaged by bombing in World War II and could well have been completely demolished afterward. However, following the 1950 destruction of the Berliner Schloss in the city center by the East Berlin authorities, the decision was made to restore Charlottenburg to its former royal glory.

The borough of Charlottenburg now extends as far as the Tiergarten and the Brandenburg Gate, but in the late 17th century this suburb of Berlin was still deep in the countryside and a suitable site for a summer palace for Sophie Charlotte, wife of Elector Frederick, later Frederick I of Prussia. She died in 1705, and Frederick changed the palace's name to Charlottenburg, in her memory.

The tone is set by the regal entrance court, with its statue of the Great Elector Frederick William (1640–1688) on horseback. Behind the palace's long facade, a succession of stunning interiors includes the sumptuous **Chapel** with its royal box, the glittering **Porcelain Cabinet,** and the **Golden Gallery,** with delicate rococo decoration. Only the almost-too-perfect state of some of the rooms reminds you that many of them were not simply restored but reconstructed from scratch. Among the paintings on display are masterworks by the French artist Antoine Watteau, one of the favorite painters of Frederick the Great. Among the exhibition's considerable assets is its collection of 18th-century French paintings, the largest outside France.

Charlottenburg's extensive grounds are a favorite place for Berliners to relax. Like the palace itself, they show the development of taste, in this case from the formal symmetry of the baroque gardens close to the castle, to the Romantic, English-style landscape extending along the banks of the River Spree. Focal points in the park include the **Mausoleum,** the burial place of Queen Luise and her husband, Frederick William III; the **Belvedere,** with a collection of porcelain; and

Charlottenburg has been restored since World War II to its former glory.

the **Schinkel-Pavillon,** an Italian-style villa designed by the Prussian architect Karl Friedrich Schinkel.

Museums: Opposite the Schloss are two museum buildings that once served as barracks for the royal guardsmen. The one on the west side is the **Museum Berggruen,** a quality collection of early 20th-century art assembled by Heinz Berggruen, a native of Berlin. It displays more than 100 paintings by Picasso, including his portrait of Georges Braque, as well as works by Paul Klee and other contemporaries. Across the street, the **Sammlung Scharf-Gerstenberg** is a fascinating trove of 250 paintings, sculptures and photos by the surrealists and their forerunners. Look out for rare works by Dalí, Ernst, Francisco Goya (1748–1828) and Man Ray (1890–1976), as well as dungeon architecture by Giovanni Battista Piranesi (1720–1778). Nearby, the **Bröhan-Museum** has fabulous examples of art nouveau and art deco porcelain, silver, glass, metalwork, and furniture.

Located near the Zoo railway station, the **Museum für Fotografie** brings together collections of the Helmut Newton Foundation and the art library of Berlin's public museums. Newton, a Jew, fled from Germany to Australia in 1938 but kept a soft spot for Berlin, his hometown. In the upstairs gallery are exhibits of contemporary and Newtonian works (such as his iconic Big Nudes), while the ground floor holds a showcase of the late photographer's personal effects.

Neighborhoods of the Former East

While some areas of the former East seem to have changed little since the days of the German Democratic Republic, others are absolutely hopping. Among them,

Bröhan-Museum
- ⓐ Map p. 52
- ✉ Schlossstrasse 1a
- ☎ 030 32 69 06 00
- 🕐 Closed Mon.
- 💲 $$
- 🚇 U-Bahn: Sophie-Charlotte-Platz, Richard-Wagner-Platz; S-Bahn: Westend; Bus: 109, 309, M45

broehan-museum.de

Museum für Fotografie
- ✉ Jebensstrasse 2
- ☎ 030 31 86 48 25
- 🕐 Closed Mon.
- 💲 $$
- 🚇 U-Bahn/S-Bahn: Zoologischer Garten

smb.museum

Kulturbrauerei

✉ Schönhauser Allee 36

🚇 U-Bahn: Eberswalder Strasse

kulturbrauerei.de

Prenzlauer Berg, once a relatively poor quarter, has become gentrified and hip. With its edginess and large Turkish community, multicultural Kreuzberg enjoys fame as a stronghold of alternative lifestyles. Farther east, Friedrichshain is winning a name for itself with a busy nightlife scene.

Prenzlauer Berg: Little more than countryside until the

and **Kollwitzplatz,** caters to their needs.

Not far from the elevated U-Bahn station at Eberswalder Strasse, the massive **Kulturbrauerei** is a masterpiece of urban recycling. Built in 1889, this dazzling complex of red-and-yellow brick was Berlin's most attractive brewery until it stopped bottling in 1967. Today it is an entertainment center, with clubs, bars, cinema, and stores.

Visitors find plenty of charming stores and cafés in Prenzlauer Berg.

Synagoge Rykestrasse

🅜 Map p. 53

✉ Rykestrasse 53

☎ 030 880 28 316

🕐 Open Thurs. 2–6 p.m., Sun. 11 a.m.–4 p.m.

💲 $$

🚇 U-Bahn: Senefelder Platz

jg-berlin.org

mid-1800s, Prenzlauer Berg had become a densely populated working-class district by the 20th century. Neglected under the GDR, it attracted East Berlin's intellectuals and artists. Since then, much has been renovated, prices have soared, and the penniless Bohemians have scattered, leaving behind a young population of go-getters. A spectrum of restaurants, bars, and shops, especially around **Kastanienallee**

The charming square Kollwitzplatz (named after noted artist Käthe Kollwitz) is the scene of a bustling Saturday market. Many Jews once lived in these parts, as the **Synagoge Rykestrasse** would suggest. The beautifully restored, redbrick structure from 1904 is one of only two to survive the Nazi era and war damage. Visible from the synagogue's entrance is the Wasserturm, a water tower known as Dicker Hermann (Fat Herman), which Hitler's storm troopers turned into a prison for local Jews. It now houses upscale apartments.

Kreuzberg: South of the River Spree, the inner-city borough of Kreuzberg revels in its boisterous, in-your-face vibe and is a favorite with students and hippies. To some extent, yuppies have now moved into the district, but there's plenty of atmosphere around the **Maybachufer,** where a colorful Turkish market is held.

Kreuzberg is also home to two impressive exhibits, including the **Jüdisches Museum** (Jewish Museum), designed by Polish-American architect Daniel Libeskind. Reached by an underground passageway from the neighboring 18th-century former courthouse, the museum was built in the 1990s to house exhibits documenting the course of Jewish history in Germany from its beginnings in the ninth century. The plan of this unique building is a deconstructed version of the star of David imposed on Germany's Jewish citizens by the Nazi regime. A central axis running through the interior is intended to evoke the terrible void left by the attempted destruction of European Jewry.

The rooftop feature of the **Deutsches Technikmuseum** (Museum of Technology)—a huge, dangling C-47 cargo plane—hints at the wondrous gadgetry inside. Plenty of interactive exhibits, as well as scads of boats and planes, will keep the keenest science buff interested. The real stars of the show, however, are the vintage locomotives and rolling stock, housed in former roundhouses.

Friedrichshain: In the far east of Berlin, the suburb of Friedrichshain is bisected by a curious experiment in 1950s Soviet-style planning and architecture, the strangely captivating Karl-Marx-Allee. Nearby **Boxhagener Platz** has become a focal point of frenetic nightlife for the restless folk who bailed out of Prenzlauer Berg.

The sprawling **Volkspark Friedrichshain** is filled with historic symbolism. Creative builders used the rubble left over after World War II to create two hills over old air-raid shelters, including the 256-foot-high (78 m) **Grosser Bunkerberg**. However, the Märchenbrunnen (Fairy-tale Fountain), fronted by a gracious colonnade in the park's northwest corner, remained unchanged. ∎

Jüdisches Museum
- 🅰 Map p. 53
- ✉ Lindenstrasse 9–14
- ☎ 030 25 99 33 00
- 💲 $$
- 🚇 U-Bahn: Hallesches Tor; Bus: 248, M29, M41

jmberlin.de

Deutsches Technikmuseum
- 🅰 Map p. 53
- ✉ Trebbiner Strasse 9
- ☎ 030 90 25 40
- 🕐 Closed Mon.
- 💲 $$
- 🚇 U-Bahn: Gleisdreieck, Möckernbrücke

sdtb.de

Viktoriapark

The "mountain" of Kreuzberg rises all of 216 feet (66 m) in Viktoriapark, a somewhat unkempt but pretty park crisscrossed with short trails, some of them quite steep. On the peak you'll find a memorial, designed by famed architect Schinkel, to the 1815 war that ejected Napoleon from Germany. The view reaches to the former Tempelhof Airport, where a huge three-pronged sculpture mimics the three air corridors used during the Berlin airlift.

EXPERIENCE: Exploring Berlin's Underworld

Things change fast in Germany's fashionably deprived capital (unofficial slogan: "Poor but Sexy"). The old East German parliament building, an icon of nostalgia, has been torn down. Visitors seeking traces of the Third Reich have to look hard: Hitler's bunker, for instance, is paved over and bears only a simple marker. To discover Berlin's deepest, darkest secrets, best take an underground tour of its bunkers, tunnels, and vaults going back to the 19th century.

Around 100 bunkers are located in, around, and under Berlin, fairly intact but nearly invisible unless you know where to look. In the latter stages of World War II, there were more than 1,000, and the Germans moved part of the war effort underground, using a railway tunnel under Tempelhof Airport to roll out fighter aircraft. As the Russians closed in on the capital, the Nazis flooded tunnels and bunkers to thwart the Allies, and untold numbers drowned. Despite that destruction, there are areas that seem remarkably undisturbed. Old schoolrooms, a "ghost" U-bahn station, and even underground vats of a brewery are visible.

The guides for **Berliner Unterwelten** (*Brunnenstrasse 105, tel 030 49 91 05 18, berliner-unterwelten.de, $$$; "Dark Worlds" tour at 11 a.m. daily April–Oct. & Thurs.–Mon. Nov.–March*), the society that runs the tours, are part historian, part archaeologist, and have turned up valuable finds, such as an IBM machine that catalogued Jewish detainees.

Most of these fascinating circuits begin a few miles north of the Brandenburg Gate, at the deepest U-Bahn station, Gesundbrunnen. It's cold, dusty, claustrophobic, and more than a bit creepy. The "Dark Worlds" tour begins just behind a sturdy steel door that hundreds of commuters normally pass unnoticed. Once inside the dark, humid entrance corridor, the guides quiz

INSIDER TIP:

Bring a sweater and sturdy shoes on your tour. The air is constantly cool, and the ground can be worn in places.

—BRIDGET A. ENGLISH
National Geographic Books editor

visitors on everything from German wartime vocabulary to the physics of air supply. The lamps are turned out to reveal luminous painted signs, important during blackouts, still aglow.

Farther inside, you begin to get an idea of everyday life during air raids: the grim, triple-bunk beds in close quarters, rows of primitive toilets without privacy, the hand-powered ventilators

to keep deadly gases at bay. The lasting images are of World War II civilians with battered suitcases, huddled in cramped, dank chambers, waiting for the walls to stop shaking from the bombing raids aboveground.

Glass cases show military uniforms, weapons, and documents. Among the prized objects is an Enigma machine that the Nazis used to encrypt secret messages until 1943, when they found the Allies had cracked the code. Remarkable, too, are photos of the chilling murals in the Fahrerbunker (chauffeurs' bunker): SS soldiers raising their shields to serve the *Volk,* painted by the guards of Hitler's chauffeur pool.

Arguably most skin-crawly is the tour "U-Bahn, Bunker, and Cold War," complete with de-radiation shower facilities and details of morale control, such as the intentional lack of exposed pipes to prevent residents from hanging themselves. But these bunkers could sustain human life for only a matter of weeks, and survivors were told little about the fleeting, irradiated lives they would be forced to lead aboveground after a nuclear strike.

More Places to Visit in Berlin

Berliner Dom (Berlin Cathedral)

The Dom is the outstanding example of the kind of overblown architecture favored by Kaiser Wilhelm II. The emperor kept an eye on every detail of the Dom's design, only accepting the architect's proposals after they had been modified again and again. The building is undeniably impressive, inside and out, even after losing some of its ornament during the extensive reconstruction that took place from 1983 onward. Perhaps the most evocative part of the building is the crypt, not for its architecture but for its contents: The coffins of 89 members of the Hohenzollern royal family are preserved.
berliner-dom.de  Map p. 53 ✉ Am Lustgarten ☎ 030 20 26 91 36 💲 $$ 🚉 S-Bahn/ U-Bahn: Alexanderplatz; Bus: 100, 200

East Side Gallery

Some of the panels along the Wall's East Side Gallery (see also p. 73) bear political images ranging from the Cold War to the present day, while others are playfully surreal and light-hearted. Despite the name, it costs nothing to see the artworks, which are best viewed on a stroll along Mühlenstrasse in the borough of Friedrichshain. At the eastern end of the gallery, at an unusually broad part of the Spree, the area's distinctly industrial character is relieved somewhat by the Oberbaum Bridge, with its redbrick faux-medieval towers and pixie-like turrets.
eastsidegallery.com  Map p. 53 🚉 S-Bahn/ U-Bahn: Warschauer Strasse

Haus der Wannsee-Konferenz

In this opulent villa on the shore of the Wannsee, the crucial decision was made in 1942 to implement the "Final Solution to the Jewish Problem." It is not easy to reconcile the tale told in the exhibits with the beauty and harmony of the surroundings. Displays cover the history of German persecution in Nazi Germany and occupied Europe from 1933 to 1945.

Directly opposite, on the other side of a lovely bay on the River Havel, lies the **Strandbad Wannsee,** a popular resort laid out in the late 1920s.
ghwk.de  Map p. 52 ✉ Am Grossen Wannsee 56–68 ☎ 030 805 0010 🚉 S-Bahn: Wannsee, then Bus 114

Kaiser Wilhelm II built the Berliner Dom in Italian Renaissance style with the intent to overawe.

Museum Dahlem

Divided into four museums spread over three floors, this ethnographic collection displays items such as painted stoneware vessels of the Maya, Aztec idols, and gold artifacts from Central America, Colombia, and Peru. The museum is noted for its periodic world music events and exotic indoor markets.
smb.museum  Map p. 52 ✉ Lansstrasse 8 ☎ 030 830 1438 🕐 Closed Mon. 💲 $$ 🚉 U-Bahn: Dahlem-Dorf; Bus: 110, X11, X83

Neue Synagoge

With its gilded cupola dominating the busy inner-city district around Oranienburger Strasse, Berlin's New Synagogue was completed in 1866. Its opulent style reflected the pride and growing status of the city's Jews. Members of the Prussian government, led by Bismarck, respectfully attended the opening ceremony. On Kristallnacht in 1938, the synagogue was one of many attacked by

INSIDER TIP:

To explore more of former East Germany, rent a bike at Pedalpower in Berlin [pedal power.de] and take a regional train to Rheinsberg [see p. 86] for a bicycle tour.

—MARKUS ZIENER
University of Applied Sciences Berlin teacher

Nazi thugs, although in this case the attackers were held off by a courageous policeman, Wilhelm Krützfeld. Although the building was largely destroyed by Allied bombs in 1943, it has been reconstructed. Today it houses displays on Berlin Jewish life. *cjudaicum.de* 🅐 Map p. 53 ✉ Oranienburger Strasse 28/30 ☎ 030 88 02 83 00 (Zentrum Judaicum) 🕐 Closed Sat. 💲 $ 🚉 S-Bahn: Oranienburger Strasse

Nikolaiviertel

Flattened in a 1943 air raid, the area around St. Nicholas Church is the oldest part of Berlin. For the city's 750th anniversary in 1987, the GDR authorities rebuilt the district in something like its old form. Architectural purists objected to the not always accurate re-creation of old buildings, but Berliners love it, and so probably will you. The area has shops and places to eat and drink. 🅐 Map p. 53 🚌 Bus: 147, 248, M48

Olympiastadion

In 1936, 110,000 spectators watched the main events of the Olympic Games in this immense stadium in the western part of the city. The Games were a propaganda coup for the Nazi regime, which managed to cover up some of the more repulsive aspects of its rule for the duration. Hitler walked out rather than have to congratulate the African-American gold-medal sprinter Jesse Owens, who had conclusively disproved the Nazis' theories of Aryan superiority. The design of the stadium was begun before the Nazis came to power, and although it shows many traces of their aesthetic preferences, it is essentially a sober and functional structure, its vast size partly concealed by its being sunk into the ground. It was completely restored in time for soccer's World Cup in 2006, when Berlin hosted the final match. *olympiastadion-berlin.de* 🅐 51 C3 & map p. 52 🚉 U-Bahn/S-Bahn: Olympiastadion

Potsdamer Platz

The old Potsdamer Platz was the busiest intersection in Berlin, but after 1945, those cafés, bars, restaurants, hotels, and stores that had survived the war were pulled down. Later the Wall was built right across what had once been Berlin's liveliest and most cosmopolitan square. Now life has returned in full, and the new Potsdamer Platz promises to be one of the focal points of 21st-century Berlin. There are apartments, theaters, cinemas, restaurants, and spacious shopping malls in abundance. Innovative building complexes extend southward from the grandiosely rebuilt S-Bahn station to the banks of the Landwehr Canal. Here you will also find the **Deutsche Kinemathek** (Filmmuseum Berlin, *Potsdamer Strasse 2, tel 030 300 90 30, deutsche -kinemathek.de, closed Mon.),* which covers the country's film history from the early days of Babelsberg studios to contemporary German cinema. 🅐 Map p. 53 🚉 S-Bahn/U-Bahn: Potsdamer Platz

Brandenburg

A sigh of relief went up from beleaguered West Berliners as the Wall came down in 1989 and, among other things, they regained their freedom to explore the hinterland of their city, the area now covered by much of the *Land* of Brandenburg. The classic destinations are the palaces and parks of Potsdam and the shady streams of the Spreewald, but there is much else to see and do in the course of a day's excursion from the capital.

The best way to explore the tranquil Spreewald area is aboard a punt.

With its woods and waterways, Brandenburg is a delight for ramblers, cyclists, and boating enthusiasts. Take local advice on footpaths, bike rental, and river trips. For a more focused outing, look beyond Potsdam, the Land capital, to Old Brandenburg, the city that gave the area its name. Despite enthusiastic industrialization by the communist regime and the slow pace of restoration, Old Brandenburg retains some of its medieval appeal with many fine buildings.

Cottbus, with one of Germany's loveliest landscaped estates at Schloss Branitz, is the country's easternmost big city. But it is Frankfurt an der Oder, on the border with Poland and split between Germany and Poland in 1945, that has become a symbol of the complex and sometimes difficult process of reconciliation between the two nations. One place of painful memory is Oranienburg; built by the Nazis as one of their main concentration camps, it was later used by the Soviets.

Potsdam

⚑ 51 C3

Visitor Information

✉ Am Neuen
Markt 1

☎ 0331 27 55 80

**potsdam-tourism
.com**

Nikolaikirche

✉ Am Alten Markt

☎ 0331 270 8602

🕐 Closed Sun. a.m.

💲 $$ (dome)

nikolai-potsdam.de

Potsdam &
the Royal Palaces

Potsdam is to Berlin what Versailles is to Paris, a royal town salubriously sited to the west of the city and dominated by palaces, parks, and gardens. Just as the château at Versailles is indissolubly linked to the Sun King, Louis XIV, so Potsdam's Sanssouci Palace reflects the personality of Frederick the Great. The city is reached swiftly by train, or in a more leisurely way by boat from Wannsee through the woods and parklands fringing the Havel River.

Visitors walking into the old town must pass the **Landtag Brandenburg,** the spanking new, and very regal, seat of regional parliament. It is a reproduction of the Stadtschloss, the onetime winter palace of the Great Elector of Brandenburg. The building segues into **Alter Markt,** the old marketplace lorded over by the early 19th-century **Nikolaikirche** and its massive dome.

Next door, that confection topped with striking green cupola and golden atlas is the **Altes Rathaus** (Old City Hall), home to the **Potsdam Museum** of art and local history. The square concludes at the 18th-century **Palast Barberini,** soon to house the private art collection of Hasso Plattner, founder of software giant SAP.

Potsdam was a residential

The royal palace of Schloss Sanssouci crowns the vine-clad terraces of Frederick the Great's park.

town, with a population dominated by high-ranking officers and senior bureaucrats. The streets are lined with fine 18th- and 19th-century homes, many of them now occupied by prosperous commuters from western Berlin.

To the north of Bassinplatz is the **Holländisches Viertel** (Dutch Quarter). Its grid of streets and brick houses dates from 1742, when Frederick William I hoped to attract industrious immigrants from the Netherlands. Not many Dutch came, and the gabled dwellings now attract visitors with shops, bookstores, and bars.

Farther north still is the **Alexandrowka,** the "Russian Colony," a group of timber chalets that provided accommodations for the members of a Russian soldiers' choir who had ended up here during the Napoleonic wars. One or two of the Siberian-style houses are still inhabited by descendants of the original choristers, and a delightful little Orthodox church tops the nearby hill. On the corner between Potsdam and Berlin stands **Schloss Glienicke,** an 1820s neoclassic palace with a magnificent landscape. The park overlooks the Havel and the steel spans of the **Glienicke Bridge** (see sidebar this page).

The Royal Palaces: Fascinating though the town of Potsdam is, it inevitably lives in the shadow of its royal palaces, above all **Sanssouci,** the supreme expression of

the Prussian rococo style. Long and low, the single-story edifice with its modest dome sits atop a plateau from which a stairway and six curving terraces descend to formal gardens below. The palace was

Spy Swap

The Glienicke Bridge linking Berlin and Potsdam over the Havel River was rebuilt in the 1950s by the East Germans and named, in what must have been a moment of black humor, Brücke der Einheit (Unity Bridge). On three occasions between 1962 and 1986, it was the stage for international spy swaps, starting on February 10, 1962, with U.S. pilot Gary Powers, who had been shot down in his U-2 spy plane over the Soviet Union; and the last on February 11, 1986, when Russian dissident Anatoli Sharansky, accompanied by three Allied spies, was exchanged for two busloads of Eastern-bloc spooks.

designed for Frederick the Great by the court architect Georg Wenzeslaus von Knobelsdorff (1699–1753), based on draft plans prepared by the monarch himself. It was intended to be a place "free of care" (*"sans souci"*), to which this cultured king could escape from affairs of state.

The main entrance to the palace is from the colonnaded court

Landtag Brandenburg
✉ Alter Markt 1
☎ 0331 966 0
landtag.brandenburg .de

Altes Rathaus (Old City Hall)/Potsdam Museum
✉ Am Alten Markt 9
☎ 0331 289 6969
🕐 Closed Mon.
💲 $$

Palast Barberini
✉ Rudolf-Breitscheid-Str. 189
☎ 0331 9799 2185
museum-barberini .com

Sanssouci
🅰 51 C3
☎ 0331 96 94 202
🕐 Palace closed Mon.
💲 $$
🚆 S-Bahn & Regional express train to Potsdam Hauptbahnhof, then Bus 695 or X15
spsg.de

to the north. The **Marble Hall** formed a dignified setting for the king's famous roundtable discussions with eminent men of letters. The finest interior is perhaps the ornate **Concert Room,** where Frederick loved to play the flute.

To the east of Sanssouci is the **Bildergalerie** (Picture Gallery), its immaculately restored rococo interior almost upstaging the old master paintings assembled by Frederick the Great. To the west are the **Neue Kammern** (New Chambers), built as guest accommodations. There is plenty more to see in the park along a nine-mile (15 km) circuit of sights. Its present appearance was dreamed up by Peter Joseph Lenné, the

The Royal Palaces

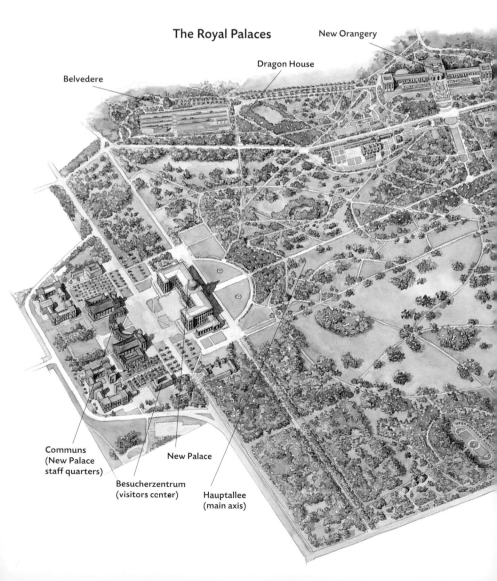

New Orangery

Dragon House

Belvedere

Communs
(New Palace
staff quarters)

New Palace

Besucherzentrum
(visitors center)

Hauptallee
(main axis)

royal landscape architect.

On the upper level, the **Neue Orangerie** (New Orangery) is an Italian-style building decorated with paintings in imitation of Raphael; beyond it are the pagoda-like **Drachenhaus** (Dragon Building) and the **Belvedere** with views over the park. Down below, the fantastical **Chinesisches Teehaus** (Chinese Teahouse) is topped by the gilded figure of a mandarin with a parasol. A little farther on are the Roman Baths (Römische Bäder), then **Schloss Charlottenhof,** a lovely little neoclassic

Neues Palais

- ⊕ Closed Tues.
- 🚇 S-Bahn: Wildpark
- 💲 $$
- 🚇 S-Bahn & Regional express train to Potsdam Hauptbahnhof, then Bus 695 or X15

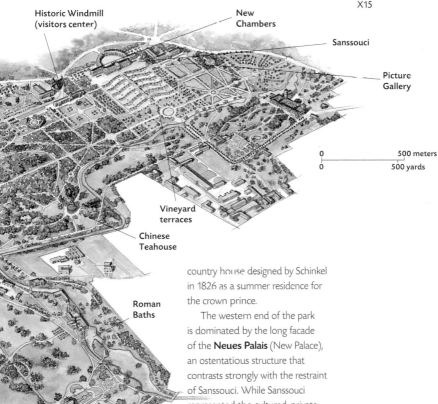

Historic Windmill (visitors center)

New Chambers

Sanssouci

Picture Gallery

| 0 | | 500 meters |
| 0 | | 500 yards |

Vineyard terraces

Chinese Teahouse

Roman Baths

Schloss Charlottenhof

country house designed by Schinkel in 1826 as a summer residence for the crown prince.

The western end of the park is dominated by the long facade of the **Neues Palais** (New Palace), an ostentatious structure that contrasts strongly with the restraint of Sanssouci. While Sanssouci represented the cultured, private life of the monarch, the New Palace expresses Prussian pride following the country's victories in the Seven Years War. Its bombast appealed to Kaiser Wilhelm II, who used it as a summer residence. The most striking interior is the Grotto Hall (Grottensaal), with an over-the-top decor of mineral fragments, shells, and semiprecious stones. ∎

More Places to Visit in Brandenburg

Cottbus

Cottbus suffered wartime damage and extensive industrialization in the GDR period. It is very proud of its theater, not only for its productions but because it is one of the finest examples of an art nouveau building in the country. However, the town is on the tourist trail mainly because of the local lord, Prince Pückler-Muskau (1785–1871). Having had to leave his family home of Muskau in 1845 through bankruptcy, the prince established himself here at **Schloss Branitz** (Robinienweg 5, tel 0355 7 51 50, pueckler-museum.de, closed Mon.). A passionate gardener, he created a fine park, which today extends to around 250 acres (100 ha). cottbus.de ⚠ 51 D2 ✉ Berlinerplatz 6 ☎ 0355 7 54 20 💲 $$

Rheinsberg

One of the most popular destinations for day trips from Berlin is Rheinsberg,

an attractive little town with a lakeside **Schloss** (tel 0339 31 72 60, spsg.de, closed Mon., $$), where Frederick the Great spent part of his youth. The future king lent his imprimatur to the place, as did writer Kurt Tucholsky (1890–1935), author of the 1912 best seller, *Rheinsberg: A Picture Book for Lovers,* in which he described how he fell in love here, both with the Schloss and with his sweetheart. The tale still draws couples to Rheinsberg for romantic weekends. ⚠ 51 C4

Spreewald

For centuries, the watery and inaccessible Spreewald, less than an hour's drive from Berlin, stayed off the beaten path. In the early 19th century, Berliners on the lookout for a rural retreat discovered the area's charms. Today more than two million visitors a year come here, some for longer vacations, some to enjoy a sociable trip aboard a many-seated punt. But it's easy enough to get away from the crowds and enjoy the natural beauties of what is now a UNESCO-designated biosphere reserve.

The most popular gateway to the Spreewald is the pleasant town of **Lübbenau** (Lubnjow); this is the northern edge of the homeland of Germany's Sorbs, a Slav nation whose language and way of life somehow survived centuries of envelopment by German culture (see pp. 240–241). You can find out about them at the open-air section of the **Spreewald-Museum** (tel 03542 24 72, spreewald-web.de, closed late Oct.–March, $), located in **Lehde** (Lehdy in Sorbian), a short punt trip or a walk of a little more than a mile (2 km) from Lübbenau. The **Gherkin Museum,** almost certainly the only one of its kind in the world, celebrates the gherkin, the area's most famous contribution to gastronomy (Bauernhaus-und Gurkenmuseum Lehde, tel 03542 8 99 90). ⚠ 51 D2

EXPERIENCE:
Bird-watching in the Oder Valley

Nestled in the northeastern corner of Brandenburg, **Lower Oder Valley National Park** (nationalpark-unteres -odertal.de) is one of Europe's great bird sanctuaries. Some 150,000 geese, ducks, and swans, and more than 3,000 cranes, gather in the unspoiled delta regions during migration time. The 160-plus species breeding here include such rare or endangered varieties as the aquatic warbler, black stork, corncrake, and white-tailed eagle. The car-free park extends nearly 40 miles (64 km) along the Polish-German border and is best explored via its network of bicycle and hiking paths.

Splendidly preserved old cities, Germany's most attractive coastline, and a glorious lake district

Mecklenburg-West Pomerania

Stylish speedster

Mecklenburg-West Pomerania

Stretching from near Lübeck in Schleswig-Holstein to the Polish border along the River Oder, Mecklenburg-Vorpommern is the most northeasterly of the German *Länder*. Along the Baltic Sea, the winds and waves modeled a shoreline of bays, spits, islands, and peninsulas, sheltering the lagoon-like inlets known as *Bodden*.

The landscapes and wildlife of the Bodden of West Pomerania are protected as a national park. Two other national parks in the region—like that of the Bodden, created since reunification—are the spectacular chalk cliffs and superb beech forests of Jasmund on the island of Rügen, and the Mecklenburg Lake District (Mecklenburgische Seenplatte). The lakes, which include the Müritz, Germany's second largest body of fresh water, are a great place for wildlife as well as for yachtsmen and canoeists. But the region's biggest magnet is the Baltic coast, with its endless sandy beaches. Two centuries ago, aristocratic entrepreneurs laid out resorts and spa facilities, and German vacationers have ever since flocked to enjoy

them. Since reunification, there has been no shortage of funds to spruce up the faded glories of resorts such as Heringsdorf and Ahlbeck on the island of Usedom, Binz on Rügen, or Kühlungsborn near Rostock.

A leading member of the Hanseatic League of trading cities (see sidebar p. 121), Rostock is the region's largest town. The city and its harbor were promoted as the German Democratic Republic's "Gateway to the World." It's a lively place, with a sense of history despite much modernization. History is even more evident in the other Hansa harbor towns: With their

NOT TO BE MISSED:

Schwerin's fantastical castle **91**

The Hanseatic trading towns of Wismar and Stralsund **94–95**

Exploring old-timey resorts along the Baltic coast **96–97**

The glorious white chalk cliffs of Rügen island **99**

An afternoon biking on the remote island of Hiddensee **101**

Imperial-style relaxation in Usedom, "Berlin's bathtub" **103–104**

Boating in lake-filled Müritz National Park **105**

heritage of fine building, Wismar and Stralsund are candidates for UNESCO World Heritage status; Greifswald preserves the memory of Caspar David Friedrich, to many the most appealing of Germany's Romantic painters; and in Güstrow is the studio of the early 20th-century expressionist sculptor Ernst Barlach. Neubrandenburg has its intact ring of medieval walls, Ludwigslust its great ducal *Schloss,* and Schwerin, the Land capital, its palaces and galleries in an unequaled lakeside setting. ∎

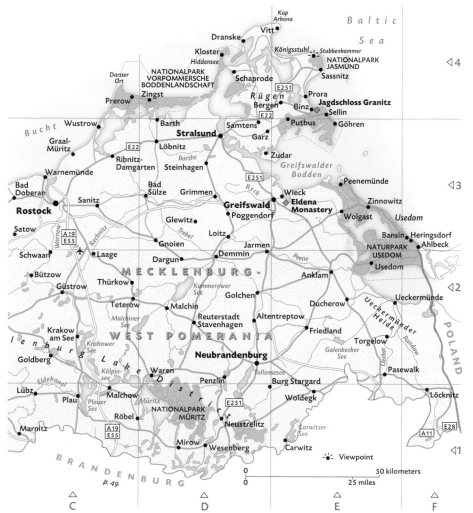

Baltic Sea

Kap Arkona
Vitt
Dranske
Königsstuhl Stubbenkammer
Kloster
Hiddensee
NATIONALPARK JASMUND
Sassnitz
Darsser Ort
NATIONALPARK VORPOMMERSCHE BODDENLANDSCHAFT
Schaprode
Zingst
Prerow
E251
Prora
Rügen
Bergen
Binz
Jagdschloss Granitz
Sellin
Bucht
Wustrow
Barth
Samtens
Putbus
Göhren
Stralsund
Graal-Müritz
E22
Löbnitz
Garz
E22
Barthe
Zudar
Ribnitz-Damgarten
Steinhagen
Greifswalder Bodden
Warnemünde
E251
Ryck
Peenemünde
Bad Doberan
Bad Sülze
Grimmen
Wieck
Zinnowitz
Sanitz
Greifswald
Eldena Monastery
Wolgast
Rostock
Glewitz
Poggendorf
Usedom
Satow
Trebel
Loitz
Bansin Heringsdorf
A19 E55
Gnoien
Jarmen
NATURPARK USEDOM
Ahlbeck
Schwaan
Laage
Dargun
Demmin
Peene
Usedom
Bützow
MECKLENBURG-
Anklam
Güstrow
Thürkow
Kummerower See
Golchen
Ducherow
Ueckermünde
Teterow
Malchin
Reuterstadt Stavenhagen
Altentreptow
Ueckermünder Heide
Krakow am See
Malchiner See
WEST POMERANIA
Friedland
Torgelow
Randow
Goldberg
Krakower See
Galenbecker See
Pasewalk
Lübz
Kölpin-see
Waren
Lake District
Penzlin
Tollensesee
Burg Stargard
Woldegk
Löcknitz
Plau
Malchow
Müritz
Neubrandenburg
Marnitz
Plauer See
Röbel
NATIONALPARK MÜRITZ
Neustrelitz
Carwitzer See
A11 E28
A19 E55
Mirow
Wesenberg
Carwitz
·Ö· Viewpoint

POLAND

BRANDENBURG
p. 49

0   50 kilometers
0   25 miles

△ C   △ D   △ E   △ F

◁4
◁3
◁2
◁1

Schwerin

When the Berlin Wall came down in 1989, West German visitors flocked to the capital of Mecklenburg-West Pomerania, drawn not only by its lakeside location but also by its ease of access: It is only an hour's drive from Hamburg. When the last Grand Duke of Mecklenburg departed in 1918, he left a legacy of fine building that may have tipped the scales when it came to choosing a capital for the new state in 1990.

The Ancestors' Gallery of Schloss Schwerin depicts more than 600 years of ducal rule.

Schwerin
🅰 88 B2
Visitor Information
✉ Am Markt 14
☎ 0385 5 92 52
12/13/14

schwerin.com

Complete with cathedral and marketplace, the city's medieval core still occupies this ancient site. You will certainly want to explore the streets and alleyways of the Altstadt, but your city tour will probably start by the lakeside, where a group of splendid public buildings makes an aristocratic backdrop to summer concerts and performances.

The **Staatstheater,** a big white neo-baroque building,

dates from the 1880s. The even grander neoclassic **Staatliches Museum** was completed around the same time. Great collectors, the grand dukes of Mecklenburg had a particular penchant for Dutch and Flemish painting, and the museum's collection by such masters as Rubens, Franz Hals, and Jan Brueghel has few equals in Germany. It also includes modern German works and 20th-century conceptual art.

INSIDER TIP:

Enge Strasse ("narrow street"), southwest of Town Hall, is lined with lovely half-timbered buildings like the former wine merchant Michaelis at No. 1.

—JEREMY GRAY
National Geographic author

The galleries are worth a visit, but if time is short, cross the bridge to the castle island. Turn left and walk clockwise around the landscaped gardens surrounding the castle with their fine views across the Schweriner See. Three-quarters of a circuit brings you to the castle entrance or to another bridge. This leads to the much larger **Schlossgarten,** a baroque park with a canal, statues, and clipped hedges.

Schloss Schwerin is a glorious confection of towers, turrets, and pinnacles, one for every day of the year according to those who have taken the trouble to count them. The first stronghold was built by the area's Slavic inhabitants in the 11th century; they burned it down rather than surrender it, but the island was soon refortified by the invading Germans. The castle's present appearance is mostly due to the 19th duke's desire for a palace that would look more medieval than the Middle Ages.

The climax of the interior is the sumptuous **Throne Room** with its frescoes, coats of arms, and columns of Carrara marble. On the second floor, you can visit the **Dining Room** and adjoining circular **Tea Room,** and in the **Ancestors' Gallery** hang the portraits of former dukes of Mecklenburg.

Back on the town side of the bridge, head toward the **Altstadt** (Old Town), using the 384-foot (117 m) cathedral tower as a landmark. The marketplace has a more jolly atmosphere than the area around the castle. The colonnaded structure on its northern side was intended as a market hall, while the **Rathaus** (Town Hall) was rebuilt in a vaguely English neo-Tudor style in the mid-19th century. Schwerin's **Cathedral** (Dom) is a grandiose example of the medieval Brick Gothic style (see p. 38), although the tower looming over the marketplace is a 19th-century addition. Climb its 220 steps for a panorama of the city. To the north is the **Pfaffenteich,** the Priests' Pond, created to supply power to the city's medieval water mills. ∎

Staatliches Museum
- ✉ Alter Garten 3
- ☎ 0385 5 95 80
- 🕐 Closed Mon.
- 💲 $$

museum-schwerin.de

Schloss Schwerin (Schlossmuseum)
- ✉ Lennéstrasse 1
- ☎ 0385 5 95 80
- 🕐 Closed Mon. mid-Oct.– mid-April
- 💲 $$

schloss-schwerin.de

EXPERIENCE: Listen to Opera in the Open Air

The highlight of the cultural calendar in Schwerin is the annual *Schlossfestspiele* (castle concert series) held June to August. It's hard to imagine a more dramatic venue: From arena seats in the royal gardens, patrons can enjoy world-class operas such as *Aida* or *The Magic Flute* performed on an open-air stage framed by the castle's magnificent turrets, the arias wafting in the summer breeze. For further details and tickets, see *theater -schwerin.de/schlossfestspiele.*

Schwerin Cathedral
- ✉ Am Dom 4
- ☎ 0385 56 50 14
- 💲 Cathedral free, $$ Schwerin Ticket gives access to the steeple tower

schwerin.com

Rostock

Rostock lost out to Schwerin when a capital city was chosen for the new Land after reunification, a slight that continues to irritate what was a proud seafaring town with one of the first universities in northern Europe. Much of the city's medieval heritage was destroyed in World War II, but enough remains to evoke a splendid past. Together with the neighboring ferry port and resort of Warnemünde, Rostock is a lively place, with good facilities and plenty of accommodations, an ideal base for your exploration of Germany's Baltic coast.

Participants in the annual Hanse Sail festival are put through their paces by a Force 6 gale.

Rostock
🅰 89 C3
Visitor Information
✉ Neuer Markt 3
☎ 0381 381 2222
rostock.travel

In its early days, Rostock was not one but three towns (Old Town to the east, Middle Town, and New Town to the west), laid out on the south bank of the broad River Warnow in the 13th century, each with its church and market square. About a mile north of the main railway station, the spacious **Neuer Markt** New Marketplace) was laid out as the focal point of the **Mittelstadt** (Middle Town) in 1232. The tramlines and broad roadway swirl around the 16th-century gateway known as the **Steintor,** part of the fortifications that once surrounded the town.

The New Market's dominant feature is the rather strange **Rathaus** (Town Hall). A fairly conventional baroque facade with a ground floor arcade is topped by a row of fierce-looking brick spikes with pointed openings below. This is the roof of the original, medieval Rathaus, one of the finest of all the Brick Gothic city halls along the Baltic coast. Its baroque front was added in the 18th century.

Overlooked by the tall spire of the **Petrikirche** (St. Peter's Church), long a familiar beacon to seafarers, the **Altstadt** (Old Town) is interesting but rather run-down, so head west along Rostock's traffic-free main street, **Kröpeliner Strasse,** which bisects the Neustadt (New Town).

Spare a few moments for the massive brick-built **Marienkirche** just to the north; fortresslike outside, the church has exceptionally rich furnishings within, including an astonishing bronze font from the late 13th century. At midday, a parade of saintly figures springs to life as the 15th-century astronomical clock strikes noon.

Continue west along Kröpeliner Strasse into the **Universitätsplatz,** lined with stately buildings. The core of the New

Town, the square is lively today with its open-air cafés, market traders shouting their wares, and children darting among the water jets and sculptures of the fountain.

Housed in an old monastery, the **Kulturhistorisches Museum** (Historical Museum; *Klosterhof 7, tel 0381 20 35 90, closed Mon.*) has artifacts and paintings—look for those of the Ahrenshoop artists, evoking the Baltic coast. It's worth climbing to the top of the lofty gateway of **Kröpeliner Tor** farther west on Kröpeliner Strasse.

As well as a sandy beach, Rostock's old seaside suburb of **Warnemünde** has elegant villas and fishermen's houses converted into restaurants. Make the 7-mile (11 km) trip to Warnemünde by the S-Bahn or, in summer, by boat from the Kabutzenhof quay.

On a moored freighter in the harbor west of town, the **Schiffbau- und Schifffahrtsmuseum** (Maritime Museum) focuses on GDR-era shipbuilding, and its large collection includes charming fleets of model vessels from Rostock's Hanseatic heyday. ■

Schiffbau- und Schifffahrts-museum

✉ IGA Rostock Schmarl-Dorf

☎ 0381 12 83 13 64

🕐 Closed Mon., open daily July–Aug.

💲 $$

schifffahrtsmuseum -rostock.de

EXPERIENCE: Setting Sail on the Baltic Sea

The River Warnow and Rostock's quayside are liveliest in early August, when vintage sailing vessels take part in the annual **Hanse Sail,** the Baltic's largest regatta, that attracts more than a million onlookers. Everywhere you look, there are tall-masted schooners, windjammers, square-riggers, and vintage yachts, all eager to strut their stuff on Sail Saturday. Traditional and museum-piece vessels from around the world (and even a handful of seaplanes) cram the harbors here and in picturesque Warnemünde. Even the local navy base gets in the act, sending its training ship *Gorch Fock* for public boarding.

During the four-day extravaganza—including fireworks, entertainment, and cultural events—dozens of captains offer day and evening trips off the Baltic coast via Hanse Sail *(Warnower Ufer 65, Rostock, tel 0381 208 52 33, hansesail.com)*. These thrilling, salt-in-your-face affairs can be surprisingly comfortable and include catering and facilities for children, who may clamber about the boat's innards under supervision. In the summer, longer cruises up to several days' journey go as far as Sweden and Denmark.

In many cases, sailors who enter the Hanse Sail races are happy to take along passengers of varying levels of experience, from landlubbers to old sea dogs. Whatever your pedigree, contact the **Tall Ship Booking Office** *(Warnower Ufer 65, Rostock, tel 0381 381 29 75, email: tallshipbooking@gmx.de)* to be matched with a suitable vessel. State your personal requirements, and expect to share in the competition's entry and mooring fees. Once you've booked, the skipper will give you details of what to expect on board. Above all, don't forget your foul-weather gear!

To learn the ropes, enroll in one of the region's many sailing courses. The experts at **Baltic Windsport** *(Stadthafen 71, Rostock, tel 0381 200 95 55, baltic-windsport.de)* offer training year-round on catamarans, yawls, and yachts. The full-service harbor-cum-hotel at **Yachhafen Hohe Düne** *(Am Yachthafen 1–8, Warnemünde, tel 0381 50 40 80 80, yachthafen-hohe-duene-de)* has courses in sailing, windsurfing, and scuba diving.

Wismar

Second only to Lübeck among the historic port cities of the Hanseatic League (see sidebar p. 121), Wismar is putting right the neglect of GDR times and sprucing itself up to welcome an ever swelling tide of visitors. Together with Stralsund, it is one of the best places to get the feel of Germany's Baltic heritage, with an intact medieval street network, an array of architecture from all periods, and an atmospheric old harbor.

Wismar
- ⚐ 88 B2

Visitor Information
- ✉ Am Markt 11
- ☎ 03841 194 33

wismar.de

Rathaus
- ✉ Am Markt
- ☎ 03841 251 30 25
- 💲 $

Schabbellhaus
- ✉ Schweinsbrücke 8
- ☎ 03841 224 31 10
- 🕐 Closed Mon.
- 💲 $

NOTE: **Boat trips** Details at visitor information center (see above)

The gently sloping cobbled **Markt** is the city centerpiece. The big draw here is the **Wasserkunst**, the little copper-domed pavilion covering the fountain that supplied the citizenry with water right up to the end of the 19th century. Among the buildings lining the east side of the square is the 14th-century high-gabled, brick house known as the **Alter Schwede** (Old Swede), a reminder that the city was handed over to Sweden after the Thirty Years War and returned to Mecklenburg only in 1803.

INSIDER TIP:

Wismar has been known for *Mumme,* a strong dark beer, since the 15th century. Try it at Brauhaus am Lohberg *(Kleine Hohe Strasse 15).*

—SANDRA MITSCHARD
Wismar Tourism Board

To discover more about Wismar's history, find the side entrance to the civic museum in the vaults of the **Rathaus** (City Hall), the serene neoclassic structure filling the northern side of the square. Or visit the town historical museum in the **Schabbellhaus,** a 16th-century mansion.

Make sure you stroll along the **Grube,** the narrow canal running past the **Nikolaikirche.** One of the grandest of Germany's Baltic Brick Gothic (see p. 38) churches, its lofty interior soars to a height of 121 feet (37 m). In this superb setting, admire the medieval altarpieces, mural paintings, and a beautiful bronze font. The city's other churches include the **Georgenkirche,** with an ornate high altar from 1430; the intimate **Heilig-Geist-Kirche** (Church of the Holy Ghost) on Lübsche Strasse; and the **Marienkirche** on St.-Marien-Kirchhof, of which only the 262-foot (80 m) tower survived wartime destruction.

Under communism, lack of care for Wismar's built heritage went hand in hand with growth and development. The city became the GDR's second most important port, after Rostock. More interesting than the modern installations is the **Alter Hafen** (Old Harbor) with the one surviving **Wassertor** (City Gate), ancient warehouses, and the chance to brave the Baltic waves aboard one of the old sailing vessels moored here. ∎

Stralsund

Almost completely surrounded by water, compact Stralsund is one of the best preserved of all the Baltic harbor towns, its skyline still dominated by the towers of three great churches, its streets still lined with houses dating from the town's glory days before the Thirty Years War. Stralsund is not only attractive in itself, but its central location along the coast also makes it an excellent base for exploration in various directions.

Views from the tower of Stralsund's Marienkirche look out over the old city.

Its strategic location and sheltered harbor helped the city to prosperity as one of the leading members of the Hanseatic League. Stralsund's former power and wealth are proudly expressed in the **Alter Markt** (Old Market), overlooked by its great central church and city hall, almost welded together into a single integrated structure incorporating several houses. The medieval **Rathaus** (City Hall) is one of the most startling civic buildings in the whole of Germany; its seven-gabled facade is exactly that—a front with nothing but air behind most of it. The adjoining **Nikolaikirche** has treasures such as the naively carved panels of bearded Russian hunters handing pelts over to a skeptical-looking merchant. Still on the square, you can admire the Gothic buildings of **Wulflamhaus,** and—in contrast—the **Commandanten-Hus,** a baroque relic of the time when the Swedes ruled Stralsund.

To the south, **Neue Markt** (New Market) boasts the **Marienkirche** rebuilt in 1416. Climb the tower for a breathtaking view of the city. The **Deutsches Meeresmuseum** (Oceanographic Museum) includes a convincingly reproduced coral reef. The aquarium has displays on North Sea marine life. ∎

Stralsund

⚑ 89 D3

Visitor Information

✉ Alter Markt 9

☎ 03831 246 90

stralsundtourismus.de

Deutsches Meeresmuseum

✉ Katherinenberg 14–20

☎ 03831 265 02 10

🕐 Closed Mon. Oct.–Dec.

$ $$$–$$$$$

www.meeresmuseum.de

A Drive Along the Baltic Coast

Old-fashioned resorts, tranquil landscapes, and intriguing inland towns feature in this two-day journey along the Baltic's sandy shores.

Leave the old Hanseatic port city of **Wismar** on the B105 toward Rostock. Ignore the "Autobahn Rostock" signs and continue on the old main road toward Rostock and Bad Doberan. After 20.5 miles (33 km), leave the main road, following signs to Kühlungsborn. The road runs north toward the coast through a short stretch of attractive, well-wooded hill country, the Kühlung.

Kühlungsborn ❶ is the biggest resort along this coast, with 2.5 miles (4 km) of sandy beach and many opulent hotels and villas (although finding somewhere to stay is not always easy if you haven't made an advance reservation). Kühlungsborn West and Kühlungsborn Ost once vied for the favors of vacationers, but they were joined in shotgun

matrimony in 1938. The main symbol of their present togetherness is the **Ostseeallee,** the long drive running parallel to the shore and separated from·it by a fine belt of trees. Drivers need to keep their eyes off its grand villas and on the road: The traffic-calming measures here include occasional solid-looking timber posts sticking up out of the carriageway. Even if you don't swim, surf, or sunbathe in Kühlungsborn, you should stroll out on to the newly built pier for the sea air.

Continue along the coast to little **Heiligendamm** ❷, Germany's very first purpose-built seaside resort, developed with splendid neoclassic buildings in the 1790s by Grand Duke Friedrich Franz I of Mecklenburg. The main road (105) now leaves the coast and

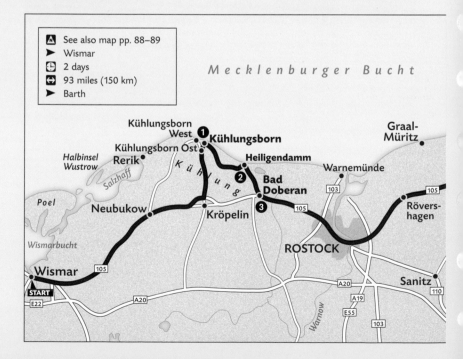

- ⓜ See also map pp. 88–89
- ► Wismar
- ⊕ 2 days
- ⬌ 93 miles (150 km)
- ► Barth

NOT TO BE MISSED:

A walk on the pier at Kühlungsborn
• The amber museum at Ribnitz-Damgarten • The harbor and seamen's church at Ahrenshoop
• The church at Prerow

heads inland on a lovely avenue of linden trees alongside the little railroad that has run the few miles between Kühlungsborn and Bad Doberan since 1886.

The Cistercians founded a monastery in **Bad Doberan** ❸, and their great Brick Gothic minster contains original furnishings, including a gilded high altar and a tabernacle carved in oak. Outside, look for the pretty ossuary (Beinhaus) where the monks' bones were preserved. The town itself bears the imprint of Duke Friedrich Franz, who made it the summer capital of his

court. His palace is now a hotel, and one of the charming Chinese-style pavilions in the middle of the Kamp, a parklike village green, is a café.

Continue on the 105, passing through the city of Rostock and on for 16 miles (26 km) to the town of **Ribnitz-Damgarten** ❹. The **Bernstein-Museum** (Im Kloster 1–3, tel 03821 46 22, closed Mon. Nov.–Feb., $$$, deutsches-bernstein museum.de) here, housed in a monastery building, has examples of amber, many containing immaculately preserved insects of long ago.

Now backtrack a few yards and find the minor road leading northwest toward Dierhagen. You are now entering the Fischland-Darss-Zingst peninsula. Much of this area is conserved as part of **Nationalpark Vorpommersche Boddenlandschaft** (National Park administration, Im Forst 5, Born, tel 038234 50 20, www.nationalpark-vorpommersche-boddenlandschaft.de), with woods, meadows, boglands, dunes, and saltwater lagoons (Bodden). It is a popular vacation area, but the old fishing villages have kept much of their character. Artists, rather than aristocrats, set the tone here, so the vacation houses are thatched cottages rather than swanky villas. The village of **Ahrenshoop** ❺ is a good place to get the feel of the Fischland. Sandy lanes lead down to the sheltered Bodden, and the harbor usually has some of the typical fishing boats known as Zeesenboote. Ahrenshoop's tiny timber church is built in the shape of an upturned boat.

The Darss area is dominated by woodland and by the resort of **Prerow** ❻, its cottages scattered among the trees. Just off the main road, Prerow's redbrick church reflects the sea, with suspended ship models and bold, colorful carvings reminiscent of ships' figureheads. Climb up onto the grassy dike for a look at the Baltic shore, and then continue along the seawall for 2.5 miles (4 km), where the road turns south back toward the mainland. The final stop is at **Barth** ❼, a little place with a long history as a harbor town. In spring and fall, countless birders flock here to admire the tens of thousands of migrating cranes.

Rügen

Rügen is Germany's largest island. In the opinion of its many visitors, it is also the most beautiful, with landscapes that range from glorious beech woods to sandy shores and spectacular chalk cliffs. Tourism here began with the creation of a spa in the early 1800s. Then came elegant seaside resorts, which saw a revival after German reunification. Even more of a paradise is traffic-free Hiddensee Island, a favorite with artists and intellectuals for more than a century.

In Jasmund National Park, sheer, beech-capped cliffs rise from the Baltic shore.

Rügen
◩ 89 D3–E4
Visitor Information
✉ Bahnhofstrasse
15, Bergen
☎ 03838 80 77 0
**www.mecklenburg
-vorpommern.eu**

A 1.5-mile (2.5 km) causeway and bridge links Rügen with the mainland at Stralsund. The main road and railroad head directly toward Bergen, the island's little capital, but you should take the side road past Gustow and Barz to **Putbus.** Centered on a ring

of white villas known as the Circus, this pretty little spa town was the brainchild in 1810 of the local lord, Prince Wilhelm Malte. He hoped to attract an exclusive clientele with landscaped gardens, theatrical entertainments, and the excitements of saltwater

INSIDER TIP:

Rügen's shores are great for beachcombing. Amber, flint stone, and fossils such as belemnites can often be found, especially after a storm.

—LINDA RICHTER
National Geographic contributor

bathing. The exotic trees he planted in his English-style park are still here, but his mansion was too redolent of feudal symbolism for the communist rulers, who demolished it in the 1960s. Other buildings survived however, among them the church, originally built as a ballroom; the orangery, guarded by stone lions saved from the mansion; and, above all, the templelike theater.

In the early 20th century, theater guests were conveyed to Putbus from their hotels on the coast aboard the dining cars of a little railroad that still runs today. Once nicknamed the *Turnip Express,* it has been rebranded *Rasender Roland (Rushing Roland),* although it dawdles rather than races the 15 miles (25 km) to its terminus at Göhren. Steam locomotives still snort in the station and depot at Putbus, which is also served by a branch off Rügen's main line.

The railroad continues one stop farther to the harbor at Lauterbach. From here you can board a boat and sail around the little island of **Vilm,** although you can land only by prior arrangement *(tel 038301 6 18 96).* No timber

has been felled on Vilm for hundreds of years, and visitor numbers to what is now a nature reserve are carefully controlled. In GDR times, the island's charms were reserved for the enjoyment of the Communist Party elite.

Binz

Rushing Roland is an entertaining way of getting to Rügen's premier resort of **Binz,** which faces the bracing Baltic breezes on the island's east coast. Binz has a promenade, a pier, and a Kurhaus (assembly rooms), and villas

Small Wonder

Tucked away in the northeast of Rügen, Germany's tiniest national park—Jasmund National Park—covers a mere 11.6 square miles (30 sq km). Tiny though it is, it harbors a lion's share of natural wealth: majestic chalk cliffs, as well as such rare plants and animals as the towering wild service tree and the white-tailed eagle, both found around the magical swamplike ponds of the Stubnitz woods.

flaunting white-painted fancy fretwork balconies and gables line its century-old streets. Although Binz has come up in the world again, its real glory days were the period just before World War I. The entertaining little **Historisches Binz Museum,** housed in the Villa Odin *(Zeppelinstrasse 8),* brings this epoch to life.

Binz
🅰 89 E4
Visitor Information
✉ Haus des Gastes, Heinrich-Heine-Strasse 7, Binz
☎ 038393 148 148
ostseebad-binz.de

Rasender Roland
🅰 89 D3–E4
✉ Bahnhofstrasse 14, Putbus
☎ 03838 01 188 4012
ruegensche -baederbahn.de

**Jagdschloss
Granitz**

- ✉ Lancken-Granitz
- ☎ 038393 667 10
- 🕐 Closed Mon.
  Nov.–March
- 💲 $$

www.granitz
-jagdschloss.de

**Documenta-
tionszentrum
Prora**

- ✉ Objektstrasse,
  Prora
- ☎ 038393 13 991

proradok.de

South from Binz, the train puffs up an incline toward the little station for the **Jagdschloss Granitz** (Granitz Hunting Lodge), a massive mock-medieval hunting lodge built on the hilltop by Prince Wilhelm. Fight any feelings of vertigo and climb the winding wrought-iron stairway inside the castle tower for a magnificent panorama of this end of the island. With its woods, flower-rich meadows, and intricate coastline, the whole area is a UNESCO-designated biosphere reserve, coexisting with small resorts such as Sellin and Baabe, their early 1930s atmosphere immortalized by novelist Christopher Isherwood in his semi-autobiographical *Goodbye to Berlin*.

EXPERIENCE:
Sleep in a Lighthouse

What goes round and round and has a bed in the middle? As historic beacons seek a new lease on life, a new experience has opened up for coastal visitors: lighthouses turned hotels. Facilities vary enormously in size, style, and furnishings, but whether you seek a youth hostel, a family hotel, or a luxury hideaway, there's something for every budget. For an overview of what's available on the north German coast, see *leuchtturmseiten.de.*

North of Binz

To the north, among the sand dunes and pine forest in the other direction from Binz, is one of Germany's most outlandish sights, a massive wall of concrete stretching more than

2.5 miles (4 km) along the curving shore. This overwhelming presence is **Prora,** a relic of the Nazis' "Strength through Joy" program, designed to keep the working masses happy. Families would vacation in the countless apartments slotted into the six-story structure, the centerpiece of which was to be a festival hall with seats for 20,000. But war intervened, and Prora's only guests were refugees from Germany's bombed-out cities. It was subsequently occupied by the Volkspolizei (People's Police) and then, until 1990, by the Nationale Volksarmee (People's Army). The building is currently being developed into private residences, but the **Documen-tationszentrum Prora,** located halfway along the complex, covers the entire story in pictures, audio, and fascinating documentary film clips.

Prora is built on a narrow strip of land separating the Baltic from the Kleiner Jasmunder Bodden, the lagoon that, together with the Grosser Jasmunder Bodden, brings salt water right into the heart of the island. To the north is Jasmund, a more substantial block of land, which was once an island in its own right. The first substantial sights here are the extensive installations of the modern ferry port of Neu Mukran. With its train ferry facilities, the harbor was built to link East Germany with Soviet ports, an alternative to the rail and road routes through Poland, which was seen as an unreliable ally in the Solidarity era in the 1980s.

Coastal Cliffs: Beyond the old harbor town of Sassnitz, much of Jasmund is covered by splendid beech forests of the **Stubbenkammer,** protected as part of a national park. The crowds mostly come here to gasp at the spectacular chalk cliffs dropping hundreds of feet into the Baltic. The drama of their jagged forms and pristine whiteness fascinated the Romantic painter Caspar David Friedrich (see p. 42); his 1818 picture of early tourists gazing in awe from the cliff edge is a frequently reproduced classic of German art.

The most adventurous way of experiencing the cliffs is on foot along the coastal path from **Sassnitz.** But this is a whole day's walk, and most visitors simply take the shuttle bus from the parking lot to the main viewpoint, known as the **Königsstuhl** (King's Seat). Those with really strong nerves should venture on to the **Viktoriasicht,** a tiny platform that projects out over the abyss. A precipitous and potentially slippery path takes you to the beach. You can also take a mini-cruise along the coastline aboard a pleasure cruiser from Sassnitz.

After the Stubbenkammer, almost anything would be an anticlimax, but it is still worthwhile continuing to Rügen's northernmost tip, **Kap Arkona,** with its two lighthouses and remains of the Slavic fortress of Jaromarsburg. Nearby is the idyllic fishing village of **Vitt,** with thatched cottages and a church containing a striking modern mural.

Hiddensee: You can also take the ferry from Schaprode on Rügen's western coast to the long, narrow island of **Hiddensee,** 10 miles (17 km) offshore. Hiddensee preserves its tranquillity by banning cars, and it is even more peaceful once the day visitors have departed. There is a bus service, but renting a bike is the best way to explore the island, with its old thatched

Kap Arkona boasts a pair of lighthouses.

houses and sandy beaches. Figures as famous as Sigmund Freud have fallen under Hiddensee's spell, but the most famous resident was the playwright and Nobel Prize winner Gerhart Hauptmann (1862–1946), who is buried in the village of Kloster. ∎

Sassnitz

⬛ 89 E4

Visitor Information

✉ Strand-
   promenade 12

☎ 038392 64 90

insassnitz.de

Greifswald

Greifswald's most famous son is the Romantic artist Caspar David Friedrich (1774–1840), and the silhouette of the ancient university town remains much as it was when he painted it in the early 19th century. The town's best known monument is the ruined monastery of Eldena, one of Friedrich's favorite subjects.

Greifswald
Ⓜ 89 E3
Visitor Information
✉ Rathaus/Markt
☎ 03834 52 13 80
greifswald.de

Eldena was founded at the mouth of the little River Ryck in 1199. The market established by the monks a short distance upstream grew into an oval-shaped town with a regular checkerboard of

Dating from 1245, the choir transept and central nave of Eldena monastery still stand.

streets. Greifswald became a member of the Hanseatic League, and in 1456 the university was founded, one of the earliest in northern Europe.

The city suffered badly in the Thirty Years War, but its surrender to the Red Army in April 1945 saved it from more destruction. Bronze relief panels commemorate these events at the entrance to the **Rathaus** (Town Hall) in the main square, Marktplatz. Here, open-air cafés mingle with a variety of fine buildings, among them the early 15th-century **Giebelhaus,** a rare example of a Baltic Brick Gothic (see p. 38) town house.

Caspar David Friedrich's paintings are scattered, but Greifswald makes the most of what it has in the **Pommersches Landesmuseum** *(Rakower Str. 9, tel 03834 83 12 0, pommersches -landesmuseum.de, closed Mon., $$),* installed in sensitively adapted turn-of-the-18th-century buildings. The Friedrich paintings on display include a much-loved depiction of Eldena.

Don't miss **Eldena monastery;** the sandstone ruins stand among fine old trees. Nearby is the fishing village of **Wieck,** reached by a Dutch-style drawbridge that could be out of a van Gogh painting. ∎

Usedom

Second only to Rügen in size, Germany's easternmost island owes its fame to the magnificent sandy beaches that stretch almost its entire length. When bathing in the sea became fashionable in the 19th century, Usedom enjoyed royal patronage, and its three most prestigious resorts style themselves imperial bathing places *(Kaiserbäder)*. However, its good rail connections with the capital earned the island the jollier nickname of Berlin's Bathtub.

Beach "baskets" by the pier at Ahlbeck protect sunbathers from Baltic breezes.

There are two approaches to Usedom from the mainland. The road and rail bridge to the northern part of the island goes from the old port of **Wolgast,** with its big brick medieval church in the upper town and a timber-framed warehouse by the quayside. Farther south, the road from **Anklam** crosses the channel on a drawbridge.

Usedom is all about the pleasures of the sea, but the island has a sinister side as well. A left turn off the main road from Wolgast will bring you to **Peenemünde** at the island's northern tip. It was here in the 1930s that Werner von Braun, the man later responsible for America's Apollo missions, toiled with teams of thousands of technicians to perfect a practical long-range missile. The fruit of his efforts was the V2, thousands of which were launched in the later stages of World War II, devastating towns and cities in southern England. The **Historisch-Technisches Informationszentrum** has displays and shows films on the place. Outside the center, there are Soviet-era aircraft and a full-size model of a V2. In GDR days, the harbor at Peenemünde was enlarged as a base for the Volksmarine. One of the

Usedom
🅜 89 E2–F3
Visitor Information
✉ Waldstrasse 1, Seebad Bansin
☎ 038378 47 710
usedom.de

Historisch-Technisches Informationszentrum
✉ Im Kraftwerk Peenemünde
☎ 038371 50 50
🕑 Closed Mon.
💲 $$
peenemuende.de

Zinnowitz

Ⓜ 89 E3

Koserower Salzhütte

✉ Off the B111, Koserow

☎ 038375 2 06 80

koserower -salzhuette.de

Heringsdorf

Ⓜ 89 F3

Villa Irmgard

✉ Maxim-Gorki-Strasse 13, Heringsdorf

☎ 038378 2 23 61

🕐 Closed Mon.

💲 $

Ahlbeck

Ⓜ 89 F3

rocket-launching vessels of the People's Navy is still here, and the site's former power station, now a technical monument, has been restored. Both are open to visitors.

Seaside resorts along the 23.5-mile (38 km) beach facing the Baltic include **Zinnowitz,** a favorite vacation spot of trade unionists and their families in communist times. The big Red October hotel

INSIDER TIP:

Near Streckelsberg Hill, Usedom's highest point, you'll find the Koserower Salzhütte, a special place in the middle of nature to dine on fish!

—DR. MANFRED NIEKISCH

National Geographic Global Exploration Fund Advisor

built in the 1970s has been privatized, modernized, renamed the Baltic, and restyled to harmonize with the region's traditional architecture. Beyond Zinnowitz, the island narrows to a thin strip of sand separating the Baltic from the great embayment of the Achterwasser, a kind of inland sea.

Kingly Resorts

Road and railroad lead southeastward to Usedom's formerly fashionable *Kaiserbäder:* Bansin, Heringsdorf, and Ahlbeck. The three resorts have kept their individual identities, despite being linked by a promenade promoted as the longest in Europe. They

are all attractive, with ravishing white villas and hotels that today attract prosperous visitors from all over German-speaking Europe and beyond.

Despite its workaday name, **Heringsdorf** (Herring Village) thinks of itself as the most gracious of the three, with a tradition going back to a visit by the King of Prussia in 1820. Within a few decades it had become, in the words of Baedeker's guidebook, the "most fashionable of the Baltic sea-bathing places." Stroll along the promenade to view prestigious residences on landscaped grounds. Kaiser Wilhelm vacationed here, as did the German-American painter Lyonel Feininger (1871–1956). Russian writer Maxim Gorki (1868–1936) stayed in the **Villa Irmgard,** hoping the fresh sea breeze would clear his congested lungs. The villa is now the local museum. Heringsdorf's **pier** is particularly elaborate, with a shopping mall, cinema, and apartments at the landward end, and a restaurant and landing stage 550 yards (500 m) out to sea.

The jaunty, red-roofed pier at **Ahlbeck,** a more middle-class resort than Heringsdorf, can claim the special distinction of being the only one of the prewar piers to have survived. Ahlbeck's eastern limit is also Germany's boundary with Poland. For the moment, only pedestrians and cyclists can cross the frontier here, but the Polish harbor town of **Swinoujscie** (formerly German Swinemünde) can also be reached by pleasure cruiser from many of the resorts along the coast. ∎

Mecklenburg Lake District

At the end of the last Ice Age, the glaciers retreated eastward across Mecklenburg, carving out lakebeds and meltwater channels and dumping sand and gravel. The landscape created consists of moorland, marsh, woodland, and innumerable bodies of water. The Mecklenburg Lake District (Mecklenburgische Seenplatte) extends from Schleswig-Holstein across southern Mecklenburg. At its heart is the glorious Müritz, Germany's second largest lake.

The lakes, connected by rivers and canals, are heaven for lovers of every kind of boating. Sailboats, motor cruisers, kayaks, and canoes crowd into the marinas and mooring places, and some of the lakes can be noisy with the activities of water-sports enthusiasts.

There are marketplaces and historic centers to explore in the area's charming villages and cities; freshly smoked fish to taste in local restaurants; and musical festivals to enjoy at ancient castles.

Among the region's many parks, the eastern shore of the Müritz is protected as part of **Müritz National Park** (pleasure boats must keep well away from its banks). Most of the national park is ancient

Boathouses at Röbel stud the shore of the vast Müritzsee.

woodland broken by heathland and flower-rich meadows grazed by rare breeds of sheep and cattle. Plentiful birdlife includes a number of endangered species; there are buzzards, cranes, and storks, as well as ospreys and mighty sea eagles, Germany's national emblem. ∎

Mecklenburg Lake District

🗺 88–89 B2–D1

Visitor Information

✉ Nationalpark-Information Federow (4.3 miles/7 km S of Waren)

☎ 03991 66 88 49

mueritz-nationalpark.de

EXPERIENCE: Paddling About Müritz National Park

Your best way of getting to know the lake district is, of course, by taking to the water. There are cruises aboard pleasure boats from the attractive old town of **Waren,** but for more invigoration, rent a canoe or raft. With a map and no sense of urgency, you could get as far as Berlin, a minimum of four days' paddling away! Landlubbers should consider renting a bicycle and circling the lake along the **Müritz-Rundweg,** a well-signed cycle route. It's farther than you might think— a total of 51 miles (82 km)—but worthwhile, with changing landscapes and plenty of places to overnight. For a shorter tour, cycle 28 miles (45 km) from Waren along the eastern shore to the picturesque Boeker Mühle, and return by bus (equipped with a bicycle trailer). For details of rental stations and water routes, contact Nationalpark-Information Federow (see above).

More Places to Visit in Mecklenburg-West Pomerania

Güstrow

This old ducal town in the middle of the Mecklenburg Lake District has an exceptionally well-preserved townscape and fine civic buildings. The **parish church** dominating the main square and the **cathedral,** tucked away in a secluded corner of the Old Town (Altstadt), have good altarpieces and other treasures, while the massive Renaissance **Schloss** *(Franz-Parr-Platz, tel 03843 75 20, closed Mon.)* has a richly decorated interior and a restored baroque garden. In addition, Güstrow was

Barlach's "Hovering Angel," one of the great religious sculptures of the 20th century

the home of Ernst Barlach (1870–1938), one of Germany's greatest 20th-century sculptors, and some of his most heartfelt and appealing work is on show here. Don't miss his "Hovering Angel," floating serenely in an aisle of the cathedral. Then move on to the **Gertrudenkapelle** *(Gertrudenplatz 1, closed Mon., combined ticket with Atelierhaus $$$),* a converted 15th-century chapel in a little park just outside the Altstadt, where archetypal figures such as "The Singer" and

"Woman in the Wind" convey the humane vision that caused the Nazis to condemn Barlach as a "degenerate artist." Finally, visit his studio, the **Atelierhaus** *(Heidberg 15, tel 03843 68 10 23, closed Mon.),* in its lovely lakeside setting 2 miles (3 km) south of the Altstadt. *guestrow-tourismus.de* 89 C2 ✉ Domstrasse 9 ☎ 03843 6810 23

Neubrandenburg

The city walls of Neubrandenburg and its four handsome gateways survived the last days of World War II, and now comprise one of the finest examples of a medieval fortification system anywhere in Germany. The 23-foot-high (7 m) walls were studded with *Wieckhäuser,* permanently manned fortlets. A few of these quaint, mostly timber-framed dwellings survive and have been restored. The four brick gateways, complex structures with an inner and outer gate and soaring gables, defy any enemy to attack. *neubrandenburg-touristinfo.de* 89 D2 ✉ Stargarder Strasse 17 ☎ 0395 1 94 33

Schloss Ludwigslust

With its 17 bays and massive central section, this monumental palace 22 miles (35 km) south of Schwerin makes an overwhelming impression, and you would certainly not guess that its construction was constantly held up by lack of funds. The stonework clads walls of common brick, and much of the interior decor is made of a patent papier-mâché (which has stood the test of time better than other more permanent-seeming materials). The palace grew out of a modest 18th-century hunting lodge built by Duke Christian Ludwig II of Mecklenburg-Schwerin, from whom it got its name, "Ludwig's Pleasure." *museum-schwerin.de* 88 B1 ☎ 03874 5 71 90 🕒 Closed Mon.

Gentle hills, shining lakes, pastoral landscapes, and the great port of Hamburg, Germany's second largest city

Hamburg & Schleswig-Holstein

Traditional trades of Lübeck

Hamburg & Schleswig-Holstein

Forming a kind of causeway linking Central Europe with Scandinavia, Schleswig-Holstein is bounded on one side by the North Sea and on the other by the Baltic (the Ostsee, or Eastern Sea, in German). Sixty miles (100 km) inland from the mouth of the Elbe, Hamburg is the country's second biggest city, after Berlin, and its greatest seaport. Its equivalent on the Baltic is Lübeck, which once dominated the Hanseatic League of trading cities.

The North Sea and Baltic coasts are quite different in character. To the west, the sea battles with the low-lying land, whose outline is continually being reshaped by the action of wind and waves, strong tides and currents. The Nordfriesische Inseln (North Frisian Islands), the area's greatest attraction, were once part of the mainland. There has been gain as well as loss, however, with much land reclaimed from the sea between the mainland and the outer islands. Hundreds of miles of dikes have been constructed to resist further encroachment.

Most of the islands' splendid beaches face west; to the east stretches the strange landscape of the Wattenmeer, a vast expanse of mud and sand exposed twice daily by the receding tide. It harbors a rich and intriguing array of wildlife,

NOT TO BE MISSED:

The sights and smells of St. Pauli's bustling Fischmarkt   **113–114**

Exploring Hamburg's canals and neo-Gothic Speicherstadt   **114**

The Kunsthalle, one of Germany's great art galleries   **115**

Shopping along fashionable Jungfernstieg   **116**

Watching masted ships race in the Kieler Förde   **119**

Lübeck's ancient port and elegant architecture   **119–121**

Wind- and kitesurfing off sandy Sylt island   **122**

Dune wandering in Schleswig-Holstein Wattenmeer National Park   **122**

nourishment for millions of seabirds, but it is a fragile ecosystem, vulnerable to pollution and other human impact. A vast swath of 1,100 square miles (2,850 sq km) stretching from the mouth of the Elbe to the northern tip of the island of Sylt, is now designated as Nationalpark Schleswig–Holsteinisches Wattenmeer.

To the east, the almost tideless Baltic is fronted for much of its length by low cliffs, interrupted by fjordlike inlets of the sea, which make good natural harbors and sites for towns and cities, such as Kiel, Schleswig, and Flensburg, Germany's northernmost city. The town's substantial Danish minority is a reminder that this is a border region, with a convoluted history, much of it spent under Danish rule.

Most foreign visitors spend their time only in ancient Lübeck and mighty Hamburg—a pity, since the rest of the region offers unique landscapes and a host of minor delights. ∎

Hamburg

Proud to call itself a "Free and Hansa City," Hamburg is a *Land* in its own right, and it has always felt itself to be at least the equal of any of its nominal rulers, whether Danish king or German kaiser. Its long-standing trading links with the rest of the world have given it a readiness to innovate not always characteristic of German cities.

Hamburg

⚑ 108 D1 &
  this page

Visitor Information

✉ Hauptbahnhof,
  Kirchenallee exit

☎ 040 30 05 13 00

hamburg-tourism.de

While it still relies on its great port, second in Europe only to Rotterdam, Hamburg is also a manufacturing and service center of the first importance. Banks, insurance companies, and media interests are based here, including the publishers of the internationally read *Stern* magazine and the weekly *Die Zeit.* There are more wealthy people here than any other German city, and its prosperity has drawn a colorful mix of immigrants.

INSIDER TIP:

Join the locals at Hamburg's tiny Park Fiction, above St. Pauli Fischmarkt, and enjoy the marvelous views over the harbor and Elbe River.

—JAN WEHBERG
National Geographic contributor

The city's general layout is easy to grasp. From the shore of the Elbe in the south, the channels of the River Alster divide the old city center roughly in half and link through to the magnificent lakelike stretches of water known as the Binnen- (Inner) and Aussen- (Outer) Alster. The line of the

long-since-demolished city walls forms a semicircular boundary to the north, followed by the broad ring road, while St. Pauli stands on slightly higher ground to the west. The high ground extends farther west along the Elbe through Altona, once under Danish rule

and quite independent of Hamburg, then on to the desirable suburb of Blankenese.

City Center

A great fire in 1842 destroyed most of Hamburg, which until then must have looked like a larger version of its Hansa partner Lübeck. The city was again devastated by bombing, particularly during the Allied air raids of July 1943, which killed 55,000 people. The city that rose from the rubble would not claim to be Germany's most beautiful, but plenty of reminders of its long past are preserved among the matrix of modern building.

Hamburg has kept its distinctive silhouette, dominated by the five towers of its great civic churches. You could start your exploration of the city at **St. Michaelis-Kirche,** built in 1762 and one of the greatest of North German baroque churches. "Der Michel" is a much-loved city symbol, its 433-foot (132 m) tower a landmark

St. Michaelis-Kirche

- Map p. 111
- Englische Planke 1
- 040 376 78 0
- $$ (tower & film)
- S-Bahn: Stadthausbrücke; Bus: 36, 37, 112

st-michaelis.de

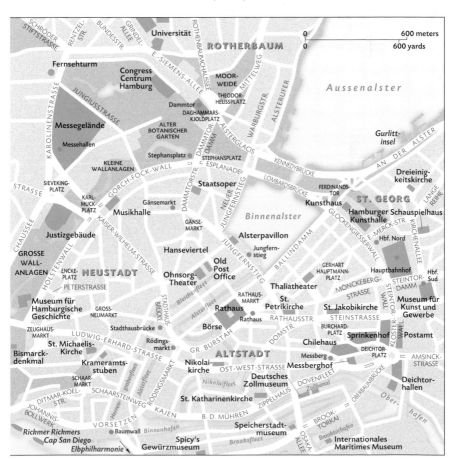

The 19th-century Rathaus, or city hall, dominates Hamburg's skyline.

Krameramtsstuben

- Map p. 111
- Krayenkamp 10
- 040 37 50 19 88
- Closed Mon.
- $
- S-Bahn: Stadt-hausbrücke

Rathausmarkt

- Map p. 111

St. Petrikirche

- Map p. 111
- Bei der Petrikirche 2
- 040 325 74 00

for sailors. Climb the tower for an unsurpassable view of river, harbor, and the town as a whole, then visit the crypt and watch the "HiStory" film for a fascinating overview of Hamburg's eventful past.

Just down from the church, the **Krameramtsstuben** (Almshouses), reached through the doorway at Nos. 10 & 11 Krayenkamp, have somehow survived to give an idea of living conditions for poor widows in the 17th century. More upscale 18th-century merchants' residences, heavily restored, line Peterstrasse. Johannes Brahms was born nearby in 1833, and No. 39, with its sign showing the bearded composer enjoying a cigar, is devoted to his memory. A short distance to

the west is the superb Hamburg History Museum (see p. 114).

Hamburg's epicenter is the **Rathausmarkt,** the spacious square in front of the monumental Nordische Renaissance (Northern Renaissance) **Rathaus** (City Hall) completed in 1897, when Hamburg prospered as imperial Germany's foremost port. Governed for centuries by patrician merchants rather than princes or nobles, Hamburg is still very careful to remind its visitors that it is a "Free and Hansa City." The mayor does not descend the steps to greet heads of state, but waits regally for them at the top (an exception being made for Queen Elizabeth II).

One side of the Rathausmarkt is bounded by the channel through which the River Alster finds its way to the Elbe from the Binnenalster to the north. On the far side, Venetian-style arcades announce the city's prestigious retail district. The area is an attractive combination of old and new; the Italianate **Old Post Office** on Poststrasse now houses one of the very first shopping arcades, which contrasts with the airy shopping galleries of the **Hanseviertel,** the largest development of its kind.

There's more shopping farther east, where department stores line **Mönckebergstrasse,** laid out early in the 20th century with the U-Bahn line running underneath. **St. Petrikirche,** on Mönckebergstrasse, is the city center's oldest place of worship, first mentioned in 1195, although the present church is a reconstruction following the great fire of 1842. Next to it, No. 9 is a charming building, to all appearances a historic Hanseatic town house but built in 1911.

To the south of Gerhart-Hauptmann-Platz, **St. Jacobikirche** dates from 1350, but the church had to be almost completely rebuilt after 1945. Many original fittings, such as the great organ of 1693, were preserved. Two blocks farther south in the **Kontorhausviertel**—a historic commercial office district—the monlumist, ingesting brick **Chilehaus** (1922–1924) has a pointed facade resembling a ship's prow.

St. Pauli & the Harbor

The notorious red-light district of St. Pauli has cleaned up its act since the sleazy days of the 1960s and '70s. Today it attracts a mixed crowd of visitors, many millions a year, who fill pubs, bars, restaurants, discos, cabarets, clubs, and theaters and keep the action going into the small hours and beyond.

St. Pauli owes its existence to the distaste felt by Hamburg's Protestant city fathers for the sort of leisure pursuits enjoyed by sailors with money in their pockets and time to spend. Those catering to their needs were forced to set up shop outside the walls, along the **Reeperbahn,** the old ropewalk that stretched from the city's western gateway to the separate borough of Altona. The ropemakers have long since gone, as have the sailors, and ships now load and unload in a matter of hours rather than weeks. Today's St. Pauli is a mixed community, with one-third of its residents non-German. Bad behavior is kept within bounds by the district's famous police station on the corner of Davidstrasse, one of the streets that is otherwise patrolled by ladies of the night. And aspiring rock musicians still make their way to St. Pauli, as did a certain up-and-coming English band (see sidebar p. 114).

St. Pauli extends down to the Elbe. Along the waterfront stands the stately **Landungsbrücken,** where ocean liners used to dock. The old **Fischmarkt** still sells fish here early on Sunday mornings, along with fruit and vegetables and much else. The colorful and

---

St. Pauli

- Map p. 110
- St. Pauli Landungsbrücken (bet. Brücke 4 & 5)
- 040 30 05 13 00

Fischmarkt

- Grosse Elbstrasse 9
- Open Sun.
- S-Bahn: Reeperbahn; U-Bahn: Landungsbrücken; Bus 112

> ## Hamburg Views
>
> Some of the best views in the city include:
>
> - **Panorama from the St. Michaelis-Kirche steeple**
> - **The grand Rathaus seen from the Alster Arcades**
> - **The towering Speicherstadt on a canal tour**
> - **The bright neon lights of the Reeperbahn**
> - **Atop Nikolaikirche's spire**
> - **Of the Elbe, as ships put out to sea at Blankensee**

---

noisy scene attracts crowds of bleary-eyed Saturday-night survivors as well as bargain hunters. Hafenstrasse, linking the market building with the ocean terminal, was the stronghold of "alternatives" in the 1980s.

As its activity expanded, Hamburg's **harbor** moved from the channels of the Alster in the city

Museum für Hamburgische Geschichte

🅰 Map p. 111

✉ Holstenwall 24

☎ 040 42 81 32 23 80

⊕ Closed Mon.

💲 $$

🚇 U-Bahn: St. Pauli; Bus: 112

hamburgmuseum.de

Speicherstadt-museum

🅰 Map p. 111

✉ St. Annenufer 2

☎ 040 32 11 91

⊕ Closed Mon.

💲 $

speicherstadt museum.de

Spicy's Gewürzmuseum

🅰 Map p. 111

✉ Am Sandtorkai 32

☎ 040 36 79 89

⊕ Closed Mon. Nov.–June

💲 $

spicys.de

A bridge leads to Hamburg's former fish hall along the harbor.

center to the Elbe waterfront, and then migrated to the far side of the river. To grasp the full magnitude of the harbor, take one of the many trips offered. As well as giving you a view of dry docks, seemingly endless quaysides, and great stacks of containers, most cruises take you around the **Speicherstadt.** This complex of beautifully decorated late 19th-century redbrick warehouses was part of the Free Port. At the western end rises the wavy-roofed **Elbphilharmonie** (Elbe Philharmonic Hall). When completed in 2017, the fanciful 110-meter (360-foot)

tower will integrate a luxury hotel, restaurants, and apartments.

Hamburg Museums & Art Galleries

Hamburg has a range of museums many capital cities might envy. The excellent **Museum für Hamburgische Geschichte** (Hamburg History Museum), which stands on parkland on the western edge of the city center, covers the general history of the city. The huge model railway, a meticulous re-creation of one of the city's principal stations, amazes most visitors.

The Beatles in Hamburg

In the summer of 1960, a fledgling band from Liverpool landed a gig at Hamburg. Their lineup included drummer Pete Best and bassist Stuart Sutcliffe, who joined John, Paul, and George in August. The Beatles opened at a sleazy club called Indra on Grosse Freiheit. When police closed the place due to noise, the group moved a block south to the Kaiserkeller, where they eventually met Ringo Starr. Over the next two years the Fab Four would play 800 hours of live performances on the seedy stages of Hamburg's red-light district. John Lennon famously recalled: "I was born in Liverpool, but I grew up in Hamburg."

In the splendid warehouse district are several museums *(take a taxi if you want to visit)*. The **Speicherstadtmuseum** deals with the history of the district, the highly aromatic **Spicy's Gewürzmuseum** is devoted to spices, and the **Deutsches Zollmuseum** is about customs and revenue. A section covers Hamburg's role as an emigration port for many Europeans.

To the east, overlooking the Brooktorhafen, the terrific **Internationales Maritimes Museum** (International Maritime Museum) is spread over ten floors of a handsome old shipping warehouse. Apart from thousands of model ships, photos, and illustrations, you'll find the baton of Nazi grand admiral Karl Dönitz and a whaler used to rescue Ernest Shackleton's Antarctic expedition in 1912. Best of all, you can take the helm on a simulated voyage of a container ship through the harbors of Rotterdam, Singapore, and Hamburg *(2 p.m. Sun. & Tues.–Wed.)*.

The city's art collections spread along an "Art Mile" that extends from the Binnenalster to the Oberhafen (Upper Harbor), where the old wholesale flower market, the **Deichtorhallen** *(Deichtorstrasse 1–2, closed Mon., $$$, deichtorhallen .de)*, has been converted into a spectacular setting for exhibitions of contemporary art.

South of the main station, the **Museum für Kunst und Gewerbe** (Art & Craft Museum) contains an exceptional array of decorative arts, among which the beautifully presented collection of historic musical instruments is outstanding. There are also rooms furnished in art nouveau or art deco style by masters such as Henry van de Velde (1863–1957), whose Weimar school of design became the Bauhaus.

North of the station, the **Hamburger Kunsthalle** is one of Germany's great art galleries, housed in a dignified 19th-century building. A highly controversial extension was specifically designed for contemporary art. The huge main collection covers works from the Middle Ages to the mid-20th century. It would take many visits to take in the important pieces.

INSIDER TIP:

One night each spring, Hamburg's museums stay open until the wee hours, from 6:00 p.m.–2:00 a.m. Visit *langenachtder museen-hamburg.de* for details.

—BRIDGET A. ENGLISH
National Geographic Books editor

If time is short, concentrate on German art of the 19th and early 20th centuries. Among the Romantics, watch for "The Sea of Ice" and "Wanderer above the Sea of Fog" by Caspar David Friedrich (1774–1840) and "Morning" by Philipp Otto Runge (1777–1810). Impressionist Max Liebermann (1847–1935) is represented with "The Netmenders" and "Ulysses and Calypso," as are modern masters Otto Dix (1891–1969) and Max Beckmann (1884–1950). ■

Deutsches Zollmuseum

- Map p. 111
- Alter Wandrahm 16
- 040 30 08 76 11
- Closed Mon.
- $

museum.zoll.de

Internationales Maritimes Museum

- Map p. 111
- Koreastrasse 1
- 040 30 09 23 00
- Closed Mon.
- $$
- U-Bahn: Überseequartier

internationales-maritimes-museum.de

Museum für Kunst und Gewerbe

- Map p. 111
- Steintorplatz 1
- 040 42 81 34 27 32
- Closed Mon.
- $$$
- S-Bahn: Hauptbahnhof

mkg-hamburg.de

Hamburger Kunsthalle

- Map p. 111
- Glockengiesserwall
- 040 42 81 3 12 00
- Closed Mon.
- $$$

hamburger-kunsthalle.de

Walk: Dryshod From Alster to Elbe

This walk starts on the Jungfernstieg, the esplanade overlooking the calm waters of the Binnenalster, and then zigzags through the city center to the busy harbor overlooking the River Elbe.

The **Jungfernstieg ❶** is a fashionable shopping boulevard as well as a good place to sit and admire the Binnenalster from a waterside café. Pleasure boats depart from here for trips around both inner and outer Alsters and farther up the river itself. The sober gray buildings along the lakeside include the prestigious Vier Jahreszeiten Hotel and the 1901 headquarters of the world's then biggest shipping line, Hapag.

The area "inland" from the Jungfernstieg is home to Hamburg's most exclusive shopping streets and arcades (see p. 112). The **Alster-arkaden** (Alster Arcades) frame the view over the channel of the Alsterfleet to the **Rathaus** (City Hall) ❷ (see p. 112). Pass

NOT TO BE MISSED:

Jungfernstieg • City Hall
• Deichstrasse & Nikolaifleet
• *Rickmer Rickmers* • St. Pauli
Landungsbrücken

through the main portal and the imposing vaulted foyer of the City Hall into the courtyard beyond. The elaborate Hygeia fountain commemorates the terrible cholera epidemic of 1892. Go out to the left, turn right, then left onto the street called Börsenbrücke. Look up the long narrow space to the left where there is a rare trace of the medieval trading city, the back of a timber-framed building with the upper floors jettied out. Cross the bridge over the Alster, with its statues of city founders Archbishop Ansgar and Graf (Count) Adolf III von Schaumburg. Take a look at the **Laeiszhof ❸**, a typical Hamburg shipping line headquarters building, put up by one of the founders of Hapag (see sidebar opposite). The poodle crowning it is a reminder of the magnate's pet name for his wife: "Poodle."

The dominant feature in this part of town is the tall spire of the bombed-out **Nikolaikirche ❹**, a memorial with a glass elevator ride to its spire. From the far end of the Hopfenmarkt square, a footbridge spans the multiple lanes of the busy east–west arterial road. Steps lead you down onto **Deich-strasse** (Dike Street), where the grand facades of the merchants' houses, dating from the 17th through 19th centuries, give a good idea of what the old Hansa town must have been

The houses lining the Nikolaifleet once served as warehouses and shops as well as residences.

like before the Great Fire of 1842. You can squeeze down a narrow passageway and walk along the pontoon on the **Nikolaifleet** **5** to get a view of the brick-built backs of the tall buildings, which combined access to the water with storerooms, offices, and living quarters. Most of the surviving buildings are now pubs and restaurants.

Cross the waterside road, and climb up on

> See also map pp. 110–111
> Jungfernstieg
> 1.75 miles (3 km)
> 1.5 hours
> St. Pauli Landungsbrücken

to the **embankment** that runs all the way west to **St. Pauli,** the city's red-light district (see pp. 113–115), giving views of the activity on the Elbe. Don't head west straight away, but cross the water of the Binnenhafen by the footbridge, and walk along the quayside for views back to the "mainland."

The **museum vessels** moored along the embankment include the classic mid-20th-century freighter *Cap San Diego* and the *Rickmer Rickmers,* a splendid East India wind-jammer of 1896, both of which are open to visitors daily. The towers and copper domes at the end of the embankment belong to the **St. Pauli Landungsbrücken** **6**, where ocean liners formerly tied up. Now it's used just by ferries and harbor cruisers, but there are plenty of places to eat, drink, and rest your legs after the walk.

Hapag of Hamburg

Hapag, a Hamburg-based transatlantic shipping company established in 1847, became the world's largest shipping line by 1901 under the direction of the young visionary Albert Ballin (1857–1918). In 1912, the company began building the first of its "Big Three" ocean liners, the *Imperator,* **followed by** *Vaterland.* **The third was completed after World War I (with the name of** *Majestic).* **Hapag has since been subsumed in a series of mergers, most recently by TUI AG in 1998, comprising a cruise line and airline in addition to the shipping line.**

Schleswig-Holstein

The two great visitor destinations of Schleswig-Holstein could hardly be more different. In the southeast, lovely Lübeck is a near-perfect example of a medieval Hansa trading city, and in the far northwest, the North Frisian Islands have been attracting crowds of vacationers in search of sun, sand, and sea for more than a century and a half. Between these two poles, there is much to see and do.

The Westerheversand lighthouse and its keeper's cottages

The Baltic coast has its share of fine beaches and seaside resorts; Travemünde is associated with Lübeck and Laboe with Kiel, the state capital. Kiel is a workaday place, but its fjord is a yachtsman's paradise. Farther north, an even longer fjord leads far inland to Schleswig, the former capital. The harbor town of Flensburg is about as far north as you can go in Germany, and it is worth the journey for its bustling harbor and Danish flavor. The more exposed western coast facing the North Sea has hardly any substantial towns, the exception being the old fishing port of Husum, a good base for exploring the smaller islands studding the Wattenmeer.

Inland Schleswig-Holstein has hardly been disturbed by international tourism. There are few trees, but this is partly compensated for by the 30,000 or so miles (50,000 km) of hedges, planted as windbreaks and stock barriers in the 18th and 19th centuries. There's little to break the force of the wind on the North Frisian mainland, where the dominant structures are the huge modern wind turbines. The great skies and bright light of the area inspired expressionist painter Emil Nolde (1867–1956), and a gallery near Niebüll housing a superb selection of his work provides a good reason for exploring this unique part of Germany. Eastward to the Baltic are the gentler landscapes of Holsteinische Schweiz (Holstein Switzerland), low wooded hills enfolding a constellation of lakes.

Kiel

The capital of Schleswig-Holstein stands at the head of its wonderful natural harbor, the Kieler Förde (Kiel Fjord) running inland from the Baltic. Every June the fjord is the scene of the world's greatest sailing event, Kieler Woche (Kiel Week), when up to three million spectators watch thousands of competitors participate in a range of thrilling events.

Kiel rose to prominence in the 19th century, when imperial Germany began to build a great navy. Shipyards and naval bases spread along the banks of the fjord, whose strategic value was immensely enhanced by the building of the **Kiel Canal** (1887–1895). Called the Nord-Ostsee-Kanal (North Sea-Baltic Canal), the 61.5-mile-long (99 km) waterway enabled ships to pass quickly between the two seas. Today the traffic consists of freighters rather than battleships, more than 43,000 of them a year, making the canal one of the world's busiest artificial waterways.

From the tower of the **Altes Rathaus** (Old City Hall), view the **Altstadt** (Old Town) and the winding fjord. A visit to the waterside **Schiffahrtsmuseum** (Maritime Museum) informs you about the city's relationship with the sea, and three historic craft are moored alongside (no

access to boats mid-Oct.–mid-April).

At the beach resort of **Laboe,** the towering **Marine-Ehrenmal,** a 280-foot-high (85 m) monument in the form of a ship's prow, was built in 1936 as Germany's principal naval war memorial. It is now dedicated to the memory of sailors of all nations who have died at sea. The top of the tower is accessible by 341 steps or elevator. At its foot is the U-995, a World War II submarine.

INSIDER TIP:

Lübeck is well worth a visit—its brick Gothic streetscapes and charming houses transport you back to the days when the city was the capital of the Hanseatic League.

—DAVID BARBER
Youth For Understanding U.S.A

Lübeck

Still surrounded by elaborate water defenses, this ancient port and trading city has preserved much of the atmosphere of its heyday when, as leader of the medieval Hanseatic League of trading cities, its influence extended all around the Baltic Sea and beyond. Lübeck remains an important harbor, with the focus of activity nowadays farther downstream toward the mouth of the River Trave. But most people come to enjoy the town's old streets and squares lined with brick buildings in

Kiel
🔼 108 D3
Visitor Information
✉ Andreas-Gayk-Strasse 31
☎ 0431 67 91 00
kiel-sailing-city.de

Altes Rathaus
✉ Fleethörn 18–24, Kiel
☎ 0431 90 10
🕐 Tower open Wed. & Sat. May–Sept.
💲 $

Schiffahrtsmuseum
✉ Wall 65, Kiel
☎ 0431 901 34 28
🕐 Closed Mon. mid-Oct.–mid-April
💲 $

Marine-Ehrenmal
✉ Strandstrasse 92, Laboe
☎ 04343 42 70 62
💲 $$
deutscher-marine bund.de

Lübeck
🔼 109 E2
Visitor Information
✉ Holstentorplatz 1
☎ 0451 88 99 700
luebeck-tourism.de

Petrikirche

✉ Am
Petrikirchhof 1

☎ 0451 39773 23

🕐 Church closed
Mon. March–
Dec.; tower
open year-round

💲 $ (tower)

st-petri-luebeck.de

**Buddenbrook-
haus**

✉ Heinrich-
und-Thomas-
Mann-Zentrum
Mengstrasse 4

☎ 0451 122 42
42/43

💲 $$

buddenbrookhaus.de

styles reflected all along the north European coasts from the Netherlands to Estonia.

Seven church towers and spires dominate Lübeck's skyline. To get to them, you must pass the city's great emblem, the massive 15th-century gateway called the **Holstentor** *(tel 0451 122 41 92, $$, die-luebecker-museen.de)*. Built of brick, like nearly every structure in the city, it consists of two sturdy cylinders topped by conical slate roofs and linked by a gabled section above the original archway. The local history museum inside displays a superb model of the town in the 17th century.

The city proper begins on the far side of the bridge beyond the gateway. Get an overall view of its oval shape and intricate street pattern by taking the elevator up the tower of the **Petrikirche,** but first take in the unsurpassed group of buildings dominating the city center. The **Rathaus** (Town Hall) and the twin-towered **Marienkirche,** both begun in the mid-13th

century, express the pride of the citizens in the independent status of their city, free from domination by prince or bishop. The bold circular openings in the upper wall of the city hall are not there for effect, but to lessen wind resistance. The church is full of artworks of the highest quality. The most poignant items, however, are probably the shattered bells beneath the south tower, left as they fell during the terrible night of March 28, 1942, when British bombs destroyed 25 percent of the city.

Just to the north of the church, the splendid white mansion of the **Buddenbrookhaus** is named after *Die Buddenbrooks,* the family saga set in Lübeck and one of the best loved novels by Thomas Mann (1875–1955), a native of the city. The building is now devoted to his memory and that of his brother and fellow-writer, Heinrich Mann.

Farther north along Breite Strasse, past the Jakobikirche, the

Lübeck's Rathaus encloses the city's brick marketplace.

The Hanseatic League

An association of trading cities, the Hansa was formed for protection against pirates and to control the lucrative trade around the Baltic Sea. Raw materials—furs, wax, amber, salt, timber, and honey—were traded for products from the west, such as textiles, wine, and metalwork. Lübeck led the way, but many other German ports, and even inland cities such as Cologne, were members with trading privileges in towns and cities as far away as England. Goods were transported by *Koggen,* broad sailing ships, some of which could carry a cargo of 600 tons. Although the league last assembled in 1669, its name lives on. The national airline is called Lufthansa (Hansa of the Air), and car license plates in Hamburg and Bremen carry the letter "H."

seamen's church, you will find the **Haus der Schiffergesellschaft** *(Breite Strasse 2, tel 0451 76776),* once the headquarters of the sea captains' guild. Today it's one of the best places to eat in town, with a carefully re-created maritime atmosphere and, of course, good fish dishes. Breite Strasse leads to another formidable gateway, the medieval Burgtor.

On Königstrasse, running parallel to Breite Strasse, the **Heiligen-Geist-Hospital** was founded about 1280 to house the less fortunate. Its elaborate facade is matched by the interior with its medieval wall paintings and great hall. Farther south, off Glockengiesserstrasse, are some little 17th-century almshouses laid out around charming courtyards.

In the quiet southern reaches of the old town, the **St. Annen-Museum** houses a great display of ecclesiastical art, including the celebrated Hans Memling Passion Altar from 1491.

Travemünde

Lübeck's location a few miles up the River Trave from the Baltic meant that in medieval times the city fathers had to pay tolls to the Holsteiners, who controlled the river mouth at Travemünde. So in 1320 the Lübeckers bought the place. Travemünde still has some old timber-framed houses where fisherfolk lived, as well as the church in which they worshipped. For some years now, however, the tone of the place has been set by its spruce casino and Kurhaus, its villas, and the long promenade. The town was one of the very first of Germany's seaside resorts, and it is still one of the most elegant.

North Frisian Islands

Before 1989, when the East German Baltic coast was closed to West Germans, West Germany's favorite seaside destination was the archipelago of the Nordfriesische Inseln off Schleswig-Holstein's North Sea coast. Of these windswept isles, Sylt was its swankiest island, dubbed the St. Tropez of the North.

The islands were once part of the mainland, but the restless sea broke in on more than one occasion, and today salt water

Heiligen-Geist-Hospital
- ✉ Am Koberg
- ☎ 0451 790 78 41
- 🕐 Closed Mon.

St. Annen-Museum
- ✉ St-Annen-Strasse 15
- ☎ 0451 122 41 37
- 🕐 Closed Mon.
- 💲 $
- **st-annen-museum.de**

North Frisian Islands
- 🅰 108 B4
- **Visitor Information**
- ✉ Strandstrasse 25
- ☎ 04651 998 351
- **westerland.de**

EXPERIENCE: (Wind)surfing on the Baltic Coast

It's easy to hang ten on Germany's North Sea coast, where surfing conditions are excellent on all levels. At the popular vacation island of **Sylt,** beginners can hone their skills in the calm sea on the east coast, while pros can grapple with the harsh winds of the west coast. Not far away, near the town of Wilhelmshaven, the man-made coastal lake of **Hooksiel** is independent of the tides and has a bay with a surfing school and opportunities for waterskiing. The German surfing and kitesurfing championships take place at the sandy resort of **St. Peter Ording,** where the outlandish stunts of freestylers draw an entourage of live musical acts, beach partiers, and entertainers. See *nordsee tourismus.de* for links to surf courses and related events.

covers the vast area designated as Schleswig-Holstein Wattenmeer National Park. The largest island, Sylt, is only 24 miles (38.5 km) long, and in places it is only a few hundred yards wide, with sand dunes rising as high as 172 feet (52.5 m). By contrast, parts of the "Halligen," the islands in the area's southern part, are actually below sea level, with farmsteads kept high and dry on artificial mounds.

The *Watten* of the Wattenmeer are the extensive slicks of sand and mud exposed by the twice-daily retreat of the sea, temporarily joining certain islands to each other or to the mainland. Watten-walking (*Wattwandern*) has become popular, preferably with an experienced guide who can explain the strange but teeming life that flourishes here and who is alert to the dangers posed as the tide sweeps in. Colonies of seals are another attraction.

People have been coming to the islands since the 19th century—for the bracing air (the sea breeze never falters), the sunshine (more of it than on the mainland), the sandy beaches,

INSIDER TIP:

The peaceful island of Amrum, near Sylt, with its sand dunes, forests, grasslands— and flat roads—is ideal for biking. Watch for the grazing horses!

—STEPHANIE BREAKMAN
National Geographic Films

the sea (beautiful breakers), and society. The social whirl began in a modest way in 1842, when the king of Denmark decided to spend his summer vacation at Wyk on the second largest island, **Föhr.** Wyk is a charming old harbor town, with a tree-lined promenade above its long sandy beach, and Föhr in general is a fine spot for family vacations.

Sylt: The center of high society action, however, shifted long ago to Sylt. Thomas Mann praised it, Marlene Dietrich loved it, and in the 1960s every swinger and jetsetter had to be seen here. The hub of the island is the substantial town of **Westerland,** the terminus of the railroad connecting Sylt with the mainland via the 7-mile (11 km) causeway of the Hindenburgdamm (there is no road access to Sylt; cars must be put aboard the train at Niebüll). Westerland likes to think of itself as terribly sophisticated. There's a classy casino and plenty of bistros, bars, and discos, but you are unlikely to meet many stars on the very ordinary shopping street linking the station to the seafront and the splendid sandy beach.

houses. **Kampen** is popular, with its 2.8-mile-long (4.5 km) Rotes Kliff, a copper-colored, 82-foot-high (25 m) cliff. Strict building regulations enforce a thatched roof on every new building, whether it be vacation home, gourmet restaurant, antique shop, or exclusive boutique.

Get off the train a couple of stops before Westerland and you are in **Keitum,** a leafy village of charming old Frisian houses. From the church, there is a vast panorama over the infinite expanse of the Wattenmeer.

**MUDFLAT WALKS
TO THE ISLANDS:**
The Watten of the Wattenmeer are extensive slicks of sand and mud exposed by the twice-daily retreat of the sea, temporarily joining certain islands to each other or to the mainland. Nature-lovers can slog their way barefoot over the mudflats to isles such as **Baltrum, Norderney** and **Langeoog.** The crossing requires an experienced guide, who will explain the strange but teeming life that flourishes here and who is alert to the possible dangers posed as the tide sweeps in. Colonies of seals are another attraction, often seen sunning themselves lazily. Guides include Eiltraut and Ulrich Kunth *(Ahornweg 7, Dornum, tel 04933 10 27, wattwanderung-kunth .de)* and Hensel/Wenten *(Bismarckstrasse 2, Hohenkirchen, tel 04463 17 16, wattwandern.de).*

Barefoot walkers follow a guide across the mudflats of the Wattenmeer.

(All visitors pay a small resort tax, the *Kurtaxe.* Hotels add it to the bill, while other guests can buy a pass from kiosks by the beach.) The victim of its popularity, Westerland has too many day-trippers and high-rise apartments destroying what character it once possessed.

The super-rich Germans have retreated elsewhere on the island, to relax in the privacy of their expensive vacation

Beyond Kampen, near the northern end of the island, is Germany's northernmost community, **List,** the harbor for ferries making the 50-minute crossing to Rømø in Denmark. This part of Sylt, just north of List, is famous for the shifting sand dunes that creep eastward at the rate of up to 23 feet (7 m) a year; they make up the largest area of this kind in Europe and have been a designated nature reserve since the 1920s. ∎

More Places to Visit in Schleswig-Holstein

Flensburg

Germany's northernmost city belonged to Denmark until 1920, and for many years its harbor was a more important port than Copenhagen's. Danes still make up some 20 percent of the population and help give Flensburg its unique atmosphere. It is an attractive place, partly built on the higher land rising steeply from both sides of the busy harbor. If you walk up the long main street leading north to the brick gateway of the Nordertor, take time to explore the intimate **Höfe,** the old merchants' courtyards running down toward the quayside. A number of historic vessels are moored near the **Schiffahrtsmuseum** (Maritime Museum; *Schiffbrücke 39, tel 0461 85 29 70, schiffahrtsmuseum.flensburg.de, closed Mon., $$*), which has a fine array of ship models, maritime paintings, and navigational instruments. A special exhibition in the basement is devoted to rum, once Flensburg's most famous product. *flensburg-tourismus.de* 🅰 108 C4 ✉ Rathausstrasse 1 ☎ 0461 9 09 09 20

Husum

"The old gray town by the sea" was how Schleswig-Holstein's greatest writer, Theodor Storm (1817–1888), described this charming harbor town on the province's western coast. Storm's home, the **Theodor-Storm-Zentrum** (*Wasserreihe 31, tel 04841 803 86 30, storm-gesellschaft .de, closed Sun., Mon., & Wed. Nov.–March, $*), was where he wrote the novella *Der Schimmelreiter (Rider on a White Horse),* a wonderful evocation of one man's struggle to keep the restless sea from reclaiming these hard-won coastlands. Husum is really rather more colorful than Storm implied. There may be no great monuments, but you could spend a very

pleasant half-day here, wandering the old streets and watching the activity in the tidal inner harbor. There are plenty of bars and fish restaurants, and the town is a good base for exploring the North Frisian coast and islands. To the south is the tiny town of **Friedrichstadt,** founded by Dutch settlers in 1621, a little bit of Holland with canals and high-gabled houses. *husum -tourismus.de* 🅰 108 B4 ✉ Grossstrasse 27 ☎ 04841 8 98 70

Schleswig

Schleswig stands on the Schlei, a fjord running 27 miles (43 km) inland from the Baltic. The finest view of the old capital of the province is across the water from the south. It was on this bank of the Schlei that the Vikings settled at the beginning of the ninth century. Among the most interesting relics of that time housed in the modern **Wikinger Museum Haithabu** (*Haddeby bei Schleswig, tel 04621 81 32 22, closed Mon. Nov.–March, $$*) is a reconstructed longship.

Even more impressive is the fourth-century Nydam Boat, one of the star exhibits in **Schloss Gottorf** (*tel 04621 81 32 22, schloss-gottorf.de, closed Mon. Nov.–March, $$*). The boat is 75 feet (23 m) long and a unique relic from the time of the great migrations of the Germanic tribes. Formerly the mighty ducal residence, the Schloss is the province's finest Renaissance building and now the regional museum. It stands apart from Schleswig's charming Altstadt (Old Town). Above the old streets rises the 19th-century tower of the **cathedral,** containing a beautiful masterpiece of late medieval carving, the Bordesholm (Bordesholmer) Altar. *ostseefjordschlei.de* 🅰 108 C4 ✉ Plessenstrasse 7 ☎ 04621 85 00 50

Varied landscapes and intriguing cities from the Dutch border to the Elbe River and south to the Harz Mountains

Lower Saxony & Bremen

Hamelin's Pied Piper

Lower Saxony & Bremen

Second in size only to Bavaria, the *Land* of Lower Saxony (Niedersachsen)
was established by the British occupation authorities after World War II.
Its northern boundary extends to the North Sea, where the dunes and sandy
beaches of the East Frisian Islands form one of Germany's favorite vacation areas.
At the eastern end of the plain is the vast Lüneburger Heide (Lüneburg Heath). To the
south the land gradually rises to form fine hill country. In the center is the fine old river
port of Bremen, not part of Lower Saxony but a separate political entity in its own right,
a recognition of its past as an independent city.

0   60 kilometers
0   30 miles

SCHLESWIG-HOLSTEIN p.107

MECKLENBURG-WEST POMERANIA p. 87

BRANDENBURG p. 49

SAXONY-ANHALT p. 211

THURINGIA p. 211

NOT TO BE MISSED:

Hanover's magnificent
Herrenhausen Gardens **130**

Reliving the Renaissance of
Hamelin's Pied Piper **131**

The amazing mummies of St. Petri's
cathedral **137**

Old-world fantasies in Bremen's
Böttcherstrasse **137–138**

Boarding historic ships and a U-boat
at Bremerhaven **138–139**

The artists' colony of rustic
Worpswede **139**

Spinning your wheels at Wolfsburg's
Autostadt park **141**

Joining in a traditional East Frisian
tea ceremony **143**

Lower Saxony's capital is Hanover, its greatest attraction not so much its rebuilt city center as the great baroque gardens at Herrenhausen. Larger than Hanover by a whisker is the city of Bremen. Bremerhaven, its modern, workaday satellite at the mouth of the River Weser, attracts hundreds of thousands of visitors to Germany's national museum of shipping.

There are more working towns to the east of Hanover: Brunswick (Braunschweig) looks back on a glorious past as the home base of the medieval duke of Saxony, Henry the Lion, while the Volkswagen town of Wolfsburg is entirely a creation of the automobile age.

The town of Hamelin is as picturesque today as when the Pied Piper led its children away to an unknown fate. Just as lovely are Lüneburg and Celle. Hildesheim and its glorious heritage of Romanesque churches is protected by its UNESCO designation, as is Goslar, a medieval mining town with an unparalleled legacy of timber-framed dwellings. And in Göttingen, Lower Saxony has one of Germany's most prestigious old university cities. ■

Hanover

The state capital of Lower Saxony is something of an upstart, certainly compared with other, far older places in the area such as Brunswick and Goslar. Hanover's importance goes back only to the mid-17th century, when it became a ducal residence of the family that was later to supply England with a ruler in the shape of George I. They also created the city's main glory, the complex of gardens at Herrenhausen in the northwest part of the town.

Opened in 1913, the grand neo-Gothic appearance of Hanover's New City Hall belies its relatively recent construction date.

Hanover

M 126 D3

Visitor Information

✉ Ernst-August-Platz 8

☎ 0511 12 34 51 11

hannover.de

Neues Rathaus

✉ Trammplatz 2

☎ 0511 16 8 0

$ $

Since then, Hanover (Hannover in German) has evolved into northern Germany's second largest city (after Hamburg), an industrial, administrative, and cultural center of first rank. On the whole, Hanover is not a place to contemplate the remains of the past; wartime bombing effectively razed the city center, and the rapid rebuilding that took place lacks any particular distinction.

However, the city hosts some of Europe's most important trade fairs. In 2000, Germany's first international expo was held here, helping to put the city firmly on the international map.

Many business visitors go straight to the extensive **Messegelände,** the trade fair grounds with their own main-line railroad station and parking for 45,000 cars. The great annual trade fair was instituted by the

INSIDER TIP:

Germany's oldest flea market takes place on Saturdays in Hanover's Altstadt—an El Dorado for lovers of art and curiosities, set against a historic backdrop.

—DANIELA BUCKMANN
National Geographic contributor

British occupation authorities in 1947. Nowadays it is supplemented by a whole series of specialist fairs, including the world's biggest computer bonanza, the CeBit.

If you are not on business, you are likely to arrive at the stately 19th-century **Hauptbahnhof,** the city-center station, from which you emerge onto spacious **Ernst-August-Platz,** with its equestrian statue of Elector Ernst August. Locals often arrange to meet *unterm Schwanz* ("under the tail") of this prominent landmark. Beyond the area of pedestrian-only shopping streets stretching southward from the station are the scant remains of Hanover's Altstadt (Old Town). They include the **Marktkirche,** with its distinctive gabled tower, together with a number of rebuilt timber-framed houses that give an idea of what the preindustrial city must have looked like.

Farther south still, the huge and flamboyant early 20th-century **Neues Rathaus** (New City Hall) marks the transition from the densely built-up city center to an extensive area of lakes and parkland. Its neo-baroque exterior conceals what at the time was an up-to-the-minute art nouveau interior. A unique inclined elevator takes you up into the dome for a fine panorama over the city and its surroundings.

Museums

The nearby **Niedersächsiches Landesmuseum** (Regional Museum of Lower Saxony) has a worthy collection of old master paintings, but the one gallery to see in Hanover is the **Sprengel Museum.** This striking modern building functions perfectly as a treasure house of 20th-century art. The star here is local artist Kurt Schwitters (1887–1948), a subversive polymath of a man who drew, painted, sculpted, wrote, published, and organized happenings.

Niedersächsiches Landesmuseum

- ✉ Willy-Brandt-Allee 5
- ☎ 0511 98 07 686
- 🕐 Closed Mon.
- 💲 $$
- 🚇 U-Bahn: Halteselle "Aegidientop-platz"; Bus: Haltestelle "Rathaus/Bleichenstrasse"

www.landesmuseum-hannover.nieder sachsen.de

Sprengel Museum

- ✉ Kurt-Schwitters-Platz
- ☎ 0511 16 84 38 75
- 🕐 Closed Mon.
- 💲 $$

sprengel-museum.de

The Party Goes North

If you feel like merrymaking for 17 days straight, head to Hanover in late September for northern Germany's largest beer festival cum fun fair. Held every year since 1957, Oktoberfest Hannover features oodles of amusement rides, try-your-luck games, feats of astonishing skill, oompah music, and plenty of food, including sausages, potato salad, and sauerkraut—not to mention two giant beer tents seating more than a thousand people each. With more than one million visitors each year, this is the second largest Oktoberfest in the world behind Munich's (see pp. 300–301). Just like in the Bavarian capital, the mayor opens proceedings by cracking the first keg and crying, "It's tapped!"

Herrenhausen Gardens

✉ 2 miles (3 km) NW of Hanover

💲 $$, free in winter

🚆 S-Bahn: 4, 5; Bus: 136

hannover.de

Wilhelm-Busch-Museum

✉ Georgengarten 1

☎ 0511 16 99 99 11/16

🕐 Closed Mon.

💲 $

🚆 S-Bahn: 4, 5

karikatur-museum.de

Herrenhausen Gardens

An avenue of lime trees links these four gardens. Walk north from the town on Nienberger Strasse, past the least interesting of the four, the **Welfengarten,** now part of the university. To the left is the Georgengarten and next to it the pride of them all, the **Grosser Garten** (Great Garden). Across Herrenhäuser Strasse to the north is the Berggarten.

Begun in 1655 and continuing until 1714, the Grosser Garten was transformed into one of Europe's most ambitious baroque gardens, largely under the direction of the wife of Elector Ernst August, Sophie von der Pfalz. Even without its Schloss, destroyed in World War II, it is a regal sight, a triumph of geometry and rationality over nature. On entering, you see the outdoor theater, which is still used for performances in summer. To the east is a great parterre, with geometric plantings of

flowers and shrubs, and in front the Great Fountain spurts an imposing jet 260 feet (80 m) into the air. The 1930s model gardens show historic styles of garden design; one reconstructs the fabled Renaissance garden of Heidelberg Castle.

The **Georgengarten** was laid out in the early 19th century. The Georgenpalais houses the **Wilhelm-Busch-Museum** of caricature. The **Berggarten,** begun in the mid-17th century, is now the university botanical garden. ∎

INSIDER TIP:

La Grotte's mosaics of mirrors, pebbles, and colored glass come together to give visitors to the Grosser Garten an absorbing, sensuous experience.

—DANIELA BUCKMANN
National Geographic contributor

House of Hanover

The Electress Sophie, granddaughter of James I of England, not only inspired one of Europe's finest gardens but also provided England with a king. In 1714 her son, Georg Ludwig, was invited to take the English throne as George I. He did so with little enthusiasm, being very attached to the sedate court at Hanover. Neither were the English very enthusiastic about him, mocking his rustic manners and his faltering attempts to speak their language.

George I and his successors ruled over both England and Hanover, gradually becoming more English in the process. On the death of William IV in 1837 a problem arose; his niece Victoria was next in succession, but Hanover's laws would not allow a woman to rule. The kingdoms had to go their separate ways, with Victoria crowned in London while an uncle became King Ernst August of Hanover.

When Victoria's son Edward VII became king of England, the House of Hanover became the House of Saxe-Coburg-Gotha (Prince Albert's family). In the feverish atmosphere of World War I, this was far too Germanic, and George V changed the name of his dynasty to the House of Windsor.

Hamelin

"A pleasanter spot you never spied," wrote British poet Robert Browning of 19th-century Hamelin (Hameln in German), and it is still the handsomest town on the River Weser, with its dignified buildings in the style known as Weser Renaissance (see p. 38).

The Brothers Grimm originally recorded the legend of the Pied Piper of Hamelin. A stranger to the town and dressed in multi-colored garb, the piper spirited the city's children away with a few notes on his flute after the citizens refused to pay him for clearing the city of rats. Vermin were a constant problem in medieval towns, but the tale of the Pied Piper probably has more to do with the forced emigration of young people from poverty-stricken areas than rat infestation.

Hamelin's great glory is its ornamented town mansions with high gables and oriel windows, the epitome of the style that developed along the Weser in the 16th and early 17th centuries. Among the most striking houses along the main street, Oster-strasse, are the **Rattenfänger-haus** (Rat-Catcher's House) of 1603, named for the Pied Piper, and the **Leisthaus** at No. 9. Together with the timber-framed **Stiftsherrenhaus** at No. 8, the Leisthaus is home to the **Museum Hamelin** (*Oster-strasse 8–9, tel 05151 2 02 12 15, closed Mon., $$*) with material on the Pied Piper legend. The story of the stingy citizens and the colorfully clad trickster is reenacted every Sunday at noon (mid-May–mid-Sept.) on the marketplace

A statue of the famous Pied Piper, a Brothers Grimm tale set in Hamelin

outside the town's massive stone-built **Hochzeitshaus** (Marriage Building). If you miss the show, the Hochzeitshaus carillon displays the story daily at 1:05, 3:35, and 5:35 p.m. ∎

Hamelin
◭ 126 D2
Visitor Information
✉ Deisterallee 1
☎ 05151 95 78 23
hameln.de

Harz Mountains

Nationalpark Harz (Harz National Park) occupies Germany's northernmost uplands, stretching across from Lower Saxony into Saxony-Anhalt and Thuringia. They include the country's highest summit outside the Alps, the Brocken (see pp. 218–219). Hikers can explore trails leading through ravines and woodlands to windswept summits.

Harz Mountains
🗺 127 E2

Oberharzer Bergwerkmuseum
✉ Bornhardt-strasse 16, Clausthal-Zellerfeld
☎ 05323 9 89 50
💲 $$

Silberbergwerk Samson
✉ Am Samson 2, St. Andreasberg
☎ 05582 12 49
💲 $$

The Harz was once Germany's foremost industrial area. More than a thousand years ago, silver was mined here, followed by copper, iron, and lead, sources of wealth that gave the mining town of Goslar (see p. 133) the status of a free imperial city. The metals have nearly all been worked out, leaving a legacy of tree-covered spoil heaps. The geographical unity of the Harz was shattered when the front line of the Cold War ran between Lower Saxony and Saxony-Anhalt.

TorfHaus (Nationalpark-Besucherzentrum TorfHaus; *Torfhaus 38B, tel 05320 331 790,*

torfhaus-harzresort.de), in the western Harz, is the starting point for many walks, including a 7.5-mile (12 km) hike up the Brocken. **Clausthal-Zellerfeld** is a double town, once the area's most important mining center. Clausthal has a huge timber church; Zellerfeld, rebuilt in baroque style in the 18th century, has the absorbing **Oberharzer Bergwerkmuseum** (Mining Museum of the Upper Harz). **St. Andreasberg,** at about 2,050 feet (630 m), is the highest town in the Harz. Here you can visit the old **Silberbergwerk Samson** (Samson Silver Mine), where once miners climbed down a 2,650-foot-deep (810 m) shaft. ∎

Founded around 1530, the silver-mining town of Lautenthal nestles among the forests of the Harz.

Goslar

Idyllically located among the wooded outliers of the Harz Mountains, Goslar has ancient churches, medieval fortifications, and a great imperial palace. Its greatest treasure, however, and the reason for its inclusion on UNESCO's World Heritage List, is its unsurpassed array of timber-framed houses.

A gilded eagle tops the 13th-century fountain in Goslar's market square.

The cobbled streets and alleyways of the old town center are lined with timber-framed houses, many built before the middle of the 16th century. Be sure not to miss highlights such as the late 17th-century **Siemenshaus,** with its charming internal courtyard, or the superb **Brusttuch** (*Hoher Weg 1, tel 05321 3 46 00*), now a hotel. It is adorned with a variety of carved figures, including the "Buttermaid," nonchalantly scratching her bare behind. The splendid **Kaiserworth,** built in 1494, shares the Marktplatz with the Gothic **Rathaus** (Town Hall).

The great stone **Kaiserpfalz** (Imperial Palace) rises majestically over grassy slopes at the edge of the town center. Originally built in the 11th century, it was restored

INSIDER TIP:

Four times a day, life-size figures on the carillon of Goslar's main square enact the legend and history of Europe's greatest silver mine.

—BO ZAUNDERS
National Geographic Traveler
magazine writer

in the 1870s as a symbol of the newly united German Empire.

The **Rammelsberg mine,** just over a mile (2 km) south, was worked continuously for at least a thousand years and closed only in 1988. You can explore the site up top or, clad in miner's gear, descend underground. ■

Goslar
- ⓜ 127 E2
- **Visitor Information**
- ✉ Markt 7
- ☎ 05321 7 80 60
- **goslar.de**

Siemenshaus
- ✉ Schreiberstrasse 12
- ☎ 05321 2 38 37
- ⏱ By guided tour only
- **siemenshaus.de**

Kaiserpfalz
- ✉ Kaiserbleek 6
- ☎ 05321 311 96 93
- $ $$

Rammelsberg mine
- ✉ Bergtal 19
- ☎ 05321 75 00
- $ $$$$ (museum & tour)
- **rammelsberg.de**

Celle

The gateway to the southern part of Lüneburg Heath, Celle—like Lüneburg in the north—has survived unscathed by war. Here, however, it is the half-timbering typical of southern Lower Saxony that prevails rather than brick. And Celle was no commercial center; it remained a ducal seat up to the mid-19th century, with its Schloss the most prominent building. Set apart from the main part of town, it neatly reflects the hierarchical social order of the old regime.

Celle

🗺 127 E3

Visitor Information

✉ Markt 14–16

☎ 05141 12 12

celle-tourismus.de

Stadtkirche

✉ Markt

☎ 05141 77 35

🕐 Closed Sun.–Mon.

💲 $ (tower)

stadtkirche-celle.de

Bomann-Museum

✉ Schlossplatz 7

☎ 05141 1 23 72

🕐 Closed Mon.

💲 $$

bomann-museum.de

Surrounded by its moat and lush parkland, the **Schloss** (tel 05141 1 23 73, closed Mon., $) stands at the western end of town, its high walls and massive towers giving it a supremely confident air. The Schlossmuseum tells the story of the Kingdom of Hanover.

Closer to the town is the **Stadtkirche,** the parish church, full of ducal tombs. A trumpeter sounds reveille from its tall tower every morning and evening. There's a great view of the town from the top. Behind the Stadtkirche is the **Rathaus** (Town Hall), a big building mostly in the Weser Renaissance style (see p. 38), with elaborate dormers and gables. The town itself has street after street of fine old houses, mostly from the 16th to the 18th centuries. Watch

Go for Baroque

Celle is home to Germany's oldest, and still operational, baroque theater. The Malersaal (*Schlosstheater Celle Schlossplatz 1, tel 05141 90 50 8 75/76*), entertaining dukes and commoners alike since the late 1600s, is a beautiful and historic setting for classical theater.

INSIDER TIP:

Celle's Zöllnerstrasse is a quaint little street that's home to the Green House (No. 32) and its whimsical crooked beam, and the Fairy-Tale House (No. 11), where a generous donkey rains cash from behind.

—JEREMY GRAY
National Geographic author

for a number of highlights such as the **Alte Lateinschule** (Old Latin School) on Kalandgasse, with its richly carved timbers, or the elaborate decoration of the **Hoppener Haus** of 1532 on the corner of Poststrasse and Rundestrasse.

Once you've strolled around town, visit the **Bomann-Museum** for the history of the region and Celle itself. It has reconstructions of town and country interiors. Finally, visit the **Niedersächsisches Landgestüt** (Lower Saxon State Stud Farm; *Spörckenstrasse 10, tel 05141 9 29 40, landgestuetcelle.de, closed Sun.*), founded in 1735. The great annual parade of the stallions takes place in late September or early October. ■

Lüneburg & Lüneburger Heide

For a thousand years, right up to 1980, salt was extracted from the ground below Lüneburg, one of northern Germany's most perfectly preserved medium-size cities. The salt trade linked Lüneburg with the Hansa towns of the coast, and their elaborate brick architecture was copied here with wonderfully picturesque results.

Overlooking the **Markt,** the main square, is the imperious baroque facade of the **Rathaus** (Town Hall; *Am Ochsenmarkt, tel 04131 30 92 30, $*), one of the largest and finest town halls in the country. Parts of the building date from the 13th century, and the Renaissance council chamber is elaborately paneled and carved. To the east is the **Wasserviertel,** the atmospheric "water town" around the River Ilmenau. An ancient crane still stands guard by the waterside.

South of the marketplace, traffic-calmed streets lead to **Am Sande,** an elongated square with some of the prettiest facades in town and the 354-foot (108 m) spire of the city's oldest church, St. Johanniskirche. West of Am Sande, on the edge of the Altstadt (Old Town), is the **Deutsches Salzmuseum** (German Salt Museum), in the old salt works. There are interactive displays on all aspects of salt—its history, production, and even a tasting.

A shepherd and his dog guard their flock on Lüneburger Heide's open expanses.

summer) and juniper; marshlands, ponds, and clear streams; and forests and farmland. The heath is now much in favor with walkers, riders, and wildlife enthusiasts; parts are designated nature parks or reserves. Leave your transport at the pretty village of **Undeloh** and climb the 554-foot (169 m) Wilseder Berg, the highest point of the heath.

On the southern edge of the heath is the location of the Nazi concentration camp at **Bergen-Belsen,** now a memorial site. Lüneburg Heath was also where Britain's Field Marshal Montgomery took the unconditional surrender of the German armed forces on May 4, 1945, which marked the final hours of World War II. ∎

Lüneburger Heide

Lüneburg has given its name to the Lüneburg Heath, a vast tract of heathland stretching southward to Celle. Its mosaic of landscapes comprises gently undulating stretches of heather (glorious when in flower in late

Lüneburg
- 127 E4

Visitor Information
- ✉ Rathaus, Am Markt 1
- ☎ 0800 220 50 05
- lueneburg.de

Deutsches Salzmuseum
- ✉ Sülfmeisterstrasse 1
- ☎ 04131 4 50 65
- $ $$
- salzmuseum.de

Bergen-Belsen
- ✉ Anne-Frank-Platz, Lohheide
- ☎ 05051 47 59 200
- bergen-belsen.de

Bremen

Bremen is proud to be a *Land* of the Federal Republic, a reminder of its independent past as Germany's first seaport and one of the country's free cities. Far inland up the estuary of the River Weser, it kept its status as a port of the first rank in the 19th century by founding a daughter town and harbor at Bremerhaven, close to the mouth of the river. Bremen's charming Altstadt (Old Town) and its wonderfully ornate town hall alone make any visit worthwhile.

The giant figure of Roland, Bremen's guardian of civic liberties, graces Bremen's central square.

Bremen's central square, the irregularly shaped Markt, is dominated by the **Rathaus** (City Hall; *Am Markt, tel 0421 36 10, $*), a grand civic structure where patrician merchants met to make political and commercial decisions about how best to ensure their trading city's prosperity. The Rathaus is medieval in origin, but the facade you see is the most elaborate example of the Weser Renaissance style, with arcade, huge windows, and elaborate gables all added in the early 17th century.

Before taking a guided tour through the interior, take a look at the two very different types of public sculpture that adorn the square. The 33-foot-tall (10 m) **figure of the knight Roland** beneath his Gothic canopy dates from 1404. As elsewhere in central Europe, Roland symbolizes civic rights and freedoms. More modest in size are the famous **figures of the Bremen Town Musicians,** cockerel, cat, dog, and donkey from a folktale retold by the Brothers Grimm.

Inside the Rathaus, one elaborately decorated room follows another, although none is quite as grand as the spacious, 130-foot-long (40 m) **Upper Hall,** with splendid ship models hanging from the ceiling. Downstairs, the cheerful **Ratskeller** (Wine Cellar) serves wine from a list featuring no fewer than 600 wines (they don't serve beer). This is no accident: Bremen has long specialized in the export of German wines.

The tall twin towers of the nearby **Cathedral** contrast with

depicting the Archangel Michael fighting a dragon. The street is one of Bremen's most intriguing sights, a joint enterprise in the 1920s and early 1930s between wealthy coffee merchant Ludwig Roselius and sculptor/architect Bernhard Hoetger. It has a cozy, old-world feel, but a closer look reveals its brick

St. Petri's Time-Warping Crypt

The cellar of Bremen's St. Petri *(Sandstrasse 10-12, tel 0421 36 50 40, closed Nov.–Easter, $)* has been the cathedral's most visited attraction for more than 300 years. Here, where lead for the roofing was originally stored, excessively dry air created the perfect conditions for preserving corpses.

The earliest interments were of workers said to have been killed during the

building's construction. Today, you can view several corpses in a well-preserved state. On display, in glass-topped coffins, you will find eight mummies, including two Swedish officers from the Thirty Years War (1618–1648), an English countess, and a student who died in a duel. The bodies of two animals, a cat and a chimpanzee, were also placed in the crypt in a study of slow decomposition.

the horizontal lines of the City Hall. The towers were added in the 19th century, but the history of the building goes back to the late eighth century, when Emperor Charlemagne sent the Anglo-Saxon bishop Willehad here to build a church and convert the heathen. Nothing remains of Willehad's timber building, but the crypt evokes the past with carved capitals from the 11th century as well as a quite superb 13th-century bronze **font** carried by figures of men riding lions.

Böttcherstrasse & Beyond

An opening on the southern side of the marketplace leads to Böttcherstrasse, a narrow street marked by a stunning relief in gold, the "Bringer of Light,"

buildings and their decoration to be of startling originality and modernity. Try to be here when Hoetger's Glockenspiel is playing (at noon, 3 p.m., and 6 p.m.).

The intimate **Museum im Roselius-Haus** is a charming assemblage of the furnishings and paintings collected by Roselius, while the adjoining **Paula Modersohn-Becker Museum** is devoted to the work of a short-lived artist who worked mainly in nearby Worpswede (see sidebar p. 139). The hotel at the end of the street, **Haus Atlantis,** is Hoetger's masterpiece. It has been much altered, but peer inside for a glimpse of his futuristic stairway.

Beyond Böttcherstrasse is the **River Weser,** quiet since docks and quays moved downstream, but the place to come in summer.

A relief sculpture adorns the entrance to the Böttcherstrasse.

Übersee Museum

- ✉ Bahnhofsplatz 13
- ☎ 0421 16 03 81 01
- ⏱ Closed Mon.
- 💲 $$

uebersee-museum.de

Focke Museum

- ✉ Schwachhauser Heerstrasse 240
- ☎ 0421 69 96 00 0
- ⏱ Closed Mon.
- 💲 $$

focke-museum.de

Kunsthalle

- ✉ Am Wall 207
- ☎ 0421 32 90 80
- ⏱ Closed Mon.
- 💲 $$$

kunsthalle-bremen.de

the pretty parkland laid out along the star-shaped baroque fortifications and moat. The windmill crowning a rise is the last of many that once stood here. Beyond the main railroad station is the **Bürgerpark,** a fine public park, with lakes, trees, woodland, waterways, and miles of footpaths, laid out in the mid-19th century.

You could spend several days exploring Bremen's many museums and galleries. The **Übersee Museum** has one of Germany's best ethnographical collections, while the **Focke Museum** is a treasure house of Bremen history. The **Kunsthalle** has paintings and sculpture from the 15th century onward. The **Neues Museum Weserburg** displays work by international contemporary artists.

There are bars, restaurants, and old ships (you can dine aboard). On the far bank is **Brauerei Beck & Co.** (Am Deich 18/19, tel 0421 50 94 55 55, closed Sun.–Wed., $$$), one of Germany's biggest breweries offering guided tours.

The most perfectly preserved part of the Old Town is the tiny **Schnoorviertel,** an old fishermen's quarter of alleyways and courtyards, and fed by the narrow Schnoor River. Threatened with demolition in the early 20th century, the area is now very trim, with many of its charming old houses occupied by gift shops and places to eat.

The Weser forms a natural boundary to one side of the Old Town, which is neatly defined to the north by the **Wallanlagen,**

Bremerhaven

The port installations at Bremerhaven stretch for more than 4 miles (7 km) along the shore of the Weser estuary, a good 37 miles (60 km) downstream from Bremen. This is one of Germany's great outlets to the seas of the world, second only to Hamburg in extent and volume handled. The fishing harbor is the biggest in Europe, and there are important shipyards, too.

The construction of this harbor at the mouth of the Weser in the 19th century was an excellent move. Bremerhaven can handle the largest vessels without trouble. Passenger traffic has almost disappeared; the Columbus Terminal through which thousands of emigrants to the New World passed now only sees the occasional cruise ship. For many years after 1945, Bremerhaven functioned as the port for U.S. forces in Germany. One of the last to come down the gangway off his troopship was GI Elvis Presley.

The dock completed in 1830 is now the **Alter Hafen** (Old Harbor), today a sleek leisure district thanks to a recent makeover. In it are moored several historic ships, including the three-master *Seute Deern,* now a restaurant. You can squeeze through the innards of the **U-boat** *Wilhelm Bauer,* which was launched in January 1945, too late to see action. She was scuttled, but later salvaged and used as a training vessel by the German navy.

At the end of the harbor winks a futuristic glass bubble, the **Klimahaus Bremerhaven** *(Am Längengrad 8, tel 0471 90 20 300, klimahaus-bremerhaven.de, $$$$).* Visitors to this full-immersion "climate center" can ponder the

INSIDER TIP:

If you enjoy the arts and the inspiring scenic vistas of the countryside, then charming Worpswede [see sidebar below] is a definite stop.

—MARK A. VIOLA
National Geographic contributor

planet's complex biospheres while wandering the different climate zones, from the Sahara to the frigid Antarctic.

Bremerhaven's great visitor attraction is the **Deutsches Schiffahrtsmuseum** (German Maritime Museum), housed in a building designed by Berlin architect Hans Scharoun. Displays illustrate every aspect of German ships and shipping. There are more than 500 models, and a few real vessels, but the star is a *Kogge,* a chunky timber sailing ship dating from around 1380. ∎

Neues Museum Weserburg
- ✉ Teerhof 20
- ☎ 0421 59 83 90
- 🕐 Closed Mon.
- 💲 $$

weserburg.de

Deutsches Schiffahrtsmuseum
- ✉ Hans-Scharoun-Platz 1, Bremerhaven
- ☎ 0471 48 20 70
- 💲 $$
- 🕐 Closed Mon. Nov.–March

dsm.museum

Worpswede

The name Worpswede became synonymous with the desire of many late 19th-century German artists to escape the city and the straitjacket of academic painting in unspoiled rustic surroundings. On the edge of a great tract of marshland, 15 miles (24 km) north of Bremen, the village of Worpswede was home for many years to a community of artists. Among them was one of Germany's most popular women painters, Paula Modersohn-Becker (1876–1907), who called it "a wonderland, a land of the gods!" Her simple but touching portraits and landscapes can be seen in the village as well as in the Kunsthalle (see opposite) and the museum named after her in Bremen (see p. 137).

With its charming mixture of thatched farmhouses and architectural oddities from the early 20th century, Worpswede has continued to be a congenial place for artists and craftspeople to live and work, and there's an abundance of galleries and studios. On a fine day, the waterways, reed beds, and meadows of the flat countryside do indeed become a wonderland, best explored by bicycle or aboard a turf-cutter's sailboat.

Wolfsburg & the Volkswagen

"This vehicle is quite unattractive to the average buyer; it's too ugly and too noisy," declared Lord Rootes, the British motor magnate, on inspecting the Volkswagen works at Wolfsburg just after World War II. By the end of 1945, the factory had turned out a few dozen vehicles. In the following year the number rose to just over 10,000. By 1972, the "Beetle" had become the world's biggest-selling automobile.

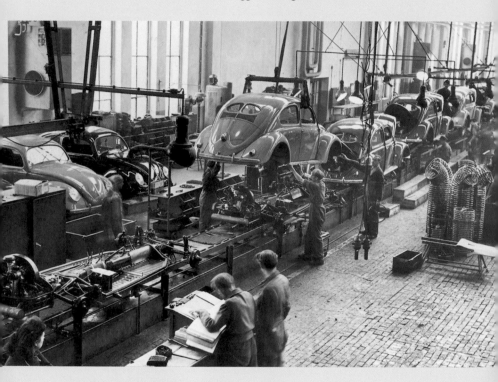

VWs roll off the production line at Wolfsburg in the 1950s.

In the 1930s, Hitler's Third Reich was busy building a network of the world's most advanced roads, the *Autobahnen,* but there was hardly any traffic to run on them. The Führer favored motoring and ordered Ferdinand Porsche to develop a car that would mobilize the masses at a price they could afford (the *Volkswagen* or People's Car), fixed at no more than the relatively modest sum of 999 marks (about $500). Drawing on the technically advanced rear-engined and streamlined vehicles designed by Hans Ledwinka for the Tatra works in Czechoslovakia, Porsche came up with the first prototype in 1935.

Hitler was enthused. A site for a factory to make the car was chosen in what is now Lower Saxony, and in 1938 the foundation stone was laid by the Führer himself. The new town, called Kraft durch Freude Stadt (Strength through Joy Town), was planned in the Nazis' favorite style, with triumphal boulevards and public buildings.

Customized Beetle, California style

War intervened before more than a few classic Volkswagens could be turned out. The design was adapted to make a jeeplike vehicle, the *Kübelwagen* (Bucket-wagon), of which some 50,000 had been produced by 1945, along with an amphibious version, the *Schwimmwagen*.

Wolfsburg

When the British arrived in 1945, the town was a dismal place consisting of barrack blocks inhabited by forced laborers from all over Europe. The British renamed it Wolfsburg, the name of the nearby castle in Weser Renaissance style, which nowadays houses the municipal museum. The barrack blocks have been replaced with mostly bland modern developments, with just a few highlights, such as the town theater, a striking design by architect Hans Scharoun. And there's an Automuseum on the appropriately named Dieselstrasse.

Having once symbolized the Nazi ideal of mass mobility, the Volkswagen came to stand for the virtues of the postwar Federal Republic—solidity, reliability, economy, endurance, and lack of ostentation. Wolfsburg itself, close to the East German border, its factory chimneys and production halls visible from the far side of the Cold War frontier, became a symbol for the achievements of capitalism.

Production of the Beetle in Wolfsburg ceased in 1974, although the car was still produced elsewhere. The last Beetle rolled off the assembly line in Mexico in 2003.

Autostadt Wolfsburg

Autostadt Wolfsburg (*Autostadt GmbH, Stadtbrücke, tel 05361 400, autostadt.de, $$$$*) is Volkswagen's own ultramodern theme park, featuring a museum, exhibits of VW Group vehicles, and a customer center for the pickup of new cars. Also worthwhile is the hour-long tour of VW's enormous factory, said to be the world's largest car plant. Visitors with a driver's licence can even take motorized spins around an obstacle course with an English-speaking instructor, and there is a mini-track where children can drive small electric Beetles.

East Frisian Islands

Strung along Lower Saxony's coast, these islands, called the Ostfriesische Inseln in German, have been attracting vacationers from the mainland for nearly 200 years, ever since the Hanoverian court decided to spend its summer vacations on Norderney.

A *Strandkorb* (beach basket) is an essential accessory on the breezy East Frisian Islands.

East Frisian Islands

📖 126 A5–C5

ostfriesische-inseln.de

Borkum

Visitor Information

✉ Am Georg-Schütte-Platz 5

☎ 04922 9330

borkum.de

Bracing breezes characterize the islands. The sun does shine on the vast sandy beaches, but to make the most of it you absolutely have to have a *Strandkorb*, one of those solid wickerwork structures that can be turned to face the warming rays and protect you from the wind blowing off the North Sea. Vacationers come here to breathe pure air, stroll or cycle among the sand dunes, watch birds, take trips to the various islands, ride one of the islands' little old railroads, or simply relax in an environment largely free of cars and traffic.

The islands are in a continuous state of evolution. Tides and currents gnaw away at their western extremities and deposit sand to the east, and the wind constantly tries to reshape the dunes. A north-facing outer rampart of the mainland, they are separated from the rest of Lower Saxony by the Wattenmeer, an area of shining mudflats that is uncovered

EXPERIENCE: Sipping Frisian Tea

In the East Frisian Islands, a necklace of sandbanks between the sea and coastal moors, lies the kingdom of Germany's ceremonial tea drinkers. The custom dates from the mid-17th century, when shipments from neighboring Holland sparked the genteel fashion of tea sipping in literary salons.

In a country of coffee lovers, the East Frisians (who consume about one-quarter of imports) take a break several times a day for a "koppke Tee," typically a strong, black variety sweetened with slow-melting rock candy sugar and a dollop of thick cream. Locals prefer not to stir the brew, resulting in three layers. Just as important is the ritual of preparation, which involves elaborate porcelain sets with tiny cups and a little cookie placed on the saucer. A shot of brown rum is added to warm the cockles in winter.

Join in a traditional East Frisian teatime at the **Ostfriesisches Teemuseum** (Am Markt 36, Norden, tel 04931 121 00, teemuseum.de., closed Mon., tea prepared Wed. & Sat. 2 p.m.).

twice daily by the receding tide and is now protected as a national park (Nationalpark Niedersächsisches Wattenmeer).

The largest and most westerly island is **Borkum,** closer to the Dutch mainland than to Germany. It rivals **Norderney,** the next in size, in its range of recreational facilities, but Norderney has the edge when it comes to character, with a Kurhaus, Kurpark, and casino as reminders of its days as an aristocratic retreat. Both islands have splendid covered swimming pools with wavemaking facilities.

Between Norderney and Borkum is **Juist,** 10.5 miles (17 km) long and only a few hundred yards across. **Baltrum** is the smallest island, like Juist completely car-free and quiet. Impressive sand dunes, carved by the wind, mark its eastern end.

Popular **Langeoog** has its tranquil spots, and seals can sometimes be spotted hauled out on the nature reserve at the island's

INSIDER TIP:

The Alte Inselkirche on Spiekeroog, built in 1696, is the oldest church on the islands. A pietà inside is said to have come from a stranded ship of the Spanish Armada.

—ANNIKA MAREK
Spiekeroog Tourism Board

eastern end. Among its modern facilities, **Spiekeroog** has preserved much of its traditional character; there's even a horse tramway! The church—Alte Inselkirche—has carvings allegedly made from the timbers of one of the ships of the Spanish Armada sent against England, wrecked here in 1588.

The easternmost island, **Wangerooge,** has a little railroad that brings vacationers to the village, with its museum of island life installed in the old lighthouse. ∎

Norderney
Visitor Information
✉ Am Kurplatz 3
☎ 04932 891 900
norderney.de

Juist
Visitor Information
✉ Kurverwaltung
☎ 04935 80 90
juist.de

Langeoog
Visitor Information
✉ Hauptstrasse 28
☎ 04972 69 30
langeoog.de

Spiekeroog
Visitor Information
✉ Noorderpad 25
☎ 04976 9 19 31 01
spiekeroog.de

Wangerooge
Visitor Information
✉ Bahnhof
☎ 04469 9 48 80
wangerooge.de

More Places to Visit in Lower Saxony

Göttingen

One of Germany's most characterful university cities, Göttingen buzzes with student life. It was founded by George II of England and Hanover in 1734 to provide his Hanoverian possessions with a reliable supply of state servants. The city's favorite statue stands in front of the medieval Rathaus; Gänseliesel ("Little Goose Girl") is the most kissed girl in Göttingen, traditionally honored by an obligatory salute from every successful doctoral student. Not so successful as a student was the future chancellor Bismarck, whose youthful roistering caused him to be banned from the town center; you can visit his undergraduate lodgings, the **Bismarckhäuschen** (Am Wall). www .goettingen-tourismus.de 🔼 127 E1 ✉ Altes Rathaus, Markt 9 ☎ 0551 49 98 00

Hildesheim

Hildesheim's importance today has been recognized by UNESCO, which put the city on the World Heritage List because of its exceptional early Romanesque art and architecture. The town has made a supreme effort to re-create its historic ambience after severe wartime destruction, and its huge main square, the **Marktplatz,** now gives a good impression of what Hildesheim was like in its heyday. The most striking building is the late medieval Knochenhaueramtshaus— literally the "Bone-Basher Building"—which, with its huge gable and five projecting upper stories, was the seat of the butchers' guild. But it is the town's churches that make it of international significance. The **Dom**'s outstanding works of art include 11th-century bronze doors (Bernward-Tür) with scenes from the Old and New Testaments, while **St. Michael's** is one of the supreme expressions of Romanesque architecture in Germany. hildesheim.de 🔼 127 E2 ✉ Rathausstrasse 18–20 ☎ 05121 1 79 80

Stade

Close to the River Elbe downstream from Hamburg, the port of Stade was once a rival to its mighty neighbor. Today Stade seeks its fortune in its heritage of fine old buildings, many of them dating from the reconstruction that took place after a terrible fire during the Swedish occupation in the mid-17th century. After a thoroughgoing restoration program, much of the town now looks as it did then. The scene by the canal-like old harbor is particularly enchanting, with gabled houses overlooking the quayside with its antique crane. Stade is the capital of the Altes Land (Old Land), the area along the Elbe reclaimed long ago from the water by settlers brought in from Holland. Hamburgers come to relax among the old farmsteads and fruit trees: This is one of the country's biggest fruit-growing areas, glorious in spring with apple and cherry blossoms. stade-tourismus.de 🔼 126 D5 ✉ Hansestrasse 16 ☎ 04141 40 91 70

Wolfenbüttel

Wolfenbüttel is a lovely example of a tiny capital city, its huge Renaissance **Schloss** (originally founded by Henry the Lion) counterbalanced by other fine public buildings and a wealth of timber-framed houses. Dwelling types were carefully graded, with high court officials living in stately homes, middle-rankers in smaller houses that were nevertheless profusely decorated, and the humblest in simpler but still pleasing two-story structures. In the 17th century the ducal library was the most richly endowed in Europe; its most famous librarian was the dramatist Gotthold Ephraim Lessing (1729–1781). A selection of its precious books, manuscripts, maps, and globes is usually on display. wolfenbuettel-tourismus.de 🔼 127 E2 ✉ Stadtmarkt 7 ☎ 05331 862 80

An extraordinary range of urban experiences, flanked by wooded uplands, tranquil landscapes, and moated castles

North Rhine-Westphalia

16th-century stained glass from Cologne Cathedral

North Rhine-Westphalia

Bounded on the west by Belgium and Holland, this is one of the most densely urbanized areas in Europe. One German in five lives in North Rhine-Westphalia, mainly in the vast industrial conurbation of the Ruhr and in the towns and cities along the River Rhine. Many people come here on business, but there is plenty to detain the more casual visitor, particularly in the cities.

Cologne (Köln), with its magnificent Gothic cathedral, is one of Germany's great historic cities. As a cultural center, it is almost matched by the state capital, Düsseldorf. Then there is Bonn, Beethoven's birthplace. An old provincial town suddenly elevated

NOT TO BE MISSED:

Cologne's iconic cathedral big and up close **150–153, 156**

Wandering Cologne's fountain-filled Old Town **154–155**

The stunning Wallraf-Richartz and Ludwig museums **156–157**

The 13th-century Shrine of Charlemagne **161**

Feeling the genius at Beethoven's birthplace **163**

Clinking glasses in Düsseldorf's stylish Mediahafen **164–165**

Skin-diving in a former Ruhr ironworks **170**

The watery castles of the Münsterland **172**

to the role of national capital after World War II, it is trying to regain its equilibrium as government moves back to Berlin. Aachen was Emperor Charlemagne's capital, while Münster, the leading city of Westphalia, has equally venerable roots.

It is easy to get around, with a dense rail network and excellent rapid transit systems. The autobahn seems to reach everywhere, but it attracts huge volumes of traffic and is frequently clogged. The most relaxing way to travel is by boat; pleasure steamers share the Rhine with great barges, or you can cruise the canals and smaller rivers. The Ruhr is proud of its network of paths and cycle tracks; you can walk or ride all along the banks of the Rhine.

On the far bank of the river from Bonn, the mountains of the Siebengebirge mark the start of the most romantic section of the Rhine. The wooded uplands and small towns of the Eifel are especially popular with the Dutch and Belgians. To the east of the Rhine, there are similar landscapes in the Sauerland, Siegerland, and the Teutoburger Wald. And the moated castles of the Münsterland are a delight. ■

Cologne

Cologne (Köln), bestriding the Rhine, is Germany's media capital, and a center of arts and learning as well as of industry and commerce. Visitors come from all parts of the world, not only to admire its many sights but also to participate in trade fairs and cultural events. The city's emblem is its twin-towered cathedral, but, although strongly Catholic, Cologne is far from pious; its people are known for their caustic humor and their love of a good time.

A city on the Rhine, Cologne's skyline is dominated by the famous cathedral.

Cologne

🅰 146 C2

Visitor Information

✉ Kardinal-Höffner-Platz 1 (opposite the cathedral)

☎ 0221 34 64 30

koelntourismus.de

Cologne was founded by the Romans as a frontier settlement called Colonia Claudia Ara Agrippinensium, which became the capital of their province of Lower Germania. In the Middle Ages it prospered from river-borne trade, becoming Germany's largest city. The vast area forming today's **Altstadt** (Old Town) was enclosed by the medieval walls, whose alignment is marked by the modern Ring boulevard. Long before the Gothic cathedral was begun, the faithful had more than 150 places of worship at their disposal, of which a dozen have survived, the finest grouping of Romanesque architecture in Germany.

Postwar Renewal

In the 19th century, industrialization set in, but Cologne, unlike the cities of the Ruhr, was never

Eau de Cologne

Europe's royalty sweet-
ened their reigns with it,
and Napoleon was said
to take a liberal sprinkle
every morning. Launched
in 1709 by Italian perfumer
Giovanni Maria Farina,
who lived in Cologne, eau
de Cologne mixes oils
drawn from lemon, orange,
lime, cedar, grapefruit,
and a scattering of herbs.
Its success prompted so
many imitators that its
name has since become a
generic term for a liquid
fragrance—cologne.

overwhelmed by industry, not least
because of the efforts of its early
20th-century lord mayor, Konrad
Adenauer. He guided Cologne's
fortunes in difficult times before
becoming first chancellor of the
postwar Federal Republic. The city
suffered terrible bomb damage
during World War II; contemporary photographs show the battered cathedral rising over a scene
of almost complete destruction.
Postwar reconstruction respected
the original street layout, and
although most buildings are new,
the city has managed to keep
much of its ancient feel.

Many visitors arrive at
Cologne's **Hauptbahnhof,** one of
the country's busiest rail stations,
sited right at the foot of the
cathedral. More than 1,200 trains
a day pass beneath the station's
arching roof and rumble over the
Hohenzollern Bridge spanning
the Rhine. The teeming life of

the city begins right here, visitors
and citizens mingling on the great
expanse of paving surrounding
the cathedral. Streets first traced in
Roman or medieval times head off
in various directions; a fragment
of Roman gateway rises from
the paving, and beneath it, in the
underground parking lot, is the
massive masonry of the Romans'
defensive wall. The line of the wall
can be traced westward along
Komödienstrasse and Zeughausstrasse. On the way it passes
the **Kölnisches Stadtmuseum**
(Municipal Museum), with its
historical memorabilia as well as a
superb model giving an overview
of the city in medieval times.

From the cathedral area, the
main flow of people is southward
along **Hohe Strasse,** Cologne's
main shopping street. To the east,
toward the Rhine, is the Altstadt,

INSIDER TIP:

**The hippest cafés, res-
taurants, and nightlife
are in the Belgisches
Viertel (Belgian Quar-
ter). Start at Rudolf-
platz and head west
down Aachener Strasse.**

—JEREMY GRAY
National Geographic author

a warren of streets, squares, and
passageways with more pubs and
restaurants than can be easily
counted. Here too are the distinctive towers of the Gothic **Rathaus**
(City Hall; see pp. 154–155) and
of the Romanesque church of

**Kölnisches
Stadtmuseum**

- Map p. 150
- Zeughausstrasse 1–3
- 0221 22 12 57 89
- Closed Mon.
- $$

museenkoeln.de

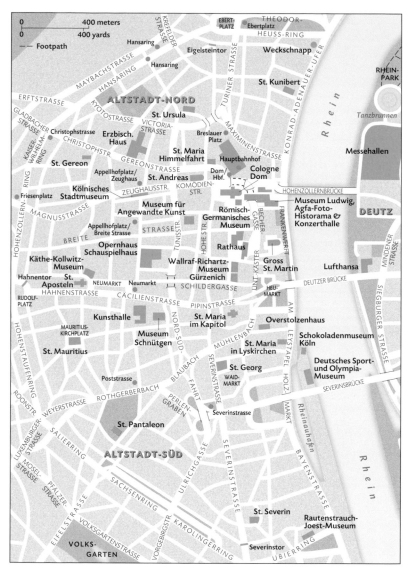

Gross St. Martin, once part of a monastery. For more exclusive wares, turn right onto Breite Strasse or follow popular Schildergasse to the **Neumarkt** and the streets around it, where boutiques, art galleries, and antique shops abound.

Cologne Dom

Its twin towers visible from far away over the Rhine plain and its lacelike stonework looming over travelers emerging from the Hauptbahnhof (main railroad station), Cologne's Gothic Dom (Cathedral) dominates the city skyline. Near at hand, the huge edifice seems like a work of nature, a vast and intricately textured cliff rearing 515 feet (157 m) over the heads of the awestruck spectators standing on the square before it.

Inspired by the cathedrals of northern France, on completion it was the tallest building in the world. But this dominance was achieved only relatively recently. Although building began in the mid-13th century, funds for the massive structure eventually ran out. By the 16th century, work on the nave had hardly begun,

INSIDER TIP:

Cologne Cathedral used to be the tallest building in the world! Check inside for the organ set into the wall way above your head. It's not too crowded if you go during the week.

—REBECCA DUPONT
National Geographic internal account representative

and the south tower had been completed only to the second level. Nineteenth-century enthusiasm for the Middle Ages inspired a new start. Work began again in 1842, and in 1880, when the finished cathedral could be seen as a symbol of a newly united Germany, a triumphant reopening took place in the presence of Kaiser Wilhelm II.

Medieval builders began Cologne's cathedral, but it wasn't completed until 1880.

After gazing at the stupendous west front, it's a good idea to savor the exterior slowly. Walk around to the right, past the south facade, regarded as one of the finest achievements of the 19th-century revival of Gothic architecture, and look down into the masons' yard; restoration work continues without pause. Facing the Rhine, the flying buttresses, soaring turrets, and pinnacles of the apse, completed about 1300, are as spectacular as the west front. On the north side of the building is the entrance to the **Schatzkammer** (Treasury). Housed in its vaults deep underground are precious liturgical items. However, the finest of the cathedral's treasures are on display in the main interior.

Cologne Dom
- Map p. 150
- Am Dom
- 0221 17 94 02 00, 0221 17 94 05 55 (treasury)
- $ (tower), $$ (treasury)

koelner-dom.de

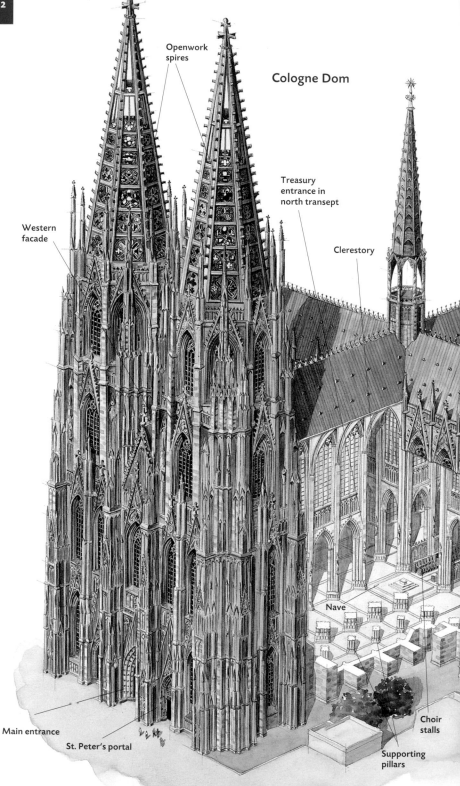

Openwork
spires

Cologne Dom

Treasury
entrance in
north transept

Clerestory

Western
facade

Nave

Main entrance

St. Peter's portal

Choir
stalls

Supporting
pillars

Once inside, allow yourself a moment again to take in the breathtaking scale of the building. From entrance to choir it stretches an astonishing 472 feet (144 m), while the vaults hang 142 feet (43 m) above the floor. Once you have recovered your equilibrium, set off to the left. The bold colors and strong designs of the windows in the north aisle are the work of master craftsmen of the early 16th century.

In the side chapel just beyond the north transept is a very different masterpiece, from an earlier, more somber age. Carved in oak toward the end of the tenth century, the **Cross of Gero** (Gerokreuz) shows the crucified Christ at the moment of death. It is the largest and oldest medieval sculpture north of the Alps.

Continue around the ambulatory with its radiating chapels; this was the very first part of the cathedral to be completed, in use as early as 1265. Much of its stained glass is of medieval date, but all eyes here are drawn toward the cathedral's greatest single treasure and the real reason for its existence: The **Dreikönigenschrein** (Shrine of the Three Magi) behind the high altar was more than 30 years in the making. It was commissioned in the 13th century to house the relics of the Three Wise Men presented to Cologne's archbishop by Emperor Frederick Barbarossa. The number of pilgrims drawn to the city by these relics in their gloriously ornate reliquary was so great that the decision was made to replace the Romanesque cathedral by a larger Gothic one. The Three Wise Men appear again in the exquisitely painted altarpiece in the last chapel of the ambulatory. The work of Stefan Lochner (ca 1400–1451), Cologne's greatest medieval artist, the **Dombild** (Cathedral Altarpiece) shows the infant Christ on his mother's knee as well as the city's patron saints, St. Ursula (to the left) and St. Gereon (right).

(continued on p. 156)

Radiating chapels

Flying buttresses supporting the south transept

Bronze doors by Mataré in south entrance

Walk: The Fountains of Cologne

Cologne abounds with fountains: ornate fountains, fountains with sparkling water jets, fairy-tale fountains, fountains carved with symbolism. Meandering from one fountain (*Brunnen*) to another, this stroll takes you through the city's oldest streets and squares.

Brunnen Fischmarkt is just one of the daedal fountains found throughout Cologne's Old Town.

The walk begins in the Domplatz, in the shadow of the great cathedral, at the delicate spiral of the **Taubenbrunnen ❶**. The Pigeon Fountain's designer, sculptor Ewald Mataré, was much involved in the postwar rebuilding and beautification of the city.

Walk diagonally across the square toward the low-slung slab of the **Römisch-Germanisches Museum** (Roman-Germanic Museum; see p. 157) on Roncalliplatz. Marking the boundary between the two squares is the 1970s concrete **Domfontäne ❷** (Cathedral Fountain). Even if you don't have time to visit the museum, peek down through the glass wall at its spectacular **Dionysus Mosaic.**

At the far southwestern end of Roncalliplatz, on Am Hof, is the charming **Heinzelmännchen-Brunnen ❸**, a fountain depicting the fairy tale of the Heinzelmännchen. Every German child knows the verses telling how the Heinzelmännchen, Puck-like beings, came out at night to

NOT TO BE MISSED:

Dionysus Mosaic • Rathaus (City Hall) • "Kallendresser" • The figures of Tünnes and Schäl

finish work left incomplete by the lazy citizens of Cologne—until they were surprised by the tailor's wife and fled, never to return.

Carry on southward along Unter Goldschmied; after the next crossing, turn left across the paved area in front of the modern part of the Rathaus. The concrete **Rathausbrunnen ❹**, the City Hall Fountain, on the left, symbolizes the rebuilding of the city after wartime destruction. Pass beneath the building into Rathausplatz. With its tall, late medieval tower and Renaissance loggia, the **Rathaus** is emblematic of the Cologne citizens' determination not to bow and scrape to any prince or archbishop. Beneath it are remains of the Prätorium, the palace of the city's Roman governor. Until the expulsion of the Jews in the 15th century, Rathausplatz was the center of Jewish life; the outline of the synagogue is traced in the paving. The 12th-century ritual bath, the **Mikwe,** is covered by a glass pyramid.

Just off the southwestern corner of the square, in front of the brick-built Haus Neuerburg, is the copper basin of the 1913 **Fastnachtsbrunnen ⑤,** the Karneval Fountain.

Go back across the square and down the steps into the Alter Markt. In the center is **Jan von Werth-Brunnen ⑥,** a statue and fountain named for a 17th-century stable lad who rose to the rank of general. Look to roof level if you want to see the bare behind of Ewald Mataré's **"Kallendresser,"** expressing his opinion of the grandees assembled in City Hall opposite.

On the east side of the square, a narrow passageway leads left into a courtyard graced by the hilarious figures of the **Ostermann-Brunnen ⑦,** a parade of Karneval characters. Turn left out of the courtyard, cross the street, and enter the area to the west of the Gross St. Martin church. Here stand Mataré's figures of **Tünnes and Schäl,** the Laurel and Hardy of Cologne. Take a look at the **Tier-Brunnen ⑧,** the Animal Fountain, to the north, then go down the steps toward the Rhine and the **Fischmarkt ⑨,** with its own distinctive cloverleaf-shaped fountain.

To get back to your starting point, go north along the riverside promenade, past the **Paolozzi-Brunnen ⑩,** a water playground, and up the broad stairway toward the cathedral.

> ⓜ See also map p. 150
> ► Domplatz
> ⏱ 2 hours
> ⟷ Just over a mile (1.8 km)
> ► Domplatz

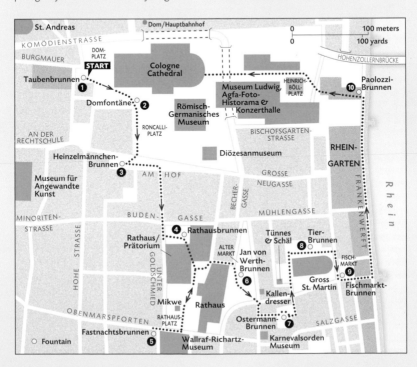

Wallraf-Richartz-Museum

🅼 Map p. 150

✉ Obenmars-
pforten

☎ 0221 22 12 11
19

🕐 Closed Mon.

💲 $$$

wallraf.museum

Käthe-Kollwitz Museum

🅼 Map p. 150

✉ Neumarkt
18–24

☎ 0221 227-2899/
-2602

🕐 Closed Mon.

💲 $$

www.kollwitz.de/en

If you leave the cathedral by the south entrance, notice the bronze doors. Local sculptor Ewald Mataré cast them to mark the cathedral's 700th year in 1948.

Museums of Cologne

If art is your thing, Cologne will keep you happy. There are collections of church art, the applied arts, and Asiatic art, and that's in addition to the internationally renowned Wallraf-Richartz-Museum and Museum Ludwig. There's even a museum, the **Käthe-Kollwitz Museum,** devoted entirely to the work of expressionist artist Käthe Kollwitz (1867–1945).

Wallraf-Richartz-Museum:

Classical European art is well represented here, with a range of

paintings by old masters, including Rubens, Rembrandt, and Claude Lorrain, as well as works by the French Impressionists and their German equivalents. For a brief visit you should perhaps concentrate on the museum's outstanding collection of German medieval art, particularly the works of Stefan Lochner (died 1451). This master of religious painting spent much of his life in Cologne, where he became an alderman of the city.

The medieval works on the first floor of the Wallraf-Richartz Museum's building in the heart of the Altstadt (Old Town) give a pretty comprehensive idea of life in the Middle Ages, with depictions of landscapes, urban scenes, interiors, and the fashions of the time. The German liking for the grim and the grotesque is given full rein, with plenty of torments, tortures, and beheadings. But with Lochner, an altogether more elevated plane is reached. Devils and monsters drag sinners to Hell in his magnificent "Last Judgment" (probably begun ca 1440), but a more typical work is his "Madonna in the Rose Garden" (ca 1440), an exquisite scene of repose and harmony.

Lochner is the undoubted star here, but don't miss the works by his successors, notably Albrecht Dürer and Lucas Cranach, or the fine collection of 19th-century German pictures, including many by the Cologne-born Wilhelm Leibl (1844–1900).

Museum Ludwig:

This gallery once shared its big redbrick building with the collections of the Wallraf-Richartz-Museum. It now

Lochner's vision of the "Madonna in the Rose Garden"

has its vast interiors to itself, ideal spaces in which to display the huge array of modern art, most of it assembled by collectors Peter and Irene Ludwig.

The museum is a good place to get acquainted with German art of the 20th century; the big names—Kirchner, Beckmann, Dix, Grosz, Kandinsky, Klee, and Beuys—are all here, as are other key European artists, including Picasso and representatives of the Russian avant-garde. But the Ludwigs' particular enthusiasm was apparently for American art, with abstracts by Rothko and de Kooning. The collection of pop art—Rauschenberg, Warhol, and Segal—is one of the largest and most comprehensive outside the United States.

In the same building is the **Agfa-Photo-Historama,** which presents a superb collection of historic photographs. Other exhibits bring to life the cultural history of the camera's art.

Römisch-Germanisches Museum: Located on the fault line separating the Roman and Germanic worlds of two millennia ago, Cologne is especially well placed to explore the encounter between these two very different cultures, and the Roman-Germanic Museum does so.

The museum's pride is the great **Dionysus Mosaic,** made up of more than a million pieces. Discovered during the construction of an air-raid bunker early in World War II, the mosaic has scenes of a drunken Dionysus attended

by dancing satyrs and maidens. The building-size tomb of the legionary soldier Poblicius stands nearby. The exquisite examples of Frankish jewelry and other items are reminders that the "barbarians" who eventually overcame the might of Rome were far from being without skills and fine taste.

Other Museums: The vast ethnographical collection of the **Rautenstrauch-Joest Museum** (Cäcilienstr. 29–33, tel 0221 221 313 01) includes a Maori funeral boat, ferocious ritual masks and an ornate rice silo from Indonesia.

INSIDER TIP:

Check out the ruins around the Roman-Germanic Museum; even if the museum is closed, you can take a look at the archaeological site.

—ANNE RANDERSON
National Geographic contributor

The modern complex adjoins a Roman basilica, now the **Museum Schnütgen** of medieval religious art and sculpture. The **Deutsches Sport & Olympia Museum** (Sport and Olympic Museum; *Im Zollhafen 1, tel 0221 336 090)* covers 3,000 years of athletic history, while nearby at the **Schokoladenmuseum,** a fountain flows with chocolate and exhibits trace the history of the cocoa bean. ∎

Museum Ludwig
- Map p. 150
- Heinrich-Böll-Platz
- 0221 22 12 61 65
- Closed Mon.
- $$$

museum-ludwig.de

Römisch-Germanisches Museum
- Map p. 150
- Roncalliplatz 4
- 0221 22 12 44 38
- Closed Mon.
- $$

museenkoeln.de

Karneval in the Rhineland

Every year as Lent approaches and the good Catholics of the Rhineland prepare for 40 days of abstemious living in the run-up to Easter, there occurs an outbreak of merrymaking rivaling that of Mardi Gras in more southern countries. All along the Rhine, Germans cast aside their serious, hardworking image and prepare for days—and nights—of unbridled (but often highly organized) fun.

The many faces of Karneval in Cologne: a clown among the crowds watching the big parade

Karneval (elsewhere in Germany called Fasching or Fastnacht) goes back to pagan rites designed to drive away the evil spirits of winter. The Christian Church was able to take over these old festivities and harness them to its own purposes, allowing the populace to indulge itself before getting down to the serious business of Lenten fasting. Each city and town has its own slant on Karneval, but there are many common elements.

Celebrations begin well in advance. All through the winter, there are dances and festivities and humorous entertainment, much of it based on folk legend. Each year produces its crop of new Karneval songs, which often become best-sellers. Costumes are elaborately stitched together, and people get together in pubs, neighborhood associations, offices, schools—in fact in every conceivable sort of grouping—to plan for the big days to come.

The real fun starts on the Thursday before Ash Wednesday. Known as *Weiberfastnacht,* the Women's Carnival is the ladies' chance to have their fling before the main events, which are traditionally dominated by men. Although it is a normal working day, festive costumes are worn and men are mercilessly teased and harassed. The action intensifies in the evening, with jollification in pubs and ballrooms.

Things quiet down on Friday as people nurse their hangovers, before engaging in more dances and entertainments on Saturday. In Cologne, the city that makes more of Karneval than anywhere else, there's a folksy preview on Saturday of the big day to follow, when schools, pubs, and neighborhood associations stage their parade through the streets.

Rose Monday

On Monday—*Rosenmontag* (Rose Monday)—the climax of Karneval is reached, with parades and pageants. The biggest of them all is the huge procession through Cologne's Altstadt (Old Town). A million spectators line the streets and squares to marvel at elaborate floats satirizing current events or prominent people in politics, sports, and the media. Marching bands provide a stirring accompaniment, while costumed

INSIDER TIP:

Fancy wearing a shirt and tie on Karneval Thursday? Watch out—tradition has it that women walk around with scissors that day to cut off men's ties!

—LINDA RICHTER
National Geographic contributor

revelers throw flowers, miniature bottles of eau de Cologne (the city's own perfume), and a total of 40 tons of candies to the spectators. Soldiers in 18th-century uniforms make fun of the military, and there's glamour in the form of long-legged *Tanzmariechen* (like 18th-century drum majorettes). Cologne's parade—indeed the whole of Karneval—is presided over by the triumvirate of Prince, referred to graciously as *Seine Tollität* (His Craziness), *Bauer Knut* (Peasant), and *Jungfrau* (Virgin). All three are men, the Virgin often flagrantly so.

Celebrations wind down on Tuesday, with smaller parades in city neighborhoods, and by Wednesday, after several sleepless nights, most people are ready to face the start of Lent, perhaps with a modest fish supper.

EXPERIENCE: Dressing up for Karneval

Dyed-in-the-wool *Kölner* (Cologne residents) take great pride in creating their own crazy get-ups and costumes for Karneval rather than buying off the rack. Enthusiasts are satisfied with nothing less than perfection. Clowns are by far the funning fools of choice, the favorite being the *Lappenclown,* a blaze of colorful scraps stitched together in a sewing-room frenzy. Evergreens such as pirates, cowboys, and lampooned politicians are sure to raise a hoot with the crowds, not to mention the many chickens, grouse, or related fowl who stomp flat-footed through the

Old Town after one too many swigs of German cheer.

For visitors carrying no more than a patch kit, Cologne teems with costume makers who tap into the city's sense of fun year-round. One excellent option is **Kostümtruhe** *(Mathiasstrasse 17, tel 0221 280 80 24, kostuemtruhe.de)* in the Old Town, a venerable dress-up shop offering a battery of rental garments at tiny prices (think $25–$65 for a three-day romp in full regalia). There you can rub shoulders with aspiring knights, goths, and poultry fetishists, or check out your alter ego online.

Aachen

In the ninth century, Germany's westernmost city rose to European prominence as the capital of the first Holy Roman Emperor, Charlemagne (Karl der Grosse in German). Few places are more redolent of the distant Germanic past than his great octagonal palace chapel (now part of Aachen's cathedral), which has miraculously survived in all its glory.

Arcades rise in tiers to the shimmering ceiling of Aachen cathedral's central octagon.

Aachen

⚑ 146 B2

Visitor Information

✉ Elisenbrunnen, Friedrich-Wilhelm-Platz

☎ 0241 1 80 29 60

aachen.de

Surrounded by later building, the ancient core of the city stands on a low hilltop, reached by charming cobbled streets and lanes. At the foot of the slope are the colonnades and rotunda of the early 19th-century **Elisenbrunnen** (Elisa Fountain), harnessing the thermal springs in which Charlemagne loved to splash and on which Aachen's reputation as a spa is founded. Fountains are a feature of the city; the **Geldbrunnen** (Money Fountain), with its satirical figures representing the circulation of money, stands in the top left-hand corner of the gardens above the Elisenbrunnen.

Rising over the Münsterplatz just beyond is the **Dom** (Cathedral), not the most harmonious of structures on the outside. Charlemagne's chapel is topped by an awkwardly elongated dome, and it appears crushed by the great Gothic choir to the east and dwarfed by the 19th-century tower to the west. A baroque chapel seems added as an afterthought. But within, all is glorious.

Charlemagne spared no effort or expense to construct a church that would proclaim his status as successor to the Roman emperors. A master architect, Odo of Metz, was employed, and Roman remains were plundered for bronze, stone, and marble. Even today, the space enclosed by the great octagon is breathtaking, its effect enhanced by the huge 12th-century circular chandelier. In the arcaded gallery stands the starkly simple throne on which more than 30 Holy Roman Emperors sat after the coronation ceremony.

Later German emperors promoted the cult of Charlemagne, and the pilgrims who swarmed here were so numerous that a Gothic chancel had to be added. Here are some of the cathedral's greatest treasures, notably the 13th-century **Karlsschrein** (Shrine of Charlemagne). The **Schatzkammer** (Treasury; *Klostergasse, closed Mon. p.m.*) also has a stunning assemblage of precious objects, without equal in northern Europe, including Charlemagne's jeweled reliquary bust.

Beyond the Cathedral

Aachen's other great building, the massive **Rathaus** (City Hall) overlooking the marketplace, incorporates stonework from Charlemagne's palace. The great emperor is difficult to escape; atop a fountain, his bronze presence even watches over your coffee break in the square. But the city has other facets to explore.

Much of medieval Aachen burned down at the end of the 17th century and was rebuilt in a sober baroque style, exemplified by the **Couven-Museum.** Its interiors evoke the comfortable life led by the merchant classes of the time. It has a shop where chocolate was first made in Aachen in 1857.

INSIDER TIP:

Of all of Aachen's fountains, be sure to visit the interactive Fountain of the Puppets and the classical Elisenbrunnen, the Aachen city emblem.

—CHRISTINA CROLLA
Aachen Tourism Board

A fortune made from chocolate enabled Peter Ludwig and his wife to establish the **Ludwig Forum für Internationale Kunst** (Ludwig Forum for International Art). Much of their huge modern art collection is in Cologne (see pp. 156–157), but there are plenty of stimulating, shocking, and entertaining works here, including pieces by German Joseph Beuys and Roy Lichtenstein's "I Know How You Must Feel, Brad!" (1963).

Aachen's nearby spa district has a lavish spa complex, **Carolus Thermen** (*Passstr. 79, tel 0241 182 74 0, carolus-thermen.de, $$*), with something of the character of decadent ancient Rome. ∎

Aachener Dom
- ✉ Münsterplatz
- ☎ 0241 47 70 91 27
- 🕐 No guided tours during services
- 💲 $$ (guided tour 2 p.m.)

aachendom.de

Rathaus
- ✉ Marktplatz
- ☎ 0241 432 73 10
- 🕐 Guided tour Sat. & Sun. 10:30 a.m.
- 💲 $$

Couven-Museum
- ✉ Hühnermarkt 17
- ☎ 0241 4 32 44 21
- 🕐 Closed Mon.
- 💲 $$

couven-museum.de

Fountain of the Puppets
- ✉ Kramerstrasse 20

Ludwig Forum für Internationale Kunst
- ✉ Jülicher Strasse 97–109
- ☎ 0241 180 71 04
- 🕐 Closed Mon.
- 💲 $$$

ludwigforum.de

Bonn

There is more to Bonn, Germany's one-time seat of government, than vacated ministries and a sense of loss. This pleasant old town is a busy city, yet on a human scale, with a cathedral, a university, several important museums, and an enviable location at the downstream end of the most romantic stretch of the Rhine.

The wooded heights of the Siebengebirge (Seven Mountains) dominate the broad Rhine.

Bonn

🗺 146 C2

Visitor Information

✉ Windeckstrasse 1 (near Münsterplatz)

☎ 0228 77 50 00

bonn.de

In the western part of the country, far from the Iron Curtain and conveniently close to the home of Konrad Adenauer, the postwar Federal Republic's first chancellor, Bonn seemed a good place to set up what all Germans hoped would be a temporary seat of government. But reunification was a long time coming, and over the decades the city fitted itself out with many of the trappings of a national capital.

Museums

The modern government quarter to the south of the old center boasts the "Museum-Mile," a series of institutions stretching along the U-Bahn line and Adenauer-Allee. The pride of the completely refurbished **Rheinisches Landesmuseum** (Rhineland Regional Museum; *Colmantstr. 14–16, tel 0228 207 00, www.landesmuseum-bonn.lvr.de, closed Mon., $$$*) is the 50,000-year-old skull of

Neanderthal Man, found near Düsseldorf. The **Kunstmuseum** (Art Museum) and the adjacent national **Ausstellungshalle** (Exhibition Hall) both have remarkably innovative architecture. The museum displays many fine works by 20th-century German artists, particularly August Macke, a resident of Bonn, while the Ausstellungshalle stages temporary exhibitions.

But the museum that cries out to be visited is the **Haus der Geschichte der Bundesrepublik Deutschland** (Museum of Contemporary History). This spacious building has a comprehensive display of well-chosen exhibits evoking the life and times of the two Germanys. Come here by U-Bahn; the museum begins in the station's underground concourse.

Bonn makes much of its most famous son, Ludwig van Beethoven (1770–1827), and you can pay your respects to him at the **Beethoven-Haus** *(Bonngasse 18–26, tel 0228 981 75 25, beethoven-haus-bonn.de, $$),* the lovely old town house that was his birthplace. It contains much fascinating Beethoven memorabilia, including his piano and some stringed instruments. The museum shop's good range of souvenirs includes reproductions of original scores and the great composer's death mask.

City Views

Before paying homage to Beethoven, wander around the city center and enjoy the fine buildings such as the baroque **Rathaus** (Town Hall), painted in gorgeous pastel colors, or the late Romanesque **Münster,** completed in the late 13th century just as the Gothic style was emerging. Walk through the city center to the riverside and take in the view of the Rhine and the enticing **Siebengebirge** (Seven Mountains) to the southeast.

The riverside promenade continues to the pleasant residential area of Bad Godesberg. There are even better views of the Seven Mountains from the hilltop ruins of the **Godesburg,** the first of many dramatically sited castles overlooking the Rhine. Actually well over seven hills in number, the wooded heights are the stumps of volcanoes that erupted 20 million years ago. Extraction of their excellent building stone began in Roman times. ∎

EXPERIENCE: Climbing the Drachenfels

One of the Rhineland's most vivid legends tells of a dragon that lurked on the flank of the Drachenfels, terrorizing virgins and sailors until dispatched by the hero Siegfried. A popular attraction, the "Dragon's Rock" makes a great excursion from Bonn. The U-Bahn runs conveniently to the foot of the hill in the riverside resort of Königswinter. From here, you can walk to the mountaintop—at 1,053 feet (321 m), it's not really very high—past the 19th-century neo-Gothic Schloss Drachenburg. Or, like most of the three million annual visitors, you can take the 1883 railroad (Drachenfelsbahn; *drachenfelsbahn-koenigswinter.de, $$$*).

Kunstmuseum

✉ Friedrich-Ebert-Allee 2

☎ 0228 77 62 60

🕐 Closed Mon.

💲 $$

kunstmuseum-bonn.de

Ausstellungshalle

✉ Friedrich-Ebert-Allee 4

☎ 0228 91 71 200

🕐 Closed Mon.

💲 $$

kah-bonn.de

Haus der Geschichte der Bundesrepublik Deutschland

✉ Willy-Brandt-Allee 14

☎ 0228 9 16 50

🕐 Closed Mon.

hdg.de

Düsseldorf

On the right bank of the Rhine, 18 miles (30 km) downstream from Cologne, is Düsseldorf, little more than half the size of its great rival, but nevertheless the capital of North Rhine-Westphalia. The city carries this status easily: For centuries it was the residence of the local dukes of Berg, whose glittering court attracted painters, musicians, and writers.

Glamorous arcades in Düsseldorf evoke a little Paris.

Industry plays an important role, too, although there are more head offices than manufacturing plants here. Much of what goes on in the Ruhr (see pp. 167–170) is administered from Düsseldorf, and much of the money made in Duisburg, Essen, and Dortmund seems to be spent in the fashionable shops lining the famous Königsallee. At the same time, Düsseldorf is very much an old Rhineland town, with a Karneval second only to Cologne's in scale and exuberance, and a raucous, pub-filled Altstadt (Old Town) proudly summed up as the "longest bar in the world."

Many visitors arrive here by Rhine cruiser, and a good spot to absorb something of the city's spirit is on the split-level riverside promenade. From here you can enjoy a breezy view of the broad river as it sweeps past the city in a great bend, crossed by a trio of elegant modern bridges. Beyond the state parliament building at the southern end of the embankment rises the **Rheinturm** (Rhine Tower), offering spectacular views from its observation platform and café some 565 feet (172 m) above the river. Nearby you'll find the old commercial harbor, which has been remolded by star architects like Frank Gehry into the **Mediahafen,** an entertainment quarter filled with beautiful people enjoying themselves in chic pubs and restaurants.

The **Schlossturm** (Castle Tower) overlooking the Burgplatz is all that is left of the old fortifications. It houses a moderately interesting little navigation museum. Just beyond it to the north is the strangely crooked spire of the **Lambertuskirche** *(Stiftsplatz),* a 14th-century church once the emblem of the city.

Inland from the riverside are the cobbled streets and alleyways of the Old Town, where entertainment is provided not only by bars, restaurants, nightclubs, and discotheques but also by cartwheeling urchins who traditionally receive a small coin per trick. Uncountable gallons of the local beer are consumed here daily; called *Altbier* or simply *Alt,* it is a very distinctive brew, in taste and hue more like British bitter than Germany's more usual light-colored lagers.

The Altstadt is not a place to come for peace and quiet at any time of the day, although it becomes progressively less busy the farther south you go. Its eastern boundary is marked by **Heinrich-Heine-Allee,** named after the German-Jewish writer born here in 1797 and best known for his haunting poem "Die Loreley" (see sidebar p. 182). The scene is dominated by large buildings, including the art nouveau Kaufhaus department store and the Wilhelm-Marx-Haus, a brick-built early skyscraper.

One block farther east is elegant **Königsallee,** known to all simply as the "Kö." Fine trees, a central canal, balustraded bridges, and a giant Triton fountain make a dignified setting for one of the most prestigious shopping experiences in all of Germany.

INSIDER TIP:

Champagne truffles, you say? Look no farther than Café Heinemann, a renowned confectioner at Bahnstrasse 16, for freshly made chocolates.

—JEREMY GRAY
National Geographic author

The Art Axis

Many of Düsseldorf's cultural attractions are organized into an "art axis" that runs north from the Altstadt. The **Kunstsammlung Nordrhein Westfalen** (North Rhine-Westphalia Art Collection), in an ultramodern building with a crisply curving facade, has a fine collection of 20th-century German and European art. Its centerpiece is a stunning body of work by Paul Klee (1879–1940), who taught at the city's art academy.

The art axis continues northward into the **Hofgarten,** the city center park first laid out in the 18th century to grace the ducal **Schloss Jägerhof** *(Jacobistr. 2, tel 0211 899 62 62, closed Mon., $$)* at its eastern end. The Schloss houses a museum of Goethe memorabilia, but looming over the trees is a structure more

Düsseldorf
 146 C3

Visitor Information
✉ Immermann-
   strasse 65b
   (opposite main
   train station)
☎ 0211 17 20 20

duesseldorf
-tourismus.de

Schlosturm
✉ Burgplatz 30
☎ 0211 899 41 95
🕐 Closed Mon.
💲 $

Kunstsammlung Nordrhein Westfalen
✉ Grabbeplatz 5
☎ 0211 83 81 204
🕐 Closed Mon.
💲 $$$

www.kunstsammlung
.de

Our European Cousins?

Mystery and intrigue have shrouded Neanderthals since German quarrymen discovered a partial Neanderthal skeleton in 1856 in a cave near Düsseldorf. The Neanderthals thrived in Europe and western Asia during the late Ice Age, dominating the landscape for 200,000 years. The last known evidence of Neanderthals, found in Spain, is dated from about 28,000 years ago.

Commonly viewed as brutish cavemen due to their protruding brow and strong, slouched physique, Neanderthals in fact may be more like our own early ancestors, with a capacity to speak, control fire, and develop stone weapons for hunting.

How did a race with all these competitive advantages die out? Recent evidence suggests a lack of ingenuity and weak social structures were to blame. The Neanderthalmuseum (Talstrasse 300, Mettmann, tel 02104 97 97 0, neanderthal .de, $$, closed Mon.) shows what they may have looked like.

Museum Kunst Palast

✉ Ehrenhof 4–5

☎ 0211 566 42 100

🗓 Closed Mon.

💲 $$$

smkp.de

emblematic of present-day Düsseldorf: the three slim slabs of the **Thyssen Building.**

The Hofgarten runs northwest toward the Rhine, where a concentration of cultural buildings includes the domed **Tonhalle,** a splendid example of expressionist brick architecture, conceived as a planetarium but converted into a concert hall. To the north is the **Museum Kunst Palast,** a combination of the old Kunstmuseum and the Kunstpalast that opened in 2001. When Napoleon's armies came this way in 1806, many of the city's art treasures were removed for safekeeping to Munich and never have been returned. But the museum still has plenty of medieval sculpture, old masters, and Romantic, Impressionist, and 20th-century German painting. And the collection of glass, particularly of art nouveau and art deco work, is outstanding.

Outside the City

With its fine shops and fashion shows, Düsseldorf likes to think of itself as a little Paris; it even has its own Versailles, 6 miles (10 km) outside town, in the shape of **Schloss Benrath** (Benrather Schlossallee 100–106, tel 0211 89 21 903, schloss -benrath.de, closed Mon., $$$). Built among the forests to the city's south between 1756 and 1771, Benrath is a perfect example of the late baroque fusion of architecture and landscape. No single structure dominates the scene; instead, the palace is split into a central section with detached wings and gatehouses. Space flows between the buildings, uniting lake, canal, and radiating avenues. It has been repainted in its original delicious pastel colors, and period furniture graces the interiors.

In the Düssel Valley lies the village of **Neandertal.** The area has been roughly treated by limestone extraction, but it was here in 1856 that the first skeleton was unearthed in a cave of that distant relative of Homo sapiens, Neanderthal Man. ∎

Ruhr Region

One of the world's foremost industrial regions, named for the river running along its southern edge, the Ruhrgebiet covers an area of some 1,800 square miles (5,000 sq km) and has a population of about 5.3 million. After the demise of its coal and steel industries, alternative employment has been found for many of those affected by the closure of pits and rolling mills, while much of the industrial heritage has been turned to advantage. Dereliction has metamorphosed into parkland, old railroad lines into bike paths, and mines, coking plants, and gasholders into visitor attractions.

For two centuries, the Ruhr was Germany's powerhouse, its days gray with a constant pall of smoke emitted by countless factories, its nights lit by the glare of blast furnaces. Deep underground lay the shafts and galleries producing the high-grade coal shipped to all parts of the country via river, canal, and railroad. But in the second half of the 20th century, decline set in; King Coal was dethroned and steel production slackened. Vigorous efforts were made to offset unemployment by promoting the service sector and attracting new industries.

From as early as the 1920s, careful control of new development protected farmland and forest. Even today much of the area is "green" along the valley of the winding River Ruhr and in the belts of countryside that penetrate throughout the conurbation, helping the individual towns and cities to maintain their own identities.

On the cultural side, the Ruhr has countless museums, as well as excellent galleries and institutions, for example, Bochum's famous Schauspielhaus.

A blast furnace at Duisburg epitomizes industry in the Ruhr.

Essen

Essen is the largest city in the Ruhr and the best place to get an overall feeling for the area's often paradoxical character. It is an old town, although the monuments of the distant past are firmly embedded in more recent developments. In 2010, the city (together with the entire Ruhr region) was designated the European Capital of Culture.

Try to see Essen's medieval **Münster** (Cathedral), which

Ruhr Region
🅐 146 C3–C4
Visitor Information
✉ Centroallee 261, Oberhausen
☎ 01806 18 16 20
ruhr-tourismus.de

Essen

🅼 146 C3

Visitor Information

✉ Am
Hauptbahnhof 2

☎ 0201 194 33

🕐 Closed Sun.

essen.de

Schatzkammer

✉ Burgplatz 2,
Essen

☎ 0201 220 42 06

🕐 Closed Mon.

💲 $$

Alte Synagoge

✉ Steeler Strasse
29, Essen

☎ 0201 884 52 18

🕐 Closed Mon.

alte-synagoge
.essen.de

Museum
Folkwang

✉ Kahrstrasse 16,
Essen

☎ 0201 884 5444

🕐 Closed Mon.

💲 $$

museum-folkwang
.de

houses a **Schatzkammer** (Treasury) containing magnificent objects of early medieval craftsmanship, including a Golden Madonna made in 980. A short distance to the east is the **Alte Synagoge,** built in 1913 by Essen's prosperous Jewish community. Although its interior was devastated on Kristallnacht in 1938, its massive walls resisted destruction, and today it houses a documentation center with displays on Jewish life and Essen during the Nazi period.

South of the city center, a single U-Bahn stop and a short walk bring you to one of the finest museums in the Ruhr. Housed in a series of striking cubes and designed by star British architect David Chipperfield, the **Museum Folkwang** has one of Germany's most important collections of 19th- and 20th-century art. There are gems scattered throughout, from the unbridled Romanticism of Caspar David Friedrich to masterpieces by Cézanne, van Gogh, Gauguin, and Matisse. These form a striking contrast to the surrealism of Salvador Dalí or the horrific images of Max Beckmann, evoked

by his experiences in World War I.

A ride south by the suburban S-Bahn reveals one of the surprises of the Ruhr—the juxtaposition of densely built-up areas with thick forests and working farmland. The branch line to Kettwig and Düsseldorf soon leaves the city streets behind to run through beautiful beech woodland. Then suddenly you see the gleam of water as the train emerges high above the **Baldeneysee,** a reservoir formed by damming the River Ruhr and a popular leisure spot. But the real reason for getting off the train here is to visit the great villa completed in 1873 by imperial Germany's foremost industrialist, Alfred Krupp (see sidebar below).

The **Villa Hügel** stands high above the valley of the Ruhr on what was a bare hillside until Krupp transformed it into parkland. He used the profits from his hugely successful works to build an enormous modern residence to accommodate not only his family but also visiting dignitaries from all parts of the world. Prominent guests included Kaiser Wilhelm II, who became a personal friend of the family. Before inspecting the villa with its vast halls and monumental

The "Cannon King"

A key figure in the history of the Ruhr region—a byword for Germany's industrial prowess—Alfred Krupp (1812–1887) was inventive, hardworking, and dedicated to the welfare of his workforce. He was also seemingly unaware of the wider impact of his success.

Krupp guns helped Prussia defeat France in 1871, and well after Alfred's

death, the monster howitzer nicknamed "Big Bertha" played a deadly role in the conflicts of World War I. Later the Krupp family helped Hitler to power, and their use of slave labor to produce weapons for his regime was one of the reasons for the imprisonment of Alfried Krupp, the last head of the firm, at the end of World War II.

staircase, pay a visit to the "Little House" alongside, where an exhibition emphasizes the achievements and public spirit of the family, through displays on their charitable activities, for example, rather than their role in producing the armaments that made killing possible on an industrial scale.

Other Ruhr Towns

The westernmost of the Ruhr's big cities is **Duisburg.** Its favorable trading location, at the point where the River Ruhr joins the Rhine, helped it to flourish at an early date, and today it is the world's largest inland port. The **Wilhelm-Lehmbruck-Museum** (Friedrich-Wilhelm-Strasse 40, tel 0203 283 2630, closed Mon.–Tues., $$$) is a museum of modern sculpture named for local artist Lehmbruck (1881–1919), one of the foremost German sculptors of the 20th century. His deeply spiritual figures inspired some of the work of Joseph Beuys (1921–1986), who is also represented here.

Bochum, in the heart of the Ruhr, was synonymous with coal, steel, and heavy engineering. Nowadays it is known more for its Opel automobile factory and its modern university. The story of coal is comprehensively told in the **Deutsches Bergbaumuseum** (German Mining Museum; Am Bergbaumuseum 28, tel 0234 5877 126, bergbau-museum.de, closed Mon., $$), the biggest of its kind in the world. The Mining Museum's buildings are dominated by a huge tower, which you can climb

for a vista of the city. Below the surface, a demonstration mine vividly re-creates life and work underground. Down by the river at Bochum-Dahlhausen, the **Eisenbahnmuseum** (Dr.-C-Otto-Strasse 191, tel 0234 49 25 16, eisenbahnmuseum-bochum.de, closed Mon. & Sat., $$$) has a collection of old steam locomotives, diesel railcars, coaches, wagons, and every kind of railroad memorabilia.

INSIDER TIP:

If you're in the Ruhr region in June, be sure to attend the ExtraSchicht festival (extraschicht.de), an imaginative all-night celebration of the region's industrial culture.

—STEFANIE DEHLER
National Geographic contributor

On the river's far bank to the south of Dortmund is the smaller city of **Hagen,** where the built-up area meets the wooded, hilly country of the Sauerland. The abundant water supply in the Sauerland was harnessed to power the very beginnings of the industrial revolution. These early stirrings of industrial activity are traced in the open-air **Westfälisches Freilichtmuseum** (Mäckingerbach, tel 02331 7 80 70, freilichtmuseum-hagen.de, closed Mon. & Nov.–March, $$). You can watch skilled smiths at work in water-driven mills or see the sails of the windmill turn. ■

Villa Hügel
✉ Hügel 15, Essen
☎ 0201 61 62 90
🕐 Closed Mon.
💲 $$ (park is free)
villahuegel.de

Duisburg
🄰 146 C3
Visitor Information
✉ Königstrasse 39
☎ 0203 285 440
duisburgnonstop.de

Bochum
🄰 146 C3
Visitor Information
✉ Huestrasse 9
☎ 0234 96 30 20
bochum-tourismus.de

Hagen
🄰 Map p. 146
Visitor Information
✉ Körnerstrasse 27
☎ 02331 809 99 80
hagen.de

EXPERIENCE: Explore the Ruhr's Postindustrial Side

The Ruhr region's unique asset is the "Route Industriekultur." This 250-mile (400 km) route threading through the region has its own distinctive signage, linking dozens of industrial heritage sites. Most are easily reached by public transportation or even along bike paths. You can descend into a coal mine, ride an old steam train, or even go diving in a former cooling tower.

Going north from Essen, the impressive pithead of the **Zeche Zollverein** (*Gelsenkirchener Strasse 181, tel 0201 24 68 10, zollverein.de*) is dominated by a giant headframe of this former colliery. When opened in 1932, the mine was the world's most advanced, its buildings fine examples of Bauhaus architecture. This multifaceted facility has changing design exhibitions, guided tours around the pithead, a steam railroad in summer, and links to foot- and bike paths. The **Ruhr Museum** (*tel 0201 884 52 00, ruhrmuseum.de, $$*) presents the region's history, geology, and archaeology in a former coal washhouse.

Imaginatively based at a former coal and steel plant, the **Landschaftspark Nord** (*tel 0203 429 19 19, landschaftspark.de*) is Duisburg's coolest postindustrial playground. You can climb to the top of the blast furnace, take a diving course in a former gas tank, free-climb the ore bunkers, or negotiate a hanging bridge over the metalworks. The lush green park is ideal for picnics.

Just outside Oberhausen, the **Gasometer** (*tel 0208 850 37 30, gasometer.de, closed Mon., $$$*) is a former gas-storage tower reborn as an exhibition space. Organizers have made the most of the silo's interior: One installation saw Swiss balloonist Bertrand Piccard inflate his 180-foot-tall (55 m) *Orbiter III* inside. Take the elevator up 384 feet (117 m) to the viewing platform for panoramas of the western Ruhr area.

North of Bochum's old center, the story of coal is told in the **Deutsches Bergbaumuseum** (see p. 169), the biggest of its kind in the world. The huge tower offers a vista of the city, and below the surface, a demonstration mine vividly re-creates life and work underground.

The impressive open-air **Westfälisches Freilichtmuseum** (see p. 169), near Hagen, tells the story of early industrial Germany. Among the many workshops and exhibits within the 60 historical buildings are demonstrations of the production of books, metal, and food.

A few miles northeast of Kalkar, a small town near the Dutch border, a decommissioned nuclear reactor has become **Wunderland Kalkar** (*tel 02824 91 00, wunderlandkalkar.eu, closed Nov.–March, $$$$$*). You can free-climb the cooling tower, or admire the Rhine from a Ferris wheel.

You can get beneath the surface at the Deutsches Bergbaumuseum.

Münster

Capital of the flat and watery Münsterland, this predominantly middle-class, 1,200-year-old cathedral city may seem a sober sort of place, but as the site of Germany's third largest university, it has its forward-looking aspect, too. The 13th-century Gothic cathedral sits well amid the burghers' elegant houses.

The numerous bicycles in Münster might make you think you have crossed into the neighboring Netherlands, an impression reinforced by the Dutch-looking high-gabled houses lining **Prinzipalmarkt,** the main street. It was in Münster's **Bürgerhalle** (Town Hall) that the Peace of Westphalia was signed on October 24, 1648. This treaty finally ended the Thirty Years War and gave independence to the Netherlands. The 12th-century woodcarving in the superb **Friedensaal** (Hall of Peace; *tel 0251 4 92 27 24*), named after the treaty, is a match for the delicate stonework of the Town Hall's soaring Gothic facade.

A short stroll northward brings you to the **Lambertikirche.** The three iron cages hanging from the church's 295-foot (90 m) tower are reminders of an earlier conflict. In the early part of the 16th century, Münster was a stronghold of the Anabaptists, a radical religious sect that took over the town. On their defeat, the sect's leaders were executed and their corpses displayed in the cages.

Münster is a staunchly Catholic city, and at its heart, a block from the Lambertikirche, stands its formidable **Cathedral** (Dom). Built in the 13th century, when the Romanesque style was giving way

High gables and arcades in Münster's Altstadt

to Gothic, the cathedral has a spacious nave and, in the ambulatory, an astronomical clock of 1540. The **Domkammer** (Cathedral Treasury) contains many marvels of medieval craftsmanship, as does the nearby **Westfälisches Landesmuseum** (Westphalian Regional Museum; *Domplatz 10, tel 0251 59 07 01, closed Mon., $*).

The River Aa wends through the city to the Aasee, a popular recreation area. Take a boat around the lake or stroll around the traditional buildings at the **Mühlenhof-Freilichtmuseum** (Open-Air Museum; *Theo-Breider-Weg I, tel 0251 981 200, muehlenhof-muenster .org, closed Sat. Nov.–Feb., $*). ■

Münster
- 🅰 146 D4

Visitor Information
- ✉ Klemensstrasse 10
- ☎ 0251 4 92 27 10
- **muenster.de**

Domkammer
- ✉ St. Paulus-Dom
- ☎ 0251 49 56 710
- 🕐 Closed Mon.
- 🆂 $
- **www.domkammer -muenster.de**

Moated Castles of the Münsterland

Instead of a conventional castle, the typical fortress in this flat land devoid of rocky crags is a *Wasserburg*, erected on an artificial mound or an island, with water as its main defense. The old province of Westphalia had more than 3,000 such moated castles; only a fraction survive, a hundred of them in the Münsterland.

Haus Rüschhaus
- 146 D4
- Am Rüschhaus 81, Münster
- 025 33 13 17
- Closed Mon. & Dec.–Feb.
- $$

Burg Hülshoff
- 146 D4
- Schonebeck 6, Havixbeck
- 025 34 10 52
- Closed Dec.–March
- $$
- burg-huelshoff.de

Burg Vischering
- 146 C4
- Berenbrock 1, Lüdinghausen
- 025 91 79 90 0
- Closed Mon.
- $
- burg-vischering.de

Schloss Nordkirchen
- 146 D4
- Nordkirchen
- 02596 93 30
- $
- www.schloss.nordkirchen.net

Haus Rüschhaus is on the outskirts of Münster. More like an elegant farmhouse than a castle, it was the playful creation in the mid-18th century of Johann Conrad Schlaun, who designed many of Münster's baroque buildings. Its main claim to fame is as the home of Annette von Droste-Hülshoff (1797–1848), Germany's greatest woman poet (see sidebar this page). Not far away, the brick-and-stone walls of her aristocratic family's ancestral home, **Burg Hülshoff,** rise sheer from the surrounding moat. Some of the interiors have been refurnished in early 19th-century style, and a small museum is devoted to the writer's memory.

About 18 miles (30 km) south of Münster at Lüdinghausen, one of the most formidable of the Wasserburgen is **Burg Vischering.** It has an outer fortress, the Vorburg, on one island, and the main residence, a Renaissance castle on medieval foundations, on another. A museum in the main building deals with the history of the Wasserburgen in general, and another, in the Vorburg, with rural life.

The Wasserburg reached the peak of its development in **Schloss Nordkirchen,** 5 miles (8 km) southeast of Lüdinghausen. Schlaun built this baroque palace in the early 18th century for Münster's ruler, Prince-Bishop Friedrich Christian von Plettenberg. The vast brick-built complex occupies a rectangular island with pepperpot towers at each corner. ■

Westphalia Poet

One of Germany's most celebrated poets, Annette von Droste-Hülshoff is perhaps most famous for her only novella, *Die Juden'buche (The Jew's Beech Tree,* 1842), which centers on two murders in rural Westphalia; featuring hints of the Gothic and the uncanny, it's also considered one of the world's first murder mysteries. Born into an aristocratic Catholic family in Westphalia, von Droste-Hülshoff lived a secluded and devout life, becoming a dominant force in German literature posthumously. Her most famous poems showcase her own internal struggle with her gender, religion, and morality.

More Places to Visit in Rhine-Westphalia

Bad Münstereifel

Still surrounded by its medieval walls and gateways, Bad Münstereifel is built along the crooked course of the River Erft, which trickles cheerfully along beside the main street, crossed by numerous flower-bedecked bridges. Cobbled streets lined with attractive old houses make leisurely exploration a sheer delight. Focal points in the townscape are created by the severe lines of the **parish church,** founded in the ninth century as the "Minster in the Eifel"; by the 12th-century **Romanische Haus,** now the local museum; and by the red-painted Gothic **Rathaus** (Town Hall) with its arcades. Among the surrounding wooded hills, at Effelsberg, is the unexpected sight of the huge white dish of the world's largest radio telescope. *bad-muenstereifel.de*

Falconry at Hellenthal in the green hills of the Eifel

▲ 146 C1 ✉ Kölner Strasse 13 ☎ 0225 3 54 22 44

The Eifel

The cool, airy uplands stretching eastward from the Belgian border to the Rhine and Moselle offer deep green woodlands and sweeping vistas rising to peaks formed by the action of ancient volcanoes. In the past, the Eifel was one of Germany's poorest and most isolated areas, and even today it is thinly populated. Visitors come here for quiet days away from the crowds, although the area is not lacking in honeypots such as wonderfully preserved old Monschau (see p. 174), the man-made lakeland of the Ruhr reservoirs, or the dramatic scenery of the Ahr Valley, famous for its red wines. *eifel.info* ▲ 146 B1–C1

Hermannsdenkmal

The gigantic Germanic figure of the Hermannsdenkmal (Hermann Monument) rises from a hilltop in the Teutoburger Wald. For nationalistic 19th-century Germany, Hermann was a great hero, the warrior who utterly crushed the Roman legions as they attempted to expand their empire east of the Rhine. It now seems that the Battle of the Teutoburger Wald in A.D. 9 took place elsewhere, but no matter—Hermann still looks fiercely westward, brandishing his 23-foot-long (7 m) sword of Krupp steel. From the plinth on which he stands, there is a fine panorama over the wooded countryside of the Lippe area. ▲ 147 E4

Lemgo

Spared wartime destruction, this old town has a wonderfully picturesque late medieval and Renaissance townscape. The historic houses you see around you are not museum pieces: People still live in them. Beauty went hand in hand with cruelty; one of the finest buildings is the **Hexenbürgermeisterhaus** *(Breite Strasse 19, tel 05261 21 32 76, hexenbuergermeisterhaus.de, closed Mon., $),* the 16th-century residence of a burgomaster who was particularly zealous in his pursuit of witches. Appropriately enough, it houses a museum

specializing in instruments of torture.
🄰 147 E4 ✉ Kramerstrasse 1 ☎ 05261 988 70

Maria Laach

Among the characteristic sights of the Eifel are the circular lakes set in the craters of extinct volcanoes. The largest of these, the Laacher See, makes a glorious setting (despite an intrusive autobahn) for one of the greatest Romanesque buildings of the Rhineland, the abbey church of Maria Laach. The austere six-towered structure is enhanced by the use of local volcanic stone in contrasting textures and colors. In the vestibule known as the Paradies, look for the intricate and often amusing carving, and at the high altar at the eastern end of the building, for the jewel-like Gothic baldachin. *maria-laach.de* 🄰 146 C1 & 177 B4 ☎ 0265 25 90

Monschau

With its timber-framed and slate-roofed buildings crowding together along the deeply incised valley of the River Ruhr, Monschau seems almost too perfect. Many of the houses were little factories, using the water to clean and dye the cloth on which the town prospered in the 18th century. Occupation by the French during the Napoleonic Wars left the town in a kind of time warp, and a stroll along the traffic-free main street, over bridges, and across little squares is pure pleasure, although you are unlikely to have the place to yourself. High above the town are two ruined castles, once needed to command views down the twisting valley. You can study the lifestyle of the richest clothier and his family in the lavishly furnished **Rotes Haus** (Red House; *Laufenstrasse 10, tel 0247 2 50 71, closed Mon. & Dec.–Easter, $*). It has a lovely spiral staircase and what looks like a picture gallery but is in fact cleverly painted wallpaper. *monschau.de* 🄰 146 B1 ✉ Stadtstrasse 16 ☎ 02472 804 80

Schloss Augustuburg

Archbishop Clemens August of Cologne, a generous patron of the arts and keen falconer, began in 1725 to build a summer residence and hunting lodge on the edge of the town of Brühl, roughly halfway between Bonn and Cologne. In its formal baroque park, the gorgeous palace demonstrates the wealth, power, and refined taste of its princely owner, a member of the Bavarian royal family. The Schloss has for many years been used as a glamorous setting for state receptions, and more than a hundred heads of state have climbed the magnificent stairway designed by the archbishop's fellow Bavarian Johann Fischer von Erlach. At the far end of the park stands the **Schloss Falkenlust** (Delight of Falconry), with charming rococo decor. It's said that it was in this secluded spot that Casanova seduced the wife of the Lord Mayor of Cologne. *schlossbruehl.de* 🄰 146 C2 ✉ Schlossstrasse 6, Brühl ☎ 0223 24 40 00 🕓 Closed Mon. & Dec.–Jan. 🟥 $$

Soest

This walled town about 37 miles (60 km) east of Dortmund shows what the Ruhr cities might have been like had the industrial revolution of the 19th century passed them by. People from the Ruhr come here on weekends to escape the pressures of urban living and to stroll the medieval streets with their timber-framed houses and buildings constructed from the attractive local greenish sandstone. Over the rooftops arise the towers and spires of churches, foremost among them the cathedral, the massive **Patroklidom.** Cathedral-like in size and beauty, the **Wiesenkirche** (Our Lady of the Meadows) has exceptionally fine stained glass, including some showing the essentials of a traditional Westphalian supper—ham, beer, and pumpernickel. *soest.de*
🄰 146 D3 ✉ Teichmühlengasse 3 ☎ 02921 66 35 00 50

A special draw for wine lovers—the romantic Rhine, the vine-clad Moselle Valley, and the classic route of the Deutsche Weinstrasse

Rhineland-Palatinate & the Saarland

The sign of a wine capital

Rhineland-Palatinate & the Saarland

Much of the Rhineland-Palatinate consists of uplands—the lonely Hunsrück, the Eifel with its remains of ancient volcanoes, and the Pfälzer Wald, one of the country's most extensive forests. But dividing the uplands are the welcoming valleys, created by the Rivers Ahr, Nahe, Moselle, and, above all, Rhine. In contrast, the Saarland is industrial, built on its huge coal deposits, but even here there are quiet forested corners.

Rhineland-Palatinate

In the southern part of the Rhineland-Palatinate, the Rhine flows smoothly past cities steeped in history: Speyer, Worms, and the *Land* capital, Mainz. Blessed by the sun, the area is warm enough to grow figs and tobacco, but it is the vine that gives the landscape its special character. Covering the plain that stretches along the left bank of the great river, the vast vineyards of the Pfalz (the old name for the Palatinate, still used in wine circles) and Rhein-Hessen produce a large proportion of all Germany's wine, best sampled in the cool cellars of the charming villages strung out along the German Wine Route (Deutsche Weinstrasse). West of Mainz, the Rhine turns north and enters its gorge, a very different sort of wine country, with vineyards climbing impossibly steep slopes to countless crag-top castles, once the aeries of robber barons preying on the river traffic far below.

As a political entity, Rhineland-Palatinate is a recent creation, formed from several old provinces by the French occupation authorities in 1946. Successive French kings, revolutionaries, and emperors have taken great interest in the territory west of the Rhine, and the area might well have been absorbed into France. The Romans liked it here, too, and the attractive city of Trier has the greatest concentration of Roman remains in Europe north of the Alps. This is also one of the heartlands of specifically German history. The rulers of Trier, Mainz, and the Palatinate were among the seven electors who chose the Holy Roman Emperor.

The Saarland

After Bremen, the Saarland is the smallest of the German *Länder,* or states. Its character has been largely determined by a heritage of heavy industry, which has furnished it with its most outstanding attraction, the great steelworks at Völklingen, the first industrial monument to feature on UNESCO's World Heritage List. ∎

NOT TO BE MISSED:

Area of map detail

Berlin ★

0   50 kilometers
0   25 miles

5▷

Wissen   Betzdorf

Altenkirchen

NORTH RHINE-WESTPHALIA   *p. 145*

Hachenburg

Wied

Remagen   Dierdorf   Rennerod

Ahrweiler   Linz   A3 E35   W e s t e r w a l d

Bad
Altenahr   Neuenahr   Montabaur

A61   Neuwied   Diez

4▷   Maria Laach   Koblenz   NATURPARK
NASSAU

Nürburg   Laacher
See   Kobern-Gondorf   Nassau   H E S S E   *p. 195*

DEUTSCH-
BELGISCHER
NATURPARK   Gerolstein   E   i   f   e   l   Schloss Stolzenfels
Vierseenblick ▲   Marksburg

Prüm   A48
E44   Thurant
Daun   Burg Eltz   Boppard

A60   Cochem   Burg Maus
Treis-   Burg   St. Goarshausen
Karden   Rheinfels   Burg Katz
R H I N E L A N D   St. Goar   Loreley
A1   Oberwesel   Kaub
Dasburg   Alf   Bacharach   Pfalz

3▷   Bitburg   Wittlich   Rhein   Mainz
Zell   Burg Sooneck
DEUTSCH-   Traben-   Burg Reichenstein   Ingelheim
LUXEMBURGISCHER   Trarbach   Burg Rheinstein   A60
NATURPARK   Bernkastel-   A61   Bingen   Selz
Schweich   Kues   Gemünden   Nierstein
Neumagen-   Bad
A1   Dhron   Morbach   Sobernheim   Bad
Kirn   Nahe   Kreuznach
Bad
Münster   Alzey

Trier   NATURPARK   P A L A T I N A T E
SAAR-HUNSRÜCK
Konz   Idar-   Meisenheim   A63   E31
Oberstein   Lauterecken   Worms
2▷   Saarburg   Zerf   Hermeskeil   Rockenhausen
Grünstadt
Nohfelden   Glan   A6
Wadern   A62   Altenglan   Ludwigshafen
Orscholz   Mettlach   Kusel   NATURPARK
Grosse   Merzig   Ramstein   PFÄLZER WALD   Bad Dürkheim
Saarschleife   S A A R L A N D   St. Wendel   E50   Deidesheim
Lebach   Kaiserslautern   P f ä l z e r
Dillingen   A1   A6   Neustadt an der   A61
Saarlouis   St. Ingbert   Homburg   A62   Weinstrasse   Speyer
Völklingen   Neunkirchen   Zweibrücken   W a l d   A65
A620   Saarbrücken   Germersheim
Blieskastel   Annweiler   Landau
1▷   Pirmasens   Rheinzabern
F   R   A   N   C   E   Bad Bergzabern   Kandel
Schweigen-
Rechtenbach   Lauter

BADEN-WÜRTTEMBERG   *p. 317*

BELGIUM

LUXEMBOURG   Mosel

Our   Prüm   Kyll   Mosel   Saar   Prims   Sauer

Winningen

△   △   △   △
A   B   C   D

Mainz

Mainz was the only possible choice of capital when the new state of Rhineland-Palatinate was created in 1946. It had been a great city in Roman times, and in the Middle Ages it was the seat of the prince-bishop of Mainz, one of seven electors who had the power to vote on who should be emperor. Johannes Gutenberg, who began a late medieval media revolution by developing printing with movable type, was born in Mainz around the end of the 14th century.

Print pioneer Johannes Gutenberg's press is re-created in the Gutenberg-Museum.

Mainz

🅰 177 D3

Visitor Information

✉ Brückenturm am Rathaus

☎ 06131 24 28 88

touristik-mainz.de

Dom- und Diözesanmuseum

✉ Domstrasse 3

☎ 06131 25 33 44

🕒 Closed Mon.

💲 $$

dommuseum -mainz.de

Mainz's grandest landmark is the **Dom** (Cathedral). City buildings crowd up against the great red sandstone edifice just as they did in medieval times, emphasizing its vast proportions. Six towers give it an unmistakable silhouette, and though it is essentially a Romanesque structure of the 12th century, construction of the cathedral was begun as early as the end of the tenth century.

The high opinion that prince-bishops held of themselves is expressed in the superb series of funerary monuments attached to the columns of the nave. But the cathedral's finest sculpture is in the **Dom- und Diözesanmuseum** (Cathedral & Diocese Museum) off the cloisters. Here fragments from a demolished 12th-century screen include scenes from the Last Judgment, while finest of all is the masterly head of a man, known as the **"Kopf mit Binde"** ("Head with Bandeau"), a medieval portrait of unique sensitivity.

Wander through the narrow streets and irregularly shaped squares around the cathedral to take in its magnificent outline from all angles. The **Markt,** with a charming Renaissance fountain at its center, fills with traders' stalls on Tuesdays, Fridays, and Saturdays. In Liebfrauenplatz, the stately

INSIDER TIP:

Note the calendar as you plan your trip— as in many German cities, nearly all of Mainz's museums are closed on Mondays.

—LARRY PORGES
National Geographic Travel Books editor

mansion called the Haus zum Römischen Kaiser is the home of the **Gutenberg-Museum.** Here you can see priceless copies of Johannes Gutenberg's 42-line Bible, as well as a reconstruction of his workshop, where there are live demonstrations of the workings of a 15th-century printing press.

A square named after the city's most famous son, Gutenbergplatz, is also home to a 19th-century statue of the printer. More public sculpture enlivens Schillerplatz at the end of Ludwigstrasse leading from the cathedral. The **Fastnacht-brunnen** (Carnival Fountain) pays riotous tribute to what Mainzers call the Fifth Season of the Year.

Make a detour southward from here to **St. Stephanskirche** (St. Stephen's Church), a restored

13th-century building. In the early 1980s, Russian-born artist Marc Chagall designed some stained-glass windows for the church. Their intense blue radiates an unearthly tranquillity.

Many of the city's Roman antiquities are in museums. They include finds in the **Römisch-Germanisches Museum** (Roman-Germanic Museum), river warships in the **Museum für Antike Schiffahrt** (Ancient Navigation Museum), and a column dedicated to Jupiter in the **Landesmuseum** (Regional Museum). ∎

Gutenberg & the Good Book

Because of disturbances in his hometown of Mainz, Gutenberg migrated to Strasbourg, where he worked in secret on a range of inventions. It was his creation of movable type that made possible the mass printing of books without any loss of the quality and beauty of the typical medieval manuscript.

Finance was always a problem: Gutenberg was continually forced to borrow considerable sums, and just as his famous Bible with 42 lines to the page was coming off the press in 1455, a creditor obtained possession of nearly all his equipment. Gutenberg was ruined. Old and nearly blind, he survived on charity until his death in 1468.

Gutenberg-Museum
⊠ Liebfrauenplatz 5
☎ 06131 12 26 40/ 44
🕐 Closed Mon.
💲 $$
gutenberg -museum.de

St. Stephanskirche
⊠ Weissgasse 12
☎ 06131 23 16 40

Römisch-Germanisches Museum
⊠ Ernst-Ludwig-Platz 2
☎ 06131 9 12 40
🕐 Closed Mon.
rgzm.de

Museum für Antike Schiffahrt
⊠ Neutorstrasse 2b
☎ 06131 28 66 30
🕐 Closed Mon.
rgzm.de

Landesmuseum
⊠ Grosse Bleiche 49–51
☎ 06131 28 57 0
🕐 Closed Mon.
💲 $$
landesmuseum -mainz.de

Rhine Gorge

The Rhine flows for 820 miles (1,320 km) through four countries, from the Alps to the North Sea. For more than 2,000 years it has been an important commercial and cultural highway. In the relatively short section between Bingen and Koblenz, the great river narrows and deepens, cutting its way through the rocks of the Rhineland massif in a winding defile whose steep, often precipitous slopes carry vineyards, woodlands, and precariously perched castles.

Strongholds such as Burg Katz (Cat Castle) stand guard at bends along the winding Rhine.

Bingen

🏛 177 C3

Visitor Information

✉ Rheinkai 21

☎ 06721 18 42 05

bingen.de

This is one of Europe's great tourist landscapes, and it has been so for more than 200 years, when it was a compulsory stop for English aristocrats on their Grand Tour southward to Italy. Poets including Byron sang its praises, and artists such as Turner attempted to catch its changing moods.

Busy roads and railroads now run along both banks, and the river itself sees a constant procession, not just of white pleasure cruisers but also of great trains of barges. You should take a trip aboard a boat, preferably heading slowly upstream so that you have time to absorb the constantly changing scene. But spend time too in some of the delightful wine towns and villages along the way, stroll among the vineyards, and climb up to a castle or two.

Bingen to Oberwesel

Fed by its great tributary the Main, the Rhine flows west past Mainz (see pp. 178–179) and Wiesbaden (see p. 208). The lovely vineyards of the Rheingau overlook the river, nearly half a mile wide (0.8 km) at this stretch. At the town of **Bingen,** where it is joined by another tributary, the Nahe, it turns north and plunges between the Taunus to the right and the 1,800-foot-high (550 m) Hunsrück uplands to the left. The hills are made of hard rocks, forming treacherous reefs in the riverbed. For centuries cargoes had to be unloaded from boats and taken around these rapids. In the 19th century explosives were used to blast out a relatively safe channel for navigation. However, what is known as the Binger Loch (Bingen Hole) still needs to be negotiated with care.

Bingen is famous as the home of the mystic St. Hildegard (1098–1179), one of the most remarkable women of the Middle Ages. A polymath, she wrote, preached, healed, and composed music with equal facility. The 900th anniversary of her birth was marked by the opening of the **Historisches Museum am Strom** (Historical Museum by the River), which documents her extraordinary life. The museum has a section on how 19th-century artists created an image of the Romantic Rhine that still persists.

A less sympathetic figure than Hildegard was Bishop Hatto of Mainz, who hoarded grain in the **Mäuseturm** (Mice Tower) standing in the stream. For this sin in a time of famine, he was, legend has it, gnawed to death by swarms of merciless mice.

The Mice Tower really was associated with the bishops of Mainz, who built it in the 13th century as a toll station. The river was a rich source of revenue for those who could control it in such a way. This explains the extraordinary number of castles along the Rhine.

Historisches Museum am Strom

- ✉ Museumstrasse 3, Bingen
- ☎ 06721 99 15 31
- 🕓 Closed Mon.
- 💲 $

landderhildegard.de

NOTE: Rhine Riverboats Several companies run boat trips on the Rhine, including **Bingen-Rüdesheimer** (Rheinkai 10, Bingen, tel 06721 308 08 10, bingen-ruedesheimer .com) and **Roessler-Line** (Lorcherstrasse 34, Assmannshausen, 06722 23 53, roesslerlinie.de).

EXPERIENCE: Celebrating the Days of Yore

Held every even-numbered year in the pretty Rhineland town of **Oberwesel,** the **Mittelalterliches Spectaculum** (spectaculum-oberwesel.de) is one of Germany's most authentic medieval festivals. A host of traditional craftsmen—cartwrights and coopers, distillers and dyers, weavers and wood-turners, among others—ply their near-forgotten arts in historical garb. Beer is quaffed from wooden barrels and "witches' bread" sold from market stalls. Popular events include duels by knights in hand-forged armor and spirited performances by Furunkulus, a well-known medieval band. The mood turns mysterious in the evening, when shadows dance on cobbled squares lit by hand-dipped candles. The locals are sticklers for realism, so later inventions such as electric lights, glass bottles, and paper napkins are strictly verboten.

The next festivals in Oberwesel are in May 2016 and 2018, but similar events take place every year across the country; see the schedule at spectaculum.de.

Burg Rheinstein

🅰 177 C3

✉ Trechtingshausen

☎ 06721 63 48

🕐 Closed Mon.–
Fri. mid-Nov.–
mid-March

💲 $$

burg-rheinstein.de

Burg Rheinfels

🅰 177 C3

✉ St. Goar

☎ 06741 77 53
(06741 3 83 in
winter)

🕐 Closed Mon.–
Fri. Nov.–March

💲 $$

st-goar.de

Immediately downstream from Bingen on the left bank are **Burg Rheinstein,** perched on a rocky spur; **Burg Reichenstein** (*Trechtingshausen, tel 06721 63 48*), a neo-medieval edifice; and the tiered **Burg Sooneck** (*Niederheimbach, tel 06743 60 64, closed Mon. & Dec.*). Another castle, Burg Stahleck, overlooks the vineyards around **Bacharach,** a delightful little town of slate roofs and cobbled streets and squares. Farther downstream, on the right bank, is Kaub with its fortress Burg Gutenfels, as well as the extraordinary **Pfalz,** a midstream toll castle breasting the river like a ship of stone. **Oberwesel** opposite is dominated by the towers of its fortifications.

flaxen-haired siren on the rock seducing sailors through the power of song may be a myth (see sidebar below), but this stretch of the river is indeed treacherous, only a third of its normal width, fast flowing, and 65 feet (20 m) deep.

Farther downstream, also on the right bank, is St. Goarshausen, with St. Goar across the river. A trio of castles compete with one another here. The greatest fortress along the Rhine, the ruined **Burg Rheinfels** above St. Goar, was originally built by the Counts of Katzenelnbogen about 1245. Strong enough to resist repeated French assaults until 1797, it epitomized patriotic German

Loreley: Legend & Reality

The implacable-looking cliff rising over the swirling waters downstream of Oberwesel was a source of legend long before Clemens von Brentano decided in 1802 to put into ballad form the story of a blond enchantress luring boatmen to their death. In the past, the rock was thought to be the abode of gnomes, guardians of the treasure of the Nibelungs. The Loreley was immortalized by Heinrich Heine in his ballad, published in 1827, beginning *"Ich weiss nicht was soll es bedeuten . . ."* ("I cannot divine what it meaneth . . ." in

Mark Twain's translation). The rock became too popular for its own good. The Nazis bulldozed the summit to make a *Thingplatz,* one of their open-air meeting places, and it became infested with kiosks and souvenir stands after the war. A kitschy statue of the Loreley stands at the foot of the cliff. Efforts have been made to tidy up the summit, which offers a superb view of the winding river in its gorge. You can walk there from St. Goarshausen, but most people get a view of it from a riverboat.

Loreley Rock to Boppard

Downstream of Oberwesel, the river is hemmed in ever more tightly between its rocky banks in order to squeeze past the legendary **Loreley rock,** a massive spur some 425 feet (130 m) above the water. The

sentiments about the "Watch on the Rhine" (Wacht am Rhein).

To challenge the Katzenelnbogens' monopoly of river tolls, the Archbishop of Trier built a castle downstream from St. Goarshausen. His rivals promptly built a bigger fortress, calling it Burg Katz and referring to the archbishop's edifice as **Burg Maus** *(open for special events only)*. More rivalries appear downstream in the adjacent castles of Liebenstein, now in ruins, and Sterrenberg, attributed to the "Warring Brothers," whose evil intentions toward each other were kept in check by a high wall built between their two castles.

Boppard to Koblenz

The valley opens out as the river approaches one of the stateliest bends along its entire course, making room for orchards and the huge vineyard called the Bopparder Hamm on the sunnier left bank. The Romans chose this inviting spot to build their fortified town of Bodobrica, the nucleus of today's Boppard, the most substantial and elegant of all the towns along this stretch of the Rhine. In the 19th century, a 2-mile-long (3 km) promenade was laid out, and wealthy pensioners were encouraged to build their retirement villas here.

Boppard is a pleasant place to break your river journey, with plenty of visitor facilities in a setting summing up all the attractions of the Rhineland— Roman walls, a castle, medieval gateways, venerable churches, fine old town mansions, timber-frame houses, and the ever changing spectacle of river traffic. You can walk up among the vines, or ride over them in a chairlift to the high point known as the **Vierseenblick** (Four Lakes View), from which the Rhine comes into sight as a series of separate lakes. A little railroad, one of the steepest and most cleverly engineered in the country, climbs up through glorious woodland to the high Hunsrück plateau in the west. Back in the town, there are plenty of taverns in which to try wine from the Bopparder Hamm.

INSIDER TIP:

Discover regional fare and mix with the locals in the small eateries in the old part of Boppard. Enjoy a glass of dry white wine made from grapes grown on the slopes just outside town.

—CONSTANCE ROELLIG
*National Geographic international
rights specialist*

Beyond the great bend in the river is **Braubach,** a smaller but equally pretty version of Boppard, and high above is the **Marksburg.** Inside the castle are displays of arms and armor and instruments of torture, while outside there is a medieval herb garden. Downstream, the restored **Burg Lahneck** guards the confluence of the Lahn with the Rhine, while on the far bank, within the Koblenz city limits, stands **Schloss Stolzenfels.** "Proud Rock" is yet another 19th-century restoration. A Prussian royal summer residence, its lavish furnishings and artworks were designed to re-create the spirit of the Middle Ages. ■

Boppard

🗺 177 C4

Visitor Information

✉ Altes Rathaus, Marktplatz

☎ 06742 38 88

🕐 Closed Sun.

boppard
-tourismus.de

Marksburg

🗺 177 C4

✉ Braubach

☎ 02627 2 06

💲 $$ (guided tours only)

marksburg.de

Schloss Stolzenfels

🗺 177 C4

☎ 0261 5 16 56

🕐 Closed Dec.

💲 $$ (tour)

schloss-stolzenfels
.de

Moselle Valley

The Moselle rises high up in the Vosges Mountains in France and has long been used as a northeastward route from France and Luxembourg into the Rhineland. The area is a vacation destination for Germans, and popular places can get very crowded at the height of the season. Stretches of the Moselle are best experienced from a riverboat, but there is also good walking among the vineyards and in the woodlands cladding the shadier slopes.

Vineyards line the hill leading to the Reichsburg in Cochem.

Koblenz

🅰 177 C4

Visitor Information

✉ Zentralplatz 1

☎ 0261 194 33

koblenz-touristik.de

Landesmuseum

✉ Ehrenbreitstein

☎ 0261 66 75 40 00

🕒 Closed Nov.– late March

💲 $$

diefestungehren breitstein.de

Some of the world's most enjoyable wines, such as Bern-kasteler Doctor and Piesporter Goldtröpfchen, are produced in the Moselle Valley. The best way to try them, and also experience Rhineland *Gemütlichkeit* (friendliness) at its jolliest, is to make your stay coincide with one of the many wine festivals held along the river. To explore the area, you can make various round-trips, combining river transport, roads, and railroads that follow the Moselle along its course.

Koblenz to Burg Eltz

The pleasant town of **Koblenz** has attractive promenades along both the Moselle and the Rhine, but its most striking feature is the great citadel of **Ehrenbreit-stein,** atop the 410-foot (125 m) cliff. Originally built by the arch-bishops of Trier, it now contains the **Landesmuseum** (Regional Museum), but the main reason for making the climb (or taking the chairlift, $$) has to be the breathtaking panorama.

Just upstream from Koblenz is the little wine town of

Winningen, followed by **Kobern-Gondorf** with two castles and **Thurant** with another.

Burg Eltz is one of the few old Rhineland castles still in its original state, including much of its furniture and fittings. Its sheer stone walls rise high above the trees on the north bank of the river. It was the long-term residence of several branches of the Eltz family. The 13th- to 16th-century interiors give you an intriguing picture of lordly life. On the slopes above stand the ruins of **Burg Trutzeltz.**

Cochem to Neumagen-Dhron

Cochem is one of the most popular destinations along the Moselle for day visitors. Here a conical, vine-clad hill rises from the river, crowned with a romantic castle, the **Reichsburg,** a mock-medieval stronghold erected in the 1870s.

At Cochem, the railroad, which so far has followed the river, takes a shortcut into a 2.5-mile (4 km) tunnel, the longest in Germany. This cuts out a whole series of bends and wine villages, but the same kind of scenery continues all the way to **Traben-Trarbach,** a double town straddling the river. Both halves are attractive, and Trarbach has an assortment of hundred-year-old art nouveau buildings, among them the imposing bridge gateway.

The mansions lining the Marktplatz on the Bernkastel side of **Bernkastel-Kues** are upstaged by the tiny **Spitzhäuschen** (Pointy House). Now a wine bar, it is one room thick and only just squeezes into its narrow site. Kues's more sober institution, the **Nikolaushospital** or **Cusanus-stift,** almshouses founded in 1458, still fulfill their intended function, with chapel, library, and dining hall. Next door, the **Mosel Wein Museum** has displays on regional wine culture, plus a Vinothek, where you can sample local varieties of wine and *Sekt,* the German sparkling wine. One of the best viewpoints over the river is from the ruined castle above the town, **Burg Landshut.**

Between Bernkastel and Trier, the wine town of **Neumagen-Dhron** is proud of the role it played in uncovering the valley's Roman past. Here, in 1884, workmen unearthed relief panels including the **Neumagen Wine Ship,** an

INSIDER TIP:

If you brave the steep climb to the Cochem castle [reichsburg -cochem.de], you'll be rewarded with a soaring falconry demonstration.

—MONICA EKMAN
National Geographic contributor

extraordinary depiction of a barge loaded with wine barrels. Originally grave markers, the panels seem to have been taken down and used to build a fort against the attacks of Germanic tribesmen. They are now in the Rheinisches Landesmuseum in Trier (see p. 188), but reproductions of the wine ship have been put up in the town. ■

Burg Eltz
- 177 C3
- ✉ Münstermaifeld
- ☎ 02672 95 05 00
- ⏲ Closed Nov.–March
- 💲 $$$

burg-eltz.de

Cochem
- 177 B3

Visitor Information
- ✉ Endertplatz 1
- ☎ 02671 6 00 40

ferienland-cochem.de

Reichsburg
- ☎ 02671 2 55
- 💲 $$

reichsburg-cochem.de

Bernkastel-Kues
- 177 B3

Visitor Information
- ✉ Gestade 6
- ☎ 06531 500190

bernkastel.de

Nikolaushospital/ Cusanusstift
- ✉ Cusanusstrasse 2
- ☎ 06531 22 60

Mosel Wein Museum
- ✉ Cusanusstrasse 2
- ☎ 06531 41 41
- 💲 $$ (tour)

moselweinmuseum.de

Neumagen-Dhron
- 177 B3

Visitor Information
- ✉ Römerstrasse 137
- ☎ 06507 65 55

EXPERIENCE: Cycling Through the Moselle Valley

As you'll quickly discover, the sumptuous curves and slopes of the Moselle Valley are absolutely perfect for exploring by bicycle. The region teems with tour options, ranging from a few hours to more than a week and affording memorable glimpses of castles, steep vineyards, and lush forests. It's incredibly accessible to any rank of cyclist and is conveniently served by bike-friendly B&Bs and hotels. Cycle tour operators abound, and there are motor services that move your gear to or from your destination.

For an afternoon of just 12.5 miles (20 km) of gentle pedaling, you might try the **Maare-Moselle Cycle Path.** This short diversion leads from the hamlet of Lieser, past the hillside sundial and Roman grape-press at Brauneberg, and concludes in popular Bernkastel-Kues, whose jumble of timber-frame houses and wine cellars make it a fixture on the oenological circuit. In fact, the surrounds are full of short, entertaining spurs for bikers, and it pays to explore lesser visited routes along the Moselle's tributaries such as the Saar and Ruwer Rivers.

A favorite four-day tour extends from Trier, the "Rome of the North," along a looping riverside path to Koblenz, some 132 miles (209 km) downstream. Soon you'll come to Schweich, where the slopes steepen and the slate-warmed earth becomes ideal for cultivating grapes. The path winds past sleepy Zeltingen, nestled on a broad hook in the river, and continues along its wider sweeps to the wine village of Trittenheim, home of some of the Middle Moselle's most sophisticated Rieslings. A bit farther on, you come to the old town and wine pubs of Bernkastel-Kues. From here

you pedal to Cochem, where you can cross the Rhine by ferry to visit Reichsburg castle, its tower mosaic of St. Christopher glinting in the sun from afar. Next up is the wine town of Karden, where vintners are happy to have you join in on the autumn grape harvest; contact the Moselle wine-growing association for details (Bernkasteler Ring; *Gestade 12–14, Bernkastel-Kues, tel 06531 97 25 22, bernkasteler-ring.de*). A few miles to the east, you come to the playful Gothic castle of Burg Eltz. Here, you follow the river's unhurried course through tiny grape-growing villages such as Kobern-Gondorf, with its own resident fortress. Before long you'll trundle into Koblenz, where the Moselle flows into the Rhine at the stolid German Corner.

For more details of guided cycle tours, planning tips, and local accommodations, check out tour operators such as **Mosellandtouristik** *(Kordelweg 1, Bernkastel-Kues, tel 06531 973 30, mosellandtouristik.de)* and **Velociped** *(Alte Kasseler Strasse 43, Marburg, tel 06421 88 68 90, velociped.de).*

Vineyards as far as the eye can see along the meandering Moselle at Trittenheim

Trier

Close to the border with Luxembourg, Trier looks back on the 2,000 years of continuous history that have left it with an exceptional architectural heritage. This, together with its fortunate location among the vineyards of the Moselle and a relaxed, mature atmosphere, make it the most appealing city in the Rhineland-Palatinate.

"Ante Romam Treveris stetit annis mille trecentis—Trier stood for 1,300 years before Rome," states the proud inscription in Latin on the Rotes Haus (Red House) in the marketplace. Trier is indeed one of the oldest towns in Germany, although not quite as old as the claim. It was about 16 B.C. that the Romans marched in, and over the next four centuries they made the place they called Augusta Treverorum into one of the finest cities north of the Alps.

In its Roman heyday, Trier had 80,000 inhabitants, a figure not reached again until recently. Emperor Constantine and his mother, St. Helena, made Trier a center of Christianity; much later the city was ruled by powerful prince-bishops. Trier's most famous son was Karl Marx (1818–1883), whose birthplace, now called the **Karl-Marx-Haus,** preserves his memory in documents, photographs, and first editions.

Trier's symbol is the colossal Roman gateway known as the **Porta Nigra,** guarding what was the northern entrance to the town. Built of massive blocks of blackened sandstone bound together by iron clamps, it is the best preserved structure of its kind anywhere in Europe. In the 11th century, a Greek hermit by the name

Relax over coffee in Trier's market square.

of Simeon lived in the eastern tower. After his death, the gateway was converted into a church, and a monastery, the Simeonstift, was built next door. The monastery's two-story galleried courtyard now houses a café, the visitor information center, and the **Stadtmuseum Simeonstift** (Municipal Museum). Here you can see a large model of Trier as it was in 1800.

From the Porta Nigra, the traffic-free Simeonstrasse runs southward more or less along the line of the Roman street to modern Trier's focal point, the **Hauptmarkt,** with cafés, market stalls, a market cross, and

Trier
- 🗺 177 B2

Visitor Information
- ✉ An der Porta Nigra
- ☎ 0651 97 80 80
- trier-info.de

Karl-Marx-Haus
- ✉ Brückenstrasse 10
- ☎ 0651 97 06 80
- 🕐 Closed Mon. a.m. Nov.–March
- 💲 $$
- fes.de/marx

Porta Nigra
- ✉ Porta-Nigra-Platz
- ☎ 0651 97 80 80
- 💲 $

Stadtmuseum Simeonstift

✉ Simeonstr. 60 (by the Porta Nigra)

☎ 0651 718 14 59

🕐 Closed Mon.

💲 $$

museum-trier.de

Kaiserthermen

✉ Weimarerallee 2

☎ 0651 97 80 80

💲 $

Rheinisches Landesmuseum

✉ Weimarerallee 1

☎ 0651 9 77 40

🕐 Closed Mon.

💲 $$

landesmuseum -trier.de

Amphitheater

✉ Olewigerstrasse

☎ 0651 73010

💲 $

amphitheater -trier.de

a Renaissance fountain. It's one of the most attractive squares in Germany, with a wonderful variety of buildings. The corner building with arcades and chisel roof is the much-restored **Steipe,** the 15th-century banqueting hall of the city notables; beside it is the Red House with its famous inscription.

From the marketplace, it's only a short step to the cathedral quarter. Pause for a few minutes in the

INSIDER TIP:

Dine at Trier's prime people-watching Ratskellar restaurant on the main square, which puts you between Marx's birthplace and some of Germany's oldest Roman ruins.

—MONICA EKMAN
National Geographic contributor

Domfreihof, the calm square in front of the **Dom** (Cathedral), and contemplate the austerely beautiful forms of the building, a marvel of early Romanesque architecture built on masonry dating from the time of Constantine. Only the taller, right-hand tower breaks the symmetry of the facade facing you. The story has it that the archbishop ordered that it be given its extra inches so that the tower of the recently built citizens' church of St. Gangolf would not overlook his cathedral. The great treasure of the Dom is the Seamless Robe worn by Christ on the Cross, one of several

relics purchased by St. Helena on a visit to Jerusalem and distributed by her around the important churches of Christendom. The robe is shown only on very special occasions, when it attracts up to two million pilgrims to the city.

A charming old street winds past the adjacent **Liebfrauen-kirche** (Church of Our Lady), a Gothic structure of great purity, one of the first to be built in Germany. Beyond is the **Konstantinbasilika,** a brick edifice of awe-inspiring size built as the emperor's throne room and now a Protestant church. It is the second largest roofed structure (after the Pantheon in Rome) remaining from Roman times.

Beyond the Cathedral

Less complete, but equally striking, are the **Kaiserthermen** (Imperial Baths) on the edge of the old city center. The site consists mainly of the foundations and basements of the Roman spa town, but the remaining walls are as imposing as the Porta Nigra.

More baths, covered by a stunning modern glass structure, can be seen in the Viehmarkt (Cattle Market), while close to the Kaiserthermen is the **Rheinisches Landesmuseum** (Regional Museum), whose great pride is the original Roman **Wine Ship** from nearby Neumagen-Dhron (see p. 185). A five-minute walk away is the **Amphitheater,** where 20,000 spectators once watched gladiatorial combats and other entertainments. It is now the venue for the city's summer drama festival. ∎

Saarbrücken & the Saarland

Industrial Saarbrücken is capital of Germany's second smallest *Land,* named after the River Saar, which rises in the Vosges Mountains in France then runs northwest to join the Moselle just above Trier. After World War I, the Saarland with its coalfields and heavy industries was ceded to France, although a 1935 plebiscite returned it to Germany. Much the same happened after 1945. The Saarland only formally became part of the Federal Republic of Germany in 1957, and there's a French flavor about the place.

The great hairpin bend formed by the Saar River near Mettlach

Together with a string of smaller rust-belt towns along the Saar, **Saarbrücken** has suffered from the demise of the coal and steel industries. However, it retains a lively regional focus; bistros abound, French words find their way into everyday speech, and there are innumerable cross-border contacts.

While the city center on the right bank of the river is largely modern, there is a fine heritage of building on the left bank from the time when the Prince of Nassau beautified his capital in baroque mode. On an elevated site above the river, the 18th-century **Schloss** was neglected for many years, but a 15-year restoration program has given it a role in city life as local government offices. Its central block is now a dramatic modern steel-and-glass structure by architect Gottfried Böhm. Adjacent to the Schloss and equally striking is the **Historisches Museum Saar** (Regional History Museum; *Schlossplatz 15, tel 0681 5 06 45 01, historisches-museum.org, closed Mon.,*

The Saarland

🗺 177 B1–B2

Visitor Information

✉ Franz-Josef-Röder Strasse 17, Saarbrücken

☎ 0681 92 72 00

tourismus.saarland.de

**Villeroy & Boch
Discovery Centre**

✉ Saaruferstrasse,
Alte Abtei,
Mettlach

☎ 06864 811 020

villeroyboch
-group.com

INSIDER TIP:

If you're into "creepy but fascinating," check out the UNESCO World Heritage site Völklingen Ironworks [see sidebar below], which operated for more than 100 years.

—MONICA EKMAN
National Geographic contributor

$$), also designed by Böhm, which relates the Saarland's convoluted recent history.

The jewel of the baroque city is the **Ludwigskirche** *(Ludwigsplatz, tel 0681 5 25 24, closed Mon.),* built between 1762 and 1775. The church is the focal point of a masterly piece of 18th-century urban design, an ensemble of mansions whose pale coloring contrasts with the rugged external stonework of the church. Enter the church to experience a further contrast, for inside, all is grace, light, and delicacy.

Elsewhere in the Saarland

For much of its course through the Saarland, the Saar is an industrial river, but the factories, old collieries, and waste dumps are seen against a backdrop of wooded hills.

Downstream from the town of Merzig, the river has a more rural character, winding through a deep valley clad at first in forest, then in vines. The late 18th-century abbey at **Mettlach** is the headquarters of the long-established ceramics firm of **Villeroy & Boch.** Its Discovery Centre stages an entertaining and instructive "Keravision" show about the firm's history and products. From here, cross the Saar and drive toward the spa town of Orscholz, following the signs to Cloef. After a 15-minute walk from the parking lot to a viewpoint high above the **Grosse Saarschleife** (Saar Bend), you can see the most spectacular natural sight in the Saarland: a dramatic hairpin bend described by the river around a densely wooded peninsula. ■

A Cathedral of Industry

The first industrial monument to be put on UNESCO's World Heritage List, the Völklinger Hütte *(Völklingen, 06898 9100 100, voelklinger-huette.org, $$$$)* is a century-old iron-and-steel works on the Saar River, 6 miles (10 km) downstream from Saarbrücken. Since it closed in 1986, it has been turned into a compelling tourist attraction. Its description as a cathedral of industry is well founded, with the awesome impact of the towering blast furnaces and the gas blower hall of more than cathedral-like proportions.

A powerful symbol of the industry that made the Saarland one of Europe's key manufacturing regions, it is a perfect example of all the processes that went into the manufacture of steel.

You can walk around the vast plant on your own, but it's much better to join a guided tour. The true scale of the installations becomes apparent only when you see the minuscule figures of your fellow visitors climbing ladders and negotiating catwalks among the monstrous coking plants and blast furnaces.

Worms

Visible from far across the Rhine plain, cathedral towers hint at this city's importance, particularly in connection with Martin Luther and the rise of Protestantism. But Worms is more than history. It is a wine town; among the vineyards to the north stands the Gothic Liebfrauenkirche (Church of Our Lady), after which a famous German blended wine, Liebfraumilch, is named.

Dom St. Peter in Worms exudes the fine points of German Romanesque architecture.

In the fifth century, the Germanic Burgundians established a short-lived kingdom at Worms before their annihilation at the hands of Attila the Hun. Their story provides some of the basis of the 12th-century epic *The Nibelungenlied (The Song of the Nibelungs)*, the inspiration for Wagner's *Ring* cycle.

Dominating the center of the Altstadt (Old Town) is the huge Romanesque **Dom St. Peter** (St. Peter's Cathedral). Here at the Imperial Assembly, or Diet, of 1521, Martin Luther was ordered to recant his heretical beliefs.

Inside, the elaborate west end was traditionally reserved for the emperor. An 18th-century altar by Balthsar Neumann enhances the east end. A five-minute walk north, the **Lutherdenkmal** (Luther Monument) shows the reformer with like-minded figures.

A Jewish community was established in Worms as early as the 11th century and became one of Germany's largest. Beyond the Altstadt, on the Lutherring, is the **Judenfriedhof Heiliger Sand,** the Jewish cemetery, thought to be Europe's oldest; some tombstones date back 900 years. ∎

Worms
- 177 D2

Visitor Information
- Neumarkt 14
- 06241 853 73 06

worms.de

Dom St. Peter
- Domplatz
- 06241 61 15
- Free (donation appreciated)

Drive: The German Wine Route

This route leads through rolling countryside at the foot of the Haardt, the eastern edge of the vast Pfälzer Wald (Palatinate Forest), giving ever changing views of the vineyards running down to the plain and passing through a succession of wine villages or small towns, each more inviting than the last.

Deidesheim's winsome Rathaus welcomes you to explore the equally charming town.

A monumental gateway marks the southern starting point of the Wine Route (Weinstrasse) at **Schweigen-Rechtenbach ❶**, on the border with Alsace. The Haardt escarpment offered fine sites for medieval castles, and there are several on the way, and also the occasional later Schloss built mainly for the wonderful views over the vineyards.

Just before reaching Eschbach, leave the Weinstrasse by turning left on Route 48 to Annweiler. The turrets and ramparts of Burg Madenburg soar on the hillside to the right. Follow signs to **Burg Trifels ❷** for superlative views over forest and plain. Trifels was an imperial castle and the prison of Richard the Lionheart of England, captured by Emperor Henry IV in 1193 on his way home from the Third Crusade.

NOT TO BE MISSED:

Burg Trifels • A walk through the vineyards to Schloss Villa Ludwigshöhe • A stroll around the old town center of Neustadt • A substantial meal in Deidesheim • Wine tasting anywhere along the route

Return to the Weinstrasse through Albersweiler and continue northward for about 6 miles (10 km). **Rhodt ❸** is a particularly enchanting village. Beautifully located above the village, where the vines give way to the forest, towers **Schloss Villa Ludwigshöhe,** a tasteful Italianate summer palace built by King Ludwig I of Bavaria in the early 19th century. A scenic side road leads from the pretty village of **St. Martin** to the **Kalmit** ❹, at 2,208 feet (673 m) the highest point in the Palatinate, with superb views all around.

Back on the Weinstrasse, as you approach Neustadt an der Weinstrasse you will see on the left the **Hambacher Schloss.** At this ancient stronghold, 30,000 patriots demonstrated for German unity and democracy in 1832 and for the first time raised the black-red-gold tricolor, since adopted as the national flag. **Neustadt** ❺ is a larger version of the wine villages on the route, with a well-preserved Altstadt (Old Town) and plenty of wine taverns.

Deidesheim ❻ is smaller, but its marketplace, lined with mansions, has a stately air; the Rathaus (Town Hall) has a splendid external staircase. It's also a center of gastronomy, with several outstanding restaurants, including ex-chancellor Helmut Kohl's favorite, Deidesheimer Hof. He used to invite visiting dignitaries here (although even his powers of persuasion failed to convince British Prime Minister Margaret Thatcher that she should eat the Palatinate specialty *saumagen*–sow's belly).

About 3.5 miles (6 km) beyond Deidesheim, **Bad Dürkheim** ❼ is the venue for the September Wurstmarkt und Weinfest, claimed to be the world's biggest wine festival. Bad Dürkheim is also a spa, with saline springs and a neoclassic *Kurhaus* set in the lovely *Kurpark*. The ruins of Kloster Limburg to the west of town are the spectacular setting for open-air performances in summer. Just east of the Weinstrasse, **Freinsheim** ❽ is a substantial place with a well-preserved town wall and gateways. The route ends at **Bockenheim,** with a counterpart to the gateway at the southern end of the route.

⚑ See also map p. 177
➤ Schweigen-Rechtenbach
🕐 53 miles (85 km)
↔ Allow at least a whole day
➤ Bockenheim

Speyer

Speyer, on the west bank of the Rhine, has one of Germany's great Romanesque cathedrals, the four towers and two domes visible from far away. The town was destroyed by the French in 1689, then slowly rebuilt. Today it is a cheerful place, happy with its location among the sun-soaked vineyards of the Palatinate. A famous center of good eating, Speyer claims to be the place where the pretzel, that essential accompaniment to a drink, was invented.

Speyer
🅜 177 D2
Visitor Information
✉ Maximilian-strasse 13
☎ 06232 14 23 92
speyer.de

The best way to approach the old town center is through its great medieval gateway, the 180-foot-high (55 m) **Altpörtel.** In front of you, the main street, Maximilianstrasse, leads to the cathedral. Usually known as the

Designed in classic Romanesque style, the Kaiserdom celebrates the apex of medieval architecture.

Kaiserdom *(Domplatz, tel 06232 10 21 18, crypt: $)* because of its imperial associations, the cathedral was begun in 1030. Now on UNESCO's World Heritage List, it is Germany's biggest Romanesque cathedral. The interior is equally imposing. In the great vaulted crypt are the tombs of kings and emperors, including the cathedral's founder, Kaiser Konrad II.

Konrad's burial crown and other precious objects are on show in the **Historisches Museum der Pfalz** (Historical Museum of the Palatinate; *Domplatz, tel 06232 1 32 50, museum.speyer.de, closed Mon., $$*), which also has a bottle of wine discovered in a third-century sarcophagus. The **Technik-Museum** (Technology Museum; *Am Technik Museum 1, tel 06232 6 70 80, speyer.technik-museum.de, $$$$*) is a light and airy industrial building expertly converted to house vintage locomotives, motor vehicles, flying machines, and even a submarine.

Like Worms, Speyer was an important center of Jewish life, and although little is left of the synagogue, the underground ritual bath, the **Mikwe**—the oldest in Germany—is perfectly preserved *(Judenbadgasse, tel 06232 29 19 71, closed Nov.–March, $).* ■

The heart of Germany, with woods, hilltop castles, and atmospheric old towns that inspired the tales of the Brothers Grimm

Hesse

"Germania" guards the Rheingau wine region.

Hesse

The *Land* of Hesse (Hessen) may be where the Brothers Grimm (see p. 203) lived and worked for the better part of their lives, but it is not all fairy tales. The large urban sprawl along the confluence of the Rhine and Main Rivers, centered on Frankfurt, has a severely practical outlook.

Everything's apples at Mr. Possmann's cider barrel.

Cosmopolitan and sophisticated, Frankfurt is Germany's financial capital and seat of the European Bank, with first-rate museums and all the attractions of a wealthy metropolis. It's a surprise to find that Frankfurters' favorite tipple is not some exotic cocktail but *Äppelwoi,* the apple wine traditionally produced from local orchards. Fruit trees grow in profusion in southwestern Hesse and make a springtime spectacle. The region's toehold in the wine-growing area along the Rhine is the Rheingau, whose south-facing slopes have some of the prettiest vineyards and most popular wine villages in the country.

Unified in the late Middle Ages, Hesse subsequently split into separate units, each with its own little capital ruled over, with luck, by enlightened rulers such as Grand Duke Ernst Ludwig, who made Darmstadt a center of European art nouveau, and Margrave Karl of Kassel, who created one of Europe's greatest landscape parks. The aristocratic imprint was also felt in Wiesbaden and in other spa towns such as Bad Homburg, while in Fulda it was prince-bishops who transformed this ancient center of German Christianity into a model baroque town.

Close to the border with Thuringia, Fulda stands in a funnel of relatively open country known as the Fulda Gap, through which the armor of the Warsaw Pact was expected to pour toward the Rhine should the Cold War ever have turned hot. They would soon have come up against American forces, concentrated in the Rhine–Main area ever since the end of World War II, when American military government carved out a new Hesse from the ruins of the Third Reich and decided the state capital would be Wiesbaden. ∎

NOT TO BE MISSED:

Basking in exhibitions on the Museum Mile **201–202**

Rediscovering the Brothers Grimm in Kassel **203**

The fancy flora at the Federal Garden Show **204–205**

Marburg's atmospheric old town **206**

Pedaling and paddling in the leafy Lahn Valley **207**

Taking the waters in Wiesbaden's soothing spas **208**

The lively artists' colony at Mathildenhöhe **209**

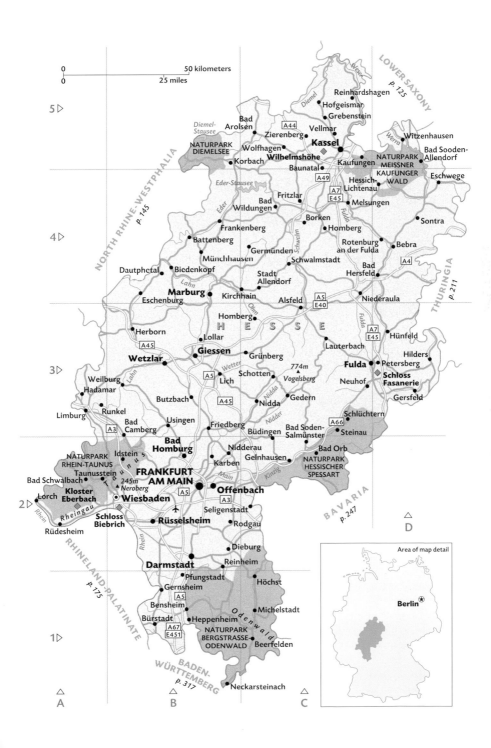

0 |————————————————| 50 kilometers
0 |————————————————| 25 miles

5▷

LOWER SAXONY *p. 125*

Reinhardshagen
Hofgeismar
Diemel-Stausee
Bad Arolsen
Grebenstein
Zierenberg
Vellmar
A44
Wolfhagen
Werra
Witzenhausen
NATURPARK DIEMELSEE
Kassel
Wilhelmshöhe
Bad Sooden-Allendorf
Korbach
Kaufungen
NATURPARK MEISSNER
Baunatal
KAUFUNGER WALD
Eschwege
A49
Hessich-Lichtenau
A7
Fritzlar
E45
Melsungen
Eder-Stausee
Bad Wildungen
Borken
Sontra
Frankenberg
Homberg
4▷
Battenberg
Rotenburg an der Fulda
Bebra
Germünden
Eder
A4
Münchhausen
Schwalmstadt
Bad Hersfeld
Dautphetal
Biedenkopf
Lahn
Stadt Allendorf
Marburg
Kirchhain
Alsfeld
Niederaula
Eschenburg
A5
E40
Schwalm
Homberg
Ohm
Fulda
Herborn
H E S S E
Lollar
Werra
A7
Hünfeld
E45
Wetzlar
A45
Giessen
Grünberg
Lauterbach
Hilders
3▷
Lahn
Wetter
Schotten
Fulda
Petersberg
Weilburg
A5
Lich
774m ▲
Vogelsberg
Schloss Fasanerie
Hadamar
Butzbach
A45
Nidda
Gedern
Neuhof
Gersfeld
Limburg
Runkel
Nidda
Nidder
Schlüchtern
A3
Bad Camberg
Usingen
Friedberg
Büdingen
A66
Steinau
Bad Soden-Salmünster
Bad Homburg
Nidderau
Bad Orb
NATURPARK RHEIN-TAUNUS
Idstein
Karben
Gelnhausen
NATURPARK HESSISCHER SPESSART
Taunusstein
Taunus
FRANKFURT AM MAIN
Bad Schwalbach
245m ▲ Neroberg
Main
Kinzig
2▷
Lorch
Kloster Eberbach
Offenbach
BAVARIA *p. 247*
Rheingau
◉ **Wiesbaden**
A5
A3
Rhein
Schloss Biebrich
✈ **Rüsselsheim**
Seligenstadt
△ D
Rüdesheim
Rhein
Rodgau
Dieburg
RHINELAND-PALATINATE *p. 175*
Darmstadt
Reinheim
Pfungstadt
Gernsheim
Höchst
A5
Bensheim
Odenwald
Bürstadt
Michelstadt
1▷
A67
Heppenheim
E451
NATURPARK BERGSTRASSE-ODENWALD
Beerfelden
BADEN-WÜRTTEMBERG *p. 317*
Neckarsteinach
△ C

△ A   △ B

Area of map detail

Berlin ★

Frankfurt am Main

The character of Frankfurt, Germany's fifth largest city, is hard to pin down. Its nickname "Mainhattan" seems particularly appropriate when you first glimpse its cluster of glittering office towers, while the epithet "Bankfurt" sums up its key role in Germany's (and continental Europe's) financial affairs. Frankfurt is the most multicultural city in Germany, yet it retains a strong sense of local patriotism, half-jokingly expressed by its addiction to apple wine.

Frankfurt's stylish skyline sparkles at night.

Some 400 financial institutions are established here, including the Börse (Stock Exchange), the Bundesbank (German Federal Bank), and the European Central Bank. But there's much more to Frankfurt than making and spending money. Its central location in western Germany, at the intersection of important routes, has long made it significant. In the Middle Ages, kings and emperors came here to be crowned, knowing that news of their glory would soon be spread around the country. Today's advertisers and publishers have built on this, and Frankfurt handles almost half of Germany's business in publishing and communications.

The city exudes modernity, especially if you come here on business, arrive at its international airport—Germany's biggest and busiest—and head straight for one of its skyscrapers such as the Messeturm, or the new innovative Commerzbank tower (see sidebar p. 202).

North of the River

Start your visit at the **Römerberg** to get the feel of old Frankfurt. This irregularly shaped square is the historical core of the city, where citizens gathered for special occasions. A coronation feast would be held in the **Römer,** Frankfurt's old city hall, a conglomerate of several houses unified by being given high Gothic gables. In its Kaisersaal are 19th-century portraits of several dozen emperors.

While World War II bombing left the Römer's facade standing, the tall timber-framed buildings on the opposite side of the square have been rebuilt from scratch, using traditional materials and methods. The southern part of the square is occupied by the red sandstone 13th-century **Nikolaikirche** (St. Nicholas's Church). From its roof platform the city fathers used to greet the crowds, and a trumpeter still salutes shoppers and stallholders from it during the big Christmas market on the square.

Explore the city's past further in the **Historisches Museum** (Historical Museum) just to the south. A model shows medieval Frankfurt in its prime, and another demonstrates the almost unbelievable extent of the devastation in 1945. The museum incorporates the city's oldest surviving building, a 12th-century

chapel that was part of the imperial palace. And there's an authentic apple wine tavern attached to the museum.

Off the Römerberg to the north is the 18th-century **Paulskirche** (St. Paul's Church). In the revolutionary year of 1848, delegates came here from Central Europe and hoped, in vain, that their deliberations would help to establish a democratic and united Germany. It's a symbol of great importance in the country's tortured progress toward unity and democracy. Public donations from all over Germany contributed

INSIDER TIP:

Peter Dünker's Weinkellerei, at Bergerstrasse 265 in the suburb of Nordend, serves delicious tipple on upended barrels in a musty, unpretentious cellar.

—JEREMY GRAY
National Geographic author

toward its postwar reconstruction in time for the centenary in 1948.

The Römerberg and the Church of St. Bartholomäus were controversially linked by the construction of the postmodern **Kunsthalle Schirn** (Schirn Art Gallery). This gallery houses changing exhibitions, mostly of contemporary art, along with the **Struwwelpeter-Museum,** with exhibits on a nightmarish children's story character ("Straw Peter" in English) and his

Frankfurt am Main
- 197 B2

Visitor Information
- Am Römerberg 27
- 069 21 23 88 00
- frankfurt-tourismus.de

Römer
- Map p. 201
- Römer, Römerberg
- 069 21 23 48 14
- $

Historisches Museum
- Map p. 201
- Saalgasse 19
- 069 21 23 55 99
- Closed Mon.
- $$
- historisches-museum.frankfurt.de

Kunsthalle Schirn
- Map p. 201
- Römerberg
- 069 2 99 88 20
- Closed Mon.
- $$
- schirn-kunsthalle.de

Struwwelpeter-Museum
- Map p. 201
- Schubertstrasse 20
- 069 74 79 69
- Closed Mon.
- $$
- struwwelpeter-museum.de

Dom

- **M** Map p. 201
- ✉ Domplatz
- ☎ 069 29 70 32 0
- 🕐 Museum closed Mon.
- 💲 $ (Dommuseum)

Goethe-Haus & Goethe-Museum

- **M** Map p. 201
- ✉ Grosser Hirschgraben 23–25
- ☎ 069 13 88 00
- 💲 $$

goethehaus
-frankfurt.de

Jüdisches Museum

- **M** Map p. 201
- ✉ Untermainkai 14–15
- ☎ 069 21 23 50 00
- 🕐 Closed Mon.
- 💲 $$

juedischesmuseum
.de

creator, 19th-century Frankfurt psychiatrist Heinrich Hoffman.

Strictly speaking, the red sandstone **Dom** (Cathedral) is "only" a parish church, the Church of St. Bartholomäus, but few parish churches have been the setting for imperial coronations. Ten emperors were crowned here, beginning with Maximilian II in 1562. Long before the coronation, the Holy Roman Empire's seven electors would meet in the church's Election Chapel (Wahlkapelle) to decide on who should be given the title of emperor. The cathedral was refurnished after a fire in 1867, but an altarpiece of 1434 survived, showing Mary on her deathbed attended by the 12 apostles. The cathedral's finest feature is its tower, completed in 1877 to the plans of a 15th-century architect, and until recently the city's tallest structure.

On an awkwardly constricted triangular site one block to the north stands another postmodern masterpiece, the **Museum für Moderne Kunst** (Modern Art Museum; *Domstrasse 10, tel 069 21 23 04 47, mmk-frankfurt.de, closed Mon., $$$*), designed by Austrian Hans Hollein. Nicknamed the

"slice of cake," it's an architectural tour de force, almost upstaging the collection of modern works by artists such as Andy Warhol and Josef Beuys.

Farther north is Frankfurt's main shopping street, the **Zeil.** Watching over the busy scene is the baroque **Hauptwache,** the city guardhouse and now a café. Still on the Zeil is **Les Facettes,** an ultramodern shopping complex worth a look.

Before returning to the river, you may want to visit the lovingly restored **Goethe-Haus,** the birthplace in 1749 of Germany's most revered writer. There are plenty of mementoes bringing to life the great man's early days before he left his native town; the **Goethe-Museum** sets his career in artistic and literary context.

Also on this side of the Main, close to the river, is the **Jüdisches Museum** (Jewish Museum), giving a fascinating account of Jewish life in Germany generally and of the Frankfurt Jewish community in particular, one of the largest in the country before 1939. Among its 30,000 members was the Frank family, whose years of hiding in Holland were so poignantly described in the diary kept by their daughter Anne. A

Frankfurt's Ill-Fated Parliament

For a short time, while the European revolutions of 1848 rippled across Germany, Frankfurt hosted the country's first freely elected national parliament. Held in the city's Paulskirche from May 1848 until May 1849, the assembly produced a draft constitution that wed the principles of monarchy with those of a parliamentary democracy. However, the liberal reformers were poorly organized and underfunded, and ultimately failed to gain military and political backing from Germany's state princes. When Prussian king Friedrich Wilhelm IV refused to become emperor, the shaky legislature collapsed. But its major ideas would later be absorbed into Germany's modern constitution, the Basic Law.

model of Judengasse (Jew Alley) shows the cramped conditions the community endured before emancipation in the early 19th century.

South of the River

On the River Main's far bank, seven major museums comprise "Museum Mile." The star is the **Städelsches Kunstinstitut** (Städel Art Institute), and not just for committed art lovers. This is one of Germany's great picture galleries, covering German painting from its beginnings to the 20th century. There are

also fine works by Dutch, Flemish, and Italian old masters, and French Impressionists.

Among the early German pictures on the top floor, look for "Paradise Garden" by an anonymous artist from the Rhineland, with a dragon no bigger or more dangerous-looking than a dachshund lying vanquished in the herb-rich grass. The other picture you should try to see is the most famous of all portraits of Goethe (on the second floor). Painted by Johann Heinrich Tischbein about 1787 and entitled "Goethe in

Städelsches Kunstinstitut

- 🅰 Map p. 201
- ✉ Schaumainkai 63
- ☎ 069 6 05 09 80
- 🕐 Closed Mon.
- 💲 $$$$

staedelmuseum.de

EXPERIENCE: Explore a Green Skyscraper

For a lofty view over Mainhattan visit the **Commerzbank Tower,** Frankfurt's tallest building, rising 850 feet (259 m) even without its striking illuminated mast. Designed by star architect Norman Foster, this eco-friendly skyscraper has a hollow core—a soaring atrium opening onto nine different levels to "sky" gardens planted with Asian, Mediterranean, or North American vegetation. The high point is the 49th-floor panorama deck with giddying vistas into the Taunus Mountains. You must reserve a free guided tour to visit; they're given on the last Saturday of each month. Email katrin.stempel@com merzbank.com with your preferred date.

Liebieghaus Skulpturen Sammlung

- 🅜 Map p. 201
- ✉ Schaumainkai 71
- ☎ 069 6 50 04 90
- ⊕ Closed Mon.
- 🅢 $$

liebieghaus.de

Museum Angewandte Kunst

- 🅜 Map p. 201
- ✉ Schaumainkai 17
- ☎ 069 21 23 40 37
- ⊕ Closed Mon.
- 🅢 $$

museumangewandte kunst.de

Weltkulturen Museum

- 🅜 Map p. 201
- ✉ Schaumainkai 29
- ☎ 069 212 315 10
- ⊕ Closed Mon.
- 🅢 $

mdw-frankfurt.de

the Roman Campagna," it shows him among ancient ruins in the Italian countryside, where he found much inspiration.

The **Liebieghaus Skulpturen Sammlung** (Liebieg Museum of Antique Sculpture) and the **Museum Angewandte Kunst** (Applied Arts Museum) are both broad in their coverage, the former featuring sculpture from ancient times to the 19th century, the latter a superb collection of European, Islamic, and Asian arts and crafts. The **Weltkulturen Museum** (Museum of World Cultures) puts on changing exhibitions relating to world folk cultures.

The **Deutsches Architekturmuseum** (German Architecture Museum; *Schaumainkai 43, tel 069 21 23 88 44, dam-online.de, closed Mon., $$*) is an imaginative amalgamation of a typical 19th-century villa with a modern structure of great purity. Its intriguing dioramas chart the history of world architecture. The **Museum für Post und Kommunikation** (*Schaumainkai 53, tel 069 6 06 00, closed Mon., $, mfk-frankfurt.de*) imaginatively covers telecommunication history. Finally, the **Deutsches Filmmuseum** (German Film Museum;

Schaumainkai 41, tel 069 9 61 22 02 20, deutschesfilmmuseum.de, closed Mon., $$) will enchant film buffs with its cinematic memorabilia.

Where the Museum Mile ends, old **Sachsenhausen** begins. If you are coming from the city center to this working-class suburb, the best approach is across the **Eiserner Steg,** an iron footbridge dating

INSIDER TIP:

Try an *Eiskaffee* (iced coffee) as a dessert. It's made with strong coffee, vanilla ice cream, loads of whipped cream, and sweet chocolate sprinkles.

—ANNE RANDERSON
National Geographic contributor

from 1869. The area is now quite trendy, although there are still cobbled alleyways, slate-roof and timber-framed houses, and, above all, dozens of *Äppelwoi* taverns. Sachsenhausen is still the place to come in the evening to sample the delicious local specialty. Whatever you do, don't ask for a beer! ∎

Kassel

Industrial Kassel is the state capital of northern Hessen. The rapid rebuilding of the old city center, which was almost completely destroyed in World War II, has not worn particularly well. But for many years it was the seat of the art-collecting *Landgraves* (local princes), who bequeathed the city its greatest asset, the Wilhelmshöhe park. Kassel is established on today's international art circuit with the *documenta*, a five-yearly aesthetic Olympics where the world's contemporary artists showcase their achievements.

The **Wilhelmshöhe** (William's Heights), west of the center, was created by Landgrave Karl. On top of the hillside terrace garden stands a huge copper statue of Hercules that has become the symbol of Kassel. Climb the steps for a great view over much of central Germany. On summer Sundays and Wednesdays, provided enough water is available, the cascade beneath the "castle" is activated: Water rushes in a torrent downhill, eventually feeding the Great Fountain of **Schloss Wilhelmshöhe** *(tel 0561 31 68 00, wilhelms hoehe.de, closed Mon., $$).* The neoclassic residence now houses the Landgraves' collection of old master paintings, notably works by Franz Hals, Rembrandt, Rubens, and Van Dyke.

In town, the **Brüder-Grimm-Museum** *(Palais Bellevue, Schöne Aussicht 2, tel 0561 787 20 33, grimms.de, closed Mon., $,)* is devoted to Jakob and Wilhelm Grimm, who, in the early 19th century, spent many years here as court librarians. They also produced grammars, language histories, and dictionaries. Because of them, characters such as Snow White and Little Red Riding Hood live on today.

Close by, the **Neue Galerie** *(Schöne Aussicht 1, tel 0561 31 68 04 00, closed Mon., $$)* is devoted to painting, sculpture and new media from the 19th century onward. Apart from canvases by cross-genre artist Lovis Corinth, there's an absorbing section on enfant terrible Joseph Beuys, who created a Volkswagen bus on skis for the museum's opening in 1976. ∎

Kassel

🅰 197 C5

Visitor Information

✉ Wilhelmsstrasse 23

☎ 0561 70 77 07

🕐 Closed Sun.

kassel.de

Vertiginous view over the Wilhelmshöhe cascade

Green Germany—
the Bundesgartenschau

German enthusiasm for everything connected with plants guarantees the success of the country's national garden festival, the Bundesgartenschau (BUGA)—literally, the Federal Garden Show—held every two years in a different location. During the months it is open (usually late April through September), the BUGA attracts millions of visitors, who come to marvel at the latest horticultural ideas and products.

Hamburg's 2013 show featured a monorail that carried visitors above 80 different gardens.

Germans are avid gardeners; even apartment-dwellers fill their rooms with plants, bedeck their balconies with flowers, and spend summer evenings and weekends tending their *Kleingärten*—garden "colonies" grouped around parks or on the edge of town. The greenness of much of the German urban scene is impressive; trees shade the streets, shrubs shelter pedestrians from traffic, and everywhere are well-planted parks.

Since its inception in 1951, the Bundesgartenschau has been used in a positive way to give the environment of the host city a significant boost. In the years following World War II, staging the show helped cities to repair the devastation that had affected parks and open spaces through bombing, cutting of trees for fuel, and clearing of flower beds and shrubbery to make way for vegetable plots. So the first postwar festivals (Hanover 1951, Hamburg 1953) were mostly about restoration. Trees were replanted, lawns resown, land reshaped, lakes cleared and refilled.

As the country prospered, emphasis was laid on adapting the urban environment to the changing conditions of modern life. There were

INSIDER TIP:

Although not nearly as polished as the Bundesgartenschau, there are many regional and state garden shows throughout the country. Check local tourist offices for information.

—LARRY PORGES
National Geographic Travel Books editor

Springtime crowds at the 2001 Potsdam garden festival

hills, woods, and lakes. Stuttgart has hosted the festival several times, using it to create a network of green, traffic-free spaces. Since reunification, the BUGA has migrated east, helping cities such as Magdeburg (1999) and Cottbus (1995) overcome environmental degradation. Lately the BUGA has embraced different cities and even entire regions in a single show (see sidebar).

traffic problems to be solved, new recreational needs to be satisfied, and a growing awareness of ecology. In 1955, Kassel used the festival to bring the run-down Karlsaue gardens by the River Fulda up to standard. By 1981, it was the city's turn again; the historic garden was further upgraded, but this time work concentrated on the far side of the river, a neglected area of gravel pits and water meadows. This was turned into a recreational lakeland, with lavish facilities for sailboats and windsurfers, as well as open areas with sunbathing lawns and children's playgrounds. Anglers were provided for, and areas were set aside for wildlife.

Recent Shows

Other cities have benefited from the show in different ways. Munich (1983) and Berlin (1985) laid out superb new parks in the suburbs. In 1979 the old capital of Bonn decided to give itself a new "green heart" joining the old center to outlying communities newly included within the city limits. Its 250-acre (100 ha) Rhine Meadows Park links both banks of the river in a new landscape of

EXPERIENCE:
Surfing the BUGA

To preview some of the world's most elaborate flowerscapes, visit the gorgeous websites of Germany's **Bundesgartenschau,** or Federal Garden Show *(bundesgartenschau.de, buga-2015-havelregion.de, iga-berlin-2017.de, and buga2019.de)* for upcoming shows. A click through the 2015 Havel Region website reveals blazing beds on display in five riverside towns—Brandenburg an der Havel, Premnitz, and Rathenow in the state of Brandenburg, and Rhinow and Havelberg in Saxony-Anhalt—linked by watery nature refuges teeming with wildlife. Visitors can travel between venues by boat.

Marburg

Marburg is one of Hesse's most atmospheric historic settlements, with steep streets and stepped alleyways linking the upper and lower parts of the town, a hilltop Schloss, a university, and a great Gothic church dedicated to the most poignant of German saints, St. Elisabeth.

The golden shrine of 13th-century St. Elisabeth rests in the church named after her, the Elisabethkirche.

Marburg

🅜 197 B4

Visitor Information

✉ Pilgrimstein 26 (Markt 8 on Sun.)

☎ 06421 9 91 20

marburg.de

Elisabethkirche

✉ Elisabethstrasse 3

☎ 06421 6 55 73

💲 $ (shrine)

elisabethkirche.de

Elisabeth (1207–1231) was a Hungarian princess, betrothed at age four to the ruler of Thuringia. Only 20 when her husband died, Elisabeth came to Marburg and devoted herself to helping the sick and needy. She died of exhaustion three years later and was canonized in 1235.

Around her tomb in the lower town, the Teutonic Knights built one of the first major Gothic buildings in Germany, the lovely **Elisabethkirche,** a treasure-house of artworks, most of which commemorate the saint. Her mausoleum has relief panels and a superb golden shrine made to contain her remains. Three centuries after Elisabeth's death, her descendant, Philip the Magnanimous (1504–1567), Landgrave of Hessen, determined to put an end to her cult, had the shrine opened and buried the bones elsewhere.

Around the church stand fine buildings erected by the Teutonic Knights. Today they house parts of the university founded by Philip the Magnanimous in 1527 as the first Protestant institution of its kind in Germany. Marburg is a lively place when the students are in residence, particularly around the **Marktplatz** in the upper town, reached by attractive but steep streets (or by elevator if you can't face the climb). The marketplace has all the right ingredients: a Gothic **Rathaus** (Town Hall), stately timber-framed houses, and a fountain featuring St. George and the dragon.

Walk west to **Marienkirche** (St. Mary's Church) with its Gothic charnel house and a terrace with a view over the old town. Enjoy more extensive views from the **Schloss** *(tel 06421 282 58 71, closed Mon., $$),* reached via steps beginning just beyond the church. Originally a ninth-century fortress, the castle was the residence of the rulers of Hessen between the 13th and 17th centuries. It has a splendid Knights' Hall and displays on the university and on Marburg's important role in the Reformation. ∎

Limburg & the Lahn Valley

Limburg, like Marburg, is one of a number of attractive towns along the Lahn Valley. Rising in the wooded uplands of the Rothaargebirge, the river winds its way below many a crag-top castle before meeting the Rhine near Koblenz.

Limburg sits at a point where the river could be easily forded or bridged. Its most prominent building is the great seven-tower **Dom** (Cathedral; Domstrasse, tel 06431 929 983, lim burgerdom.de, $ tower). You climb up to it through narrow streets and squares lined with restored timber-framed houses.

The cathedral was built in the first half of the 13th century just as masons were beginning to abandon the massive round-arched Romanesque style in favor of more elegant Gothic forms, and it combines elements of both styles. The building's massive presence is enhanced by the restoration of its original colors, the bright orange bringing out the bold lines of its construction and contrasting wonderfully with white walls and gray roofs. The sober interior has kept some original wall paintings, including a striking depiction of Samson. Outside, take a moment to enjoy the idyllic scene of river, wooded islands, and ancient bridge.

Farther upstream is **Runkel,** where the walls and towers of the ruined medieval castle rise majestically over the little town. Almost enclosed by a loop in the river, baroque **Weilburg** is dominated by its Renaissance Schloss (tel 06471 9 12 70, closed Mon.), complete with terraced garden.

From the river at **Wetzlar,** old slate-roofed houses step up the slope topped by the collegiate church known as the Dom. Wetzlar is famed for its Goethe associations—he fell in love with local girl Lotte Buff—and for its industries, notably the Leitz factory. Oskar Barnack invented the 35mm camera here. ∎

Limburg
- 🄰 197 A3

Visitor Information
- ✉ Hospitalstrasse 2
- ☎ 06431 228 81

limburg.de

Wetzlar
- 🄰 197 B3

Visitor Information
- ✉ Domplatz 8
- ☎ 06441 99 77 50

wetzlar.de

EXPERIENCE: Navigating the Lahn

The Lahn River flows through a pretty wooded valley that forms a natural border between the Taunus and Westerwald hills. The valley is popular with nature-lovers, who are drawn to this 85-mile (135 km) stretch of unspoiled beauty that is well removed from industry and urban areas. The course of the river is delightfully varied, taking in gentle rapids and a number of locks (some hand-operated) as it passes many cultural points of interest, such as Weilburg's Schloss and Limburg Cathedral. Tour companies catering to the area include **Velociped** (velociped.de), specializing in cycle tours for individuals, and **Lahntours** (lahntours.de), which has options for cycling, kayaking, and hiking, as well as a combination of all three over a week's journey. Both offer rentals and extra services such as the pickup and delivery of your baggage to your next destination.

Wiesbaden

This stately spa town just north of the Rhine was chosen as the capital of Hesse in 1946. In the late 19th and early 20th centuries, Wiesbaden was perhaps the most fashionable of German spas, when Kaiser Wilhelm II was a regular summer visitor, and some 200 millionaires lived in the sumptuous villa districts laid out between the old center and the Taunus foothills.

Wiesbaden's casino, part of the Kurhaus, retains its 1907 elegance.

Wiesbaden
 197 B2
Visitor Information
✉ Marktplatz 1
☎ 06151 1729 930
wiesbaden.de

Museum Wiesbaden
✉ Friedrich-Ebert-Allee 2
☎ 0611 3 35 22 50
🕐 Closed Mon.
💲 $$
museum-wiesbaden.de

The focal point is the porticoed and domed **Kurhaus** (Assembly Rooms), completed in 1907. To the north, a colonnade houses part of the casino, while the colonnade to the south forms the approach to the neo-baroque **Staatstheater.**

West of the Kurhaus, older buildings include the 19th-century Stadtschloss, former home of the dukes of Nassau and now the seat of the local parliament. To the north is the **Kochbrunnen,** where you can sample the hot salty water of the local springs. For the full experience, try the Roman-Irish steam bath in the luxuriously appointed art nouveau **Kaiser-Friedrich-Bad** (Langgasse 38–40, tel 0611 1 72 96 60, $ per hour).

Wiesbaden was popular with the elite of tsarist Russia, and it has an Orthodox church. The **Museum Wiesbaden** has a gallery full of paintings by Alexej Jawlensky (1864–1941), a Russian member of the Blaue Reiter group of artists (see p. 43).

Popular short trips out of town are to the Rhine-side summer castle of the Nassau rulers, **Schloss Biebrich,** and a ride up the local hill, the **Neroberg,** in the water powered funicular that has been doing the trip since 1888. ■

Darmstadt

A single air raid in 1944 saw the virtual destruction of Darmstadt, yet a visit here is well worth-while. The town has a particular distinction in the world of architecture and arts and crafts as one of the great centers of art nouveau.

Until 1918, Darmstadt was the seat of the grand dukes of Hessen-Darmstadt, a line of enlightened rulers who supported literature and the arts and instituted traditions that have lived on long after them. The last and greatest ruler was the energetic modernizer Ernst Ludwig, who ruled from 1892 to 1918. His initials (EL) are carved into many monuments.

In the town center's **Marktplatz** is the ducal **Schloss** *(Marktplatz 15, tel 06151 2 40 35, closed Mon.–Thurs., $$)*. Given a baroque appearance in the early 18th century, it is basically much older. The Schlossmuseum's great treasure is the "Darmstadt Madonna" by Hans Holbein the Younger. There's much more to see just to the north in the **Hessisches Landesmuseum** *(Friedensplatz 1, tel 06151 16 57 03, closed Mon., $)*. This above-average regional museum contains superb works by Loch-ner, Cranach, Rembrandt, and Rubens; modern art, including the biggest collection anywhere of works by Joseph Beuys; and—above all—art nouveau items.

In 1901, Grand Duke Ernst Ludwig assembled some expo-nents of *Jugendstil,* the German version of art nouveau, gave them space to work and live, and organized a great exhibition, "A Document of German Art." Take

the tram to the eastern part of town and the **Mathildenhöhe.** "Mathilda's Heights" was the site of the artists' colony and is an architectural shrine to art nouveau. Some of the idiosyn-cratic villas still stand, and the **Ausstellungsgebäude** (Exhibi-tion Building; *Olbrichweg 13, tel 06151 13 33 50, closed Mon., $$)* is still in use. The center where

Darmstadt

◮ 197 B2

Visitor Information

✉ Darmstadt Shop im Luisencenter, Luisenplatz 5

☎ 06151 134 513

darmstadt -marketing.de

EXPERIENCE:
Learn Free-Form Painting

If the masterpieces in Darmstadt's muse-ums inspire you to creative heights, you can pick up a brush at **Atelier Freifarbe** *(Odenwaldstrasse 162A, Ober-Ramstadt, tel/fax 06167 14 27, atelier-freifarbe.de, email: freifarbe@gmx.de),* based 6 miles (11 km) southeast of town. Run by artists and gallery owners Heidi Schrickel and Horst Benz, this roomy, comfortable studio draws people from around the country (including many beginners) to take week-end courses in free-form painting—mostly with easy-to-use acrylic, but also by apply-ing finer oils, shellac, or wax.

---

artists had their studios is now the **Künstlerkolonie** (Artist Colony; *Olbrichweg/Bauhausweg, tel 06151 13 33 85, closed Mon.)*. Extraordinary sights are the 157-foot-high (48 m) **Hoch-zeitsturm** (Wedding Tower) and a gold-encrusted Russian orthodox chapel. ∎

More Places to Visit in Hesse

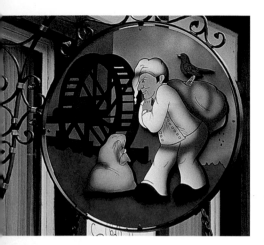

An inn sign in Rüdesheim's Drosselgasse

Bad Homburg

The Kurpark and the surroundings of this spa town on the edge of the Taunus uplands still have much of the allure of the glory days before World War I. The Homburg, a soft felt hat with a dented crown and a narrow upturned brim, was invented here and made popular by Britain's King Edward VII, a frequent visitor. Of course the town has a **Hat Museum** *(Tannenwaldweg 102, tel 06172 3 76 18, closed Mon.). bad-homburg-tourismus.de* 197 B2 ✉ Kurhaus ☎ 06172 178 37 10

Fulda

The principal town of eastern Hesse has long been one of the great strongholds of Christianity in Germany. Its origins go back to the foundation of a monastery in the eighth century by the Englishman St. Boniface, whose relics are kept in the cathedral museum. Part of **Michaelskirche** (St. Michael's Church) dates from the ninth century, but the overall character of the town was created by powerful and prosperous prince-bishops of the 18th century, who built superlative baroque edifices, such as the cathedral, the palace,

and their summer castle, Schloss Fasanerie, in the nearby countryside. *tourismus-fulda.de* ⚐ 197 C3–D3 ✉ Bonifatiusplatz 1, Palais Buttlar ☎ 0661 102 1813/14

Kloster Eberbach

The Cistercian monks who founded this monastery in 1136 chose a remote spot in a beautiful setting. By contrast, the church where they worshipped is simple and austere. Among the other buildings is a 236-foot-long (72 m) vaulted dormitory that provides a vivid picture of monastic life. The wine-growing tradition established by the monks continued after the monastery was secularized in 1803, and products can be sampled on site. *kloster-eberbach.de* ⚐ 197 A2 ☎ 06723 60 460

Michelstadt

The little town of Michelstadt in the heart of the Odenwald uplands has one of the most photographed street scenes in Germany. The almost too-perfect composition focuses on the **Rathaus** (Town Hall), a timber-framed structure on stilts with corner towers and spiky roofs. ⚐ 197 C1 ✉ Marktplatz 1 ☎ 06061 979 41 10

Rüdesheim

Crowds gather in this wine village at the southern end of the Rhine Gorge, the most popular place in the Rheingau. The narrow main street is called Drosselgasse, meaning Thrush Lane or Throttle Alley—and the press of people can indeed be choking. But no one comes to Rüdesheim for peace and quiet, so join in the fun, drink some Riesling, then perhaps take a cable-car ride up through the vineyards to the **Niederwalddenkmal,** a statue of "Germania," commemorating German unification in 1871. *ruedesheim.de* ⚐ 197 A2 ✉ Rheinstrasse 29a ☎ 06722 906 15 0

Weimar, Wittenberg, Wartburg Castle, and other historic sites in eastern Germany's long-time favorite vacation area

Thuringia & Saxony-Anhalt

A decorated column in the Wartburg

Thuringia & Saxony-Anhalt

Lying on the former border of East and West Germany, once part of the German Democratic Republic (GDR), Thüringen and Sachsen-Anhalt are at the geographical heart of the country. Its diverse range of scenery includes the forested uplands of the Harz and the Thuringian Forest, fertile lowlands, and industrial landscapes based on the varied mineral resources beneath the ground.

Thuringia, with Bavaria to the south, is one of the original provinces of Germany, whereas Saxony-Anhalt, north of Thuringia, is a much more recent creation. Set up as a temporary measure in the immediate aftermath of World War II, it was abolished in GDR times, then given new life after reunification. Much of the Harz Mountains, including the Brocken, the highest summit in the northern half of Germany, lies within Saxony-Anhalt. The Thuringian Forest to the south offers equally fine hiking trails and winter sports.

In the rain shadow of the hills stretches low-lying countryside blessed with some of Germany's most productive agricultural land.

The favorable climate even allows vines to be cultivated along the valley of the Saale, the river running northward from the Thuringian Forest to the Elbe. The city of Halle profited from the extraction and merchandising of salt, while lignite mining helped the area's chemical industry rise to world importance. Nowadays, however, the industrial dinosaurs promoted by communist planners are extinct, and promising sectors such as green technology and tourism are growing apace.

In the early Middle Ages, the area lay on the frontier between the Germanic and Slavic worlds, and consequently it has many castles, churches, and monasteries. Magdeburg, the newly designated capital of Saxony-Anhalt, has the finest cathedral in eastern Germany, while Eisenach in Thuringia is overlooked by what many claim is the country's most romantic and history-laden stronghold, the Wartburg. In the 16th century, the fortress provided a refuge for Martin Luther. Eisenach, like Erfurt (Thuringia's capital) and Gotha—other old towns whose heritage of fine building is largely intact—grew up along the Via Regia, the great trading route linking Western and Eastern Europe.

Political fragmentation characterized much of the region's later history as petty principalities vied with one another from their capital cities, some of which, most notably Weimar, became cultural centers of European importance. Other ancient places—Quedlinburg, Tangermünde—are just as picturesque. ∎

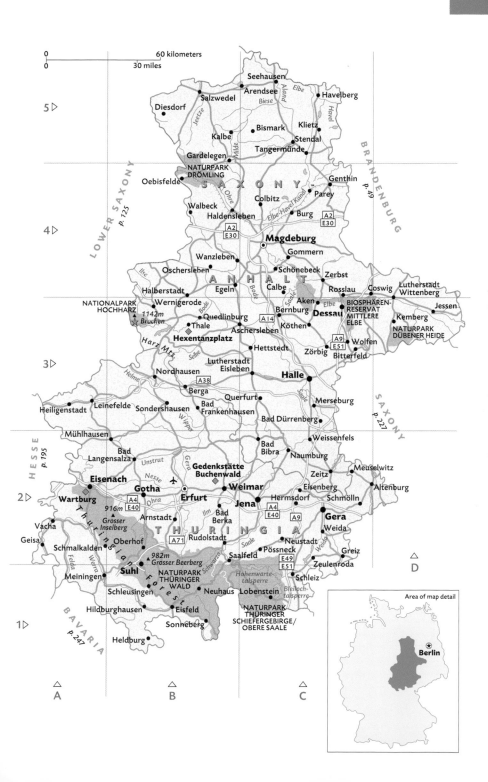

Weimar

Small and provincial it may be, but Weimar occupies a unique place in German hearts, standing as it does for a golden age in the country's cultural history known as Weimar Classicism. The exponents of this late 18th-century literary movement took an essentially optimistic view of the individual's place in the world and strove for a balance between restraint and humanity. A harmonious atmosphere still pervades the mansions, streets, and squares of the town.

The market trades briskly beneath the neo-Gothic Rathaus of 1842.

Weimar

 213 B2

Visitor Information

✉ Markt 10

☎ 03643 74 50

weimar.de

In the late 18th and early 19th centuries Weimar's ducal court attracted some of the finest minds of the time. The greatest of them was Johann Wolfgang von Goethe (1749–1832), but his fellow poet and dramatist Friedrich von Schiller (1759–1805), the influential philosopher Johann Gottfried Herder (1744–1803), and poet

Christoph-Martin Wieland (1733–1813) all flourished in the enlightened atmosphere promoted by Goethe and his patron, Grand Duke Carl August.

Weimar's artistic life did not begin or end with Goethe and Classicism. Painter Lucas Cranach the Elder (died 1553) worked here, Johann Sebastian Bach was court organist and choirmaster from 1708 to 1717, and Franz Liszt was appointed to Bach's position in 1848. Philosopher Friedrich Nietzsche (1844–1900) spent his last years in Weimar.

New ideas came to Weimar early in the 20th century, when the great Belgian designer Henri van de Velde founded a school of applied art here. Then, in 1919, Walter Gropius became the first director of a state school of architecture, the Bauhaus, the pioneering institution of modernist design that taught the integration of all the arts and crafts.

In the aftermath of World War I, Germany's parliament met in Weimar's theater in 1919 and drew up the constitution for a republic. Until its demise in 1933, the regime was known as the Weimar Republic. However, the innovative, left-wing ideas of the Bauhaus were disliked in Weimar, and in 1926 the institution was forced to move to Dessau.

In 1932, Thuringia became the first German state to have a Nazi government., and in 1937, one of the most notorious concentration camps—Buchenwald—was established 5 miles (8 km) northwest. By 1945, more than 50,000 people had perished there, followed by a further 10,000 during the camp's subsequent Stalinist reincarnation. The mass graves and buildings are now a memorial site, **Gedenkstätte Buchenwald,** and a museum charts the history of the camp.

Visiting Weimar

Begin at the **Marktplatz,** with its neo-Gothic Rathaus and the gabled Renaissance Cranach-Haus, where the painter had his studio *(not open to the public).* The historic, although much rebuilt, **Hotel Elephant** (see Travelwise p. 371) is one of Germany's most luxurious establishments.

INSIDER TIP:

Visiting Weimar's opulent Hotel Elephant is a must. The carved staircase spiraling up from the lobby is amazing.

—LARRY PORGES
*National Geographic
Travel Books editor*

Walk east to Platz der Demokratie, where an equestrian statue celebrates Grand Duke Carl August. The stately buildings around the square include the **Grünes Schloss** (Green Palace), containing a superb rococo library, the construction of which was supervised by Goethe. Many of its million-plus volumes relate to the literature of Weimar Classicism, but it also contains the largest collection of works by and about Shakespeare on the continent of Europe. Named for Grand Duchess Anna Amalia, this historic library was badly damaged (and 50,000 books destroyed) by fire in 2004, but it has since been restored.

Weimar's Cultural Sites:

The Platz der Demokratie looks north to the highly variegated

Gedenkstätte Buchenwald

☎ 03643 43 00
🕐 Closed Mon.
buchenwald.de

Weimar's Cultural Sights

☎ 03643 545 400
klassik-stiftung.de

NOTE: Same contact information (telephone and website) for all cultural sites listed

Schlossmuseum

⊠ Burgplatz 4

🕒 Closed Mon.

💲 $$

Goethes Gartenhaus

⊠ Park an der Ilm

💲 $$

Goethes Wohnhaus

⊠ Frauenplan 1

🕒 Closed Mon.

💲 $$$

group of buildings that make up the ducal **Schloss.** The medieval origins of the palace can be seen in the solid stone base of the tower, although most of the building dates from the 18th and 19th centuries. The Schlossmuseum's art collections include paintings by Dürer and Cranach. The latter's finest picture in Weimar, however, is the altarpiece completed by his son that is the pride of the nearby **Herderkirche** *(Herderplatz)*.

The palace overlooks the English-style **Park an der Ilm.** The kernel of this park laid out along the valley of the River Ilm was a plot of land on the far bank given by Carl August to Goethe, together with a retreat subsequently known as **Goethes Gartenhaus.** The poet spent much of his time while at Weimar in this rustic dwelling. A stroll through the greenery is enlivened by mock ruins, a fanciful house made of tree bark, and the duke's own retreat,

the neoclassic **Römisches Haus.**

No tour of Weimar would be complete without a visit to Goethe's main residence, **Goethes Wohnhaus,** on the little square known as Frauenplan. Linked to it is a lavish, modern museum chronicling the events of his life in Weimar. Much will be of interest only to those with a scholarly bent, but there are intriguing items such as a model of the pioneering steam locomotive *Rocket* acquired by Goethe. The main attraction is the house itself, much as Goethe and his family left it after 50 years of residence. Particularly evocative are his private quarters, including his library with its makeshift shelving, his collections of mineral specimens, and his small bedroom.

Schiller, too, lived for a while on Frauenplan, and the pedestrian-only street named after him leads westward from there toward Theaterplatz. Goethe's residence was granted to him by

Goethe's Women

When the 26-year-old Goethe was first summoned to Weimar in 1775 by his friend and admirer, the teenage Grand Duke Carl August, he was something of a rough diamond, quite unschooled in the refined ways of a provincial court. His coarse manners offended Charlotte von Stein, wife of a minor aristocrat and court official, but she was to become his friend, mentor, and platonic lover. They expressed their passion for each other in innumerable letters, although only those written by Goethe have survived. Charlotte made the uncouth young man *salonfähig* (presentable in polite

society) and helped him lay the foundations of his career as a high-ranking court official, the essential counterpoint to his prolific poetic and scientific activity. But Goethe eventually tired of this cerebral relationship, and in 1788 he fell for the more robust charms of Christiane Vulpius, a cheerful and hearty town girl. Weimar society was shocked that the great man should consort with such a vulgar creature, and while Goethe adored his "bedroom treasure," he kept her in the background and only married her 18 years after their first meeting.

The sparsely furnished study in Goethe's Gartenhaus

ducal favor, but the perennially hard-up Schiller was plunged into debt by his purchase in 1802 of what is now known as the **Schillerhaus.** Like Goethe's house, it has a modern annex where the poet's life and times are evoked.

Schiller chose to live here in order to be near Goethe, his friend and idol. Their relationship is celebrated in the **Theaterplatz** by one of Germany's best known statues. The two poets, here equal in height (although Goethe was several inches shorter in real life), stand side by side. Behind them, the much rebuilt **Deutsches Nationaltheater** was the scene of many a premiere, including Goethe's *Faust,* Schiller's *Wilhelm Tell,* and Richard Wagner's *Lohengrin.* A plaque recalls the building's political role in 1919 (see p. 215).

Other buildings on the square include the **Wittumspalais** (closed Mon., $$) and the **Bauhaus-Museum** (Theaterplatz, $$). In the latter you'll find exhibits from the Bauhaus years of the 1920s and from the earlier School of Applied Arts. Architecture enthusiasts will want to look at the building named for van de Velde where the revolutionary ideas of the Bauhaus were taught. Now part of the university, it is in the southern part of town, not far from the **LisaZthaus** (Marienstrasse 17, closed Tues., $$), the composer's home from 1869 to 1886. Close by is the **Historischer Friedhof** (Historic Cemetery), where Grand Duke Carl August and Goethe are buried in the classical mausoleum called the **Fürstengruft.** In 2006, DNA tests proved that the remains in Schiller's coffin here were not his, and now no one is sure where he's buried. ■

Schillerhaus
✉ Schillerstrasse 12
☎ 03643 54 54 00
🕐 Closed Mon.
💲 $$

Walk: To the Summit of the Brocken

The rounded summit of the Brocken, the highest point in the Harz Mountains in northern Germany at 3,747 feet (1,142 m), is visible from far away with its array of towers and masts. It enjoys great prominence in the minds of Germans because of its legendary associations with the supernatural dating back to medieval times and earlier, and also because of its place in literature from Goethe onward.

The Witches' Altar is the name given to this granite tor crowning the summit of the Brocken.

On the eve of May 1, witches are supposed to gather on the crags atop the windswept summit of the Brocken to consort with the devil and celebrate the festival of Walpurgisnacht, events immortalized by Goethe in his *Faust*. Goethe himself came here several times. The best way of experiencing the special appeal of this distinctive mountain is to do as he did and make the climb on foot.

You can take the easy way up by horse and carriage or aboard the *Brockenbahn,* the steam train that first chugged up the steep grade to the summit in 1899. It's tempting to take the train up and walk down, but the ascent, although hard work and slow, allows you to savor the glorious scenery to the full.

NOT TO BE MISSED:

The sight and sound of the *Brockenbahn* steam train pounding up the grade • Brockenhaus • Views from the summit • Devil's Pulpit and Witches' Altar

On the way down, the ruggedness of the path jars the joints and requires your full attention. The Brocken is a real mountain, with a harsh and variable climate. Wear tough shoes or boots and get local advice about weather conditions, perhaps from the visitor information bureau at the mountain resort of **Schierke** *(Brockenstrasse 10, tel 039455 55 86 80, schierke-am-brocken.de).*

Reaching the Summit

Begin the walk at the parking lot by the church in Schierke. The houses and hotels along the main street eventually give way to woodland. Turn right off the road at a waterworks where a sign announces "Brocken über Eckerloch 5 km," and follow the path that climbs alongside a stream, crosses the road, and meets it again at a bridge named after Goethe. Keep to the path, which crosses the Brockenbahn and then traverses a stream on a bridge. The going gets more difficult beyond **Eckerloch shelter;** the path is steep, rocky, and wet in places, although sections of boardwalk help out. Eventually you emerge onto the road again, turning left and crossing the railroad once more before arriving at the summit.

The Bahnhof

Refreshments await the crowds here, most of whom will have made their way up by train. You may feel inclined to join them before visiting the **Brockenhaus** *(tel 03945 55 00 05, nationalpark-brockenhaus.de),* with exhibits explaining the history and ecology of the mountain. Find out how the Brocken, on the border between East and West Germany, was a restricted military area under the GDR and had its own version of the Berlin Wall.

If you follow the 1.2-mile (2 km) circuit around the top of the mountain, you can enjoy the stupendous views over the wooded ridges of the Harz and the plain beyond, and admire the fantastically weathered granite tors known as **Teufelskanzel** (Devil's Pulpit) and **Hexen-altar** (Witches' Altar). If you feel that you have walked enough, take the train down to Schierke station, then walk 550 yards (500 m) down a wooded path back to your starting point.

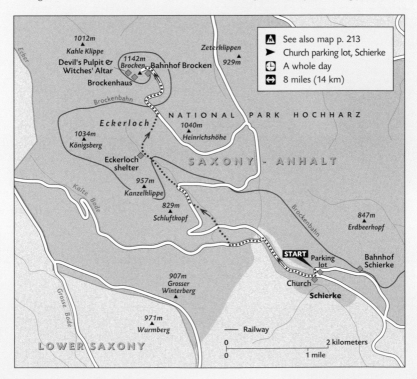

Halle

Saxony-Anhalt's biggest city has not had good press. It was, after all, home to 40 percent of the GDR's environmentally unfriendly chemical industry. Yet Halle is also an ancient place, proud of its past and well worth a day or two of your time. Its university was one of the centers of the Enlightenment, and its vibrant tradition of music culminated in the great Georg Friedrich Handel (1685–1759).

The buildings of Halle's saltworks museum symbolize the city's long industrial tradition.

Halle

⚠ 213 C3

Visitor Information

✉ Marktplatz 13

☎ 0345 122 99 84

halle.de

Händel-Haus

✉ Grosse Nikolaistrasse 5

☎ 0345 50 09 00

🕓 Closed Mon.

💲 $$

haendelhaus.de

Wartime damage was minimal, so something of the atmosphere of historic Halle remains, despite neglect of the physical fabric of the **Altstadt** (Old Town) and the inner suburbs during the communist period. City life revolves around the **Marktplatz,** reached from the main railroad station via the **Leipziger Turm,** the only surviving town gate, and bustling, traffic-free **Leipziger Strasse.** The large market square is dominated by towers, four belonging to the **Marktkirche,** which was cobbled together in the 16th century from two separate churches. The tallest structure is

the 15th-century **Roter Turm** (Red Tower), which you can climb for a view of the city.

A figure of Roland—traditional guardian of civic rights—stands at the foot of the Red Tower, but the square's most prominent statue is that of Handel, erected in 1859 on the centenary of the composer's death. **Händel-Haus,** the baroque mansion that was Handel's birthplace in 1685, is now a museum evoking his life and work, with exhibits of period musical instruments. Occasional performances of his music using contemporary instruments take place in the small concert hall or the inner courtyard.

Art lovers will want to visit the **Moritzburg** (*Friedemann-Bach-Platz 5, tel 0345 21 25 970, stiftung-moritzburg.de, closed Mon., $$*), the palace built by the archbishops in the late Middle Ages to keep the turbulent townsfolk in check.

More unusual is the **Technisches Halloren- und Saline-museum** (Saltworks Museum; *Mansfelderstrasse 52, tel 0345 209 32 30, salinemuseum.de, closed Mon., $$*), set up in the old saltworks on which Halle's medieval prosperity was built and which eventually led to the establishment of its vast chemical industries. ■

Dessau

The historic capital of Anhalt, Dessau has seen a remarkable turn in its fortunes over the past century. Pummelled by Allied bombs in 1945, under the GDR the city was rebuilt in grim Stalinist style. But it never forgot its role as a hothouse of modernist ideas during the Bauhaus movement, based here in 1925–1932. The Bauhaus buildings are now listed as a World Heritage site, as is gorgeous Wörlitz, a baroque landscaped park nearby.

Situated just south of the confluence of the Elbe and Mulde Rivers, Dessau's old town is anchored by its Gothic-towered **Rathaus.** But most visitors make a beeline to the ensemble of Bauhaus structures, located a short walk west of the train station. The headquarters of the school was the **Bauhausgebäude,** designed by Walter Gropius when the movement relocated from Weimar.

Unveiled in 1926, the simplicity of its functional lines set off a seismic wave in architectural circles and exerts an influence on contemporary design even today. Badly damaged in World War II, the sprawling complex was given a proper face-lift in the 1990s. One-hour guided tours (in German) are given daily at 11 a.m. and 2 p.m. The Cubist wing with the huge plate-glass windows houses the **Bauhaus Kolleg** for postgraduate study, but rooms of this former workshop section are kept open for exhibitions.

Heading north from the Bauhausgebäude, it's a ten-minute stroll to the **Meisterhäuser,** a collection of houses built for senior staff of the school. Leading lights of the art and design world rubbed shoulders here. Three of the surviving houses are open to visitors. The **Feiningerhaus,** the former residence of artist Lyonel Feininger, is home to the **Kurt-Weill-Zentrum** (tel 0340 619 595), with displays on the Dessau-born Weill, best known for *The Threepenny Opera* and other collaborations with Bertolt Brecht. The interior of the **Kandinsky/ Klee Haus** (tel 0340 661 09 34) features the pastel hues prominent in those artists' works. Followers of the Bauhaus legacy can visit the attractive **Törten** housing estate in Dessau's south, where the **Stahlhaus** (Südstrasse 5, tel 0340 858 14 20, closed Mon.) contains a Bauhaus information center. ∎

Dessau
- 213 C3

Bauhausgebäude
- Gropiusallee 38
- 0340 65 08 250
- $$ (exhibitions)
- bauhaus-dessau.de

Meisterhäuser
- Ebertallee 63–71
- 0340 65 08 250
- Closed Mon.
- $$
- meisterhaeuser.de

Dessau's Garden Realm

Dessau is embraced by a girdle of lush parkland, dubbed the "Garden Realm" in the 18th century. Some 11 miles (18 km) east of the city lies Wörlitz Park (*Förstergasse 26, tel 034905 202 16, closed Sat.–Sun. Nov.–Feb.*), a fanciful tract with a string of palaces. The grounds, linked by a delightful tangle of footpaths, hedges, and lakes, were meant to reflect the Age of Enlightenment. Close to Wörlitz village, the neo-Palladian Schloss (*woerlitz-information.de, closed Mon., $$*) displays antique statues, including the noted Amazon of Wörlitz, a Roman copy of the Greek original. In summer, a series of classical concerts is held on the verdant lawns next to the lake.

Magdeburg

History has not always been kind to Magdeburg, one of Germany's great historic cities. The baroque town that arose from the ashes of the Thirty Years War was bombed to bits in early 1945, and the rebuilding that took place under communism was typically insensitive. But in 1990 the city emerged victorious over Halle in the contest to become the capital of the newly created *Land* of Saxony-Anhalt.

Magdeburg

🅰 213 C4

Visitor Information

✉ Ernst-Reuter-Allee 12

☎ 0391 83 80 402

🕐 Closed Sun.

magdeburg-tourist.de

Kloster Unser Lieben Frauen

✉ Regierungsstr. 4–6

☎ 0391 56 50 20

🕐 Closed Mon.

💲 $$

kunstmuseum -magdeburg.de

Germany's 1999 Federal Garden Show (see pp. 204–205) held in Magdeburg transformed land once occupied by the Soviet garrison into a new 250-acre (100 ha) park to add to the city's other open spaces. These include the **Elbe promenade** and the **Stadtpark Rotehorn,** laid out on an island in the river. City life centers on the **Alter Markt,** with its baroque **Rathaus** (Town Hall) and golden reproduction statue of the 13th-century **Magdeburg Rider,** thought to be Emperor Otto I. The original is in the town's Kulturhistorisches Museum.

Magdeburg's greatest jewel is the lovely Gothic **Dom** (Cathedral), begun in the early 13th century. It stands on the left bank of the Elbe River, where German merchants had settled early in the ninth century to trade with their Slav neighbors on the far shore. Inside is the modest tomb of Emperor Otto I, together with a striking 13th-century statue of a seated couple. This almost certainly represents the emperor and his Anglo-Saxon wife, Edith. The facade of the porch known as the Paradise Portal is graced with ten expressive figures representing the Wise and Foolish Virgins.

The cathedral interior has superbly carved capitals and representations of the Apostles, as well as the masterpiece of Nuremberg sculptor Peter Vischer the Elder, the bronze tomb of Archbishop Ernst (1495). Dating from about 1245, the damaged statue of St. Maurice is an unusual European representation of a black African. For more fine sculpture—both medieval and modern—visit the nearby **Kloster Unser Lieben Frauen,** a monastery founded about 1017, but now a museum. ∎

EXPERIENCE: Riding Horses in the Altmark

In north Saxony-Anhalt lies the **Altmark** (Old March), a comely region in the Elbe Valley known for quaint brick churches and Hanseatic trading towns. Horse shows and major eventing tournaments are a familiar feature here, particularly around the towns of **Stendal** and **Salzwedel.** The gentle landscape is ideal for horseback holidays, and the dense network of riding trails (hundreds of sandy, field, and forest paths) is a wonderful way to see the sights. Accommodation ranges from delightfully rustic *Heulager* (hay beds) to "riding hotels" with stables and opulent castle inns, and hosts cater to every equestrian need. See *sternreiten-altmark.de* for details.

Eisenach

Most of the visitors to Eisenach come to climb up to the Wartburg, a castle so steeped in history that it was given global recognition by its inclusion on UNESCO's World Heritage List. The steep ascent to the castle can be made on foot from the town in about half an hour; alternatively, you can drive most of the way and complete the climb by donkey. But first give the town itself its due, perhaps entering through the severe Stadttor gateway.

The **Bachhaus** (Bach's Birthplace; *Frauenplan 21, tel 03691 7 93 40, bachhaus.de, $$$*), a few minutes' walk south of the Markt, celebrates a famous son of Eisenach, Johann Sebastian Bach (1685–1750). Furnishings evoke the period around 1700. In the Music Room, museum staff give short performances on original keyboard instruments.

The late Gothic **Lutherhaus** (*Lutherplatz 8, tel 03691 2 98 30, lutherhaus-eisenach.de, $$*), northwest of the Bachhaus, is where Martin Luther may have lodged between 1498 and 1501. Twenty years later, he preached in the **Georgenkirche,** the church where the infant Bach was baptized in 1685. It stands on the **Markt,** along with the 16th-century **Rathaus** (Town Hall) and the **Stadtschloss,** once a ducal residence and now the regional museum.

In GDR times, Eisenach was famous for another kind of Wartburg, the country's prestige car. The last model came off the assembly line in 1991. Look for it, along with other historic vehicles, at the **Automobile-Welt** (*Friedrich-Naumann-Strasse 10, tel 03691 7 72 12, closed Mon., $$*).

Perched on a crag above the town, **Wartburg** is everything a German castle should be, with

Half-timbered buildings enclose a homey courtyard inside the Wartburg.

sentry walks, timber-framed upper stories rising from massive stone foundations, and vaulted interiors. Go through the outer courtyard to the 12th-century **Palais,** a rare surviving example of a Romanesque palace *(guided tour).* Beside the authentically medieval structures are parts that were romantically restyled in the 19th century. Medieval balladeers assembled in the Wartburg for a famous singing competition, an episode re-created by Richard Wagner in *Tannhäuser.* Martin Luther lived here in the **Lutherstube** from 1521 to 1522 while he translated the Bible into German. ∎

Eisenach
🅜 213 A2
Visitor Information
✉ Markt 24
☎ 03691 7 92 30
eisenach.info

Wartburg
✉ Auf der Wartburg
☎ 03691 25 00
💲 $$$
wartburg-eisenach.de

Erfurt

The Thuringian capital was one of the great cities of medieval Germany, and Erfurt's Altstadt (Old Town), with its buildings of all periods, survived World War II relatively intact. A walk along any street in the center will reveal delights, and few sights compare with the city's two great churches rising high above the vast main square, scene of one of Germany's largest Christmas markets.

Erfurt

🅰 213 B2

Visitor Information

✉ Benediktsplatz 1

☎ 0361 6 64 00

erfurt-tourismus.de

West of the town center, **Petersberg** (Peters Hill) provides fine views over the town. At the foot of the hill is the **Domplatz.** The spacious square sets off to perfection the breathtaking architecture of the great Gothic **Dom** (Cathedral) and the **Severi-Kirche** (Church of St. Severus) on the rising ground to the west. The change in level is accentuated by a monumental flight of steps and by the massive buttresses of the *Cavaten,* structures supporting the stonework of the cathedral choir.

The treasures inside the cathedral include a baroque altar and the strange Romanesque sculpture known as "Wolfram," adapted for use as a candleholder. The triangular porch is adorned with figures of the Wise and Foolish Virgins, and the central tower houses one of the largest church bells in Europe, the "Gloriosa." The plainness of St. Severus is offset by its trio of spiky spires. The saint's sarcophagus inside has carvings telling the tale of how the humble weaver Severus was raised to the rank of bishop.

The **Krämerbrücke** (Merchants' Bridge) over the Gera River is unique for its rows of shops and claims to be the only inhabited bridge north of the Alps. On your way, make sure you see the central square called **Fischmarkt,** where the neo-Gothic **Rathaus** (Town Hall) competes with equally elaborate Renaissance mansions. Complete your tour with a stroll along **Anger,** a broad, curving street that is a virtual museum of 19th-century city architecture. ∎

Colorful shops adorn the Krämerbrücke in Erfurt.

Great Little Steam Railroads

One of the pleasures of visiting eastern Germany is to travel on its steam railroads. More than just visitor attractions, they are working railroads, providing everyday passenger (and sometimes freight) service, and manned not by amateur enthusiasts but by career railroad workers.

Once Germany's trunk rail network had been completed toward the end of the 19th century, innumerable connecting local lines were built. These lines went up hill and down dale, even through village streets, on narrow gauge (usually 3 feet/1 m) track. They took farmers to market, children to school, and tourists to the seaside; they also hauled all kinds of freight.

The last to be built, these local lines were the first to be closed down in West Germany, where competition from cars and trucks made them uneconomical. In the GDR, however, steam power flourished on the main lines well into the 1970s. In the post-reunification period, the importance of these lines to the local economy was recognized, and with ingenious methods of privatization, most have survived.

The most extensive narrow-gauge system, the **Harzquerbahn** (hsb-wr.de), winds its way for 70 miles (113 km) through the Harz Mountains. Its principal lines link towns such as Wernigerode and Gernrode on the northern flank of the massif to Nordhausen in the south, and there are several branches. One is the **Brockenbahn** (see p. 218), which leaves the main line at Drei Annen Hohne and climbs through the forest to the open summit of the Brocken, the highest station in Germany. From the open coaches, you can hear the throaty roar of the locomotive as it pounds up the grade. The locomotives, formidable-looking 2-10-2 machines, were specially built for the job in the 1950s and seem well set to carry it out competently for another half-century. For 30 years, the Brockenbahn was closed to the public. Its reopening in 1991 aroused great controversy, with environmentalists arguing

Cars share the street with the narrow-gauge Molli in Bad Doberan.

that the line should remain closed. The needs of tourism prevailed, but the company is limited to operating no more than five trains a day.

Another mountain line is the **Fichtelbergbahn** (Fichtel Mountain Railway; fichtel bergbahn.de), which climbs to the country's topmost town, Oberwiesenthal, through some of Saxony's most glorious countryside. Saxony is home to several other railroads, including the little **Lössnitzgrundbahn** (loessnitzgrundbahn .de), which threads its way through the Lössnitz Valley near Dresden to the country castle of Augustus the Strong at Moritzburg.

On the Baltic coast, the **Molli** steams through the streets of Bad Doberan before delivering vacationers to the seashore at Kühlungsborn, while on the island of Rügen this duty is performed by the **Rügensche BäderBahn** (ruegensche-baederbahn.de).

More Places to Visit in Thuringia & Saxony-Anhalt

Eastern Harz Mountains

Within **Nationalpark Hochharz** (national park-harz.de), the Brocken is the highest summit (see pp. 218–219). Elsewhere, the mantle of dark spruce forest gives way to glorious woods of beech and other deciduous trees, best seen in the **Bodetal,** the dramatic valley of the River Bode. From the little spa of **Thale** you can take a cable car up to the Hexentanzplatz (Witches' Dance Floor) or a chairlift up to the **Rosstrappe** for vertiginous views down into the rocky cleft. A good way to get around the eastern Harz is by the wonderful **Harzquerbahn,** the 70-mile (113 km) railroad system linking many of the towns and visitor sights (see p. 225). One of the railway's main stations is at **Wernigerode.** Ideally located at a point where the valleys running down from the mountains emerge onto the plain, this is a beautifully preserved town of neat, timber-frame burghers' houses and an impossibly picturesque Rathaus (Town Hall). *wernigerode-tourismus.de* 🅜 213 B3 ✉ Markt-platz 10, Wernigerode ☎ 03943 55 378 35

Naumburg

Set in the attractive countryside of the Saale Valley, Naumburg is an exquisite little town whose greatest asset is the **medieval sculpture** in its cathedral. The western rood screen and the figures of benefactors, all by the late 13th-century sculptor known as the Master of Naumburg, are works of an extraordinary emotional realism and human-ity, unparalleled in medieval times. *naumburg-tourismus.de* 🅜 213 C2 ✉ Markt 6 ☎ 03445 27 31 25

Quedlinburg

Quedlinburg's appeal resides in its legacy of more than 1,600 timber-framed buildings

of all periods, which have put the town on UNESCO's World Heritage List. First visit the **Burgberg** (literally "castle-mountain"), an imperial stronghold dating from as early as the tenth century. Its Romanesque church contains exquisite carvings and a fine treasury. Then stroll through the cob-bled streets, squares, and alleyways. *quedlinburg.de* 🅜 213 B3 ✉ Markt 4 ☎ 03946 9 05 624

Thuringian Forest

Cool green uplands stretch southeastward from Eisenach for more than 60 miles (100 km). The **Rennweg** long-distance footpath follows their ridgeline. This is one of eastern Germany's most important year-round vacation areas, with summer hiking giving way to winter sports centered on the 2,600-foot-high (800 m) resort of **Oberhof.** At 3,222 feet (982 m) the range's highest point is the Grosser Beerberg. The most popular peak, however, is the **Grosser Insel-berg** (3,005 feet/916 m), with its fabulous views and easy accessibility by road. *oberhof.de* 🅜 213 A2–B1 ✉ Crawinkler-strasse 2, Oberhof ☎ 036842 26 90

Wittenberg

Now also known as Lutherstadt Wittenberg, this attractive town was the powerhouse of Protestantism. It was to the door of the **Schlosskirche** that Martin Luther nailed his 95 Theses in 1517, and his tomb is inside. An oak tree marks the spot where he pub-licly burned the Papal Bull threatening him with excommunication. The **Lutherhalle** has a rich selection of documents, pictures, and other items evoking Luther's life and the rise of Protestantism. *wittenberg.de* 🅜 213 D4 ✉ Schlossplatz 2 ☎ 03491 49 86 10

An eastern German *Land* with castles galore, spectacular scenery, and a resplendent royal past

Saxony

The royal crown of Saxony tops
a Dresden roof.

Saxony

Sachsen was a proud kingdom until 1918. The munificence of its rulers left its most imposing imprint on Dresden, one of Europe's great centers of art and culture. Although heir to very different traditions, Leipzig also resounds in European culture. Its reputation was made by the musical genius of Bach and Mendelssohn, by printers and publishers, by traders, merchants, and inventors. And Leipzig is justly proud of the role it played in the events leading up to the fall of communism.

Industry came early to this part of Germany. The cities built many of their monuments on the profits earned from the medieval mines of the Erzgebirge (Ore Mountains). In the early 18th century, it was in the little city of Meissen that a European first discovered how to use china clay to make porcelain, which was until then only produced in China. In the next century Germany's first long-distance rail line linked Leipzig and Dresden, and smoke rose from Chemnitz's

NOT TO BE MISSED:

Marveling at the incredible comeback of the Frauenkirche **231**

The jewel-encrusted objects of Dresden's Neues Grünes Gewölbe **233**

The crags of the medieval fortress Bastei **236–237**

Experiencing the Sorbian traditions of Bautzen **238, 240–241**

The delicate artistry of Meissen's famed porcelain **239**

A concert by Leipzig's renowned Gewandhaus Orchestra **244**

Grasping the sinister methods of East Germany's secret police **245**

Seeing the Erzgebirge's master woodcarvers at work **246**

Area of map detail

Berlin

many chimneys as industry grew.

Remains of early industrialization abound, none grander than the Göltzschtalbrücke, the world's highest railroad viaduct, built in brick and rivaling the aqueducts of ancient Rome. The town of Zwickau looks back on a century of automobile manufacture, its most famous, or rather notorious, product being the East German people's car, the Trabant.

The most exciting scenery in Saxony is that of Saxon Switzerland in the upper valley of the Elbe, where 1,000-foot-high (300 m) sandstone cliffs have been eroded into fantastic shapes. The woods and valleys of the Erzgebirge, cross-ing the south of the state to form the border with Bohemia in the Czech Republic, make fine walking country, and in the far southeast is the wooded Zittau range.

Saxony is the heartland of Germany's Slav minority, the Sorbs, whose capital, Bautzen, is a charming little city in its own right. Of Ger-many's many ethnic minorities, the Sorbs have been around the longest. ■

Dresden

Hailed as "Florence on the Elbe," the Saxon capital has doggedly rebuilt much of its glorious heritage since February 1945, when its historic center was destroyed by Allied bombing. Today visitors flock to Dresden to explore its museums and galleries—among the most richly stocked in Germany—and to enjoy some of Saxony's loveliest scenery nearby in the valley of the Elbe.

Baroque architecture at its most extravagant: the Zwinger, pleasure palace of Augustus the Strong

Dresden

⚑ 228 D3

Visitor Information

✉ Neumarkt 2

☎ 0351 501 501

dresden.de

Zwinger

⚑ Map p. 232

☎ 0351 49 14 20 00

🕐 Closed Mon.

💲 $$$$$ (combination ticket for all collections)

skd.museum

Dresden's rebuilt **Altstadt** (Old Town) lies on the river's left bank, but the silhouette of its famous skyline is best viewed from the **Neustadt** (New Town) on the far side of the river. The rebuilding of the Frauenkirche (see sidebar p. 231) and the restoration of the Schloss (see pp. 233–234) are part of the process begun in the early postwar years aimed at re-creating at least some of the Altstadt's historic character. These efforts have been borne out, refuting the critics who thought the ruined city should be abandoned.

Zwinger

Most visitors begin their exploration of the city at the Zwinger in the city center. Intended as an impressive setting for courtly ceremonies and festivals, this fabulous architectural creation is now a museum complex. It was built by architect Matthäus Daniel Pöppelmann (1662–1736) to the orders of the most colorful of Saxony's kings, Augustus the Strong, who came to the throne in 1694. Consisting of a series of buildings arranged around a spacious grassy courtyard with pools and fountains, the Zwinger is considered by many to be the supreme expression of German baroque architecture. It is also the repository of Dresden's outstanding collection of old master paintings.

The best way to approach the Zwinger is through the gateway of the **Glockenspielpavillon,** with its carillon of bells made from Meissen porcelain. In the center of the wing to the left is the **Kronentor** (Crown Gate), topped by sculptures of eagles guarding the crown of Poland (Augustus also ruled Saxony's neighbor to the east for a time). To the right, the massive **Semper Gallery** designed by Gottfried Semper was added to the complex in 1847, but the structure that commands most attention is the **Wallpavillon,** on the far side of the courtyard. This is Pöppelmann's masterpiece, its bravura beauty enhanced by the lively and expressive sculptures carved by his collaborator, Balthasar Permoser (1651–1732). Even greater exuberance is on view in the adjoining **Nymphenbad,** a sunken grotto in which stone nymphs disport themselves.

Inside the Zwinger are varied treasures that rival the building's architectural and sculptural delights. With so much to see, don't try to get around to everything; it's best to choose what interests

you and follow the signs. The **Mathematisch-Physikalischer Salon** (Mathematical-Physical Salon) displays an extraordinary array of scientific instruments dating from the 16th to 19th centuries. Then there is the extensive **Porzellansammlung** (Porcelain

Collection), with superb examples of porcelain from the royal collections. Augustus the Strong was fascinated by porcelain. By experimenting in the vitrification of clays with heat, his alchemist, Johann Friedrich Böttger, discovered how to make fine china, thereby laying the foundation of an industry that

Mathematisch-Physikalischer Salon
🕐 Closed Mon.
$ $$

Porzellansammlung
🕐 Closed Mon.
$ $$

INSIDER TIP:

Visit the Zwinger at night. The buildings are beautifully lit and there are "Zwinger & Mehr" classical concerts in the courtyard on summer evenings.

—LINDA RICHTER
National Geographic contributor

The Fall & Rise of the Frauenkirche

Before 1945, Dresden's skyline was dominated by the monumental dome of the baroque Frauenkirche, completed in 1743 as the central place of Protestant worship. Amazingly, the dome survived the 1945 firestorm (see sidebar p. 235) but collapsed after a few days as the stonework cooled. The heap of blackened rubble stood for decades, a monument to the folly of war.

Then, in 1994, the decision was made to rebuild. The surviving stonework, each piece carefully numbered, was stored in an on-site depot ready for reuse. Fragments were turned into souvenirs—they appeared in watch faces, for example—all helping to finance the mammoth operation. After more than a decade of work, the reconstructed church was ready for the 800th anniversary of Dresden.

Gemäldegalerie Alter Meister

🕐 Closed Mon.

💲 $$$

skd.museum

is still inseparable from the names of Dresden and Meissen.

The **Gemäldegalerie Alter Meister** (Gallery of Old Masters) is also based largely on the enthusiasms of Augustus the Strong and his successor, Friedrich Augustus II. The gallery's most celebrated painting is Raphael's "Sistine Madonna" (1512–1513), loved not only for its exquisite representation of Mother and Child but also for the delightful pair of bored cherubs at the base of the picture. Another renowned painting from the Italian Renaissance is Giorgione's "Sleeping Venus," which remained unfinished at his death in 1510. There are also important works by many of the great names of Western European art—Rembrandt and Vermeer, Claude Lorrain and Poussin, El Greco and Velazquez, Cranach

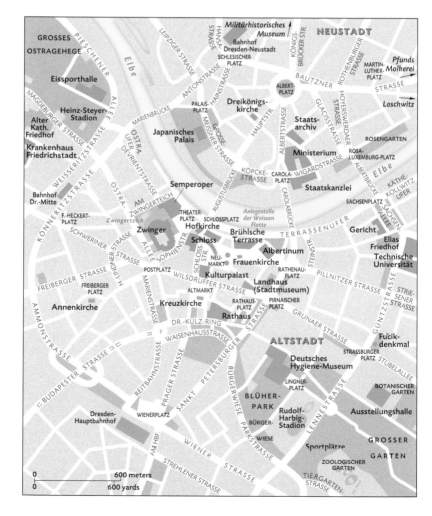

and Dürer. Canaletto's townscapes are uncannily exact depictions of Dresden and Pirna as they were in the 18th century.

Altstadt

The northeastern facade of the Gallery of Old Masters looks out over the **Theaterplatz,** an imposing square bounded by some of Dresden's outstanding historic landmarks: Even the visitor center is a neoclassic temple, originally a guardhouse built by Berlin architect Karl Friedrich Schinkel in 1830–1832.

Home to both the Saxon State Opera and the State Orchestra, the grandiose **Semperoper** is named for architects Gottfried Semper and his son, Manfred. Gottfried Semper's first opera house burned down in 1869. Banned from the city because of his involvement in the abortive 1848 revolution, he entrusted its rebuilding to his son. Its sumptuous interior saw the premieres of several operas by Richard Wagner and Richard Strauss. Left a shell in 1945, the opera house was saved from demolition by its world reputation—and its architect's revolutionary credentials. The complex task of rebuilding it and providing it with modern facilities was completed in 1985, on the 40th anniversary of its destruction.

With its 100-foot-high (30 m) tower, the nearby great **Schloss** is where the rulers of Saxony resided for centuries until 1918. Located on the outer wall facing Schlossstrasse, an extraordinary frieze made of Meissen tiles depicts a succession of princely figures glorifying the

dynasty's 800-year rule. The palace, now being restored to its former splendor, houses a number of museums, including the **Rüstkammer** (Armory), one of the world's great collections of arms and armor. But most riveting is the **Neues Grünes Gewölbe** (New Green Vault), a dazzling treasury of some of the most spectacular creations of the jeweler's and goldsmith's art. Don't miss the wildly

INSIDER TIP:

In the Neustadt north of the Elbe, stop by Pfunds Molkerei at Bautzner Strasse 79. This dairy shop is decked out in hand-painted tiles and sculptures by Villeroy & Boch.

—JEREMY GRAY
National Geographic author

extravagant piece known as the "Court of Delhi on the Birthday of the Great Moghul." Augustus the Strong's court jeweler, Johann Melchior Dinglinger, worked with his brothers for seven years to make what is a thinly veiled exaltation of the Saxon king's own ostentatious court. They created 137 gilded and enameled figures and used countless precious stones. The eventual cost outstripped that of Augustus's grand palace at Moritzburg (see p. 246). Thousands more items from Augustus's day are housed in the **Historisches Grünes Gewölbe**

Semperoper
- Map p. 232
- Theaterplatz 2
- 0351 49 11 705
- $$$ (guided tours)

semperoper.de

Schloss
- Map p. 232
- Taschenberg 2
- 0351 491 42 000
- Closed Tues.
- $$$$ (combination ticket including Rüstkammer & Neues Grünes Gewölbe)

Historisches Grünes Gewölbe
- 0351 491 42 000
- $$$$

A glittering array of treasures is displayed in the Albertinum.

Albertinum

- Map p. 232
- Tzschirnerplatz 2
- 0351 491 42 000
- $$$

skd.museum

Galerie Neue Meister

- Closed Mon.
- $$$

skd.museum

(Historic Green Vault) in the west wing, with visitors required to enter via a "dust lock" to protect the artwork.

Along the River: Linked to the palace by a bridge enabling the royal family to attend Mass without crossing the street, the Roman Catholic Hofkirche caused a stir in this ultra-Protestant city when the Catholic convert Augustus the Strong ordered it built in 1739. The king's architect was Italian Gaetano Chiaveri, who imported many of his countrymen to carry out the work, housing them on the Elbe embankment in what is still called the Italienisches Dörfchen. (The "Italian Village" is now a restaurant with a riverside terrace.) Statues of saints parade on the balustrade of Chiaveri's church, and the interior has baroque furnishings. The remains of Saxon rulers lie in the crypt.

The classic view of the mighty Elbe River is from the **Brühlsche Terrasse,** the promenade laid out in the 18th century over the redundant riverside fortifications by Count Brühl as part of his private garden. It's a wonderful place to sit or stroll and watch the pleasure craft and paddleboats coming and going from the quayside below. On the far bank of the river, reached via the Augustusbrücke of 1910, is the **Neustadt** (New Town), laid out on planned lines in the 18th century. It was less affected than the Altstadt by the 1945 bombing and, with its shops and cafés, has a genuinely lived-in feeling about it.

The 1,600-foot (500 m) terrace is reached from near the Hofkirche by a magnificent flight of steps decorated with sculptures representing the seasons. It leads to the **Albertinum,** the onetime royal arsenal. Following a devastating flood in 2002, the building was fitted with a watertight depot—an "ark for art"—and now houses two fine collections. The Sculpture Collection covers five millennia but shines brightest in the past two centuries. Gems here include "The Thinker" by Auguste Rodin (1840–1917), works from the Fin de Siècle school by Max Klinger (1857–1920), and a draft of the Goethe-Schiller monument in Weimar, by Dresden sculptor Ernst Rietschel (1804–1861).

Galerie Neue Meister: Within the Albertinum, the Gallery of New Masters is an excellent place to get a grip on German 19th- and 20th-century painting. Two of the most important figures in Romantic painting, Caspar David Friedrich (1774–1840) and Ludwig Richter (1803–1884), thrived in Dresden and found inspiration in the landscapes of Saxony and nearby Bohemia. Both are represented by atmospheric works. Few are unmoved by Richter's "Crossing by the Schreckenstein," a metaphor for the river of life as passengers are ferried across the Elbe.

A century later, expressionism took root in Dresden with the founding in 1905 of a branch of the movement known as *Die Brücke* (The Bridge; see p. 43). Between 1929 and 1932 one of its members, Otto Dix (1891–1969), painted perhaps the most searing evocation of the horrors of the trench warfare of 1914–1918, a triptych simply entitled "Der Krieg" ("War"), based deliberately on the great altarpieces of the Middle Ages. Similar shock value is offered by another triptych, "Das tausendjährige Reich" ("The Thousand-Year Reich"), completed in 1938 by Hans Grundig (1901–1958). The moving work accurately foretells the even greater horrors about to be perpetrated by the Hitler regime.

Other Sights

North across the Elbe lies the city's boldest old-new hybrid, the **Militärhistorisches Museum** (Military History Museum) designed by American architect Daniel Libeskind. A glass-and-steel arrowhead pierces the facade of a 19th-century Saxon armory; inside, exhibits trace the evolution of German war-making from the Middle Ages to the present. Far from a parade of weaponry, the museum sheds light on the causes and effects of armed conflict.

History may have been a priority along the riverfront after World War II, but to the south a new, socialist city arose from the rubble. The "New" Dresden created by East German planners is seen at its best around the **Altmarkt,** where establishments such as McDonald's occupy mock-baroque buildings of the 1950s.

One of Dresden's most unusual museums is the **Deutsches Hygiene-Museum** (German Hygiene Museum), devoted to the human body and its relationship to the environment. The "Glass Woman" reveals our inner workings in astonishing detail. ∎

Militärhistorisches Museum

- 🅰 Map p. 232
- ✉ Olbrichtplatz 2
- ☎ 0351 823 28 03
- 💲 $$

mhmbw.de

Deutsches Hygiene-Museum

- 🅰 Map p. 232
- ✉ Lingnerplatz 1
- ☎ 0351 48 46 400
- 🕐 Closed Mon.
- 💲 $$

dhmd.de

February 1945

The last weeks of World War II saw Dresden packed with refugees from the advancing Red Army. Its population clung to the mistaken belief that their city of art and culture with its long-standing connections with Britain and America would be spared from bombing. Sharing this misconception, the German High Command had stripped its air defenses and deployed them elsewhere. At the peak of their deadly efficiency on the night of February 13, the Allied bomber fleets thus met little opposition, and the firestorm they unleashed destroyed 75 percent of the city and killed tens of thousands of people, perhaps even as many as perished at Hiroshima, Japan, in August of that same year.

Drive: The Valley of the Elbe & Saxon Switzerland

This relatively short journey along the banks of the Elbe takes in palaces and castles, fine old towns, and the dramatic sandstone scenery of the Nationalpark Sächsische Schweiz (Saxon Switzerland).

Leave Dresden on the busy B172 to **Pirna ❶**. The historic center of this ancient riverside town focuses on the marketplace. Peek inside the town church and marvel at its intricate vaulting. Continue along the B172, turning right to **Festung Königstein ❷** *(tel 035021 6 46 07, festung-koenigstein.de, $$).* This mighty fortress rising sheer from the crags is all the more impressive if you climb up to it on foot, but the shuttle from the parking lot is the easy way to the top, which offers views down to the river and over the strange landscape of Sächsische Schweiz. Continue along the main road and over the river into the charming spa town of **Bad Schandau ❸**, where the **Nationalparkzentrum Sächsische Schweiz** *(Dresdner Strasse 2b, tel 035022 502 40, closed Mon. Nov.– March, $)* has exhibits on the national park.

National Park

From Bad Schandau a funny little tramway runs up the valley known as the Kirnitzschtal, the heart of the eastern section of the national park, but unless you have plenty of time to spare, turn back toward Dresden. Don't go back across the bridge over the Elbe, but keep straight on along the minor road through the village of Rathmannsdorf, then straight on at a road junction. The narrow road up through the woods brings you to the hilltop town and castle of **Hohnstein.** Beyond it, follow signs to Bastei, eventually turning off the main road to the left.

Walk up to the **Bastei ❹**, a great natural curiosity. Its weather-sculpted sandstone cliffs, crags, and pillars tower more than 1,000 feet (300 m) above the curve of the Elbe far below. The Bastei (bastion) has long been a visitor attraction, and paths, viewpoints, and

NOT TO BE MISSED:

Festung Königstein and the views from the ramparts • The views from the Bastei • A stroll on the grounds of Schloss Pillnitz

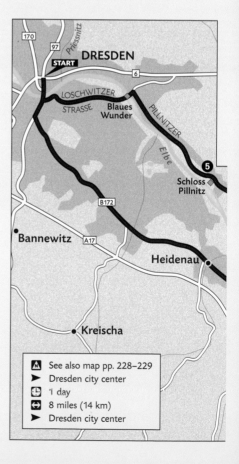

🅜 See also map pp. 228–229
▶ Dresden city center
🕒 1 day
🔁 8 miles (14 km)
▶ Dresden city center

catwalks enable you to wander around it, protected by railings from the abysses suddenly opening up beneath your feet.

Riverside Palace

Return to the main road and continue toward Dresden, stopping at **Schloss Pillnitz** ⑤ *(tel 0351 261 32 60, closed Mon., $ garden)*. This riverside palace in mock-Chinese style was begun on the orders of Augustus the Strong in 1720 as a summer residence. Guests were borne up the Elbe from Dresden to disembark at the splendid waterside stairway. The palace's exquisite decoration includes some of Europe's earliest examples of chinoiserie. The park, a fusion of French formality and English naturalism, is dotted with delightful structures such as the Palmenhaus, the Orangerie, and the Kamelienhaus, built especially to protect a 200-year-old camellia.

The palace houses the **Kunstgewerbe-museum** *(closed Mon., $$$)*, with fine examples of furniture, silverware, wood carving, and other crafts from medieval to modern times. Pillnitz sits among vineyards that rise up the slopes to wooded hilltops. Among the vines

Bastei bridge, in Nationalpark Sächsische Schweiz, was built in 1851.

stands a lovely little church, the **Weinberg-kirche,** which, like the palace, was the work of Augustus's court architect, Daniel Pöppelmann.

Continue along the main road toward Dresden, crossing the Elbe via the **Blaues Wunder;** the "Blue Miracle" is a steel suspension bridge dating from 1893, a considerable technical achievement for its time.

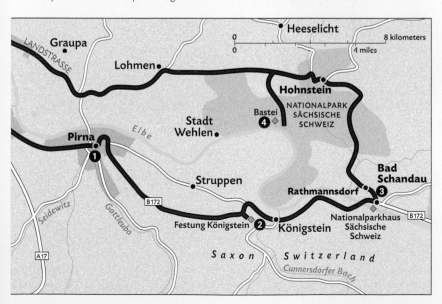

Bautzen

Occupying a fine and easily fortified site high above a bend in the River Spree, Bautzen owes its striking silhouette to its many towers. It is a stately old place, largely rebuilt in baroque style after being burned down more than once during the Thirty Years War.

Bautzen

🅐 229 E3

Visitor Information

✉ Hauptmarkt 1

☎ 03591 4 20 16
or
03591 1 94 33

bautzen.de

Alte Wasserkunst

✉ Wendischer Kirchhof 7

☎ 03591 4 15 88

🕐 Closed Mon.– Fri. Jan.

💲 $

In addition to those of its well-preserved medieval fortifications, Bautzen's towers include church spires, the tall slender tower of the Rathaus (Town Hall), and two curiosities: Saxony's own leaning tower, the 184-foot (56 m) **Reichenturm** (*Reichenstrasse, tel 03591 46 04 31, $*), which tilts 4.75 feet

INSIDER TIP:

Sorbian tradition and culture team up in the "wedding dish," a tasty union of braised beef, horseradish, and parsley potatoes. Sample it at Wjebik, an old-world eatery in Bautzen at Kornstrasse 7.

—JEREMY GRAY
National Geographic author

(1.44 m) out of the vertical; and the **Alte Wasserkunst,** a water tower that supplied the city with fresh water for more than 400 years before being taken out of commission in 1965. If you can face its 135 steps, the late 15th-century Reichenturm provides a splendid panorama

over the town. The wheel of the Alte Wasserkunst was used to pump water from the Spree up into a cistern, from where it was distributed in wooden pipes. The workings are explained in the museum inside. You can admire the tower (and enjoy the best view of Bautzen) from the **Friedensbrücke** (Bridge of Peace), which leads into town from the west.

Buildings on the central square, the **Hauptmarkt,** include the 18th-century Rathaus, a Gothic apothecary, and the Jahreshaus (House of the Year), so called because it has four staircases, 12 chimneys, 52 rooms, and 365 windows. The square known as Fleischmarkt, to the north, is dominated by **Petridom** (St. Peter's Cathedral), where both Roman Catholics and Protestants worship—Catholics in the choir, Protestants in the nave.

Old streets lead west to the **Ortenburg,** Bautzen's castle, dating from about 1000. It was rebuilt in Gothic style by King Matthias of Hungary, who ruled here in the late 16th century; there is a relief portrait of him on a tower. Colorful traditional costumes are among the highlights of the **Serbski Musej** (*Ortenburg 3, tel 03591 27 08 700, $*), the museum of the Sorbian people with a huge photo collection (see pp. 240–241). ■

Meissen

Meissen's international fame rests on the prestige of its porcelain, but there is more to it than that. With the closely packed red-roofed dwellings of its Altstadt (Old Town) overlooked by the Burgberg—the rock spur crowned by castle and cathedral—Meissen is arguably the best preserved of Saxony's smaller towns.

Meissen's citadel, the Burgberg, on its rock outcrop above the Elbe River

On arrival, pause in the riverside parking lot on the right bank of the Elbe to view the harmonious grouping of town and citadel. Cross the bridge into the Altstadt, centered on the sloping **Markt** with stately burgher houses, town apothecary, and late 15th-century Rathaus (Town Hall). The tower of the **Frauenkirche** dominates one side of the square; close by is a famous tavern, the Gasthaus Vincenz Richter.

Narrow streets, steps, and alleyways climb up the castle hill. At the center of an enclosure of buildings is the glorious Gothic **Dom** (Cathedral; *Domplatz 7, tel 03521 45 24 90, $$*). Its twin spires were added in the early 20th century, but its interior is almost entirely medieval. The castle itself, the **Albrechtsburg,** was mostly built between 1471 and 1525, with striking features such as a cleverly engineered spiral staircase.

In 1709, Augustus the Strong's court alchemist, Johann Friedrich Böttger, discovered the technique of making perfect porcelain (see pp. 231–232). Commercial production began within the walls of Meissen's fortress. The factory moved to its present site in the Triebisch Valley in the 1860s. Today the **Staatliche Porzellan-Manufaktur** offers guided tours and demonstrations. Pieces from the factory's past are displayed in the exhibition halls, and there is a well-stocked shop. ■

Meissen
🅰 228 D3
Visitor Information
✉ Markt 3
☎ 03521 4 19 40
touristinfo-meissen .de

Albrechtsburg
✉ Domplatz 1
☎ 03521 4 70 70
$ $$$
albrechtsburg -meissen.de

Staatliche Porzellan- Manufaktur
✉ Talstrasse 9
☎ 03521 46 82 08
$ $$$
meissen.com

Germany's Slav Minority

Of modern Germany's many ethnic minorities, no group has been around longer than the Sorbs of Saxony and Brandenburg. The Sorbs were one of a number of Slavic peoples who moved westward around the sixth century A.D. and occupied what is now eastern Germany.

Sorbian girls in traditional dress lead a procession during the Feast of Corpus Christi.

Lacking any central political organization, the Sorbs put up little resistance when the Germans began to colonize the lands to the east of the Elbe. In the face of this advance, most of their fellow Slavs retreated, were slaughtered, or became assimilated into the German population.

Somehow the Sorbs survived, preserving their language and culture, although today their numbers have been much reduced. Some 50,000 members of this minority live in Oberlausitz (Upper Lusatia), the area centered on the town of Bautzen (see p. 238) in eastern Saxony, and in Niederlausitz (Lower Lusatia), around Cottbus in southeastern Brandenburg. They have their own press and schools.

The Sorb presence is most obvious in the town of Bautzen, where their central cultural and political organization, the Domowina, has its headquarters, and where many aspects of their distinctive culture are presented in the Serbski Musej (Sorbian Museum). Watch for

For the Birds

The mysterious Sorbian custom of the *Vogelhochzeit* (Marriage of the Birds) can be traced back to pre-Christianity, when food sacrifices kept the gods happy. The custom was tweaked over time, so that now, on the eve of January 25—historically, the start of the nesting season—children set out plates that our feathered friends then fill with bird-shaped pastries, a "thank you" for feeding them during their winter nuptials.

bilingual road signs; Bautzen becomes Budysin in Sorbian, Cottbus changes to Chosebuz, Weisswasser to Bela Woda. You may come across a village where the older women wear traditional costume on an everyday basis.

The Sorbs continue to celebrate their special feast days, mostly to do with life and work on the land. For the *Vogelhochzeit* (Marriage of the Birds; see sidebar above) on January 25, empty plates are set out to be filled with treats by thankful birds. On Easter, there are horseback processions as well as intricately painted eggs. Harvest time is celebrated, too. The biggest festival is probably the one held in alternate odd years in the village of Crostwitz near Bautzen.

Culture Threatened

Today's Sorbs have claimed and been granted the rights that every civilized country accords its minorities. This does not guarantee the survival of their culture, which in any case is not a homogeneous one—the Sorbian spoken in Lower Lusatia is akin to Polish and quite distinct from the Upper Lusatian dialect, which is closer to Czech. However, the prospect for Sorbian culture is more hopeful than it has often been in the past. When medieval German rulers tried to stamp out the language and force the Sorbs to assimilate into the German majority, Sorbian became confined to the villages where, paradoxically, it flourished. The community was

threatened again when industrialization began in the 19th century, when Sorbian speakers became bilingual for the sake of their jobs and many villages lost their Slav identity altogether. The worst time was under the Slav-hating Nazi regime, which not only forbade the use of the language but also plotted to expel the Sorbs to some remote corner of Europe. Many leading members of the community were imprisoned or exiled to other parts of Germany. In GDR times, the Sorbs had many privileges on paper, but all cultural life was strictly controlled and the regime's enthusiasm for large-scale open-cast brown coal mining destroyed dozens of Sorb villages in Lower Lusatia. The biggest threat today is assimilation and emigration because of lack of local employment. Nevertheless, the Sorbs remain a lively—and welcoming—presence in eastern Germany.

An expert egg painter

Leipzig

Saxony's second city is known for its musical and intellectual traditions and for its trade fairs. Since the overthrow of the GDR regime in 1989, in which its citizens played a leading role, the city has moved swiftly to recover its former place as one of the country's star cities. Leipzig's go-ahead spirit is expressed in a wealth of new buildings and in what is arguably the liveliest "scene" in eastern Germany, with an unequaled choice of restaurants, bars, and cabarets.

On the far side of Willy-Brandt-Platz and the ring road, Leipzig's historic core, the **Innenstadt**, is quite small and easily explored

The Thomaner choirboys perform in the Nikolaikirche.

on foot. The covered shopping arcades called **Passagen** add to the pleasure of a city stroll with their boutiques, places of refreshment, and refined decor. **Steibs Hof** is a contemporary example of one of these arcades, while the early 20th-century **Specks Hof** has been brilliantly modernized.

Opposite the entrance to Specks Hof is the **Nikolaikirche.** Beginning in 1982 the regular Monday prayer meetings for peace held here became an institution, and in 1989 they were a rallying point for demonstrators against the government. The church was originally built in Romanesque times. Its sober exterior belies the interior, renewed at the end of the 18th century with soaring white columns terminating in pale green palm leaves reaching high into the elaborate vaulting.

Mädlerpassage, the most splendid of the Passagen, is three stories high, but its most famous establishment is belowground. **Auerbachs Keller** (tel 0341 21 61 00) owes its world reputation to Goethe's *Faust*, in which Faust and Mephistopheles descend into the cellar tavern to carouse with students. Most visitors to Leipzig follow in their footsteps, to

EXPERIENCE: Visiting the Old Spinning Mill

In the late 19th century, the Leipziger Baumwollspinnerei was the largest cotton-spinning mill on the European continent. After the decline of cotton yarn production in the early 1990s, the factory, which is located in the southwestern district of Plagwitz, adopted a new motto ("from cotton to culture") and the building was repurposed as an artists' colony, studio complex, and exhibition space dubbed the **Alte Spinnerei** *(Spinnereistrasse 7, tel 03 41 498 02 00, spinnerei.de, closed Sun.–Mon.).*

Today more than 100 professional artists, including such Leipzig School stars as Neo Rauch and Matthias Weischer, ply their trade here, and works from all over the world are presented in 15 galleries. You can peruse the displays on your own or join guided tours on Fridays and Saturdays. Art instruction on different techniques is available at galleries such as **Halle 14** *(halle14.org),* a nonprofit exhibition center that offers workshops with artists and creative drawing courses for both children and adults.

---

enjoy a glass of Saxon wine from the barrel or a substantial meal among the Faustian memorabilia. In nearby **Naschmarkt** is a statue of Goethe himself. The freshly restored small baroque building in Naschmarkt was built as a produce exchange and now serves as a concert hall.

At the center of the Innenstadt stands the **Altes Rathaus** (Old Town Hall), built in 1557, one of the first typical German Renaissance town halls, with high roof, tall tower, stepped gables, and arcaded ground floor facing the marketplace. It is now the **Stadtgeschichtliches Museum** (Municipal History Museum), with an imposing reception hall hung with portraits of princes and city fathers. One room is devoted to composer Felix Mendelssohn-Bartholdy (1809–1847), who spent the last 12 years of his life in the city.

Musical Legacy

Just along the Thomasgasse is Leipzig's second great civic church,

the **Thomaskirche** *(Thomaskirchhof 18, tel 0341 222 24 200).* Founded in 1212, the church was rebuilt in Gothic style at the end of the 15th century. It is best known as the home of the Thomaner, a celebrated boys' choir. The choir is as old as the church; its members attend a boarding school where they receive an academic education and rigorous musical training.

From 1723 until his death in 1750, Johann Sebastian Bach was Cantor (choirmaster) of St. Thomas's and also Leipzig's director of music. He is now buried in the church, and a statue of him stands outside. Opposite, the **Bachmuseum** *(Thomaskirchhof 16, tel 0341 9 13 72 02, bach-leipzig .de, $$$)* has documents and musical instruments. The best way to honor the great musician and the choir he led, however, is to attend one of the regular services at which the Thomaner perform.

If the Thomaskirche represents one pole of Leipzig's musical life, the other is the vast

Leipzig
🅰 228 B3

Visitor Information
✉ Richard-Wagner-Strasse 1
☎ 0341 7104 260/265
leipzig.travel

Nikolaikirche
🅰 Map p. 244
✉ Nikolaikirchhof 3
☎ 0341 12 45 380

Stadtgeschichtliches Museum
🅰 Map p. 244
✉ Altes Rathaus, Markt 1
☎ 0341 965 13 20
🕐 Closed Mon.
💲 $$

stadtgeschichtliches-museum-leipzig.de

Neues Gewandhaus

🅜 Map p. 244

✉ Augustplatz 8

☎ 0341 127 02 80

gewandhaus.de

Augustusplatz, on the far side of the Innenstadt. On one side of the square is the **Opernhaus** (Opera House) of 1960, and on the other is the **Neues Gewandhaus** (New Concert Hall), home base of the city's great orchestra, whose origins go back to the mid-18th century. Felix Mendelssohn was appointed director of the orchestra at the age of 26 in 1835. The present building is a far cry from the upper floor of the clothmakers' guildhall (Gewandhaus), where a concert hall was improvised in 1781. One of the prestige projects of GDR times, the concert hall was built in 1981. Both opera house and concert hall have excellent acoustics and a wealth of ornament and decoration. Another example of the

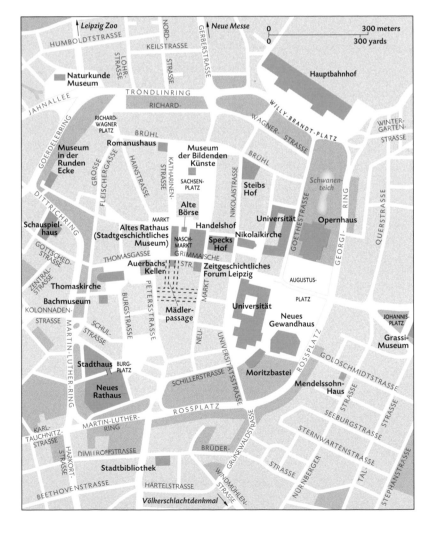

communist regime's architectural aspirations is the 31-story university tower close by.

Museums & More

Built in Bauhaus style in the late 1920s, the **Grassi-Museum,** east of the city center, contains three separate museums: **Völkerkunde** (Ethnology; *tel 0341 973 19 00*), **Musikinstrumente** (Musical Instruments; *tel 0341 973 07 50*), and **Angewandte Kunst** (Decorative Arts; *tel 0341 213 37 19*), the last based on a huge collection dating back to medieval times. In its new gallery on Sachsenplatz, the **Museum der Bildenden Künste** (Fine Arts Museum) has an impressive selection of works by early German masters and German Romantics.

Two fascinating exhibits deal with the historic upheavals. The **Zeitgeschichtliches Forum Leipzig,** near the Nikolaikirche, evokes the challenges of daily life in the GDR. Out on the city's outskirts, Napoleon suffered a crushing defeat at the hands of the allied armies of Prussia, Austria, and Russia. Known as the Völkerschlacht (Battle of the Nations), the battle of October 1813 is commemorated by the **Völkerschlachtdenkmal** (*Prager Strasse, tel 0341 241 68 70*). Climb the steps of this colossal pyramidlike structure to the viewing platform 300 feet (91 m) above the crypt for the definitive view over Leipzig.

Enjoy the film *Jurassic Park*? One of Germany's best animal parks, the **Leipzig Zoo** recently opened "Gondwanaland," a domed jungle habitat with 17,000 plants and 300 rare animal species such as Komodo dragons, Malaysian tapirs and pygmy rhinos. You can explore via jungle paths, treetop bridges, or boat.

Many businesspeople flying into Leipzig head straight for the **Neue Messe,** a bright modern trade fair center on the northern outskirts. Linked by a rapid transit line to Leipzig's breathtaking **Hauptbahnhof**—the largest rail terminus in Europe, completed in 1915—the complex consists of five exhibition halls and centers on the 985-foot-long (300 m) Glashalle, a tribute to the city's 800-year tradition of markets and trade fairs. ■

Grassi-Museum
- ▲ Map p. 244
- ✉ Johannisplatz 5–11
- ☎ 0341 22 29 100
- 🕐 Closed Mon.
- 💲 $$
- **grassimuseum.de**

Museum der Bildenden Künste
- ▲ Map p. 244
- ✉ Katharinenstrasse 10
- ☎ 0341 21 69 90
- 🕐 Closed Mon.
- 💲 $$
- **mdbk.de**

Zeitgeschichtliches Forum Leipzig
- ▲ Map p. 244
- ✉ Grimmaische-Strasse 6
- ☎ 0341 22 200
- 🕐 Closed Mon.
- **hdg.de**

Leipzig Zoo
- ▲ Map p. 244
- ✉ Pfaffendorfer Strasse 39
- ☎ 0341 593 33 85
- 💲 $$$$$
- **zoo-leipzig.de**

The Sinister Stasi

The GDR's Ministry for State Security was one of the world's most repressive secret police forces. Commonly known as the Stasi, it infiltrated almost every aspect of East German life. By the time the Wall fell in 1989, it numbered 91,000 full-time employees and at least 180,000 unofficial "coworkers." West of Leipzig's city center, the Museum in der Runden Ecke (see map p. 224; *Dittrichring 24, tel 0341 9 61 24 43, runde-ecke-leipzig.de, $$*) documents the extraordinary lengths to which the rulers of the GDR went in order to control their subjects. Apart from agents' disguises, surveillance devices, and propaganda, the displays include odor samples taken from suspected dissidents so that dogs could track them down.

More Places to Visit in Saxony

Nutcrackers are a traditional Erzgebirge craft, as well as other hand-carved wooden toys.

Colditz

An impregnable-looking stronghold rising high above the Mulde River dwarfs the pleasant little town of Colditz. Between 1940 and 1945, the **Schloss** was an "escape-proof" prisoner-of-war camp for Allied officers. Of the more than 300 attempts made to break out, about 10 percent were successful. The most ambitious, a glider laboriously assembled beneath the castle roof, was never put to the test as the war ended before it could be launched. Guided tours take place when a large enough group has gathered. *schloss-colditz.com* 228 C3 ⊠ Schlossgasse 1 ☎ 034381 437 77 $ $$

Erzgebirge (Ore Mountains)

Southern Saxony consists largely of these forested uplands, which rise gently from north to south then culminate in an almost clifflike drop at the Czech frontier. In the Middle Ages, this was the heartland of German industry, the place where mining techniques were invented and refined to release the treasures hidden beneath the surface: silver, tin, and iron. When the mineral resources were exhausted, the inhabitants turned to crafts to make a living. Erzgebirge woodcarvers are famous for their skill, and

the area has a long tradition of toymaking. One place to see the masters chipping away is Seiffen, a museum-piece hamlet renowned for its open workshops.

There are plenty of signs of past prosperity in towns such as **Annaberg-Buchholz,** with a sumptuously furnished and exquisitely vaulted church, and **Freiberg,** where the cathedral has one pulpit in the form of a giant tulip and another held aloft by the figure of a silver miner. Old mines in both towns are now visitor attractions.

The resort of **Oberwiesenthal,** 15 miles (24 km) from Annaberg-Buchholz, lies at the foot of the highest point in the Erzgebirge, the Fichtelberg (3,983 feet/1,214 m). Climb to the top on foot, or take the easy way up by chairlift. The most enjoyable way of making the trip to Oberwiesenthal is aboard one of the steam-hauled trains of the Fichtelbergbahn, which chugs its way up the scenic valley from its terminus at Cranzahl (see p. 225). 228 C2–D2 ⊠ Buchholzer Strasse 2, Annaberg-Buchholz ☎ 03733 1 94 33

Schloss Moritzburg

Augustus the Strong had his country home to the north of Dresden, where his predecessor, Duke Moritz, had built a modest hunting lodge in Renaissance style in 1546. Augustus's alterations to Schloss Moritzburg turned it into an imposing baroque palace, its corner towers reflected in the huge artificial lake on which extravagant naval pageants were held. The palace is now the **Baroque Museum,** containing porcelain, furniture, paintings, wall hangings, and hunting trophies. Outside the palace, there are great fishponds, the rococo Pheasantry Pavilion rising over a miniature harbor, and the Saxon State Stud Farm. *schloss-moritzburg.de* 228 D3 ☎ 035207 87 30 🕒 Closed Mon. Nov.–Dec. $ $$

Tranquil river valleys, gloriously forested uplands, and a wealth of historic towns and cities richly stocked with art and culture

Northern Bavaria

St. Christopher as depicted in the Vierzehnheiligen basilica

Northern Bavaria

From the town of Aschaffenburg in the far northwest to Passau on the Austrian border, and the Czech Republic frontier to the northeast, this region is one of the most rewarding for vacationers. Much of the area—the old provinces of Franconia in the north and part of Swabia in the southwest—was incorporated into the former kingdom of Bavaria (Bayern) in the early 19th century, and it is far removed from the typical Bavarian stereotypes of lederhosen, beer halls, and cow-filled Alpine meadows.

Nuremberg combines modernity and big-city dynamism with medieval charm. But for a trip back in time, Rothenburg ob der Tauber reigns supreme. Perfectly preserved, Rothenburg is the jewel of the Romantische Strasse (Romantic Road), Germany's foremost tourist road. Starting in the north at Würzburg, the route runs south past Dinkelsbühl and Nördlingen to Augsburg and the Alps.

Every city in the region has something: Regensburg has an almost Italian character, as does Passau; Bamberg's matchless architecture

NOT TO BE MISSED:

The seductive aromas of Nuremberg's Christmas market **253**

Whiling away the hours on Bamberg's Venetian-style canals **254–255**

The over-the-top baroque of Vierzehnheiligen church **256–257**

Following Wagner's footsteps in his festival town, Bayreuth **259–260**

Sampling delicate Riesling wines in wonderful Würzburg **262**

Dark medieval passages, and tasty sausage, in Regensburg **268–269**

Paddling down the leafy Altmühl River **269**

Gentle skiing, and glass-blowing, in the Bavarian Forest **274–275**

has survived untouched by war; Wagner's Bayreuth hosts one of the world's great music festivals; and Coburg has a unique past, linking it with many of Europe's royal families.

Northern Bavaria has been home to some of Germany's finest artists and craftsmen. Albrecht Dürer (1427–1528) was from Nuremberg, and the city has a wealth of work by his contemporaries. Superlative works of art can be found throughout the region, not least in the baroque monasteries, abbeys, and pilgrimage churches. Vierzehnheiligen, overlooking the broad valley of the upper Main, is the loveliest. Kloster Weltenburg stands guard over the narrow limestone gorge formed by the Danube before it joins the Altmühl. One of the country's largest protected nature parks, the valley of the Altmühl is a favorite with German vacationers. There is more peace and quiet in the countryside running up to the wooded ridges of the Bavarian Forest along the border with the Czech Republic. ■

Nuremberg

Lovingly rebuilt after wartime devastation, Nuremberg (Nürnberg) remains the archetypal German medieval city, encircled by mighty defensive walls, its red-roofed buildings with their row upon row of dormer windows overlooked by the Kaiserburg, the imperial castle on its sandstone outcrop. The undisputed capital of northern Bavaria is a city for all seasons: As well as museums of national significance, it has a colorful street life from spring to fall, and Germany's oldest and biggest Christmas market.

The railing surrounding Nuremberg's **Schöner Brunnen** dates from the 16th century.

Although it covers a considerable area—almost 1.5 square miles (4 sq km)—Nuremberg's **Altstadt** (Old Town) is a delight to explore on foot, with its ancient, irregular street pattern surviving intact on both banks of the River Pegnitz. Heavy traffic is kept outside the walls, where the ring road along the line of the old moat is graced by grand buildings such as the opera house and the main railroad station (Hauptbahnhof).

A good starting point is **Loren-zerplatz,** the square named after one of the city's great churches, the **Lorenzkirche.** Inside the church, works of art depict the city at its late medieval zenith of prestige, prosperity, and creative excellence. The two outstanding works are by artists closely associated with Nuremberg: Adam Krafft created the great 66-foot-high (20 m) tabernacle in the 1490s, and the great wood-carver Veit Stoss (died 1533) painted the limewood depiction of the Annunciation hanging in the choir.

The church's 266-foot (81 m) twin towers may dominate the scene, but as impressive in its own way is the **Nassauer Haus** opposite. This fortified town house with its corner turrets and oriel window dates to the 13th century, and it nicely symbolizes the wealth of a leading citizen and his determination to defend it. Also on the square is the **Tugendbrunnen,** a Renaissance fountain spouting water from the figures of the Seven Virtues.

The bridges crossing the Pegnitz offer many enticing views. From the Museumsbrücke (Museum Bridge), you can get a good view of the **Heilig-Geist-Spital** (Hospital of the Holy Ghost). A medieval almshouse and hospital, the building was faithfully reconstructed in the 1950s after its destruction in World War II. It now houses a restaurant.

Frauenkirche & Around

On the far bank is **Hauptmarkt,** the site of a daily market since the Middle Ages and the hub of city life. The Christmas market (see sidebar p. 253) takes place here against the incomparable backdrop of the **Frauenkirche,** one of the most exquisite churches in Germany. Below its steep and spiky gable covered in sculptures is an oriel with a clock; automata, the so-called Männleinlaufen, perform daily at noon. The church, built in the 14th century for Emperor Charles IV, for many years housed the crown jewels. Among its proudest possessions today are the high altar and the triptych known as the Tucher Altar. Even more spectacular than these is the fountain in the northwest corner of the marketplace; the Gothic **Schöner Brunnen** resembles a medieval space probe, 62 feet high (19 m), manned by 40 figures representing allegorical and

biblical characters and the seven imperial electors.

From the square, Burgstrasse leads northward toward the castle height. Before beginning the climb, however, glance at the splendid Renaissance **Rathaus** (Town Hall) and perhaps spend some time exploring the 30 or so rooms of the **Fembohaus** (Burgstrasse 15, tel 0911 2 31 25 95, closed Mon., $$), a stately 16th-century mansion and now a multimedia museum of the city's history. Take the elevator to the top floor with its superb city model, then work your way down.

The complex silhouette of the **Kaiserburg** on the city's northern rim is the result of demolitions and rebuildings spread over many centuries. The most striking internal feature is the Imperial Chapel built on two levels. A climb up the 113 steps in the tower,

---

EXPERIENCE: Sampling Sausage in Bavaria

The nation's love of pork sausage is elevated to a science in Bavaria, where cities enjoy a friendly rivalry over the grilled links. The most famous is Nuremberg's midget Rostbratwurst, seasoned with marjoram in gossamer-thin casings and fiercely protected under European law. Legend has it that prisoners got the slender morsels through keyholes from visiting relatives. Stiff resistance comes from Regensburg's Bratwurstl, grilled over beechwood at an ancient sausage BBQ. Veal or beef is mixed into the coarser bratwurst of Coburg, whose butchers unusually add raw eggs. For a shortlist of sausage spots, consult the **Bavarian Tourist Board** (Arabelliastrasse 17, Munich, tel 89 212 3970, bavaria.by).

Nuremberg
- 249 C3

Visitor Information
- ✉ Hauptmarkt 1 & Königstrasse 93
- ☎ 0911 2336 132

tourismus.nuernberg.de

Lorenzkirche
- Map p. 252
- ✉ Lorenzerplatz 10
- ☎ 0911 244 699 30

lorenzkirche.de

Frauenkirche
- Map p. 252
- ✉ Hauptmarkt 14
- ☎ 0911 20 65 60

Kaiserburg
- Map p. 252
- ✉ Auf der Burg 13
- ☎ 0911 2 44 65 90
- $ $$

kaiserburg-nuernberg.de

NOTE: Nuremberg
Museums
museums.nuremberg.de

Albrecht-Dürer-Haus

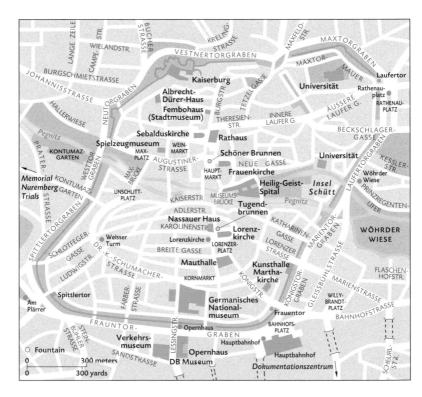

Map p. 252

✉ Albrecht-Dürer-
Strasse 39

☎ 0911 2 31 25 68

🕐 Closed Mon.

💲 $$

Sebalduskirche

Map p. 252

✉ Albrecht Dürer
Platz 1

☎ 0911 214 25 00

sebalduskirche.de

the Sinwellturm, affords a view over the whole city, while a penny tossed into the Deep Well takes six seconds to splash down. Just down from the castle is the **Albrecht-Dürer-Haus.** Furnished in late medieval style, it gives a good idea of the life and domestic circumstances of the great artist.

The last of Nuremberg's trio of great churches is **Sebalduskirche** (St. Sebald's). Its austere Romanesque west front dates from the early 13th century, while the soaring east end of the church was completed in High Gothic style toward the end of the 14th century. The sumptuous furnishings include a Christ carrying the Cross by Adam Krafft, relief panels

by Veit Stoss, and St. Sebald's elaborate bronze tomb by master craftsman Peter Vischer the Elder (1455–1529), who incorporated a self-portrait of himself at work. This level of skill was exceptional, but Nuremberg was always famous for inventiveness and meticulous workmanship.

Museums

Toymaking was another skill that flourished here. The exhibits in the **Spielzeugmuseum** (Toy Museum, *Karlstrasse 13–15, tel 0911 2 31 31 64, closed Mon., $$*) will appeal to adults as much as to children. Toy trains feature here, but the real thing stars in the **DB Museum** (Transportation

Museum). Germany's national museum of public transportation is located here not least because the country's very first steam railroad was opened between Nuremberg and the nearby town of Fürth in 1835. A reproduction of the original locomotive, the *Adler* ("eagle"), occupies pride of place, but there is much more, including the luxurious state carriage of Bavaria's Mad King Ludwig and what must be one of the world's largest and most realistic model railway layouts.

Birds." His portraits, such as his painting of Michael Wolgemut, his former teacher, reveal character with equal skill.

Nazi History: On the city's southeastern outskirts are the remains of a darker era: the Zeppelinhaupttribüne, the podium where Hitler addressed mass Nazi party rallies. It is the focal point of the never-completed Kongresshalle, which was modeled on Rome's Colosseum. Inside, the extent of Nazi megalomania

DB Museum
- Map p. 252
- ✉ Lessingstrasse 6
- ☎ 0180 4 44 22 33
- 🕐 Closed Mon.
- 💲 $$

dbmuseum.de

Germanisches Nationalmuseum
- Map p. 252
- ✉ Kartäusergasse 1
- ☎ 0911 1 33 10
- 🕐 Closed Mon.
- 💲 $$$

gnm.de

Germany's Christmas Markets

From late November to Christmas Eve, more than two million visitors flock to Nuremberg's Christmas market, far and away the country's most impressive. On the Friday before the first Advent Sunday, the long-locked Christmas Angel opens the market with a prologue from the Frauenkirche gallery. Some 200 wooden stalls present handmade toys, spicy

Lebkuchen, crèches, and Christmas ornaments as the tantalizing aromas of mulled wine and bratwurst hang in the air.

While Nuremberg hogs the limelight, the custom is echoed in dozens of cities such as Erfurt (particularly delightful), Cologne, Hamburg, Munich, and Stuttgart, each boasting a distinct flavor and tradition.

The **Germanisches Nationalmuseum** (Germanic National Museum), just to the north, dates from 1852 and has expanded to include craft objects of every kind, paintings, sculptures, arms and armor, costumes, and folklore. Its original home, an old Carthusian monastery, is now embedded in an attractive modern extension. Don't miss the painting galleries on the second floor, where Dürer's genius becomes fully apparent. Germany's greatest Renaissance artist, Dürer had a masterly ability to depict anatomical detail; look for his "Hercules Slaying the Stymphalian

is cast into sharp relief at the **Dokumentationszentrum** (Documentation Center), which elaborates on Nuremberg's key role in the Third Reich.

Göring, Keitel, von Ribbontrop, and other Nazi henchmen received their last judgement at the Nuremberg Trials, held in 1945–1949. The original venue, Courtroom 600, is open to visitors as part of the **Memorium Nürnberger Prozesse** (Nuremberg Trials Memorial), located in the attic of the Palace of Justice. Audio tapes and films give a compelling account of the historic event. ∎

Dokumentationszentrum
- Map p. 252
- ✉ Bayernstrasse 110
- ☎ 0911 231 75 38
- 💲 $$

Memorium Nürnberger Prozesse
- Map p. 252
- ✉ Bärenschanzstrasse 72
- ☎ 0911 321 79 372
- 🕐 Closed Tues.
- 💲 $$

memorium-nuremberg.de

Bamberg

A wonderful synthesis of nature and architecture, Bamberg sits at the point where low hills converge on the valley of the Regnitz River. Old residential districts and market gardens have survived in the city center, and streets and squares have suffered neither wartime destruction nor insensitive redevelopment. Yet Bamberg is very much a modern city, a commercial and cultural center with a harbor on the Main-Danube Canal and a recently refounded university.

Built in Gothic, baroque, and rococo styles, the Altes Rathaus crowds its little island in the Regnitz River.

Bamberg

🅰   249 C3

Visitor Information

✉   Geyerswörth-strasse 5

☎   0951 297 62 00

bamberg.info

NOTE: Bamberg Museums
museum.bamberg.de

Bamberg's outstanding buildings are those on the land rising steeply from the river's left bank—the great cathedral and the bishop's palace, the Residenz. But start your exploration in the **lower town,** modeled by citizens rather than clergy.

The **Altes Rathaus** (Old Town Hall) is built on an islet in the river. An odd but endearing structure, it consists of three

incongruously unrelated parts: a fairly conventional 18th-century section adorned with colorful frescoes; an elaborate baroque tower penetrated by the carriageway of the bridge; and what looks like a timber-framed house perched precariously above the rushing stream. Inside is an exceptional porcelain collection, the **Sammlung Ludwig.**

Linger by the river, admiring the statuary and absorbing the atmosphere of the riverside scene, with its old weirs, ancient cranes, and the pleasingly irregular fishermen's houses all making up Bamberg's "Little Venice."

The lower town has many more treasures. Two of Bavaria's finest baroque architects, Georg Dientzenhofer (1643–1789) and Balthasar Neumann (1687–1753), worked here, designing the great Jesuit church of **St. Martin** and the **Neues Rathaus** (New Town Hall), respectively. There are also whole streets of lovely 18th-century houses. Some of *The Tales of Hoffmann,* the basis for the opera by Offenbach, were written in the little **E.T.A.-Hoffmann-Haus,** which between 1808 and 1813 was the home of this much-loved musician and storyteller.

Steep streets and stairways climb to the **upper town,**

bringing you up on the sloping, cobbled **Domplatz**, a space of breathtaking impact. The square is lined by the glorious four-towered **Dom** (Cathedral), the late medieval palace known as the Alte Hofhaltung, and the imperious 18th-century Neue Residenz. The Dom, the third cathedral to occupy the site, took most of the 13th century to build. During that time, the prevailing style changed from Romanesque to Gothic, but this shift does not affect the building's overall harmony.

Inside are masterpieces of medieval sculpture. The best known is the **"Bamberger Reiter,"** a noble figure on horseback who seems to embody the virtues of medieval Germanic chivalry. He may, in fact, be a representation of King Stephen of Hungary, the brother-in-law of Emperor Henry II who is buried here with his empress, Kunigunde. Their tomb is the work of Tilman Riemenschneider (ca 1460–1531), one of the greatest late-medieval sculptors. With its elaborate scenes from the couple's lives, it took 14 years to complete. Other outstanding sculpture includes female figures representing the triumphant Church ("Ecclesia") and misguided Judaism (the blindfolded "Synagogue"); the lindenwood Nativity Altar is the last major work by Veit Stoss.

Opposite the cathedral on Domplatz, the **Alte Hofhaltung** was originally built as an imperial palace and later converted into the bishop's residence. Beyond the Renaissance gateway is an irregular courtyard overlooked by charming timber-framed buildings. In 1693, Prince-Bishop Schönborn commissioned Leonhard Dientzenhofer (ca 1655–1707) to design the **Neue Residenz.** However, money ran out, and only two wings of his new baroque palace were completed. Inside are magnificent state rooms and the **Staatsgalerie,** with a collection of paintings by German masters such as Grien and Cranach. From the terrace of the Rosengarten, you can look out over the whole town. ■

Sammlung Ludwig
- ✉ Altes Rathaus, Obere Brücke 1
- ☎ 0951 87 18 71
- 🕐 Closed Mon.
- 💲 $$

E.T.A.-Hoffmann-Haus
- ✉ Schillerplatz 26
- ☎ 0951 955 03 10
- 🕐 Closed Mon. & Nov.–April
- 💲 $$

Dom
- ✉ Domplatz 5
- ☎ 0951 502 25 12

Alte Hofhaltung
- ✉ Domplatz 7
- ☎ 0951 87 11 42
- 🕐 Closed Mon.; special exhibits only, Nov.–April
- 💲 $

Neue Residenz
- ✉ Domplatz 8
- ☎ 0951 51 93 90
- 💲 $$
- residenz-bamberg.de

EXPERIENCE: Brewing Bavarian Style

Franconia has Germany's greatest concentration of breweries, mostly intimate, family-run affairs with output a tiny fraction of a Löwenbräu or Beck's. The art of Bavarian brewing is presented by Bierland Oberfranken, an industry association for Upper Franconia's brewers with a flair for palatable public relations. The masters give a one-day seminar (serious business!) in the hallowed halls of the **Bayerisches Brauereimuseum** (Bavarian Brewery Museum), explaining the history, different varieties, and, of course, tasting and brewing techniques. The two- and three-day events (in English on request) include a visit to a local brewery, and all participants are awarded a "beer diploma" for their efforts. The courses are held in **Kulmbach,** 39 miles (64 km) northeast of Bamberg. To reserve a spot, contact Kulmbach visitor information (Sutte 2, Kulmbach, tel 09221 958 80, email: touristinfo@stadt-kulmbach .de; see also bierland-oberfranken.de).

Vierzehnheiligen

Crowning a hillside in the lovely upper valley of the Main River, the great pilgrimage church dedicated to the Fourteen Saints (Vierzehnheiligen) is one of the architectural wonders of Germany.

Vierzehnheiligen

 249 C4

✉ Wallfahrtskirche Vierzehnheiligen

☎ 09571 9 50 80

 Donation requested

vierzehnheiligen.de

For centuries, the church has attracted crowds of pilgrims, and you will not be disappointed if you follow their footsteps up the gentle slope to this rococo masterpiece. It was designed by Balthasar Neumann, one of the most creative architects of the 18th century.

The Fourteen Saints, among them St. Barbara, St. Catherine, St. Christopher, and St. Vitus, had long been the subject of a popular cult in southern Germany, where they are called *Nothelfer* (Helpers in Time of Need). In 1446 they appeared in a vision, along with a figure of the Infant Jesus, to Hermann, a simple Franconian shepherd. Miracles were soon reported, and a pilgrimage chapel was erected on the spot.

Rebuilt more than once to accommodate growing crowds of pilgrims, it received the ultimate in architectural expression on the orders of Prince-Bishop Friedrich Carl von Schönborn, already engaged in transforming the face of his episcopal city, nearby Bamberg (see pp. 254–255). Neumann, who had won fame as court architect at Würzburg (see pp. 261–262), was the natural choice. The foundation stone was laid in 1741, and the building was completed in 1772, well after Neumann's death but in faithful compliance with his plans.

The Church Today

The twin **towers** of the church act as a beacon, signaling across the floor of the Main Valley to the baroque abbey of **Kloster Banz,** its counterpart on the opposite slope. From the outside, Vierzehnheiligen looks like a conventional church, with walls of coarse sandstone apparently enclosing the typical layout of nave, aisles, transepts, and choir. Only the undulating west front gives some hint of the pleasures to come.

The radiant glory inside is revealed as soon as you walk through the doors—the space seems less like a logical work of architecture than the inside of some fantastical coral reef. Light streams through the many windows to illuminate exuberant, curvilinear forms in pink, white, and gold. Structure seems to disappear entirely beneath ornamentation, the culmination of which is reached in the oval-shaped marble and stucco **Gnadenaltar** (Altar of Mercy), dedicated to the Fourteen Saints and placed at the center of

North transept

Twin towers with cupolas

the church. Surrounded by a balustrade, it reproduces the shepherd's vision in the most extravagant way. No other artifact expresses quite so vivaciously the playful and sensual spirit of the rococo. ■

South transept

High altar

Centrally placed Gnadenaltar by Johann Michael Feichtmayer

Conventional exterior in coarse sandstone

Coburg

For centuries, this town was the capital of a ducal dynasty whose mastery at marriage arrangements influenced half the royal families of Europe. The dignified buildings lining its streets and squares, and its fine heritage of parks and gardens, reflect Coburg's aristocratic past.

Coburg's downtown ducal palace, the Ehrenburg, overlooks the landscaped Schlossplatz.

Coburg
🗺 249 C4
Visitor Information
✉ Herrngasse 4
☎ 09561 89 8000
coburg-tourist.de

Veste Coburg
✉ Veste Coburg
☎ 09561 8 79 0
🕐 Closed Mon. Nov.–March
💲 $$
kunstsammlungen-coburg.de

Life in Coburg centers on the bustling **Marktplatz,** where the late 16th-century Rathaus (Town Hall) faces the grand three-gabled Stadthaus. The statue in the marketplace is of Albert von Sachsen-Coburg-Gotha, who in 1840 married his cousin Victoria, Queen of England.

When she visited, Victoria stayed in the **Ehrenburg** (*Schlossplatz 1, tel 09561 80 88 32, schloss-ehrenburg.de, closed Mon., $$),* an early 19th-century ducal palace. The interior highlight is the Riesensaal, a stuccoed ballroom, its ceiling held up by a bevy of giants (*Riesen*). The palace looks out over

Schlossplatz, with arcades and the neoclassic Staatstheater.

You can climb up to the old castle, **Veste Coburg,** by road or walk through the parkland of the Hofgarten to the baroque portal. Because of its dominant position, triple ring of walls, and towers, the stronghold is known as the "Crown of Franconia." In the Steinerne Kemenate building are two rooms where Martin Luther stayed in 1530; medieval and early modern art are now on display. Decorative arts and glassware are shown in the Carl Eduard building. Look for the ducal family's sleighs and coaches in the Duchess's Wing. ∎

Bayreuth

This old town dates back to the 12th century, but it remained essentially unnoticed until the 19th century, at the time of the rising fame of composer Richard Wagner (1813–1883), who lived and worked here. His reputation is still celebrated every July and August, when visitors from all over the globe come to enjoy the famous Festspiele—the Wagner opera festival.

The foundations for the city's fame were laid in the 17th century, when Bayreuth became the seat of the margraves of Kulmbach, who began to rebuild it in a style befitting a small princely city. The life of the court was given a great boost

INSIDER TIP:

Bayreuth's Sommernachtsfest in early August celebrates midsummer with bands, fireworks, and entertainers dressed in 17th-century costumes.

—SONJA HAAS
Bayreuth Tourism Board

a century later, when Margrave Friedrich, a dull man, succeeded in winning the hand of Princess Wilhelmine, favorite sister of Frederick the Great of Prussia.

Energetic and talented, with a passion for music, theater, architecture, and landscape gardening, Wilhelmine attracted leading artists, designers, and musicians to the town and spent her husband's money on projects such as the luxurious **Markgräfliches Opernhaus** (Margraves' Opera House).

One of five theaters built during her reign, this is the most splendid, with one of Germany's great baroque interiors. It is said that it was this theater that first attracted Wagner to Bayreuth, and it was here that he conducted a triumphal performance of Beethoven's Ninth Symphony on taking up residence in the town.

The Markgräfliches Opernhaus hosts Bayreuth's "other" music

Bayreuth

🅰 249 C3

Visitor Information

✉ Luitpoldplatz 9
☎ 0921 8 85 88

bayreuth-tourismus.de

Markgräfliches Opernhaus

✉ Opernstrasse 14
☎ 0921 7 59 69 22
💲 $$

A rehearsal of *Siegfried* for the 2013 Bayreuth Wagner opera festival

Birth of a Cult

At an early age, Richard Wagner stated his intention to create a truly national Germanic opera that would be as great a cultural achievement as the symphonies of Beethoven. Deliberately turning his back on Germany's infatuation with Italy and the world of classical antiquity, he found inspiration in the country's medieval past and the deeds of the gods of Norse mythology. He also revolutionized and enriched musical language to create a web of sound of astonishing intensity and emotional power. He was saved from an erratic personal life by the generosity of one of his admirers, King Ludwig II of Bavaria. It seemed that the theater needed for Wagner's epic productions would be built in the Bavarian capital, Munich, but the composer preferred a site in Bayreuth.

Wagner's style of opera, called "musical drama," attracts near-fanatical enthusiasm. But not all are entranced; it has been called "an avalanche of sound." Wagner's anti-Semitism and overblown nationalism endeared him to the Nazis (Hitler was a regular guest at the Festspiele), but has detracted from his personal stature.

Neues Schloss
✉ Ludwigstrasse 21
☎ 0921 759 69 0
💲 $$

bayreuth-wilhelmine.de

Haus Wahnfried (Richard Wagner Museum)
✉ Richard-Wagner-Strasse 48
☎ 0921 75 72 80
💲 $

wagnermuseum.de

Festspielhaus
✉ Festspielhügel
☎ 0921 7 87 80
💲 $$ (guided tour)

bayreuther-festspiele.de

Richard Wagner in stone

festival, the Fränkische Festwoche in May, which showcases the works of 18th-century composers. Also in the old town center, the rococo **Schlosskirche** holds the tombs of Wilhelmine and her husband. Close by is the **Altes Schloss** (Old Palace) rebuilt in baroque style at the end of the 17th century, although its core is older. Its most striking feature is the octagonal Renaissance tower, with a spiral staircase big enough to ascend on horseback.

Not happy about living in an old castle, Wilhelmine ordered a new palace to be built, supervising much of the work herself. The delicious interiors of the **Neues Schloss** (New Palace) show her taste at its most inventive, with a Japanese room, a palm room, an extraordinary mirror room, and the splendid Cedar Room, a fine setting for the official opening of the Festspiele. Guided tours are available. Beyond is the **Hofgarten,** a park landscaped in the informal English style at the end of the 18th century.

Wagner's residence, **Haus Wahnfried,** stands on the edge of the Hofgarten, an essential visit not only for opera fans but for anyone interested in this controversial genius. A short distance from the center of town, the **Festspielhaus** (Festival Theater), where his "musical dramas" are staged, was inaugurated with a performance of his colossal *Ring* cycle in 1876. ∎

Würzburg

The history of this ancient city began in the eighth century, when a church was erected over the bones of the Irish missionary St. Kilian, martyred here when he fell foul of the local ruler. Later, the city was a center of the Counter-Reformation, and in 1895, physicist Wilhelm Konrad Röntgen discovered the secrets of X-rays here. Although badly bombed in World War II, many buildings survived or have been restored; the baroque Residenz alone justifies a visit.

After living for some 500 years in the Marienberg fortress high up on the west bank of the Main, the prince-bishops aspired to more spacious quarters. The man chosen to design their new, prestigious palace was the virtuoso architect Balthasar Neumann (see p. 38). Built between 1720 and 1744, his magnificent **Residenz** is one of Germany's great baroque buildings.

As you enter the central wing, you can't miss the spectacular grand staircase, adorned with the world's largest ceiling painting, the work of Venetian artist Giovanni Battista Tiepolo (1696–1770). After the restraint of the stucco-decorated Weisser Saal (White Room) comes the opulent, oval Kaisersaal (Imperial Chamber) with trompe l'oeil scenes from Würzburg's history on the ceiling also painted by Tiepolo. The sumptuous Sala Terrena connects the palace with the terraced garden, a perfect setting for the early-summer Mozart festival.

The Romanesque **Dom** (Cathedral) west of the Residenz, badly damaged in 1945 but since rebuilt, contains tombs of the Schönborns, the most prominent of the prince-bishops. The adjacent **Neumünster** is a Romanesque basilica lavishly rebuilt in baroque

style, the resting place of the saintly Kilian. To the rear, in the tiny green space of the **Lusamgärtchen,** is a memorial to the much loved troubadour Walther von der Vogelweide. The nearby Marktplatz is

Würzburg

🗺 248 B3

Visitor Information

✉ Marktplatz 9

☎ 0931 37 23 98

wuerzburg.de

Tiepolo's fresco in Würzburg's Residenz shows the four known continents paying homage to the prince-bishop.

Residenz
- ✉ Residenzplatz 2
- ☎ 0931 35 51 70
- 💲 $$$ (garden free)

residenz-wuerzburg .de

Würzburg Dom
- ✉ Domstrasse 43
- ☎ 0931 3866 2800
- 💲 $ tour

Marienkapelle
- ✉ Marienplatz 7
- ☎ 0931 3866 2800

Festung Marienberg & Mainfränkisches Museum
- ✉ Festung Marienberg
- ☎ 0931 20 59 40
- 🕐 Closed Mon.
- 💲 $$

mainfraenkisches -museum.de

graced by the gorgeous rebuilt rococo mansion known as the **Haus zum Falken** *(Marktplatz 9, tel 0931 372 335)* and by the graceful Gothic **Marien-kapelle,** with its depiction of the Annunciation above the northern entrance. This chapel in honor of the Virgin Mary was built on the site of the ghetto, burned down in 1349 when its Jewish residents were held responsible for bringing bubonic plague to the city.

The **Alte Mainbrücke,** the stone bridge over the Main, dates from 1133, although floods, ice, and other misfortunes have necessitated much rebuilding. It was embellished in the 18th century with baroque statuary, dramatically posturing figures of bishops and saints. Locks allow very large barges to pass the weir.

Climb up to the **Festung Marienberg** (Marienberg Fortress) on foot or take one of the infrequent buses. The medieval castle, the first residence of the prince-bishops, was enlarged into a Renaissance palace before they moved to the Residenz. The superb view of river and city is best appreciated from the terrace below the castle. Inside are the unusual eighth-century circular church, the **Marienkirche,** and the **Mainfränkisches Museum,** the regional museum. Do not miss the collection of very delicate lindenwood carvings by Tilman Riemenschneider, whose career took off in Würzburg about 1478.

On roughly the same level as the Marienberg, but reached separately via a stepped passageway with Stations of the Cross, is the **Käppele.** This onion-domed pilgrimage church was the final work in Würzburg of Balthasar Neumann. From the terrace, admire the splendid view of the town and the Marienberg. ∎

EXPERIENCE: Tasting Franconia's Wines

The northern part of Würzburg's old town is an appropriate place to sample the products of Franconian vineyards—particularly the delicate, prize-winning Rieslings, sold in teardrop Bocksbeutel bottles and served in traditional "Roman" wineglasses. For tastings, a convenient first port of call is the **Haus des Franken-weins** *(Kranenkai 1, tel 0931 390 11 20, haus-des-frankenweins.de),* occupying the building beneath a riverside loading crane from 1573. Organized tastings are offered in the cozy paneled chambers of two medieval hospices, which have always gained much of their income from the vines planted by their founders: the

Bürgerspital *(Theaterstrasse 19, tel 0931 3503 441, buergerspital.de),* established in 1319, and the **Juliusspital** *(Klinikstrasse 1, tel 0931 3 93 14 00, juliusspital.de)* from 1576, which has a fine courtyard and an 18th-century pharmacy with original furnishings. The many vineyards nearby are also pleased to whet your whistle, often in showrooms but sometimes directly in the master's own cellar, pleasantly reeking of fermentation. Rules of thumb: Move from dry to sweet, avoid the region's thin reds, and try to save your palate for a splash of excellent *Eiswein,* a dessert variety produced from grapes harvested after an early frost.

Rothenburg ob der Tauber

The countryside sweeps right up to Rothenburg's ring of medieval ramparts, inside which exists a medieval townscape of great perfection. Monuments are few, but the narrow streets and charming squares seem not to have changed since Burgomaster Nusch saved his city from destruction in the Thirty Years War by winning a wager, the *Meistertrunk* (see sidebar p. 265). If you can, come out of season or get up early before the streets fill with fellow visitors.

One of Rothenburg's medieval gateways guards the approach to the cobbled Plönlein.

The first fortification built on this headland overlooking the River Tauber a thousand years ago was on the spot where the Burggarten now stands. A small town spread out on the plateau to the east, protected by a long-since-demolished line of walls. By 1300, growing prosperity brought expansion and a second line of walls and towers, more than 1.5 miles (2.5 km) long with a sentry walk that can still be followed today.

After the Thirty Years War, the tide of trade ebbed, and the

Rothenburg ob der Tauber

🅰 248 B3

Visitor Information

✉ Marktplatz 2

☎ 09861 40 48 00

**tourismus
.rothenburg.de**

Perfectly preserved, the old walls of Rothenburg still hold the modern world at bay.

St.-Jakobs-Kirche

✉ Klostergasse 15

☎ 0931 20 57 70 60

rothenburgtauber -evangelisch.de

town—fortunately for visitors today—became a backwater. Many of its inhabitants lived as simple peasants, driving their animals into the fields during the day.

In the mid-19th century, Rothenburg was "discovered" by sentimental painters such as Carl Spitzweg and Ludwig Richter, who saw in it the epitome of the Romantic German past. It became a stopping point for British travelers heading south to Switzerland and Italy, and the townsfolk soon realized where their future lay: in tourism.

For many years, Rothenburg has operated one of the most stringent preservation policies of any town in Germany, banning modern intrusions such as shop signs that might detract from its medieval image. After an air raid in the last days of World War II, J. J. McCloy, a civilian with the advancing U.S. forces, successfully argued against further raids on Rothenburg, and thereafter the town was restored and preserved.

Marktplatz & Around

At the very center of town is the **Marktplatz,** dominated by the stately Renaissance wing of the Rathaus (Town Hall), its steps a favorite sitting place for weary sightseers. On the north side of the square is the crinkly baroque gable of the **Ratsherrentrink- stube,** the tavern where the city councillors once met. Adorned with three clocks, it features the figures of Tilly and Nusch (see sidebar p. 265), who appear on the hour several times a day to reenact their historic encounter.

Just north of the Marktplatz in **St.-Jakobs-Kirche** is Rothenburg's finest church treasure. The Altar of the Holy Blood is a masterpiece of delicacy and expressiveness carved in linden wood by Tilman Riemenschneider (1504). Housed in an old convent behind the church, the **Reichsstadtmuseum's** most famous exhibit is the original *Humpen* of the *Meistertrunk* legend.

The best view of Rothenburg is from the **Rathaus** (Town Hall). You pass through the spacious **Kaisersaal** (Imperial Hall) and climb the steep stairway in the oldest, Gothic part of the building, to emerge onto a narrow platform at the top of the tower. Two hundred feet (60 m) below are the patterned cobblestones of the marketplace, while beyond the crowded, red-tiled roofs and the ramparts stretch the beautiful woods and fields of Franconia.

Some of the finest old houses are on **Herrngasse,** the street leading west to the Burgtor. This was the gateway to the castle, now a park, the **Burggarten,** with idyllic views over the valley of the Tauber. South of the marketplace, **Schmiedgasse** is lined with more splendid houses, including the

step-gabled **Baumeisterhaus.** Statues on the second floor represent figures of the Seven Virtues, and those above depict the Seven Deadly Sins. Just off Schmiedgasse, the **Puppen- und Spielzeugmuseum** (Puppet & Toy Museum) has one of the country's largest collections of old toys and dolls. The **Mittelalterliches Kriminalmuseum** will make you shudder with its array of torture instruments, including an example of the cruel Iron Maiden. Schmiedgasse ends in the tiny triangular square known as the **Plönlein,** a much photographed spot. ∎

INSIDER TIP:

Walk the ramparts around the city's perimeter; it's an opportunity to escape most of the tourists and see some beautiful medieval architecture.

—NICHOLAS ROSENBACH
National Geographic contributor

Reichsstadtmuseum

- ✉ Klosterhof 5
- ☎ 09861 93 90 43
- 💲 $$

reichsstadtmuseum.rothenburg.de

Rathaus

- ✉ Marktplatz 1
- ☎ 09861 404 177
- 💲 $ (tower)
- 🕐 Open daily April–Oct.; Sat.–Sun. Jan.–March & Nov.

Puppen- und Spielzeugmuseum

- ✉ Hofbronnengasse 13
- ☎ 09861 73 30
- 💲 $$

www.spielzeugmuseum.rothenburg.de

Mittelalterliches Kriminalmuseum

- ✉ Burggasse 3
- ☎ 09861 53 59
- 💲 $$

www.kriminalmuseum.rothenburg.de

The *Meistertrunk*

Rothenburg fell to the imperial army of General Tilly on October 30, 1631. The merciless warlord had decided to level the town to the ground because of its impertinent resistance, but nevertheless he accepted the offer of a drink from a *Humpen*, a capacious vessel holding some seven pints (3.25 L) of the good local wine. Mellowing slightly, Tilly proposed sparing the town if someone could empty the vessel in one draft—an

almost unheard-of *Meistertrunk* (masterly drinking feat). Former Mayor Nusch accepted the challenge, and he succeeded in downing the wine without pausing, although it took him ten minutes.

Tilly was as good as his word, and, after three days of blissful oblivion, Nusch revived to live to the ripe old age of 80. A colorful re-creation of this event is staged several times a year in the Kaisersaal of the Rathaus.

Drive: The Romantic Road

Tranquil countryside, the memory of great battles, natural curiosities, and, above all, an incomparable succession of historic towns make the Romantische Strasse, stretching 220 miles (350 km) from Würzburg in the Main Valley to Füssen in the Alps, Germany's most popular vacation route.

Start in the north on the first section of the specially signposted route leading from Würzburg (see pp. 261–262) along the B27 to **Tauberbischofsheim ❶**, a lovely medieval wine village located in the valley of the Tauber River. Follow the river upstream on the B290 to the spa town of **Bad Mergentheim ❷**, where the modern district contrasts with the old town and the Renaissance residence of the Grand Master of the Order of Teutonic Knights. From here,

NOT TO BE MISSED:

Riemenschneider altarpiece at Creglingen • A stroll in Rothenburg ob der Tauber • Deutsches Haus in Dinkelsbühl • View from the church tower in Nördlingen • Neuschwanstein Castle

the route brings you to **Weikersheim,** with the moated castle of the Hohenlohe family, and on to **Creglingen,** where the Herrgottskirche has the superb Altarpiece of the Virgin Mary carved in linden wood by Tilman Riemenschneider. The church in **Detwang** also has an altarpiece by Riemenschneider. Stop for a stroll in peerless **Rothenburg ob der Tauber ❸** (see pp. 263–265).

To the south of Rothenburg, medieval **Feuchtwangen ❹** has a fine old marketplace and Romanesque cloisters used for open-air performances in summer. Next, perfectly preserved within its tightly drawn ring of walls and towers, **Dinkelsbühl ❺** can still be entered only through one of its four gates. Within are grand old merchant houses such as the **Deutsches Haus** (Am Weinmarkt), with seven projecting stories reaching into its immense gable. The 15th-century **St. George's,** one of the finest town churches in southern Germany, has a wonderfully calm and lofty interior. Take a horse-drawn carriage tour through the town streets, then promenade around the ramparts. Dinkelsbühl's deliverance from destruction in the Thirty Years War is commemorated every year in July by a pageant, the Kinderzeche, celebrating the successful appeal made to the besieging commander by the town's children.

Taking a rest along the Romantische Strasse in Dinkelsbühl, a taste of the Middle Ages

Bavaria

As the route nears Nördlingen, it passes through a landscape almost devoid of woodland. This is the **Ries**, a circular crater 15.5 miles (25 km) across, formed by a giant meteorite some 15 million years ago. You can survey the area from the top of the 300-foot-high (90 m) tower of St. George's church in **Nördlingen** ❻, or find out more about the cosmic event that created it in the town's **Rieskrater-Museum** (Eugene-Shoemaker-Platz 1, tel 09081 84 710, closed Mon., $$). The tower also gives the best view over the oval-shaped town, whose glory days were between the 14th and 16th centuries, when its huge Whitsun fair attracted traders from all over Germany. A mighty ring of ramparts, with 16 towers and five gateways, still protects the streets radiating out from the central Markt-platz with its 13th-century Rathaus (Town Hall). In the **Municipal Museum** (Vordere Gerbergasse 1, tel 09081 84 810, stadtmuseum-noerdlingen.de, closed Mon., $$), 6,000 tin sol-diers still fight one of the great battles of the Thirty Years War, which took place outside the town in 1634.

From Nördlingen, the route reaches the Danube at **Donauwörth** ❼ then beyond Augsburg crosses the **Lechfeld**. In 955, this was the site of one of Europe's most decisive battles, when Otto the Great ended the pagan Hungarians' incursions and drove them back east. Beyond Landsberg, the foothills of the Alps begin, but before you reach the Aus-trian border at Füssen you will come to one of Germany's greatest romantic sights: King Lud-wig II's dreamlike castle of **Neuschwanstein** ❽, perched on its crag amid forests and waterfalls (see p. 307).

🇦 See also maps pp. 248–249, 280

➤ Würzburg

🕐 Minimum 3 days

↔ 220 miles (350 km)

➤ Füssen

Regensburg

This handsome city at the confluence of the Danube and Regen Rivers enjoys the atmosphere of a mellow provincial capital. The pace of life is leisurely, despite the presence of a university with more than 20,000 students. The city center suffered little wartime damage, and Regensburg was one of the first German cities to banish through-traffic, create pedestrian districts, and rehabilitate old buildings. In 2006, UNESCO declared the old town a World Heritage site.

Sturdy cutwaters protect the ancient arches of Regensburg's 12th-century Steinerne Brücke.

Regensburg

🅰 249 D2

Visitor Information

✉ Altes Rathaus, Rathausplatz 4

☎ 0941 507 44 10

regensburg.de /tourismus

As Castra Regina, Regensburg guarded the Roman Empire's northern frontier, and the labyrinthine pattern of narrow streets still reflects the grid traced by Roman surveyors.

In the Middle Ages, the city was the most important town in southern Germany. The wealthiest families built fortified tower houses in competition with one another. Some 30 of these unusual structures survive today.

Spanning the two arms of the Danube and 1,014 feet (309 m) long, the pedestrian **Steinerne Brücke** (Stone Bridge) was completed in the 12th century. It was said that only the help of the Devil made such a structure possible, and his fee was to claim the first soul to venture across. The wily citizens first sent across a dog, a cat, and a chicken.

The bridgehead on the city side is a fine sight: a gateway and clock tower flanked by solid-looking, high-roofed buildings, both of them storehouses for the salt on which much of the city's prosperity depended in the Middle Ages. The mouthwatering aroma in the area emanates from the **Historische Wurstküche** (*Thundorferstrasse 3, tel 0941 466 210, wurstkuchl.de*), the sausage kitchen whose tasty products are supposed to have fed the masons working on the bridge. You can still get sausages and sauerkraut there today.

To the west of the Dom is one of the grandest of the city's merchant houses, the **Heuporthaus,** now a restaurant, and farther west are fine examples of tower houses such as the **Goldener Turm** on Wahlenstrasse, the city's oldest named street. The Gothic and very picturesque **Altes Rathaus** (Old Town Hall) is where the German Reichstag met until it was dissolved by Napoleon in 1806.

To the east of the city center, the **Historisches Museum** (Historical Museum) has extensive collections relating to local history, but of greater interest are the paintings by Albrecht Altdorfer (ca 1480–1538), one of the first artists to treat landscape as a subject.

Dom
- ✉ Domplatz
- ☎ 0941 597 16 60
- 💲 $$ (guided tour)

Altes Rathaus
- ✉ Rathausplatz
- ☎ 0941 507 34 42 (guided tours)
- 💲 $$$

Historisches Museum
- ✉ Dachauplatz 2–4
- ☎ 0941 507 24 48
- 🕐 Closed Mon.
- 💲 $$

EXPERIENCE: Canoeing & Kayaking

About 25 miles (40 km) west of Regensburg lies the prettiest stretch of the Altmühl River. Between Pappenheim and Kipfenberg (see pp. 270–271) is a 35-mile (55 km) section of gentle bends that you can canoe or kayak. Drift past towering cliffs, oak forest, and lovely elderberry meadows, with castles peeking from the hilltops. There are occasional rapids and little dams. Virtually every town along the way has a boat rental, and for a small fee, staff will move you and your vessel to or from your point of departure. Among the best tour companies is **San-Aktiv Tours** (*Otto-Dietrich-Strasse 3, Gunzenhausen, tel 09831 49 36, san-aktiv-tours.de*).

Beyond the bridgehead soar the twin spires of Regensburg's Gothic **Dom** (Cathedral). Work began in the 13th century, but the lacelike stonework of the towers is a 19th-century addition. Art lovers come to admire the stained glass, the "laughing angel," and the other figures in the group of lovely late 13th-century statues depicting the Annunciation.

The southern part of the Altstadt (Old Town) is dominated by the **Schloss Thurn und Taxis,** the residence of the princely family that amassed a fortune in the 16th century by pioneering Europewide postal services. The palace has medieval cloisters, fine examples of the decorative arts, and a nice collection of coaches, carriages, sleighs, and sedan chairs. ■

Schloss Thurn und Taxis
- ✉ Emmeramsplatz 5
- ☎ 0941 504 81 33
- 🕐 Closed Dec.–March
- 💲 $$$–$$$$

thurnundtaxis.de

A Drive Along the Altmühl Valley

This full-day drive takes you along one of Germany's most unspoiled river valleys. The winding Altmühl has cut deeply into a limestone plateau, creating an ecologically rich and varied landscape of sheep-grazed pastures overlooked by limestone cliffs and interspersed with lovely villages, small towns, and crag-top castles.

Essing's timbered bridge across the Danube adds to the village's charm.

The drive begins at **Ellingen ❶**, 33.5 miles (54 km) south of Nuremberg just off the B2. The tiny town was largely rebuilt in the 18th century. Dominating the town is the great baroque Schloss, the former residence of the former commander of the Teutonic Knights. Continue along the old main road south to medieval **Weissenburg ❷**, which is bigger and has a nearly complete set of ramparts and gateways, and Roman remains (it guarded the northern frontier of the Empire's province of Rhaetia).

Continue south on the B2 for 7 miles (11 km), and turn left after a railway bridge onto the road through the Altmühl Valley. From here to Kelheim, the road follows the course of the river and forms part of the designated Ferienstrasse Alpen-Ostsee

NOT TO BE MISSED:

Jura-Museum in the Willibaldsburg
• Sight of Prunn castle perched
on its cliff • Essing's riverside
• Befreiungshalle at Kelheim

(Alps-to-Baltic Vacation Route). Almost completely surrounded by a bend in the river, well-preserved **Pappenheim ❸** is overlooked by its castle. Near Esslingen, the river curves past a series of rocks known as the Twelve Apostles, once part of a great reef on the edge of an ancient sea.

On your approach to the elegant Episcopal town of **Eichstätt ❹**, you will see the shining white Willibaldsburg standing on a wooded hill above town. The castle houses the **Jura-Museum** *(Willibaldsburg, tel 08421 47 30, closed Mon., $$)*, chronicling the geological history of the valley. You should also visit the **Informationszentrum Naturpark Altmühltal** *(Notre-Dame-Weg 1, tel 08421 9 87 60, naturpark-altmuehltal.de)*, located in a former monastery.

Main-Donaul-Kanal

Continue along the road toward Pfünz, past limestone cliffs around Arnsberg and beneath the A9 autobahn near Kinding. Beyond the town of **Beilngries ❺** and its hilltop palace of Hirschberg, the Altmühl becomes part of the Main-Danube waterway, the latest attempt to connect the North Sea river systems with those feeding southeastern Europe and the Black Sea.

The valley's spectacularly sited castle at **Prunn ❻** *(tel 09442 33 23, burg-prunn.de, closed Mon. winter, $$ guided tour)* is on a sheer cliff above the river. Just downstream, at **Essing ❼**, the idyllic riverside scene of village, watchtower, and ancient timber bridge has been perfectly preserved. But it is a stage set: The canalized Altmühl bypasses the village, and the "river" is an artificially fed lake.

The drive ends at **Kelheim ❽**, where the Altmühl joins the Danube. On the hilltop above the two rivers stands the **Befreiungshalle** or Hall of Liberation *(Auf dem Michelsberg, tel 09441 68 20 70, $)*, a neoclassic rotunda built by Ludwig I to mark the German victory over Napoleon in 1813. Inside, figures of the goddesses of Victory are flanked by shields made from melted-down French cannon.

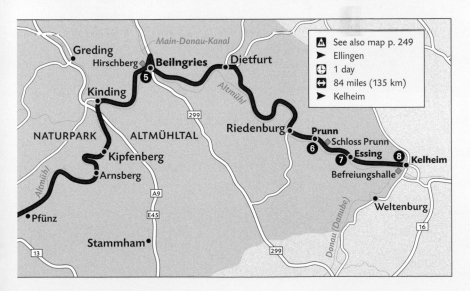

Augsburg

Founded in 15 B.C., this stately city was named after the Roman emperor Augustus. Between the 15th and 17th centuries, its banking dynasties dominated the finances of Central Europe, and the city was rebuilt, importing design ideas from Renaissance Italy. Martin Luther was active here, and it was also home to artists Hans Holbein the Elder and Younger, musician Leopold Mozart, and writer Bertolt Brecht. At the end of the 19th century, a revolutionary motor was perfected in the factory owned by one Rudolf Diesel.

The Herkulesbrunnen (Hercules Fountain) and Basilika St. Ulrich und Afra on Maximilianstrasse

Augsburg

🗺 249 C1

Visitor Information

✉ Rathausplatz

☎ 0821 50 20 70

augsburg-tourismus .de

The city's greatest son was financier Jakob Fugger (1459–1529), whose **Fuggerei,** an old people's housing project, was the first establishment of its kind in the world. A town within a town consisting of several dozen steep-roofed buildings, it still accommodates deserving old folk. Remember that the

Fuggerei is home to its residents and not a theme park; the only interiors open to the public are those of the little church and the Fuggerei-Museum.

Much fine architecture is in evidence around the central square, **Rathausplatz,** including the Renaissance **Augustusbrunnen,** one of the city's elaborate

INSIDER TIP:

Reserve an evening for König von Flandern, the oldest gastropub in Augsburg. This cavernous beer hall offers fresh brews and sumptuous fare.

—MELANIE IGNACIO
National Geographic contributor

fountains. In 1602, Elias Holl became city architect, and the Renaissance **Rathaus** (Town Hall) is his most ambitious creation, its pediment topped by a pinecone (part of the city arms) and flanked by onion-domed towers. Inside, the Goldener Saal (Golden Hall) is also redolent of municipal pomp. Holl gave a Renaissance gloss to the tall **Perlachturm** overlooking the square, disguising its Romanesque origins. Climb the 230-foot (70 m) tower for a view over the city.

Walk north from the square to Augsburg's **Dom** (Cathedral), which has Romanesque bronze doors and stained glass. The same distance westward is

St.-Anna-Kirche (St. Anne's Church), where the Fuggers are buried. Their chapel is one of the first examples of Italian Renaissance design in Germany.

The Fuggers lived on broad Maximilianstrasse running north–south through the city center. The **Fuggerhäuser** include a private bank and a luxury hotel. Farther along the street, by one of the city's finest fountains, the **Herkulesbrunnen,** is the **Schaezlerpalais.** Step inside this rococo palace to admire the gilded and painted plasterwork in the Festsaal (Banqueting Hall). In the palace are paintings of the 16th to 18th centuries, and earlier masterworks in the **Staatsgalerie** beyond *(same ticket),* among them a portrait of Jakob Fugger the Rich by Albrecht Dürer. The **Basilika St. Ulrich und Afra** (Church of Sts. Ulrich & Afra) closes off Maximilianstrasse to the south. Its Gothic nave leads to the tombs of the two local saints to whom the church is dedicated.

Augsburg's glorious art nouveau **Synagogue** complex survived the Nazi era. The museum deals with the history of the city's Jewish community. ∎

Fuggerei
- ✉ Fuggerei 56
- ☎ 0821 31 98 81 14
- $ $$ (incl. museum)
- **fugger.de**

König von Flandern
- ✉ Karolinestrasse 12
- ☎ 0821 15 80 50

Rathaus
- ✉ Rathausplatz 2
- ☎ 0821 324 91 96
- $ $

Perlachturm
- ✉ Rathausplatz
- ☎ 0821 502 07 0
- ⌚ Closed Nov.–April
- $ $

Staatsgalerie im Schaezlerpalais
- ✉ Maximilianstr. 46
- ☎ 0821 324 41 02
- ⌚ Closed Mon.
- $ $$
- **schaezlerpalais-augsburg.de**

Synagogue
- ✉ Halderstrasse 6–8
- ☎ 0821 51 36 58
- ⌚ Closed Mon. & Sat.
- $ $$ (museum)
- **jkmas.de**

Bavaria's Beers

Brewing in Germany has a long and illustrious tradition, and nowhere is it taken more seriously than in Bavaria. In 1156, when King Friedrich Barbarossa granted town rights to Augsburg, he stipulated that beer brewers would be punished for making poor suds. The German beer purity law (see p. 23) was later passed in Bavaria.

Some popular local varieties are *Weizenbier* or *Weissbier,* available as *Hefeweizen* (with a yeasty flavor) and the clear *Kristallweizen.* Seasonal beers include strong *Märzenbier,* a favorite at Munich's Oktoberfest. Northern Bavaria is known for its lightly carbonated, unfiltered *Kellerbier* and for *Rauchbier,* a dark brew with a smoky flavor.

Bavarian Forest

Between the valley of the Danube and Germany's border with the Czech Republic, the land rises gradually through lovely rolling farming countryside to the densely wooded ridges of the Bavarian Forest on the German side, and the Bohemian Forest on the Czech side. This is "Europe's Green Roof," reaching 4,777 feet (1,456 m) at the bare summit of the Grosser Arber and covering a total area of some 2,300 square miles (6,000 sq km).

A stream meanders through the thick Bavarian Forest near the Czech border.

Bavarian Forest
🅰 249 E2

Schnupftabak-museum
✉ Spitalstrasse, Grafenau
☎ 08552 21 00
🕐 Closed Mon. & Nov.–Dec.
💲 $

The heart of the forest is the **Nationalpark Bayerischer Wald** (Bavarian Forest National Park), where commercial woodland management has been halted. The harsh climate and poor soils forced the people of this peripheral region to supplement the traditional activities of timber-growing and upland farming with mining, metalworking, and—above all—glassmaking. Today tourism plays a vital role.

Most visitors are Germans looking for quiet and inexpensive vacations with fresh air and many opportunities to enjoy healthy pursuits such as walking, cycling, or, in winter, skiing. Follow their example and book accommodations in one of the villages with an onion-domed church and convenient swimming pool, rent a bike, and take your time to explore the local trails and towns.

INSIDER TIP:

In the Nationalpark Bayerischer Wald, be sure to wander through the virgin forest experience area of Mittelsteighütte and follow the canopy trails near Mount Lusen.

—KARL BARTHMANN
Nationalpark Bayerischer Wald

Most of the towns have a museum, though few are as quirky as Grafenau's **Schnupftabakmuseum:** It's devoted to the pleasures of snuff taking!

If possible, make your stay in the Bavarian Forest coincide with one of the folk festivals; the most spectacular is the Drachenstich—dragon-sticking—at Furth im Wald (just north of the park) during the second week in August.

If time is short, visit the national park interpretive center known as the **Hans-Eisenmann-Haus.** Then stop by the **Glasmuseum** at Frauenau, a wonderful collection of glass spanning three millennia and a celebration of a living local craft.

With the surrounding conifer-clad slopes reflected in its dark waters, the **Grosser Arbersee** seems to sum up the mystery and majesty of the region. Near the lake, a cable car (*arber.de*) whisks you up through the trees to the top of the Grosser Arber. The short walk to the summit is rewarded with fabulous views over the forested ridges. ∎

Hans-Eisenmann-Haus
- ✉ Böhmstrasse 35, Neuschönau
- ☎ 08558 9 61 50
- 🕐 Closed mid-Nov.–Dec.

nationalpark
-bayerischer-wald.de

Glasmuseum
- ✉ Am Museumspark 1, Frauenau
- ☎ 09926 94 10 20
- 🕐 Closed Mon.

glasmuseum
-frauenau.de

EXPERIENCE: Getting a Natural High

Billed as the "world's longest treetop trail," the stunning **Baumwipfelpfad** (*Biosphärenhaus, Königsbruch 1, Fischbach bei Dahn, tel 06393 92100, baumwipfelpfad .by, $$–$$$, limited access in winter*) near the Hans-Eisenmann-Haus (see above) lends new meaning to a walk in the woods. Running the best part of a mile (1.6 km), and rising as high as 82 feet (25 m) above the forest floor, this wide, elevated walkway is perched on a series of angular wooden stilts that blend seamlessly with the rich stock of spruce, beech, and firs of the Nationalpark Bayerischer Wald.

During the gentle but breathtaking ascent—the path zigzagging among the leafy crowns—you're treated to a crash course in the biosphere via a series of English-enabled information screens and a rush of natural wonder.

The undisputed highlight comes at the end, the celebrated viewing platform looking much like the chassis of a courtly skirt, but held aloft by a giant spring—it's a showcase of German engineering, although most of the technology is tastefully hidden away. A bridge from the treetop trail leads into the lower reaches of this fantastic structure. Here, a walkway corkscrews 131 feet (40 m) toward the clouds, affording a top-down view of the mighty firs within the dome's arched frame and panoramas reaching as far as the Alps in southern Bavaria.

Unveiled with great fanfare in 2009, the path is open daily year-round.

Passau

Few German cities have as distinctive a setting as Passau. Right on the border with Austria and overlooked by wooded heights, the old town stretches out on a narrow spit of land at the point where the Danube, the Inn, and the Ilz converge. The effect looks like some fantastical ocean liner, its prow breasting the waters of the triple rivers, its portholes the windows of the brightly painted houses, and its superstructure formed by the great cathedral. Visitors are invited aboard across a series of bridge-gangways.

A Danube riverboat makes its way upstream from the landing stage at Passau.

Passau

🅰 249 E1

Visitor Information

✉ Rathausplatz 3

☎ 0851 95 59 80

passau.de

Veste Oberhaus

✉ Oberhaus 125

☎ 0851 49 33 50

🕐 Closed early Jan.–mid-March

💲 $$ (museum)

oberhausmuseum.de

Drive or make the steep walk up to the **Veste Oberhaus,** the fortress cum palace built by Passau's powerful prince-bishops in the 13th century to keep an eye on the often unruly citizenry in the town below. The fortress contains an excellent regional museum, but the view of the three rivers is the star here.

There will probably be some activity on the water. Passau long ago lost its importance as a freight port, trading salt, cereals, and wine, but it is a starting point for riverboats going downstream to Vienna and on to Budapest, Belgrade, and the Black Sea.

The riverboats tie up by the **Rathaus** (Town Hall), with its tall tower and elaborately painted facade. Next door, in the Wilder Mann building, is the superlative **Glasmuseum** (Am Rathausturm, tel 0851 3 50 71, glasmuseum.de, $$), celebrating the traditional craft of the Bavarian Forest; it has an unsurpassed collection of Bohemian glass.

Walk east to the point where the rivers meet, then west past the bishops' neoclassic **Residenz** to the **Dom** (Cathedral), rebuilt in baroque style in the late 17th century; it reputedly contains the world's biggest organ. ■

More Places to Visit in Northern Bavaria

Aschaffenburg

The most northwesterly town in Bavaria, Aschaffenburg became part of the kingdom only in the early 19th century. Its previous rulers, the archbishops of Mainz, left a massive mark in the shape of their local residence. The red sandstone **Schloss Johannesburg** (*Schlossplatz 4, tel 06021 38 65 70, closed Mon., $$*), with four uncompromising-looking corner towers, was one of the most ambitious Renaissance buildings in Germany.

The archbishops were also enthusiastic landscapers, and their more modest summer residence of **Schönbusch** stands in an English-style park just outside town. King Ludwig I of Bavaria liked his new acquisition and came here often, calling it a "northern Nice." His particular contribution, reflecting his classical enthusiasms, was the **Pompejanum,** a re-creation of a Roman villa from Pompeii.

On the square known as **Stiftskirche** is an oddly appealing mishmash of Romanesque, Gothic, and baroque styles. The attached museum (*tel 06021 44 47 950, closed Mon., $*) is home to a 13th-century cloister and intriguing relics such as Germany's oldest chessboard. *info-aschaffenburg.de* 🅜 248 A4 ✉ Schlossplatz 1 ☎ 06021 39 58 00

Ingolstadt

Modern outskirts with an oil refinery and Audi factory give little hint of a distinguished old walled city with fine churches and civic buildings. Its ancient university—the setting for Mary Shelley's *Frankenstein*—was moved to Munich, but Ingolstadt upholds proud Bavarian traditions with its fascinating **Bayerisches Armeemuseum** (*Neues Schloss, Paradeplatz 4, tel 0841 9 37 70, armeemuseum.de, closed Mon., $*). The emphasis in this military museum, housed in the city's ducal palace, is on the glory and pageantry of long-forgotten battles.

About a mile north of town, very different hardware is on show at the **Audi Forum** (*Ettinger Strasse, tel 0800 283 44 44, $$*), where a high-tech museum traces the car's evolution from dainty 1899 jalopies to the latest sleek models. You can also join a factory tour. *ingolstadt-tourismus.de* 🅜 249 C2 ✉ Im Alten Rathaus, Rathausplatz 2 ☎ 0841 305 30 30

Schloss Weissenstein

Built between 1711 and 1718, the exquisite baroque palace Schloss Weissenstein (map 249 C3; *tel 09548 98180, pommersfelden.de, closed Nov.– March, $$ guided tours*) dominates the village of Pommersfelden. It continues to proclaim the wealth, power, and taste of Prince-Bishop Lothar Franz von Schönborn, ecclesiastical ruler of nearby Bamberg. A gifted amateur architect, he employed the very best designers of the day, Johann Dientzenhofer and Johann Lukas von Hildebrandt, court architect to the Hapsburgs. He himself may have been responsible for the palace's most original feature, the grandiose staircase that gives access to a series of splendid state rooms. The other most intriguing interior is the grottolike garden room, a fantasy of seashells and stucco figures.

Kloster Weltenburg

Unspoiled nature and sophisticated architecture join in supreme harmony at Kloster Weltenburg, Bavaria's oldest monastery, founded in the seventh century at the entrance to the Danube gorge above **Kelheim** (*kelheim.de*). Here, limestone cliffs squeeze the broad river into a channel one-quarter of the river's normal width and correspondingly deep; glorious beech woods complete the primeval-seeming scene. The Asam brothers, architect and painter Cosmas Damian (1686–1739) and sculptor Egid Quirin (1692–1750), rebuilt the monastery, outbuildings and all, in the early 18th century. The church is an unrivaled example of baroque theatricality. A mounted figure of St. George combating the dragon presides over the interior, the action enhanced by virtuoso use of natural lighting effects.

The ideal way of visiting the monastery, as well as its renowned beer garden is to walk the 3 miles (5 km) through the woods from Kelheim and then return by riverboat. But even if you arrive by car, get the boatman to ferry you to the far bank, so that you can climb the wooded slope to the ramparts of the Celtic stronghold high above and absorb the wonderful view. *klosterschenke-weltenburg.de* 🔼 249 D2 ✉ Asamstrasse 32, Kelheim/Donau ☎ 09441 20 40

Landshut

Little seems to have changed in this old provincial capital on the Isar River, once the seat of a branch of the powerful Bavarian Wittelsbach family (see p. 281), since its peak of fame in 1475. In that year, the wedding took place here between the ruler's son and Jadwiga, daughter of the King of Poland. Few nuptials have ever been celebrated on such a scale; with banquets, pageants, processions, feasts, and tournaments, the revelries lasted for days. In the early 20th century, the celebrations were revived, and since then, the **Landshuter Hochzeit,** one of Germany's biggest and most lavish popular festivals, has been held here every four years. The next one will take place in the summer of 2017. The town provides a perfect backdrop; high gabled

and arcaded houses line its gently curving main street, Altstadt. The scene is presided over by the 436-foot (133 m) brick-built tower (the tallest of its kind in the world) of the cathedral and by the ducal castle, **Burg Trausnitz,** on its crag above the town. But you don't need to come at festival time to fall under the spell of one of southern Germany's best preserved medieval towns. *landshut.de* 🔼 249 D1 ✉ Altstadt 315 ☎ 0871 92 20 50

Walhalla

A gleaming copy of the Parthenon in Athens, Greece, this temple high above the Danube is a monument to the great and good of German history, busts of whom adorn the sober interior. Like the **Hermannsdenkmal** in the Teutoburger Wald (see p. 173) and **Germania** above the Rhine at Rüdesheim (see p. 210), it is a key monument to the growth of German national feeling in the 19th century. However, Walhalla is less bombastic than these other creations, perhaps because it dates from an earlier phase. The brainchild of King Ludwig I of Bavaria (r. 1825–1848), it was conceived when he was a young man, begun in 1830, and completed in 1842. The name Walhalla is taken from Nordic mythology and refers to the resting place for the souls of battle heroes. Every German who visits here is able to find fault with the selection of "heroes"; some dubious characters are honored, and there are inexplicable omissions. In all, about 120 busts of famous soldiers, artists, scientists, and statesmen are here, along with 64 plaques of lesser known figures. Far from being a historical curiosity, Walhalla's pantheon is still being added to: The late Chancellor Konrad Adenauer (died 1967) has recently found a place of honor here. *walhalla-regensburg.de* 🔼 249 D2 ✉ Donaustauf bei Regensburg ☎ 09403 96 16 80 💲 $

Germany's most glamorous city, set against the rampart of the Bavarian Alps, with their crags, castles, and cozy mountain resorts

Munich & the Alps

Porcelain beer steins from Bavaria

Munich & the Alps

The Bavarian heartland of Munich and its Alpine background are the most beguiling part of the country. The Alps and their foothills are Germany's foremost vacation area, while the popularity of Munich has pushed house prices to an impossible height. Here alphorns and brass bands play in beer gardens, and you'll see men in lederhosen and buxom girls in dirndls. The landscape offers rocky peaks, rushing torrents, upland lakes, and grazing pastures; the village churches have onion domes, and people live in timber chalets.

The chalets, of course, are triple-glazed and well equipped, for Bavaria is far from being backward. BMW—Bavarian Motor Works—is not alone in standing for the advanced products and services characteristic of the region, and people migrate to Munich not just because of its beauty and its ideal location but also for hard-nosed career reasons. To convince yourself that Bavaria represents progress just as much as picturesqueness, arrange to arrive at Munich's Franz-Josef Strauss Flughafen, the most spectacularly modern airport in the country.

Bavaria now calls itself Freistaat Bayern, a Free State rather than a kingdom, but its strong

and distinctive identity can in part be attributed to the Wittelsbach dynasty, which reigned here for centuries, a far longer rule than any other German royal or noble family enjoyed. Its influence still pervades this core area of its domain; Munich is very obviously a royal capital, its Residenz crammed with treasures, its townscape shaped by kingly command.

Palaces and castles stud the landscape elsewhere, a good proportion of them the fantasies set in stone by "Mad" Ludwig II (1845–1886). He may have bankrupted the royal finances at the time, but he left Bavaria with a legacy of some of its most lucrative visitor attractions: the castles of Hohenschwangau, Linderhof, Herrenchiemsee, and above all Neuschwanstein, the very essence of a romantic crag-top stronghold. ∎

NOT TO BE MISSED:

The Bavarian dynasty's treasure trove at the Residenz **287**

A millennium of art at Munich's Pinakothek museums **291–297**

A stroll in the sprawling, folly-filled Englischer Garten **302**

King Ludwig's castles **305–307**

A trip on the Königssee **308–309**

The view from the Kehlsteinhaus **309**

The majestic solitude of the Deutsche Alpenstrasse **310–311**

Taking a breathless cable-car ride to the towering Zugspitze **314–315**

Munich

München, as the city is known in German, is situated within sight of the Alps. It is a handsome city, happily combining metropolitan facilities and sophisticated lifestyle with a small-town, homey atmosphere, symbolized to perfection by its smoky beer halls and cheerful beer gardens. It may not have quite as many millionaires as Hamburg, but some of its most stylish residents, male and female, are not ashamed to show themselves in city-slicker versions of *Tracht*, the characteristic Bavarian folk costume.

"*Eins, zwei, suffe!*"–a seasoned drinker makes a toast at Oktoberfest.

Munich
Ⓜ 281 E3

Visitor Information

✉ Hauptbahnhof (Main railway station, S side of main entrance); Marienplatz (Neues Rathaus)

☎ 089 23 39 65 00

muenchen-tourist.de

Munich benefited enormously from the presence of the Wittelsbach family (see p. 281). In addition to the spreading courtyards of their urban stronghold, the Residenz, the Wittelsbachs built out-of-town palaces at Nymphenburg and Schleissheim, decorating and furnishing them regardless of cost. In the 19th century, they turned Munich into one of Europe's great cities, endowing it with stately suburbs, grandiose public buildings, and world-class art galleries.

The superlative collections of the Alte and Neue Pinakotheken (Old and New Picture Galleries) continue to draw crowds and are occasionally supplemented by the

Pinakothek der Moderne (Gallery of Modernism), Germany's largest gallery of 20th-century and contemporary art. Art lovers will need more than one stay to see the treasures of these and the host of other collections and commercial galleries.

There are museums and institutions to suit every taste and interest. With its incomparable technical and scientific exhibits, the Deutsches Museum alone is enough to justify a visit, while other establishments cover the range from A (Anthropology Museum) to Z (the Zoo, one of the finest in Europe).

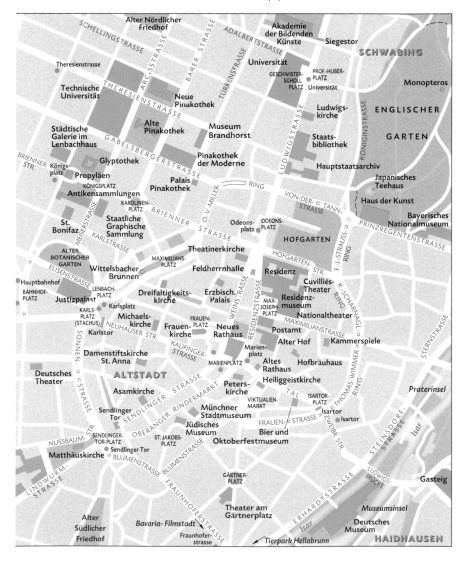

Munich's Marienplatz, center of city life

Visitors come here in huge numbers for the gargantuan Oktoberfest (see pp. 300–301), but festivals and events fill the calendar year-round. The city is maybe at its best in very early summer, when the sun shines brightly (but not too hotly) as you enjoy your half-liter of foaming beer in the shade of the chestnut trees and work up an appetite for a plateful of tasty Munich veal sausages, *Weisswurst.*

The Altstadt (Old Town)

Within its three remaining gateways—Isartor, Karlstor, and Sendlinger Tor—Munich's Altstadt is easily explored on foot; in the late 1960s and early 1970s, the city led the way in excluding unnecessary traffic and creating an attractive environment for pedestrians. Strolling through the tastefully repaved streets,

with their fountains, statuary, and immaculately restored buildings, is an experience you cannot fail to enjoy.

Start in busy **Marienplatz,** named for the Virgin Mary, whose lovely gilded statue stands atop the column erected in 1638 in the middle of the square. Throngs of tourists gather here (*at 11 a.m., noon, &, in summer, 5 p.m.*) to admire the **Glockenspiel.** It is set into the main facade of the **Neues Rathaus** (New City Hall), built in mock-Gothic style in the late 19th to early 20th centuries. After the bells of the carillon have played, mechanical figures appear and reenact two events: the traditional coopers' dance originally performed to ward off the plague, and a famous wedding celebrated in the square in 1568. The Rathaus has an elevator that will whisk you most of the way up its 262-foot-high (80 m) tower for a great view of the city.

The **Altes Rathaus** (Old City Hall) on the eastern side of the square is a genuine if much rebuilt Gothic structure; its tower has several floors of toys from times past. A taller tower looms over the square from the south; this is the belfry of Alter Peter ("Old Peter"), more properly known as **Peterskirche** (St. Peter's Church), Munich's oldest place of worship, with a wonderful baroque altar. The catwalk around the top of the tower gives a rooftop panorama, but note there are 306 steps to climb.

Hidden away in the lanes to the northeast of Marienplatz is the **Hofbräuhaus** (Court Brewery). It was established by Duke Wilhelm V in 1589 with orders to produce a beer to suit his personal palate. Only in the early 19th century were members of the public permitted to share his taste in ale. The cavernous beer hall, with its oompah band and dirndl-clad waitresses bearing an impossible number of giant mugs in both hands, still has its complement of local boozers. Nearby, the **Bier- und Oktoberfestmuseum** sheds light on two cornerstones of Bavarian culture and offers tastings.

To the west of the square is another sight: the brick-built **Frauenkirche** (Church of Our Lady), whose domed twin towers symbolize the city. From nearby, the scale of the building is almost overwhelming, with improbably tall, slim Gothic windows soaring skyward. Signs warn you not to stand too close in winter to avoid minor avalanches cascading from the roof. An elevator takes you up one of the church towers for another view of the city (closed for repairs until 2016).

To descend from these lofty heights into the belly of the city, walk south from Marienplatz to the **Viktualienmarkt.** This is probably Germany's most lively and colorful food market, its stalls peopled by square-jawed harpies with a great line in Bavarian banter. Don't even think of squeezing the goods or questioning the prices. The produce may not be cheap, but nearly all of it is of excellent quality and a feast for the eye as

Fashion Faves

Munich's sophisticated fashion scene routinely one-ups Berlin, Düsseldorf, and Hamburg, and the city center is stuffed with shops making cutting-edge statements in must-have apparel. Be on the lookout for venerable names like Bogner and Escada (see Travelwise p. 384), as well as some of the younger newcomers, such as the outdoors specialist Peak Performance, the top-end trends of Very Poolish, the Gypsy-inspired garments of Virmani, and the wild styles of Stierblut. All have outlets in Munich's fashion district in and around Maximilianstrasse, Theatinerstrasse, Residenzstrasse, and Briennerstrasse.

Altes Rathaus
- Map p. 283
- Marienplatz 15
- 089 29 40 01
- $$

spielzeugmuseum-muenchen.de

Peterskirche
- Map p. 283
- Rindermarkt 1
- 089 210 237 760

Bier- und Oktoberfestmuseum
- Map p. 283
- Sternecker Strasse 2
- 089 242 316 07
- Closed Mon.
- $$

Frauenkirche
- Map p. 283
- Frauenplatz 1
- 089 2 90 08 20
- Tower closed Sun. Elevator not operating Nov.–March
- $ (tower)

muenchner-dom.de

Barrelmakers perform as the Glockenspiel springs to life.

**Münchner
Stadtmuseum**

🗺 Map p. 283

✉ St-Jakobs-Platz
1

☎ 089 23 32 23 70

🕐 Closed Mon.

💲 $$

**stadtmuseum
-online.de**

Jüdisches Museum

🗺 Map p. 283

✉ St-Jakobs-Platz
13

☎ 089 233 96 096

🕐 Closed Mon.

💲 $$

**juedisches-museum
-muenchen.de**

well as the stomach. There are
plenty of places to snack.

Not far away is the superlative
Münchner Stadtmuseum (City
Historical Museum), where the
imaginatively presented exhibits
tell the story of the city in fascinating detail. The stars here are
the *Moriskentänzer,* wonderfully
contorted and expressive figures
of dancers carved in the late 15th
century, but it also has one of
the world's largest collections of
musical instruments; museums
dedicated to film, marionettes,
and beer; and a photographic
department.

In the modern cube opposite,
the **Jüdisches Museum** (Jewish
Museum) lays out the tapestry

of Munich's Jewish community.
Opened only in 2007—well
behind developments in other
German cities—it is geared toward
daily life, history, and culture
rather than the Holocaust. The
local Jewish community numbers
around 9,500, second in Germany
only to Berlin's.

Nearby on Sendlinger Strasse
stands the **Asamkirche,** a glorious
confection of a church named
not after a saint, but after the
Asam brothers who built it, Egid
Quirin (1692–1750) and Cosmas
Damian (1686–1739).

Residenz

Munich's Residenz, set around
seven courtyards in the northeastern part of the Old Town,
demonstrates the power, wealth,
and taste of Bavaria's Wittelsbach rulers. Employing the best
architects, designers, and deco-
rators, they built and rebuilt
their palace over the centuries,
lavishly decorating it and filling it with the results of their
collecting mania. Successful
restoration after World War II
bomb damage conceals the fact
that much of the Residenz is a
re-creation. Fortunately, most
of the contents, including the
interior of the Cuvilliés-Theater,
had been taken to safety.

In 1385 the Wittelsbachs
moved from their old home, the
Alter Hof, to the Residenz, then
a moated fortress on the edge of
town. Two hundred years later,
under Duke Albrecht V, it was
a setting for courtly life rather
than a fortress. In 1568, Albrecht
ordered the construction of the

Antiquarium, one of the largest, most extravagant Renaissance interiors north of the Alps. Its tunnel vault pierced by window openings allows natural light to illuminate the collection of antique sculpture. It is decorated with fantastical frescoes and views of Bavarian scenes to remind the rulers of their realm. Outside, the **Grottenhof** (Grotto Courtyard), presided over by a bronze Perseus fountain, was completed in 1591.

By the early 17th century, the Wittelsbachs were electors of the Holy Roman Empire, and Elector Maximilian I celebrated by creating a series of magnificent interiors around the **Kaiserhof** (Imperial Courtyard); these include the splendid **Kaisersaal** (Imperial Chamber), a great hall designed for the most prestigious state occasions.

To reinforce the status of his line, Elector Karl Albrecht commissioned 121 family portraits, even including such "ancestors" as the great Charlemagne. The pictures are displayed in the **Ahnengalerie** (Ancestors' Gallery), a rococo version of the Antiquarium with much stuccowork and elaborate carving. The equally sumptuous **Reiche Zimmer** (Rich Rooms) and **Grüne Galerie** (Green Gallery) are also in rococo style. These were largely the work of François Cuvilliés, Elector Maximilian III Joseph's court dwarf, who doubled as both architect and interior designer.

Following the demise of the monarchy in 1918, the complex passed to the Bavarian state and much of it is now open to the public. The Residenzmuseum entrance is on Max-Joseph-Platz, and you need most of a day to take everything in. Further highlights include the Royal Apartments, Porcelain Rooms, Court Chapel, and the Reliquary, Silver and Stone Rooms.

Treasury: Many of the treasures assembled by the Wittelsbachs over the centuries can be seen in the Schatzkammer (Treasury), one of the finest such collections of precious objects in the world. Among the most venerable items is an *altar ciborium* (Communion chalice) made a thousand years before the Bavarian crown jewels and commissioned from Napoleon's Parisian goldsmith in 1806.

Cuvilliés-Theater: Cuvilliés's greatest achievement was the court theater, which *(continued on p. 290)*

Residenz
 Map p. 283
✉ Residenzstrasse 1
☎ 089 29 06 71
💲 $$ (single tour), $$$ (combined tour), $$$$ (with Cuvilliés-Theater)
residenz-muenchen .de

Cuvilliés-Theater
🗺 Map p. 283
✉ Residenzstrasse 1
☎ 089 218 501

Munich Views

The Bavarian capital looks her best from these spots:

- **The bird's-eye panorama from Peterskirche (see p. 285)**
- **The Old Town's rooftops from the Frauenkirche (see p. 285)**
- **Englischer Garten sunbathers from the Monopteros (see p. 289)**
- **The Isar River from atop the Deutsches Museum (see pp. 295–297)**
- **The snowcapped Alps from the Olympiapark tower (see p. 304)**

A Walk from the Altstadt to Schwabing

This introduction to the historic core of Munich and its finest open space can be anything from a brisk stroll to a full day's exploration, with plenty of refreshment stops and time to take in some major attractions more fully.

A spectacular modern sculpture strides out along Schwabing's Leopoldstrasse.

The 14th-century **Karlstor** (Charles' Gate) ❶ and the crescent around it are almost like a piece of stage scenery, encouraging you to enter the old city center with a theatrical spring in your step. Before you stretches **Neuhauser Strasse,** traffic free since the 1970s and so full of activity that you wonder how it ever accommodated trams and cars. Among the delightful and unusual items you pass are the **Brunnenbuberl** (a fountain featuring a satyr and a naked boy) and the **Richard Strauss fountain** (with scenes from the Munich-born composer's opera *Salome*). Commercial buildings mix with noble edifices such as the **Bürgersaal** (Civic Hall); **Michaelskirche** (St. Michael's Church) ❷, the first Renaissance church of this size north of the Alps; and the Augustinerkirche, now home of the Deutsches Jagd- und Fischereimuseum (German Museum of Hunting and Fishing).

NOT TO BE MISSED:

Rathaus Glockenspiel • View from the Monopteros • A beer and pretzel at the Chinesischer Turm • Watching the action on Leopoldstrasse

Just to the north of St. Michael's rise the towers of the great symbol of Munich, the **Frauenkirche** ❸ (see p. 285).

Continue along the pedestrian-only precinct, now named Kaufingerstrasse, into the epicenter of the city, **Marienplatz** ❹. There's standing room only when the **Glockenspiel** in the Rathaus (City Hall) tower puts on its regular performances (see p. 284). Push through the crowd and turn left onto Dienerstrasse, which runs along the side of the Rathaus past, on the right, Dallmayers, one of the country's finest delicatessens. Beyond Max-Joseph-Platz with the Nationaltheater (state opera) and the **Residenz** (see pp. 286–287 & 290), Residenzstrasse leads to **Odeonsplatz** ❺, dominated by the graceful three-arched **Feldherrnhalle** (Commanders' Hall; see p. 298) and the swelling, ocher-colored forms of the baroque **Theatinerkirche** (see p. 298).

The café just ahead of you is one of the oldest in Munich. Just by it, a neoclassic archway leads into the arcaded **Hofgarten** ❻, the formally laid-out Renaissance garden of the Residenz. Cross it diagonally, past the black granite cube commemorating members of the anti-Nazi resistance, and go through the broad underpass to the **Englischer Garten** (see p. 302). Here you could explore the Japanese

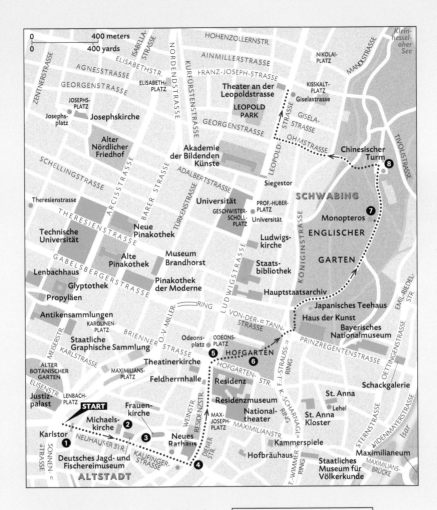

garden with its teahouse (Japanisches Teehaus), find a cool place by the river channel, or even strip off and enjoy some nude sunbathing on the meadow! Otherwise keep to the main path and walk up the spiral path to the top of the mound where the temple of the **Monopteros** ❼ offers a classic panorama of the city skyline rising over the trees.

Back at meadow level, continue by walking a short distance northward to one of the city's liveliest beer gardens, laid out around the pagoda-like **Chinesischer Turm** (Chinese Tower) ❽. From the upper floor, a brass band blares out on occasion.

- 🗺 See also map pp. 282–283
- ▶ Karlsplatz
- 🕐 Minimum half a day
- 🔄 3 miles (4.5 km)
- ▶ Leopoldstrasse

A little cheating is now allowed; take the No. 154 bus (every few minutes) two stops to **Leopoldstrasse,** the main artery of the **Schwabing** student district. There are many places here to sit and watch the scene, including the famous Roxy café, before taking the Metro home from Giselastrasse station.

Königsplatz
🅰 Map p. 283

Glyptothek
🅰 Map p. 283
✉ Königsplatz 3
☎ 089 28 61 00
🕐 Closed Mon.
💲 $$
www.antike-am-koenigsplatz.mwn.de

Antikensammlungen
🅰 Map p. 283
✉ Königsplatz 1
☎ 089 59 98 88 30
🕐 Closed Mon.
💲 $$
www.antike-am-koenigsplatz.mwn.de

now immortalizes his name. Reopened in the summer of 2008 after a lengthy makeover, the Cuvilliés-Theater is a jewel casket in red, white, and ivory, encapsulating in architectural form the rigors of court etiquette, with seating according to the exact rank and social status of the audience. The centerpiece is not really the stage, but the electors' box facing it from the far end of the auditorium. In this sublime space, Mozart's opera *Idomeneo* was given its first performance in 1781. The building could be used for more than performances, since its floor could be raised to create a magnificent ballroom.

Residenz Additions: The final large-scale extensions to the Residenz were made after Ludwig I acceded to the throne in 1825. Ludwig's architect, Leo von Klenze, added wings to north (the Festsaalbau facing the Hofgarten) and south (the Königsbau facing Max-Joseph-Platz). Klenze was also responsible for the apartments reserved for Ludwig and his queen, some of which are decorated with dramatic murals based on the Nibelung legends.

Königsplatz

Surrounded by the neoclassic buildings that proclaim Munich as an "Athens on the Isar," this square was laid out in the mid-19th century as the focal point of the museum district.

While still crown prince, Ludwig I collected Greek and Roman

sculpture, which was housed in Leo von Klenze's porticoed **Glyptothek** (1830), open to the public from the outset. One of the most moving pieces in the museum is the "Barberini Faun" (ca 220 B.C.), a study of a youngster overcome by drowsiness. Others range from figures controversially acquired from the Aphaia Temple of Aegina (fifth century B.C.) to busts of Roman notables.

The building opposite the Glyptothek now houses the **Antikensammlungen** (State Collections of Greek & Roman Antiquities). Its displays of Greek vases are unequaled elsewhere, and there are also fine Roman and Etruscan ceramics and jewelry.

The most striking structure on the square is Klenze's **Propyläen** gateway, modeled on one guarding the approach to the Acropolis at Athens and completed in 1862. The relief sculptures evoke the Greek wars of independence and commemorate the accession to the Greek throne of Otto, Ludwig's son.

The Nazis turned the square into a parade ground and location for mass ceremonies. A building at the eastern end of the square, now the College of Music, was the scene in 1938 of the signing of the Munich Agreement, which delivered up the Sudetenland to Hitler and sealed the fate of independent Czechoslovakia.

To the northwest of the Propyläen is the **Städtische Galerie im Lenbachhaus** (City Gallery in the Lenbach House). Built in 1889 as residence and studio by the successful society portraitist Franz von Lenbach, the Florentine villa is set in an authentic-looking Italian garden.

Marc, August Macke, and Alexei Jawlensky.

Alte Pinakothek

Many of Munich's finest museums and galleries lie northwest of the Altstadt, in the area now called **Kunstareal München** (Art Area Munich). In the first half of the 19th century, a district of streets and squares was laid out here as a dignified setting for the institutions that were to transform Munich into a world-class city of art. The royal collection of old master paintings was given a new home in the purpose-built

Städtische Galerie im Lenbachhaus
- Map p. 283
- Luisenstrasse 33
- 089 23 33 20 00
- Closed Mon.
- $$$

lenbachhaus.de

Alte Pinakothek
- Map p. 283
- Barer Strasse 27
- 089 23 80 52 16
- Closed Mon.
- $$$ ($$ during renovations)

pinakothek.de

EXPERIENCE: Becoming an Artist in Munich

Generations of artists, including members of the renowned Blaue Reiter group, have been inspired by the mind-opening architecture and expanses of the Bavarian capital. The tradition is still very much alive, and there are about as many art courses on offer as lederhosen.

Short-breakers are best served by two go-ahead art studios, **MachWerk** (Schulstrasse 1, tel 089 552 919 72, mach werk-muenchen.de) and **Atelierprojekt**

(Landwehrstrasse 39, tel 089 59 66 48, atelierprojekt.de). Both cater to beginners and advanced students and have an extensive range of courses lasting from a day or weekend to the entire summer. Costs cover tools and materials for painting, drawing, and sculpture and field trips for landscapes. Inquire about instruction conducted in English. Longer courses can culminate in a local exhibition of your best pieces.

The gallery presents the story of painting in Munich from the 18th century onward. Among the most appealing pictures are droll scenes of small-town life by Carl Spitzweg, and there are, of course, portraits by Lenbach. But the gallery's great draw are works by members of the Blaue Reiter group, with many colorful canvases by their leader, Wassily Kandinsky (1866–1944), and works by Paul Klee, Franz

palace of the **Alte Pinakothek** (Old Picture Gallery).

Here is one of the world's great collections of European art from the Middle Ages to the 18th century. Acquired over the centuries by the Wittelsbachs, the paintings are now on show in this Italian Renaissance-style palazzo. Commissioned by Ludwig I in 1822, the palazzo was built by architect Leo von Klenze and restored in the 1990s.

Neue Pinakothek

- 🅼 Map p. 283
- ✉ Barer Strasse 29 (enter Theresienstrasse)
- ☎ 089 23 80 51 95
- 🕐 Closed Tues.
- 💲 $$

pinakothek.de

Rooms XI–XIII on the lower floor hold **early German painting,** such as the "Nativity" by Hans Baldung Grien (1484–1545), with its cherubs and farm animals. Works of the **Brueghel family** occupy Rooms XVI–XXIII. Pieter Brueghel the Elder's "Land of Cockayne" fascinates visitors, with its sated guzzlers sleeping off their gluttony in a landscape of roast pigs and boiled eggs on legs.

On the upper floor, you can trace the development of **Italian Renaissance art** in Rooms IV–V from its beginnings to the achievements of Botticelli, Raphael, and Titian. Rooms XI and XIIa hold **French works** by Poussin, Claude Lorrain, and a lovely "Nude" by Boucher, and the **Spanish masters** El Greco, Murillo, and Goya hang in Room XIII. There are outstanding paintings by **Flemish and Dutch masters,** particularly Rubens, in Rooms VI–IX.

If time is limited, concentrate on the great **German artists** (Rooms II–III), often less well represented in galleries outside Germany. Of several pictures by Albrecht Dürer, the most striking is the "Self-portrait in a Fur Coat," while an ideal of feminine beauty seems to obsess Lucas Cranach the Elder in "The Death of Lucretia." No one has depicted the dynamics of human suffering and cruelty with more feeling than Matthias Grünewald in his "Mocking of Christ" (1503), and there are few more evocative depictions of the German forest than Albrecht Altdorfer's tiny picture of "St. George and the Dragon" deep in the beech woods. Altdorfer worked on a grander scale in the "Battle of Alexander" (1529), where countless combatants fight in an apocalyptic landscape.

Neue Pinakothek

A 1981 monumental concrete, granite, and sandstone structure, sometimes called the "Palazzo Branca" after its architect Alexander von Branca, more than matches the older buildings in the museum district as a setting for the **Neue Pinakothek** (New Picture Gallery) and its fine art. It's worthwhile spending a few minutes strolling around the outside of this outstanding building, set off by fine trees, the modern equivalent of a moat, and some choice sculpture.

Museum Brandhorst

Focusing on 20th-century art, especially in illustrated books and literature, the Museum Brandhorst (Theresienstrasse 35a, tel 089 238 052 286, museum-brandhorst.de, closed Mon., $$, $ on Sun.), next to the Pinakothek der Moderne, has 112 editions illustrated by Picasso, as well as pieces by Joan Miró and Kurt Schwitters. Among the hundreds of paintings, sculptures, and drawings, you'll find works by Andy Warhol, calligraphic artist Cy Twombly, and modernists Damien Hirst and Gerhard Richter.

Albrecht Dürer's "Self-Portrait in a Fur Coat" (1500) at the Alte Pinakothek

The suggested route around the collection takes you in more or less chronological order from late 18th-century paintings to the work of the French Impressionists. But the emphasis is on German art of the 19th and early 20th centuries. This is the place to admire Romantic works by artists such as Caspar David Friedrich (1774–1840; Room 9), best represented by his picture of the mysteriously fogbound Giant Mountains on the borders of Silesia and Bohemia.

More soberly factual, yet equally compelling, are the carefully composed pictures by Wilhelm von Kobell (1766–1853),

such as his "Siege of Kosel" of 1808. Ludwig Richter's (1803–1884) "Watzmann" (Room 5) contains the essential ingredients of Alpine scenery, including crashing waterfalls, upland pastures, and rustic peasants. In Room 10a you'll find evocations of small-town life and human eccentricity by Carl Spitzweg (1808–1885), among them the "Poor Poet" and the "Nightly Round," in which a pot-bellied officer leads his platoon through the dusk of an obviously law-abiding little place.

In contrast are large history and landscape paintings (Rooms 12, 13, 14/14a) by, for example, Karl von Piloty (1826–1886).

Pinakothek der Moderne

- 🅰 Map p. 283
- ✉ Barer Strasse 40
- ☎ 089 23 80 53 60
- 🕐 Closed Mon.
- 💲 $$$ (Sun. $)

pinakothek.de

Palais Pinakothek

- 🅰 Map p. 283
- ✉ Türkenstrasse 4
- ☎ 089 23 80 51 98
- 🕐 Varies by program
- 💲 $$–$$$

pinakothek.de

There are interesting works by German contemporaries of the French Impressionists in Rooms 18–20: Take time to look at pictures such as realist Wilhelm Leibl's (1844–1900) "Interior with Peasants," and the cheerful "Munich Beer Garden" by Max Liebermann (1847–1935), leader of the German Impressionists. But don't let yourself be seduced by the snake-entwined, extremely sexy "Sin" by Franz von Stuck (1863–1928).

INSIDER TIP:

Have a budding Monet in the family? The Palais Pinakothek is a delightful hands-on arts center that gets kids painting while you peruse the nearby Pinakothek museums.

—JEREMY GRAY
National Geographic author

Pinakothek der Moderne

Opened in 2002, the Gallery of Modernism is the country's largest gallery of modern and contemporary art, a conscious rival to the Centre Pompidou in Paris and London's Tate Modern. A superb new home for several previously separate collections, it has been designed to act as an architectural link between the city center and the buildings and squares of the museum district.

This latest of the Pinakotheken may have a bland exterior, but

few visitors quibble with its cool, elegant display spaces, all wonderfully lit by natural light. The core of the building is a 46-foot (14 m) rotunda, celebrating the unity in diversity of the arts.

The main collection is that of the **Staatsgalerie Moderner Kunst** (Bavarian State Gallery of Modern Art), a world-class array of 20th- and 21st-century painting, sculpture, photography, new media, and installations. It is rich in paintings by German artists of the early 20th century, such as Max Beckmann, Wassily Kandinsky, and Paul Klee. There are also works by surrealists such as René Magritte, examples of American abstract expressionism, minimal and concept art, an Andy Warhol collection, video works, and a huge installation by Joseph Beuys entitled "The End of the Twentieth Century."

The vast number of items assembled in the gallery's **Neue Sammlung** (New Collection) is claimed to be the most comprehensive collection of design and craft objects in the world. Among the treasures of the **Architekturmuseum** (Architecture Museum) are original drawings by Frank Lloyd Wright, as well as countless photographs and 500 models tracing the development of contemporary architecture.

Finally, the **Staatliche Graphische Sammlung** (Bavarian State Graphic Collection) comprises an outstanding array of more than 400,000 drawings and prints from the 15th century to the present day.

Deutsches Museum

On its island site between two arms of the Isar River, this enormous and interactive museum of science and technology is one of the most popular attractions in the country and the most visited museum in Munich.

At every turn there are chances to press a button, set a model in motion, watch a film, or take part in a demonstration. Children will not want to tear themselves away, but the "masterpieces of science and technology" to enlighten and stimulate the public. Kaiser Wilhelm II laid the foundation stone of the museum in 1904, but the great institution opened only in 1925. Since then its buildings have become one of Munich's landmarks, not least the distinctive tower overlooking the Isar, complete with barometer.

There are a number of highlights you should not miss. The **Aeronautics Halls** on the first

Deutsches Museum

🅰 Map p. 283
✉ Museumsinsel 1
☎ 089 2 17 91
💲 $$$

deutsches-museum.de

A 1932 Junkers Ju-52 is one of dozens of original airplanes on display in the Deutsches Museum.

well-stocked gift shop stays open an hour after closing.

The floor plan on p. 296 may help you decide priorities. Details of daily demonstrations and film showings are given in the foyer, and you could use these as a starting point to structure your visit.

The museum was the brainchild of visionary engineer Oskar von Miller. In 1903 he founded an association to showcase the and second floors are filled with flying machines, such as Otto Lilienthal's revolutionary gliders and the monoplanes and biplanes (even triplanes!) that fought above the trenches from 1914 to 1918. There are fighters from World War II as well.

Everybody thrills to the 800,000-volt flash of lightning produced in the **Electrical Power** department in Hall 9, first

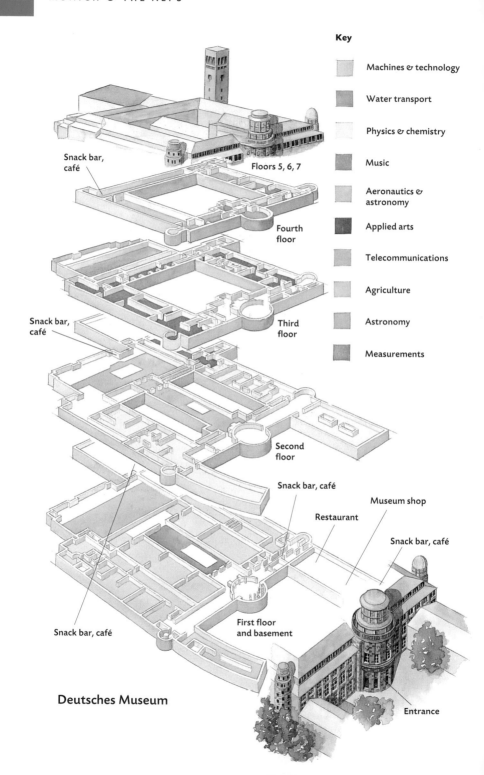

Key

- Machines & technology
- Water transport
- Physics & chemistry
- Music
- Aeronautics & astronomy
- Applied arts
- Telecommunications
- Agriculture
- Astronomy
- Measurements

Snack bar, café

Floors 5, 6, 7

Fourth floor

Snack bar, café

Third floor

Second floor

Snack bar, café

Snack bar, café

Museum shop

Restaurant

Snack bar, café

Snack bar, café

First floor and basement

Deutsches Museum

Entrance

floor, even if it lasts for only two microseconds. In the **Power Machinery** room, you can see a working reproduction of Rudolf Diesel's first engine (1897) and some early motors by Gottlieb Daimler. You can also see Germany's first submarine, the U1, in the **Navigation Department** or peer into the crowded interior of a 19th-century emigrant boat, lit by kerosene lamps. The basement holds a popular **reconstruction of a mine** and the **Kid's Kingdom,** with such hands-on fun as an electric light cinema, a giant guitar, and a canal with moveable locks.

On the second floor, the **Musical Instruments** section has a "Phonolizt," a player piano contraption with violins, and some of the first synthesizers. The sound booths allow you to listen to simulations of famous concerts and analyze your own voice. This section extends to the third floor, which houses whiz-bang displays of **Astronautics** and **Technical Toys.** Then it's up through the remaining floors, with **Telecommunications** on the fourth, the **Planetarium** on the seventh, and much, much more.

The museum's rolling stock has been shifted to the **Deutsches Museum Verkehrszentrum** (German Transport Center), an airy, ever expanding gallery in a historic former trade fair hall overlooking the Theresienwiese. Among the **railway vehicles** on display, the pioneering *Puffing Billy* of 1814 contrasts with the resplendent green locomotives

of the Royal Bavarian Railways built a century later, which hauled the Rhinegold Express. Germany was in the forefront of electric traction, although the first electric locomotive of 1879 looks more like a mobile park bench.

INSIDER TIP:

Don't miss the mining section in the Deutsches Museum; you'll enter tunnels and shafts that appear true to life.

—BARBARA A. NOE
National Geographic Travel Books senior editor

The **motor vehicles** section is stuffed with gems, including the Benz Motorwagen of 1886, the first motor vehicle powered by a gasoline engine and the forerunner of today's automobiles. Only a hundred or so models were made of the gorgeous 1929 Mercedes-Benz Tourenwagen Super-Sport, and for sheer oddity you can't beat the weird Krupp three-wheeled street-cleaner of around the same time. The small-fry will enjoy the pint-size **indoor racetrack,** where the roadsters are self-assembled from toy kits.

North Along Ludwigstrasse

Much of the vibrant life of Munich's city center is in the area beyond the Residenz, where elegant Ludwigstrasse heads north toward the old

Deutsches Museum Verkehrszentrum

✉ Am Bavariapark 5

☎ 089 500 806 762

💲 $$

🚇 U-Bahn: Schwanthaler Höhe

deutsches-museum .de

Englischer Garten sunbathers cool off in the Isar.

suburb of Schwabing. A variety of establishments serves this fashionable area's highly variegated population, from antiquarian bookshops to experimental galleries, and there are cafés, "alternative" eating places, and every possible kind of bar.

From Odeonsplatz, beside the Residenz, **Ludwigstrasse** runs north. Named after that indefatigable city improver King Ludwig I, whose statue stands on the western side of Odeonsplatz, Ludwigstrasse is the grandest thoroughfare in Munich. At its southern end stand the three great arches of the **Feldherrnhalle** (Commanders' Hall). Modeled on the famous Loggia dei Lanzi in Florence, it was built on Ludwig's orders to honor the Bavarian army and its generals. History remembers it more as the focus

of Hitler's failed Putsch in 1923, when the march he was leading was dispersed by rifle-fire from the police. After the Nazis' rise to power it became a place of sacred memory. Anti-Nazis would avoid giving the obligatory raised-arm salute by detouring through little Viscardigasse, henceforth known as Shirkers' Alley.

West of the Feldherrnhalle rises the resplendent baroque **Theatinerkirche,** one of Munich's best loved places of worship. The church is named after the order of Theatine monks founded in the 16th century to oppose Lutheranism. A landmark with its bold ocher facade, dome, and twin towers, it was built to celebrate the birth in 1662 of a son and heir to the Bavarian elector, and the gorgeously decorated interior surely reflects the parents' joy.

University & Around

Farther north on Ludwigstrassse, the Theatinerkirche's towers are echoed by the twin towers of the 1844 **Ludwigskirche**. Inside, the mural painting of the Last Judgment by Peter Cornelius (1783–1867) is only exceeded in size by Michelangelo's treatment of the same subject in the Vatican's Sistine Chapel. The church's neighbor to the south is the immensely long **Staatsbibliothek** (Bavarian State Library). To the north, where Ludwigstrasse opens out into a kind of forum with fountains, is the **university,** one of the biggest in Germany, transferred from Landshut (see p. 278) by Ludwig I in 1826. Among those who have taught within its walls have been physicist Wilhelm Konrad Röntgen, discoverer of X-rays, the groundbreaking 19th-century chemist Justus von Liebig, humanist philosopher Ludwig Andreas Feuerbach, and sociologist and political economist Max Weber. Its most famous students were the members of the White Rose, a group of anti-Nazi activists executed in 1943. The **Siegestor** arch, topped by four lions, makes a fitting climax to Ludwigstrasse.

Prinzregentenstrasse

A busy road cuts across Ludwigstrasse just north of the Residenz, becoming to the east **Prinzregentenstrasse.** The last royal boulevard to be built in Munich, it was laid out in the 1890s on the orders of Luitpold, the prince regent. Its formerly pleasing relationship with the Englischer Garten was spoiled when the **Haus der Kunst** (House of Art) was built in typical Third Reich style in the 1930s. Once the home of the State Gallery of Modern Art (now in the Pinakothek der Moderne), it is used for temporary exhibitions.

Its much jollier neighbor, in an exuberant variety of styles, is the **Bayerisches Nationalmuseum,** Bavaria's state museum of arts and crafts from the Middle Ages to the 19th century.

(continued on p. 302)

Ludwigskirche
- Map p. 283
- Ludwigstrasse 22
- 089 287 799

Haus der Kunst
- Map p. 283
- Prinzregentenstrasse 1
- 089 2 11 27 113
- $$$$

hausderkunst.de

Bayerisches Nationalmuseum
- Map p. 283
- Prinzregentenstrasse 3
- 089 2 11 24 01
- Closed Mon.
- $$

bayerisches
-nationalmuseum.de

EXPERIENCE: Rafting on the Isar River

In the good old days, log rafts in Bavaria were used to transport bulky goods, but that tradition has passed firmly into the hands of recreation seekers. Fed by Alpine streams, the pristine, frigid Isar River has a long history of log rafting, and the simple vessels are built much as they were a century ago. From May to September, tour operators run rafting trips from the town of Wolfratshausen, 23 miles (37 km) south of Munich, back to the Bavarian capital. The grand day out typically involves a Bavarian breakfast (think weisswurst and big pretzels), draft beer, and a few musicians drafted to play oompah tunes.

The fun is orchestrated by firms like **Isar Flossfahrten** (*Münchner Freiheit 6, tel 089 340772 300, isarflossfahrten.biz*). One of the most imaginative options is available from **Montevia** (*Bergbahnstrasse 1, Lenggries, tel 08042 972400, montevia .de*), which helps you strap together your own raft before taking the crew down the river.

Oktoberfest

"Eins, zwei, suffe"—roughly, "One, two, swallow"—is the joyous refrain of the best known Bavarian drinking song. You're likely to hear it more than once if you attend what is claimed to be the biggest folk festival in the world.

The Bavarian state colors, blue and white, bedeck one of Oktoberfest's huge beer tents.

Oktoberfest begins on the last Saturday in September and lasts for 16 beery days into October. More than six million drinkers pour into the city, cramming into the tents set up on the great meadow known as the Theresienwiese and consuming around 1.8 million gallons (7 mL) of beer, over half a million roast chickens, 150,000 pairs of sausages, more than a hundred oxen, nearly 70,000 pork knuckles, and an incalculable number of pretzels. And it's all accompanied by

raucous brass bands called *Blaskapellen*.

Like so much else about Munich, all this can be blamed on King Ludwig I. In 1810, while still crown prince, he marked his marriage to Princess Therese von Sachsen-Hildburghausen by inviting the citizenry to celebrations. These culminated in a horse race in what was then open countryside, but was subsequently named "Theresa's Meadow" in the bride's honor. The festivities became an annual event, expanding to fairground attractions and beer-drinking.

INSIDER TIP:

Munich's Oktoberfest is one of the world's best loved festivals— and one of the most crowded. You can beat the throngs by reserving a table in a tent— check out *oktoberfest.de/en /navitem/Tents* for details.

—JEANNE HORAK-DUFF
National Geographic contributor

A brass band, the musical backdrop behind every good Oktoberfest

Celebrating Oktoberfest

Nowadays things begin on the opening Saturday with a parade of splendidly bedecked horse-drawn wagons carrying brewery landlords, brass bands, and dirndl-clad waitresses. At the stroke of noon, the Lord Mayor of Munich broaches the first barrel with a cry of *"O'zapft is!"* (Bavarian for "It's tapped!"). In the evening, there is a folklore concert that serves as a warm-up for another, much bigger procession the following day. This is the International Costume and Riflemen's Parade, which winds through the city center to the Theresienwiese in a seemingly never-ending succession of spectacularly costumed bands, mountain marksmen, jesters, folklore groups, and carriages drawn by horses, oxen, and goats. Once the parade has reached its destination, the fortnight's drinking can really get under way, presided over by the statue of "Bavaria," a 100-foot-high (30 m) bronze figure of a female clad in a bearskin.

Oktoberfest is still a quintessentially Bavarian celebration, and the majority of your fellow drinkers will be shouting in a dialect that even other Germans find incomprehensible. The beer tents are no place for the fainthearted: The benches are packed, the noise level is high, and the exuberance increases as the evening advances. If you consider venturing on to any of the fairground's white-knuckle rides, you are strongly advised to consider the state of your stomach—even though most Bavarian beer is not particularly strong.

The city of Munich fills up for Oktoberfest. If you intend to come, book accommodations well in advance, and think seriously about reserving a seat for the Saturday evening folklore concert or a grandstand place for the opening ceremony and the Sunday parade *(München Ticket GmbH, tel 0180 54 81 81 81 or 089 54 81 81 81 from abroad, muenchenticket.de)*.

Other German Festivals

All are celebrated with gusto:
- Karneval foolery in the Rhineland (see pp. 158–159)
- Bonn's concert extravaganza, the Beethoven Festival (see p. 162)
- Summer wine festivals along the Rhine and Moselle (see pp. 180–185)
- The witches' sabbath on Walpurgisnacht (see p. 218)
- The bombastic charm of Bayreuth's Wagner Festival (see p. 259)
- For those who miss Oktoberfest, the revelry in Bad Cannstatt (see p. 323)

Schloss Nymphenburg

🅰 281 E3

✉ Schloss- und Gartenver- waltung Nymphenburg

☎ 089 17 90 80

💲 $$$$ (combined ticket for all buildings)

schloss -nymphenburg.de

The lovingly carved Nativity scenes are a highlight.

East of Ludwigstrasse and north of Prinzregentenstrasse, the beautiful **Englischer Garten,** 3 miles (5 km) long and covering just over 1,000 acres (417 ha), was laid out in the 18th century. Today people come here from all over the city to breathe fresh air, row a boat, ride a bike or horse, enjoy a drink in the huge beer garden, or perhaps strip for an allover tan.

Perfect Porcelain

Schloss Nymphenburg's delicate porcelain is deservedly famous. The Marstall's upper rooms contain more than a thousand examples made between the 1740s and the 1920s. Some of the most appealing are the winsome, witty figures from the Italian comme- dia dell'arte, created in the mid-18th century.

Schloss Nymphenburg

This palace on the western out- skirts of Munich was originally conceived as a hunting lodge and later expanded on a grand scale to become an embodi- ment of the Bavarian rulers' status and style. While its exte- rior is fashioned in a subdued baroque style, the interior features rococo colors and flamboyant frescoes that are a delight to the eye. And don't miss a tour of the 500-acre

(200 ha) park, a virtual history of landscape gardening.

The Schloss is easily accessible from Munich's center by U-Bahn and tram. As you arrive from the east, Nymphenburg is a long line of harmoniously related buildings facing a formal lake and a semicircular road bor- dered with what were once the residences of court officials. The central palace building grew out of a much smaller structure of 1664, a cubelike summer residence erected, like the Theatinerkirche in town, to celebrate the birth to Electress Henriette Adelaide of a son, Max Emanuel. On his accession to power, Max enlarged the build- ing, endowing it with the **Stein- erner Saal,** one of Germany's most opulent rococo interiors.

Ludwig I added the most popular interior feature to the Schloss; his **Schönheitengalerie,** with its portraits of three dozen women, was intended to pres- ent a definitive view of ideal femininity. It was no coincidence that it included a representation of Lola Montez, the "Spanish dancer" whose affair with the king forced his abdication.

The Park: From the double stairway on the palace's far side you can enjoy a view of Nymphenburg's park. A French- style parterre occupies the foreground, while a rectilinear canal leads the eye into the far distance. These are remnants of the original geometrical garden. In the early 19th century it was relandscaped in the informal

English style, with winding pathways, serpentine lakes, and "naturalistic" planting.

The **Amalienburg,** a perfectly proportioned miniature rococo palace by Cuvilliés, is to the left. The interior, especially the Hall of Mirrors, is a masterpiece of rococo fantasy, with writhing silver stuccowork running riot everywhere. Beyond is the **Badenburg,** built to house a lavishly decorated heated indoor swimming pool. North of the canal is the **Pagodenburg,** containing exquisite interiors reflecting European courtly interest in chinoiserie. Max Emanuel built the Pagodenburg with parties in mind, but the later **Magdalenenklause** reflects the aging ruler's preoccupation with more serious matters. It is an artificial ruin, designed for the contemplation of mortality and eternal verities.

Two quadrangles flank the central palace buildings. To the south is the **Marstall.** Built as the stables, it now houses the vehicles used by the Wittelsbachs. In winter, sleighs were used; one of the most spectacular examples here is a fabulous rococo creation of 1740. The state coaches are even more stylish, notably the one made for Elector Karl Albrecht when he was promoted to Holy Roman Emperor in 1742. Here, too, you'll find a display of the palace's famous porcelain (see sidebar opposite).

A very different museum occupies the northern quadrangle; the **Museum Mensch und Natur** uses multimedia and hands-on techniques to tell the tale of Earth's history and mankind's evolution.

Visit the adjacent **Botanischer Garten** to see one of Europe's finest botanical collections. ∎

Museum Mensch und Natur

- ✉ Schloss Nymphenburg
- ☎ 089 179 58 90
- 🕐 Closed Mon.
- 💲 $

musmn.de

Botanischer Garten

- ✉ Menzinger Strasse 61–65
- ☎ 089 178 61 310
- 💲 $$

botmuc.de

The modest baroque exterior of Schloss Nymphenburg fronts formal gardens and a lake.

More Places to Visit in Munich

BMW Museum

The gleaming metallic BMW headquarters building in the shape of a four-cylinder engine has been a Munich landmark since the 1970s. At its foot, the famous automobile manufacturer has installed its museum in an equally distinctive structure, a great silver chalice. No expense has been spared to create an exhibit with the same standard of technical excellence as the vehicles themselves, with all kinds of presentational wizardry to repeat the message of mobility as progress. *bmw-museum.de* Map p. 282 ✉ Am Olympiapark 2 ☎ 089 1250 160 01 🕐 Closed Mon. 💲 $$$

INSIDER TIP:

While access to Dachau is free, consider renting the audio tour in English, which provides in-depth historical information.

—ELIZABETH BARRETT

National Geographic international rights specialist

Dachau

In Renaissance times, the Wittelsbachs built a summer castle in this pretty town 12 miles (19 km) northwest of Munich. In the 19th century an artists' colony thrived here, attracted by the picturesque streets and the special light effects of the countryside around. Later, ordinary Munich residents would take the suburban train and escape the city's stuffy air in these peaceful surroundings. In March 1933 the rural idyll was grotesquely interrupted when the Nazis built their first concentration camp just outside the town. It is now a memorial to the tens of thousands who suffered and died here, and a tour of the site with its execution ground, crematoria, rebuilt

barracks, and museum is an experience not easily forgotten. *kz-gedenkstaette-dachau.de* 🗺 281 E4 ✉ Pater-Roth-Strasse 2a, Dachau ☎ 08131 66 99 70 �e S-Bahn 2

Olympiapark

The Oberwiesenfeld on the northern edge of town was originally an army parade ground, then the site of Munich's first airport. In 1972, after being relandscaped and linked to the Metro, it hosted the 20th Summer Olympics, leaving the city with a new park and superb sporting and recreational facilities. The 69,250-seat stadium, the Olympic Hall, and the swimming pool sit beneath a tentlike transparent roof tethered by cables *(tel 089 30 67 27 07, tours)*. For an incomparable panorama that on a good day takes in a 250-mile (400 km) sweep of the Alps, ride the elevator to the viewing platform of the 950-foot (290 m) Olympic Tower. *olympiapark -muenchen.de* 🗺 281 E3 ✉ Spiridon-Louis-Ring 21 ☎ 089 30 670 💲 $$ (tower) 🚇 U-Bahn 3

Schleissheim

Nine miles (15 km) north of Munich await the village of Schleissheim and the palace and park complex of Schloss Schleissheim. Behind the long facade of the **Neues Schloss** *(Max-Emanuel-Platz 1, Oberschleissheim, tel 089 3 15 87 20, schloesser-schleisheim.de, closed Mon., $$$)* are sumptuous interiors and baroque paintings. The smaller **Altes Schloss** houses a collection of religious folk art, while at the far end of the gardens, **Schloss Lustheim** is now the setting for a collection of mostly 18th-century Meissen porcelain. Nearby **Flugwerft Schleissheim** is an airfield *(tel 089 3 15 71 40, deutsches-museum.de, $$)* with 50 or so historic aircraft on display. 🗺 281 E4 �e S-Bahn 1 to Oberschleissheim

The Alps

Germany possesses only a small section of the Alps, a relatively narrow strip running the 200 miles (300 km) or so from the Berchtesgadener *Land* in the east through the Allgäuer Alpen in Bavarian Swabia to the Bodensee (Lake Constance) in the west. But, rising from the Bavarian lowlands, this band of mountains has a dramatic impact out of proportion to its height, which nowhere quite breaks the 9,840-foot (3,000 m) barrier.

The best way to taste the pleasures of the Bavarian Alps to the full is to hike some of the hundreds of miles of way-marked footpaths. There are walks for the after-lunch stroller as well as the experienced hill walker wanting a high-level hike of several days. A number of recognized routes cater to the latter, some of them requiring familiarity with ropes, although the Heilbronner Weg in the Allgäu is an exception. Local visitor information centers will have good maps of their areas.

The Bavarian Alps are not a remote or isolated region. Attractive towns, villages, and mountain resorts crowd around the foot of the mountains. From ancient times, busy trade routes penetrated the Alps, linking Central Europe with the Mediterranean and the cities of Italy. Their equivalents today are the electrified railroads and autobahns that have made the Alps more accessible than ever.

View Austria, Switzerland, Italy, and the Bavarian lowlands from the summit of Germany's highest peak, the Zugspitze.

Royal Castles

The obsessively romantic vision of the Middle Ages held by Ludwig II, the "Dream King," still captures the imagination today. More than a million visitors a year make the pilgrimage to his spectacularly sited Schloss Neuschwanstein, prototype of all theme park castles, together with neighboring Schloss Hohenschwangau.

Visit Hohenschwangau first: Its impact is less dramatic than

Schloss Neuschwanstein, in all its faux-medieval glory, perches on an Alpine crag.

Schloss Hohenschwangau & Schloss Neuschwanstein

- 🅰 280 C2
- ✉ Ticketcenter Hohenschwangau, Alpseestrasse 12
- ☎ 08362 93 08 30
- 💲 $$$$$ ($$$$ one castle). Guided tours only, available in English.

ticket-center-hohen schwangau.de

that of Neuschwanstein, and it makes sense to save the best for last. The great popularity of Neuschwanstein causes congestion, and you may have quite a long wait between finding a space for your car in one of the parking areas, buying your timed ticket in the pavilion in the village, and beginning your visit. Schloss Hohenschwangau is a 15-minute walk west from the pavilion, Neuschwanstein a stiff 25-minute hike up the hill opposite. You can take a bus or horse-drawn carriage.

Hohenschwangau: Near the old town of Füssen just over 60 miles (100 km) southwest of Munich, the Ammergebirge mountains separate Bavaria from the Austrian Tyrol. The approach to this Alpine frontier was

guarded by a string of medieval castles, among them Schwanstein. A ruin by the 1830s, it was rebuilt between 1832 and 1836 by Crown Prince Maximilian, in a style influenced by an idealized view of Gothic and Tudor England, and renamed Hohenschwangau (High Schwangau).

For all the medievalism of Hohenschwangau, with its wall paintings of troubadours and chivalrous deeds and repeated swan motifs, it has a lived-in feeling about it. It was, indeed, often in use as a Wittelsbach family residence. Young Ludwig spent much of his childhood here, and it was at Hohenschwangau that a meeting with Richard Wagner led to friendship. You can see the piano on which they played together in the Hohenstaufensaal, along with items of their correspondence. Ludwig's bedroom ceiling reproduced the night sky, and from here he could watch the progress of work on his dream castle on the crag far above.

Neuschwanstein: In a wildly romantic location, Neuschwanstein crowns a rock spur above the deep Pöllat gorge, with its plunging waterfall, eroding cliffs, and primeval forest. You can immerse yourself in this wilderness by walking to the **Marienbrücke,** a footbridge spanning the torrent nearly

inspiration for its creation, notably the Minstrels' Hall, in the Wartburg (see p. 223), supposedly the setting for the singers' contest in Wagner's opera *Tannhäuser.* The *Lohengrin* story is alluded to in the swan motifs in the sitting room. The Byzantine **Throne Room** is modeled on the Court Chapel in the Munich Residenz. In the end, however, it is a rather melancholic place; having more or less emptied the royal coffers to build it, Ludwig spent less than six months here.

If by this time, your thirst for local regalia still isn't quenched, stop by the **Museum der**

Museum der Bayerischen Könige

✉ Alpseestrasse 27
☎ 08362 92 64 640
$ $$$

museumderbayer ischenkoenige.de

Berchtesgaden
🗺 281 G2
Visitor Information
✉ Königsseer Strasse 2
☎ 08652 96 70

berchtesgadener -land.com

"Mad" King Ludwig (1845–1886)

Ludwig came to the throne at the early age of 18. He preferred dreams to reality, a propensity reinforced by disastrous misjudgments in the complex events leading to German unification, with Bavaria giving way to Prussia on all counts. Thereafter, Ludwig turned away from affairs of state and concentrated on realizing his fantasies. At Neuschwanstein, these were inspired by Wagner's operas and his own idealized view of the Middle Ages. His castles at Linderhof and

Herrenchiemsee (see p. 316) drew on the extravagant age of Louis XIV in France. In 1886, increasingly concerned by Ludwig's neglect of his duties, waste of royal resources, and eccentric personal behavior, the Bavarian government declared him insane. He was arrested and taken to Schloss Berg on Lake Starnberg south of Munich. Two days later he was dead, drowned in the waters of the lake. To this day the manner of his death remains a mystery.

---

300 feet (90 m) below. Ludwig would come here at night to gaze at his castle, and it is the point from which the building and its setting can best be appreciated. The castle appears to grow out of the rock, its solid mass broken by fantastical crenelated towers, turrets, oriel windows, and various projections.

Work began on the castle in 1869, and Ludwig found

Bayerischen Könige (Museum of Bavarian Kings) to inspect Ludwig's collection of toy soldiers, a walk-through Wittelsbach family tree and a 69-foot-long (21 m) long panorama window giving a fabulous view over the Alpsee.

Berchtesgaden

Ringed by mountain peaks, the little town of Berchtesgaden sits on a natural balcony overlooking

Nationalpark Berchtesgaden

- 🅰 281 G2
- ✉ Nationalpark-Haus Franziskanerplatz 7
- ☎ 08652 6 43 43

www.nationalpark -berchtesgaden .bayern.de

Königliches Schloss

- ✉ Schlossplatz 2
- ☎ 08652 94 79 80
- ⊘ Closed Sat.
- 💲 $$$

schloss-berchtes gaden.de

The church of St. Bartholomä sits at the edge of Königssee, at the foot of the mighty Watzmann.

Salzbergwerk

- ✉ Bergwerkstrasse 83
- ☎ 08652 600 20
- 💲 $$$$$

salzzeitreise.de

an idyllic valley. In the surrounding area you'll find some of the most glorious sights in the Bavarian Alps, foremost among them the fjordlike Königssee in the shadow of towering Watzmann, Germany's second highest summit.

Coming to this mountain fastness from the north is almost like entering another country—not surprising, when you remember that for centuries the Berchtesgadener region was independent. Augustinian priors first settled the valley in the 12th century and their successors later ruled the state.

After 1810, when their domain joined Bavaria, Berchtesgaden became a favorite summer retreat for the Bavarian royal family. Others followed them, especially when a rail line was opened in 1888, and today it is one of Germany's most popular vacation spots, attracting crowds in summer and winter.

Visiting Berchtesgaden: A good place to take in the panorama from Berchtesgaden is the garden of the Nationalpark-Haus, the interpretive center of **Nationalpark Berchtesgaden.** Much of the sublime landscape visible from here is protected. An outer area of farmland and forest continues to be managed under strict environmental regulations, while in the inner, core area, natural processes are being allowed to take their course. Visit the Nationalpark-Haus for information about the area's heritage, its extraordinarily rich and varied wildlife, and its almost endless possibilities for walks or more challenging hikes.

A stroll through the attractive streets of old painted houses will bring you to the town's showpiece, the **Schlossplatz.** Facing the sturdy arcaded building on the left are the church and priors' residence from the old monastery, parts of which are from the 12th century. The residence is now the **Königliches Schloss,** from 1923 until 1933 the home of Crown Prince Ruprecht, head of the deposed Bavarian royal family. It now displays items from the Wittelsbach collections—paintings, sculptures, carvings, furniture, hunting trophies, and weapons.

The town's other great attraction is the **Salzbergwerk,** the underground saltworks on which Berchtesgaden's early prosperity was founded and which is still in operation. Clad in traditional miner's garb, you whiz underground on a heart-stopping but perfectly safe slide, explore galleries and grottoes, and are

EXPERIENCE: Roughing It in Alpine Huts

For outdoor enthusiasts, the organized network of Alpine hikers' huts are the ideal refuge after a day of trekking or climbing. Numbering more than 1,300, the majority are managed by live-in staff, while a few simple huts are available for self-caterers (members of various Alpine clubs can get a skeleton key). In recent years, back-to-nature holidays have enjoyed a boom, and paradoxically, some "huts" are more like villas, with comforts that rival those of luxury hotels.

Quite a few hikes with planned hut-stops begin in Berchtesgadener Land, where you have the option of hiring an experienced guide before you go. A popular six-day journey from the Königssee makes a well-marked arc through the mountains, returning to the lakeside church of St. Bartholomä. For further details and hut bookings, contact the **German Alpine Club** (*Von-Kahr-Strasse 2–4, Munich, tel 089 140 0317, fax 089 140 03 23, alpenverein.de*).

rafted across a sparkling salt lake.

The classic Berchtesgaden experience is a trip on the **Königssee** into the heart of the mountains. A silently gliding, electrically powered launch slips through the clear water to the endearing little church of **St. Bartholomä**. Disembark here and stroll by the lakeside or take a 90-minute walk up to the **Ice Chapel** at the foot of the east face of the Watzmann. A farther ride on the boat brings you close to the southern tip of the lake; a short walk leads up to the tiny lake of Obersee and the 1,542-foot (470 m) Röthbach waterfall.

Obersalzberg: The name of Berchtesgaden is associated with the Berghof, Hitler's mountain chalet on the **Obersalzberg,** one of the foothills of the 6,017-foot (1,834 m) **Kehlstein.** The future Führer first came here in 1923, and it was later an alternative headquarters to Berlin. Allied bombers destroyed the complex in the last days of the war, and most

of the remains were blown up in the 1950s. An excellent information center, the **Dokumentation Obersalzberg** (*Salzbergstrasse 41, tel 08652 94 79 60, obersalzberg.de, closed Mon. Nov.–March, $*), relates events in and around Berchtesgaden to the wider history of the Third Reich.

Once the snow has cleared, you can take a bus (mid-May–Oct.) from the parking lot at Obersalzberg-Hintereck up the 4-mile (6.5 km) **Kehlsteinstrasse,** Germany's most spectacular mountain road, to Hitler's other chalet, the **Kehlsteinhaus** (Eagle's Nest), atop the Kehlstein. The final stage of the trip, from the bus terminus to this example of National Socialist architecture (now a restaurant), is conducted via a tunnel and a brass-lined elevator (included in the bus fare). The Alpine panorama is unsurpassed.

Garmisch-Partenkirchen

The Garmisch-Partenkirchen resort stands in a broad valley (continued on p. 312)

Kehlsteinhaus
- ✉ Bergwerkstrasse 83
- ☎ 08652 20 29
- 🕐 Closed Nov.– mid-May
- 💲 $$$$$ (incl. bus)

kehlsteinhaus.de

Garmisch-Partenkirchen
- 🅰 280 D2

Visitor Information
- ✉ Richard-Strauss-Platz 2
- ☎ 08821 18 07 00

gapa.de

Drive: The German Alpine Road

With a few interruptions, the Deutsche Alpenstrasse—begun in the 1930s—runs for nearly 200 miles (300 km) between Berchtesgaden and Lindau on Lake Constance. Few travelers set out nowadays to drive its whole length; the section described is a less frantic alternative to the final section of the autobahn, between Berchtesgaden and Munich, introducing you gently to the delights of the foothills and to the Alps themselves.

Christmas scene at Ramsau

Southeast of Munich, leave the autobahn E52/E60 at exit 106 and follow Route 305 south past Bernau to **Grassau ❶**. This old place, with a classic onion-domed church, is now a vacation resort, overlooked by a 5,204-foot (1,586 m) peak, the Hochplatte.

Continue south to **Marquartstein ❷**, with its 11th-century castle and a ski lift up to the Hochplatte. Composer Richard Strauss lived in the town, and it was here that he composed his opera *Salome*. Carry on along the winding 305 to the resort of **Reit im Winkl ❸**, with its Tyrolean-style houses. In a sunny valley on the Austrian border and almost surrounded by forest-mantled mountains rising to 6,500 feet (2,000 m), its reliable snowfall makes it as popular in winter as in summer. The 305 now turns east, then

north through the protected landscape of the Chiemgauer Alpen (Chiemgau Mountains) with their chain of little lakes.

After 15 miles (24 km) you arrive in **Ruhpolding ❹**. This busy little town has grown in popularity with visitors since Duke Wilhelm V built his Renaissance-style hunting lodge here in 1597. However, it maintains many of its traditions and still has much of the atmosphere of an Alpine village. Its fine baroque parish church houses a

NOT TO BE MISSED:

A short stroll in Ruhpolding • The "Ruhpolding Madonna" in Ruhpolding • Ramsau's church • Hintersee

great treasure, the **"Ruhpolding Madonna."** A wood carving dating from about 1230, it is a fine example of Upper Bavarian craftsmanship.

Deutsche Ferienstrasse Alpen-Ostsee

Drive east, still on the 305, to the village of **Inzell** ⑤, with its onion-domed church. The road, which now also becomes part of the Alps-to-Baltic Vacation Route, runs southeast along the well-wooded Schwarzbach Valley. It crosses the watershed at the pass known as Schwarzbachwacht-Sattel and goes

downhill through forest and pastureland with wonderful mountain views.

Turn right off the main road into the village of **Ramsau** ⑥. Although now almost a suburb of Berchtesgaden, the village has kept plenty of its original charm, and it has one incomparable asset: the parish church of 1512 standing on a rise against a dramatic background of snow-capped Alps. Get out of the car and follow the sign that will lead you across the stream to the spot providing the perfect shot. Ramsau also has a baroque pilgrimage church known as Maria Kunterweg, dating from 1733, with a lovingly decorated interior.

Keep going west 2.5 miles (4 km) to the little lake called the **Hintersee** ⑦, above which the clifflike slopes rise to the peaks and a glinting glacier, the northernmost one in the Alps. Go back the way you came and rejoin 305, which brings you to your destination, **Berchtesgaden** ⑧ (see pp. 307–309).

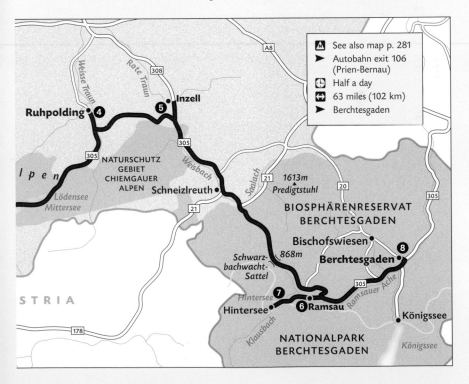

among mountains. Beautiful forest covers the lower slopes all around, but to the south arise the rocky ramparts of the Wetterstein Mountains, reaching their peak (9,721 feet/ 2,963 m) at the Zugspitze. Not much more than an hour by road and rail from Munich, it is both a winter sports mecca and Bavaria's prime summer resort, with all the facilities to be expected.

EXPERIENCE: Gliding Along the Alpine Rim

On warm summery days, the sky in southern Germany fills with hang- and paragliders who literally soar with the hawks. Paragliding has taken the lead for practical reasons: The inflatable wing easily fits into a backpack, and design advances mean they can fly almost as far as a hang-glider. Beginners can take tandem flights with an instructor from launch points near Garmisch-Partenkirchen and elsewhere along the Alpine rim. For courses and rental, try **Fly for Fun** (*Ehrengutstrasse 15, Munich, tel 089 74 68 81 87, flyforfun.com*) **or Jochen Schweizer** (*Rosenheimer Strasse 145, tel 089 708 090 90, jochen-schweizer.de*).

Yet it is still on an intimate scale, with a friendly atmosphere and local traditions. The cultural program ranges from the summer music festival, named for long-term resident Richard Strauss, to zither sessions in smoky bars and folklore performances in a pair of "peasant theaters."

The two communities of Garmisch and Partenkirchen joined forces in 1935 to host the Winter Olympics the following year. The first-rate winter sports facilities built for the occasion consolidated the town's reputation internationally, and Garmisch-Partenkirchen was selected again for the never-to-be-held 1940 Games. The town continues to attract those in search of challenging skiing as well as the more gentle pursuits of *Langlauf* (cross-country skiing), skating, curling, and exploring the wild countryside on skis or snowshoes. In summer, chairlifts and cableways help hikers enjoy hundreds of miles of way-marked trails.

Partenkirchen: Partenkirchen is the more venerable of the partners, with a history going back to the Romans. The stately main street, **Ludwigstrasse,** is lined with fine old houses, some of them with exuberant *Lüftl-malerei,* the folksy murals that are a specialty of the region. Even the mid-20th-century **Rathaus** (Town Hall) has been given this colorful treatment. Partenkirchen's principal inheritance from the 1936 Olympics is the **Olympische Skistadion,** with ski jump, slalom course, and space for 80,000 spectators.

To the northeast stands **St. Anton,** an early 18th-century pilgrimage church idyllically located on the lower slopes of the Wank (5,840 feet/1,780 m). It's the starting point of an easy-graded 7-mile (11 km) walk called the **Philosophenweg** (Philosophers' Trail), giving superb views of the Wettersteins and the Zugspitze. You can climb a zigzag path to the summit of the Wank, or take the Wankbahn cable car *($$$$).*

Ride a cable car up the Zugspitze for a bird's-eye view of Garmisch-Partenkirchen and the Wetterstein Mountains beyond.

Garmisch: Compared with Partenkirchen, Garmisch is an upstart, having first made its appearance in the records in A.D. 802. Garmisch's modern main street may not have the ancient allure of Partenkirchen's Ludwigstrasse, but its shops are full of sophisticated merchandise and souvenirs. Activity centers on the **Richard-Strauss-Platz,** with casino, *Kurhaus* (spa rooms), and attractive *Kurpark* (spa gardens).

The old core of the place is to the west around **St. Martin's Church,** where there are plenty of attractive old painted buildings. There are even more of them on the far side of the river, close to the other church (also dedicated, confusingly, to St. Martin): Look particularly

for the **Restaurant Husar** inn, with its bold decoration in the Bavarian colors of blue and white and trompe l'oeil figures leaning from the window.

Richard Strauss lived in the town for many years until his death in 1949, and the **Richard-Strauss-Institut** is in Partenkirchen. It has a changing program of exhibitions and a "sound museum," where you can listen to extracts from the composer's work.

Not the least of Garmisch-Partenkirchen's advantages is its proximity to many other attractions. A cable car ride to the top of the **Zugspitze** (see pp. 314–315) is almost obligatory, as is the spectacular walk through the narrow gorge known as the **Partnachklamm.**

Richard-Strauss-Institut

✉ Schnitzschulstrasse 19

☎ 08821 91 09 50

🕒 Closed Sat.–Sun.

💲 $

www.richard-strauss-institut.de

Oberammergau
 280 D2

Visitor Information

✉ Eugen-Papst-
Strasse 9

☎ 08822 92 27 40

Zugspitze
🚠 280 D1

zugspitze.de

NOTE: See website for information on the railroad, cable cars, and other transportation around the mountain.

A two-hour walking trail leads around one of the loveliest lakes in the Alps, the **Eibsee** at the foot of the Zugspitze. A 12-mile (20 km) drive to the east of Garmisch is **Mittenwald,** "a living picture book" of a village as Goethe described it, famous for its tradition of violinmaking. A similar drive north brings you past the great baroque abbey at **Ettal** to world-famous **Oberammergau,** home to countless woodcarvers of variable ability and scene of the world-renowned Passion Play (next performance 2020; see sidebar opposite). An excursion here can be combined with a visit to one of Ludwig II's castles, his own favorite, **Linderhof** (see p. 316).

Zugspitze

Half a million people a year make it to the 9,721-foot (2,963 m) summit of Germany's highest mountain, the hardy on foot, the vast majority by cable car and railway. They are rewarded by a magnificent panorama over peaks in Germany, Austria, Switzerland, and Italy and into the Bavarian lowlands. Before you set out, check the weather report; the summit is atmospheric, even when shrouded in mist, but you will never forget the views if you take the trip on a clear day.

The Zugspitze was long thought to be the abode of witches, a place to avoid. In 1820, Lt. Josef Naus of the Royal

Sightseers crowd the Zugspitzplatt, with its observation platforms and breathtaking view.

EXPERIENCE: Taking in the Passion Play

In the 17th century, when the tiny village of Oberammergau was spared the ravages of the plague, its grateful citizens vowed to stage a play illustrating the miracle. Since then, the famous *Passionsspiele* (Passion Play) has been held once nearly every ten years, drawing thousands of spectators from around the globe. The huge open-air theater was built in the 1890s and constructed so that every audience member enjoys a full view. The performers are all locals, and they must abide by strict rules:

Costumes are all hand-sewn, and men begin growing beards for their roles months ahead of time. The part of Mary traditionally goes to a presumed virgin under 35; a scandal erupted in 1990, when, against the grain, the job went to an older, and married, mother of two. The next performance of the multi-hour play takes place between May and October in 2020. Book early, as obtaining tickets is always a challenge. See *oberammergau-passion.com* for details.

Bavarian Army struggled to the top. He was carrying out an order from King Maximilian I of the newly created Kingdom of Bavaria to survey this part of his realm. In 1851 a golden cross was erected on the summit, and an Alpine hut was built in 1897. A weather station followed three years later. The demand for easier access grew, and in 1928, 2,000 men started work on the construction of the rack railroad to the Zugspitzplatt, the plateau just below the peak.

The popular **railroad** was completed in two years. You can board it at its station in Garmisch-Partenkirchen *(Zugspitzbahn, Garmisch-Partenkirchen, Olympiastrasse 27, tel 08821 79 70, zugspitze.de, $$$$$)*, or drive up to the station at Eibsee and leave your vehicle in the parking lot there. Make sure you buy a round-trip ticket and allow half a day or longer to make the most of the experience.

From Eibsee, the real climb begins, with the train grinding its way up, first in forest, then in tunnels, to its 8,530-foot (2,600 m)

terminus. Reliable snow cover means that you can ski here from October to May. To reach the very top, take the **Gletscherbahn cableway,** opened in 1992.

The rocky wilderness found by Lieutenant Naus has long since disappeared under the steel and concrete of the extended weather station, the **observatory,** and the visitor facilities (including an art gallery). But the view is the thing, and it's worth a good stay up here to absorb it, particularly in changing weather conditions.

A passageway at the end of the observation deck leads from German territory to the upper station of the Austrian Zugspitzbahn. However, your recommended way down is via the Eibsee cable car, preferably with a window view. This is one of the most impressive rides in the Alps; the gondola swings out from the sheer rock face into the abyss, swaying slightly as it passes over the pylons holding up the cables, giving ever closer views of the Eibsee in its glorious setting. ∎

More Places to Visit in the Alps

Landsberg am Lech

A handsome medieval town and an important stop on the Romantic Road linking Northern Bavaria with the Alps, Landsberg owes part of its fame to the political prison where Adolf Hitler, an inmate after the failed Putsch in 1923 (see p. 298), dictated *Mein Kampf* to his acolyte Rudolf Hess. The great 18th-century church architect Dominikus Zimmermann, who was burgomaster here, gave the Rathaus (Town Hall) its richly decorated facade. *ammerseelech.de* 🅰 280 D3 ✉ Hauptplatz 152 ☎ 08191 12 82 47

Oberstdorf

Despite its wealth of sports and recreation facilities (ski jump, several cable cars), this mountain resort in the Allgäu Alps has kept much of its village character. The most popular excursion is to the top of the 7,297-foot (2,224 m) **Nebelhorn,** the highest peak in the Allgäu, from where the panorama takes in more than 400 Alpine peaks. *oberstdorf.de* 🅰 280 B1 ✉ Prinzregenten-Platz 1 ☎ 08322 70 00

Ottobeuren

The little town of Ottobeuren in Bavarian Swabia is dominated by its **monastery church.** Founded in the eighth century, the abbey was rebuilt a millennium later by one of the greatest architects of the 18th century, Johann Michael Fischer. The vast interior, richly decorated with stuccowork and frescoes, is one of the finest creations of the baroque style in Germany. *ottobeuren.de* 🅰 280 C3 ✉ Marktplatz 14 ☎ 08332 92 19 50

Schloss Herrenchiemsee

Bavaria's biggest lake, the Chiemsee, is a favorite spot for weekenders from Munich as well as for admirers of Ludwig II, who built his last and most expensive palace here.

Schloss Herrenchiemsee was intended to be a facsimile of Versailles, but it was far from finished at Ludwig's death in 1886. It is nevertheless worth seeing, with a 320-foot (100 m) Hall of Mirrors and a French-style formal park. The royal apartments of the **Neues Schloss** (New Palace) can be visited by guided tour only, but you can spend as long as you like in the south wing, which houses the **König Ludwig II-Museum** with much fascinating material about the life of this strange but appealing figure. The baroque **Altes Schloss** (Old Palace) contains a museum celebrating the foundation of the Federal Republic of Germany. It was here in 1948 that its constitution was drawn up. *herrenchiemsee.de* 🅰 281 F3 ☎ 08051 6 88 70 💲 $$$

Schloss Linderhof

Lost in a quiet side valley in the heart of the Ammergebirge mountains, Schloss Linderhof is perhaps the most appealing of King Ludwig II's castles. More villa than palace, it is set on grounds that combine Italian terrace gardens, French parterres, and English-style parkland. Intriguing garden buildings include a Moroccan House, a Moorish Kiosk with a peacock throne, and an artfully contrived Venus Grotto, simulating a scene from Wagner's *Tannhäuser. schlosslinderhof.de* 🅰 280 D2 ☎ 08822 9 20 30 💲 $$$

Wieskirche

Harmonizing perfectly with its setting, the Wieskirche ("church in the meadow") marks the place where an abandoned carving of Christ miraculously shed real tears. In 1746, rococo designer Dominikus Zimmermann was commissioned to erect a church on the spot. The church interior is a blissful confection of luxuriant stuccowork and lively ceiling frescoes. *wieskirche.de* 🅰 280 D2 ☎ 08862 93 29 30

Vineyards and orchards, successful industries, and scenery ranging from the Black Forest to Germany's biggest lake, Constance

Baden-Württemberg

Black Forest couple

Baden-Württemberg

This *Land* in Germany's southwestern corner has a dual character. The climate in the Rhine Valley and around the Bodensee has a touch of the south about it, perhaps explaining the area's easygoing lifestyle. On the other hand, the Swabians, as Württembergers prefer to be called, are a bit more determined—their contributions to the German economic miracle helped make the region one of the country's most prosperous.

Enjoying the cure at Baden-Baden's Friedrichsbad spa

Of the wonderful landscapes in Baden-Württemberg, the Schwarzwald (Black Forest) is supreme, with its cloak of dark and mysterious conifers, green meadows, and farmsteads. The region's other main upland range, the Schwäbische Alb (Swabian Jura), is more austere. Rivers cut into its series of limestone plateaus, leaving dramatic rock spurs crowned by picture-book castles.

There are castles almost beyond counting along the lower River Neckar, including that of the ancient university town of Heidelberg, most visited of all Baden-Württemberg's cities. The state capital, Stuttgart, is one of Germany's most progressive cities, proud of the technical excellence of its products and its cultural attractions. The city was the royal seat of the rulers of Württemberg, whose kingdom extended to the shores of Lake Constance.

NOT TO BE MISSED:

Stuttgart's fine museums **320–323**

The magnificent ruined castle and surrounds in Heidelberg **325–326**

The sumptuous Schloss and royal gardens of Karlsruhe **328–329**

Baden-Baden's fancy spas **332–333**

Exploring the charming university town of Freiburg **334–335**

Hiking up the Feldberg, the tallest Black Forest summit **338–339**

The dramatic scenery along Lake Constance's shores **340–342**

Strolling in Ulm's delightful Fisherman's Quarter **343**

Until 1918, Baden had been a grand duchy with its capital at Karlsruhe, and Badeners see themselves as quite distinct from Swabians. Perhaps influenced by the long line of vineyards cladding the sunny western slopes of the Black Forest, they are not quite so dedicated to work as their compatriots just to the east. And nowhere is a place more dedicated to pleasure and relaxation than that archetypal spa town, Baden-Baden. ∎

Stuttgart

The symbols of Swabian Stuttgart are not venerable churches or civic buildings, but the Mercedes star and the Fernsehturm, Germany's first TV tower. The city has plenty of other firsts to its credit, not least the internal combustion engine patented by Gottlieb Daimler in 1883. Daimler amalgamated with Mercedes in 1926, forming one of Stuttgart's world-class enterprises. On the arts scene, the Staatsgalerie has become an icon of postmodern design.

Stuttgart
🅰 319 C3
Visitor Information
✉ Königstrasse 1A
☎ 0711 22 28 253
stuttgart-tourist.de

The city center spreads out along a valley surrounded by wooded hills. Some of the slopes are covered with vineyards, while from the summit of one of the hills rises the **Fernsehturm.** Its observation

platform gives a commanding view over the city (closed until mid-2015). The lavish provision of parks and pedestrian spaces means that you can walk unhindered by traffic from chic city center shopping arcades to the riverside several kilometers away.

Stuttgart's name comes from the stud farm ("Stutengarten") established by the local dukes in the tenth century (a black horse still features on the city's coat of arms). When Napoleon redrew the map of Germany in 1802, the dukes were promoted to royal status, and Stuttgart became the capital of the kingdom of Württemberg. The origins of the **Altes Schloss** (Old Castle) go back to the days of the stud farm, although the present building, with its courtyard and towers, is mostly Renaissance in date. It houses the **Landesmuseum** (Regional Museum), with wonderful examples of religious works by local master carvers and also the Württemberg crown jewels.

A much more expansive structure, the baroque **Neues Schloss** (New Castle) is big enough to dominate the huge Schlossplatz that, with its formal lawns and Jubilee column, is the city's main meeting place. Built by the dukes in the second half of the

The Calwer Passage, a fashionable shopping arcade

18th century, the Neues Schloss now houses some departments of the state government.

Off the southwest corner of the square, an illuminated glass cube makes a modernist statement for the renowned **Kunstmuseum Stuttgart** (Stuttgart Museum of Art), the cutting edge among local galleries. Works by *Neue Sachlichkeit* (New Objectivity) artist Otto Dix (1891–1969) are prominent here, above all the tremendous "Metropolis" triptych. With its parade of crippled war veterans and strutting creatures of the night, it sums up the splendors and miseries of the Weimar years. To the west, Schlossplatz is bounded by broad **Königstrasse,** Stuttgart's principal shopping street, running straight down to the main station (Hauptbahnhof). A controversial, €6.5 billion ($9 billion) project, dubbed Stuttgart 21, will shift all rail traffic to an underground terminus by 2022.

Best Stuttgart Views

Lovely spots to admire:
- Vineyards and velvety forests seen from the Fernsehturm
- Neues Schloss from lovely lawns around the Jubilee column
- Stately buildings along manicured paths in the Schlossgarten
- From the viewing platform atop the massive Hauptbahnhof
- The high-tech Mercedes-Benz Museum

INSIDER TIP:

Don't leave Stuttgart without tasting a favorite regional dish, *Maultaschen*. Similar to ravioli, it's stuffed with meat and veggies and served in broth.

—HOLGER SIEGLE
Stauferland Tourism Association

For a hint of old Stuttgart, return to the Altes Schloss, which shares **Schillerplatz** with other old buildings. Beyond is a web of old streets around the **Markthalle** (Market Hall), a stylish art nouveau establishment with fruit, vegetables, and spices, as well as great places to eat and drink.

To see how Stuttgart has won a reputation as an immaculately landscaped city, walk north to the **Schlossgarten** to find the modern Baden-Württemberg **Landtag** (Parliament Building) and the cultural complex of the **Staatsoper and Staatstheater** (State Opera and State Theater).

Staatsgalerie

Opposite the Staatstheater is the Staatsgalerie. Part of the collection is housed in a neoclassic building of 1843, the rest in the world-renowned extension designed by British architect James Stirling and completed in 1984. Stonework contrasts with gaudy green, blue, and pink piping and metalwork. It's a puzzle trying to work out where external spaces end and the gallery

---

Fernsehturm
- Map p. 323
- Jahnstrasse 120, Stuttgart-Degerloch
- 0711 23 25 97
- $$

fernsehturm
stuttgart.com

Landesmuseum
- Map p. 323
- Altes Schloss, Schillerplatz 6
- 0711 89 535 111
- Closed Mon.
- $$

landesmuseum
-stuttgart.de

Kunstmuseum Stuttgart
- Map p. 323
- Kleiner Schlossplatz 1
- 0711 216 196 00
- Closed Mon.
- $$

kunstmuseum
-stuttgart.de

Staatsgalerie
- Map p. 323
- Konrad-Adenauer-Strasse 30–32
- 0711 47 04 00
- Closed Mon.
- $$$

staatsgalerie.de

Schloss Rosenstein

- Map p. 323
- Rosenstein 1
- 0711 8 93 60
- Closed Mon.
- $$

naturkunde museum-bw.de

Wilhelma

- Map p. 323
- Neckartalstrasse
- 0711 5 40 20
- $$$$

wilhelma.de

A Latin American *colectivo* (minibus) is one of the more colorful exhibits at the Mercedes-Benz Museum.

begins; in fact, you can follow a public walkway right through the building.

Appropriately, the older building houses artworks from medieval times to the 19th century. Paintings by Dutch and Italian old masters are here, and there is a good selection of early German works. Look for the Herrenberg altarpiece by the visionary Jörg Ratgeb, a Swabian painter from Gmünd who died fighting in the Peasant Wars in 1526. Good examples of the work of 19th-century German Romantic painters include Caspar David Friedrich's particularly evocative "Bohemian Landscape." Anselm Feuerbach's "Iphigenie" of 1872 may intrigue you with her enigmatic thoughts. The gallery also has many first-rate canvases by French Impressionists, including Claude Monet's "Fields in Spring" (1887).

In the new extension, Stirling's highly varied interior spaces make a superb setting for Stuttgart's outstanding collection of early 20th-century German art. Among works by Otto Dix, look for his grotesquely disabled yet moving "Matchseller." Apocalyptic scenes by George Grosz and Ludwig Meider foretell the horrors of war and the chaos of the Weimar years. Don't miss the beautifully lit costumes designed by Bauhaus teacher Oskar Schlemmer for his "Triadic Ballet." Here, too, is the Picasso collection, the largest in Germany.

If you have time, take the footpaths north through the Schlossgarten to reach Rosensteinpark. Here, **Schloss Rosenstein,** the summer palace of **Württemberg** royalty, is home to the city's museum of natural history, and the old royal grounds of the **Wilhelma** have been adapted as a first-rate zoo and botanical gardens.

Farther Afield

Cross the river and you find yourself in **Bad Cannstatt,** once an independent town and famous spa, now a suburb of Stuttgart. The place is best known for its September Volksfest, a worthy rival to Munich's Oktoberfest (see pp. 300–301).

Gottlieb Daimler lived and carried out his early experiments with internal combustion engines here. Some of the fruits of his inventiveness are on display at Stuttgart's two outstanding motor museums. In the suburb of Unter-türkheim south of Cannstatt, the lavish **Mercedes-Benz Museum** celebrates more than a century of automobile manufacture by this great company and its predecessors. The Japanese limousine used by Emperor Hirohito is here, as is Chancellor Adenauer's official car and the first of the "Popemobiles."

In the interwar years, Ferdinand Porsche was technical director of Stuttgart's Daimler works, but his fame rests on his association with the early development of the Volkswagen and then on his conquest of the upper end of the automobile market with his roadsters. These superlative machines are turned out by the factory in the suburb of Zuffenhausen, where the **Porsche Museum** has about 80 historic examples on display. ∎

Mercedes-Benz Museum

- ⓜ Map p. 323
- ✉ Mercedesstrasse 100
- ☎ 0711 173 00 00
- ⏱ Closed Mon.
- 💲 $$

mercedes-benz
-classic.com

Porsche Museum

- ⓜ Map p. 323
- ✉ Porscheplatz 1, Stuttgart-Zuffenhausen
- ☎ 0711 911 20 911
- ⏱ Closed Mon.
- 💲 $$$

porsche.com
/museum

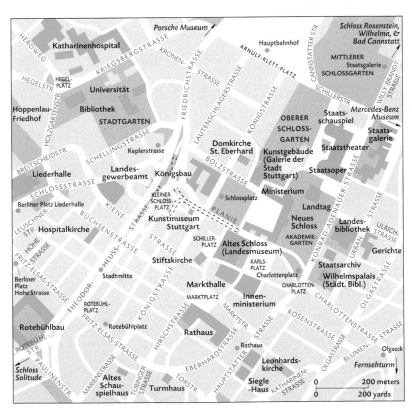

Heidelberg

Enticingly located among steep wooded hills just upstream from where the Neckar River flows out into the Rhine plain, this famous university city has been immortalized by writers, musicians, and artists. Mark Twain wrote about it with affection in *A Tramp Abroad;* the image of student life created by Sigmund Romberg in his musical *The Student Prince* lives on; and generations of military personnel have lived here ever since it was chosen as the headquarters of U.S. forces in Germany.

Heidelberg appears a quintessential Rhine Valley town from atop the Philosophenweg.

Heidelberg

⚑ 319 B4

Visitor Information

✉ Hauptbahnhof (Main station), Willy-Brandt-Platz 1, & Marktplatz (Rathaus)

☎ 06221 58 44 444

heidelberg -marketing.de

Heidelberg's story could be said to begin half a million years ago. The jawbone of Europe's oldest known inhabitant, *Homo heidelbergensis,* was found nearby. However, the town itself developed only in the Middle Ages under the rulers of the Rhineland-Palatinate, a territory extending on both sides of the Rhine. In 1386 the first

university on purely German soil was founded here, and in later years Heidelberg flourished, becoming a center of Humanism and Protestantism.

Its greatest benefactor was also its nemesis: Elector Frederick V (1596–1632) beautified the castle for his bride, Elizabeth Stuart, daughter of James I of England, and laid out magnificent gardens.

But he also helped provoke the disasters of the Thirty Years War, when the city was sacked and plundered. In 1693, the French invaded, laying waste to town and castle. Heidelberg emerged from obscurity only when it was "discovered" by the poets of the Romantic movement at the end of the 18th century, when ruins came into fashion.

The city has never looked back, but despite its immense popularity, Heidelberg has not sold its soul to tourism. Most visitors come on business; the city is a focus of the new economy based on brainpower, with many research and scientific institutions and a thriving university.

Castle Ruins

Start your exploration at the **Schloss,** perhaps more lovely in its ruined state than it ever was before. You can take the funicular up, but the climb on foot, albeit steep, isn't all that far. If you arrive by funicular, turn left once you reach the castle grounds and enjoy a classic view over the city from the promontory where cannon once stood. The way to the courtyard is via the Elisabethentor, a gateway Frederick V had built in a single night to surprise his bride. Beyond a fortified bridge, the courtyard gateway is decorated with the formidable figure of a knight in armor.

While buildings from all periods of the castle's construction line the courtyard, the most striking are the elaborately decorated Renaissance facades of the eastern and northern wings,

the Ottheinrichsbau and the Friedrichsbau. The Ottheinrichsbau is home to the **Deutsches Apotheken-Museum** (German Museum of Pharmacy), with reconstructed historical pharmacies as well as an alchemist's laboratory located deep underground.

What attracts the crowds into another of the courtyards is the monster wine barrel known as the **Grosses Fass,** as big as a two-story building. Built to hold the portion of the wine harvest traditionally surrendered to the

Badges of Honor

From the mid-19th century through the 1930s, members of Germany's fencing fraternities inflicted ceremonial cheek scars on their dueling partners. Known as a *Schmiss,* **the dueling scar was an elite symbol of courage and honor, and recipients took steps to preserve it by rubbing salt in the open wound. The custom lives on today in a handful of fencing fraternities, such as those in Heidelberg and Tübingen. In public you can occasionally spot a Schmiss on the visage of prominent Germans.**

electors, it has an unbelievable capacity of about 58,000 gallons (222,000 L).

Make sure you walk around the Schloss's perimeter to get an idea of the strength of its fortifications. The most spectacular

Schloss
☎ 06221 53 84 72
💲 $$ (audioguide)
schloss-heidelberg.de

Deutsches Apotheken-Museum
☎ 06221 258 80
💲 $$ (incl. in Schloss ticket)
deutsches-apotheken -museum.de

**Kurpfälzisches
Museum**

 Hauptstrasse 97

 06221 583 40 20

Closed Mon.

 $

**www.museum
-heidelberg.de**

Studentenkarzer

Augustinergasse 2

06221 54 35 54

Closed Mon.
April–Oct.,
& Sun.–Mon.
Nov.–March

$

feature is the **Gesprengter Turm** (Blown-Up Tower); most of its masonry lies in the moat, leaving much of its interior exposed. Of Frederick V's great garden, with its fountains, grottoes, mazes, conservatories, and pavilions, the only remains are the high retaining walls and terraces.

Around Town

Heidelberg's **Altstadt** (Old Town) squeezes in between the Neckar River and the wooded slope to the south. The long main street, Hauptstrasse, runs parallel to the river from the cobbled **Marktplatz.** The square, lined by fine town houses and the baroque Rathaus (Town Hall), is dominated by the **Heiliggeistkirche,** a church built from the same red sandstone as the castle. Market stalls surround the church's outer walls, just as in medieval times. Don't leave the square without peeking at the

ornate facade of the **Haus zum Ritter** in the far southwestern corner, the only building to survive the disasters of the 17th century.

Leave the Marktplatz by Steingasse, which leads to the **Alte Brücke** (Old Bridge). It is approached through an archway flanked by medieval towers topped by jaunty little caps added in the 18th century. There's a fine view of the castle and the city from the bridge.

Back in town, you might now explore the smaller streets leading off busy Hauptstrasse, along with **Untere Strasse,** an attractive street that runs parallel to the main one. On Hauptstrasse you'll find the city's most important museum, the **Kurpfälzisches Museum** (Regional Museum of the Palatinate). Exhibits here show what Heidelberg was like before the destruction of the Thirty Years War; there is also a cast of the jawbone of *Homo heidelbergensis.*

Many of the university institutions are grouped around Universitätsplatz, among them the **Studentenkarzer,** Heidelberg's student prison. Until 1914, students were under the jurisdiction of the university, and misbehavior was punished by incarceration here—although prisoners were allowed to attend lectures and take their exams! Read the graffiti to see how they spent their time here. The **Marstall,** the former arsenal, is now the university refectory and gathering place. You might also lift a stein in one of the local old taverns nearby such as the Sepp'l or the Roter Ochs just off Karlsplatz. ■

EXPERIENCE: Exploring the Philosophenweg

For the very best panorama over Heidelberg, especially in the alluring late afternoon light, cross to the north bank of the Neckar River and steel yourself for a steep climb up to the Philosophenweg (Philosophers' Way). Ostensibly, this leafy footpath commemorates brainy Heidelbergers who walked these slopes to clear their thoughts or ponder the mysteries of time and decay. More likely, the path was named for amorous philosophy students who sought solitude here with their sweethearts. Once you pass house number 21, the trail levels out at the **Philosopher's Garden,** the best vantage point.

Neckar Valley

Forcing its way through the upland massif of the Odenwald upstream from Heidelberg, the Neckar forms an attractive, steep-sided valley. Winding among woods, orchards, and vineyards, it offers a rapid succession of hilltop castles, small towns, and villages.

Neckarsteinach, 7 miles (12 km) east of Heidelberg, has four castles, mostly in ruins, while the remains of another fortress, **Burg Dilsberg,** crown the heights opposite, giving a superb view over the river and the Odenwald forest. Another panorama awaits a few miles farther upstream from the terrace or tower of **Burg Hirschhorn,** now a hotel and restaurant.

Eberbach, 6 miles (10 km) farther east, where the river turns west, has a reconstructed castle, remains of its town walls, timber-frame houses, and a rare medieval bathhouse, now a restaurant, the Altes Badehaus. Once the seat of nobles who made a living extracting tolls from river traffic, the **Burg Zwingenberg** is the next castle upstream. Careful restoration has preserved it as perhaps the most picture-perfect medieval stronghold along the Neckar. Beyond the **Minneburg,** the valley widens, giving more space for agriculture.

Rising through the vines above Neckarzimmern is **Burg Hornberg** (tel 06261 50 01, $, burg-hornberg.de), home of the Knight of the Iron Hand, Götz von Berlichingen, the subject of a play by Goethe. Farther on, the castle of **Burg Guttenberg** (tel 06266 2 28, burg-guttenberg.de) is a birds-of-prey center (tel 06266 3 88, $$$).

A typical timber-framed building in Bad Wimpfen, with the turreted Blauer Turm in the background

The valley's highlight is **Bad Wimpfen.** A Gothic church dominates the lower town, Bad Wimpfen im Tal. In the upper town, Bad Wimpfen am Berg, a watchtower of bluish limestone, **Blauer Turm,** overlooks winding streets of timber-framed houses. On Sunday at noon, a trumpeter plays from the top of the tower. ■

Bad Wimpfen
△ 319 C3
Visitor Information
✉ Carl-Ulrich-Strasse 1
☎ 07063 972 00
badwimpfen.de

Karlsruhe

The city of Karlsruhe is laid out in the shape of a fan, its principal streets radiating out from the main facade of its baroque Schloss. This feat of urban design was conceived by Karl Wilhelm, Margrave of Baden, in 1715, to reflect the absolutist ideas of the age. At the epicenter of the plan he placed his palace, the focal point of nine city streets and a further 23 avenues cut through the forest. No building was permitted to upstage the three-story Schloss by being more than two stories high. The town was given the name of "Carols Ruhe" (Charles's Rest).

Karlsruhe's baroque Schloss and the grounds of the Schlosspark

Karlsruhe

 319 B3

Visitor Information

✉ Bahnhofplatz 6

☎ 0721 37 20 53 83

karlsruhe-tourism.de

Modern Karlsruhe has developed into an important university city with science-based industries and a rich cultural life. No longer a state capital, it is the home of two national institutions, the Federal Supreme Court and the Federal Constitutional Court. Many buildings taller than two stories have gone up since Karl Wilhelm's time, but his plan is still intact. Its bold design is best seen from the air; the next best view is from the Schloss's central tower.

Rebuilt after wartime damage, the margraves' palace now houses the **Badisches Landesmuseum.** As the regional museum of the Grand Duchy of Baden, it contains the Baden crown jewels, prehistoric objects, archaeological finds from the Mediterranean, and medieval and Renaissance art. Take a look at the **Türken-beute,** the booty assembled by Margrave Ludwig Wilhelm during his campaigns against the Turks. Its weapons, armor, textiles, jewelry, and other items make it one of the most important collections of Islamic arts and crafts in the world.

The area around the palace has a botanical garden with exceptionally fine 19th-century greenhouses. The vast **Schlosspark,** beautified in 1967 in the course of the Federal Garden Show (see pp. 204–205), merges gradually with the forest. Housed in the **Orangerie** is part of the city's outstanding art gallery, with fine examples of German and European 20th-century painting. In the main gallery, the **Staatliche Kunsthalle,** are superb French, Dutch, and German old masters, including works by Dürer, Cranach, and Holbein the Younger. The "Crucifixion" by Grünewald is unequaled in the intensity of its depiction of pain and horror. You can find relief in the appealing portraits and landscapes of Hans Thoma (1839–1924), a former director of the gallery.

Marktplatz & Around

A century or so after Karl Wilhelm's reign, his successor, Archduke Karl Friedrich, employed Friedrich Weinbrenner, a local architect, to transform the city. View his results by walking from the Schloss along the axial route that leads due south. Weinbrenner laid out a new **Marktplatz,** gracing it with fine neoclassic public buildings: Stadtkirche (City Church) to the east, Rathaus

(Town Hall) to the west. The red sandstone **Pyramid** stands over the grave of Karl Wilhelm.

Farther south is Rondell-platz flanked by the neoclassic **Markgräfliches Palais.** The central obelisk commemorates the constitution granted by the grand duke to his realm in 1818. Always the most progressive German state, Baden abolished serfdom and torture early and introduced compulsory schooling. This 1818 constitution served as a model for the liberal revolutionaries of 1848 when they assembled in Frankfurt.

INSIDER TIP:

Discover Karlsruhe's sights at your own pace using the audio city iGuide. The starting point is Marktplatz, where you can rent iGuides from the City Information Office.

—YVONNE HALMICH
Karlsruhe Tourism Board

Located in an old munitions factory in the city's southwestern suburbs, the **Zentrum für Kunst-und Medientechnologie** (Center for Art & Media Technology) shows the potential of contemporary art and new media in an entertaining and instructive way. You can admire works by the likes of Andy Warhol and Roy Lichtenstein and also create your own art in an interactive gallery. ■

Badisches Landesmuseum
- ✉ Schloss, Schlossbezirk 10
- ☎ 0721 9 26 65 14
- 🕐 Closed Mon.
- 💲 $$

landesmuseum.de

Staatliche Kunsthalle
- ✉ Hans-Thoma-Strasse 2–6
- ☎ 0721 9 26 33 59
- 🕐 Closed Mon.
- 💲 $$–$$$

kunsthalle-karlsruhe.de

Zentrum für Kunst- und Medientechnologie
- ✉ Lorenzstrasse 19
- ☎ 0721 8 10 00
- 🕐 Closed Mon.–Tues.
- 💲 $$

zkm.de

Mannheim

Mannheim was planned in the 18th century as a grid of intersecting streets. Uniquely in Germany, the streets were not given names, but were defined with letters and numbers, making it easy to find one's way around. The town's location at the confluence of the Rhine and Neckar guaranteed its prosperity; its port is now one of the biggest inland harbors in Europe. The city, which in the 18th century was a byword for courtly culture, is now a stronghold of industry and the commercial center for much of the region.

Mannheim
🗺 319 B4
Visitor Information
✉ Willy-Brandt-Platz 3 (at main train station)
☎ 06221 65 88 80
🕐 Closed Sun.

tourist-mannheim.de

Mannheim's baroque **Schloss** (*Bismarckstrasse, tel 0621 65 57 18, schloss-mannheim.de, closed Mon., $$ guided/audio tour*) was built by Elector Carl Philipp when he moved his court here in 1720 from Heidelberg. The biggest building of its kind in Germany, it was the scene of the city's golden age, a center of the arts and music. It now houses the university, but you can visit the **Rittersaal** (Knights' Hall).

Best visited on market day (*Tues., Thurs., & Sat.*), **Marktplatz** is graced by the architecture of the Rathaus (Town Hall) and the Stadtkirche (City Church). **Paradeplatz** is dominated by a pyramid dedicated to Elector Johann Wilhelm.

The most interesting square is **Friedrichsplatz,** lined with fine art nouveau buildings and centered on the city's other landmark, the 200-foot (60 m) **Wasserturm.** Built in 1886, this is probably the most splendid of all German water towers.

The city's museums include the **Reiss-Engelhorn-Museum** (*Zeughaus C5, tel 0621 2 93 31 50, rem-mannheim.de, closed Mon., $$$*), with displays about city history; the **Städtische Kunsthalle** (*Friedrichsplatz 4, tel 0621 93 64 52, kunsthalle-mannheim.de closed Mon., $$*), with 19th- and 20th-century European art; the outstanding **Landesmuseum für Technik und Arbeit** (Regional Museum for Technology & Work; *Museumstrasse 1, tel 0621 42 98 9, technoseum.de, closed Mon., $$*); and the **Museumsschiff Mannheim** (*Am Museumsufer [Neckar], tel 0621 42 98 9, open daily p.m., $*), which features displays about navigation on the Rhine and Neckar Rivers. ∎

The Jesuitenkirche is one of the finest baroque churches in southwest Germany.

Tübingen

Dominated by its ancient university, Tübingen is a near-perfect example of a southern German medieval town, with a hilltop castle, a wealth of timber-framed houses, and an idyllic location on the banks of the River Neckar.

The river is divided into two channels by a long, narrow artificial island. Here, magnificent plane trees form a splendid avenue, the **Platanenallee.** Among the old houses and weeping willows on the north bank stands a gazebo-like yellow tower. The **Hölderlinturm** is where poet Friedrich Holderlin (1770–1843), one of the university's illustrious alumni, spent the last 36 years of his life after being declared insane.

Just behind this tower is the oldest part of the town, centered on two squares. In **Holzmarkt** stands the Gothic **Stiftskirche,** with the elaborate tombs of many of the rulers of Württemberg, among them Duke Eberhard the Bearded, who founded the university in 1477. You can climb the church tower (*tel 07071 43 151, closed Mon.–Thurs., $*) for a fine view over the rooftops. The charmingly irregular cobbled **Marktplatz** has a Neptune fountain and a picturesque 15th-century **Rathaus** (Town Hall) with an astronomical clock in its gable.

Laid out around a courtyard with a portal in the form of a Roman arch, the present **Schloss Hohentübingen** is a Renaissance structure built on 11th-century foundations. It houses various university departments, a museum, and a Heidelberg-style giant barrel.

Unfortunately it is no longer possible to visit the cellars where the barrel is situated, as they also contain south Germany's biggest bat colony! The **museum** contains the university's eclectic collections of antiquities and prehistoric items, such as the tiny figure of a horse carved from bone in Paleolithic times.

INSIDER TIP:

Seek out Tübingen's tower, overlooking the beautiful Neckar River, where the poet Hölderlin was confined during the troubled last years of his life.

—BETTINA ARNOLD
National Geographic grantee

Don't leave the castle area without enjoying the fine views over the Neckar and the town. The lower part of the old town has interesting old buildings, among them the Kornhaus (Corn Store), now home to the **Stadtmuseum** (City Museum), with its model of the old town. Tübingen also has its prison for unruly students, the **Studentenkarzer** (*Münzgasse 20, tel 07071 9 13 60, by appt. only*), which you can visit by guided tour only. ∎

Tübingen
🅰 319 C2
Visitor Information
✉ An der Neckarbrücke
☎ 07071 9 13 60
tuebingen-info.de

Hölderlinturm
✉ Bursagasse 6
☎ 07071 2 20 40
🕐 Closed Mon.
💲 $
hoelderlin -gesellschaft.de

Schlossmuseum
✉ Schloss Hohentübingen, Burgsteige 11
☎ 07071 2 97 73 84
🕐 Closed Mon.–Tues.
💲 $$

Stadtmuseum
✉ Kornhausstrasse 10
☎ 07071 204 17 11
🕐 Closed Mon.
💲 $

Baden-Baden

Synonymous with the fashionable pastime of "taking the cure," Baden-Baden remains the quintessential spa town. Here, quasi-medical pampering is only one element in the pleasurable round of strolling, eating, seeing and being seen, concerts, casino visits, and entertainment of all kinds.

Spa guests luxuriate in the sumptuous surroundings of the 19th-century Friedrichsbad.

Baden-Baden

🇦 319 B3

Visitor Information

✉ Schwarzwald-strasse 52 (off main road into town)

☎ 07221 27 52 00

baden-baden.de

The virtues of the waters that well up from deep underground at a temperature of 156°F (60°C) were recognized by the Romans, particularly by Emperor Caracalla. Nearly two thousand years later, the ultramodern spa facilities now bear his name. People came here to be cured throughout the Middle Ages and later, but it was the 19th century that made Baden-Baden into a legend. The town has very cleverly maintained the allure it had then, when kings and emperors, composers and artists, flocked

to what was deservedly called the "summer capital of Europe."

The town has a mild climate and an attractive setting in the wooded valley of the little Oos River running down from the Black Forest. But it benefits even more from the vision of the early 19th-century French entrepreneur Jacques Bénazet, the uncrowned "King of Baden-Baden." He and his son Edouard invested huge sums in the town, turning the ailing casino into a gaming palace.

Even if you prefer not to risk your hard-earned dollars at roulette, poker, or baccarat, it's well worth looking inside the **casino** of the Kurhaus, where fortunes are lost and won in surroundings worthy of the finest French châteaux. Outside, the stately neoclassic colonnade is the work of architect Friedrich Weinbrenner, who rebuilt much of nearby Karlsruhe (see pp. 328–329).

Town Center

An elegant parade of little single-story shops leads from the Kurhaus toward the town center. To the south is **Lichtentaler Allee,** which was Baden-Baden's most fashionable promenade. Originally an avenue of oaks, it is now the jewel of the town's immaculately maintained heritage of parks and gardens. Here is the **Theater** (Goetheplatz 1, tel 07221 93 27 51), built in 1860. Beautifully restored and staging performances again, it's an exuberant example of French neo-baroque design, a fitting setting for the 1862 premiere of Hector Berlioz's Shakespearean opera *Béatrice et Bénédict.* To the north is more parkland, with the **Trinkhalle,** a colonnaded pump room decorated with frescoes of local legends.

Stairways and narrow streets climb north to the Marktplatz and the Gothic **Stiftskirche.** The church's many treasures include a superb sandstone late-medieval crucifix and an over-the-top monument to "Türkenlouis"—the "Terror of the Turk," Margrave Ludwig Wilhelm.

Farther up the hill looms the **Neues Schloss** (New Castle), until 1918 the summer residence of the grand dukes of Baden, with fine views from its terrace. It's being converted into a luxury hotel, but you can visit the lobby.

On the same level as the Stiftskirche, you'll find the spa quarter. It begins with the most opulent of all Baden-Baden's spa establishments, the **Friedrichsbad.** Intended to replicate the luxury of ancient Rome, it opened in 1877 and created a sensation with its up-to-the-minute facilities in palatial surroundings. It has been unobtrusively modernized to accommodate a "Roman-Irish spa," which offers a three-hour treatment that is highly recommended. The remains of the real Roman spa installations are beyond, upstaged by the **Caracalla-Therme** (*tel 07221 27 59 40, $$$$*), a state-of-the-art complex of indoor and outdoor pools completed in 1985.

Among the reminders of Baden-Baden's heyday are its churches. Romanian Prince Michael Stourdza commissioned the great Munich architect Leo von Klenze (1784–1864) to design the domed **Stourdza-Kapelle** in the parkland high above the Trinkhalle in memory of his son. In the 19th century and the years immediately before World War I, members of the Russian aristocracy were among the most enthusiastic visitors to Baden-Baden. The connection was strengthened when Prince Wilhelm of Baden married the sister of Tsar Alexander II. The **Russian Orthodox Church,** with its onion domes, strikes an exotic note in the southern part of town. ∎

Casino
- ✉ Kurhaus, Kaiserallee 1
- ☎ 07221 302 40
- 💲 $

casino-baden-baden.de

Friedrichsbad
- 🅰 319 B2
- ✉ Römerplatz 1
- ☎ 07221 27 59 20
- 💲 $$$$$

carasana.de

Russian Orthodox Church
- ✉ Lichtentaler Strasse 76
- ☎ 07221 37 32 138
- 💲 $

Bare Treatment

In the 19th century, "taking the waters" became a fashionable means of recreation, as the many German town names prefixed by *Bad* (spa) might suggest. Apart from special sessions one or two days a week, today's continental bathhouses and spa pools are resolutely mixed-sex, and no clothing is permitted. More modest patrons can discreetly wrap themselves in the towel that is provided along with shoes and basic cosmetics, such as shampoo and skin cream. Children under 14 are not allowed, but older teenagers can go in with a parent. Lasting two to three hours, a full cycle of treatment consists of a timed series of hot and cold showers, sometimes with perfumed water, as well as visits to the sauna, steam bath, and whirlpool. If that's not enough, the in-house masseur is sure to hit the right spots.

Freiburg im Breisgau

Freiburg has an enviable sunny location where one of the main valleys running down from the Black Forest meets the Rhine plain. The city has a sunny temperament, too; its citizens, and the students at its venerable university, seem more cheerful and relaxed than many of their fellow countrymen. It's a good center for exploring the surrounding region: The Black Forest, the Rhine Valley, France, and Switzerland are not far distant. Within sight of Freiburg is the Kaiserstuhl (Emperor's Seat), an ancient, vine-clad volcano.

Freiburg im Breisgau

🅰 319 A1

Visitor Information

✉ Rathausplatz 2–4

☎ 0761 3 88 18 80

freiburg.de

The city's greatest treasure is its red sandstone cathedral, the **Münster Unserer Lieben Frau** (Minster of Our Lady) on Münsterplatz. It's hard to believe that this magnificent Gothic structure with its 377-foot (115 m) tower was built simply as a parish church, being elevated to the rank of cathedral only in the 19th century. It was begun in Romanesque style about 1200, but from this first period only the transepts remain, flanked by towers with openwork caps added later. These imitate the lacelike structure of the spire that crowns the western end of the cathedral. This was a pioneering effort, a great technical achievement when it was completed around 1350. You can climb to the tower's viewing platform for a vista of the city.

To appreciate the richness and complexity of the cathedral's exterior, with its flying buttresses and droll gargoyles, walk around the square; the color and bustle of the market stalls add an authentically medieval note. Pause at the north door, where the sculpture includes a figure of God resting on the seventh day of the Creation. On the west portal Satan is shown as a smooth seducer leading on a lady clad only in a goatskin. You can take a guided tour of the cathedral, but the highlights are the 13th-century stained glass and a superb altarpiece by Hans Baldung Grien depicting the Coronation of the Virgin.

A word of warning: The streets and squares are seamed with channels, originally built to water animals and flush away filth, a hazard for the unwary. With this in mind, don't miss the other

A Gothic doorway and oriel window enliven the street scene.

EXPERIENCE: Hiking Through Hell's Valley

Spectacularly vertiginous and at times forbidding, the 5.5-mile (9 km) trail through the Höllental, or Hell's Valley, is perhaps the most romantic in all of the Black Forest. The valley, the result of a glacier or tectonic fault, begins about 9 miles (15 km) east of Freiburg. You can pick up the trail here, or in town, and walk all the way to the picturesque waters of **Titisee Lake.** The trail runs along the Rotbach stream, sometimes above the hairpins of the B31, and shadows the tracks of the Höllentalbahn

(Hell's Train), which passes through a series of tunnels on the way to **Donaueschingen.** Below the village of **Hinterzarten,** the trail winds downhill to a glacial bowl called **Spoon Valley,** where wooden spoons were once the local craft. The narrowest part of the valley is the 25-foot-wide (7.5 m) **Hirschsprung,** where you'll see the likeness of the stag said to have saved itself by leaping across the gorge. At this point the canyon is so steep that sunlight penetrates only for a short time around midday.

buildings around Münsterplatz. Note especially the arcaded, steep-roofed, and oxblood-red **Historisches Kaufhaus,** the early 16th-century Merchants' Hall. The statues and coats of arms adorning its facade represent the city's Austrian rulers.

To the west of Münsterplatz, the commercial heart of Freiburg is a pleasing mixture of old and new. During World War II, accidental German bombing destroyed a good portion of the city, and further destruction occurred during an Allied air raid in 1944; much rebuilding has occurred since.

Beyond Kaiser-Joseph-Strasse is **Rathausplatz,** with its two town halls converted from once-separate buildings. The **Neues Rathaus** (New Town Hall) has a carillon, which plays at noon. Behind St. Martin's Church in the middle of the square is one of the city's finest old houses, the **Haus zum Walfisch,** with an exuberant Gothic doorway.

Kaiser-Joseph-Strasse leads south to the restored 13th-century city gateway called the **Martinstor.** To the left, alongside a broad water channel, is **Fischerau,** once the district of fishermen, tanners, and others who needed water for their work. In the old Augustinian monastery, the **Augustiner-museum** has excellent examples of medieval religious art, including original gargoyles from the cathedral. The **Schwabentor,** the medieval gateway guarding the southeastern approach to the city, still stands. Close by is the 14th-century **Zum Roten Bären** (Ober-linden 12, tel 0761 38 78 70, closed Sun.), said to be Germany's oldest inn. Leading north is a pretty old street, **Konviktstrasse.**

Freiburg has its own mountain within the city limits. The **Schau-insland** (4,213 feet/1,284 m), meaning "look into the country," gives great views over the city, Black Forest, and Rhine plain. It is accessible by cable car from Stüble, a short bus ride from the city center. ∎

Münster Unserer Lieben Frau

- ✉ Münsterplatz
- ☎ 0761 21 88 243
- 🕐 Tower closed Mon.
- 💲 $ (tower)

freiburger
muenster.info

Augustiner-museum

- ✉ Am Augustiner-platz 1–3
- ☎ 0761 2 01 25 31
- 🕐 Closed Mon.
- 💲 $$

museen.freiburg.de

Black Forest

Running north for about 100 miles (160 km) from the Swiss border and extending some 37 miles (60 km) from east to west, the mountainous Black Forest region boasts dark masses of spruce and fir, clear streams and waterfalls, great timber farmhouses, and extravagant folk costumes. A superb network of footpaths has long attracted walkers. Today, visitors can stay in a wide range of accommodations, ranging from farmstead self-catering apartments to luxury lakeside hotels.

Beautifully located Titisee makes a good base for exploring the Black Forest.

Black Forest
- 319 A1, B1–B2

Titisee
- 319 B1
Visitor Information
- ✉ Strandbadstrasse 4
- ☎ 07652 1206 8120

hochschwarzwald.de

The Black Forest reaches its highest point in the southwest, where the **Feldberg** tops out at 4,898 feet (1,493 m). The Feldberg, like other summits in this area, is bare, but coniferous forest covers the higher ground almost everywhere else. This dark cover gives way to more varied deciduous woodland and meadows on the lower slopes and in the valleys. The uplands drop gently in most directions, but in the west they fall steeply to the Rhine Valley. Along the crest, the viewpoints include the

Feldberg itself and the **Schauinsland** (see p. 335), reached by cable car ($$$) from **Freiburg im Breisgau.** Views extend over the valley, where the forest cover gives way to a line of wine villages and orchards, toward the great river, and beyond to the Vosges Mountains in Alsace. On clear days, the distant line of the Alps comes into sight.

One good base for exploration is **Titisee,** a resort on the lake of the same name, centrally located in the southern Black Forest and within reach of many of the highlights in the region. Titisee can be very crowded, but there are many places to stay in the surrounding area.

To the west, you can follow the spectacular deep cleft of **Höllental** (Hell's Valley) along a main road or an ingeniously engineered railroad that links the interior of the Black Forest to Freiburg. To the north, the clock-making town of **Furtwangen** is home to the wonderful **Deutsches Uhrenmuseum** (German Clock Museum), featuring timepieces of all kinds—including cuckoo clocks.

Triberg, farther north still, is also famous for clockmaking. Its **Schwarzwaldmuseum** has displays of local costumes and crafts. A half-hour's walk away is the country's highest waterfall (535 feet/163 m).

For more traditional Black Forest culture, continue up the road to the **Schwarzwälder Freilichtmuseum** (Black Forest Open-Air Museum). Here you'll find a collection of farm buildings and learn how all farming activities took place beneath their massive hipped roofs.

INSIDER TIP:

Hike up to Hochfirst, Titisee's highest look-out, for magnificent views of the Black Forest, Rhine Valley, and Vogesen Mountains, as well as the Alps.

—JÜRGEN HÖRMANN
Titisee Tourism Board

You could take a drive along one of Germany's finest scenic roads, the **Schwarzwald-Hochstrasse,** which joins Freudenstadt with Baden-Baden. However, you are likely to have the most memorable experiences on foot. Visitor centers have information about local paths, but make sure you climb to at least one classic viewpoint (see pp. 338–339). In the Titisee area, a rewarding walk takes you from the village of Hinterzarten into the Höllental and the Ravenna Gorge. Long-distance trails crisscross the Black Forest. (Arrange at a visitor center or travel agent to have your luggage transported between hotels.) ∎

Deutsches Uhrenmuseum
- ✉ Robert-Gerwig-Platz, Furtwangen
- ☎ 07723 920 28 00
- 💲 $$

deutsches-uhren
museum.de

Schwarzwald-museum
- 🅰 319 B2
- ✉ Wallfahrtsstrasse 4, Triberg
- ☎ 07722 44 34
- 🕐 Closed Mon.
- 💲 $$

schwarzwald
museum.de

Schwarzwälder Freilichtmuseum
- 🅰 319 B2
- ✉ Gutach
- ☎ 07831 9 35 60
- 🕐 Open April–early Nov.
- 💲 $$$

vogtsbauernhof.org

Black Forest Clocks

In the 1949 film *The Third Man*, Orson Welles may have scornfully attributed cuckoo clocks to the Swiss, but they are a quintessential Black Forest product. Clockmaking began in the region in the 17th century, as impoverished farmers looked for alternative ways of making a living. In this well-forested region, their familiarity with wood proved invaluable, and clock mechanisms were expertly carved from wood until well into the 19th century. Millions of clocks were exported, to America and the rest of Europe, until the industry drastically declined in the 1970s. A modest revival has since taken place. Souvenir shops are stocked with clocks to suit all budgets, while individual timepieces can be ordered to personal specifications from highly skilled specialists.

The Feldberg: A Walk to the Black Forest's Highest Summit

The Black Forest rises grandly in its southwestern corner to its highest elevation, culminating in the 4,898-foot (1,493 m) Feldberg. Virtually all visitors to this magical place feel an obligation to climb the great block of granite and gneiss, scraped into its final shape by the glaciers of the last ice age. Extensive and spectacular views reaching as far as the Swiss Alps are the reward.

Black Forest views fan out from the Feldberg's summit.

A road leads most of the way up the Feldberg, terminating at a huge parking lot with hotels, kiosks, souvenir shops, and an interpretive center, the **Haus der Natur ❶** (Nature House). This is an excellent place to find out more about local history and ecology before striking out. You will learn that although trees rise from the lower slopes, the top is clear, with the grasses and bog vegetation the result of the exceptionally harsh climate and centuries of cattle grazing.

The summit receives nearly 80 inches (2,000 mm) of precipitation a year, much of it falling as snow. The first flakes can descend as

NOT TO BE MISSED:

Haus der Natur • View down to the Feldsee • Panoramic views from the summit

early as September, and snow covers sheltered spots on the northern slopes until well into summer. The reliability of snowfall led to the Feldberg's early popularity as a place for winter sports, the first ski enthusiasts appearing in 1890. Walkers come year-round; the most

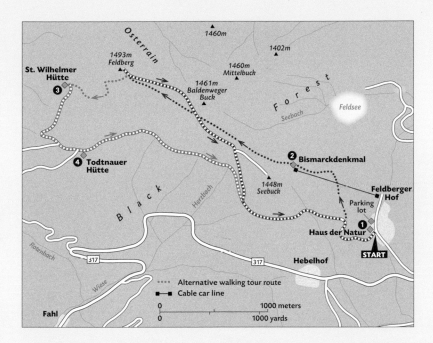

favorable conditions can occur in fall or early winter, when temperature inversions fill the valleys with fog and leave the upper air clear.

Reaching the Summit

Even if you dislike walking uphill, resist the temptation to take the Feldbergbahn cable car. It saves a climb of only 575 feet (175 m) and will diminish your sense of achievement! Set off along the surfaced road to the left of the Haus der Natur and, after about 330 yards (300 m), turn right onto a path. This is the only mildly strenuous part of the walk, climbing up to the granite obelisk of the **Bismarckdenkmal ②**, erected in 1896. There are stupendous views in all directions, including down to the **Feldsee,** a small lake formed by a glacier. Panels help identify distant features such as the Schwäbische Alb to the northeast and the ridge of the Vosges Mountains beyond the Rhine to the west. If conditions are exceptionally clear, you may be able to identify peaks such as the Eiger, Mönch, and Jungfrau, and even Mont Blanc, 150 miles (250 km) away.

> 🅼 See also map p. 319
> ➤ Feldberghof parking lot
> 🔁 4.7 miles (7.5 km), or 5.6 miles (9 km) via the chalets
> 🕑 2 hours (2.5 hours via the chalets)
> ➤ Feldberghof parking lot

From the Bismarckdenkmal, follow the path across the airy, gently undulating top of the mountain toward the high point at its western end. The Feldberg has suffered serious erosion in the past from the pressure of countless pairs of feet, and its mantle of vegetation is still vulnerable. The towers rising from the peak include a weather station and modern radio and television installations. From here you can return to the starting point by the service road.

If you have time, descend the southwestern flank of the mountain to the chalet called the **St. Wilhelmer Hütte ③**. A road runs down to a mountain hut, **Todtnauer Hütte ④**, after which it continues on an almost level alignment to rejoin the service road.

Lake Constance

A serene vacation destination sharing borders with Switzerland and Austria, Lake Constance (Bodensee) is not a lake but a great swelling of the Rhine as it leaves the Alps. Gouged by an Ice Age glacier, the body of water is divided into the upper lake, between Bregenz in Austria and German Konstanz, and smaller sections to the northwest, cut by the Bodanrück Peninsula.

A pleasure boat leaves Lindau harbor and its resident Bavarian lion.

Lindau

📍 280 A2 & 319 C1

Visitor Information

✉ Alfred-Nobel-Platz 1 (opposite main station)

☎ 08382 26 00 30

lindau-tourismus.de

NOTE: If you are staying several days, purchase the Lake Constance Experience ticket (*BodenseeErlebniskarte*), which buys you use of lake cruisers and entry to most attractions in the area.

Lindau

At the lake's northeast end, the island city of Lindau is actually in Bavaria, but it forms such an integral part of the Lake Constance region that it is included here. Linked to the mainland by a road bridge and a causeway carrying the railroad, it's a magical place, with a harbor looking south to the mountains of Appenzell in Switzerland and the Vorarlberg range rising over the Austrian lakeside town of Bregenz.

Walk east along the quayside, past the 13th-century **Mangturm,** a relic of the medieval fortifications, and then turn inland. The

old town center is full of charm, its unspoiled streets and squares lined with timber-framed and gabled houses. The Gothic **Altes Rathaus** (Old Town Hall) on Kanzleistrasse was modernized in Renaissance times with an external staircase and murals.

Go east along the main street, Maximilianstrasse, and you will come to **Marktplatz,** Lindau's loveliest square. The town began here with the founding of a ninth-century convent. The most striking building in the square is the **Haus zum Cavazzen,** an imposing baroque mansion that now serves as the municipal museum.

EXPERIENCE: Cycling Around Lake Constance

The alluring shoreline of one of Europe's largest lakes is tailor-made for bicycling. The well-signposted, 172-mile (273 km) path of the **Lake Constance Cycle** bike route circumnavigates the lake, leading you through picturesque patches of Germany, Austria, and Switzerland. The route passes between the lake's glimmering waters on one hand, and leafy forests and vineyards on the other. Sights in the Germany section include the historic town of

Konstanz (a good departure point), the garden island of Mainau, the pilgrimage church in Birnau, the vineyards of Meersburg, and lovely Lindau. Maps and details of bike rental and hotels are available from **Bodensee-Radweg Service** *(Fritz Arnold Strasse 16a, Konstanz, tel 07531 81 99 30, bodensee-radweg.com)*. The region's ferries and trains take bicycles on board, so you can pedal out and take public transportation back.

Other North Shore Towns

Still in Bavaria, **Wasserburg** *(280 A1 & 319 C1)* is an island settlement reached by causeway. Packed together are its castle, onion-domed church, and the gabled courthouse, the **Malhaus,** where witches were tried in the 17th century. On view is the "Wasserburg Pear," a steel bridle used to torture them. **Schloss Montfort,** in the next settlement along the lake, **Langenargen,** is a Moorish-style summer residence of the Württemberg royal family.

The second largest lake town after Konstanz, **Friedrichshafen** *(319 C1)* is a businesslike place with modern industries carrying on the traditions established by Ferdinand Graf von Zeppelin (1838–1917). In 1900, Zeppelin oversaw the maiden flight of the first of the airships that bears his name. The **Zeppelin-Museum,** housed in a gleaming 1930s building, has a full-scale reconstruction of part of the ill-fated *Hindenburg,* whose demise at Lakehurst, New Jersey, in 1937 brought their era to a tragic end.

Perched high above the lake, the little town of **Meersburg** has two castles. The lower town by the harbor is linked by the steep Steigstrasse to the upper town, full of sloping streets and squares lined by flower-bedecked houses. The **Weinbaumuseum's** *(Vorburgasse 11, tel 07532 44 04 00, open 2–6 p.m. Tues., Fri., & Sun.; closed Nov.– March, $)* historic exhibits include a monster barrel with a capacity of about 13,000 gallons (50,000 L).

Farther along the shore, the life of earlier inhabitants of the Bodensee is displayed in the open-air **Pfahlbaumuseum** (Stilt House Museum; *Strandpromenade 6, tel 07556 92890 0, pfahlbauten.de, closed Dec.–March, $$$)* at Unteruhldingen. The museum has convincing reconstructions of a number of ancient dwellings.

High among the vineyards between here and Überlingen is the pilgrimage church of **Birnau** *(normally open daily),* a little masterpiece of rococo architecture and interior decoration. The most famous feature is the "Honig-schlecker," a cherub sucking honey from his finger, a reference to the

Haus zum Cavazzen
- ⊠ Marktplatz 6, Lindau
- ☎ 08382 27 75 65 14
- 🕐 Closed Mon. & Nov.–March
- 💲 $

Malhaus
- ⊠ Halbinselstr. 77, Wasserburg
- ☎ 08382 750 457
- 🕐 Closed Mon. & Nov.–March
- 💲 $

Zeppelin-Museum
- ⊠ Seestrasse 22, Friedrichshafen
- ☎ 07541 38 01 0
- 🕐 Closed Mon. Nov.–April
- 💲 $$$
- zeppelin-museum.de

Meersburg
- 🅰 319 C1
- **Visitor Information**
- ⊠ Kirchstrasse 4
- ☎ 07532 440 400
- meersburg.de

Überlingen

⚑ 319 C1

Visitor Information

✉ Landungsplatz 5

☎ 07551 947 15 22

ueberlingen.de

Reichlin-Meldegg-Haus

✉ Krummeberg-
strasse 30,
Überlingen

☎ 07551 99 10 79

🕑 Closed Mon.

💲 $$

**museum-
ueberlingen.de**

Konstanz

⚑ 319 C1

Visitor Information

✉ Fischmarkt 2

☎ 07531 13 30 30

konstanz-tourismus.de

Mainau

⚑ 319 C1

Visitor Information

✉ Insel Mainau

☎ 07531 30 30

🕑 Closed late
Oct.–late March

💲 $$$$$

mainau.de

"honeyed eloquence" of Bernard of Clairvaux, founder of the church's Cistercian Order.

Overlooking the Bodanrück peninsula is the lovely old imperial town of **Überlingen**. In the 19th century it reinvented itself as a health resort. Unlike many similar places, its people realized that the town walls and their towers were a visual asset and preserved them.

Walk up from the lakefront to **Münsterplatz,** with its Rathaus (Town Hall) and Gothic minster church, and continue to the local museum. Housed in the 15th-century **Reichlin-Meldegg-Haus,** it has the country's biggest collection of dollhouses and a fine view of town from its garden.

Konstanz

The busiest ferry service on the lake links Meersburg to the city of Konstanz, the region's largest town. On the south bank, the Altstadt (Old Town) has kept much of its medieval charm. Konstanz was founded by the Romans, but the city's moment of glory came in 1414–1418, when the Council of Konstanz met here to heal the great crisis of medieval Christendom, the rift between rival popes called the Great Schism.

The delegates are popularly said to have met in the massive **Konzilgebäude** by the harbor. They actually assembled in the city's cathedral, the **Münster,** with its magnificent 13th-century Holy Sepulchre.

The historical figure most closely associated with the city is the radical Czech preacher Jan Hus (ca 1372–1415), who denounced the corruption of the Church. In 1414, he was summoned to Konstanz, where he was tried, condemned, and burned at the stake. To learn more, pay a visit to the **Hus Museum** *(Hussenstrasse 64, Konstanz, tel 07531 290 42, closed Mon.).*

Islands in the Lake

From Konstanz, it is only a short distance to the Bodensee's two islands. You'll find two ancient monastery churches in quiet **Reichenau:** In Oberzell, **St. Georg** has thousand-year-old wall paintings, while the **Münster St. Maria und Markus** *(tel 07534 9 20 70)* in Mittelzell is a marvel of architectural simplicity.

The garden island of **Mainau** is Lake Constance's most popular destination. This subtropical paradise is laid out around the 18th-century Schloss. Other attractions include a lovely baroque church, medieval watchtower, and butterfly garden. ∎

EXPERIENCE: Ballooning in a Zeppelin

Those who recall the *Hindenburg* going down in flames over New Jersey may have their doubts, but thanks to nonflammable helium, the airships cruising around Lake Constance are a safe and singular delight. Flights aren't cheap, starting at around $270 (€200) for a half-hour spin, but the experience is unforgettable. During the slow and easy ride at 1,000 feet (300 m), the panorama windows of the Zeppelin NT give an incomparable view of the Alps. For tickets, contact **Zeppelin Luftschifftechnik** *(Allmansweilerstrasse 132, Friedrichshafen, tel 07541 590 00, zeppelinflug.de).*

Ulm

With its ancient fortifications and houses, all lorded over by the minster's great spire, Ulm creates a picturesque scene on the Danube. Before exploring its narrow lanes, take a stroll along the riverbank's south (Bavarian) side to take it all in.

Stepped gables, elaborate Gothic windows, and murals adorn Ulm's Rathaus.

Start with the well-preserved **Fischer-Viertel** (Fishermen's Quarter). There's a good view of the onetime houses of riverside residents—tanners, dyers, ferrymen—from the promenade atop the fortifications. The **Metzgerturm** (Butchers' Tower) leans at an angle some 6 feet (2m) off center, while the 15th-century **Schiefes Haus** (Crooked House) lives up to its name, cast askew by piles sagging into the soft riverbed underneath. The picturesque **Fischerplätzle** (Fishermen's Square) affords a great view of the 15-century **Zunfthaus** (the fishermen's guildhall) and the

Schönes Haus (Pretty House), adorned with a proud scene of shipping on the Danube. A key trading post as early as the 12th century, the town would dispatch *Ulmer Schachteln*, or flat boats, laden with goods down the waterway as far as the Black Sea.

On the first Monday in June, the mayor addresses the burghers from the balcony of the 18th-century **Schwörhaus** (Oath House), swearing on the 1397 constitution that rich and poor should be treated equally—a bold statement in a society run by wealthy patricians. From here, you can wander down **Kussgasse**

Ulm
🄰 319 D2
Visitor Information
✉ Münsterplatz 50, im Stadthaus
☎ 0731 1 61 28 30
tourismus.ulm.de

Although work began on Ulm's massive Münster in the 14th century, it was not completed until 1890.

Ulmer Museum

- ✉ Marktplatz 9
- ☎ 0731 161 43 30
- ⏱ Closed Mon.
- 💲 $$

museum.ulm.de

(Kissing Alley), where opposing eaves nearly touch each other overhead, and cross over the **Lügner-Brücke** (Liar's Bridge), where shady dealers were thought to make their getaway.

Ulm's **Rathaus** (Town Hall) is a Gothic cum Renaissance building

---

Ulm's Best Views

Marvel in wonder at the following vantage points:
- The panorama from the Münster, the world's tallest church spire
- Fischer-Viertel's half-timbered houses along the tiny Blau River
- The old town walls seen from the Danube's south shore
- The off-kilter perspective of the Metzgerturm from below

---

adorned with figures of Charlemagne and the kings of Hungary and Bohemia, and a dazzling astrological clock. In the foyer, Albrecht Berblinger's attempt at manned flight is commemorated by a full-size copy of his machine, now considered more a visionary than foolhardy venture. On Marktplatz, the brightly colored **Fischkastenbrunnen** (Fish Crate Fountain) is where fishmongers kept their catch alive on market days.

The giant **Münster** is not a cathedral but a parish church. Its nave can hold 20,000 people—nearly twice the town's population when work began in 1377. The spire rises 525 feet (161 m), making it the world's tallest church tower. Climb the 768 steps ($) to the top on a clear day, and you will see not only a close-up of the spire's openwork construction but also the Alps more than 60 miles (100 km) away to the south.

Medieval builders conceived the tower's idea, but its completion had to await late 19th-century technology. The finest work of art is inside: Carved by two 15th-century locals, the choir stalls are ornamented with figures from the ancient world and the Bible.

The **Ulmer Museum** has carvings by Daniel Mauch, the last of the city's great disciples of Italianate sculpture. Upstairs is a fascinating section on the four centuries of thought and toil that went into erecting the Münster. The treasures include the renowned Kurt Fried collection of works from the 1950s to '80s, by artists including Kandinsky, Klee, Liechtenstein, and Picasso. ■

More Places to Visit in Baden-Württemberg

Burg Hohenzollern

In the early 19th century, Prussian Crown Prince Friedrich Wilhelm inspected the ruins of the ancestral castle of the Hohenzollern dynasty and decided to rebuild it. Between 1850 and 1867, a new building arose from the old foundations, more spectacularly medieval than the old castle ever was. Its dramatic outline visible from far and wide, Burg Hohenzollern is one of the great monuments of the rising German nationalism of the 19th century, with fascinating interiors and many reminders of the ill-fated local family. *burg-hohenzollern.com* 🚠 319 C2 ✉ Hechingen ☎ 07471 24 28 💲 $$$ (guided tour)

Haigerloch

The point where a pair of rock spurs forces the Eyach River into tightly constricted bends makes a picturesque but impractical urban site. Haigerloch has a castle and the **Atomkeller-Museum** *(Pfluggasse 5, tel 07474 6 97 27, closed Dec.–Feb., $)*, a real curiosity. In the spring of 1945, scientists evacuated from Berlin worked feverishly in underground chambers on the development of a nuclear reactor, and the museum tells the story of their vain efforts. *haigerloch.de* 🚠 319 B2 ✉ Oberstadtstrasse 11 (Rathaus) ☎ 07474 69 727

Maulbronn

The 12th-century Cistercian monastery at Maulbronn has been granted UNESCO World Heritage status as a perfectly preserved example of the architectural setting for medieval monastic life. The austere Cisterican order chose remote locations for their monasteries, where they could live a self-sufficient life apart from the temptations of the world. Inside Maulbronn's walls and towers is a complete world, with all the structures necessary to sustain a considerable community—smithies, stables, storehouses, a bakery, a guesthouse—all grouped picturesquely around a courtyard. At the far end, the church originally reflected the Cistercian love of simplicity but later was enhanced with artworks and decorative features such as elaborate vaulting. The monastic quarters around the cloister include a lovely washing fountain used by the monks before and after meals in the great refectory. Maulbronn was also a school; its pupils included astronomer Johannes Kepler, poet Friedrich Hölderlin, and writer Hermann Hesse. *maulbronn.de* 🚠 319 B3 ✉ Ehemaliges Zisterzienserkloster Maulbronn ☎ 07043 92 66 10 🕑 Closed Mon. Nov.–Feb. 💲 $$

Strange figures stroll the streets during Rottweil's *Fastnet* celebrations.

Rottweil

In Germany, Rottweil is synonymous with particularly spectacular pre-Lenten *Fastnet* celebrations, whose high point is the *Narrensprung,* a parade of colorfully costumed and masked fools. This takes place in the setting of Rottweil's unspoiled townscape, with its elaborately decorated old houses, Renaissance fountains, and intact fortifications. *rottweil.de* 🚠 319 B2 ✉ Hauptstrasse 21–23 ☎ 0741 49 42 80

EXPERIENCE: Hiking With the Foresters

While any tenderfoot will be smitten by Germany's lush forests, a qualified warden can really help you see what's in the woods. **Meeting Point Forests,** a grass-roots campaign, binds together forestry offices all over the country that devote a good part of their time explaining log habitats, bird species, and fields of mushrooms to curious visitors. For instance, in the Tauber River valley town of Tauberbischofsheim in northeastern Baden-Württemberg, hikes led by felt-capped foresters explore nature trails every Thursday afternoon (book at Lieblices Taubertal, Gartenstrasse 1, tel 07941 825 806, liebliches-taubertal.de).

Treffpunkt Wald (Büsgenweg 1, Göttingen, tel 0551 379 62 65, treffpunkt wald.de, email: info@idwald.de) will marry a learned warden with your destination in virtually any German province. Beyond the leafy wanderings, activities available include balloon rides, mountain biking, walking tours, and gently supervised "survival" camps for kids.

Schloss Bruchsal

The baroque Schloss at Bruchsal is one of the most ambitious of its kind, with some 50 individual buildings and a French-style formal garden whose main avenue once led to the Rhine 10 miles (16 km) away. The grand palace was built for one of the most extravagant of Germany's 18th-century prince-bishops, Cardinal Damian Hugo von Schönborn. He is flatteringly portrayed in one of the frescoes on the upper floor, benevolently approving the plan of his palace. Behind him stands the figure of Balthasar Neumann, perhaps the greatest architect of the German baroque, responsible here at Bruchsal for the spectacular staircase. The Schloss houses the **Deutsche Musikautomaten Museum** (German Automata Museum), with musicmaking apparatus from pianolas to jukeboxes (separate ticket). schloss-bruchsal.de 🄰 319 B3 ☎ 07251 74 26 61 🕓 Closed Mon. 💲 $$ (combined Schloss & museum ticket)

Schloss Schwetzingen

His town palace at Mannheim gave Elector Palatine Carl Theodor (1724–1799) little scope for his passion for landscape. He turned his attention to his summer residence at nearby Schwetzingen, and over a 30-year period laid out one of the most fabulous 18th-century gardens in Europe. This mixture of French formality and English naturalism is peppered with an array of buildings, including Roman temples, artificial ruins, a bathhouse, and a mosque with twin minarets and a "Turkish" garden. The palace is also worth visiting for its rococo theater and authentically furnished interiors. Schwetzingen is a center for growing Germany's favorite vegetable, the asparagus. A bronze asparagus seller greets you as you near the palace. schloss-schwetzingen.de 🄰 319 B4 ☎ 06221 65 88 80 🕓 Closed Mon. 💲 $$$ (guided tour)

Schwäbisch Hall

Schwäbisch Hall minted silver coins called Häller (or Heller), and like today's euro, they were valid throughout Europe. (Hellers are still part of the currency in the Czech Republic and Slovakia.) Schwäbisch Hall's timber-frame houses rise over the River Kocher, crossed by covered bridges. The townscape is dominated by the church of **St. Michael,** reached by an enormous stairway leading up from the sloping marketplace, one of the finest urban spaces in Germany. schwaebischhall.da 🄰 319 C3 ✉ Am Markt 9 ☎ 0791 75 12 46

Travelwise

Intercity express train

TRAVELWISE

PLANNING YOUR TRIP

Climate

Germany's climate is temperate with continental extremes. Marine influences from the north and west make for cool summers and mild, damp winters. Eastern and southern parts of the country experience hotter summers and harsher winters. The region along the Alpine rim gets the most precipitation.

Average daytime temperature:

Berlin 35°F (2°C) in winter; 65°F (18°C) in summer

Hamburg 32°F (0°C) in winter; 64°F (18°C) in summer

Munich 30°F (−1°C) in winter; 63°F (17°C) in summer

Insurance

It pays to take out a travel insurance policy. Make sure you have adequate coverage for medical treatment and expenses including repatriation, and also for baggage and money loss. It's also a good idea to take photocopies of important documents and keep them separate from the originals, in case the latter are stolen.

Main Events

Easter and Christmas both offer fascinating glimpses of traditional local events. The southern Catholic regions are alive with religious festivals, especially in the springtime.

January

Six-day cycle race in Berlin, Jan. 1, sechstagerennen-berlin.de

Grüne Woche in Berlin, mid-Jan., a consumer fair for agriculture, gruenewoche.de

February

Berlin International Film Festival, 2nd & 3rd week, berlinale.de

Carnival celebrations in Cologne, Düsseldorf, and Mainz, from the Thurs. of the week before Ash Wednesday, karneval.de

March

Cebit computer expo, early March, cebit.de

Book Fair in Leipzig, mid-March, leipziger-buchmesse.de

April

Easter celebrations in Catholic villages

Hanover International Industrial Trade Fair, early/mid-April, hannovermesse.de

Walpurgisnacht, a witches' sabbath in the Harz Mountains, April 30–May 1, harzinfo.de

May

Ruhrfestspiele in Recklinghausen, exhibitions, concerts, and theater, May 1–mid-June, ruhrfestspiele.de

Hamburger Hafengeburtstag, sailing regattas and street entertainment, mid-May, hamburger-hafengeburtstag.de

June

Festival of Classical Music in Mecklenburg, June–Sept., festspiele-mv.de

Kieler Woche yachting regatta, 3rd week in June, kielerwoche.de

Festival of Classical Music in Bad Kissingen, kissingersommer.de

Open-Air Opera Festival in Potsdam, 2 weeks in late June, musikfestspiele-potsdam.de

Christopher Street Day, gay & lesbian parades in Berlin & Cologne, mid-June, deutschland.de

Burgfestspiele Jagsthausen, theater and classical music festival in a romantic castle, jagsthausen.de

documenta in Kassel, June–Sept. 2017, documenta.de

Karl-May Festival in Bad Segeberg, reenactment of Apache tales from the American West, late June–early Sept., karl-may-spiele.de

July

Festival of Classical Music in Schleswig-Holstein, early July–late Aug., shmf.de

Richard Wagner Festival in Bayreuth, late July–late Aug., bayreuther-festspiele.de

August

Mainfest in Frankfurt, celebrations of the River Main, early Aug., frankfurt-tourismus.de

Rhein in Flammen in Koblenz, fireworks from boats and river banks, early Aug., rhein.feuerwerk-info.de

September

Wine Festival in Bensheim an der Bergstrasse, nine days from 1st week Sept., www.verkehrs verein.bensheim.de

Musikfest Berlin, with guest orchestras, ensembles, and choirs; first 3 weeks of Sept., berlinerfest spiele.de

Beethoven Festival in Bonn, early Sept.–early Oct., beethovenfest.de

Cannstatter Volksfest in Stuttgart, the world's second largest beer festival, late Sept.–mid-Oct., cannstatter-volksfest.de

Ruhr-Triennale Arts Festival, mid-Aug.–late Sept., ruhrtriennale.de

Oktoberfest in Munich, 16 days in late Sept.–mid-Oct., oktoberfest.de

October

Zwiebelmarkt in Weimar, a colorful street market, early/mid-Oct., weimar.de

Frankfurt Book Fair, early to mid-Oct., buchmesse.de

Kassel Music Days, classical concerts, late Oct.–early Nov., kasseler-musiktage.de

November

St. Martin's Day, Nov. 11, children's procession with lanterns and singing in Catholic areas

December
Christmas Markets, until Christmas Eve; the prettiest are held in Baden-Württemberg and Bavaria, with the most renowned in Nuremberg, *christmasmarkets.com*

Tourist Information
Regional tourist offices *(Verkehrsamt)* provide information on attractions and accommodations, and sell guidebooks and maps. Helpful websites include:
German Government Website
   deutschland.de
German National Tourist Board
   germany.travel
Historic Highlights of Germany
   hhog.de

What to Take
Whether you're going to admire Germany's historic monuments or its natural wonders, be sure to pack comfortable footwear. The weather can change quickly, so even in summer bring along a waterproof jacket and layers of clothing. A hat and sunscreen are good ideas if you're going to be outdoors for long periods.

Don't forget any prescription drugs you might need, and a second pair of glasses if you wear them. Everything else is readily available. Pharmacies *(Apotheke,* recognizable by the patent red "A" sign) are open during normal business hours, and, in large towns, at least one is open evenings and Sundays. Drugstores *(Drogerien)* sell a limited range of nonprescription medicines, but for anything stronger than toothpaste, you'll have to hit the pharmacy.

Lastly, don't forget the essentials: passport, driver's license, ATM cards (or traveler's checks), and insurance documents.

When to Go
See sidebar p. 10

HOW TO GET TO GERMANY
Entry Formalities
Visitors from the U.S., Canada, Australia, New Zealand, Israel, Hong Kong, Japan, South Korea, and most European countries may visit Germany for three months without a visa. People visiting from other countries need to apply for a visa in advance from the German embassy in their own countries. To stay more than three months, you should apply to the German Embassy in your own country for a residence permit.

Airlines
All the major airlines have flights to Germany and many arrange package tours and budget-price flights. Continental and American Airlines offer direct scheduled flights from North America to Frankfurt am Main; Continental and Delta fly to Berlin; Air Canada flies to Frankfurt and Munich. Connecting flights can be made to other cities. Lufthansa offers frequent flights from the U.S., together with its partners in the Star Alliance, and has booking offices abroad.

From the U.K. and Ireland, British Airways operates hundreds of flights a week to German destinations. The no-frills airlines EasyJet and Ryanair fly to several German cities from the U.K. Be aware that some of their destination airports may be some distance from the named city.

Useful numbers in the U.S. & Canada:
Air Canada, tel 888/247 2262, *aircanada.com*
American Airlines, tel 800/433 7300, *aa.com*
Delta, tel 888/750 3284, *delta.com*
Lufthansa, tel 800/645 3880, *lufthansa.com*
United, tel 800/864 8331, *united.com*

Useful numbers in Germany:
American Airlines, tel 069 2999 3234, *aa.com*
British Airways, tel 0421 5575 758, *britishairways.com*
Delta, tel 01806 805 872, *delta.com*
EasyJet, tel 01806 060 606, *easyjet.com*
Germanwings, tel 01806 320 320, *germanwings.com*
Lufthansa, tel 069 867 99 799, *lufthansa.com*
United, tel 069 5098 5010, *united.com*

Airports
The largest German airport is Frankfurt Rhein-Main, the busiest in Europe after London's Heathrow. The country's other main airports are at Munich, Düsseldorf, Hamburg, and Berlin, which in fact has two: Tegel and Schönefeld (both for international traffic). A much delayed supraregional hub, Berlin-Brandenburg Airport is expected to open around 2017.

Frankfurt Rhein-Main Airport
Tel 01806 372 46 36
frankfurt-airport.de
This gigantic airport comprises two terminals and two railroad stations. Passengers arrive at Terminal 2 and are taken via a Skyline transfer to Terminal 1 (20 minutes). Terminal 1 has a long-distance railroad station (the AIRail Terminal, from where you can reach all major cities in Germany) as well as a local station for the S-Bahn. A journey by taxi to Frankfurt center (7 miles/12 km) takes 20 minutes.

Munich Franz-Joseph Strauss Airport
Tel 089 975 00
munich-airport.de
The S-Bahn (lines S-1 and S-8, every 20 minutes) goes directly from the airport to Munich

central rail station (Hauptbahnhof) and takes 45 minutes. The bus or taxi journey to the center (22 miles/35 km) also takes 45 minutes.

Berlin Tegel & Schönefeld Airports
Tel 030 6091 1150
berlin-airport.de
From Tegel, the frequent buses 109, X9, 128, and TXL Express link to stops in the city center (5 miles/8 km), where you can switch to the U-Bahn or S-Bahn. From Schönefeld (11 miles/18 km away), take the S-Bahn RE Airport Express train. The journey by bus or taxi takes about 25 minutes from Tegel and 25–40 minutes from Schönefeld.

Düsseldorf Rhein-Ruhr Airport
Tel 0211 42 10
dus.com
A sky train or bus takes passengers from the terminal to the airport's railroad station in five minutes. From there an efficient S-Bahn system (line 7), which leaves every 20–30 minutes, gets you to the main station in 13 minutes. A taxi journey to Düsseldorf center (6 miles/10 km) takes 20 minutes.

Hamburg Fuhlsbüttel Airport
Tel 040 507 50
ham.airport.de
S-Bahn and subway links to Hamburg city center (8 miles/13 km) take 25 minutes. There are good bus services at 20-minute intervals. Journeys by bus or taxi take 30 minutes.

GETTING AROUND
By Air
There are domestic flights to most major cities in Germany. Some of the main routes are operated by:
Air Berlin, tel 030 3434 3434,
airberlin.com

Germanwings, tel 0900 19 19 100,
germanwings.com
Lufthansa, tel 069 8679 9799,
lufthansa.de

By Train
Germany's excellent national railway network is run by **Deutsche Bahn** (DB, *bahn.de*). The InterCity-Express (ICE), InterCity (IC), and EuroCity (EC) services link major towns and cities, usually on an hourly basis. InterRegio lines have good connections to regional centers. Flagship of DB is the super high-speed ICE3 between Cologne and Frankfurt, with its own dedicated track and tickets nearly a third more expensive. All these trains have restaurant or buffet cars. Some services require a seat reservation as well as a ticket.

DB runs a night train service, **City Night Line** (*tel 069 265 21 357*), on long German and European routes. Sleeper trains go as far as Amsterdam and Copenhagen in the north, Paris in the west, Prague in the east, and Rome to the south. Options run from plush private berths on down to the cheapest fares with reclining seats in shared compartments. You can load your vehicle onto a railroad car and have it waiting for you at the other end.

Timetables and service information are available at all stations; every large station has a service center (*Reisezentrum*). You can buy train tickets in advance either online from the service center or from a travel agency (*Reisebüro*) in Germany. Deutsche Bahn offers a variety of reduced rates that are constantly changing. Foreign visitors to Germany can buy a special vacation pass before traveling. The **DB information line** (*tel 08000 99 66 33*) is a free service with recorded information in German. For details in English, call 01806 99 66 33 from anywhere in Germany.

By Bus or Tram
Throughout Germany, tightly-woven networks of buses, trams, subway (U-Bahn), and commuter rail (S-Bahn) will get you where you want to go fast. Buses go to villages and small towns that are not plugged into the rail network. Within a city, a local transport ticket is valid simultaneously on buses, trams, and the U-Bahn. If there is no conductor, get your ticket from one of the vending machines at stops, or in some cases from onboard machines. Before you travel, you must validate your ticket in one of the time-stamping devices installed at the entrance of every bus, U-Bahn, and S-Bahn.

By Car
Germany has a huge network of toll-free expressways (*Autobahnen*). If you are not in a hurry, secondary roads (*Landstrassen* or *Bundesstrassen*) are usually more picturesque. Roads are typically in excellent shape with clear signage to European standards.

Car rentals To explore places Germany's trains and buses don't go, renting a vehicle is the way to go. Arranging a deal before leaving home can be cheaper, and there are fly-drive options with most flights. Otherwise, seek out the on-site desks in airports and major railroad stations in Germany.
Central offices:
Avis, tel 01806 21 77 02,
avis.de
EasyCar, *easycar.de*
Hertz, tel 01806 33 35 35,
hertz.de
Sixt, tel 01806 25 25 25,
sixt.de

To rent a car in Germany you must be at least 18 years old and have a current driver's license.

Driving information & licenses
U.S. and Canadian driving licenses are valid in Germany. Although

an international driving license is not legally required, it can be quite useful—obtain one before you leave home. Visitors bringing cars from non-European countries should carry an international driving license and vehicle registration document. Non-German vehicles require a nationality sticker on the back of the vehicle.

Breakdown assistance In the event of a breakdown on the autobahn, Road Patrol Assistance can be called from emergency telephones on the shoulder. They can also be contacted directly via motoring organizations:

ACE, tel 0711 530 34 35 36, *ace-online.de*
ADAC, tel 01802 22 22 22, *adac.de*
AvD, tel 0800 990 9909, *avd.de*

Children Children under the age of 8 or under 5 feet (1.5 m) in height must sit in the back seat of a vehicle. Child seats are required for children under 4, and children under 12 must use a booster cushion.

Distances All distances on signposts in Germany are shown in kilometers (1 km = 0.62 mile).

Drunk driving The legal blood alcohol limit is 0.05 percent.

Fines Heavy fines can be imposed on the spot, e.g., for driving without a seat belt or while using a cell phone. For serious incidents, the police can confiscate the driving license and vehicle of foreign motorists, even if the vehicle is a German rental.

First aid Every vehicle is required to carry a first-aid kit on board. Rental cars always come equipped with them.

Fuel All gasoline in Germany is unleaded. At the pumps, you will find Normal (regular) and Super, as well as diesel and *Flüssiggas* (LPG). Gas and service stations are open 24 hours on autobahns and in bigger

cities. Most gas stations accept credit cards.

Highway code Driving is on the right-hand side. At crossings, priority is given to traffic approaching from the right unless a sign (a yellow diamond) indicates you have the right of way. Buses leaving stops have priority. At traffic lights, a green arrow to the right indicates you may turn right on red. Pedestrians always have the right of way.

Parking Parking is not allowed up to 16 feet (5 m) in front of or behind a pedestrian crossing, up to 33 feet (10 m) in front of traffic lights, or up to 49 feet (15 m) in front of or behind stop signs and exits.

Most towns have on-street parking meters (*Parkuhren*), from which you can buy a ticket to display in your car. Multistory parking lots are common, but check the closing times—some close overnight and many are shut by 8 p.m.

Road conditions For details of current road conditions, tune into the local radio frequency (often indicated on signs beside the road), or call 224 99 for a recording in German.

Road signs
• *Baustelle*: roadworks
• *Einbahnstrasse*: one-way traffic
• *Fussgängerübergang*: pedestrian crossing
• *Halt*: stop
• *Keine Einfahrt*: no entry
• *Licht anmachen*: switch on lights
• *Parkverbot*: no parking
• *Stau*: traffic jam

Seat belts Seat belts must be worn by all passengers in the car. The penalty for not wearing one is €30.

Speed limits Different speed limits apply for different weather conditions and times of poor visibility (heavy rain and fog). Autobahns have a recommended limit of 110–130 kph (75–85 mph). In cities, towns, and villages the limit is 50

kph (30 mph). The limit on all other roads is 100 kph (70 mph).

Studded tires & snow chains Studded tires are generally not allowed. In the winter you should buy or rent snow chains before traveling to regions with medium or higher altitudes.

Tolls All autobahns and main roads are toll-free for passenger vehicles. However, a charge is levied on some sightseeing roads in Bavaria.

Transportation in Berlin

Taxi stands are located at airports, train and subway stations, and throughout the city. Taxis can also be hailed in the street. There are two rates: one for short journeys from taxi stands and another for journeys ordered by telephone. The rate remains the same at night.

Public transportation Berlin's buses, trams, and local rail network is run by the **Berlin Transport Authority** (BVG, *tel 030 19 44 9, bvg.de*). The U-Bahn (underground trains) and S-Bahn (commuter network) operate from 4 a.m. until at least 12:30 a.m., with some lines running until 1:30 a.m., when a nighttime bus network takes over.

The city is divided into three travel zones: Zones A and B include the urban area, and Zone C (including Potsdam) is farther away from the center of Berlin. Most destinations can be reached with a single A + B ticket.

The **WelcomeCard** (available at ticket offices, Berlin hotels, and BVG ticket machines) is a public transportation ticket valid for 72 hours on all buses, trams, and trains within the A, B, and C fare zones. In addition, WelcomeCard holders are entitled to free admission, or up to 50 percent reduction, on guided tours or walks, boat trips, museums, theaters, and leisure facilities in

Berlin and Potsdam. For a good rolling tour of the city, bus lines 100 and 200 take you past all the main sights (see sidebar p. 66).

PRACTICAL ADVICE
Communications
Post Offices

In large towns, post offices (Post-amt) are usually open from 8 a.m. until 6 p.m. weekdays, and from 8 a.m. until noon on Saturdays. Branches at airports and railroad stations keep longer hours. Buy stamps from the post office counter and automatic vending machines. Sample rates: Postcards to Germany/rest of world—€0.45/0.75; letters—€0.60/0.75.

Telephones

Public telephones run by Deutsche Telecom are dwindling as virtually every German owns a Handy (cell phone). Phone cards (Telefonkarten) can be bought at any post office or newspaper shop for €15, €20, or €30. Some booths still take coins.

If you bring a mobile phone it must be compatible with the European GSM network. After arriving, you can buy a basic handset and benefit from cheap local rates. Check with your home provider for international "roaming" packages, and know that companies such as Ortel also have good-value prepaid plans for visitors to Germany.

To call a German number from abroad, dial the international code (011 from the United States and Canada, 00 from the U.K.), then the code for Germany (49), followed by the number, omitting the first 0.

To make an international call from Germany, dial 00 followed by the country code and the rest of the telephone number, deleting the initial 0 if there is one. Country codes include: Australia 61; Canada 1; United Kingdom 44; United States 1.

Useful Telephone Numbers

International inquiries 11834
National inquiries 11837
(in English)

Wireless Internet

Owners of mobile devices can access the Web in bars, cafés, department stores, hotels, service stations and some public places across Germany. Berlin alone has more than 400 such WLAN (Wi-Fi) hot spots. Many are free of charge, although you may be required to buy something to log in. Deutsche Bahn gives you up to 30 minutes of free daily surf time at 105 train stations across the country.

Conversions

1 kilo = 2.2 lbs
1 liter = 0.26 U.S gallons
1 kilometer = 0.62 mile

Women's clothing

U.S.	8	10	12	14	16	18
European	36	38	40	42	44	46

Men's clothing

U.S.	36	38	40	42	44	46
European	46	48	50	52	54	56

Women's shoes

U.S.	6	6.5–7	7.5–8	
	8.5–9	9.5		
European	37	38	39	40

Men's shoes

U.S.	8	8.5	9.5	10.5	11.5	12
European	41	42	43	44	45	46

Electricity

German sockets are of the round, Continental two-pin variety, so you'll need a converter to use equipment with U.S. or U.K. plugs. Airport shops routinely carry them.

Etiquette & Customs
See p. 10

Holidays

All banks and post offices, and many museums, galleries, and stores, close on public holidays. Many stores and businesses are also shut on Carnival Rose Monday (Cologne and Rhine region), Christmas Eve, and New Year's Eve.

January 1 New Year's Day
January 6 Epiphany (in Bavaria, Baden-Württemberg, Saxony-Anhalt)
March/April Good Friday
March/April Easter Monday
May 1 Labor Day
May/June Ascension Day
May/June Pentecost Monday
June Corpus Christi (in Baden-Württemberg, Bavaria, Hesse, North Rhine-Westphalia, Rhineland-Palatinate)
August 15 Ascension of the Virgin Mary (Saarland, Catholic areas of Bavaria)
October 3 Day of Unity
October 31 Day of Reformation (Brandenburg, Mecklenburg-West Pomerania, Saxony, Saxony-Anhalt, Thuringia)
November 1 All Saints' Day (Baden-Württemberg, Bavaria, North Rhine-Westphalia, Rhineland-Palatinate, Saarland, Catholic areas of Thuringia)
November 20 Repentance Day (only in Saxony)
December 25 & 26 Christmas

Media
Newspapers

Serious daily newspapers are the liberal Sueddeutsche Zeitung (SZ), the conservative Frankfurter Allgemeine Zeitung (FAZ), the left-of-center Frankfurter Rundschau, and the conservative Die Welt. Popular tabloids are Bildzeitung—Germany's best-selling paper—and Express. Weekly magazines also play an important role. The hard-hitting news magazine Der Spiegel is published on Saturdays, its rival Focus on Mondays, and the sophisticated Die Zeit as well as entertainment-oriented titles Stern and Bunte appear on Thursdays. All these periodicals have online editions. Regional newspapers cover national and international as well as local news and are as widely read as the national press.

American & British newspapers American (*International New York Times, USA Today, Washington Post*) and British (*Times, Telegraph, Independent, Guardian*) newspapers are available in airports, major railroad stations, the more important vacation resorts, and most large hotels. On Fridays, the *Sueddeutsche Zeitung* carries an English-language summary of the *New York Times*.

TV Channels

German television relies heavily on the two national networks ARD and ZDF, which form the parent networks for a host of regional public channels. Stiff competition comes from the private channels, above all RTL and SAT 1. The most authoritative news broadcasts are the ZDF evening news *Heute* at 7 p.m. and the ARD *Tagesschau* at 8 p.m. Channels available in English include CNN, NBC, MTV Europe, and BBC World.

Money Matters

In 2002 the euro (€) replaced the beloved deutsche mark as Germany's official currency. There are 100 cents to 1 euro. Banknotes come in denominations of 5, 10, 20, 50, and 100, as well as the rarer 200 and 500 bills. Coins consist of €1 and €2 as well as 1, 2, 5, 10, 20, and 50 cents.

Most banks have ATMs for bank cards and international credit cards, with instructions in a number of languages. Cash and traveler's checks can be exchanged in the larger banks and at currency booths at railroad stations and airports.

Opening Times

Banks 9 a.m. or 10.a.m.–4 p.m. or 6 p.m. Monday to Thursday, and no later than 4 p.m. on Friday. Smaller branches close for a lunch break. All banks are shut on weekends, but ATMs operate 24/7.

Museums Generally 9 a.m.–6 p.m. Many museums are closed on Mondays, but some in large cities will have extended opening hours on one night a week.

Pharmacies Open during normal shop hours. In cities a few outlets (usually one per district) stay open all night and weekends for urgent cases.

Post Offices Mostly 8 a.m.–6 p.m. weekdays and until at least noon on Saturdays.

Stores Weekdays 9 or 9:30 a.m.–7 p.m. (until 10 p.m. for many department stores and large supermarkets). On Saturdays, hours are 8:30 a.m.– 8 p.m., although many smaller shops close by 2 p.m. With a few exceptions, stores are closed on Sundays.

Pets

Bringing a pet has to be organized well in advance. Contact your local veterinarian for information about vaccinations and other requirements. Visitors from the U.S. and Canada must bring documentation with them in order to bring a pet to Germany; a certificate of permission will be issued by customs at the airport/port of entry.

Restrooms

Self-cleaning toilet cabins are usually located near the big railroad and bus stations. Large department stores have public restrooms, but charge a small fee (like €0.20). You can also slip into a bar or café, keeping an eye out for the doors marked *Herren* (men) and *Damen* (women).

Time Differences

Germany runs on CET (Central European Time), one hour ahead of Greenwich Mean Time and six hours ahead of Eastern Standard Time. Noon in Germany is 6 a.m. in New York. Remember that Germany uses the 24-hour clock, so 8 p.m. becomes "20 Uhr" in German.

Tipping

By law, sales tax and a service charge are included in your bill. It is customary, though, to add a small gratuity if you are happy with the service. The amount widely varies—in bars, restaurants and taxis, some customers round up to the nearest euro, while others might pay an extra 5 to 10 percent. Bellhops typically get €1 per bag in the top-end hotels.

Tourist Offices

The **German National Tourist Office** (*germany.travel*) has branches with helpful staff in North America and the U.K.

United States

New York
112 East 42nd St., 52nd floor
New York, NY 10168
Tel 212/661-7200
Fax 212/661-7174
germanyinnyc.org

Canada

Toronto
480 University Ave., Suite 1410
Toronto, Ontario M5G 1V2
Tel 416/968-1685
Fax 416/968-0562

Great Britain

London
P.O. Box 2695
London W1A 3TN
Tel 020 7317 0908
Fax 020 7317 0917

Travelers With Disabilities

Germany is fairly well equipped for the needs of disabled travelers, especially the wheelchair-bound. There are access ramps and lifts in many public buildings, including restrooms, train stations, museums, theaters, and cinemas. On public transportation, some buses, trams, and commuter trains have special wheelchair ramps, but it varies. The national association for the disabled will send you details free of charge:

Bundesverband Evangelischer Behindertenhilfe
Invalidenstrasse 29
10115 Berlin
Tel 030 83 00 12 70
Fax 030 83 00 12 75
beb-ev.de

EMERGENCIES

Embassies

U.S. Embassy
Clayallee 170
14191 Berlin
Tel 030 83 05 0 (emergencies), 030 83 29 23 3 (routine calls, 2–4 p.m., Mon.–Fri.)
Fax 030 8305 1215
germany.usembassy.gov

Canadian Embassy
Leipziger Platz 17
10117 Berlin
Tel 030 20 31 20
Fax 030 20 31 25 90
berlin.gc.ca

British Embassy
Wilhelmstrasse 70
10117 Berlin
Tel 030 20 45 70
Fax 030 20 45 75 94
ukingermany.fco.gov.uk

Emergency Phone Numbers

Fire department & ambulance *(Feuerwehr)* 112
Police *(Polizeinotruf)* 110

What to Do in a Car Accident

You must switch on the hazard warning lights. All cars driven in Germany must carry a red warning triangle, to be placed on the road to warn approaching traffic of a stationary vehicle or accident. Position the warning triangle on an autobahn about 165 yards (150 m) behind the vehicle. Next, exchange names, addresses, telephone numbers, and registration details, and ask to see the other party's driver's license to confirm. You should also make a note of the events leading to the accident, with drawings that you may need for your insurance claim. The police must always be called, regardless of whether injuries have occurred or not.

Lost Property

Your travel insurance should cover the loss or theft of your property if you are not already covered by your home insurance. Theft must be reported to the police so you can obtain a certificate saying that the crime was reported. For lost property, ask at the lost property office *(Fundbüro)* in any German city. The national railway DB and urban transportation systems have their own offices, if you forget something on a train.

Health

In the case of minor health problems, the qualified staff of any pharmacy can offer expert advice. Doctors' hours are normally 9 a.m.–noon and 3–5 p.m., except weekends. For urgent attention outside office hours, simply go to the nearest hospital *(Krankenhaus)*. German medical treatment and facilities are generally excellent. In Berlin the best known of several hospitals with a 24-hour emergency ward is the **Charité** *(Luisenstrasse 65/66, tel 450 531 000).*

FURTHER READING

Fiction

The Buddenbrooks by Thomas Mann (1901). Charts the decline of a North German mercantile family over four generations.
The Danzig Trilogy (The Tin Drum [1959], Cat and Mouse [1961], Dog Years [1963]) by Günther Grass. The three novels by the Nobel Prize winner are an inventive mix of fantasy and reality, set in the Nazi era.
Elective Affinities by Johann Wolfgang von Goethe (1809). Classic 19th-century novel about the emotional turmoil of two couples and the weighty issue of free will.
The Lost Honor of Katharina Blum by Heinrich Böll (1974). A young woman's association with a hunted man leads her into a web of sensationalism and character assassination.
The Reader by Bernhard Schlink (1997). Love and secrets, compassion and horror in postwar Germany.

Nonfiction

A Concise History of Germany by Mary Fulbrook (1990). A crisply written account starting with medieval Germany and ending with reunification in 1990.
The Harz Journey by Heinrich Heine (2007). These travel vignettes are a poetic and ironic critique of man and society.
Steppenwolf by Hermann Hesse (1927). An autobiographical work that blends Eastern mysticism with Western culture.

Hotels & Restaurants

Germany offers a variety of accommodations, from traditional grand hotels and palaces converted into hotels to moderately priced chain hotels. Small, privately owned hotels are more easily found in small towns. There are two visible trends in German hotels: ultramodern hotels and a growing number of hotels that offer spa treatments. Some of the newest are in the east, and after generations of communism, they are working hard to match the standards of the rest of Germany. The tourist offices can supply lists of accommodations and book rooms (sometimes for a small fee). Cheaper hotels may not have private baths. As everywhere, prices vary depending on the season and special events. Taxes are included, but parking and telephone often cost extra.

HOTELS

Hotels are graded by the German hospitality association with one to four stars. In reality, the stars say little about the overall quality of an establishment, which is why we omit them here.

Many hotels have their own restaurants, and in the countryside the "bed-and-breakfast" formula is a common feature. Half-board, or *Halbpension,* includes breakfast and dinner, while *Vollpension* throws in lunch as well. If a hotel is a *Garni,* this means there is no restaurant but breakfast is (probably) served. A B&B is called a *Pension* or *Privatquartier;* addresses are best obtained from local tourist offices. They are inexpensive and bring you in contact with locals, but do not expect facilities like private bathrooms.

The following is a selection of quality hotels throughout the country listed by location and price, then in alphabetical order. The choice is meant to be individual and typical of the area, perhaps with links to local culture or history. For that special occasion, Gast im Schloss (*gast-im-schloss.de*) has information about hotels in former monasteries, palaces, castles, and mansions.

Please note that in the listings, unless otherwise stated:
• Breakfast is not included in the price.
• The hotel has a restaurant. Notable hotel restaurants are given an icon or a reference to a separate entry.
• All rooms have a telephone

and television. Many hotels also provide guests with Internet access, and wireless links (Wi-Fi or WLAN) are increasingly standard in mid- to top-end establishments.
• Room price categories are no more than a rough guide and do not take into account seasonal variations. Local taxes (such as *Kurtaxe,* which is commonly levied in health resorts) may be added to the bill. Prices are per double room.

In high season, always try to book in advance and confirm your reservation by fax or e-mail. You may be asked for a deposit or credit card number.

Hotel Chains & Groups

Contact numbers in/from the U.S. are:

Dorint, tel 49 221 48 567 444 (in Germany), *dorint.com*

Golden Tulip, tel 800/448 8355, *goldentulip.com*

Hilton, tel 800/445 8667, *hilton.com*

Leading Hotels of the World, tel 800/745 8883, *lhw.com*

Relais & Chateaux, tel 800/735 2478, *relaischateaux.com*

Steigenberger, tel 866/991 1299, *en.steigenberger.de*

All of the following hotel chains can be booked online from the U.S. and Canada via the Hotel Reservation Service (HRS; *hrs.de*) or by calling a central reservation number, tel 866/839 9731: Best Western, Comfort Inns, Crowne Plaza, Design Hotels, Hyatt, Marriott, Novotel,

Quality Inns, Radisson , Ramada, Ritz Carlton, and Sorat.

RESTAURANTS

Germany has a bewildering variety of restaurants, ranging from the humble *Gasthof* with everyday fare to vaunted temples of gourmet cuisine. In most *Kneipen* or *Bierstuben* (drinking pubs), you can enjoy simple dishes over a foaming mug of beer. A *Weinstube* is a wine bar, usually serving local specialities. And in many towns you will find an atmospheric *Ratskeller* in the basement of the town hall, a reliable bet for a tasty meal. Traditionally, the main meal of the day in Germany was lunch, but changing habits have shifted the balance toward the evening. The lunch menu *(Mittagstisch)* tends to be the best deal of the day.

German food is not as heavy as its reputation says, although most dishes are anchored by a large helping of meat. Pork roast with crackling is a stereotype of Bavaria. Classic dishes from the Black Forest include ham, venison, trout, and black cherry gateau.

Many regions have their own favorite sausage; in Munich the specialty is *Weisswurst,* a bulging veal sausage flecked with parsley, while Nuremberg and Regensburg are renowned for their little grilled links. Tasty *Mettwurst* (soft smoked sausages) are popular in Westphalia. More than 500 years old, the *Frankfurter* lays a plausible claim to being the original hot dog.

The cultivation of asparagus is taken very seriously, and in season (spring) the "king of vegetables" turns up in dishes all over Germany.

Sole, plaice, and shrimp come from the North Sea coasts. Oysters are very good on the island of Sylt, and Helgoland is famous for its lobster soup. The Baltic Sea smokehouses supply tender *Kieler Sprotten* (smoked sprats).

In the Lower Rhine area, mussels come fresh from the coast. An old-fashioned but still popular dish is *Biersuppe* (soup made of milk, beer, cinnamon, raisins, and egg whites).

This selection (listed by city, price, then in alphabetical order) focuses on regional eateries offering local dishes, as well as some of the great stars of German cuisine.

L = lunch **D** = dinner

Eating in Germany

Breakfasts are substantial enough to see you through until dinnertime. A full breakfast can consist of various types of bread, accompanied by marmalade, eggs, cold cuts, cheese, and perhaps a bowl of fruit-filled *quark* (white yogurt). Lunch usually starts around midday and continues until 2 p.m. Dinner starts at 6 p.m. to 8 p.m., while in smaller places or in the countryside you may be too late after 9 p.m. Dinner tends to start earlier in the north of the country, and later as you go south. In high season, or anytime if you have a particular place in mind, be sure to make a reservation.

Restaurants often have tables for alfresco dining. Such facilities are mentioned here only where the view or setting is of particular note. Most restaurants offer a fixed-price menu for lunch and dinner.

In Germany, salad is usually eaten with the main course rather than as an appetizer. Tap water (*Leitungswasser*) is safe to drink.

Local wines tend to dominate wine lists. Most restaurants have a *Nichtraucher* (nonsmoking) section or ban smoking altogether.

Cafés

Cafés are a German institution for morning coffee, leisurely drinks, a light lunch, and definitely for afternoon *Kaffee und Kuchen* (coffee and cake). In small towns they are the center of local life.

Tipping

A service charge is always included in the bill, but it is customary to add 5 to 10 percent if the service has been particularly good. Give the server the tip upon payment, rather than leaving it on the table. If your bill is €14, you might hand the server a 20 and say "15."

CREDIT & DEBIT CARDS

Many hotels and restaurants accept all major cards, but smaller ones may only accept those shown in their entry. Abbreviations used are: **AE** American Express, **DC** Diners Club, **MC** Mastercard, **V** Visa.

■ BERLIN & BRANDENBURG

BERLIN

CHARLOTTENBURG

🏨 **HOTEL Q!**
$$$–$$$$
KNESEBECKSTRASSE 67
TEL 030 810 06 60
FAX 030 810 066 666
loock-hotels.com
A cool gray facade signals your arrival at the Q, an ultra-chic retreat named for the nearby Ku'Damm. Hardwood floors curve up the walls, and you can literally slide from the tub into bed. The spa has its own self-contained "beach" complete with heated sand and aromatherapy.

🛈 77 🅿 🚇 S5, S7, S9

Savignyplatz 🚇 🍴
🍴 All major cards

🏨 **ASKANISCHER HOF**
$$$
KURFÜRSTENDAMM 53
TEL 030 881 80 33/34
FAX 030 881 72 06
askanischer-hof.de
For a dose of Berlin history, stay at this delightfully intimate abode on the city's most famous shopping avenue. Furnished in roaring '20s style, rooms are individually designed with plenty of high-tech features. Rock star David Bowie was a regular guest here in the 1970s.

🛈 15 + 1 suite 🅿 🚇 S5, S7
Savignyplatz 🍴
🍴 All major cards

SOMETHING SPECIAL

🏨 **PROPELLER ISLAND CITY LODGE**
$$$
ALBRECHT-ACHILLES-STRASSE 58

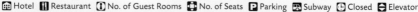

TEL 030 891 90 16

FAX 030 892 87 21

propeller-island.com

Get ready for a surprise—nothing about this place can be described as ordinary. This 19th-century apartment block has been rewired as an eccentric hotel where every room is an inhabitable work of art. Most draw on fantasies: The Flying Bed hovers in the air, while the Two Lions features a pair of caged mattresses 5 feet (1.5 m) above the ground. Every stick of furniture was crafted by the owner-artist himself.

🛏 42 🚇 U7 Adenauerplatz
💳 All major cards

🍴 **CAFE IM LITERATURHAUS**
$$

FASANENSTRASSE 23

TEL 030 882 54 14

literaturhaus-berlin.de

This café-restaurant in an old villa a heartbeat from the main Kurfürstendamm shopping artery provides a well-stocked bookshop in the basement, plus food from breakfast to supper in the first-floor salon. Supper dishes—perhaps roast lamb with rosemary or trout with new potatoes—are strictly seasonal. The regulars have a worldly sophistication that comes from a lifetime of intellectual debate over coffee.

🍴 100 🚇 U1 Uhlandstrasse
💳 No credit cards

🍴 **DICKE WIRTIN**
$$

CARMERSTRASSE 6

TEL 030 312 49 52

dicke-wirtin.de

An earthy pub-restaurant, the "Fat Landlady" has been serving Berlin comfort food for more than 80 years. Specialties include tender beef roulade, seared Havel pike-perch, and the legendary schnitzel, big enough to feed two. Wash it all

down with a tasty shot of mirabelle, one of a dozen home-made schnapps on offer.

🍴 220 🚉 S5, S7 Savignyplatz
💳 No credit cards

MITTE & POTSDAMER PLATZ

🏨 **ADLON KEMPINSKI**
🍴 **$$$$$**

UNTER DEN LINDEN 77

TEL 030 22 61 11 11

FAX 030 22 61 22 22

hotel-adlon.de

British club meets art deco at this portal of German history, where Marlene Dietrich was discovered and Joseph Goebbels chased his mistress down the corridor. The grand dame of Berlin hotels has been restored to its pre-WWII splendor, complete with grandstand views of the Brandenburg Gate and a first-class restaurant, **Lorenz Adlon Esszimmer.** All rooms have flat-screen TVs and WLAN.

🛏 304 + 78 suites 🅿 🚉 S1, S2 Unter den Linden 🚭 ❄ 🏋 💳 All major cards

🏨 **GRAND HYATT**
🍴 **$$$$$**

MARLENE-DIETRICH-PLATZ 2

TEL 030 25 53 12 34

FAX 030 25 53 12 35

hyatt.com

A favorite haunt of movie stars, this temple of luxury on Potsdamer Platz has matte-black surfaces and fashioned hardwood that exude a Euro-Japanese elegance. Rooms have perks like heated bathroom floors and Bauhaus art, and on the rooftop you'll find a gym, pool and beauty center.

🛏 326 + 16 suites 🅿 🚉 S1, S2, U2 Potsdamer Platz 🚭 🚰 🏊 ❄ 🏋 💳 All major cards

🏨 **CIRCUS HOTEL**
🍴 **$$–$$$**

ROSENTHALERSTRASSE 1

TEL 030 20 00 39 39

FAX 030 28 39 14 84

circus-berlin.de

Handily situated on Rosenthaler Platz in the hub of the Mitte district, the bright, modern Circus is like a luxury youth hostel for grown-ups. The garden courtyard (and the rear quarters overlooking it) is a great place to relax, and there are hip little amenities, such as iPods loaded with Berlin music. Rooms are clean, stylish, and imaginatively furnished, and there's Wi-Fi throughout. Breakfast is included.

🛏 60 🚇 U8 💳 MC, V

🏨 **MONBIJOU HOTEL**
🍴 **$$–$$$**

MONBIJOUPLATZ 1

TEL 030 616 20 300

monbijouhotel.com

Steps from Hackescher Markt, this stylish boutique hotel features plush, modernist decor, hardwood floors, a well-stocked library, and large windows overlooking the nearby Mitte neighborhood—some rooms have unobstructed views of Berliner Dom. There's a pleasant bar area and lounge with fireplace, and the Parisian-style bistro offers a menu of international-style tapas—Irish beef entrecote, wiener schnitzel on roasted potatoes, tuna steak with green curry sauce. In summer enjoy snacks and drinks on the rooftop terrace. Fitness center and free wifi.

🛏 101 🅿 🚉 S5, S7 Hackescher Markt 🚭 ❄ 💳 All major cards

🍴 **WEINBAR RUTZ**
$$$$

CHAUSSEESTRASSE 8

TEL 030 24 62 87 60

rutz-weinbar.de

An oenophile's dream, the Rutz has more than 1,000 different wines and a terrific choice of contemporary cuisine. You can nibble on tapas in

---

the bistro or go straight to the elegant upstairs restaurant. The show-stopper is the entrecôte from milk-fed Kobe cattle served in a truffle gravy.

🍴 110 🚇 U6 Oranienburger Tor 🕐 Closed Sun. ⬥ All major cards

SOMETHING SPECIAL

🍴 **VAU**

$$$–$$$$$

JÄGERSTRASSE 54–55

TEL 030 202 97 30

vau-berlin.de

Chef Kolja Kleeberg once aspired to acting, and his Michelin-starred restaurant in a courtyard near Gendarmenmarkt is something of a movie set, with screaming orange walls, wooden floors, and halogen spots. You might start with a chestnut soup before moving on to breast of pigeon with blackroot and a lemon-grass-chili sherbet. Reserve ahead.

🍴 115 🚇 U6 Französische Strasse 🕐 Closed Sun. ⬥ All major cards

🍴 **GANYMED**

$$$

SCHIFFBAUER DAMM 5

TEL 030 28 59 90 46

ganymed-brasserie.de

This hair-down riverside brasserie exudes the spirit of *la belle France* on vacation. The gutsy forté of chef Attila Konrad is seafood—mussels from Brittany, shrimp, crabs, and oysters prepared in a bewildering number of ways. You can dine on the dreamy terrace or in the candlelit dining room.

🍴 75 🚇 S1, S2, S5, S7, U6 Friedrichstrasse ⬥ All major cards

🍴 **MUTTER HOPPE**

$$

RATHAUSSTRASSE 21

TEL 030 241 56 25

prostmahlzeit.de
/mutterhoppe

This old-fashioned restaurant in the Nikolai quarter is named for a formidable cook who used to whip up mountains of food for her family and friends. Tuck into a serving of *Eisbein* (pork knuckle) or oversized schnitzel while you savor music hits from the 1920s (live on weekends).

🍴 90 🚇 U2, S3, S5, S7 Alexanderplatz ⬥ MC, V

PRENZLAUER BERG

🏨 **HOTEL ADELE**

🍴 **$$$**

GREIFSWALDER STRASSE 227

TEL 030 44 32 43 10

FAX 030 44 32 43 11

adele-berlin.de

From the street, this cool "lounge hotel" is nearly invisible, fronted by separate coffee and wine shops as well as a fine Mediterranean-inspired restaurant. Rooms feature dark hardwoods and leathers set off by hand-picked colors.

ℹ️ 14 🅿️ 🚇 U2 Senefelder Platz ⬌ 🚫 ⬥ All major cards

🏨 **HOTEL KASTANIENHOF**

$$$

KASTANIENALLEE 65

TEL 030 443 050

FAX 030 443 05 111

kastanienhof.biz

This guesthouse, one of east Berlin's first after reunification, has an enviable spot on Prenzlauer Berg's hippest strip. The furnishings are simple pinewood but have a genuine charm thanks to the historic photos which pepper the rooms and common areas.

ℹ️ 35 🅿️ 🚇 M1 Kastanienallee, U8 Rosenthaler Platz ⬌ 🚫 ⬥ All major cards

🍴 **ODERQUELLE**

$$$

ODERBERGER STRASSE 27

TEL 030 44 00 80 80

oderquelle.de

This hidden gem lends German classics a Franco-Italian accent.

The seasonal menu changes daily and might include lamb filet served with Sicilian eggplant and pastry, or tender braised beef on parsley potatoes. Service is impeccable, and the laid-back staff speaks English. You can dine in paneled chambers with antique fittings and a gorgeous wooden bar, or on the shady front terrace. Save room for the homemade chocolate-pear cake.

🍴 120 🚇 U2 Eberswalder Strasse 🕐 Closed L ⬥ MC, V

🍴 **WEINSTEIN**

$$$

LYCHENER STRASSE 33

TEL 030 441 18 42

Roy Metzger and his brother Marc serve up an eclectic mix of cuisines at this cozy wine bar–restaurant. Mixed salad with Brandenburg veal, potato dumplings stuffed with goat cheese, and marinated tuna are typical of the fare.

🍴 65 🚇 U2 Eberswalder Strasse 🕐 Closed L ⬥ MC, V

🍴 **ARS VINI**

$$–$$$

SREDZKISTRASSE 27

TEL 030 547 14 182

arsvini.de

The specialty here is fondue in every variety imaginable, from Tex-Mex, Chinese, and fish to more conventional cheese fondues (eight varieties), all served in bubbling cauldrons at your table. The knowledgeable staff will match your meal with a wine (tastings offered before ordering). Save room for the kicky chocolate banana fondue.

🍴 40 🚇 U2 Eberswalder Strasse 🕐 CLosed L ⬥ MC, V

SCHÖNEBERG & KREUZBERG

🏨 **HOTEL RIEHMERS**
🍴 **HOFGARTEN**

$$$

🏨 Hotel   🍴 Restaurant   ℹ️ No. of Guest Rooms   🍴 No. of Seats   🅿️ Parking   🚇 Subway   🕐 Closed   ⬌ Elevator

YORCKSTRASSE 83
TEL 030 78 09 88 00
FAX 030 78 09 88 08
riehmershofgarten.de
This romantic small hotel near Viktoriapark was built by Wilhelm Riehmers, a renowned 19th-century architect. French double doors open into spacious rooms with high ceilings and tasteful contemporary decor. Its fine restaurant, **ETA Hoffmann,** serves patrons in a cobblestone courtyard.
🅘 22 🅿 🏨 U6, U7 Mehringdamm 🔁 🛇 🅰 All major cards

🍴 LE COCHON BOURGEOIS
$$$
FICHTESTRASSE 24
TEL 030 693 01 01
lecochon.de
Chef-owner Hannes Behrmann puts his je ne sais quoi into classy French game and seafood dishes, such as monkfish in bacon sauce on green lentils. Every night, a pianist entertains in this former showroom of a colonial-goods dealer.
🏨 55 🏨 U7 Südstern
🕐 Closed L & Sun.– Mon.
🛇 No credit cards

🍴 DER GOLDENE HAHN
$$
PÜCKLERSTRASSE 20
TEL 030 618 80 98
goldenerhahn.de
This gem of a Tuscan restaurant has old farm implements and an apothecary's cabinet behind the bar. Stuffed pearl hen with anise sauce and pumpkin gnocchi in Parma butter are a couple of highlights that the owner will pair with an excellent Italian wine.
🏨 110 🏨 U1 Görlitzer Bahnhof 🕐 Closed L 🛇 MC, V

🍴 ZUR HENNE
$
LEUSCHNERDAMM 25
TEL 030 614 77 30
henne-berlin.de
In 1963, President John F.

Kennedy declined an invitation to visit this earthy bar-café just yards away from the Wall, and the president's signed letter now hangs over the bar. The menu is simple: delicious roast chicken, sauerkraut, and *bouletten* (meatballs). Reserve ahead.
🏨 80 🏨 U1, U8 Kottbusser Tor 🕐 CLosed L & Mon.
🛇 No credit cards

POTSDAM

SOMETHING SPECIAL

🏨 SCHLOSSHOTEL CECILIENHOF
$$$
NEUER GARTEN
TEL 0331 3 70 50
FAX 0331 3 70 52 21
relexa-hotel.de
Situated in a park on the shore of the Wannsee, this grand, half-timbered mansion was the setting for the Potsdam Conference, where Truman, Churchill, and Stalin met in 1945 to discuss the fate of a defeated Germany. The hotel is close to Potsdam but has a tranquil country atmosphere.
🅘 35 + 6 suites 🅿 🏨 S1, S7 Wannsee or Potsdam, then taxi 🛇 All major cards

🍴 SPECKERS LANDHAUS
$$$–$$$$
JÄGERALLEE 13
TEL 0331 280 43 11
speckers.de
Enjoy country food such as eel soup or roast rabbit filled with black pudding at this elegant restaurant in historic surroundings. Much of the produce is from local farmers. If you can't move afterward, stylish guest rooms are available.
🏨 70 🏨 S7 Potsdam
🕐 Closed Sun. 🛇 AE, MC, V

■ MECKLENBURG-WEST POMERANIA

KRAKOW

SOMETHING SPECIAL

🏨 ICH WEISS EIN HAUS 🍴 AM SEE
$$–$$$
ALTES FORSTHAUS 2,
KRAKOW/SEEGRUBE
TEL 038457 232 73
FAX 038457 232 74
hausamsee.de
Five miles (8 km) outside Krakow, half hidden between a forest and a lake, this hotel offers an idyllic hideaway. Rooms are large, light, and furnished in country style; most have a view of the park and lake. Under the auspices of owner-chef Michael Laumen, the modern European cuisine has earned Lower Pomerania its first Michelin star. Specials include bouillabaisse of local fish and wild herb risotto. Serious wines are on offer.
🅘 10 🅿 🕐 Restaurant closed L & Mon. 🛇 No credit cards

ROSTOCK

🏨 HOTEL NEPTUN
$$–$$$
SEESTRASSE 19,
ROSTOCK-WARNEMÜNDE
TEL 0381 777 77 77
FAX 0381 77 78 00
hotel-neptun.de
All rooms have balconies at this seaside hotel, the better to enjoy the magnificent ocean views.
🅘 325 + 4 suites + 8 apts. 🔁 🖼 🎽 🛇 All major cards

🏨 HOTEL SONNE
$$–$$$
NEUER MARKT 2
TEL 0381 4 97 30
FAX 0381 4 97 33 51
www.rostock.steigenberger.de
An efficient modern hotel in

the new wing of the historic town hall. Well-planned rooms, health and beauty facilities, a good restaurant, a café with excellent cakes, and two bars make this a popular hotel.

🛈 112 + 9 suites 🅿 🛗 🕲
🍽 ♿ All major cards

🍴 ZUR KOGGE
$$
WOKRENTER STRASSE 27
TEL 0381 493 44 93
zur-kogge.de
This old seaman's locale oozes atmosphere with model ships, a giant swordfish and a 150-year-old bar (if it could only talk!). Seasonal fish dishes, simple but well prepared, dominate the menu. Upper and lower decks overlook the harbor.

🪑 64 🕐 Closed L Mon.–Fri.
♿ No credit cards

RÜGEN

🏨 VIER JAHRESZEITEN
🍴 $$$
ZEPPELINSTRASSE 8, BINZ
TEL 038393 5 00
FAX 038393 5 04 30
vier-jahreszeiten.eu
A classic example of Binz resort architecture, this smartly renovated hotel has a fancy indoor pool, a health and beauty center, and several fine restaurants. In its newest gourmet temple, **Freustil,** celebrated chef Ralf Haug gives his creations a distinctly Nordic accent. A first-class breakfast buffet is included in the room rates.

🛈 74 + 5 suites 🅿 🚇 🍽
♿ AE, MC, V

🏨 PANORAMA HOTEL LOHME
$$–$$$
AN DER STEILKÜSTE 8,
LOHME
TEL 038302 911 0
FAX 038302 911 132
lohme.com
High on the white cliffs of

Rügen Island, the Panorama Hotel has stunning views from its beautiful terrace and absolutely romantic rooms. Watch the sun set from the veranda while enjoying salmon marinated in fennel, or herring with a crunchy lentil-potato ragout. Room rates include a generous breakfast.

🛈 41 + 2 suites + 2 apts. 🅿
♿ No credit cards

SCHWERIN

🏨 ARTE
🍴 $$$
DORFSTRASSE 6,
SCHWERIN-KREBSFÖRDEN
TEL 0385 6 34 50
FAX 0385 6 34 51 00
hotel-arte.de
Just outside town, an exquisite country hotel in an extended old farmhouse with a fine on-site restaurant, the **Fontane.** The hotel has a solarium, plenty of nonsmoking rooms, and a sauna (which, like breakfast, is included).

🛈 41 🅿 🍽 ♿ All major cards

🍴 SCHRÖTER'S
$$$
SCHLIEMANNSTRASSE 2
TEL 0385 550 76 98
This intimate restaurant in the historic quarter has views of Pfaffenteich Lake and offers regional cuisine with a French accent, including caramelized duck liver with asparagus and Frisian beef.

🪑 40 🕐 Closed L. & Sun.
♿ All major cards

STRALSUND

🏨 HANSEDOM HOTEL
$$$
GRÜNHOFER BOGEN 18–20
TEL 0800 1010 88 0
FAX 03831 37 73 900
wyndhamstralsund.com
Close to the beautiful Hanse Dom-Park, the hotel offers large rooms with pastel-colored

walls, lots of polished wood, and wicker chairs.

🛈 109 + 5 suites 🕲 🚇 🛗
🍽 ♿ All major cards

🍴 TAFELFREUDEN IM SOMMERHAUS
$$$
JUNGFERNSTIEG 5A
TEL 03831 29 92 60
Ambitious chef Axel Müller offers fusion cuisine at moderate prices in a pretty yellow country villa. Try the mussels, St. Pietro fish with polenta, and avocado salad with a special vinaigrette.

🪑 50 🅿 🕐 Closed Mon.; open D Tues.–Sun. ♿ AE, MC, V

TIMMENDORFER STRAND

🏨 LANDHAUS CARSTENS
🍴 $$$–$$$$$
STRANDALLEE 73
TEL 04503 60 80
FAX 04503 6 08 60

landhauscarstens.de
A country house hotel beside the sea. Local fish with a champagne sauce or pigeon with Madeira sauce will restore your strength after a beach walk.

ⓘ 30 + 3 suites 🅿 🎇 🌡
🅢 All major cards

USEDOM

SOMETHING SPECIAL

🏨 GUTSHAUS STOLPE
🍴 $$$
PEENSTRASSE 33,
STOLPE BEI ANKLAM
TEL 039721 55 00
FAX 039721 55 09
gutshaus-stolpe.de
Occupying a 19th-century manor house and surrounded by a beautiful park, the intimate Gutshaus Stolpe emulates the small country inns of England or France. Guest rooms and the cozy public areas are tastefully furnished with antiques. The Michelin-starred cuisine of chef Andre Münch changes with the seasons and caters to individual wishes (vegetarians welcome). Dinner guests have raved about meals on the terrace, with its views of the splendid oaks.

🛏 32 + 4 suites 🅿 🕒 Closed Mon. & Sun.–Mon. Nov.–March 🌡 🅢 MC, V

HAMBURG & SCHLESWIG-HOLSTEIN

HAMBURG

🏨 VIER JAHRESZEITEN
🍴 $$$$$
NEUER JUNGFERNSTIEG 9–14
TEL 040 34 94 31 51
FAX 040 34 94 26 00
hvj.de
Hamburg's traditional grand hotel presents rooms in classic style. The restaurant **Haerlen** has exquisite Biedermeier

furniture. Favorites on the menu include four variations of goose liver, and juicy lamb in a pecorino crust with haricot beans and onion confit. The restaurant boasts excellent wines.

ⓘ 156 🅿 🖨 🌡
🅢 All major cards

🏨 KEMPINSKI ATLANTIC
🍴 $$$$–$$$$$
AN DER ALSTER 72–79
TEL 040 2 88 80
FAX 040 24 71 29
atlantic.de
This Hamburg institution displays great elegance throughout. The best of the luxurious suites, of course, have views of Alster Lake.

ⓘ 215 + 30 suites 🅿 🖨
🎇 🅢 All major cards

🏨 SIDE HOTEL HAMBURG
🍴 $$$$–$$$$$
DREHBAHN 49
TEL 040 30 99 90
FAX 040 30 99 93 99
side-hamburg.de
A striking Hamburg landmark, this 12-story glass tower was designed by local architect Jan Störmer. Italian designer Matteo Thun continues the minimalist theme from the reception area into the bedrooms. Sushi is a big feature in the restaurant.

ⓘ 168 + 10 suites 🅿 🖨
🎇 🌡 🅢 All major cards

🏨 SOFITEL AM ALTEN
🍴 WALL
$$$$
ALTER WALL 38–46
TEL 040 36 95 00
FAX 040 36 95 010 00
sofitel.com
Big rooms and an exciting mix of materials—glass, felt, wooden floors, stone—characterize this central hotel. Eight studio rooms have views of the canals.

ⓘ 223 + 18 suites 🅿 🖨 🎇
🅢 All major cards

🏨 GRAND ELYSEE
$$$–$$$$
ROTHENBAUMCHAUSSEE 10
TEL 040 41 41 20
FAX 040 41 41 27 33
grand-elysee.com
A Hamburg favorite with light comfortable rooms, a cheerful lobby, two restaurants, a café, and a bar.

ⓘ 511 + 19 suites 🅿 🖨 🎇
🅢 All major cards

🏨 WIDENA GALERIE HOTEL
$$$–$$$$
LANGE REIHE 50
TEL 040 280 89 00
FAX 040 280 38 94
hotelwedina.de
This boutique pension features East Asian ink-wash paintings and bright, contrasting color schemes in four suite-like rooms with excellent amenities. Refurbished with state funds, the 18th-century building is superbly located on a lively street teeming with cafés and art galleries, and it's a five-minute walk to Alster Lake. The owner's three guest cottages opposite are geared to literature and architecture.

ⓘ 18 🅿 🅢 MC, V

SOMETHING SPECIAL

🏨 ÖKOTEL HAMBURG
$$$
HOLSTEINER CHAUSSEE 347
TEL 040 55 97 30 0
FAX 040 55 97 30 99
oekotel.de
This "ecological hotel" matches personal comforts with the well-being of the planet. The light, spacious rooms—many with balcony views of a leafy suburb—have been infused with a Far Eastern flavor, with oiled wood floors taken from environmentally friendly forests and linens made of organic cotton. Antiallergenic materials such as latex mattresses feature throughout. The in-house

Bio-Restaurant serves healthy regional dishes and, of course, organic wines.
[I] 25 + 2 apts. [P]
[&] No credit cards

🍴 LE CANARD
$$$$$
ELBCHAUSSEE 139
TEL 040 88 12 95 31/32
lecanard-hamburg.de
It's still hard to quibble with the finely honed recipes of chef Ali Güngörmüs, a Bavarian-born Turk. The Michelin-starred menu excels in seafood dishes such as monkfish with bouillabaise potatoes, or North Sea turbot with polenta soufflé. The elegant, sunlit dining room overlooks the Elbe.
[🔢] 70 [P] [🕐] Closed Sun.–Mon.
[&] All major cards

🍴 FISCHEREIHAFEN RESTAURANT
$$$–$$$$
GROSSE ELBSTRASSE 243
TEL 040 38 18 16
fischereihafenrestaurant.de
A Hamburg tradition with a classic fish menu (haddock with mustard sauce, plaice fried in bacon, broiled sole) plus sushi. Usually crowded.
[🔢] 150 [P] [&] All major cards

🍴 LANDHAUS SCHERRER
$$$–$$$$$
ELBCHAUSSEE 130
TEL 040 88 30 700 30
landhausscherrer.de
North German cuisine comes with an exotic twist here: bean soup with scallops, North Sea fish with saffron, caipirinhia parfait with mangos. One Michelin star and plenty of return customers.
[🔢] 95 [P] [🕐] Closed Sun.
[&] All major cards

KIEL

🏨 ROMANTIK HOTEL KIELER KAUFMANN
$$$$
NIEMANNSWEG 102
TEL 0431 881 10
FAX 0431 881 11 35
kieler-kaufmann.de
Quietly located in a leafy park, this picturesque villa dates back to the turn of the last century, but it also has a modern annex.
[I] 33 + 6 suites [P] [🚇]
[&] All major cards

🍴 LÜNEBURG-HAUS
$$$–$$$$
DÄNISCHE STRASSE 22
TEL 0431 98 26 00 0
lueneburghaus.com
Confident Mediterranean cuisine served in a beautiful early 20th-century house. Try the turbot with a sorrel-tomato ragout.
[🔢] 65 [🕐] Closed Sun.
[&] All major cards

🍴 SEPTEMBER
$$$
ALTE LÜBECKER CHAUSSEE 27
TEL 0431 68 06 10
september-kiel.de
The beautiful winter garden is a feature of this second-floor restaurant in the city center. Service can be slow, but the Holstein beef in red wine sauce is worth the wait. There are 170 liqueurs and a huge wine list.
[🔢] 70 [🕐] Closed Sun. D
[&] No credit cards

LÜBECK

🏨 KLASSIK ALTSTADT HOTEL
$$$
FISCHERGRUBE 52
TEL 0451 70 29 80
FAX 0451 7 37 78
klassik-altstadt-hotel.de
You can explore picturesque Lübeck on foot from this traditionally decorated hotel. Breakfast is included.
[I] 22 + 3 suites [P]
[&] All major cards

🍴 WULLENWEVER
$$$$
BECKERGRUBE 71
TEL 0451 70 43 33
wullenwever.de
A splendid restaurant in a town-center patrician villa. Choose from dishes such as sautéed lobster with herb salad, perch with foie gras, and pigeon carpaccio. The wine list has more than 350 entries.
[🔢] 79 [🕐] Closed L [&] DC, V

SYLT

🏨 DORINT SÖL'RING HOF
🍴 $$$$$
AM SANDWALL 1,
RANTUM
TEL 04651 83 62 00
FAX 04651 83 62 020
soelring-hof.de
Enjoying a great location in the dunes, this vacation hotel offers guests light, modern rooms, some with ocean views. The very popular restaurant run by renowned chef Johannes King boasts two Michelin stars. Breakfast, minibar, and beach chair are included in the rate.
[I] 15 + 2 suites [P] [🔵] [🚇] [📺]
[&] All major cards

SOMETHING SPECIAL

🍴 SANSIBAR
$$$–$$$$
HÖRNUMER STRASSE 80,
RANTUM
TEL 04651 96 46 56
FAX 04651 96 46 47
sansibar-sylt.de
Watch the sun set from a beach chalet as evocative as its exotic name. Offerings include large portions of fried turbot and other fish, afternoon coffee, and cakes. Reserve in advance.
[🔢] 95 [&] AE, MC, V

■ LOWER SAXONY & BREMEN

BRAUNLAGE

SOMETHING SPECIAL

▥ ROMANTIK HOTEL
▯ ZUR TANNE
$$$

HERZOG-WILHELM-STRASSE 8
TEL 05520 931 20
FAX 05520 931 24 44
tanne-braunlage.de
A well-preserved 18th-century inn, now a family-owned hotel. Rooms are furnished in cozy country style in the main hotel and the modern annex. The restaurant specializes in Harz Mountain classics such as *Harzer Bachforelle* (local trout), followed by a plum or apple tart. The room rate includes use of the sauna and a generous breakfast.
① 18 + 3 suites 🅿 ⊕ Restaurant closed Mon. ▯
⬥ All major cards

BREMEN

▥ PARK HOTEL
▯ $$$$–$$$$$

IM BÜRGERPARK
TEL 0421 3 40 80
FAX 0421 3 40 86 02
park-hotel-bremen.de
Bremen's premier hotel looks like a stately home with a domed central lobby. Room styles range from Japanese to Italian. Chef Norman Fischer's team proffers dishes such as marinated rabbit with rose petals or roast perch in almond sauce.
① 155 + 20 suites 🅿 ⊖
🏊 ▯ ⬥ All major cards

▯ KAFFEEMÜHLE AM WALL
$$$$

AM WALL
TEL 0421 144 66
muehle-bremen.de
Enjoy dishes such as herring with sour cream and fried

potatoes in unique surrounds: a 19th-century windmill.
➕ 90 ⬥ All major cards

▯ L'ORCHIDEE IM BREMER RATSKELLER
$$$

AM MARKT 1
TEL 0421 32 16 76
ratskeller-bremen.de
This restaurant located in the 600-year-old town hall cellar (Ratskeller) serves haute cuisine—such as roasted fish soup, veal filled with lobster, and passion fruit tart with raspberries—as well as such down-home fare as *Sauerbraten (boeuf à la mode)*.
➕ 83 ⬥ DC, MC, V

▯ GRASHOFF'S BISTRO
$$

CONTRESCARPE 80
TEL 0421 147 49
grashoff.de
Paris-trained chef Oliver Schmidt has made this one-Michelin-star bistro into an institution. Haddock with mustard sauce, caramel ice cream with almonds—no disappointments.
➕ 42 ⊕ Closed Sun. & holidays ⬥ All major cards

CELLE

▥ FÜRSTENHOF
▯ $$$$

HANNOVERSCHE STRASSE 55–56
TEL 05141 20 10
FAX 05141 20 11 20
fuerstenhof.de
Near the medieval town center, this former palace (built in 1670) with annex is furnished with antiques and oil paintings. The restaurant, **Endtenfang**, features chicken with truffles and lobster with curry-cauliflower couscous. Breakfast is included.
① 68 + 5 suites 🅿 🏊 ▯
⬥ All major cards

GOSLAR

▥ DER ACHTERMANN
▯ $$$

ROSENTORSTRASSE 20
TEL 05321 7 00 00
FAX 05321 7 00 09 99
hotel-der-achtermann.de
Part of this town-center hotel dates to 1501. The annex is less atmospheric but has a good fitness center. The restaurant, **Altdeutsche Stuben**, specializes in local food. Breakfast and sauna use are included.
① 152 ⊖ 🏊 ▯
⬥ All major cards

GÖTTINGEN

▥ ROMANTIK HOTEL GEBHARDS
$$$–$$$$

GOETHEALLEE 22/23
TEL 0551 4 96 80
FAX 0551 4 96 81 10
gebhardshotel.de
This beautiful historic house near the station is now a splendid hotel, furnished with antiques.
① 48 + 2 suites 🅿 ▯
⬥ All major cards

▥ FREIZEIT IN
▯ $$$

DRANSFELDER STRASSE 3
TEL 0551 9 00 10
FAX 0551 9 00 11 00
freizeit-in.de
Up-to-date rooms make this a popular business hotel. Best of the three restaurants is the bistro, which serves regional cuisine with a Mediterranean slant: minestrone with pesto to start, sole with spinach and roast potatoes to follow. Breakfast is included.
① 212 🅿 ⊖ 🏊 ▯
⬥ All major cards

▯ GAUSS
$$$–$$$$

OBERE KARSPÜLE 22
TEL 0551 566 16

restaurant-gauss.de
Owner Jacqueline Amirfallah,
a well-known cook on German
television, takes her inspirations
from France: sole with saffron
rice, poached chicken with
herb sauce, lamb in thyme *jus.*
You eat in a vaulted cellar or
outside in summer.
🛈 85 🕒 Closed Sun.–Mon., *&*
L 🖾 AE, MC, V

HANOVER

🏨 **KASTENS HOTEL**
🍴 **LUISENHOF**
$$$$
LUISENSTRASSE 1–3
TEL 0511 3 04 40
FAX 0511 3 04 48 07
kastens-luisenhof.de
Between the main station and
the Opera House, Hanover's
grand hotel is furnished with
antiques. Enjoy pan-global
cuisine in the restaurant **Luise:**
Main courses include breast
of pigeon with caramelized
apples and veal in a curry-
saffron sauce.
🛈 138 + 8 suites 🅿 ⬍ Ⓢ 🖵
🖾 All major cards

🏨 **SHERATON PELIKAN**
🍴 **HOTEL HANNOVER**
$$$
PELIKANPLATZ 31
TEL 0511 9 09 30
FAX 0511 9 09 35 55
sheratonpelikanhannover.com
Converted from some hand-
some early 20th-century
industrial buildings, this busi-
ness hotel has its best and
largest rooms on the second
and third floors. The restau-
rant, **5th Avenue,** prepares
top-notch dishes from around
the globe and does a terrific
iced whisky parfait.
🛈 138 + 9 suites 🅿 ⬍ Ⓢ
🖵 🖾 All major cards

🍴 **PIER 51**
$$$
RUDOLF-VON-
BENNINGSEN-UFER 51

TEL 0511 807 1800
pier51.de
Here you can dine on the terrace and look at the sunset
over the Maschsee. Unfussy
Mediterranean dishes such
as pasta with mushrooms in
cream sauce or salad with scallops and scampi.
🍴 70 🅿 🖾 AE, MC, V

🍴 **WEINSTUBE LEONARDO**
$$$
SOPHIENSTRASSE 6
TEL 0511 32 10 33
weinstube-leonardo.de
This basement restaurant
serves solid regional food, such
as lamb with a purée of beans.
Good wines.
🍴 70 🕒 Closed Sun.
🖾 MC, V

HILDESHEIM

🏨 **VAN DER VALK HOTEL**
HILDESHEIM
$$–$$$
MARKT 4
TEL 05121 3000
FAX 05121 300 444
hildesheim.vandervalk.de
This modern hotel in the
medieval market square sits
right next to Germany's most
beautiful half-timbered house.
English-style interior and
modern conference facilities.
All rooms have Wi-Fi and air-
conditioning, a relative novelty
in this price category.
🛈 110 + 2 junior suites 🅿 ⬍
Ⓢ 🖾 🖵 🖾 All major cards

🍴 **KUPFERSCHMIEDE**
$$
AM STEINBERG 6
TEL 05121 697 79 31
gasthof-kupferschmiede.de
A delightful setting in a forest south of Hildesheim and
32 varieties of champagne
at attractive prices are good
reasons to come here. French
cuisine of good quality.
🍴 90 🕒 Closed Mon. 🅿
🖾 MC, V

JUIST

🏨 **ROMANTIK &**
WELLNESS HOTEL
ACHTERDIEK
$$$$$
WILHELMSTRASSE 36
TEL 04935 80 40
FAX 04935 17 54
hotel-achterdiek.de
Art and antiques in the
entrance hall lend a whiff
of grandeur to this hotel.
If the wind blows too hard,
retreat to the sauna or
beauty spa.
🛈 49 + 21 apts. 🕒 Closed
Nov. 22–Dec. 22 🖾 🖵
🖾 No credit cards

LÜNEBURG

🏨 **BARGENTURM**
$$$
ST. LAMBERTIPLATZ
TEL 04131 72 90
FAX 04131 72 94 99
hotel-bargenturm.de

In the historic center, the rather pedestrian facade belies the sumptuous furnishings inside, like bathtubs of Turkish marble. Health club with Finnish sauna.
🛈 40 🅿 🛡 🕲 All major cards

🍴 ZUM HEIDKRUG
$$$
AM BERGE 5
TEL 04131 2 41 60
zum-heidkrug.de
Lüneburg's top-rated restaurant is often booked solid. The cuisine—for example, vegetable soup with black truffles or crepinette of venison—is modern international with a Mediterranean accent. Excellent desserts; don't miss the Black Forest cherry ice cream.
🍴 56 🕒 Closed Sun.–Tues. 🕲 MC, V

NORDERNEY

🏨 VILLA NEY
🍴 $$$
GARTENSTRASSE 59
TEL 04932 91 70
FAX 04932 917 31
villa-ney.de
This whitewashed modern villa has good-size bedrooms with comfortable armchairs and marble bathrooms. Owner Peter Mackel inspires admiration for his imaginative treatment of fresh local fish.
🛈 14 studios & suites
🕒 Closed 2 weeks Nov. & 2 weeks Jan. 🕲 MC, V

SCHNEVERDINGEN

SOMETHING SPECIAL
🏨 CAMP REINSEHLEN
🍴 $$$
REINSEHLEN
TEL 05198 98 30
FAX 05198 983 99
campreinsehlen.de
An ecologist's dream on Germany's oldest nature reserve, only 40 minutes from Hamburg.

Clean, modern design contrasts with rustic, traditional features. All rooms have terraces. The restaurant, **Gasthaus,** uses only organic ingredients.
🛈 51 🅿 🕲 AE, MC, V

WOLFSBURG

SOMETHING SPECIAL
🏨 RITZ-CARLTON
$$$$$
PARKSTRASSE 1
TEL 05361 60 70 00
FAX 05361 60 80 00
ritzcarlton.com
Designed by renowned French interior guru Andrée Putman, the hotel is right in the middle of the 6-acre (2.4 ha) Autostadt (Auto City)—a theme park northeast of town (see p. 141). Only the best furnishings grace the rooms, from the finest Frette linens to Eileen Gray sofas in the suites.
🛈 153 + 21 suites 🅿 🍴 🕲
🕲 🛡 🕲 All major cards

WORPSWEDE

🏨 EICHENHOF
🍴 $$$$
OSTENDORFER STRASSE 13
TEL 04792 26 76
FAX 04792 44 27
eichenhof-worpswede.de
The fusion of rustic North German architecture with modern interiors works well at this country hotel. The restaurant serves modern European dishes such as chervil soup with shreds of salmon.
🛈 15 + 2 suite + 3 apts.
🕒 Open D only 🕲 DC, MC, V

■ NORTH RHINE-WESTPHALIA

AACHEN

🏨 PULLMAN AACHEN QUELLENHOF

$$$$
MONHEIMSALLEE 52
TEL 0241 913 20
FAX 0241 913 21 00
pullmanhotels.com
Rooms in the premier hotel in Charlemagne's ancient capital are furnished in classical taste.
🛈 182 + 3 suites 🕲 🛡
🕲 All major cards

🍴 ST BENEDIKT
$$$$
BENEDIKTUSPLATZ 12, KORNELIMÜNSTER
TEL 02408 28 88
stbenedikt.de
Aachen's best restaurant, and one of its coziest, is in a picturesque little town to the southeast. Owner-chef Maximilian Kreus pulls out all the stops in four- to six-course meals fit for royalty. One Michelin star. Daytime bistro next door.
🍴 68 🕒 Closed Sun.–Mon. 🕲 No credit cards

SOMETHING SPECIAL
🍴 CAFE VAN DEN DAELE
$
BÜCHEL 18
TEL 0241 357 24
van-den-daele.de
A coffeehouse in a 17th-century building with beautifully preserved rooms. You can have breakfast, brunch, and afternoon coffee and cake. The specialties here are the *Reisfladen* (rice cake) and Aachen's famous *Printen* (ginger cakes).
🍴 95 🕒 Closed D 🕲 MC, V

BONN

🏨 DORINT VENUSBERG
🍴 $$$$
AN DER CASSELSRUHE I
TEL 0228 28 80
FAX 0228 28 82 88
hotel-bonn.dorint.com
In a quiet and beautiful spot beside a forest with a view of the Siebengebirge

(Seven Mountains) and the Rhine. Ambitious restaurant **Basilico** offers Mediterranean specialties.

ⓘ 75 + 10 suites 🅿 🔁 🔲 🔳
🔳 All major cards

COLOGNE

🏨 EXCELSIOR HOTEL
🍴 ERNST
$$$$$
TRANKGASSE 1–5 (DOMPLATZ)
TEL 0221 27 01
FAX 0221 270 33 33
excelsior-hotel-ernst.de
Located directly opposite the cathedral and railroad station, the rooms and foyer of the 140-year-old hotel are replete with antiques. Minibar use is included in the room price. The restaurant, **Hanse Stube**, offers creative French cuisine: sole with a citrus-fruit salad, tournedos of beef with marrow bones, and cassis-chicory. The second restaurant, **taku**, serves Asian dishes such as Thai fish curry with bamboo sprouts, or perch with asparagus tempura.

ⓘ 108 + 34 suites 🔁 🔳
🔳 All major cards

SOMETHING SPECIAL

🏨 HOTEL IM
🍴 WASSERTURM
$$$$$
KAYGASSE 2
TEL 0221 2 00 80
FAX 0221 200 81 44
hotel-im-wasserturm.de
A flamboyant hotel by French designer Andrée Putman behind an old water tower. Chic rooms, some with African hardwoods, others in a yellow-and-blue color scheme, and even more elegant suites. The restaurant, **W**, has city views from the 12th-floor roof terrace. Here, French cuisine comes with a twist: salmon pâté with sturgeon mousse, loin of rabbit roulade, fillet of sea bass with tomato fondu,

and a beurre blanc sauce.

ⓘ 54 + 34 suites
🔳 All major cards

🏨 DOM-HOTEL
$$$$–$$$$$
DOMKLOSTER 2A
TEL 0221 202 42 50
FAX 0221 202 42 51
domhotel.com
Cologne's finest address, the Dom-Hotel has elegant rooms, some with views of the cathedral. The terrace is strictly for seeing and being seen.

ⓘ 124 🔁 🔳 🔳 AE, MC, V

🍴 ALFREDO
$$$$
TUNISSTRASSE 3
TEL 0221 257 73 80
ristorante-alfredo.com
An exclusive Italian eatery next to the Opera House, specializing in fish. Don't miss the langoustines with fennel.

🔳 58 🕐 Closed Sat.–Sun.
🔳 AE, MC, V

🍴 L'ESCALIER
$$$$
BRÜSSELER STRASSE 11
TEL 0221 205 39 98
lescalier-restaurant.de
Run by rising culinary star Maximilian Lorenz, this gourmet temple prides itself on superbly inventive German-French crossovers. Excellent service and wine list, snug bistro tables.

🔳 32 🕐 Closed Sun.–Mon.
🔳 AE, MC, V

DÜSSELDORF

🏨 AUSZEIT HOTEL
$$$
AUF'M HENNEKAMP 71
TEL 0211 30 20 59 0
FAX 0211 30 20 59 99
auszeit-hotel.de
Skillful lighting brings out the best in the elegant ruby-and-slate color scheme of this refined, modern hotel near the

Volksgarten, southeast of the center. A favorite with the business crowd, the Wi-Fi-equipped rooms are generously sized and filled with designer touches. Rates include breakfast as well as use of the sauna and fitness room.

ⓘ 54 🅿 🔁 🔳
🔳 All major cards

🍴 NÖTHEL'S
$$$$$
BONIFATIUSSTRASSE 35
TEL 0211 59 44 02
hummerstuebchen.de
One of Düsseldorf's top restaurants, located in a small hotel. Specialties are sautéed lobster with marinated glass noodles, *ris de veau* with braised fennel and parsley sauce. Excellent wines.

🔳 49 🅿 🕐 Closed Sat. L, Sun., & Thurs. 🔳 DC, MC, V

🍴 MARUYASU
$$
SCHADOWSTRASSE 11
TEL 0211 13 21 57
www.maruyasu.de
Düsseldorf is well known for its good Japanese food. This chic sushi temple in the bowels of the Schadow shopping arcades prides itself on its 70 varieties of excellent sushi.

🔳 75 🕐 Closed Sun. 🔳 No credit cards

🍴 ROBERTS BISTRO
$$
WUPPERSTRASSE 2
TEL 0211 30 48 21
robertsbistro.de
A popular bistro with plain decor, pleasant food, and a trendy young clientele. Expect big portions of sausages, salads, and veal kidney in mustard sauce.

🕐 Closed Sun.–Mon.
🔳 No credit cards

ESSEN

🏨 SCHLOSS HUGENPOET
$$$$$
AUGUST-THYSSEN-STRASSE 51,
ESSEN-KETTWIG
TEL 02054 1 20 40
FAX 02054 1 204 50
hugenpoet.de
This baroque castle in the middle of a large park is stylish and restful. Suitably, the rooms are stuffed with antiques.
ℹ️ 19 + 6 suites + 1 villa 🅿️
🏧 All major cards

🍴 KÖLNER HOF
$$$
DUISBURGER STRASSE 20,
ESSEN-FROHNHAUSEN
TEL 0201 76 34 30
restaurant-koelner-hof.de
Creative cooking inspired by the Mediterranean, with starched linens and personable service. Try the tender lamb with a pine nut crust, beef medallions in red wine sauce, and hazelnut nougat with caramelized apples.
🍴 48 🕐 Closed Sat. L & Mon.–Tues. 🏧 No credit cards

KÖNIGSWINTER

SOMETHING SPECIAL

🏨 STEIGENBERGER
🍴 GRANDHOTEL PETERSBERG
$$$$–$$$$$
PETERSBERG
TEL 02223 7 40
FAX 02223 7 44 43
en.steigenberger.com
On a plateau high above Königswinter, a few miles south of the former capital of Bonn, this imposing early 20th-century mansion acted as a guesthouse for state visits to Chancellor Helmut Kohl's government. The timeless elegance of the hotel is matched by the classic cuisine of its restaurant, **Rheinterrassen.**
ℹ️ 87 + 12 suites 🅿️ 🔁 🟩 🏊
🩺 🏧 All major cards

MÜNSTER

🏨 HOF ZUR LINDE
🍴 $$$–$$$$
HANDORFER WERSEUFER 1,
MÜNSTER-HANDORF
TEL 0251 327 50
FAX 0251 327513
hof-zur-linde.de
A romantic old building on the banks of the River Werse with canopied beds, fireplaces, and decoration veering from hunting lodge to French royal. The best rooms are in the adjacent *Spieker* house.
ℹ️ 49 + 4 suites 🅿️
🏧 All major cards

🍴 RESTAURANT FREIBERGER
$$$
SIRKSFELD 10,
COESFELD IN WESTFALEN
TEL 02541 3930
restaurant-freiberger.de
This sprawling *Gasthof* in the Westfalian backwoods offers no-nonsense German regional fare. In its countrified dining chambers you can enjoy wild boar or roast venison alongside "lighter" fare like bacon pancakes or braised pike-perch.
🍴 120 🅿️ 🕐 Closed Mon.–Tues. 🏧 DC, V

■ RHINELAND-PALATINATE & THE SAARLAND

BOPPARD

🏨 BEST WESTERN BELLEVUE RHEINHOTEL
$$–$$$
RHEINALLEE 41
TEL 06742 10 20
FAX 06742 10 26 02
bellevue-boppard.de
Stylish art nouveau house on the promenade overlooking the rushing waters of the Rhine River. The rooms come in different shapes and sizes, some with antiques and balconies.

ℹ️ 93 + 1 suite 🅿️ 🔁 🟩 🏊
🩺 🏧 All major cards

🍴 GASTHAUS HIRSCH
$$
RHEINSTRASSE 17,
BOPPARD-HIRZENACH
TEL 06741 26 01
gasthaus-hirsch.net
Family-owned restaurant known for its very good game and regional cooking. In summer, dine in the courtyard.
🍴 36 🅿️ 🕐 Closed Mon.–Tues. 🏧 All major cards

KNITTLESHEIM

🍴 STEVERDING'S ISENHOF
$$$–$$$$
HAUPTSTRASSE 15A
TEL 06348 57 00
isenhof.de
This restaurant is a rising star on the culinary scene, run by chef Peter Steverding in a handsome timber-framed house from the 15th century. The sea bass with potato and spinach tart is especially good.
🍴 60 🕐 Closed Sun.–Tues.; D only 🏧 No credit cards

KOBLENZ

🏨 DIEHL'S HOTEL
🍴 $$$
RHEINSTEIGUFER 1
TEL 0261 970 70
FAX 0261 970 72 13
diehls-hotel.de
Set at the foot of the fortress Ehrenbreitstein, this family-oriented hotel has comfortable quarters in both modern and traditional style. Panorama views abound, and the indoor pool and sauna offer peeks at the mighty Rhine. The restaurant, **ClemenS**, puts a modern spin on German cuisine.
ℹ️ 53 + 4 suites 🅿️ 🔁 🏊 🩺
🏧 All major cards

MAINZ

🏨 HILTON MAINZ CITY
🍴 $$$–$$$$
MÜNSTERSTRASSE 11
TEL 06131 27 80
hilton.de/mainzcity
Blessed with a pretty Rhine-side location, this Hilton has been redone top to bottom and offers cut-above, well-equipped quarters with lots of perks and fine views of the old town. All guests enjoy free access to the fitness areas, while air conditioning, Wi-Fi, and satellite TV are standard in all rooms. Summer terrace overlooking the river.
🛏 126 + 1 suite 🅿 🚇 🛗
🚭 All major cards

🍴 WEINHAUS ZUM BEICHTSTUHL
$$
KAPUZINERSTRASSE 30
TEL 06131 23 31 20
In this cozy, paneled drinking hole—a onetime hangout of Rhine River sailors—students mingle with grizzled locals over beveled glasses of Riesling and portions of Mainzer Käse mit Musik, a cheese smothered in onions. In summer, grab a streetside table.
🪑 80 🕐 Closed L
🚭 No credit cards

NEUSTADT AN DER WEINSTRASSE

🍴 BECKER'S GUT
$$$
WEINSTRASSE 507
TEL 06321 21 95
Delicate interior hues contrast with powerful regional cooking from chef Harry Becker, who makes excellent *Schupfnudeln* (Swabian potato noodles) and venison with mushrooms.
🪑 60 🅿 🕐 Closed Mon.–Tues. & L 🚭 All major cards

SAARBRÜCKEN

🍴 KUNTZE'S HANDELSHOF
$$$$
WILHELM-HEINRICH-STRASSE 17
TEL 0681 569 20
kuntzes-handelshof.de
Good cooking in a region renowned for it. Warm and cold chicken dishes, veal kidneys in champagne-mustard sauce, and rustic potato soup. Chandelier-lit baroque rooms.
🪑 56 🕐 Closed Sat. L, Sun. D, & Mon. 🚭 AE, MC, V

STROMBERG

SOMETHING SPECIAL

🏨 STROMBURG
🍴 $$$$–$$$$$
SCHLOSSBERG
TEL 06724 931 00
FAX 06724 93 10 90
johannlafer.de
This castle dating from the 11th century set beside the Nahe River is pure elegance, from the grand lobby to guest rooms furnished in different styles. Most of the rooms have a view over the romantic Soon Forest. Owner-chef Johann Lafer runs the restaurant, **Le Val D'Or**, and cooks classic French haute cuisine. One Michelin star.
🛏 13 + 1 suite 🅿
🕐 Restaurant closed Mon.–Tues. 🚭 All major cards

TRIER

🏨 MERCURE HOTEL TRIER PORTA NIGRA
$$$
PORTA-NIGRA-PLATZ 1
TEL 0651 270 1 0
FAX 0651 270 1 1 70
mercure.com
The view of the Roman Porta Nigra is a major selling point for this business hotel just a few steps from the Old Town

and its imposing cathedral. Fresh waffles for breakfast.
🛏 104 + 2 suites 🅿 🛗
🚇 🚭 All major cards

🍴 WEINSTUBE KESSELSTADT
$$
LIEBFRAENSTRASSE 10, TRIER
TEL 0651 411 78
A strange bedfellow in the baroque Kesselstadt Palais, this wine pub-restaurant prides itself on fine Riesling wines and earthy regional fare such as wild boar, smoked trout and creamed chanterelles. Nice front terrace with views of the cathedral.
🪑 120 🚭 No credit cards

ZWEIBRÜCKEN

🏨 ROMANTIK HOTEL
🍴 LANDSCHLOSS FASANERIE
$$$$–$$$$$
FASANERIE 1
TEL 06332 97 30
FAX 06332 97 31 11
landschloss-fasanerie.de
Built in 1714 by Polish king Stanislaus Lescynski, this onion-domed villa sits in a flower-filled park. Rooms are in country style. French cooking in the restaurant **ESSlibris.** Try the venison, followed by pear-vanilla ice cream. Breakfast is included.
🛏 37 + 13 apts. 🅿
📞 📺 🚭 AE, MC, V

◼ HESSE

BAD HOMBURG

🏨 STEIGENBERGER
$$$–$$$$
KAISER-FRIEDRICH-PROMENADE 69–75
TEL 06172 18 10
FAX 06172 18 16 30
en.steigenberger.com
A gracious establishment notable for its art deco furnishings.

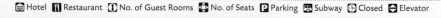

🏨 Hotel 🍴 Restaurant 🛏 No. of Guest Rooms 🪑 No. of Seats 🅿 Parking 🚇 Subway 🕐 Closed 🛗 Elevator

This is where assorted royalty stayed while taking the rejuvenating spa waters or playing the nearby casino.

🛏 148 + 21 suites 🅿 ⬌
❄ 🏋 ⚄ All major cards

🍴 ZUM WASSER-WEIBCHEN

$$–$$$

AM MÜHLBERG 57

TEL 06172 302 553

wasserweibchen.de

Set in a sturdy Kaiser-era building, this traditional eatery never fails to please with local evergreens like boiled beef with Frankfurt green sauce and crisp roast potatoes. Save space for the plum pancake and vanilla ice cream.

🍴 52 🕐 Closed Sat. & L
⚄ All major cards

DARMSTADT

🛏 JAGDSCHLOSS KRANICHSTEIN

$$$$

KRANICHSTEINER STRASSE 261

TEL 06151 130 670

FAX 06151 130 67 99

**hotel-jagdschloss
-kranichstein.de**

This enormous Renaissance-era palace has been converted to a traditional hotel with two restaurants and grand halls filled with hunting trophies. Tours of the grounds and museum. Breakfast and mini-bar are included.

🛏 48 🅿 ⚄ ⚄ All major cards

🍴 EINSIEDEL

$$$

DIEBURGER STRASSE 263

TEL 06159 244

www.restaurant-einsiedel.de

Another former hunting lodge, now a sprawling restaurant with art deco touches. Roast venison with Spätzle and rabbit with a tomato-basil sauce are local favorites.

🍴 110 🅿 🕐 Closed Tues.–Wed. & L ⚄ AE, MC

ELTVILLE

🛏 🍴 KRONEN-SCHLÖSSCHEN

$$$$

RHEINALLEE,

ELTVILLE-HATTENHEIM

TEL 06723 640

FAX 06723 76 63

kronenschloesschen.de

A beautiful small castle with stylish rooms set in a leafy park. The French-inspired restaurant serves foie gras on a fig confit, sea bass with saffron paella, and chocolate soufflé.

🛏 8 + 10 suites 🅿
⚄ All major cards

SOMETHING SPECIAL

🛏 GÄSTEHAUS KLOSTER EBERBACH

$$$

TEL 06723 99 30

FAX 06723 99 31 00

klostereberbach.com

A dramatic mélange of Romanesque, Gothic, and baroque buildings on the grounds of a former monastery where Augustinian monks once cultivated their vines. Scenes from the medieval thriller *The Name of the Rose* were shot here. The restaurant offers venison and other regional dishes. Breakfast, sauna, and Wi-Fi included.

🛏 28 🅿 ⚄ AE, MC, V

FRANKFURT AM MAIN

🛏 HESSISCHER HOF

$$$$$

FRIEDRICH-EBERT-ANLAGE 40

TEL 069 754 00

FAX 069 75 40 29 24

hessischer-hof.de

Old-fashioned traditional hotel near the financial district and trade fair grounds. Its elegant rooms are furnished with plenty of fine art and antiques. New health club with sauna, climbing wall, and a roof terrace with views of

Frankfurt's skyline.

🛏 107 + 10 suites 🅿 ⬌
⚄ All major cards

🛏 🍴 STEIGENBERGER FRANKFURTER HOF

$$$$$

AM KAISERPLATZ 1

TEL 069 215 02

FAX 069 21 59 00

en.steigenberger.com

All the elegantly furnished rooms in this 125-year-old hotel are wired with Wi-Fi and flat-screen TVs. **Restauarant Français,** with chandeliers and tapestries, has French haute cuisine.

🛏 286 + 46 suites 🅿 ⬌ ⚄
❄ 🏋 ⚄ All major cards

🛏 TURM HOTEL

$$$

ESCHERSHEIMER

LANDSTRASSE 20

TEL 069 15 40 50

FAX 069 55 35 78

turmhotel-fra.de

Frescoes from Italian palazzos grace the rooms in this hotel near the banking district. Rooms have eclectic themes, from Mona Lisa to avant-garde to Oriental hip.

🛏 74 🅿 ⚄ All major cards

🍴 ERNO'S BISTRO

$$$$$

LIEBIGSTRASSE 15

TEL 069 72 19 97

ernosbistro.de

Specialties at this rustically decorated restaurant, one of Frankfurt's finest (and most expensive), include *tete de veau,* carpaccio with a caper-onion vinaigrette, and beef roulade. Copious wine list.

🍴 60 🕐 Closed Sat.–Sun. & holidays ⚄ MC, V

🍴 HOLBEIN'S

$$$$

HOLBEINSTRASSE 1

TEL 069 66 05 66 66

meyer-frankfurt.de

Chic, modern, and conveniently located near the pubs and beer gardens in the suburb of Sachsenhausen, Holbein's serves its creative international dishes from a rear annex of the Städelsches Kunstinstitut. Flagship dishes here include halibut and lobster.

🕐 Closed Mon. L 💳 AE, MC, V

KASSEL

🏨 KURFÜRST WILHELM 1
$$–$$$
WILHELMSHÖHER ALLEE 257
TEL 0561 318 70
FAX 0561 31 87 77
kurfuerst.bestwestern.de
Modern facilities in a handsome late 19th-century building, located on a plateau high above Kassel. All quarters have 10-foot (3 m) ceilings and state-of-the-art designer furnishings. Breakfast is included.

🛏 42 + 1 suite 🅿 💳
💳 All major cards

🍴 ZUM STEINERNEN SCHWEINCHEN
$$$
KONRAD-ADENAUER-STRASSE 117
TEL 0561 94 04 80
steinernes-schweinchen.de
The "little stone pig" has a view that complements some of Kassel's best cuisine. Try the beef in Bordeaux sauce with braised onions.

🍽 55 🅿 💳 All major cards

LIMBURG

🏨 ZIMMERMANN
🍴 $$$
BLUMENRÖDERSTRASSE 1
TEL 06431 46 11
FAX 06431 4 13 14
hotelzimmermann.de
An intimate, atmospheric hotel stuffed with precious antiques and classy furniture, with Wi-Fi throughout. Bathrooms have fine Italian marble, while some quarters are in English country style. Breakfast is included in the stylish breakfast room.

🛏 16 + 4 suites 🅿 💳
💳 All major cards

MARBURG

🍴 DAS KLEINE RESTAURANT
$$$
BARFÜSSERTOR 25
TEL 06421 222 93
das-kleine-restaurant.de
Halfway up the path to Marburg's castle (see p. 206), this intimate little eatery poses a question. Do you stop now to test the skills of chef Markus Fuchs, in his braised lamb shoulder in bulgur or sea bream fillet with asparagus risotto? Or do you save it for your return? Think it over while sampling one of the restaurant's 450 wines.

🍽 30 🕐 Closed Mon.
💳 MC, V

WIESBADEN

🏨 NASSAUER HOF
🍴 $$$$$
KAISER-FRIEDRICH-PLATZ 3–4
TEL 0611 13 30
FAX 0611 13 36 32
nassauer-hof.de
A grand hotel with elegant rooms with what's reputed to be Wiesbaden's best restaurant, **ENTE.** The Euro-Asian cuisine thrills: perch with aubergines, roast chicken with langoustines.

🛏 129 + 30 suites 🅿 💳
💳 💳 💳 All major cards

■ THURINGIA & SAXONY-ANHALT

DESSAU

🏨 NH HOTEL
$$$
ZERBSTER STRASSE 29
TEL 0340 251 40
FAX 0340 251 41 00
nh-hotels.de
The rooms at this sleek Spanish-owned chain hotel are spacious and smartly furnished, and the friendly staff is happy to cater to individual wishes. All rooms have Wi-Fi. There's an in-house bar and restaurant, and a generous breakfast buffet is included.

🛏 120 🅿 💳 All major cards

🍴 KORNHAUS
$$
KORNHAUSSTRASSE 146
TEL 0340 640 41 41
kornhaus-dessau.de
Built as a dance hall in the Bauhaus era, this striking 1930s edifice now houses a cozy restaurant that serves well-prepared traditional German dishes. In fine weather, the best seats are on the balcony overlooking the Elbe.

🍽 80 🅿 🕐 Closed Thurs.
💳 MC, V

EISENACH

SOMETHING SPECIAL

🏨 AUF DER WARTBURG
🍴 $$$$
AUF DER WARTBURG
TEL 03691 79 70
FAX 03691 79 71 00
wartburghotel.de
This is a truly romantic hotel located at the foot of the legendary Wartburg castle. Enjoy the country-house furniture, quiet atmosphere, and views of the courtyard or the Thuringian Forest. Local specialties are served in the restaurant **Landgrafenstube**: venison with Thuringian potato salad, sautéed trout with tomato-bean ragout. Breakfast is included in the rate.

🛏 30 + 5 suites 🅿 💳
💳 All major cards

🏨 HOTEL KAISERHOF
🍴 $$–$$$
WARTBURGALLEE 2
TEL 03691 8 88 90

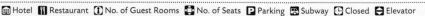

🏨 Hotel 🍴 Restaurant 🛏 No. of Guest Rooms 🍽 No. of Seats 🅿 Parking 🚇 Subway 🕐 Closed 💳 Elevator

FAX 03691 88 89 599
kaiserhof-eisenach.de
Downtown hotel replete with
English-style furnishings. Chef
Ulrich Rösch combines regional
traditions with the latest trends
in the **Turmschänke** restaurant.
Breakfast is included.
ℹ️ 96 🅿️ 🗞️ All major cards

ERFURT

🏨 **MERCURE HOTEL
ERFURT ALTSTADT**
$$$
MEIENBERGSTRASSE 26–27
TEL 0361 594 90
FAX 0361 594 91 00
mercure-hotel-erfurt.de
The oldest part of this hotel
dates from 1450. Most of the
rooms, however, are located
in the 1995 annex. All rooms
have free Wi-Fi, and breakfast
is included.
ℹ️ 141 + 2 suites 🅿️ 🔄
🗞️ All major cards

MAGDEBURG

🏨 **HERRENKRUG
🍴 PARKHOTEL**
$$$–$$$$
HERRENKRUG 3
TEL 0391 850 80
FAX 0391 850 85 01
herrenkrug.de
Historic house in a park where
large, well-furnished rooms
embrace art deco furnishings
and a wonderful view. The
restaurant, **Die Saison,** has a
winter garden and serves ambi-
tious European dishes.
ℹ️ 126 + 21 suites 🅿️ 🔄
🏊 🗳️ 🗞️ All major cards

WEIMAR

🏨 **HOTEL ELEPHANT
🍴 $$$–$$$$**
MARKT 19
TEL 03643 80 20
FAX 03643 80 26 10
hotelelephantweimar.com
Weimar's oldest (dating from
1696) and most renowned

hotel, with Bauhaus and art
deco touches. Artists and poets
were frequent guests, and paint-
ings by George Baselitz and
Rainer Fetting are on display.
For Mediterranean fare, visit the
restaurant, **Anna Amalia.**
ℹ️ 82 + 17 suites 🅿️ 🔄
🗞️ All major cards

🏨 **ALT WEIMAR**
$$$
PRELLERSTRASSE 2
TEL 03643 861 90
FAX 03643 86 19 10
alt-weimar.de
This attractive 18th-century
building behind the theater has
quiet, airy rooms, furnished
with Bauhaus designs. A small
but exquisite hotel.
ℹ️ 17 🅿️ 🗞️ All major cards

🏨 **DORINT AM
GOETHEPARK**
$$$
BEETHOVENPLATZ 1–2
TEL 03643 87 20
FAX 03643 87 21 00
hotel-weimar-dorint.com
Behind the Goethehaus, the
hotel consists of two 18th-
century villas and a contem-
porary building. The rooms,
furnished in classic style of the
era, are complemented by a
restaurant and beer cellar.
ℹ️ 143 + 6 suites + 3 apts. 🔄
🗞️ All major cards

■ SAXONY

BAUTZEN

🏨 **SPREE-HOTEL BAUTZEN**
$$
AN DEN STEINBRÜCHEN 9
TEL 03591 213 00
FAX 03591 21 30 10
spreehotel.de
A lakeside hotel in this baroque
town. Comfortable guest
rooms and a restaurant with
regional cooking. Breakfast
is included.
ℹ️ 70 🅿️ 🔄 🗳️ 🗞️ AE, MC, V

DRESDEN

🏨 **HOTEL TASCHENBERG-
PALAIS KEMPINSKI
DRESDEN**
$$$$$
TASCHENBERG 3
TEL 0351 491 20
FAX 0351 491 28 12
kempinski-dresden.de
Dresden's number-one hotel,
between the Zwinger and
the palace, displays its old-
fashioned luxury behind a
baroque facade.
ℹ️ 182 + 32 suites 🅿️ 🔄
🏊 🏊 🗳️ 🗞️ All major cards

🏨 **ART'OTEL DRESDEN
🍴 $$–$$$**
OSTRAALLEE 33
TEL 0351 492 20
FAX 0351 492 27 77
artotels.de
Snazzy, Wi-Fi-equipped rooms
a 10-minute walk from the
Semperoper and the historic
old town. The stylish interior is
the product of a Milan designer,
and the in-house gallery features some challenging works
by Dresden artist A. R. Penck.
ℹ️ 164 + 19 suites 🅿️ 🔄 🏊
🏊 🗳️ 🗞️ All major cards

🍴 **ITALIENISCHES
DORFCHEN**
$$$
THEATERPLATZ 3
TEL 0351 49 81 60
italienisches-doerfchen.de
The name recalls the Italian
builders who lived here in the
mid-1700s while working on
the Catholic Hofkirche. During
the day, tourists sip beer and
coffee on the shady terrace
overlooking the Elbe; later, the
baroque *ristorante* teems with
patrons filling up for a night at
the Semperoper. The cuisine is
regional Saxon and Italian.
🪑 300 🗞️ All major cards

🍴 KUPPEL RESTAURANT
$$

WEISSERITZSTRASSE 3
TEL 0351 490 59 90
kuppelrestaurant.de
Located in the former Yenidze cigarette factory, serving Middle Eastern and Saxon specialties under a terrific stained-glass dome. The building is styled after an oriental mosque with a smokestack disguised as a minaret. You can dine on the rooftop.
🔲 130 ⬧ MC, V

LEIPZIG

🏨 HOTEL
🍴 FÜRSTENHOF
$$$

TRÖNDLINRING 8
TEL 0341 140 0
FAX 0341 140 37 00
hotelfuerstenhofleipzig.com
Luxury in an old aristocratic palace that has been opulently renovated. Elegant restaurant Villiers has competent, if erratic, French cuisine. On the menu: souffléed fillet of turbot with fennel fondue, roast breast of pigeon with truffled bananas.
ℹ 80 + 12 suites 🅿 ⬧ 🚫
🏨 ⬧ All major cards

🏨 LEIPZIGER HOF
$$$

HEDWIGSTRASSE 1–3
TEL 0341 697 40
FAX 0341 697 41 50
leipziger-hof.de
This 19th-century private residence has been transformed into a sleek hotel equipped with the latest technology. True to its sobriquet of "art hotel," there are paintings by local artists throughout. Breakfast is included.
ℹ 67 + 1 suite + 4 apts. 🅿
🏨 📺 ⬧ All major cards

🍴 AUERBACHS KELLER
$$

MÄDLER-PASSAGE

GRIMMÄISCHE STRASSE 2–4
TEL 0341 21 61 00
auerbachs-keller-leipzig.de
One of Germany's classic restaurants, founded in 1525, Auerbachs Keller has earned kudos for its contemporary European cuisine. The historical section depicts a scene from Goethe's *Faust*.
🔲 700 🕐 Weinstube closed Sun. ⬧ AE, V

🍴 BARTHELS HOF
$$

HAINSTRASSE 1
TEL 0341 141 310
barthels-hof.de
This historic eatery—Leipzig's oldest—has a bar, wine cellar, and restaurant serving Saxon dishes such as *Heubraten* (marinated lamb roasted on hay). Waitresses wear traditional costume. The courtyard nestles among Leipzig's oldest Renaissance buildings.
🔲 180 ⬧ All major cards

MEISSEN

🏨 WELCOME PARKHOTEL MEISSEN
$$$

HAFENSTRASSE 27–31
TEL 03521 722 50
FAX 03521 72 29 04
mercure.com
Once a rich industrialist's villa, this hotel close to the river and the historic center has art deco bedrooms in the old building, modern ones in the extension. Meissen porcelain decorates the restaurant.
ℹ 92 + 5 suites
⬧ All major cards

◼ NORTHERN BAVARIA

AUGSBURG

🏨 STEIGENBERGER DREI MOHREN
$$$–$$$$

<table>
<tr><td colspan="2"><strong>PRICES</strong></td></tr>
<tr><td colspan="2"><strong>HOTELS</strong></td></tr>
<tr><td colspan="2">An indication of the cost of a double room in the high season is given by $ signs.</td></tr>
<tr><td>$$$$$</td><td>Over $270</td></tr>
<tr><td>$$$$</td><td>$200–$270</td></tr>
<tr><td>$$$</td><td>$120–$200</td></tr>
<tr><td>$$</td><td>$80–$120</td></tr>
<tr><td>$</td><td>Under $80</td></tr>
<tr><td colspan="2"><strong>RESTAURANTS</strong></td></tr>
<tr><td colspan="2">An indication of the cost of a three-course meal without drinks is given by $ signs.</td></tr>
<tr><td>$$$$$</td><td>Over $80</td></tr>
<tr><td>$$$$</td><td>$50–$80</td></tr>
<tr><td>$$$</td><td>$35–$50</td></tr>
<tr><td>$$</td><td>$20–$35</td></tr>
<tr><td>$</td><td>Under $20</td></tr>
</table>

MAXIMILIANSTRASSE 40
TEL 0821 503 60
FAX 0821 15 78 64
en.steigenberger.com
This venerable hotel in the center dates from 1723, although inside everything is a showcase of modern design. Replace the highlighted sentence with: All rooms have free Wi-Fi, satellite TV, and minibars. There are a bistro, a bar, and a formal restaurant serving Mediterranean dishes.
ℹ 99 + 6 suites 🅿 ⬧ 🚫
⬧ All major cards

🍴 BAYERISCHES HAUS AM DOM
$$

JOHANNESGASSE 4
TEL 349 79 90
bayerischeshaus.de
This cavernous, traditional eatery offers regional favorites and earthy Bavarian cheer. The barrelled ceilings and nooks make for relaxed chatting, and tables upstairs give fine views of the

Obstmarkt below. There's a
beer garden, too.
🛏 300 🚫 No credit cards

BAMBERG

🏨 WELCOME HOTEL RESIDENZSCHLOSS BAMBERG
$$$–$$$$
UNTERE SANDSTRASSE 32
TEL 0951 609 10
FAX 0951 609 17 01
residenzschloss.com
A historic palace and former
hospital on the banks of the
Regnitz River, only a few
minutes from the medieval
center of Bamberg. The clas-
sically styled bedrooms have
Wi-Fi and scads of amenities,
and the range of wellness
facilities is superb. Breakfast
is included.
🛏 180 + 4 suites 🅿 ♿ 🛇 🎽
🚫 All major cards

🍴 BRAUEREI SPEZIAL
$–$$
OBERE KONIGSTRASSE 10
TEL 0951 243 04
brauerei-spezial.de
Popular since 1536, this
Franconian brewery inn
serves the smoked beer
that Bamberg is famous for.
Mainstays of the menu
include delicious sausages
and crispy roast pork. It also
has a handful of guest rooms
that are spartan, but clean
and quiet.
🛏 120 🛇 7 🕐 Closed Sat.
🚫 No credit cards

BAYREUTH

🏨 RAMADA HOTEL
🍴 RESIDENZSCHLOSS BAYREUTH
$$–$$$
ERLANGER STRASSE 37
TEL 0921 75 850
FAX 0921 75 856 01
h-hotels.com/bayreuth
Situated in the historic center,

this comfortable modern
hotel is a favorite with guests
visiting the annual Wagner
festival. A former brewery
hosts an atmospheric bar
serving traditional Franconian
beers, while the restaurant,
Sudhaus, serves excellent
local cuisine in a bright, airy
conservatory. All guests get
free use of the fitness facilities
and Wi-Fi.
🛏 101 + 3 suites 🅿 🛇
🚫 All major cards

🍴 GOLDENER LÖWE
$
KULMBACHER STRASSE 30
TEL 0921 74 60 60
goldener-loewe-bayreuth.de
Enjoy homemade beer, sau-
sages, or schnitzel in a restful
country atmosphere. The restaurant is attached to a brewery.
🛏 75 🕐 Closed L & Sun.–
Tues. 🚫 AE, MC, V

HEROLDSBERG

🍴 FREIHARDT
$$–$$$
HAUPTSTRASSE 81
TEL 0911 518 08 05
freihardt.com
A country inn northeast of
Nuremberg where owner
Hans-Jürgen Freihardt whips
up an array of sausages, steaks,
and pork fillets. As well as traditional fare, he makes a good
fish with green curry and other
modern dishes.
🛏 68 🕐 Closed Mon.–Tues.
🚫 All major cards

NUREMBERG

🏨 LE MERIDIEN GRAND
🍴 HOTEL NÜRNBERG
$$$–$$$$
BAHNHOFSTRASSE 1–3
TEL 0911 232 20
FAX 0911 232 24 44
lemeridiennuernberg.com
Opposite the railroad station on
the edge of the old town, this
grandest of Nuremberg's hotels

has accommodated plenty of
celebrities over the years such
as Bob Dylan and the Beatles.
The palatial rooms have tons of
marble and chandeliers.
🛏 178 + 4 suites 🅿 🛇 🎽
🚫 All major cards

🏨 ROTTNER
$$$
WINTERSTRASSE 17
TEL 0911 65 84 80
FAX 0911 65 84 82 03
rottner-hotel.de
This traditional half-timbered
hotel with colorful rooms is
situated in a peaceful suburb
southwest of Nuremberg.
Savor excellent regional cooking in the restaurant, including
sautéed goat with buttered
vegetables and pigeon in aspic.
Good selection of Franconian
wines. Breakfast is included.
🛏 33 + 4 family rooms 🅿
🚫 All major cards

🍴 ESSIGBRÄTLEIN
$$$$–$$$$$
WEINMARKT 3
TEL 0911 22 51 31
Nuremberg's premier restaurant located in the historic
quarter. Andree Kothe and
Yved Ollech draw on fresh
local ingredients in dishes such
as lamb with carrot *jus*, or
breast of pigeon served with
nuts, arugula, and figs. Tables
are harder to come by due to
its latest acquisition, a second
Michelin star.
🛏 30 🕐 Closed Sun.–Mon.
🚫 DC, MC, V

🍴 ALTE POST
$$
KRAFTSHOFER
HAUPTSTRASSE 164
TEL 0911 30 58 63
altepost.net
Just north of Nuremberg,
this old village inn has a lively
atmosphere. Tables are situated
around a tiled stove or on a
small terrace. Regional cuisine
includes fish with potato

dumplings and Wesling sauce, wild duck, or salads.

⊞ 210 💳 All major cards

SOMETHING SPECIAL

🍴 HISTORISCHE BRATWURSTKÜCHE ZUM GOLDENEN STERN

$

ZIRKELSCHMIEDSGASSE 26

TEL 091 1 205 92 88

bratwurstkueche.de

A must for every visitor to Nuremberg, this ancient restaurant (founded in 1419) is the oldest purveyor of sausages in the world. The famous Nürnberger Bratwürstchen (small fried sausages) are roasted over a beech fire and served on a pewter plate with horseradish, sauerkraut, and potato salad.

⊞ 220 💳 All major cards

PASSAU

🏨 SCHLOSS ORT

$$$

IM ORT 11

TEL 0851 340 72/73

FAX 0851 318 17

hotel-schloss-ort.de

This intimate palace hotel, located in a quiet spot near the confluence of the Danube, Iltz, and Inn, offers large rooms in faux-rustic styles. The pretty restaurant with a terrace and river vistas serves regional specialties like Passau fish soup and suckling pig in a dark beer sauce. Breakfast is included.

ⓘ 18 🅿 💳 MC, V

🏨 WILDER MANN

$$

AM RATHAUSPLATZ 1

TEL 0851 350 71

FAX 0851 317 12

wilder-mann.com

Occupying four houses in the historic quarter of Passau, this ex-medieval court building has storied rooms where countless celebrities have slumbered, including Austrian empress Elizabeth and Count Zeppelin. It's attached to the renowned glass museum next door.

ⓘ 47 + 2 historical rooms

💳 All major cards

REGENSBURG

🏨 HOTEL ORPHEE

$$–$$$

UNTERE BACHGASSE 8

TEL 0941 596 020

FAX 0941 596 021 99

hotel-orphee.de

A world of unparalleled charms in the historic center of Regensburg, with an uncommonly high standard at reasonable prices. The careful floor designs, wrought-iron beds, and exposed beams convey a sense of easy luxury; some rooms have views of the cathedral. Patrons come from miles around to breakfast in its renowned art deco café.

ⓘ 59 🅿 🎪 💳 All major cards

SOMETHING SPECIAL

🍴 ROSENPALAIS

$$$

MINORITENWEG 20

TEL 0941 599 75 79

rosenpalais.de

A beautiful, pint-size baroque castle built in 1730 and now owned by Christian Graf von Walderdorff, an ambitious fusion chef and avowed Italophile. The handsome restaurant serves delicious lobster minestrone, venison with celeriac purée, and salad with marinated artichokes. The ground-floor bistro is more relaxed but equally good.

⊞ 40 🕐 Closed Sun.–Mon.

💳 MC, V

🍴 KNEITINGER

$–$$

ARNULFSPLATZ 3

TEL 0941 524 55

knei.de

This legendary 16th-century inn serves solid food such as Regensburg sausages, roast pork with potato dumplings, and a huge *Brotzeit* (selection of breads and hams), not to mention its own Kneitinger Pils. The brewery gives tours every Wednesday at 3 p.m.

⊞ 140 💳 No credit cards

ROTHENBURG OB DER TAUBER

🏨 EISENHUT

$$$

HERRNGASSE 3–5

TEL 09861 70 50

FAX 09861 705 45

eisenhut.com

This hotel in one of Germany's most romantic towns consists of several historic buildings (dating from the 15th and 16th centuries) on the market square. Rooms in front have a view of the old town hall.

ⓘ 76 + 2 suites

💳 All major cards

🏨 VILLA MITTERMEIER

$$–$$$

VORM WÜRZBURGER TOR 9

TEL 09861 945 40

FAX 09861 94 54 94

villamittermeier.de

The Mittermeier family has modernized two houses, one dating from 1892, and turned them into a friendly hotel. The wine restaurant **Die Blaue Sau** (The Blue Sow) tackles a handful of quality dishes— rib-eye steak, corn-fed chicken, beef tatar, and of course pork.

ⓘ 14 + 13 suites 🅿

💳 All major cards

🍴 DIE POST

$$

ROTHENBURGER STRASSE, SCHILLINGSFÜRST

TEL 09868 95 00

FAX 09868 950 250

---

flairhotel-altepost.de
An old inn southeast of
Rothenburg with just a few
dining rooms. After you have
sampled the *Schweinshaxe* (leg
of pork) in beer sauce, sample
one of the schnapps from the
house distillery.
🛏 40 🕙 DC, MC, V

WÜRZBURG

🏨 HOTEL REBSTOCK
🍴 $$$$
NEUBAUSTRASSE 7
TEL 0931 309 30
FAX 0931 309 31 00
rebstock.com
This elegant hotel with Wi-Fi
brings a touch of the Mediterranean to northern Bavaria.
The restaurant, **KUNO 1408,**
is popular for its modern
take on Franconian cooking;
a favorite is the roast chicken
stuffed with goose liver. Breakfast is included.
ℹ 49 + 20 suites + 1 apt. 🅿
🕙 All major cards

🍴 ZUM STACHEL
$$
GRESSENGASSE 1
TEL 0931 527 70
weinhaus-stachel.de
The specialty in this traditional
wine restaurant is fresh fish,
and in winter, the poached
carp is a must. On summer
evenings it's a delight to linger
in the courtyard over a local
vintage, poured from a distinctive *Bocksbeutel* flask.
🛏 63 🕙 Closed Sun. 🕙 MC, V

◼ MUNICH & THE ALPS

ALTÖTTING

🍴 GRAMINGER WEISSBRÄU
$$
GRAMING 79
TEL 08671 961 40
graminger-weissbraeu.de

For distinctive Austro-Bavarian
cooking, this venerable
country inn is just the ticket.
The *Tafelspitz* (boiled rump of
beef) is a local specialty, best
washed down with the home-
brewed Weissbier.
🛏 380 🕙 Closed Thurs.
🕙 MC, V

ASCHAU

SOMETHING SPECIAL

🏨 RESIDENZ HEINZ
🍴 WINKLER
$$$$$
KIRCHPLATZ 1
83229 ASCHAU IM CHIEMGAU
TEL 08052 179 90
FAX 08052 17 99 66
residenz-heinz-winkler.de
Classic cuisine with an Italian
accent. Whether you choose
lasagna with scallops and white
truffle sauce or roast lamb in
a potato crust, the result is
always magnificent. The beautiful guest rooms, located in the
1405 country manor between
the Chiemsee and Chiemgau
Mountains, are a welcome
blend of floral-filled antiques
and modern comforts.
ℹ 15 rooms + 17 suites 🛏 80
🎴🎴 🕙 All major cards

BAD FÜSSING

🏨 KURHOTEL HOLZAPFEL
$$$$
THERMALBADSTRASSE 5
TEL 08531 95 70
FAX 08531 95 72 80
hotel-holzapfel.de
In this modern health-resort
hotel near Austria, beauty,
health, and relaxation are
taken seriously. Three restaurants, one serving Bavarian
specialties. Breakfast included.
ℹ 73 + 6 suites 🅿🎴🎴🎴
🕙 MC, V

🍴 GASTHOF ZUR POST
$$
POSTSTRASSE 1, STUBENBERG

TEL 08571 60 00
FAX 08571 600 230
hotel-post-prienbach.de
Located a few miles south of
Bad Füssing, this cozy wood-
paneled restaurant prides
itself on its salads with organic
herbal dressing, trout straight
from the river, and juicy steaks
from local farms. Don't miss
the hazelnut ice cream. There
are a few guest rooms upstairs.
🛏 85 🕙 Closed Mon. L
🕙 No credit cards

BAD REICHENHALL

🏨 WYNDAM GRAND
🍴 AXELMANNSTEIN
$$$$
SALZBURGER STRASSE 2–6
TEL 0800 101 08 80
FAX 08651 59 32
wyndamgrand
badreichenhall.com
This famous health resort is
situated in a beautiful park not
far from Salzburg and Berchtesgaden. Everything here is old
school, from the Alpine-style
rooms to the welcoming service
in traditional Bavarian garb.
Many patrons come for the
excellent beauty treatments.
Breakfast is included.
ℹ 143 + 3 suites 🅿🎴🎴🎴
🎴🎴 🕙 All major cards

BAD TÖLZ

🏨 JODQUELLENHOF-ALPAMARE
$$$$$
LUDWIGSTRASSE 13–15
TEL 08041 50 90
FAX 08401 50 95 55
jodquellenhof.com
Lodged in the valley of this picturesque spa town, this modern
hotel offers a warm atmosphere
with scads of health and sports
facilities. The gigantic indoor
pool is amazing.
ℹ 89 + 1 suite 🅿🎴🎴
🎴 🕙 All major cards

GASTHAUS BAIERNRAIN

$$

LEHRER-VOGL-WEG 1, DIETRAMSZELL

TEL 08027 91 93

gasthaus-baiernrain.de

A country idyll in a village northeast of Bad Tölz with fine Tirolean cooking at knockdown prices. The *Schweinsbraten* (roast pork) is succulent and tender, and there's locally brewed beer on tap.

60 MC, V

BERCHTESGADEN

ALPENHOF

$$$–$$$$

RICHARD-VOSS-STRASSE 30, SCHÖNAU AM KÖNIGSSEE

TEL 08652 60 20

FAX 08652 6 43 99

alpenhof.de

A short drive south of Berchtesgaden, this big hotel near the sparkling Königssee has tons of amenities with large rooms furnished in Alpine style. The indoor pool has panoramic views of the mountains. Breakfast is included.

53 Closed Nov. MC, V

BERGHOTEL REHLEGG

$$$

HOLZENGASSE 16 , RAMSAU

TEL 08657 988 40

FAX 08657 988 44 44

rehlegg.bestwestern.de

This amiable Swiss-style chateau is perched on a flowery slope above the pretty village of Ramsau, a few miles southwest of Berchtesgaden. The decor is traditional hunting lodge, the atmosphere homey. Breakfast is included.

77 + 10 suites All major cards

FRAUENCHIEMSEE

SOMETHING SPECIAL

ZUR LINDE

$$

HAUS NR. 1

TEL 08054 903 66

FAX 08054 72 99

linde-frauenchiemsee.de

After visiting King Ludwig's island castle on Herrenchiemsee (see p. 316), replenish your reserves on the smaller island, Frauenchiemsee. The informal eatery here dates from 1396, located next to a former Benedictine convent. The highlight of the menu is fresh local fish served with roasted vegetables.

100 Closed mid-Jan.–mid-March MC

GARMISCH-PARTENKIRCHEN

STAUDACHERHOF

$$$–$$$$

HÖLLENTALSTRASSE 48

TEL 08821 92 90

FAX 08821 92 93 33

staudacherhof.de

This towering villa in the town center looks like something out of a Grimms' fairy tale. Expect large and cozy country-style rooms decked out in quality linens. It offers first-class views of the Alps. You'll leave its renowned beauty center feeling brand new. Breakfast is included.

21 + 5 suites + 7 apts. MC, V

REINDL'S PARTENKIRCHNER HOF

$$$

BAHNHOFSTRASSE 15

TEL 08821 94 38 70

FAX 08821 94 38 72 50

reindls.de

This venerable hotel is a prime stop for visiting royalty or sports celebrities. Expect oil paintings with hunting motifs and exquisite Bavarian-style

carved bedsteads. **Reindls Restaurant** features a rotating menu of regional cuisine with the occasional nod to the French. Breakfast is included.

25 + 30 suites + 7 apts. All major cards

LANDSHUT

ROMANTIK HOTEL FÜRSTENHOF

$$$

STETHAIMER STRASSE 3

TEL 0871 9 25 50

FAX 0871 92 55 44

fuerstenhof.la

A romantic hotel with medieval flair. The large breakfast buffet includes homemade jams. The **Fürstenzimmer** restaurant specializes in organic regional cuisine, such as hearty duck sausage with bread-dumpling carpaccio and honey-glazed suckling pig. Breakfast and sauna included.

22 + 1 suite + 1 historic room All major cards

🍽 BERNLOCHNER
$$$
LANDTORPLATZ 2–5
TEL 0871 899 90
restaurant-bernlochner.de
Fine Bavarian and Austrian
dishes served in a building
dating from 1841. Recom-
mended dishes include game,
poultry, and *Tafelspitz* (boiled
rump of beef); the *Mehlspeisen*
(sweet pancakes with a variety
of fillings) are irresistible.
🚫 No credit cards

MITTENWALD

🏨 HOTEL ALPENROSE
$$
OBERMARKT I
TEL 08823 92700
FAX 08823 3720
hotel-alpenrose-mittenwald.de
This baroque villa is decorated
with Bavaria's *Lüftlmalerei*, or
facade painting. The rooms
tend to be on the snug side,
but the ones overlooking the
square are more spacious. The
wine cellar hosts live oompah
bands. Breakfast is included.
🛏 18 🅿 💟 🚫 All major cards

MUNICH

SOMETHING SPECIAL

🏨 BAYERISCHER HOF
$$$$$
PROMENADEPLATZ 2–6
TEL 089 212 00
FAX 089 212 09 06
bayerischerhof.de
This traditional grand hotel is
the favorite of visiting celebrities, with true Bavarian charm
and the glamour of times past.
Rooms vary from classic to
modern, and the huge suites
have fantastic views of the
Alps. The basement jazz club is
one of Munich's finest. Despite
its enormity, it is still a family-
run hotel. Breakfast included.
🛏 303 + 60 suites 🅿
🚇 Marienplatz 🔄 🕃 🏢
💟 🚫 All major cards

🏨 HOTEL MÜNCHEN
🍽 PALACE
$$$$$
TROGERSTRASSE 21
TEL 089 41 97 10
FAX 089 41 97 18 19
hotel-palace-muenchen.de
A fine town-house hotel,
with Wi-Fi, furnished in Louis
XIV style and decorated with
antiques. The garden is a
peaceful oasis and a perfect
spot for breakfast (included).
🛏 67 + 7 suites 🅿
🚇 Prinzregentenplatz 💟
🚫 All major cards

🏨 KEMPINSKI VIER
JAHRESZEITEN
$$$$$
MAXIMILIANSTRASSE 17
TEL 089 212 50
FAX 089 21 25 20 00
**kempinski-vierjahreszeiten
.com**
A grand hotel close to the
best shopping in Munich. The
lobby bustles with international guests; the rooms are
exquisitely decorated. Rooms
are customizable down to the
choice of pillows.
🛏 238 + 65 suites 🅿
🚇 Marienplatz 🔄 🕃 🏢
🏢 💟 🚫 All major cards

🏨 KÖNIGSHOF
🍽 $$$$$
KARLSPLATZ 25
TEL 089 55 13 60
FAX 089 55 13 61 13
koenigshof-hotel.de/en
A family-owned treasure
overlooking busy Karlsplatz. Its
modern facade belies the interiors, a mélange of modern and
traditional styles. The classy
restaurant serves up great
Mediterranean cuisine. Try the
tuna tartare or sea bass with
arugula risotto.
🛏 74 + 13 suites 🚇 Karlsplatz
💟 🚫 All major cards

🏨 SHERATON ARABELLA-
PARK HOTEL
$$$$
ARABELLASTRASSE 5
TEL 089 923 20
FAX 089 930 01 6837
sheratonarabellapark.com
This modern luxury hotel close
to the business district draws
a large corporate clientele.
Rooms have high-tech perks
and decor from modern to
traditional Bavarian.
🛏 405 + 41 suites 🅿
🚇 Arabella Park 🔄 🕃 🕃
🏢 💟 🚫 All major cards

🏨 GÄSTEHAUS
ENGLISCHER GARTEN
$$$
LIEBERGESELLSTRASSE 8
TEL 089 383 94 10
FAX 089 38 39 41 33
hotelenglischergarten.de
A well-run, small, simple hotel
in the trendy neighborhood
of Schwabing, famous for its
village atmosphere and café
life. The rooms are furnished in
an agreeable rustic style; ones
at the rear overlook the Englischer Garten. It's very popular,
so book ahead.
🛏 12 + 20 apts. 🅿 🚇 Münchner Freiheit 🚫 All major cards

🍽 TANTRIS
$$$$$
JOHANN-FICHTE-STRASSE 7
TEL 089 361 95 90
tantris.de
Munich's finest and most creative chefs perform their magic
here. Dishes include terrine of
beetroot or sautéed sea bass
with pepperoni and spinach.
The wine list and service are
first-class. The zany '70s decor
is part of the allure.
🍴 120 🚇 Didlindenstrasse
🕐 Closed Sun.–Mon.
🚫 All major cards

🍽 BÖTTNER'S
$$$$
PFISTERSTRASSE 9
TEL 089 22 12 10
boettners.de
Opposite the famous Hof-
bräuhaus, Bottner's simple

ambience draws bigwigs from Munich's business and media districts. The menu is reliably trend-free. Pumpkin risotto, parfait of goose liver, pheasant with sauerkraut, and lobster tartare with caviar and chive sauce are among the favorites.

🍴 97 🚇 Marienplatz 🕐 Closed Sun. 🏧 All major cards

🍴 HIPPOCAMPUS

$$$–$$$$

MÜHLBAURSTRASSE 5

TEL 089 47 58 55

hippocampus-restaurant.de

Munich's many beautiful people flock to this trendy Italian restaurant in the upscale Bogenhausen area. Try the pumpkin risotto, squid carpaccio with capers, and delicious tiramisu. There is a little garden discreetly surrounded by a hedge for privacy.

🍴 75 🚇 Prinzregentenplatz 🕐 Closed Sat. L 🏧 DC, MC, V

🍴 BRASSERIE TRESZNJIEWSKI

$$$

THERESIENSTRASSE 72

TEL 089 282 349

tresznjewski.com

A Munich institution, the "Trezi" draws loads of artsy types associated with ad agencies and the Pinakothek museums nearby. Waiters in full-length aprons dish up quick repartee and heaping portions of tasty Italian food. A breakfast fixture with the after-party crowd.

🍴 200 🚇 Universität 🏧 AE, MC, V

🍴 KÄFER SCHÄNKE

$$$

PRINZREGENTENSTRASSE 73

TEL 089 416 82 47

www.feinkost-kaefer.de

A fabulous delicatessen plus a series of dining rooms in Bavarian style. Tasty dishes are the vegetable lasagna, mushroom risotto, and venison with

chanterelles in a pear sauce. As much a part of Munich as Marienplatz.

🍴 150 🕐 Closed Sun. & holidays 🚇 Prinzregentenplatz 🏧 All major cards

🍴 LENBACH

$$$

OTTOSTRASSE 6

TEL 089 549 13 00

lenbach.de

This gourmet temple offers lightweight and trendy meals (e.g., bean ravioli with calamari and spinach, or mango mousse with banana salad) for the cool, youthful crowd that dine here before hitting the nightclubs.

🍴 95 🚇 Karlsplatz 🕐 Closed Sun. 🏧 DC, MC, V

🍴 MESSAGE IN A BOTTLE

$$$

MAXIMILIANSTRASSE 35

TEL 089 24 21 77 78

This lively Italian restaurant has become a favorite haunt of Munich's smart set. Daily specialties include pasta with tomatoes and zucchini, roast veal, and sautéed scallops.

🍴 60 🚇 Isartorplatz 🕐 Closed Sun. 🏧 MC, V

🍴 ALTES HACKERHAUS

$$

SENDLINGER STRASSE 14

TEL 089 260 50 26

hackerhaus.de

This rustic central inn with a beer garden and typical old-fashioned atmosphere is one of Munich's classic locales. The traditional Bavarian menu features classics like suckling pig in dark beer sauce.

🍴 543 🚇 Marienplatz 🏧 All major cards

🍴 HOFBRÄUHAUS

$

AM PLATZL 9

TEL 089 22 16 76

hofbraeuhaus.de

World-famous beer hall

where you can expect strong dark Weissbier and authentic *Schweinshax'n* and *Knödel* (knuckle of pork with potato dumplings). Locals never eat *Weisswurst* (veal sausage) after noon, to be sure it's still fresh.

🍴 1,770 🚇 Marienplatz 🏧 MC, V

MURNAU

🏨 ALPENHOF MURNAU

$$$$$

RAMSACHSTRASSE 8

TEL 08841 49 10

FAX 08841 49 11 00

alpenhof-murnau.com

This Relais & Châteaux hotel northeast of Oberammergau has rooms in two sections: a Bavarian-style main building and a modern extension. It boasts extensive spa facilities, and most rooms afford breathtaking views of the Alps. Breakfast is included.

🛏 64 + 5 suites + 2 apts. 🅿 🚫 🎽 🏧 AE, MC, V

OBERAUDORF

SOMETHING SPECIAL

🍴 GASTHAUS WALLER

$–$$

URFAHNSTRASSE 10

TEL 0833 14 73

waller-reisach.de

Set in the middle of a fruit orchard, this country restaurant features antlers on the walls, checkered tablecloths, and dirndl-clad staff. Try the excellent roast meats, dumplings, *Zwetschgenwasser* (plum schnapps), and local Weissbier.

🍴 58 🕐 Closed Mon. 🏧 No credit cards

SCHWANGAU

🏨 RÜBEZAHL

🍴 $$$

AM EHBERG 31

TEL 08362 88 88

FAX 08362 8 17 01
hotelruebezahl.de
A typical family-run Alpine hotel, conveniently located in a busy little valley between two Bavarian royal palaces. Some of the modern quarters have a view of Schloss Neuschwanstein (see p. 306), the inspiration for Walt Disney's castles.
[i] 25 + 6 suites + 4 apts.
MC, V

BADEN-WÜRTTEMBERG

BADEN-BADEN

BELLE EPOQUE
$$$$$
MARIA-VIKTORIA-STRASSE 2C
TEL 07221 30 06 60
FAX 07221 30 06 66
hotel-belle-epoque.de
If you prefer a more intimate atmosphere, this graceful small hotel is ideal. Rooms are in the dainty period style.
[i] 10 + 10 suites P
All major cards

BRENNER'S PARKHOTEL & SPA
$$$$$
SCHILLERSTRASSE 4–6
TEL 07221 90 00
FAX 07221 3 87 72
brenners.com
Luxury is evident everywhere in this palatial 19th-century pile, from the enormous rooms furnished with exquisite antiques to the lavish spa area with every imaginable amenity. The swimming pool rivals anything in Hollywood.
[i] 71 + 29 suites P S
All major cards

RADISSON BADISCHER HOF
$$$$
LANGE STRASSE 47
TEL 07221 93 40
FAX 07221 93 44 70

hotel-badischerhof-badenbaden.de
This luxury spa hotel occupies a former Capuchin convent. Guest rooms exude a historic elegance in the old section, while the modern extension has more amenities. The bathtubs dispense thermal spring water. Breakfast is included.
[i] 135 + 4 suites P S
All major cards

ALDE GOTT
$$$$
WEINSTRASSE 10
TEL 07223 5513
zum-alde-gott.de
The imaginative food here includes dishes such as beans and cauliflower in a curry vinaigrette, and Charolais beef with savoy cabbage in a Burgundy sauce. It's just south of Baden-Baden.
60 Closed Thurs.
MC, V

BAIERSBRONN

SOMETHING SPECIAL

BAREISS
$$$$$
GARTENBÜHLWEG 14, BAIERSBRONN-MITTELTAL
TEL 07442 470
FAX 07442 473 20
bareiss.com
A sanctuary of peace in the Black Forest, this is surely one of Germany's best run hotels, with meticulous attention paid to details. Flower-decked balconies grace the modern facade, and the stylish rooms are packed with perks. You can dine in the restaurant with three Michelin stars or one of the pair of smart bistros. The main menu features blue-ribbon fare like warm lobster with a honey-thyme vinaigrette or mille-feuille of goose liver with celery purée and truffle-glace. Breakfast is included.
[i] 89 + 10 suites P
DC, MC, V

TRAUBE TONBACH
$$$$$
TONBACHSTRASSE 237
TEL 07442 49 20
FAX 07442 49 26 92
traube-tonbach.de
This traditional family-run hotel dates back to 1778, and some of the public areas positively ooze history. The four restaurants include the outstanding **Schwarzwaldstube** (see below) and the **Köhlerstube,** which serves international food such as crustaceans in Chablis aspic and river fish with gnocchi. Breakfast included.
[i] 171 + 4 suites + 57 apts.
P All major cards

SOMETHING SPECIAL

SCHWARZWALDSTUBE
$$$$–$$$$$
TONBACHSTRASSE 237
TEL 07442 49 26 62
This place belongs among Germany's culinary elite, rating three whole Michelin stars for chef Harald Wohlfahrt's masterful creations. Restaurant critics come from far-flung corners to sample his goose liver in salt crust, the braised veal with truffle *jus*, and sautéed duck with rosemary and juniper berries. Superb wines and faultless service round out an unforgettable experience.
40 Closed Mon.–Tues. & Jan. & Aug.
All major cards

FELDBERG

COLOMBI HOTEL
$$$$$
ROTTECKRING 16
TEL 0761 210 66 17
FAX 0761 210 60
colombi.de
This distinguished and welcoming hotel blends soft colors and well-chosen materials. The grand entrance hall looks like something out of a movie set, and you couldn't ask for a finer

location in the heart of the old town. Excellent fare at restaurant **Zirbelstube.**

ⓘ 59 + 53 suites 🅿 🔄 🅢
🔲 📺 🅢 All major cards

🏨 ADLER
$$
FELDBERGSTRASSE 4,
FELDBERG-BÄRENTAL
TEL 07655 933 933
FAX 07655 930 521
adler-feldberg.de
This is a traditional Black Forest holiday hotel, located between the Feldberg and the pretty lakes Titisee and Schluchsee. The rooms are rustic but comfortable.

ⓘ 9 + 7 apts. 🅿 🅢 MC, V

HEIDELBERG

🏨 DER EUROPÄISCHE HOF
$$$$$
FRIEDRICH-EBERT-ANLAGE 1
TEL 06221 51 50
FAX 06221 51 55 06
europaeischerhof.com
Originally built in 1865 but updated over time, the Europäischer Hof is a Heidelberg landmark. The handsome, thoughtfully planned rooms are truly the lap of luxury, and there are an up-to-date fitness center and a wood-paneled restaurant.

ⓘ 100 + 14 suites + 3 apts. 🅿
🔄 🔲 📺 🅢 All major cards

🏨 ZUM RITTER ST. GEORG
$$$
HAUPTSTRASSE 178
TEL 06221 13 50
FAX 06221 13 52 30
ritter-heidelberg.de
This 16th-century house in the historic quarter is now a traditional hotel with terrific period rooms. Breakfast included.

ⓘ 37 + 2 suites 🅿 🅢
🅢 All major cards

🍴 SIMPLICISSIMUS
$$$–$$$$
INGRIMSTRASSE 16

TEL 06221 673 25 88
simplicissimus-restaurant.de
A study in contrasts, lately this venerable French eatery in the old quarter got a makeover with bold colors and sleek designer furnishings. The oft-changing menu might include marinated aubergines, sautéed octopus with herbs, or fillet of beef with wild mushrooms.

🔳 60 🕐 Closed Sun. 🅢 V

🍴 WEISSER BOCK
$$–$$$
GROSSE MANTELGASSE 24
TEL 06221 90 00 0
weisserbock.de
This highly recommended eatery has an excellent international menu. The dining area exudes an old world feel, with lots of dark wood. The maître d' can recommend gems from the splendid wine list. Reservations are advised.

☎ 85 🅢 MC, V

INZLINGEN

🍴 INZLINGER WASSERSCHLOSS
$$$$
RIEHENSTRASSE 5
TEL 07621 470 57
inzlinger-wasserschloss.de
Situated in a delightful moated castle, this restaurant offers modern European cuisine such as venison with chanterelles and celeriac purée, pigeon de Bresse with risotto, and turbot with artichokes.

🔳 75 🕐 Closed Tues.–Wed.
🅿 🅢 MC, V

KARLSRUHE

🏨 SCHLOSSHOTEL
$$$$
BAHNHOFSPLATZ 2
TEL 0721 3 83 20
FAX 0721 3 83 23 33
schlosshotelkarlsruhe.de
Set conveniently between the railroad station and city park, this hotel has a broad range of

individually decorated rooms, some in a contemporary vein, others more traditional. Breakfast is included.

ⓘ 93 + 3 suites 🅿 🔄 📺
🅢 All major cards

🍴 OBERLÄNDER WEINSTUBE
$$$$
AKADEMIESTRASSE 7
TEL 0721 250 66
oberlaender-weinstube.de
This cozy little wine bar has a charming courtyard for drinking and dining. Solid regional dishes include lamb with chanterelles and pigeon with fried potatoes, celeriac purée, and beans. Delicious sorbets.

🔳 45 🕐 Closed Sun.–Mon.
🅢 DC, MC, V

🍴 NAGEL'S KRANZ
$$
NEUREUTER HAUPTSTRASSE 210
KARLSRUHE-NEUREUT
TEL 0721 70 57 42
nagels-kranz.de
This lovely country restaurant just outside Karlsruhe serves local specialties such as turbot with a potato crust, pork braised in red wine, and sea bass in Riesling.

🔳 70 🅿 🕐 Closed Sat. L &
Sun. 🅢 No credit cards

KONSTANZ

🏨 GRAF ZEPPELIN
🍴 **$$$**
ST. STEPHANSPLATZ 15
TEL 07531 691 36 90
FAX 07531 691 369 70
hotel-graf-zeppelin.de
This is a dyed-in-the-wool German inn with an ornate Gothic-style facade that dates back to 1835. Most rooms are modern and rather generic, but the restaurant gushes atmosphere and has a respectable wine list. It's in a nice spot near the minster. Breakfast is included.

ⓘ 49 + 3 suites 🅿 🅢 MC, V

🏨 Hotel 🍴 Restaurant ⓘ No. of Guest Rooms 🔳 No. of Seats 🅿 Parking 🚇 Subway 🕐 Closed 🔄 Elevator

LINDAU

SOMETHING SPECIAL

🏨 VILLINO
🍴 $$$$
HOYERBERG 34
TEL 08382 934 50
FAX 08382 93 45 12
villino.de
This enchanting house with a Tuscan flavor towers at the end of a steep lane overlooking Lindau. It has pretty rooms, a small health club, and a wonderful rolling garden. The restaurant, which has a Michelin star, carefully marries the regional with the international in dishes such as tuna sashimi with sesame spaghettini, or fresh river fish stuffed with ricotta. Breakfast is included.
🛏 15 + 7 suites 🅿 🔽
🏧 AE, MC, V

STUTTGART

SOMETHING SPECIAL

🏨 HOTEL AM
🍴 SCHLOSSGARTEN
$$$$$
SCHILLERSTRASSE 23
TEL 071 12 02 60
FAX 071 12 02 68 88
hotelschlossgarten.com
Grand style and tradition are writ large at this venerable institution, located near the opera house and the elegant boutiques along Königstrasse. Many rooms have a view of the Schlosspark, the sprawling municipal park. The atmosphere is warm and welcoming, more like someone's home than a hotel. There's a gourmet restaurant, the **Zirbelstube.**
🛏 106 + 10 suites 🔵
🏧 All major cards

🏨 STEIGENBERGER
🍴 GRAF ZEPPELIN
$$$$
ARNULF-KLETT PLATZ 7

TEL 071 12 04 80
FAX 071 12 04 85 42
en.steigenberger.com
This distinguished hotel near the railroad station contains large rooms with either neoclassic or modern touches. Nico Burkhardt, chef of the **Olivo** restaurant, is an aficionado of all things Mediterranean, as suggested by dishes like pappardelle pasta with wild boar ragoût or braised shoulder of lamb with artichokes.
🛏 117 + 38 suites 🅿 🔵 🔵
🏠 🔽 🏧 All major cards

🍴 SPEISEMEISTEREI
$$$$$
AM SCHLOSS HOHENHEIM,
STUTTGART-HOHENHEIM
TEL 0711 34 21 79 79
speisemeisterei.de
If you feel like a well-deserved splurge, head over to the castle of Schloss Hohenheim and its legendary Michelin-starred restaurant run by Chef Frank Oehler. His skill is evident in everything he serves, be it potato soup (from La-Ratte potatoes, served with imperial caviar) or crepinette of chicken with poached goose liver. And the heated chocolate cake is to die for.
🪑 65 🅿 🕐 Closed Tues.
🏧 AE, MC, V

🍴 WIELANDSHÖHE
$$$$–$$$$$
ALTE WEINSTEIGE 71,
STUTTGART-DEGERLOCH
TEL 0711 640 88 48
wielandshoehe.de
Owner-chef Vincent Klink excels in dishes such as *Maultaschen* (a kind of stuffed ravioli) as well as combinations of Asian and Mediterranean cuisine. The lunch menus offer tremendous value.
🪑 52 🕐 Closed Sun.–Mon.
🏧 All major cards

🍴 EMPORE
$–$$
DOROTHEENSTRASSE 4
TEL 0711 245 97 9
empore-markthalle.de
You'll find this Italian restaurant on the second floor of Stuttgart's art deco market halls. Treat yourself to a cappuccino, glass of bubbly, or dish of pasta, then browse through the array of alluring produce stands and shops downstairs.
🪑 45 🕐 Closed Sun.
🏧 No credit cards

TÜBINGEN

SOMETHING SPECIAL

🏨 KRONE
$$$
UHLANDSTRASSE 1
TEL 07071 133 10
FAX 07071 13 31 32
krone-tuebingen.de
This tasteful and soigné hotel, owned by the same family since 1885, is typical of this delightful medieval town with a large student population. Look for Swabian specialties in the restaurant, **Uhlandstube.** Breakfast is included.
🛏 43 + 2 suites
🏧 All major cards

🍴 WALDHORN
$$$$–$$$$$
SCHÖNBUCHSTRASSE 49,
TÜBINGEN-BEBENHAUSEN
TEL 07071 612 70
waldhorn-bebenhausen.de
About 3 miles (5 km) north of Tübingen, the Waldhorn has a rustic interior and authentic Swabian cooking. Few have managed to copy its delectable *Hägenmarkeis-bömble* (rose hip ice cream).
🪑 65 🕐 Closed Mon.–Tues.
🏧 No credit cards

Shopping

Germany is renowned for its high-tech, high-quality goods. Form follows function, and molds the designs of everything from sleek roadsters to elegant Wagenfeld lamps. But the traditional crafts live on, in the cuckoo clocks, porcelain, and wood carvings that emerge from artisans' workshops.

Most towns have central, shop-filled *Fussgängerzonen* (pedestrian districts) that were made to check the advance of shopping malls. In the main cities, leading *Einkaufsstrassen* (shopping streets) include Kurfürstendamm and Friedrichstrasse in Berlin, Königsallee in Düsseldorf, Maximilianstrasse in Munich, and arcades around Jungfernstieg, Neuer Wall, and Mönckebergstrasse in Hamburg.

Famous German products such as marzipan, Christmas ornaments, and Steiff teddy bears make terrific gifts. Cameras by Leica and lenses or binoculars with Zeiss glass are often cheaper in Germany. In Bavaria, lederhosen and dirndl dresses are available in traditional and updated versions. But the most popular souvenir is the beer mug, graced at times with a hinged pewter lid.

Markets

A weekly market, known as *Wochenmarkt,* is held in towns throughout Germany. In smaller communities, stalls are set up in the market square, while in larger towns and cities the market is held in specially designated squares. You will find fresh fruit and vegetables, cheeses, a full range of sausages, cheeses, and regional specialties, as well as many useful everyday items. Every large town also has its *Flohmarkt* (flea market), where you might find something rare and unusual.

Opening Hours

Under German law, stores can operate 24 hours a day from Monday to Saturday. Few do so, however. Smaller retailers open

their doors at 9:30 or 10 a.m. and close by 7 p.m., while department stores might keep going until 10 p.m. Newsagents and bakeries open as early as 6 a.m. On Sundays, everything is closed, with a few exceptions such as shops in train stations, airports, and service stations. Some cities have introduced an economy-boosting "shopping Sunday" once a month.

Payment

Cash is still king in Germany. Department and luxury-goods stores will take credit cards and traveler's checks, but supermarkets and smaller shops usually do not; look at the door stickers. Most Germans pay by either cash or EC direct debit cards.

Exports

Except for EU citizens, visitors to Germany are entitled to a refund on value-added (sales) tax for all nonedible goods bought in German stores. The usual minimum is €50 in a single store. Ask for a special form at stores displaying the tax-free sign. When you leave Germany, the form must be stamped by customs and you'll have to present goods in their original packaging. The tax can be refunded on the spot or sent on, which requires patience.

BADEN-WÜRTTEMBERG

Black Forest

Hubert Herr, Hauptstrasse 8, Triberg, tel 07722 42 68, *hubert herr.de.* In the town that claims the world's largest cuckoo clock, this workshop, now in its fifth generation of craftsmen, has

carved out a formidable reputation. Orders can be shipped.

Stuttgart

Steiff Galerie, Calwer-Strasse 17, tel 0711 220 0472, *steiff.de.* Credited with the first mass-produced teddy bear, Steiff stocks an animal kingdom of stuffed toys ranging from tiny bees to giant African elephants made of mohair.

BAVARIA

Nuremberg

Christkindlesmarkt (Christmas Market), *christkindlesmarkt.de.* Held late November to December 24, the highlight is the opening ceremony at 5:30 p.m., when the Christ Child speaks to the masses from the Frauenkirche (Church of Our Lady) gallery.

Lebkuchen Schmidt, Zollhausstrasse 30, tel 0911 896 60, *lebkuchen-schmidt.com.* Traditionally eaten at Christmas, Nuremberg's celebrated *Lebkuchen* (ginger spice cookies) are sold here year-round.

Oberammergau

Josef Albl, Verlegergasse 12, tel 08822 94 51 85, *albl-oberammer gau.com.* One of the premier carvers of religious icons, Herr Albl's workshop is open for viewing.

Rothenburg ob der Tauber

Käthe Wohlfahrt Weihnachtsdorf, Herrngasse 1, tel 09861 40 90, *wohlfahrt.com.* An eye-popping display of Yuletide decorations and ornaments at the year-round "Christmas Village." Entry fee of €1 in the jolly season.

BERLIN

Books

Bücherstube Marga Schöller, Knesebeckstrasse 33, Charlottenburg, tel 030 881 11 12, *235750 .umbreitwebshop.de.* This venerable bookshop has an impressive English-language section.
Dussmann, Friedrichstrasse 90, Mitte, tel 030 20 25 11 11, *kulturkaufhaus.de.* Three spacious floors with padded armchairs inviting you to sit and read. Sections include a huge CD department, a café cum events stage, and a separate English bookshop.

Department Stores

Galeries Lafayette, Friedrichstrasse 76-78, tel 030 20 94 80, *galerieslafayette.de.* An upscale French department store offering quality designer apparel, cosmetics, and accessories.

KaDeWe, Tauentzienstrasse 21–24, Schöneberg, tel 030 21 21 0, *kadewe.de.* "If we don't have it, it probably doesn't exist" is the motto of Germany's largest department store. The lavish sixth-floor food hall stocks global delicacies.

Karstadt, Kurfürstendamm 231, Charlottenburg, tel 030 88 00 30, *karstadt.de.* Second only to the KaDeWe in size, this emporium is a good stop for souvenirs. Enjoy views of the Gedächtniskirche from the rooftop café.

Fashion & Accessories

Bramigk, Niebuhrstrasse 1, Charlottenburg, tel 030 882 73 73, *bramigk-breer.com.* Dresses and trousers made of fine Italian fabrics, plus hand-painted scarves and felt slippers.

Budapester Schuhe, Kurfürstendamm 43 + 199, Charlottenburg, tel 030 88 62 42 06, *budapester-schuhe.net.* Ladies' shoes from Prada and Jimmy Choo. Gentlemen's from classic English

brogues to Gucci loafers.
Hut up, Oranienburger Strasse 32, Heckmann-Höfe, Mitte, tel 030 28 38 61 05, *hutup.de.* Stylish hats, clothes, and accessories made from felt with organza or chiffon.

Killerbeast, Schlesische Strasse 31, Kreuzberg, tel 030 99 26 03 19, *killerbeast.de.* Cool urban streetware rolled out anew almost every week.

Thatchers, Hackesche Höfe, Hof IV, Rosenthaler Strasse 40–41, Mitte, tel 030 27 58 22 10, and Kastanienalle 21, tel 030 24 62 77 51, *thatchers.de.* Trendy lines for both men and women, inspired by music, digital art, and architecture.

Food Markets

Turkish Market, Maybachufer, Neukölln. This lively, crowded market has delicious feta cheeses, teas, fresh breads and olives. Open noon–6:30 p.m. Tues. & Fri.

Winterfeldt Markt, Winterfeldtplatz, Schöneberg. A beautiful array of cheeses, sausages, flowers, and handmade designer clothes. Open 8 a.m.–2 p.m. Wed. & Sat.

Gifts

Ampelmann, Hackesche Höfe, Hof V, Mitte, tel 030 44 72 64 38, *ampelmann.de.* The East German "crosswalk man" graces all items in this unusual souvenir shop.

Erzgebirgskunst Original, Sophienstrasse 9, Mitte, tel 030 2804 5130, *original-erzgebirgs kunst.de.* Traditional wooden handicrafts from the eastern Ore Mountains.

Meissener Porzellan, Unter den Linden 39b, Mitte, tel 030 22 67 90 28, *meissen.de.* Fine plates, sculptures, and chandeliers from the Saxon china maker.

HAMBURG

Art

Galerie Deichstrasse, Deichstrasse 28, 20459, tel 040 36

51 51, *galerie-deichstrasse.de.* Paintings and drawings with Hamburg as their theme.

Books

Sautter & Lackmann, Admiralitätsstrasse 71–72, tel 040 37 31 96, *sautter-lackmann.de.* Specialists in art, art history, photography, film, architecture. Many English-language titles.

Department Stores

Alsterhaus, Jungfernstieg 16, tel 040 359 010, *alsterhaus.de.* Shopping arcades along Neuer Wall and Jungfernstieg boulevard teem with upmarket stores for designer dresses, jewelry, and beauty products. The 1912 Alsterhaus towers over all, with four floors of exclusive wares and a gourmet restaurant overlooking the harbor.

Fashion & Accessories

Annette Rufeger Mode, Bartelsstrasse 2, tel 040 43 25 36 65, *annetterufeger.de.* Exclusive mix-and-match wardrobes of timeless elegance are the highlight at this intimate boutique.

Kaufrausch, Isestrasse 74, tel 040 4808 313, *kaufrausch-hamburg .de.* Clothes, shoes, costume jewelry, and much more, all exquisite one-offs. Popular café.

Schuhsalon Grabbe Meets Moneypenny, Marktstrasse 100, tel 040 43 25 04 84, *schuhsalon.de.* Shoes by German designers such as Stefi Talmann, Trippen, and Ludwig Reiter. Also handbags and home and fashion accessories.

Nautical items

A.W. Niemeyer, Holstenkamp 58, tel 040 89 96 97 300, *awn.de.* Serious outfitter with everything from sextants to foul-weather gear.

Buddel-Bini, Barmbeker Strasse 171, tel 040 46 28 52, *buddelbini.com.* Maritime doodads and a huge selection of ships-in-bottles.

MUNICH

Books

Hugendubel, Karlsplatz 12 (Stachus), tel 089 3075 7575, *hugen dubel.de.* The flagship of the national bookstore chain with comfy couches for browsing. Good English-language section.

Words' Worth, Schellingstrasse 3, tel 089 290 91 41, *wordsworth.de.* Situated in the university's humanities building, this store has a large selection of English paperbacks.

Delicatessens

Alois Dallmayr, Dienerstrasse 14–15, tel 089 213 50, *dallmayr.de.* Founded in 1870, a deli famous for its tea and coffee selection.

Käfer, Prinzregentenstrasse 73, tel 089 416 82 47, *www.feinkost -kaefer.de.* In-demand caterer with foods from all corners of the Earth.

Department Stores

Ludwig Beck, Marienplatz 11, tel 089 236 910, *ludwigbeck.de.* A haven of style, occupying a tasteful niche between cutting-edge and mainstream.

Oberpollinger, Neuhauser Strasse 18, tel 089 290 230, *ober pollinger.de.* A reliable source for souvenirs like beer mugs, household goods, and fabrics.

Fashion & Accessories

Bogner, Residenzstrasse 15, tel 089 290 70 40, *bogner.com.* Fabulous sports clothes for both men and women.

Eduard Meier, Brienner Strasse 10, tel 089 22 50 02, *edmeier.de.* Its exquisitely made shoes, felt hats, hunting bags, and Bavarian-style suspenders are classics.

Escada, Maximilianstrasse 27, tel 089 219 96 50, *escada.com.* A German designer label with classic couture for every occasion.

Exatmo, Tengstrasse 25, tel 089 33 57 61, *exatmo.de.* Over-the-top

Bavarian style with plenty of humor. Handwoven linens and accessories.

Loden Frey, Maffeistrasse 7–9, tel 089 21 03 90, *lodenfrey.com.* Wide choice of distinctive Bavarian folk costumes, not exactly cheap but made to last forever.

Trachtenmoden Guth, Plinganserstrasse 50, tel 089 26 69 69. Bavarian country fashion: lederhosen (leather shorts), dirndl (dresses), and loden (brushed wool).

Gifts

Bayerischer Kunstgewerbe-Verein, Pacellistrasse 6–8, tel 089 290 14 70, *kunsthandwerk-bkv.de.* Handcrafted Bavarian pottery, jewelry, and Carnival masks.

Manufactum im Alten Hof, Dienerstrasse 12, tel 089 23 54 59 00, *manufactum.de.* Germany's premier vendor of prime-quality goods of nostalgia is inessential but easy to fall for.

Obletter Spielwaren, Karlsplatz 11, tel 089 55 08 95 10, *obletter.de.* Classic German toys such as Steiff teddy bears, Märklin model trains, and hand-painted wooden playthings.

Prantl Schreibwaren, Brienner Strasse 11, tel 089 22 34 36, *prantl .de.* Exquisite writing tools and materials from silver cedarwood pens to writing paper.

Herbs

Dehner, Frauenstrasse 8, tel 089 24 23 99 80, *dehner.de.* For garden lovers: Take a packet of Alpine flower seeds home.

Kräuterparadies Lindig, Blumenstrasse 15, tel 089 26 57 26, *phytofit.de.* Germany's oldest herb specialist with more than 400 varieties, including oils, teas, organic medicines, and beauty products.

Markets

Viktualienmarkt. Munich's largest food market, located near the central Marienplatz, is the source

for Bavarian tidbits—Alpine herbs, mouthwatering *Weisswurst* (veal-parsley sausage), and Allgäu cheeses. Open Mon.–Sat.

Photographic

Foto-Video-Media-Sauter, Sonnenstrasse 26, tel 089 551 5040, *foto-video-sauter.de.* Great stock of leading manufacturers, and the place to look for new and used gear by Leica or Hasselblad.

Porcelain

Porzellan Manufaktur Nymphenburg, Odeonsplatz 1, tel 089 28 24 28, *nymphenburg.com.* Founded in 1747, the manufacturer became famous for its exclusive tableware created for the Bavarian royal court.

Rosenthal Studio-Haus, Theatinerstrasse 1, tel 089 22 26 17, *rosenthal.de.* Contemporary designs in glass, china, and cutlery, from conservative classics to lines by designers like Versace.

SAXONY

Dresden

Elbe-Team GmbH, Spenerstrasse 35, tel 0800 220 33 02. A huge warehouse selling cult items from former East Germany—records, glassware, postcards, and more.

Weihnachtsland am Zwinger, Kleine Brüdergasse 5, tel 0351 215 38 88, *weihnachtsland-dresden.com.* Traditional Christmas handicrafts, notably from the Ore Mountains—incense-puffing "smoking men," Christmas pyramids, nutcrackers, and more.

SCHLESWIG-HOLSTEIN

Marzipan

Fa Niederegger Holger Strait, Breite Strasse 89, Lübeck, tel 0451 530 11 27, *niederegger.de.* Their famous almond-filled confection comes in all shapes and colors.

Entertainment

Germany has a great tradition of drama, music, and performing arts. The country boasts more than 120 opera houses, and in almost every town you'll find a choir and one or more orchestras giving regular recitals. Berlin enjoys world repute for its experimental theater and cabaret, a form with more than a whiff of 1920s decadence. Apart from its three big opera houses and world-class symphony orchestras, the German capital has a vibrant scene at its nightclubs and discotheques, many of which stay open until dawn. Berlin, Hamburg, and Munich have the top jazz venues, with performers from across the globe.

BALLET & OPERA

Bayreuth

Bayreuth Wagner Festival, tel 069 212 49 49 4, *bayreutherfest spiele.de.* Opera lovers make a pilgrimage to the Richard Wagner Festival in July and August. The Festspielhaus (festival theater) was built in 1872–1875 specifically for Wagner's operas.

Berlin

Deutsche Oper Berlin, Bismarck-strasse 35, Charlottenburg, tel 030 343 84 343 (tickets), *deutscheoperberlin.de.* The major opera house of the West during the Cold War, which fended off communism with a repertoire of grand 19th-century operas. Traditional ballet is still a forte.

Staatsoper Unter den Linden, Unter den Linden 7, Mitte, tel 030 20 35 45 55, *staatsoper-berlin .org.* Built in 1742, this grand opera house stages great classics of ballet and opera, such as Tchaikovsky's *Swan Lake.*

Cologne

Oper der Stadt Köln, Offen-bachplatz, tel 0221 221 28 256, *buehnenkoeln.de.* Classical as well as modern performances, composed by both established and up-and-coming talent.

Dresden

Semperoper, Sächsische Staat-soper, Theaterplatz 2, tel 0351 4911 705 (tickets), *semperoper.de.* Damaged during World War II

and by severe floods, this classic opera house has been restored to its original splendor. Home to the renowned Staatskapelle Dresden.

Frankfurt

Oper, Willy-Brandt-Platz, tel 069 21 13 40 400 (tickets), *oper-frankfurt.com.* Lavish, experimental productions, with spectacular scenery and budgets.

Hamburg

Hamburger Staatsoper, Grosse Theaterstrasse 25, tel 040 35 68 68, *hamburgische-staatsoper.de.* Germany's oldest opera house, with headline productions, concerts, and *Lieder* recitals.

Munich

Bayerische Staatsoper, Max-Joseph-Platz 2, tel 089 21 85 19 20, *bayerische.staatsoper.de.* Chief venue of the summer opera festival. Early booking essential.

CABARET

Berlin

Bar jeder Vernunft, Spiegelzelt, Schaperstrasse 24, Wilmersdorf, tel 030 883 15 82, *bar-jeder -vernunft.de.* Berlin's best known entertainers and artists perform in an atmosphere of 1920s abandon.

Chamäleon Varieté, Rosen-thaler Strasse 40–41, Mitte, tel 030 40 00 590, *chamaeleonberlin.com.* Seats stageside in this lovely old theater treat you to a tour de force of singers, comedians, and acrobats.

Tipi am Kanzleramt, Grosse Queralle, tel 030 39 06 65 50, *tipi -am-kanzleramt.de.* This big-top circus tent on the fringe of the Tier-garten presents musicals, cabaret, and stand-up comedy.

CINEMA

Berlin

Arsenal, Potsdamer Strasse 2, Potsdamer Platz, Tiergarten, tel 030 269 55 100, *arsenal-berlin.de.* Shows fine German, Russian, and other European films, often with English subtitles. Hosts the annual Berlin International Film Festival (Feb.).

Cinestar Sony Center, Pots-damer Strasse 4, Tiergarten, tel 030 26 06 64 00, *cinestar.de.* Plush multiplex shows movies in their original language without subtitles—a rarity in Berlin.

Sommerkino Kulturforum, Matthäikirchplatz 4–6, tel 030 893 71 431. Cult, oldie, and independent movies are shown on the forecourt of the museum complex (June–early Sept.), with subtitles. Deck chairs are provided.

Munich

Atlantis, Schwanthaler Strasse 2, tel 089 55 51 52. Arty films in their original language.

Cinema, Nymphenburger Strasse 31, tel 089 55 52 55, *www .cinema-muenchen.com.* The best pick for English-speakers, with salty popcorn, sound tracks in English, and the occasional film-maker's chat.

City & Atelier 1 + 2, Sonnenstrasse 12, tel 089 59 19 83, *city-kinos.de.* Subtitled and original American and European art films.

CONCERTS

Berlin

Berliner Philharmonie, Herbert-von-Karajan-Strasse 1, Mitte, tel 030 25 48 80, *berliner-phil harmoniker.de.* The best place in Berlin to hear world-class classical performances, conducted by Sir Simon Rattle.

Konzerthaus Gendarmenmarkt, Berlin-Mitte tel, 030 2030 92101, *konzerthaus.de.* Home to the Berlin Symphony Orchestra, the handsomely restored Konzerthaus holds more than 550 concerts every year.

Cologne

Philharmonie, Bischofsgartenstrasse 1, tel 0221 280 280, *koelner-philharmonie.de.* This huge concert hall close to the cathedral does seminal classical, but also jazz and pop.

Hamburg

Musikhalle, Johannes-Brahms-Platz, tel 040 357 666 66, *elbphil harmonie.de.* Built in 1908, this storied venue hosts jazz, blues, world, and classical concerts.

Leipzig

Neues Gewandhaus, Augustusplatz 8, tel 0341 12 70 280, *gewandhaus.de.* Home of Europe's oldest orchestra, with a tradition dating back to 1743 when Mendelssohn was a conductor.

Munich

Münchner Kammerorchester, Oskar-von-Miller Ring 1, tel 089 46 13 64 0, *m-k-o.de.* A smaller hall with wonderful chamber music and formidable voices.

Philharmonie im Gasteig, Rosenheimer Strasse 5, tel 089 54 81 81 81, *gasteig.de.* Home to the city's celebrated Philharmonic Orchestra, conducted by James Levine and featuring a fine pedigree of world talent. The Bavarian Radio Symphony Orchestra performs every Sunday.

JAZZ

Berlin

A-Trane, Bleibtreustrasse 1, Charlottenburg, tel 030 313 25 50, *a-trane.de.* Blue-ribbon talent plays contemporary jazz on a regular basis in this cozy little club. Special Afro-Cuban nights are a regular feature. Book ahead.

Badenscher Hof, Badensche Strasse 29, Wilmersdorf, tel 030 861 00 80, *badenscher-hof.de.* An intimate club with a garden open in summer. African-American bands, modern jazz.

B Flat, Rosenthaler Strasse 13, Mitte, tel 030 283 31 23, *b-flat -berlin.de.* The best jazz club in Mitte, with live concerts most nights. The program covers everything from blues and mainstream jazz to world crossover and even tango dance nights.

Quasimodo, Kantstrasse 12A, Charlottenburg, tel 030 318 045 60, *quasimodo.de.* A favorite venue for visiting performers from the U.S.

Munich

Café am Beethovenplatz, Goethestrasse 51, tel 089 552 91 00, *mariandl.com.* Old-style café-restaurant near the train station, with live music most nights and a piano brunch on Sunday.

Jazzbar Vogler, Rumfordstrasse 17, tel 089 294 662, *jazzbar-vogler .com.* Ex-journalist Vogler has built this club into a top jazz venue without losing the intimate ambience.

Jazzclub Unterfahrt im Einstein, Einsteinstrasse 42, tel 089 448 27 94, *unterfahrt.de.* One of the most important jazz clubs in all of Germany, with musicians from all over the world.

Nightclub Hotel Bayerischer Hof, Promenadeplatz 2–6, tel 089 212 09 94, *bayerischerhof.de.* Top talent from Chick Corea to Kenny Barron stop off here, in the cellar of the grand Hotel Bayerischer Hof.

NIGHTLIFE

Berlin

Berghain & Panorama Bar, Friedrichshain, tel 030 29 36 02 10, *berghain.de.* Berlin's hottest bastion of electro and techno dance parties, housed in an old Communist-era power station with rooftop bar.

Cassiopeia, Revaler Strasse 99, tel 030 4738 5949, *cassiopeia -berlin.de.* Everything's here but the kitchen sink: a dance club, beer garden, skating hall, and a funky climbing tower, Der Kegel, converted from an air-raid shelter.

Club der Visionäre Am Flutgraben 1, tel 030 6951 8942, *clubder visionaere.com.* An old boathouse on a Spree canal is the final destination of many a pleasure captain and dancing fool. Between numbers, grab a brew and dangle your toes in the river.

Newton Bar, Charlottenstrasse 57, Mitte, tel 030 202 95 421, *new ton-bar.de.* Named for Berlin-born photographer Helmut Newton, whose "big nudes" grace the walls of the downstairs bar. Upstairs are a well-stocked humidor and comfy lounge.

Sage Club, Köpenicker Strasse 76, Mitte, tel 030 278 98 30, *sage -club.de.* One of the trendiest clubs in Berlin, the Sage features three dance floors with a high celebrity quotient and outdoor swimming pool.

Spindler & Klatt in der Heeresbäckerei, Köpenicker

Strasse 16–17, Kreuzberg, tel 030 319 88 18 60, *spindlerklatt.com*. The beautiful guests at this sprawling waterfront club pose on cool white dining futons and nibble on pan-Asian cuisine.

Hamburg

China Lounge, Nobistor 14, tel 040 31 97 66 22, *china-lounge.de*. Four areas offering electro, house, hip-hop, or R&B. Attracts students on Thurs. and beautiful people Fri. and Sat.

Die Fabrik, Barnerstrasse 36, tel 040 39 10 70, *fabrik.de*. This old machinery factory with exposed beams and two levels of spectator galleries is the scene of high-octane jazz and rock concerts.

Golden Pudel Club, Am St. Pauli Fischmarkt 27, tel 040 31 97 99 30, *pudel.com*. A rickety fisher-man's hut now plays host to this waterfront club with a mongrel program of indie and punk.

Prinzenbar, Kastanienallee 20, tel 040 3178 8311, *docks-prinzenbar .de*. Indiepop, acoustic, and elec-tronica played in a quirky little space hung with baroque cherubs and chandeliers.

Munich

Atomic Café, Neuturmstrasse 1, tel 089 228 30 54, *atomic.de*. Ameri-can DJs play electro and acid-jazz, supplemented by top bands. The entrance is in a back alley.

Call Me Drella, Maximilianplatz 5, tel 089 5700 4957, *drella.de*. Bizarre blend of Dracula's living room and Cinderella's castle, where bartenders are zombie sailors and neon-painted Indians dance on the counter.

Kultfabrik, Grafinger Strasse 6, tel 089 499 49170, *kultfabrik .de*. Based in an old food factory, this supermarket of bars and clubs caters to every possible taste and age group.

P1, Prinzregentenstrasse 1, tel 089 211 114 0, *p1-club.de*. Disco for a fashionable crowd out to join obscure celebrities or pro football players let-ting their hair down. Expect a picky door and expensive drinks.

Stuttgart

Perkins Park, Stresemannstrasse 39, tel 0711 256 00 62, *perkins -park.de*. This is a massive place with two dance floors, a restau-rant, pool table, and a personality that veers from rock 'n' roll to funk to techno.

THEATER

Berlin

Berliner Ensemble, Theater am Schiffbauerdamm, Bertolt-Brecht-Platz 1. Mitte, tel 030 28 40 81 55, *berliner-ensemble.de*. On the banks of the Spree, this theater is renowned for its contempo-rary drama and connection with Bertolt Brecht, whose pieces are performed here.

Schaubühne, Kurfürstendamm 153, Charlottenburg, tel 030 89 00 23, *schaubuehne.de*. Berlin's cutting edge of drama and choreography, featuring some of the country's most accomplished actors.

Volksbühne am Rosa-Luxem-burg-Platz, Linienstrasse 227, Mitte, tel 030 24 065 777, *volksbuehne -berlin.de*. Provocative, satirical politi-cal plays and cabarets held in a his-toric venue from the GDR era.

Hamburg

Deutsches Schauspielhaus, Kirchenallee 39, tel 040 248 713, *schauspielhaus.de*. Classic plays in a 100-year-old theater with deep pockets for stage design and the occasional radical outburst.

Munich

Münchner Kammerspiele, Maxi-milianstrasse 26–28, tel 089 23 39 66 00, *muenchner-kammerspiele .de*. Once a private theater, now a showplace for living writers and directors.

Prinzregententheater, Prinz-regentenplatz 12, tel 089 21 85 28 99, *prinzregententheater.de*.

Residenztheater, Max-Joseph-Platz 1, tel 089 21 85 19 40, *residenztheater.de*. Commissioned by Elector Maximilian Joseph in the 18th century, this stage remains a leading fixture on the Bavarian arts scene.

Theater am Gärtnerplatz, Gärtnerplatz 3, tel 089 21 8519 60, *gaertnerplatztheater.de*. Fashionable venue specializing in light operettas, ballets, and musicals.

Oberammergau

Oberammergau Passion Play, tel 08822 923 10, *passionstheater .de*. Every ten years, the Passion Play reenacts a scenario thanking God for sparing the village from the plague in the 17th century (see sidebar p. 315). In between, the theater hosts modern reli-gious dramas and the Heimat-soundfestival of Bavarian music.

Stuttgart

Staatstheater Stuttgart, Oberer Schlossgarten 6, tel 0711 20 20 90, *www.staatstheater.stuttgart.de*. Since choreographers John Cranko and Marica Haydée made it world famous in the 1960s, the dancing has been an almost greater draw than the drama.

Wuppertal

Tanztheater, Kurt-Drees-Strasse 4, tel 0202 56 34 253, *pina-bausch.de*. Now led by Lutz Förster, this touchstone of expres-sionist dance was founded by one of Germany's most influential choreographers, Pina Bausch (1940–2009). Productions are renowned for their flowing forms and emotionally jarring visuals.

Activities

With its treasure trove of natural riches, Germany has myriad choices for anyone seeking an active vacation. The mountains lure for their climbing, hiking, or winter skiing, and the lake districts have near-perfect conditions for sailing and other water sports. Pleasure boaters are drawn to the North and Baltic Seas, as well as to the large freshwater lakes like the Chiemsee in Bavaria. Windsurfing and water-skiing are also extremely popular. Idyllic areas for cycling with clearly marked trails can be found just about everywhere. Detailed information such as maps, cycle guides, local sports options, and activity holidays are available from the regional tourist offices.

Boating & Sailboarding

Germany's north coast is heaven for sailboating and sailboarding. The Baltic and North Seas provide delightful harbors, steady wind, and plenty of whitecaps. For Baltic Sea details, contact: **Ostseebäderverband Schleswig-Holstein,** Strandallee 75a, Timmendorfer Strand, tel 04503 888 525, *ostsee-schleswig-holstein .de.* For details on the North Sea: **Nordsee-Tourismus-Service** Zingel 5, Husum, tel 04841 89 750, *nordseetourismus.de.*

Water sport enthusiasts will be drawn to the larger lakes such as Lake Constance, the Starnberger See, and Chiemsee, all in southern Germany within a stone's throw of the snowcapped Alps.

Berlin has 113 miles (182 km) of navigable rivers, with the Wannsee at its spiritual hub. For a popular boat tour through the canals of central Berlin, try **Reederei Bruno Winkler,** Mierendorffstrasse 16, Charlottenburg, tel 030 349 95 95, *reedereiwinkler.de.* Most lines depart from Friedrichstrasse Bridge. In surrounding Brandenburg you can spread out on 3,000 lakes and 18,640 miles (30,000 km) of rivers. Contact the sailing association **Berliner Segler-Verband,** Müggelseedamm 74, tel 030 641 97 875, *berliner-segler-verband.de,* for details.

Climbing

Germany has plenty of climbing opportunities. Its Alpine mountaineering is world famous, but the rock formations found at lower altitudes provide challenges even for skilled climbers. Try to spend the night in one of the many rough hikers' cabins in the Alps, a wonderful experience. Details and reservations: **Deutscher Alpenverein,** Von Kahr Strasse 2–4, Munich, tel 089 14 00 30, *alpenverein.de.*

Cycling

Specially designated cycling routes are well signposted and maintained by local authorities. For general information, contact the German national cycling club **ADFC,** Friedrichstrasse 200, Berlin, tel 030 209 14 980, *adfc.de.*

Baden-Wurttemberg

There are 17 routes to choose from—from leisurely tours along flat riverbanks to the challenging Central German Highlands Route. One of the most popular options is around Lake Constance, a trail which takes you through sections of Austria and Switzerland. For more details: **Freiburg Tourist Information,** Rathausplatz 2–4, Freiburg, tel 0761 388 18 80, *freiburg.de.*

Baltic Sea Route

Extending 529 miles (836 km) along the north German coast, from Flensburg to Usedom Island, the route is not particularly hilly, but the winds can be strong. You pass through the city of Kiel and traditional fishing villages to reach Lübeck, then cross the Trave River on a ferry and pedal through the Baltic seaside resorts. **Tourismusverband Mecklenburg-Vorpommern,** Platz der Freundschaft 1, Rostock, tel 0381 403 05 00, *auf-nach-mv.de.*

Berchtesgaden

This region has several cyclist "service stations" that look after your bike and distribute maps and brochures listing bike-friendly hotels and inns. For details, contact the **Berchtesgadener Land tourist office,** Bahnhofplatz 4, Berchtesgaden, tel 08652 656 500, *berchtesgadener-land.com.*

Chiemgau, Bavaria

A relaxing tour through the villages of the south German plains in sight of the Alpine foothills. The local tourist office can organize tours, while Urlaub auf dem Bauernhof (farm holidays) has a register of farmhouses for a charming overnight stay. For more information: **Chiemsee Alpenland,** Felden 10, Bernau am Chiemsee, tel 08051 965 550, *chiemsee-alpenland.de.* **Urlaub auf dem Bauernhof,** Kirchplatz 3, St. Georgen, tel 08669 40 01, *chiemgau-bauern hofurlaub.de.*

Franconia

A romantic 150-mile (241 km) tour along the beautiful gorge of the River Altmühl, stretching from Rothenburg ob der Tauber to Kelheim. It's flat almost the whole way. Contact: **Altmühl Valley Nature Reserve**

Information, Notre Dame 1, Eichstätt, tel 08421 98 76 0, *naturpark-altmuehltal.de.*
Romantic Franconia Tourist information, Am Kirchberg 4, Colmberg, tel 09803 941 41, *romantisches-franken.de.*

Hesse

Cycling routes in Hesse take you through secluded forests, villages, the valleys of the Fulda, and mountain ranges. For information: **Hessen Tourismus,** Konradinerallee 9, Wiesbaden, tel 0611 9501 781 91, *hessen -tourismus.de.*

Mecklenburg Lakes

For 373 miles (600 km) from Lüneburg to the town of Waren on Usedom Island, the route curls around the lakes of the Mecklenburg plain. A great way to ease into some of the more challenging routes. For information: **Tourismusverband Mecklenburgische Schweiz,** tel 03994 29 97 81, *mecklenburgische-schweiz.com,* and **Tourismusverband Mecklenburgische Seenplatte,** tel 03993 153 80, *mecklenburgische -seenplatte.de.* Both organizations are located at Turmplatz 2, Röbel/Müritz.

North Sea

This 560-mile (900 km) route along the North Sea coast starts in Leer and travels alongside the top of dykes, with views out across the sea. Remember to take into account the wind, which always seems to be in your face. See *www.northsea-cycle.com* for information resources. Contact: **Nordsee Tourismus Service,** Zingel 5, Husum, tel 04841 897 50, *nordseetourismus.de.*

Rhine Valley

Beginning in Koblenz, the route heads across the Moselle to Andernach and on to vineyards by the mouth of the Ahr River. You follow the Rhine through the Siebengebirge (Seven Mountains) region, ending at Bonn. For more details, contact the **Romantischer Rhein** via **Koblenz Touristik,** Bahnhofplatz 7, Koblenz, tel 0261 30 38 80, *koblenz-touristik.de.*

Golf

Many of Germany's golf courses are for members only, but for nonmembers there's a selection of clubs and specialized golf hotels. Contact the **Deutscher Golfverband (DGV),** Viktoriastrasse 16, Wiesbaden, tel 0611 99 02 00, *golf.de.*

Hiking

Germany has a network of well-signposted and meticulously cared-for hiking paths. The proximity to nature and the local people make for an intimate encounter with Germany. Along the routes, you will find quite a few hotels and inns that specialize in accommodation for hikers. Many trip organizers offer packages that send your luggage on to your next destination.

Popular routes include the **Hochsauerland-Path,** which weaves through the valleys of Hesse and North Rhine-Westphalia; the nearby **Hoher Westerwald trail,** which traces the mountain ridges; and the **Northern Black Forest trail** through pristine forests. In Bavaria, the **Maximilian Hiking Path** follows the footsteps of 19th-century nature buff King Maximilian, from the Allgäu region to the Königssee.

For more information, contact: **Deutscher Volkssportverband,** Fabrikstrasse 8, Altötting, tel 086 71 963 10, *dvv-wandern.de.*
Naturfreunde Deutschlands, Warschauer Strasse 58a, Berlin, tel 030-29 77 32 60, *naturfreunde.de.*
Verband Deutscher Gebirgsund Wandervereine, Warschauer Strasse 58a–59a, Berlin, tel 030 29 77 32 60, *wanderverband.de.*

Horseback Riding

Wherever you go in Germany, you will find an abundance of riding stables, farmhouses, and hotels catering to riding enthusiasts of all experience levels, from beginners to the advanced. If you like western riding with a German accent, try the **Clearwater Ranch,** tel 0157 8508 6085, *clearwaterranch.de,* in the wilds of the central state of Hesse. Also, *reiten.de* offers details on national competitions and hunting parties.

Skiing

Germany has plenty of resorts to enjoy downhill and cross-country skiing, snowboarding, and other winter sports. The Bavarian Alps grab the headlines, but some of the lesser known ranges can be just as exciting. The gentle peaks of the Bavarian Forest have the most reliable snow conditions, and cross-country skiers here appreciate the diversity of the trails. Germany's northernmost winter sports area is in the Harz Mountains, for Alpine-style or cross-country skiing as well as old-fashioned sleigh rides. You will find an extensive network of ski lifts, cable cars, and pistes. For details: **Deutscher Skiverband,** Hubertusstrasse 1, Munich-Planegg, tel 089 85 79 00, *deutscherskiverband.de.* **Harzer Tourismusverband,** Markttrasse 45, Goslar, tel 05321 340 40, *harzinfo.de*

Menu Reader

General

Abendessen dinner
Brot bread
Guten Appetit Enjoy your meal
Imbiss snack
Käse cheese
Messer/Gabel/Löffel knife/fork/
  spoon
Mittagessen lunch
Prost Cheers
Salz/Pfeffer salt/pepper
Senf mustard
Speisekarte menu
Weinkarte wine list
Zucker sugar

Drinks

Kaffee coffee
Tee tea
Apfelsaft apple juice
Orangensaft orange juice
Milch milk
Bier beer
Rotwein red wine
Weisswein white wine
Sekt sparkling wine

Frühstück/Breakfast

Brötchen bread roll
(Rühr)eier (scrambled) eggs
Schwarzbrot dark brown rye
  bread
Speck bacon
Spiegelei fried egg
Weissbrot white bread

Suppe/Soup

Erbsensuppe pea soup
Gemüsesuppe vegetable soup
Hühnersuppe chicken soup
Linsensuppe lentil soup
Ochsenschwanzsuppe oxtail soup
Spargelcremesuppe cream of
  asparagus soup

Fleisch/Meat

Blutwurst black pudding
Bockwurst large frankfurter
Brathuhn roast chicken
Bratwurst grilled sausage
Currywurst curried sausage

Eintopf stew
Eisbein knuckle of pork
Ente duck
Gebratene Gans roast goose
Hackbraten meatloaf
Kalbsbrust breast of veal
Kassler Rippen smoked pork chops
Lammkeule roast lamb
Leberknödel liver dumplings
Leberwurst liver sausage
Rehkeule roast venison
Döner Kebap pocket sandwich
  with roast veal or chicken
Sauerbraten braised beef, mari-
  nated in spiced red wine
Schinken ham
Schlachtplatte mixed grill
Schweinebraten roast pork
Tafelspitz boiled rump of beef
Wiener Schnitzel veal escalope
Wildschweinkeule roast wild boar
Wurst sausage

Fisch/Fish

Aal eel
Austern oysters
Karpfen carp
Forelle trout
Garnelen prawns
Heilbutt halibut
Hummer lobster
Jakobsmuscheln scallops
Kabeljau cod
Krabben shrimps
Lachs salmon
Makrele mackerel
Matjes pickled herring
Schellfisch haddock
Seebarsch sea bass
Seelachs pollack
Seezunge sole
Tintenfisch squid
Zander pike-perch

Gemüse/Vegetables

Aubergine eggplant
Blumenkohl cauliflower
Bohnen beans
Champignons/Pilze mushrooms
Erbsen peas
Feldsalat lamb's lettuce

Fenchel fennel
Gurke cucumber
Kartoffeln potatoes
Kohl cabbage
Kürbis pumpkin
Lauch leek
Linsen lentils
Möhren carrots
Maiskolben sweet corn
Pfifferlinge chanterelles
Reis rice
Rosenkohl brussels sprouts
Rotkohl red cabbage
Sauerkraut pickled cabbage
Sellerie celery
Spargel asparagus
Spinat spinach
Tomaten tomatoes
Zwiebeln onions

Obst/Fruit

Ananas pineapple
Apfel apple
Apfelsine/Orange orange
Aprikose apricot
Birne pear
Blaubeeren blueberries
Brombeeren blackberries
Erdbeeren strawberries
Himbeeren raspberries
Kirschen cherries
Pfirsich peach
Johannisbeeren currants
Stachelbeeren gooseberries
Weintrauben grapes
Zitrone lemon

Nachspeisen/Desserts

Apfelkuchen apple cake
Bienenstich honey almond cake
Gebäck pastry
Kaiserschmarrn sweet pancake
Käsekuchen cheesecake
Kompott stewed fruit
Krapfen/Berliner doughnuts
Mandelkuchen almond cake
Obstkuchen fruit tart
Rote Grütze red fruit jelly
Sachertorte chocolate cake
Schlagsahne whipped cream
Schwarzwälder Kirschtorte Black
  Forest cake

Language Guide

Useful Words & Phrases

Yes *Ja*
No *Nein*
Please *Bitte*
Thank you *Danke*
Excuse me *Entschuldigen Sie bitte*
Sorry *Entschuldigung*
Good-bye *Auf Wiedersehen*
Good-bye *Tschüs* (informal)
Good morning *Guten Morgen*
Good day *Guten Tag* (after noon)
Good evening *Guten Abend*
Good night *Gute Nacht*
here *hier*
there *dort*
today *heute*
yesterday *gestern*
tomorrow *morgen*
now *jetzt*
later *später*
this morning *heute morgen*
this afternoon *heute nachmittag*
this evening *heute abend*
large *gross*
small *klein*
hot *heiss*
cold *kalt*
good *gut*
bad *schlecht*
left *links*
right *rechts*
straight ahead *geradeaus*
Do you speak English? *Sprechen Sie Englisch?*
I am American *Ich bin Amerikaner (m)/Amerikanerin (f)*
I don't understand *Ich verstehe Sie nicht*
Please speak more slowly *Bitte sprechen Sie langsamer*
Where is/are...? *Wo ist/sind...?*
I don't know *Ich weiss nicht*
My name is... *Ich heisse...*
At what time? *Wann?*
What time is it? *Wieviel Uhr ist es?*

Numbers

one *eins*
two *zwei*
three *drei*
four *vier*
five *fünf*
six *sechs*
seven *sieben*
eight *acht*
nine *neun*
ten *zehn*
twenty *zwanzig*

Days of the Week

Monday *Montag*
Tuesday *Dienstag*
Wednesday *Mittwoch*
Thursday *Donnerstag*
Friday *Freitag*
Saturday *Samstag/Sonnabend*
Sunday *Sonntag*

Months & Seasons

January *Januar*
February *Februar*
March *März*
April *April*
May *Mai*
June *Juni*
July *Juli*
August *August*
September *September*
October *Oktober*
November *November*
December *Dezember*
spring *Frühling*
summer *Sommer*
fall *Herbst*
winter *Winter*

In the Hotel

Do you have a vacancy? *Haben Sie noch ein Zimmer frei?*
a single room *ein Einzelzimmer*
a double room *ein Doppelzimmer*
with/without bathroom/shower *mit/ohne Bad/Dusche*
key *Schlüssel*
porter *Pförtner*

Emergencies

Help *Hilfe*
I need a doctor/dentist *Ich brauche einen Arzt/Zahnarzt*
Can you help me? *Können Sie mir helfen?*
Where is the hospital?/police station?/telephone? *Wo finde ich das Krankenhaus?/die Polizeiwache?/Wo kann ich telefonieren?*

Shopping

Do you have...? *Haben Sie...?*
How much is it? *Wieviel kostet es?*
Do you take credit cards ? *Akzeptieren Sie Kreditkarten?*
When do you open/close? *Wann machen Sie auf/zu?*
size (clothes) *Kleidergrösse*
size (shoes) *Schuhgrösse*
color *Farbe*
cheap *billig*
expensive *teuer*
I'll take it *Ich nehme es*
too much *zu viel*
check/bill *Rechnung*

Shops

bakery *Bäckerei*
bookshop *Buchhandlung*
pharmacy *Drogerie*
delicatessen *Feinkostladen*
department store *Kaufhaus*
fishmonger *Fischhändler*
grocery *Gemüseladen*
antique shop *Antikladen*
library *Bibliothek*
supermarket *Supermarkt*
newspaper kiosk *Zeitungskiosk*
shoe shop *Schuhgeschäft*
clothes shop *Bekleidungsgeschäft*
special offer *Sonderangebot*
stationery *Schreibwaren*

Sightseeing

visitor information *Touristen-Information*
exhibition *Ausstellung*
open *geöffnet*
closed *geschlossen*
daily *täglich*
all year *ganzjährig*
all day long *den ganzen Tag*
entry fee *Eintrittspreis*
free *frei/umsonst*
church *Kirche*
castle *Schloss/Burg*

INDEX

ILLUSTRATIONS CREDITS

National Geographic

TRAVELER
Germany

Published by the National Geographic Society

Gary E. Knell, *President and Chief Executive Officer*

John M. Fahey, *Chairman of the Board*

Declan Moore, *Executive Vice President; President, Publishing and Travel*

Melina Gerosa Bellows, *Executive Vice President; Publisher and Chief Creative Officer, Books, Kids, and Family*

Lynn Cutter, *Executive Vice President, Travel*

Keith Bellows, *Senior Vice President and Editor in Chief, National Geographic Travel Media*

Prepared by the Book Division

Hector Sierra, *Senior Vice President and General Manager*

Janet Goldstein, *Senior Vice President and Editorial Director*

Jonathan Halling, *Creative Director*

Marianne R. Koszorus, *Design Director*

Barbara A. Noe, *Senior Editor, National Geographic Travel Books*

R. Gary Colbert, *Production Director*

Jennifer A. Thornton, *Director of Managing Editorial*

Susan S. Blair, *Director of Photography*

Meredith C. Wilcox, *Director, Administration and Rights Clearance*

Staff for This Book

Karen Carmichael, *Project Editor*

Elisa Gibson, *Art Director*

Ruth Ann Thompson, *Designer*

Carl Mehler, *Director of Maps*

Mike McNey & Mapping Specialists, *Map Production*

Marshall Kiker, *Associate Managing Editor*

Michael O'Connor, *Production Editor*

Galen Young, *Rights Clearance Specialist*

Katie Olsen, *Production Design Assistant*

Hannah Lauterback and Marlena Serviss, *Contributors*

Production Services

Phillip L. Schlosser, *Senior Vice President*

Chris Brown, *Vice President, NG Book Manufacturing*

Nicole Elliott, *Director of Production*

George Bounelis, *Senior Production Manager*

Rachel Faulise, *Manager*

Robert L. Barr, *Manager*

Map illustrations drawn by Chris Orr Associates, Southampton, England.

Cutaway illustrations drawn by Maltings Partnership, Derby, England.

The information in this book has been carefully checked and to the best of our knowledge is accurate. However, details are subject to change, and the National Geographic Society cannot be responsible for such changes, or for errors or omissions. Assessments of sites, hotels, and restaurants are based on the author's subjective opinions, which do not necessarily reflect the publisher's opinion.

The National Geographic Society is one of the world's largest nonprofit scientific and educational organizations. Founded in 1888 to "increase and diffuse geographic knowledge," the member-supported Society works to inspire people to care about the planet. Through its online community, members can get closer to explorers and photographers, connect with other members around the world, and help make a difference. National Geographic reflects the world through its magazines, television programs, films, music and radio, books, DVDs, maps, exhibitions, live events, school publishing programs, interactive media, and merchandise. *National Geographic* magazine, the Society's official journal, published in English and 38 local-language editions, is read by more than 60 million people each month. The National Geographic Channel reaches 440 million households in 171 countries in 38 languages. National Geographic Digital Media receives more than 25 million visitors a month. National Geographic has funded more than 10,000 scientific research, conservation, and exploration projects and supports an education program promoting geography literacy. For more information, visit www.nationalgeographic.com.

For more information, please call 1-800-NGS LINE (647-5463) or write to the following address:

National Geographic Society
1145 17th Street N.W.
Washington, D.C. 20036-4688 U.S.A.

For information about special discounts for bulk purchases, please contact National Geographic Books Special Sales: ngspecsales@ngs.org

For rights or permissions inquiries, please contact National Geographic Books Subsidiary Rights: ngbookrights@ngs.org

National Geographic Traveler: Germany
(Fourth Edition)
ISBN: 978-1-4262-1367-0

Printed in Hong Kong
14/THK/1

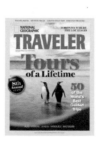